Fifteenth Edition

CRAFTING& EXECUTING STRATEGY

The Quest for Competitive Advantage
CONCEPTS AND CASES

ARTHUR A. THOMPSON, JR.
UNIVERSITY OF ALABAMA.

J. STRICKLAND III
UNIVERSITY OF ALABAMA

JOHN E. GAMBLE
UNIVERSITY OF SOUTH ALABAMA

BRYANT UNIVERSITY • BUS 400
Policy and Strategy

 **Learning Solutions**

Boston   Burr Ridge, IL   Dubuque, IA   New York   San Francisco   St. Louis
Bangkok   Bogotá   Caracas   Lisbon   London   Madrid
Mexico City   Milan   New Delhi   Seoul   Singapore   Sydney   Taipei   Toronto

The McGraw-Hill Companies

Crafting & Executing Strategy
The Quest for Competitive Advantage: Concepts and Cases, Fifteenth Edition
Bryant University • BUS 400 • Policy and Strategy

This book is a McGraw-Hill Learning Solutions textbook and contains select material from the following sources:

Crafting & Executing Strategy: The Quest for Competitive Advantage, Concepts and Cases, Fifteenth Edition by Arthur A Thompson, Jr., A.J. Strickland III, and John E. Gamble. Copyright © 2007 by The McGraw-Hill Companies, Inc.

"Apple Computer, 2006," prepared by David B. Yoppie and Michael Slind Harvard Business School Cases – Competitive Strategy 9-706-496. Copyright © 2006 by the President and Fellows of Harvard College.

"Southwest Airlines 2002: An Industry Under Siege," prepared by James L. Heskett Harvard Business School Cases – Service Management 9-803-133. Copyright © 2003 by the President and Fellows of Harvard College.

"Vivendi: Revitalizing a French Conglomerate," prepared by John M. Turner Harvard Business School Cases – Competitive Strategy 9-799-019. Copyright © 1998 by the President and Fellows of Harvard College.

"Johnson & Johnson: The Tylenol Tragedy," prepared by Stephen A. Greyser Harvard Business School Cases – Marketing 9-583-043. Copyright © 1982 by the President and Fellows of Harvard College.

"What is Strategy?," by Michael E. Porter Harvard Business Review – Industry and Competitive Strategy Articles Nov.-Dec. 1996. Copyright © 1996 by the President and Fellows of Harvard College.

"Understanding Industry Structure," prepared by Michael E. Porter Harvard Business School Cases – Competitive Strategy 9-707-493. Copyright © 2006 by the President and Fellows of Harvard College.

"Creating Corporate Advantage," by David J. Collis and Cynthia A. Montgomery Harvard Business Review – Industry and Competitive Strategy Articles May-June 1998. Copyright © 1998 by the President and Fellows of Harvard College.

"Introduction to Financial Ratios and Financial Statement Analysis," prepared by William Bruns Harvard Business School Cases – Accounting and Control 9-193-029. Copyright © 1992 by the President and Fellows of Harvard College.

"The Social Responsibility of Business is to Increase its Profits," by Milton Friedman The New York Times Magazine Copyright © 1970 by The New York Times Magazine.

All are reprinted with permission of the publisher. Many custom published texts are modified versions or adaptations of our best-selling textbooks. Some adaptations are printed in black and white to keep prices at a minimum, while others are in color.

1 2 3 4 5 6 7 8 9 0 BLA BLA 0 9 8 7

ISBN 13: 978-0-697-77629-7
ISBN-10: 0-697-77629-8

Custom Publishing Specialist: Nada Mraovic
Production Editor: Nina Meyer
Printer/Binder: Perfect Printing

CONTENTS

Chapters

Cases

Articles

chapter one

What Is Strategy and Why Is It Important?

Strategy means making clear-cut choices about how to compete.

—Jack Welch
Former CEO, General Electric

A strategy is a commitment to undertake one set of actions rather than another.

—Sharon Oster
Professor, Yale University

The process of developing superior strategies is part planning, part trial and error, until you hit upon something that works.

—Costas Markides
Professor, London Business School

Without a strategy the organization is like a ship without a rudder.

—Joel Ross and Michael Kami
Authors and Consultants

Managers face three central questions in evaluating their company's business prospects: What's the company's present situation? Where does the company need to go from here? How should it get there? Arriving at a probing answer to the question "What's the company's present situation?" prompts managers to evaluate industry conditions and competitive pressures, the company's current performance and market standing, its resource strengths and capabilities, and its competitive weaknesses. The question "Where does the company need to go from here?" pushes managers to make choices about the direction the company should be headed—what new or different customer groups and customer needs it should endeavor to satisfy, what market positions it should be staking out, what changes in its business makeup are needed. The question "How should it get there?" challenges managers to craft and execute a strategy capable of moving the company in the intended direction, growing its business, and improving its financial and market performance.

In this opening chapter, we define the concept of strategy and describe its many facets. We shall indicate the kinds of actions that determine what a company's strategy is, why strategies are partly proactive and partly reactive, and why company strategies tend to evolve over time. We will look at what sets a winning strategy apart from ho-hum or flawed strategies and why the caliber of a company's strategy determines whether it will enjoy a competitive advantage or be burdened by competitive disadvantage. By the end of this chapter, you will have a pretty clear idea of why the tasks of crafting and executing strategy are core management functions and why excellent execution of an excellent strategy is the most reliable recipe for turning a company into a standout performer.

WHAT DO WE MEAN BY *STRATEGY?*

A company's **strategy** is management's action plan for running the business and conducting operations. The crafting of a strategy represents a managerial *commitment to pursue a particular set of actions* in growing the business, attracting and pleasing customers, competing successfully, conducting operations, and improving the company's financial and market performance. Thus a company's strategy is all about *how—how* management intends to grow the business, *how* it will build a loyal clientele and outcompete rivals, *how* each functional piece of the business (research and development,

> **Core Concept**
>
> A company's **strategy** consists of the competitive moves and business approaches that managers are employing to grow the business, attract and please customers, compete successfully, conduct operations, and achieve the targeted levels of organizational performance.

supply chain activities, production, sales and marketing, distribution, finance, and human resources) will be operated, *how* performance will be boosted. In choosing a strategy, management is in effect saying, "Among all the many different business approaches and ways of competing we could have chosen, we have decided to employ this particular combination of competitive and operating approaches in moving the company in the intended direction, strengthening its market position and competitiveness, and boosting performance." The strategic choices a company makes are seldom easy decisions, and some of them may turn out to be wrong—but that is not an excuse for not deciding on a concrete course of action.[1]

In most industries companies have considerable freedom in choosing the hows of strategy.[2] Thus, some rivals strive to improve their performance and market standing by achieving lower costs than rivals, while others pursue product superiority or personalized customer service or the development of competencies and capabilities that rivals cannot match. Some target the high end of the market, while others go after the middle or low end; some opt for wide product lines, while others concentrate their energies on a narrow product lineup. Some competitors position themselves in only one part of the industry's chain of production/distribution activities (preferring to be just in manufacturing or wholesale distribution or retailing), while others are partially or fully integrated, with operations ranging from components production to manufacturing and assembly to wholesale distribution or retailing. Some competitors deliberately confine their operations to local or regional markets; others opt to compete nationally, internationally (several countries), or globally (all or most of the major country markets worldwide). Some companies decide to operate in only one industry, while others diversify broadly or narrowly, into related or unrelated industries, via acquisitions, joint ventures, strategic alliances, or internal start-ups.

At companies intent on gaining sales and market share at the expense of competitors, managers typically opt for offensive strategies, frequently launching fresh initiatives of one kind or another to make the company's product offering more distinctive and appealing to buyers. Companies already in a strong industry position are more prone to strategies that emphasize gradual gains in the marketplace, fortifying the company's market position, and defending against the latest maneuvering of rivals and other developments that threaten the company's well-being. Risk-averse companies often prefer conservative strategies, preferring to follow the successful moves of pioneering companies whose managers are more entrepreneurial and willing to take the risks of being first to make a bold and perhaps pivotal move that reshapes the contest among market rivals.

There is no shortage of opportunity to fashion a strategy that both tightly fits a company's own particular situation and is discernibly different from the strategies of rivals. In fact, a company's managers normally attempt to make strategic choices about the key building blocks of its strategy that differ from the choices made by competitors—not 100 percent different but at least different in several important respects. A strategy stands a better chance of succeeding when it is predicated on actions, business approaches, and competitive moves aimed at (1) appealing to buyers in ways that set a company apart from rivals and (2) carving out its own market position. Simply copying what successful companies in the industry are doing and trying to mimic their market position rarely works. Rather, there needs to be some distinctive "aha" element to the strategy that draws in customers and produces a competitive edge. Carbon-copy strategies among companies in the same industry are the exception rather than the rule.

For a concrete example of the actions and approaches that comprise strategy, see Illustration Capsule 1.1, which describes Comcast's strategy to revolutionize the cable TV business.

Illustration Capsule 1.1

Comcast's Strategy to Revolutionize the Cable Industry

In 2004–2005 cable TV giant Comcast put the finishing touches on a bold strategy to change the way people watched television and to grow its business by introducing Internet phone service. With revenues of $18 billion and almost 22 million of the 74 million U.S. cable subscribers, Comcast became the industry leader in the U.S. market in 2002 when it acquired AT&T Broadband, along with its 13 million cable subscribers, for about $50 billion. Comcast's strategy had the following elements:

- *Continue to roll out high-speed Internet or broadband service to customers via cable modems.* With more than 8 million customers that generated revenues approaching $5 billion annually, Comcast was already America's number one provider of broadband service. It had recently upgraded its broadband service to allow download speeds of up to six megabits per second—considerably faster than the DSL-type broadband service available over telephone lines.

- *Continue to promote a relatively new video-on-demand service that allowed digital subscribers to watch TV programs whenever they wanted to watch them.* The service allowed customers to use their remotes to choose from a menu of thousands of programs, stored on Comcast's servers as they were first broadcast, and included network shows, news, sports, and movies. Viewers with a Comcast DVR set-top box had the ability to pause, stop, restart, and save programs, without having to remember to record them when they were broadcast. Comcast had signed up more than 10 million of its cable customers for digital service, and it was introducing enhanced digital and high-definition television (HDTV) service in additional geographic markets at a brisk pace.

- *Promote a video-on-demand service whereby digital customers with a set-top box could order and watch pay-per-view movies using a menu on their remote.* Comcast's technology enabled viewers to call up the programs they wanted with a few clicks of the remote. In 2005, Comcast had almost 4000 program choices and customers were viewing about 120 million videos per month.

- *Partner with Sony, MGM, and others to expand Comcast's library of movie offerings.* In 2004, Comcast agreed to develop new cable channels using MGM and Sony libraries, which had a combined 7,500 movies and 42,000 TV shows—it took about 300 movies to feed a 24-hour channel for a month.

- *Use Voice over Internet Protocol (VoIP) technology to offer subscribers Internet-based phone service at a fraction of the cost charged by other providers.* VoIP is an appealing low-cost technology widely seen as the most significant new communication technology since the invention of the telephone. Comcast was on track to make its Comcast Digital Voice (CDV) service available to 41 million homes by year-end 2006. CDV had many snazzy features, including call forwarding, caller ID, and conferencing, thus putting Comcast in position to go after the customers of traditional telephone companies.

- *Use its video-on-demand and CDV offerings to combat mounting competition from direct-to-home satellite TV providers.* Satellite TV providers such as EchoStar and DIRECTV had been using the attraction of lower monthly fees to steal customers away from cable TV providers. Comcast believed that the appeal of video-on-demand and low-cost CDV service would overcome its higher price. And satellite TV providers lacked the technological capability to provide either two-way communications connection to homes (necessary to offer video-on-demand) or reliable high-speed Internet access.

- *Employ a sales force (currently numbering about 3,200 people) to sell advertising to businesses that were shifting some of their advertising dollars from sponsoring network programs to sponsoring cable programs.* Ad sales generated revenues of about $1.6 billion, and Comcast had cable operations in 21 of the 25 largest markets in the United States.

- *Significantly improve Comcast's customer service.* Most cable subscribers were dissatisfied with the caliber of customer service offered by their local cable companies. Comcast management believed that service would be a big issue given the need to support video-on-demand, cable modems, HDTV, phone service, and the array of customer inquiries and problems such services entailed. In 2004, Comcast employed about 12,500 people to answer an expected volume of 200 million phone calls. Newly hired customer service personnel were given five weeks of classroom training, followed by three weeks of taking calls while a supervisor listened in—it cost Comcast about $7 to handle each call. The company's goal was to answer 90 percent of calls within 30 seconds.

Sources: Information posted at www.comcast.com (accessed August 6, 2005); Marc Gunter, "Comcast Wants to Change the World, But Can It Learn to Answer the Phone?" *Fortune,* October 16, 2004, pp. 140–56; and Stephanie N. Mehta, "The Future Is on the Line," *Fortune,* July 26, 2004, pp. 121–30.

Strategy and the Quest for Competitive Advantage

The heart and soul of any strategy are the actions and moves in the marketplace that managers are taking to improve the company's financial performance, strengthen its long-term competitive position, and gain a competitive edge over rivals. A creative, distinctive strategy that sets a company apart from rivals and yields a competitive advantage is a company's most reliable ticket for earning above-average profits. Competing in the marketplace with a competitive advantage tends to be more profitable than competing with no advantage. And a company is almost certain to earn significantly higher profits when it enjoys a competitive advantage as opposed to when it is hamstrung by competitive disadvantage. Furthermore, if a company's competitive edge holds promise for being durable and sustainable (as opposed to just temporary), then so much the better for both the strategy and the company's future profitability. It's nice when a company's strategy produces at least a temporary competitive edge, but a **sustainable competitive advantage** is plainly much better. What makes a competitive advantage sustainable as opposed to temporary are actions and elements in the strategy that cause an attractive number of buyers to have a *lasting preference* for a company's products or services as compared to the offerings of competitors. Competitive advantage is the key to above-average profitability and financial performance because strong buyer preferences for the company's product offering translate into higher sales volumes (Wal-Mart) and/or the ability to command a higher price (Häagen-Dazs), thus driving up earnings, return on investment, and other measures of financial performance.

> **Core Concept**
> A company achieves **sustainable competitive advantage** when an attractive number of buyers prefer its products or services over the offerings of competitors and when the basis for this preference is durable.

Four of the most frequently used and dependable strategic approaches to setting a company apart from rivals, building strong customer loyalty, and winning a sustainable competitive advantage are:

1. *Striving to be the industry's low-cost provider, thereby aiming for a cost-based competitive advantage over rivals.* Wal-Mart and Southwest Airlines have earned strong market positions because of the low-cost advantages they have achieved over their rivals and their consequent ability to underprice competitors. Achieving lower costs than rivals can produce a durable competitive edge when rivals find it hard to match the low-cost leader's approach to driving costs out of the business. Despite years of trying, discounters like Kmart and Target have struck out trying to match Wal-Mart's frugal operating practices, super-efficient distribution systems, and its finely honed supply chain approaches that allow it to obtain merchandise from manufacturers at super-low prices.

2. *Outcompeting rivals based on such differentiating features as higher quality, wider product selection, added performance, value-added services, more attractive styling, technological superiority, or unusually good value for the money.* Successful adopters of differentiation strategies include Johnson & Johnson in baby products (product reliability), Harley-Davidson (bad-boy image and king-of-the-road styling), Chanel and Rolex (top-of-the-line prestige), Mercedes-Benz and BMW (engineering design and performance), L. L. Bean (good value), and Amazon.com (wide selection and convenience). Differentiation strategies can be powerful so long as a company is sufficiently innovative to thwart clever rivals in finding ways to copy or closely imitate the features of a successful differentiator's product offering.

3. *Focusing on a narrow market niche and winning a competitive edge by doing a better job than rivals of serving the special needs and tastes of buyers comprising*

the niche. Prominent companies that enjoy competitive success in a specialized market niche include eBay in online auctions, Jiffy Lube International in quick oil changes, McAfee in virus protection software, Starbucks in premium coffees and coffee drinks, Whole Foods Market in natural and organic foods, CNBC and The Weather Channel in cable TV.

4. *Developing expertise and resource strengths that give the company competitive capabilities that rivals can't easily imitate or trump with capabilities of their own.* FedEx has superior capabilities in next-day delivery of small packages. Walt Disney has hard-to-beat capabilities in theme park management and family entertainment. Over the years, Toyota has developed a sophisticated production system that allows it to produce reliable, largely defect-free vehicles at low cost. IBM has wide-ranging expertise in helping corporate customers develop and install cutting-edge information systems. Ritz-Carlton and Four Seasons have uniquely strong capabilities in providing their hotel guests with an array of personalized services. Very often, winning a durable competitive edge over rivals hinges more on building competitively valuable expertise and capabilities than it does on having a distinctive product. Clever rivals can nearly always copy the attributes of a popular or innovative product, but for rivals to match experience, know-how, and specialized competitive capabilities that a company has developed and perfected over a long period of time is substantially harder to duplicate and takes much longer.

The tight connection between competitive advantage and profitability means that the quest for sustainable competitive advantage always ranks center stage in crafting a strategy. The key to successful strategy making is to come up with one or more differentiating strategy elements that act as a magnet to draw customers and yield a lasting competitive edge. Indeed, what separates a powerful strategy from a run-of-the-mill or ineffective one is management's ability to forge a series of moves, both in the marketplace and internally, that sets the company apart from its rivals, tilts the playing field in the company's favor by giving buyers reason to prefer its products or services, and produces a sustainable competitive advantage over rivals. The bigger and more sustainable the competitive advantage, the better the company's prospects for winning in the marketplace and earning superior long-term profits relative to its rivals. Without a strategy that leads to competitive advantage, a company risks being outcompeted by stronger rivals and/or locked in to mediocre financial performance. Hence, company managers deserve no gold stars for coming up with a ho-hum strategy that results in ho-hum financial performance and a ho-hum industry standing.

Identifying a Company's Strategy

The best indicators of a company's strategy are its actions in the marketplace and the statements of senior managers about the company's current business approaches, future plans, and efforts to strengthen its competitiveness and performance. Figure 1.1 shows what to look for in identifying the key elements of a company's strategy.

Once it is clear what to look for, the task of identifying a company's strategy is mainly one of researching information about the company's actions in the marketplace and business approaches. In the case of publicly owned enterprises, the strategy is often openly discussed by senior executives in the company's annual report and 10-K report, in press releases and company news (posted on the company's Web site), and in the information provided to investors at the company's Web site. To maintain the confidence of investors and Wall Street, most public companies have to be fairly open about their strategies. Company executives typically lay out key elements of their strategies in

Figure 1.1   **Identifying a Company's Strategy—What to Look for**

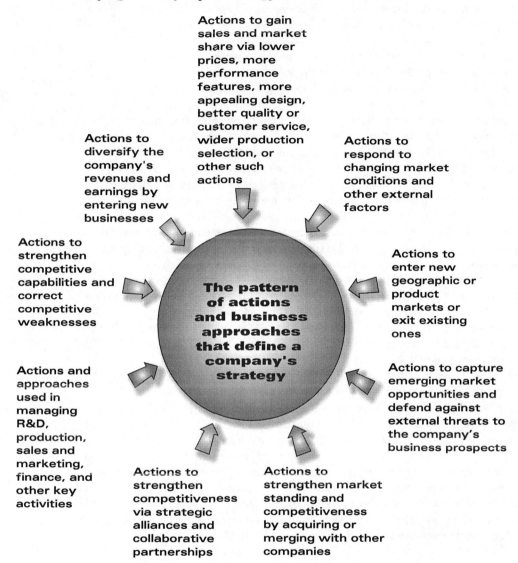

presentations to securities analysts (the accompanying PowerPoint slides are sometimes posted in the investor relations section of the company's Web site), and stories in the business media about the company often include aspects of the company's strategy. Hence, except for some about-to-be-launched moves and changes that remain under wraps and in the planning stage, there's usually nothing secret or undiscoverable about a company's present strategy.

Why a Company's Strategy Evolves over Time

Irrespective of where the strategy comes from—be it the product of top executives or the collaborative product of numerous company personnel—it is unlikely that the strategy, as originally conceived, will prove entirely suitable over time. Every company must be willing and ready to modify its strategy in response to changing market conditions, advancing technology, the fresh moves of competitors, shifting buyer needs and preferences, emerging market opportunities, new ideas for improving the strategy, and mounting evidence that the strategy is not working well. Thus, *a company's strategy is always a work in progress.*

Most of the time a company's strategy evolves incrementally from management's ongoing efforts to fine-tune this or that piece of the strategy and to adjust certain strategy elements in response to unfolding events. But, on occasion, major strategy shifts are called for, such as when a strategy is clearly failing and the company faces a financial crisis, when market conditions or buyer preferences change significantly, or when important technological breakthroughs occur. In some industries, conditions change at a fairly slow pace, making it feasible for the major components of a good strategy to remain in place for long periods. But in industries where industry and competitive conditions change frequently and in sometimes dramatic ways, the life cycle of a given strategy is short. Industry environments characterized by *high-velocity change* require companies to rapidly adapt their strategies.[3] For example, companies in industries with rapid-fire advances in technology—like medical equipment, electronics, and wireless devices—often find it essential to adjust one or more key elements of their strategies several times a year, sometimes even finding necessary to reinvent their approach to providing value to their customers. Companies in online retailing and the travel and resort industries find it necessary to adapt their strategies to accommodate sudden bursts of new spending or sharp drop-offs in demand, often updating their market prospects and financial projections every few months.

But regardless of whether a company's strategy changes gradually or swiftly, the important point is that a company's present strategy is always temporary and on trial, pending new ideas for improvement from management, changing industry and competitive conditions, and any other new developments that management believes warrant strategy adjustments. Thus, a company's strategy at any given point is fluid, representing the temporary outcome of an ongoing process that, on the one hand, involves reasoned and creative management efforts to craft an effective strategy and, on the other hand, involves ongoing responses to market change and constant experimentation and tinkering. Adapting to new conditions and constantly learning what is working well enough to continue and what needs to be improved is consequently a normal part of the strategy-making process and results in an evolving strategy.

> **Core Concept**
> Changing circumstances and ongoing management efforts to improve the strategy cause a company's strategy to evolve over time—a condition that makes the task of crafting a strategy a work in progress, not a one-time event.

> A company's strategy is shaped partly by management analysis and choice and partly by the necessity of adapting and learning by doing.

A Company's Strategy Is Partly Proactive and Partly Reactive

The evolving nature of a company's strategy means that the typical company strategy is a blend of (1) proactive actions to improve the company's financial performance and secure a competitive edge and (2) as-needed reactions to unanticipated developments and fresh market conditions (see Figure 1.2).[4] The biggest portion of a company's current strategy flows from previously initiated actions and business approaches that are working well enough to merit continuation and newly launched initiatives aimed at boosting financial performance and edging out rivals. Typically, managers proactively modify this or that aspect of their strategy as new learning emerges about which pieces of the strategy are working well and which aren't, and as they hit upon new ideas for strategy improvement. This part of management's action plan for running the company is deliberate and proactive, standing as the current product of management's latest and best strategy ideas.

Figure 1.2   **A Company's Strategy Is a Blend of Proactive Initiatives and Reactive Adjustments**

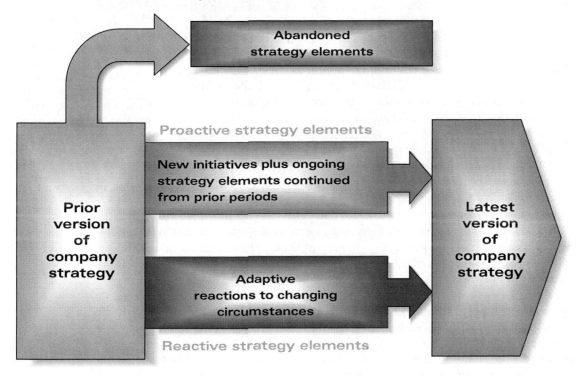

But managers must always be willing to supplement or modify all the proactive strategy elements with as-needed reactions to unanticipated developments. Inevitably, there will be occasions when market and competitive conditions take an unexpected turn that calls for some kind of strategic reaction or adjustment. Hence, a portion of a company's strategy is always developed on the fly, coming as a response to fresh strategic maneuvers on the part of rival firms, unexpected shifts in customer requirements and expectations, fast-changing technological developments, newly appearing market opportunities, a changing political or economic climate, or other unanticipated happenings in the surrounding environment. These adaptive strategy adjustments form the reactive strategy elements.

As shown in Figure 1.2, a company's strategy evolves from one version to the next as managers abandon obsolete or ineffective strategy elements, settle upon a set of *proactive/intended strategy elements*, and then adapt the strategy as new circumstances unfold, thus giving rise to *reactive/adaptive strategy elements*. A company's strategy thus tends to be a *combination* of proactive and reactive elements. In the process, some strategy elements end up being abandoned because they have become obsolete or ineffective.

STRATEGY AND ETHICS: PASSING THE TEST OF MORAL SCRUTINY

In choosing from among strategic alternatives, company managers are well advised to embrace actions that are aboveboard and can pass the test of moral scrutiny. Just keeping a company's strategic actions within the bounds of what is legal does not mean the strategy is ethical. Ethical and moral standards are not governed by what is legal. Rather, they involve issues of both right versus wrong and *duty*—what one *should* do. A strategy is ethical only if (1) it does not entail actions and behaviors that cross the line from "should do" to "should not do" (because such actions are unsavory, unconscionable, or injurious to other people or unnecessarily harmful to the environment) and (2) it allows management to fulfill its ethical duties to all stakeholders— owners/shareholders, employees, customers, suppliers, the communities in which it operates, and society at large.

Admittedly, it is not always easy to categorize a given strategic behavior as definitely ethical or definitely unethical. Many strategic actions fall in a gray zone in between, and whether they are deemed ethical or unethical hinges on how clearly the boundaries are defined. For example, is it ethical for advertisers of alcoholic products to place ads in media having an audience of as much as 50 percent underage viewers? (In 2003, growing concerns about underage drinking prompted some beer and distilled spirits companies to agree to place ads in media with an audience at least 70 percent adult, up from a standard of 50 percent adult.) Is it ethical for an apparel retailer attempting to keep prices attractively low to source clothing from foreign manufacturers who pay substandard wages, use child labor, or subject workers to unsafe working conditions? Many people would say no, but some might argue that a company is not unethical simply because it does not police the business practices of its suppliers. Is it ethical for the makers of athletic uniforms, shoes, and other sports equipment to pay coaches large sums of money to induce them to use the manufacturer's products in their sport? (The compensation contracts of many college coaches include substantial payments from sportswear and sports equipment manufacturers, and the teams subsequently end up wearing the uniforms and using the products of those manufacturers.) Is it ethical for manufacturers of life-saving drugs to charge higher prices in some countries than they charge in others? (This is a fairly common practice that has recently come under scrutiny because it raises the costs of health care for consumers who are charged higher prices.) Is it ethical for a company to turn a blind eye to the damage its operations do to the environment even though its operations are in compliance with current environmental regulations—especially if it has the know-how and the means to alleviate some of the environmental impacts by making relatively inexpensive changes in its operating practices?

Senior executives with strong ethical convictions are generally proactive in linking strategic action and ethics: They forbid the pursuit of ethically questionable business opportunities and insist that all aspects of company strategy reflect high ethical standards.[5] They make it clear that all company personnel are expected to act with integrity, and they put organizational checks and balances into place to monitor behavior, enforce ethical codes of conduct, and provide guidance to employees regarding any gray areas. Their commitment to conducting the company's business in an ethical manner is genuine, not hypocritical.

Instances of corporate malfeasance, ethical lapses, and fraudulent accounting practices at Enron, WorldCom, Tyco, Adelphia, HealthSouth, and other companies leave no room to doubt the damage to a company's reputation and business that can result from ethical misconduct, corporate misdeeds, and even criminal behavior on the part of company personnel. Aside from just the embarrassment and black marks that accompany headline exposure of a company's unethical practices, the hard fact is that many customers and many suppliers are wary of doing business with a company that engages in sleazy practices or that turns a blind eye to illegal or unethical behavior on the part of employees. They are turned off by unethical strategies or behavior and, rather than become victims or get burned themselves, wary customers will quickly take their business elsewhere and wary suppliers will tread carefully. Moreover, employees with character and integrity do not want to work for a company whose strategies are shady or whose executives lack character and integrity. There's little lasting benefit to unethical strategies and behavior, and the downside risks can be substantial. Besides, such actions are plain wrong.

THE RELATIONSHIP BETWEEN A COMPANY'S STRATEGY AND ITS BUSINESS MODEL

Core Concept
A company's **business model** explains the rationale for why its business approach and strategy will be a moneymaker. Absent the ability to deliver good profitability, the strategy is not viable and the survival of the business is in doubt.

Closely related to the concept of strategy is the concept of a company's **business model.** While the word *model* conjures up images of ivory-tower ideas that may be loosely connected to the real world, such images do not apply here. A company's business model is management's story line for how the strategy will be a moneymaker. The story line sets forth the key components of the enterprise's business approach, indicates how revenues will be generated, and makes a case for why the strategy can deliver value to customers in a profitable manner.[6] A company's business model thus explains why its business approach and strategy will generate ample revenues to cover costs and capture a profit.

The nitty-gritty issue surrounding a company's business model is whether the chosen strategy makes good business sense. Why is there convincing reason to believe that the strategy is capable of producing a profit? How will the business generate its revenues? Will those revenues be sufficient to cover operating costs? Will customers see enough value in what the business does for them to pay a profitable price? The concept of a company's business model is, consequently, more narrowly focused than the concept of a company's business strategy. A company's strategy *relates broadly to its competitive initiatives and action plan for running the business* (but it may or may not lead to profitability). However, a company's business model zeros in on *how and why the business will generate revenues sufficient to cover costs and produce attractive profits and return on investment.* Absent the ability to deliver good profits, the strategy is not viable, the business model is flawed, and the business itself is in jeopardy of failing.

Companies that have been in business for a while and are making acceptable profits have a proven business model—because there is hard evidence that their strategies are capable of profitability. Companies that are in a start-up mode or that are losing money have questionable business models; their strategies have yet to produce good bottom-line results, putting their story line about how they intend to make money and their viability as business enterprises in doubt.

Magazines and newspapers employ a business model based on generating sufficient subscriptions and advertising to cover the costs of delivering their products to readers. Cable TV companies, cell-phone providers, record clubs, satellite radio companies, and Internet service providers also employ a subscription-based business model. The business model of network TV and radio broadcasters entails providing free programming to audiences but charging advertising fees based on audience size. McDonald's invented the business model for fast food—economical quick-service meals at clean, convenient locations. Wal-Mart has perfected the business model for big-box discount retailing—a model also used by Home Depot, Costco, and Target. Gillette's business model in razor blades involves selling a "master product"—the razor—at an attractively low price and then making money on repeat purchases— the razor blades. Printer manufacturers like Hewlett-Packard, Lexmark, and Epson pursue much the same business model as Gillette—selling printers at a low (virtually break-even) price and making large profit margins on the repeat purchases of printer supplies, especially ink cartridges. Companies like Dell and Avon employ a direct sales business model that helps keep prices low by cutting out the costs of reaching consumers through distributors and retail dealers. Illustration Capsule 1.2 discusses the contrasting business models of Microsoft and Red Hat.

WHAT MAKES A STRATEGY A WINNER?

Three questions can be used to test the merits of one strategy versus another and distinguish a winning strategy from a so-so or flawed strategy:

1. *How well does the strategy fit the company's situation?* To qualify as a winner, a strategy has to be well matched to industry and competitive conditions, a company's best market opportunities, and other aspects of the enterprise's external environment. At the same time, it has to be tailored to the company's resource strengths and weaknesses, competencies, and competitive capabilities. Unless a strategy exhibits tight fit with both the external and internal aspects of a company's overall situation, it is likely to produce less than the best possible business results.

> **Core Concept**
> A winning strategy must fit the enterprise's external and internal situation, build sustainable competitive advantage, and improve company performance.

2. *Is the strategy helping the company achieve a sustainable competitive advantage?* Winning strategies enable a company to achieve a competitive advantage that is durable. The bigger and more durable the competitive edge that a strategy helps build, the more powerful and appealing it is.

3. *Is the strategy resulting in better company performance?* A good strategy boosts company performance. Two kinds of performance improvements tell the most about the caliber of a company's strategy: (*a*) gains in profitability and financial strength, and (*b*) gains in the company's competitive strength and market standing.

Once a company commits to a particular strategy and enough time elapses to assess how well it fits the situation and whether it is actually delivering competitive advantage and better performance, then one can determine what grade to assign that strategy. Strategies that come up short on one or more of the above questions are plainly less appealing than strategies that pass all three test questions with flying colors.

Managers can also use the same questions to pick and choose among alternative strategic actions. A company evaluating which of several strategic options to employ can evaluate how well each option measures up against each of the three questions. The strategic option with the highest prospective passing scores on all three questions can be regarded as the best or most attractive strategic alternative.

Other criteria for judging the merits of a particular strategy include internal consistency and unity among all the pieces of strategy, the degree of risk the strategy poses as compared to alternative strategies, and the degree to which it is flexible and adaptable to changing circumstances. These criteria are relevant and merit consideration, but they seldom override the importance of the three test questions posed above.

Illustration Capsule 1.2

Microsoft and Red Hat: Two Contrasting Business Models

The strategies of rival companies are often predicated on strikingly different business models. Consider, for example, the business models for Microsoft and Red Hat in operating system software for personal computers (PCs).

Microsoft's business model for making money from its Windows operating system products is based on the following revenue-cost-profit economics:

- Employ a cadre of highly skilled programmers to develop proprietary code; keep the source code hidden so as to keep the inner workings of the software proprietary.

- Sell the resulting operating system and software package to PC makers and to PC users at relatively attractive prices (around $75 to PC makers and about $100 at retail to PC users); strive to maintain a 90 percent or more market share of the 150 million PCs sold annually worldwide.

- Strive for big-volume sales. Most of Microsoft's costs arise on the front end in developing the software and are thus fixed; the variable costs of producing and packaging the CDs provided to users are only a couple of dollars per copy—once the break-even volume is reached, Microsoft's revenues from additional sales are almost pure profit.

- Provide a modest level of technical support to users at no cost.

- Keep rejuvenating revenues by periodically introducing next-generation software versions with features that will induce PC users to upgrade the operating system on previously purchased PCs to the new version.

Red Hat, a company formed to market its own version of the Linux open-source operating system, employs a business model based on sharply different revenue-cost-profit economics:

- Rely on the collaborative efforts of volunteer programmers from all over the world who contribute bits and pieces of code to improve and polish the Linux system. The global community of thousands of programmers who work on Linux in their spare time do what they do because they love it, because they are fervent believers that all software should be free (as in free speech), and in some cases because they are anti-Microsoft and want to have a part in undoing what they see as a Microsoft monopoly.

- Collect and test enhancements and new applications submitted by the open-source community of volunteer programmers. Linux's originator, Linus Torvalds, and a team of 300-plus Red Hat engineers and software developers evaluate which incoming submissions merit inclusion in new releases of Linux—the evaluation and integration of new submissions are Red Hat's only upfront product development costs.

- Market the upgraded and tested family of Red Hat products to large enterprises and charge them a subscription fee that includes 24/7 support within one hour in seven languages. Provide subscribers with updated versions of Linux every 12–18 months to maintain the subscriber base.

- Make the source code open and available to all users, allowing them to create a customized version of Linux.

- Capitalize on the specialized expertise required to use Linux in multiserver, multiprocessor applications by providing fees-based training, consulting, software customization, and client-directed engineering to Linux users. Red Hat offers Linux certification training programs at all skill levels at more than 60 global locations—Red Hat certification in the use of Linux is considered the best in the world.

Microsoft's business model—sell proprietary code software and give service away free—is a proven moneymaker that generates billions in profits annually. In contrast, the jury is still out on Red Hat's business model of selling subscriptions to open-source software to large corporations and deriving substantial revenues from the sales of technical support (included in the subscription cost), training, consulting, software customization, and engineering to generate revenues sufficient to cover costs and yield a profit. Red Hat posted losses of $140 million on revenues of $79 million in fiscal year 2002 and losses of $6.6 million on revenues of $91 million in fiscal year 2003, but it earned $14 million on revenues of $126 million in fiscal 2004. The profits came from a shift in Red Hat's business model that involved putting considerably more emphasis on getting large corporations to purchase subscriptions to the latest Linux updates. In 2005, about 75 percent of Red Hat's revenues came from large enterprise subscriptions, compared to about 53 percent in 2003.

Source: Company documents and information posted on www.microsoft.com and www.redhat.com. (accessed August 10, 2005).

WHY ARE CRAFTING AND EXECUTING STRATEGY IMPORTANT?

Crafting and executing strategy are top-priority managerial tasks for two very big reasons. First, there is a compelling need for managers to *proactively shape*, or *craft*, how the company's business will be conducted. A clear and reasoned strategy is management's prescription for doing business, its road map to competitive advantage, its game plan for pleasing customers and improving financial performance. Winning in the marketplace requires a well-conceived, opportunistic strategy, usually one characterized by strategic offensives to outinnovate and outmaneuver rivals and secure sustainable competitive advantage, then using this market edge to achieve superior financial performance. A powerful strategy that delivers a home run in the marketplace can propel a firm from a trailing position into a leading one, clearing the way for its products/services to become the industry standard. High-achieving enterprises are nearly always the product of astute, creative, proactive strategy making that sets a company apart from its rivals. Companies don't get to the top of the industry rankings or stay there with imitative strategies or with strategies built around timid actions to try to do better. And only a handful of companies can boast of strategies that hit home runs in the marketplace due to lucky breaks or the good fortune of having stumbled into the right market at the right time with the right product. There can be little argument that a company's strategy matters—and matters a lot.

Second, a *strategy-focused enterprise* is more likely to be a strong bottom-line performer than a company whose management views strategy as secondary and puts its priorities elsewhere. There's no escaping the fact that the quality of managerial strategy making and strategy execution has a highly positive impact on revenue growth, earnings, and return on investment. A company that lacks clear-cut direction, has vague or undemanding performance targets, has a muddled or flawed strategy, or can't seem to execute its strategy competently is a company whose financial performance is probably suffering, whose business is at long-term risk, and whose management is sorely lacking. In contrast, when crafting and executing a winning strategy drive management's whole approach to operating the enterprise, the odds are much greater that the initiatives and activities of different divisions, departments, managers, and work groups will be unified into a *coordinated, cohesive effort*. Mobilizing the full complement of company resources in a total team effort behind good execution of the chosen strategy and achievement of the targeted performance allows a company to operate at full power. The chief executive officer of one successful company put it well when he said:

> In the main, our competitors are acquainted with the same fundamental concepts and techniques and approaches that we follow, and they are as free to pursue them as we are. More often than not, the difference between their level of success and ours lies in the relative thoroughness and self-discipline with which we and they develop and execute our strategies for the future.

Good Strategy + Good Strategy Execution = Good Management

Crafting and executing strategy are core management functions. Among all the things managers do, nothing affects a company's ultimate success or failure more fundamentally than how well its management team charts the company's direction, develops

Core Concept
Excellent execution of an excellent strategy is the best test of managerial excellence—and the most reliable recipe for turning companies into standout performers.

competitively effective strategic moves and business approaches, and pursues what needs to be done internally to produce good day-in, day-out strategy execution and operating excellence. Indeed, *good strategy and good strategy execution are the most trustworthy signs of good management*. Managers don't deserve a gold star for designing a potentially brilliant strategy but failing to put the organizational means in place to carry it out in high-caliber fashion—weak implementation and execution undermine the strategy's potential and pave the way for shortfalls in customer satisfaction and company performance. Competent execution of a mediocre strategy scarcely merits enthusiastic applause for management's efforts either. The rationale for using the twin standards of good strategy making and good strategy execution to determine whether a company is well managed is therefore compelling: *The better conceived a company's strategy and the more competently it is executed, the more likely that the company will be a standout performer in the marketplace.*

Throughout the text chapters to come and the accompanying case collection, the spotlight is trained on the foremost question in running a business enterprise: What must managers do, and do well, to make a company a winner in the marketplace? The answer that emerges, and that becomes the message of this book, is that doing a good job of managing inherently requires good strategic thinking and good management of the strategy-making, strategy-executing process.

The mission of this book is to provide a solid overview of what every business student and aspiring manager needs to know about crafting and executing strategy. This requires exploring what good strategic thinking entails; presenting the core concepts and tools of strategic analysis; describing the ins and outs of crafting and executing strategy; and, through the cases, helping you build your skills both in diagnosing how well the strategy-making, strategy-executing task is being performed in actual companies and in prescribing actions for how the companies in question can improve their approaches to crafting and executing their strategies. At the very least, we hope to convince you that capabilities in crafting and executing strategy are basic to managing successfully and merit a place in a manager's tool kit.

As you tackle the following pages, ponder the following observation by the essayist and poet Ralph Waldo Emerson: "Commerce is a game of skill which many people play, but which few play well." If the content of this book helps you become a more savvy player and equips you to succeed in business, then your journey through these pages will indeed be time well spent.

Key Points

The tasks of crafting and executing company strategies are the heart and soul of managing a business enterprise and winning in the marketplace. A company's strategy is the game plan management is using to stake out a market position, conduct its operations, attract and please customers, compete successfully, and achieve organizational objectives. The central thrust of a company's strategy is undertaking moves to build and strengthen the company's long-term competitive position and financial performance and, ideally, gain a competitive advantage over rivals that then becomes a company's ticket to above-average profitability. A company's strategy typically evolves and reforms over time, emerging from a blend of (1) proactive and purposeful actions on the part of company managers and (2) as-needed reactions to unanticipated developments and fresh market conditions.

Closely related to the concept of strategy is the concept of a company's business model. A company's business model is management's story line for how and why the company's product offerings and competitive approaches will generate a revenue stream and have an associated cost structure that produces attractive earnings and return on investment—in effect, a company's business model sets forth the economic logic for making money in a particular business, given the company's current strategy.

A winning strategy fits the circumstances of a company's external situation and its internal resource strengths and competitive capabilities, builds competitive advantage, and boosts company performance.

Crafting and executing strategy are core management functions. Whether a company wins or loses in the marketplace is directly attributable to the caliber of a company's strategy and the proficiency with which the strategy is executed.

Exercises

1. Go to Red Hat's Web site (www.redhat.com) and check whether the company's recent financial reports indicate that its business model is working. Is the company sufficiently profitable to validate its business model and strategy? Is its revenue stream from selling training, consulting, and engineering services growing or declining as a percentage of total revenues? Does your review of the company's recent financial performance suggest that its business model and strategy are changing? Read the company's latest statement about its business model and about why it is pursuing the subscription approach (as compared to Microsoft's approach of selling copies of its operating software directly to PC manufacturers and individuals).

2. From your perspective as a cable or satellite service consumer, does Comcast's strategy as described in Illustration Capsule 1.1 seem to be well matched to industry and competitive conditions? Does the strategy seem to be keyed to maintaining a cost advantage, offering differentiating features, serving the unique needs of a niche, or developing resource strengths and competitive capabilities rivals can't imitate or trump (or a mixture of these)? Do you think Comcast's strategy has evolved in recent years? Why or why not? What is there about Comcast's strategy that can lead to sustainable competitive advantage?

3. In 2003, Levi Strauss & Company announced it would close its two remaining U.S. apparel plants to finalize its transition from a clothing manufacturer to a marketing, sales, and design company. Beginning in 2004, all Levi's apparel would be produced by contract manufacturers located in low-wage countries. As recently as 1990, Levi Strauss had produced 90 percent of its apparel in company-owned plants in the United States employing over 20,000 production workers. With every plant closing, Levi Strauss & Company provided severance and job retraining packages to affected workers and cash payments to small communities where its plants were located. However, the economies of many small communities had yet to recover and some employees had found it difficult to match their previous levels of compensation and benefits.

    Review Levi Strauss & Company's discussion of its Global Sourcing and Operating Guidelines at www.levistrauss.com/responsibility/conduct. Does the company's strategy fulfill the company's ethical duties to all stakeholders—owners/shareholders, employees, customers, suppliers, the communities in which it operates, and society at large? Does Levi Strauss's strategy to outsource all of its manufacturing operations to low-wage countries pass the moral scrutiny test given that 20,000 workers lost their jobs?

chapter two

The Managerial Process of Crafting and Executing Strategy

Unless we change our direction we are likely to end up where we are headed.

—Ancient Chinese proverb

If we can know where we are and something about how we got there, we might see where we are trending—and if the outcomes which lie naturally in our course are unacceptable, to make timely change.

—Abraham Lincoln

If you don't know where you are going, any road will take you there.

—The Koran

Management's job is not to see the company as it is . . . but as it can become.

—John W. Teets
Former CEO

C rafting and executing strategy are the heart and soul of managing a business enterprise. But exactly what is involved in developing a strategy and executing it proficiently? What are the various components of the strategy-making, strategy-executing process? And to what extent are company personnel—aside from top executives—involved in the process? In this chapter we present an overview of the managerial ins and outs of crafting and executing company strategies. Special attention will be given to management's direction-setting responsibilities—charting a strategic course, setting performance targets, and choosing a strategy capable of producing the desired outcomes. We will also examine which kinds of strategic decisions are made at which levels of management and the roles and responsibilities of the company's board of directors in the strategy-making, strategy-executing process.

WHAT DOES THE STRATEGY-MAKING, STRATEGY-EXECUTING PROCESS ENTAIL?

The managerial process of crafting and executing a company's strategy consists of five interrelated and integrated phases:

1. *Developing a strategic vision* of where the company needs to head and what its future product/market/customer technology focus should be.
2. *Setting objectives* and using them as yardsticks for measuring the company's performance and progress.
3. *Crafting a strategy to achieve the objectives* and move the company along the strategic course that management has charted.
4. *Implementing and executing the chosen strategy efficiently and effectively.*
5. *Evaluating performance and initiating corrective adjustments* in the company's long-term direction, objectives, strategy, or execution in light of actual experience, changing conditions, new ideas, and new opportunities.

Figure 2.1 displays this five-phase process. Let's examine each phase in enough detail to set the stage for the forthcoming chapters and give you a bird's-eye view of what this book is about.

Figure 2.1 **The Strategy-Making, Strategy-Executing Process**

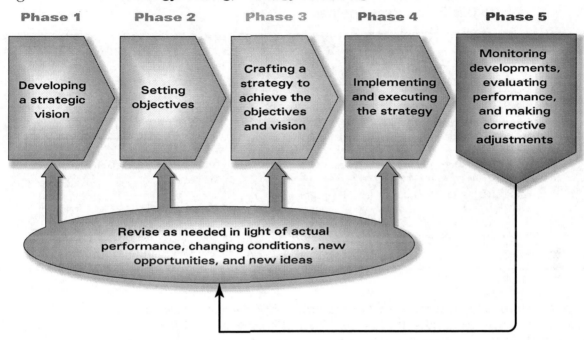

DEVELOPING A STRATEGIC VISION: PHASE 1 OF THE STRATEGY-MAKING, STRATEGY-EXECUTING PROCESS

Very early in the strategy-making process, a company's senior managers must wrestle with the issue of what path the company should take and what changes in the company's product/market/customer/technology focus would improve its market position and future prospects. Deciding to commit the company to one path versus another pushes managers to draw some carefully reasoned conclusions about how to modify the company's business makeup and what market position it should stake out. A number of direction-shaping factors need to be considered in deciding where to head and why such a direction makes good business sense—see Table 2.1.

Top management's views and conclusions about the company's direction and future product/market/customer/technology focus constitute a **strategic vision** for the company. A strategic vision delineates management's aspirations for the business, providing a panoramic view of "where we are going" and a convincing rationale for why this makes good business sense for the company. A strategic vision thus points an organization in a particular direction, charts a strategic path, and molds organizational identity.A clearly articulated strategic vision communicates management's aspirations to stakeholders and helps steer the energies of company personnel in a common direction. For instance, Henry Ford's vision of a car in every garage had power because it captured the imagination of others, aided internalefforts to mobilize the Ford Motor Company's resources, and served as a reference point for gauging the merits of the company's strategic actions.

Core Concept
A *strategic vision* describes the route a company intends to take in developing and strengthening its business. It lays out the company's strategic course in preparing for the future.

Table 2.1   **Factors to Consider in Deciding to Commit the Company to One Path versus Another**

External Considerations	Internal Considerations
• Is the outlook for the company promising if it simply maintains its product/market/customer/technology focus? Does sticking with the company's current strategic course present attractive growth opportunities? • Are changes under way in the market and competitive landscape acting to enhance or weaken the company's prospects? • What, if any, new customer groups and/or geographic markets should the company get in position to serve? • Which emerging market opportunities should the company pursue? Which ones should not be pursued? • Should the company plan to abandon any of the markets, market segments, or customer groups it is currently serving?	• What are the company's ambitions? What industry standing should the company have? • Will the company's present business generate sufficient growth and profitability in the years ahead to please shareholders? • What organizational strengths ought to be leveraged in terms of adding new products or services and getting into new businesses? • Is the company stretching its resources too thin by trying to compete in too many markets or segments, some of which are unprofitable? • Is the company's technological focus too broad or too narrow? Are any changes needed?

Well-conceived visions are *distinctive* and *specific* to a particular organization; they avoid generic feel-good statements like "We will become a global leader and the first choice of customers in every market we choose to serve"—which could apply to any of hundreds of organizations.[1] And they are not the product of a committee charged with coming up with an innocuous but well-meaning one-sentence vision that wins consensus approval from various stakeholders. Nicely worded vision statements with no specifics about the company's product/market/customer/technology focus fall well short of what it takes for a vision to measure up. A strategic vision proclaiming management's quest "to be the market leader" or "to be the first choice of customers" or "to be the most innovative" or "to be recognized as the best company in the industry" offers scant guidance about a company's direction and what changes and challenges lie on the road ahead.

For a strategic vision to function as a valuable managerial tool, it must (1) provide understanding of what management wants its business to look like and (2) provide managers with a reference point in making strategic decisions and preparing the company for the future. It must say something definitive about how the company's leaders intend to position the company beyond where it is today. A good vision always needs to be a bit beyond a company's reach, but progress toward the vision is what unifies the efforts of company personnel. Table 2.2 lists some characteristics of an effectively worded strategic vision.

A sampling of strategic visions currently in use shows a range from strong and clear to overly general and generic. A surprising number of the visions found on company Web sites and in annual reports are vague and unrevealing, saying very little about the company's future product/market/customer/technology focus. Some are nice-sounding but say little. Others read like something written by a committee to win the support of different stakeholders. And some are so short on specifics as to apply to most any company in any industry. Many read like a public relations statement—high-sounding words that someone came up with because it is fashionable for companies to have an official vision statement.[2] Table 2.3 provides a list of the most

Table 2.2 **Characteristics of an Effectively Worded Strategic Vision**

Graphic	Paints a picture of the kind of company that management is trying to create and the market position(s) the company is striving to stake out.
Directional	Is forward-looking; describes the strategic course that management has charted and the kinds of product/market/customer/technology changes that will help the company prepare for the future.
Focused	Is specific enough to provide managers with guidance in making decisions and allocating resources.
Flexible	Is not a once-and-for-all-time statement—the directional course that management has charted may have to be adjusted as product/market/customer/technology circumstances change.
Feasible	Is within the realm of what the company can reasonably expect to achieve in due time.
Desirable	Indicates why the chosen path makes good business sense and is in the long-term interests of stakeholders (especially shareowners, employees, and customers).
Easy to communicate	Is explainable in 5–10 minutes and, ideally, can be reduced to a simple, memorable slogan (like Henry Ford's famous vision of "a car in every garage").

Source: Based partly on John P. Kotter, *Leading Change* (Boston: Harvard Business School Press, 1996), p. 72.

common shortcomings in strategic vision statements. The one- or two-sentence vision statements most companies make available to the public, of course, provide only a glimpse of what company executives are really thinking and the strategic course they have charted—company personnel nearly always have a much better understanding of where the company is headed and why that is revealed in the official vision. But the real purpose of a strategic vision is to serve as a management tool for giving the organization a sense of direction. Like any tool, it can be used properly or improperly, either clearly conveying a company's strategic course or not.

Table 2.3 **Common Shortcomings in Company Vision Statements**

Vague or incomplete	Is short on specifics about where the company is headed or what the company is doing to prepare for the future.
Not forward-looking	Does not indicate whether or how management intends to alter the company's current product/market/customer/technology focus.
Too broad	Is so umbrella-like and all-inclusive that the company could head in most any direction, pursue most any opportunity, or enter most any business.
Bland or uninspiring	Lacks the power to motivate company personnel or inspire shareholder confidence about the company's direction or future prospects.
Not distinctive	Provides no unique company identity; could apply to companies in any of several industries (or at least several rivals operating in the same industry or market arena).
Too reliant on superlatives	Does not say anything specific about the company's strategic course beyond the pursuit of such lofty accolades as *best, most successful, recognized leader, global or worldwide leader,* or *first choice of customers.*

Sources: Based on information in Hugh Davidson, *The Committed Enterprise: How to Make Vision and Values Work* (Oxford: Butterworth Heinemann, 2002), Chapter 2, and Michel Robert, *Strategy Pure and Simple II* (New York: McGraw-Hill, 1992), Chapters 2, 3, and 6.

Illustration Capsule 2.1

Examples of Strategic Visions—How Well Do They Measure Up?

Using the information in Tables 2.2 and 2.3, critique the following strategic visions and rank them from 1 (best) to 7 (in need of substantial improvement).

RED HAT

To extend our position as the most trusted Linux and open source provider to the enterprise. We intend to grow the market for Linux through a complete range of enterprise Red Hat Linux software, a powerful Internet management platform, and associated support and services.

WELLS FARGO

We want to satisfy all of our customers' financial needs, help them succeed financially, be the premier provider of financial services in every one of our markets, and be known as one of America's great companies.

HILTON HOTELS CORPORATION

Our vision is to be the first choice of the world's travelers. Hilton intends to build on the rich heritage and strength of our brands by:

- Consistently delighting our customers
- Investing in our team members
- Delivering innovative products and services
- Continuously improving performance
- Increasing shareholder value

- Creating a culture of pride
- Strengthening the loyalty of our constituents

THE DENTAL PRODUCTS DIVISION OF 3M CORPORATION

Become THE supplier of choice to the global dental professional markets, providing world-class quality and innovative products.
[*Note:* All employees of the division wear badges bearing these words, and whenever a new product or business procedure is being considered, management asks "Is this representative of THE leading dental company?"]

CATERPILLAR

Be the global leader in customer value.

eBAY

Provide a global trading platform where practically anyone can trade practically anything.

H. J. HEINZ COMPANY

Be the world's premier food company, offering nutritious, superior tasting foods to people everywhere. Being the premier food company does not mean being the biggest but it does mean being the best in terms of consumer value, customer service, employee talent, and consistent and predictable growth.

Sources: Company documents and Web sites.

Illustration Capsule 2.1 provides examples of strategic visions of several prominent companies. See if you can tell which ones are mostly meaningless or nice-sounding and which ones are managerially useful in communicating "where we are headed and the kind of company we are trying to become".

A Strategic Vision Covers Different Ground than the Typical Mission Statement

The defining characteristic of a well-conceived *strategic vision* is what it says about the company's *future strategic course*—"the direction we are headed and what our future product/market/customer/technology focus will be."

In contrast, the *mission statements* that one finds in company annual reports or posted on company Web sites typically provide a brief overview of the company's *present* business purpose and raison d'être, and sometimes its geographic coverage or standing as a market leader. They may or may not single out the company's present products/services, the buyer needs it is seeking to satisfy, the customer groups it serves, or its technological and business capabilities. But rarely do company mission statements say anything about where the company is headed, the anticipated changes in its business, or its aspirations; hence, they lack the essential forward-looking quality of a strategic vision in specifying a company's direction and *future* product/market/customer/technology focus.

Consider, for example, the mission statement of Trader Joe's (a specialty grocery chain):

> The mission of Trader Joe's is to give our customers the best food and beverage values that they can find anywhere and to provide them with the information required for informed buying decisions. We provide these with a dedication to the highest quality of customer satisfaction delivered with a sense of warmth, friendliness, fun, individual pride, and company spirit.

Note that Trader Joe's mission statement does a good job of conveying "who we are, what we do, and why we are here," but provides no sense of "where we are headed." (Some companies use the term *business purpose* instead of *mission statement* in describing themselves; in practice, there seems to be no meaningful difference between the terms *mission statement* and *business purpose*—which one is used is a matter of preference.)

> The distinction between a strategic vision and a mission statement is fairly clear-cut: A strategic vision portrays a company's *future* business scope ("where we are going"), whereas a company's mission typically describes its *present* business and purpose ("who we are, what we do, and why we are here").

There is value in distinguishing between the forward-looking concept of a strategic vision and the here-and-now theme of the typical mission statement. Thus, to mirror actual practice, we will use the term *mission statement* to refer to an enterprise's description of its *present* business and its purpose for existence. Ideally, a company mission statement is sufficiently descriptive to *identify the company's products/services and specify the buyer needs it seeks to satisfy, the customer groups or markets it is endeavoring to serve, and its approach to pleasing customers.* Not many company mission statements fully reveal *all* of these facets (and a few companies have worded their mission statements so obscurely as to mask what they are about), but most company mission statements do a decent job of indicating "who we are, what we do, and why we are here."

An example of a well-formed mission statement with ample specifics is that of the U.S. government's Occupational Safety and Health Administration (OSHA): "to assure the safety and health of America's workers by setting and enforcing standards; providing training, outreach, and education; establishing partnerships; and encouraging continual improvement in workplace safety and health." Google's mission statement, while short, still captures the essence of the company: "to organize the world's information and make it universally accessible and useful." Likewise, Blockbuster has a brief mission statement that cuts right to the chase: "To help people transform ordinary nights into BLOCKBUSTER nights by being their complete source for movies and games."

An example of a not-so-revealing mission statement is that of the present-day Ford Motor Company: "We are a global family with a proud heritage passionately committed to providing personal mobility for people around the world. We anticipate consumer need and deliver outstanding products and services that improve people's lives." A person who has never heard of Ford would not know from reading the company's mission statement that it is a global producer of motor vehicles. Similarly, Microsoft's mission statement—"to help people and businesses throughout the world realize their full potential"—says nothing about its products or business makeup and could apply to many companies in many different industries. Coca-Cola, which markets nearly 400 beverage brands in over 200 countries, also has an overly general mission statement: "to benefit and refresh everyone it touches." A mission statement that provides scant indication of "who we are and what we do" has no substantive value.

Occasionally, companies couch their mission statements in terms of making a profit. This is misguided. Profit is more correctly an *objective* and a *result* of what a company does. Moreover, earning a profit is the obvious intent of every commercial enterprise. Such companies as BMW, McDonald's, Shell Oil, Procter & Gamble, Nintendo, and Nokia are each striving to earn a profit for shareholders; but plainly the fundamentals of their businesses are substantially different when it comes to "who we are and what we do." It is management's answer to "Make a profit doing what and for whom?" that reveals a company's true substance and business purpose. *A well-conceived mission statement distinguishes a company's business makeup from that of other profit-seeking enterprises in language specific enough to give the company its own identity.*

Communicating the Strategic Vision

Effectively communicating the strategic vision down the line to lower-level managers and employees is as important as choosing a strategically sound long-term direction. Not only do people have a need to believe that senior management knows where it's trying to take the company and understand what changes lie ahead both externally and internally, but unless and until frontline employees understand why the strategic course that management has charted is reasonable and beneficial, they are unlikely to rally behind managerial efforts to get the organization moving in the intended direction.

Winning the support of organization members for the vision nearly always means putting "where we are going and why" in writing, distributing the written vision organizationwide, and having executives personally explain the vision and its rationale to as many people as feasible. Ideally, executives should present their vision for the company in a manner that reaches out and grabs people. An engaging and convincing strategic vision has enormous motivational value—for the same reason that a stonemason is more inspired by "building a great cathedral for the ages" than by "laying stones to create floors and walls." When managers articulate a vivid and compelling case for where the company is headed, organization members begin to say, "This is interesting and has a lot of merit. I want to be involved and do my part to helping make it happen." The more that a vision evokes positive support and excitement, the greater its impact in terms of arousing a committed organizational effort and getting company personnel to move in a common direction.[3] Thus executive ability to paint a convincing and inspiring picture of a company's journey and destination is an important element of effective strategic leadership.

> **Core Concept**
> An effectively communicated vision is a valuable management tool for enlisting the commitment of company personnel to actions that get the company moving in the intended direction.

Expressing the Essence of the Vision in a Slogan
The task of effectively conveying the vision to company personnel is assisted when management can capture the vision of where to head in a catchy or easily remembered slogan. A number of organizations have summed up their vision in a brief phrase:

- Levi Strauss & Company: "We will clothe the world by marketing the most appealing and widely worn casual clothing in the world."
- Nike: "To bring innovation and inspiration to every athlete in the world."

- Mayo Clinic: "The best care to every patient every day."
- Scotland Yard: "To make London the safest major city in the world."
- Greenpeace: "To halt environmental abuse and promote environmental solutions."
- Charles Schwab: "To provide customers with the most useful and ethical financial services in the world."

> Strategic visions become real only when the vision statement is imprinted in the minds of organization members and then translated into hard objectives and strategies.

Creating a short slogan to illuminate an organization's direction and purpose and then using it repeatedly as a reminder of "where we are headed and why" helps rally organization members to hurdle whatever obstacles lie in the company's path and maintain their focus.

Breaking Down Resistance to a New Strategic Vision   It is particularly important for executives to provide a compelling rationale for a dramatically *new* strategic vision and company direction. When company personnel don't understand or accept the need for redirecting organizational efforts, they are prone to resist change. Hence, reiterating the basis for the new direction, addressing employee concerns head-on, calming fears, lifting spirits, and providing updates and progress reports as events unfold all become part of the task of mobilizing support for the vision and winning commitment to needed actions.

Just stating the case for a new direction once is not enough. Executives must repeat the reasons for the new direction often and convincingly at company gatherings and in company publications, and they must reinforce their pronouncements with updates about how the latest information confirms the choice of direction and the validity of the vision. Unless and until more and more people are persuaded of the merits of management's new vision and the vision gains wide acceptance, it will be a struggle to move the organization down the newly chosen path.

Recognizing Strategic Inflection Points   Sometimes there's an order-of-magnitude change in a company's environment that dramatically alters its prospects and mandates radical revision of its strategic course. Intel's former chairman Andrew Grove has called such occasions *strategic inflection points*—Illustration Capsule 2.2 relates Intel's two encounters with strategic inflection points and the resulting alterations in its strategic vision. As the Intel example forcefully demonstrates, when a company reaches a strategic inflection point, management has some tough decisions to make about the company's course. Often it is a question of what to do to sustain company success, not just how to avoid possible disaster. Responding quickly to unfolding changes in the marketplace lessens a company's chances of becoming trapped in a stagnant or declining business or letting attractive new growth opportunities slip away.

Understanding the Payoffs of a Clear Vision Statement   In sum, a well-conceived, forcefully communicated strategic vision pays off in several respects: (1) it crystallizes senior executives' own views about the firm's long-term direction; (2) it reduces the risk of rudderless decision making; (3) it is a tool for winning the support of organizational members for internal changes that will help make the vision a reality; (4) it provides a beacon for lower-level managers in forming departmental missions, setting departmental objectives, and crafting functional and departmental strategies that are in sync with the company's overall strategy; and (5) it helps an organization prepare for the future. When management is able to demonstrate significant progress in achieving these five benefits, the first step in organizational direction setting has been successfully completed.

Illustration Capsule 2.2
Intel's Two Strategic Inflection Points

Intel Corporation has encountered two strategic inflection points within the past 20 years. The first came in the mid-1980s, when memory chips were Intel's principal business and Japanese manufacturers, intent on dominating the memory chip business, began cutting their prices 10 percent below the prices charged by Intel and other U.S. memory chip manufacturers. Each time U.S. companies matched the Japanese price cuts, the Japanese manufacturers responded with another 10 percent price cut. Intel's management explored a number of strategic options to cope with the aggressive pricing of its Japanese rivals— building a giant memory chip factory to overcome the cost advantage of Japanese producers, investing in research and development (R&D) to come up with a more advanced memory chip, and retreating to niche markets for memory chips that were not of interest to the Japanese.

At the time, Gordon Moore, Intel's chairman and cofounder, and Andrew Grove, Intel's chief executive officer (CEO), jointly concluded that none of these options offered much promise and that the best long-term solution was to abandon the memory chip business even though it accounted for 70 percent of Intel's revenue. Grove, with the concurrence of both Moore and the board of directors, then proceeded to commit Intel's full energies to the business of developing ever more powerful microprocessors for personal computers. Intel had invented microprocessors in the early 1970s but had recently been concentrating on memory chips because of strong competition and excess capacity in the market for microprocessors.

Grove's bold decision to withdraw from memory chips, absorb a $173 million write-off in 1986, and go all out in microprocessors produced a new strategic vision for Intel—becoming the preeminent supplier of microprocessors to the personal computing industry, making the personal computer (PC) the central appliance in the workplace and the home, and being the undisputed leader in driving PC technology forward. Grove's new vision for Intel and the strategic course he charted in 1985 produced spectacular results. Since 1996, over 80 percent of the world's PCs have been made with Intel microprocessors and Intel has become the world's most profitable chip maker.

Intel encountered a second inflection point in 1998, opting to refocus on becoming the preeminent building-block supplier to the Internet economy and spurring efforts to make the Internet more useful. Starting in early 1998 and responding to the mushrooming importance of the Internet, Intel's senior management launched major new initiatives to direct attention and resources to expanding the capabilities of both the PC platform and the Internet. It was this strategic inflection point that led to Intel's latest strategic vision of playing a major role in getting a billion computers connected to the Internet worldwide, installing millions of servers, and building an Internet infrastructure that would support trillions of dollars of e-commerce and serve as a worldwide communication medium.

Source: Andrew S. Grove, *Only the Paranoid Survive* (New York: Doubleday-Currency, 1996), company documents and press releases, and information posted at www.intel.com.

Linking the Vision/Mission with Company Values

Many companies have developed a statement of values to guide the company's pursuit of its vision/mission, strategy, and ways of operating. By **values** (or *core values,* as they are often called), we mean the beliefs, traits, and ways of doing things that management has determined should guide the pursuit of its vision and strategy, the conduct of company's operations, and the behavior of company personnel.

Values, good and bad, exist in every organization. They relate to such things as fair treatment, integrity, ethical behavior, innovation, teamwork, top-notch quality, superior customer service, social responsibility, and community citizenship. Most companies have built their statements of values around four to eight traits that company personnel are expected to display and that are supposed to be mirrored in how the company conducts its business.

> **Core Concept**
> A company's **values** are the beliefs, traits, and behavioral norms that company personnel are expected to display in conducting the company's business and pursuing its strategic vision and strategy.

At Kodak, the core values are respect for the dignity of the individual, uncompromising integrity, unquestioned trust, constant credibility, continual improvement and personal renewal, and open celebration of individual and team achievements. Home Depot embraces eight values (entrepreneurial spirit, excellent customer service, giving back to the community, respect for all people, doing the right thing, taking care of people, building strong relationships, and creating shareholder value) in its quest to be the world's leading home improvement retailer by operating warehouse stores filled with a wide assortment of products at the lowest prices with trained associates giving absolutely the best customer service in the industry. Toyota preaches respect for and development of its employees, teamwork, getting quality right the first time, learning, continuous improvement, and embracing change in its pursuit of low-cost, top-notch manufacturing excellence in motor vehicles.[4] DuPont stresses four values—safety, ethics, respect for people, and environmental stewardship; the first three have been in place since the company was founded 200 years ago by the DuPont family. Heinz uses the acronym PREMIER to identify seven values that "define to the world and to ourselves who we are and what we stand for":

- *P*assion . . . to be passionate about winning and about our brands, products and people, thereby delivering superior value to our shareholders.
- *R*isk Tolerance . . . to create a culture where entrepreneurship and prudent risk taking are encouraged and rewarded.
- *E*xcellence . . . to be the best in quality and in everything we do.
- *M*otivation . . . to celebrate success, recognizing and rewarding the achievements of individuals and teams.
- *I*nnovation . . . to innovate in everything, from products to processes.
- *E*mpowerment . . . to empower our talented people to take the initiative and to do what's right.
- *R*espect . . . to act with integrity and respect towards all.

Do companies practice what they preach when it comes to their professed values? Sometimes no, sometimes yes—at runs the gamut. At one extreme are companies with window-dressing values; the values statement is merely a collection of nice words and phrases that may be given lip service by top executives but have little discernible impact on either how company personnel behave or how the company operates. Such companies have values statements because such statements are in vogue and are seen as making the company look good. At the other extreme are companies whose executives take the stated values very seriously—the values are widely adopted by company personnel, are ingrained in the corporate culture, and are mirrored in how company personnel conduct themselves and the company's business on a daily basis. Top executives at companies on this end of the values-statement gamut genuinely believe in the importance of grounding company operations on sound values and ways of doing business. In their view, holding company personnel accountable for displaying the stated values is a way of infusing the company with the desired character, identity, and behavioral norms—the values become the company's equivalent of DNA.

At companies where the stated values are real rather than cosmetic, managers connect values to the pursuit of the strategic vision and mission in one of two ways. In companies with long-standing values that are deeply entrenched in the corporate culture, senior managers are careful to craft a vision, mission, and strategy that match established values, and they reiterate how the values-based behavioral norms contribute to the company's business success. If the company changes to a different vision or strategy, executives take care to explain how and why the core values continue to be relevant. Few companies with sincere commitment to established core values ever undertake strategic moves that conflict with ingrained values.

In new companies or companies with weak or incomplete sets of values, top management considers what values, behaviors, and business conduct should characterize the company and that will help drive the vision and strategy forward. Then values and behaviors that complement and support vision are drafted and circulated among managers and employees for discussion and possible modification. A final values statement that incorporates the desired behaviors and traits and that connects to the vision/mission is then officially adopted. Some companies combine their vision and values into a single statement or document, circulate it to all organization members, and in many instances post the vision/mission and values statement on the company's Web site. Illustration Capsule 2.3 describes the connection between Yahoo's mission and its core values.

Of course, a wide gap sometimes opens between a company's stated values and its actual business practices. Enron, for example, touted four corporate values—respect, integrity, communication, and excellence—but some top officials engaged in dishonest and fraudulent maneuvers that were concealed by "creative" accounting; the lack of integrity on the part of Enron executives and their deliberate failure to accurately communicate with shareholders and regulators in the company's financial filings led directly to the company's dramatic bankruptcy and implosion over a six-week period, along with criminal indictments, fines, or jail terms for over a dozen Enron executives. Once one of the world's most distinguished public accounting firms, Arthur Andersen was renowned for its commitment to the highest standards of audit integrity, but its high-profile audit failures and ethical lapses at Enron, WorldCom, and other companies led to Andersen's demise—in 2002, it was indicted for destroying Enron-related documents to thwart investigators.

SETTING OBJECTIVES: PHASE 2 OF THE STRATEGY-MAKING, STRATEGY-EXECUTING PROCESS

The managerial purpose of setting **objectives** is to convert the strategic vision into specific performance targets—results and outcomes the company's management wants to achieve. Objectives represent a managerial commitment to achieving particular results and outcomes. Well-stated objectives are *quantifiable,* or *measurable,* and contain a *deadline for achievement.* As Bill Hewlett, cofounder of Hewlett-Packard, shrewdly observed, "You cannot manage what you cannot measure. . . . And what gets measured gets done."[5] Concrete, measurable objectives are managerially valuable because they serve as yardsticks for tracking a company's performance and progress—a company that consistently meets or beats its performance targets is generally a better overall performer than a company that frequently falls short of achieving its objectives. Indeed, the experiences of countless companies and managers teach that precisely spelling out *how much* of *what kind* of performance *by when* and then pressing forward with actions and incentives calculated to help achieve the targeted outcomes greatly improve a company's actual performance. Such an approach definitely beats setting vague targets like "maximize profits," "reduce costs," "become more efficient," or "increase sales," which specify neither how much nor when. Similarly, exhorting

> **Core Concept**
> **Objectives** are an organization's performance targets—the results and outcomes management wants to achieve. They function as yardsticks for measuring how well the organization is doing.

Illustration Capsule 2.3

The Connection between Yahoo's Mission and Core Values

Our mission is to be the most essential global Internet service for consumers and businesses. How we pursue that mission is influenced by a set of core values—the standards that guide interactions with fellow Yahoos, the principles that direct how we service our customers, the ideals that drive what we do and how we do it. Many of our values were put into practice by two guys in a trailer some time ago; others reflect ambitions as our company grows. All of them are what we strive to achieve every day.

EXCELLENCE

We are committed to winning with integrity. We know leadership is hard won and should never be taken for granted. We aspire to flawless execution and don't take shortcuts on quality. We seek the best talent and promote its development. We are flexible and learn from our mistakes.

INNOVATION

We thrive on creativity and ingenuity. We seek the innovations and ideas that can change the world. We anticipate market trends and move quickly to embrace them. We are not afraid to take informed, responsible risk.

CUSTOMER FIXATION

We respect our customers above all else and never forget that they come to us by choice. We share a personal responsibility to maintain our customers' loyalty and trust. We listen and respond to our customers and seek to exceed their expectations.

TEAMWORK

We treat one another with respect and communicate openly. We foster collaboration while maintaining individual accountability. We encourage the best ideas to surface from anywhere within the organization. We appreciate the value of multiple perspectives and diverse expertise.

COMMUNITY

We share an infectious sense of mission to make an impact on society and empower consumers in ways never before possible. We are committed to serving both the Internet community and our own communities.

FUN

We believe humor is essential to success. We applaud irreverence and don't take ourselves too seriously. We celebrate achievement. We yodel.

WHAT YAHOO DOESN'T VALUE

At the end of its values statement, Yahoo made a point of singling out 54 things that it did not value, including bureaucracy, losing, good enough, arrogance, the status quo, following, formality, quick fixes, passing the buck, micromanaging, Monday morning quarterbacks, 20/20 hindsight, missing the boat, playing catch-up, punching the clock, and "shoulda coulda woulda."

Source: http://docs.yahoo.com/info/values (accessed August 20, 2005).

company personnel to try hard or do the best they can, and then living with whatever results they deliver, is clearly inadequate.

The Imperative of Setting Stretch Objectives   Ideally, managers ought to use the objective-setting exercise as a tool for *stretching an organization to perform at its full potential and deliver the best possible results.* Challenging company personnel to go all out and deliver "stretch" gains in performance pushes an enterprise to be more inventive, to exhibit more urgency in improving both its financial performance and its business position, and to be more intentional and focused in its actions. Stretch objectives spur exceptional performance and help companies guard against contentment with modest gains in organizational performance. As Mitchell Leibovitz, former CEO of the auto parts and service retailer Pep Boys, once said, "If you want to have ho-hum results, have ho-hum objectives." *There's no better way to avoid ho-hum results than by setting stretch objectives and*

Setting stretch objectives is an effective tool for avoiding ho-hum results.

using compensation incentives to motivate organization members to achieve the stretch performance targets.

What Kinds of Objectives to Set: The Need for a Balanced Scorecard

Two very distinct types of performance yardsticks are required: those relating to *financial performance* and those relating to *strategic performance*—outcomes that indicate a company is strengthening its marketing standing, competitive vitality, and future business prospects. Examples of commonly used **financial objectives** and **strategic objectives** include the following:

> **Core Concept**
> **Financial objectives** relate to the financial performance targets management has established for the organization to achieve. **Strategic objectives** relate to target outcomes that indicate a company is strengthening its market standing, competitive vitality, and future business prospects.

Financial Objectives	Strategic Objectives
• An *x* percent increase in annual revenues • Annual increases in after-tax profits of *x* percent • Annual increases in earnings per share of *x* percent • Annual dividend increases • Larger profit margins • An *x* percent return on capital employed (ROCE) or return on equity (ROE) • Increased shareholder value—in the form of an upward trending stock price and annual dividend increases • Strong bond and credit ratings • Sufficient internal cash flows to fund new capital investment • Stable earnings during periods of recession	• Winning an *x* percent market share • Achieving lower overall costs than rivals • Overtaking key competitors on product performance or quality or customer service • Deriving *x* percent of revenues from the sale of new products introduced within the past five years • Achieving technological leadership • Having better product selection than rivals • Strengthening the company's brand-name appeal • Having stronger national or global sales and distribution capabilities than rivals • Consistently getting new or improved products to market ahead of rivals

Achieving acceptable financial results is a must. Without adequate profitability and financial strength, a company's pursuit of its strategic vision, as well as its long-term health and ultimate survival, is jeopardized. Furthermore, subpar earnings and a weak balance sheet not only alarm shareholders and creditors but also put the jobs of senior executives at risk. However, good financial performance, by itself, is not enough. Of equal or greater importance is a company's strategic performance—outcomes that indicate whether a company's market position and competitiveness are deteriorating, holding steady, or improving.

The Case for a Balanced Scorecard: Improved Strategic Performance Fosters Better Financial Performance   A company's financial performance measures are really *lagging indicators* that reflect the results of past decisions and organizational activities.[6] But a company's past or current financial performance is not a reliable indicator of its future prospects—poor financial performers often turn things around and do better, while good financial performers can fall on hard times. The best and most reliable *leading indicators* of a company's future financial performance and business prospects are strategic outcomes that indicate whether the

> **Core Concept**
> A company that pursues and achieves strategic outcomes that boost its competitiveness and strength in the marketplace is in much better position to improve its future financial performance.

company's competitiveness and market position are stronger or weaker. For instance, if a company has set aggressive strategic objectives and is achieving them—such that its competitive strength and market position are on the rise, then there's reason to expect that its *future* financial performance will be better than its current or past performance. If a company is losing ground to competitors and its market position is slipping—outcomes that reflect weak strategic performance (and, very likely, failure to achieve its strategic objectives), then its ability to maintain its present profitability is highly suspect. Hence, the degree to which a company's managers set, pursue, and achieve stretch strategic objectives tends to be a reliable leading indicator of whether its future financial performance will improve or stall.

Consequently, a *balanced scorecard* for measuring company performance—one that tracks the achievement of both financial objectives and strategic objectives—is optimal.[7] Just tracking a company's financial performance overlooks the fact that what ultimately enables a company to deliver better financial results from its operations is the achievement of strategic objectives that improve its competitiveness and market strength. Indeed, *the surest path to boosting company profitability quarter after quarter and year after year is to relentlessly pursue strategic outcomes that strengthen the company's market position and produce a growing competitive advantage over rivals.*

Roughly 36 percent of global companies and over 100 nonprofit and governmental organizations used the balanced scorecard approach in 2001.[8] A more recent survey of 708 companies on five continents found that 62 percent were using a balanced scorecard to track performance.[9] Organizations that have adopted the balanced scorecard approach to setting objectives and measuring performance include Exxon Mobil, CIGNA, United Parcel Service, Sears, Nova Scotia Power, BMW, AT&T Canada, Chemical Bank, DaimlerChrysler, DuPont, Motorola, Siemens, Wells Fargo, Wendy's, Saatchi & Saatchi, Duke Children's Hospital, U.S. Department of the Army, Tennessee Valley Authority, the United Kingdom's Ministry of Defense, the University of California at San Diego, and the City of Charlotte, North Carolina.[10]

Illustration Capsule 2.4 shows selected objectives of five prominent companies—all employ a combination of strategic and financial objectives.

Both Short-Term and Long-Term Objectives Are Needed   As a rule, a company's set of financial and strategic objectives ought to include both near-term and longer-term performance targets. Having quarterly and annual objectives focuses attention on delivering immediate performance improvements. Targets to be achieved within three to five years prompt considerations of what to do *now* to put the company in position to perform better later. A company that has an objective of doubling its sales within five years can't wait until the third or fourth year to begin growing its sales and customer base. By spelling out annual (or perhaps quarterly) performance targets, management indicates the *speed* at which longer range targets are to be approached. Long-term objectives take on particular importance because it is generally in the best interest of shareholders for companies to be managed for optimal long-term performance. When trade-offs have to be made between achieving long-run objectives and achieving short-run objectives, long-run objectives should take precedence (unless the achievement of one or more short-run performance targets have unique importance). Shareholders are seldom well-served by repeated management actions that sacrifice better long-term performance in order to make quarterly or annual targets.

Strategic Intent: Relentless Pursuit of an Ambitious Strategic Objective
Very ambitious companies often establish a long-term strategic objective that clearly

Illustration Capsule 2.4
Examples of Company Objectives

NISSAN

Increase sales to 4.2 million cars and trucks by 2008 (up from 3 million in 2003); cut purchasing costs 20% and halve the number of suppliers; have zero net debt; maintain a return on invested capital of 20%; maintain a 10% or better operating margin.

McDONALD'S

Place more emphasis on delivering an exceptional customer experience; add approximately 350 net new McDonald's restaurants; reduce general and administrative spending as a percent of total revenues; achieve systemwide sales and revenue growth of 3% to 5%, annual operating income growth of 6% to 7%, and annual returns on incremental invested capital in the high teens.

H. J. HEINZ COMPANY

Achieve 4–6% sales growth, 7–10% growth in operating income, EPS in the range of $2.35 to $2.45, and operating free cash flow of $900 million to $1 billion in fiscal 2006; pay dividends equal to 45–50 percent of earnings; increase the focus on the company's 15 power brands and give top resource priority to those brands with number one and two market positions; continue to introduce new and improved food products; add to the Heinz portfolio of brands by acquiring companies with brands that complement existing brands; increase sales in Russia, Indonesia, China and India by 50 percent in fiscal year 2006 to roughly 6 percent of total sales; and by the end of fiscal 2008, derive approximately 50 percent of sales and profits from North America, 30 percent from Europe, and 20 percent from all other markets.

SEAGATE TECHNOLOGY

Solidify the company's No. 1 position in the overall market for hard-disk drives; get more Seagate drives into popular consumer electronics products; take share away from Western Digital in providing disk drives for Microsoft's Xbox; maintain leadership in core markets and achieve leadership in emerging markets; grow revenues by 10 percent per year; maintain gross margins of 24–26 percent; hold internal operating expenses to 13–13.5 percent of revenue.

3M CORPORATION

To achieve long term sales growth of 5–8% organic plus 2–4% from acquisitions; annual growth in earnings per share of 10% or better, on average; a return on stockholders' equity of 20%–25%; a return on capital employed of 27% or better; double the number of qualified new 3M product ideas and triple the value of products that win in the marketplace; and build the best sales and marketing organization in the world.

Sources: Information posted on company Web sites (accessed August 21, 2005); and "Nissan's Smryna Plant Produces 7 Millionth Vehicle," *Automotive Intelligence News,* August 2, 2005, p. 5.

signals **strategic intent** to be a winner in the marketplace, often against long odds.[11] A company's strategic intent can entail unseating the existing industry leader, becoming the dominant market share leader, delivering the best customer service of any company in the industry (or the world), or turning a new technology into products capable of changing the way people work and live. Nike's strategic intent during the 1960s was to overtake Adidas; this intent connected nicely with Nike's core purpose "to experience the emotion of competition, winning, and crushing competitors." Canon's strategic intent in copying equipment was to "beat Xerox." For some years, Toyota has been driving to overtake General Motors as the world's largest motor vehicle producer—and it surpassed Ford Motor Company in total vehicles sold in 2003, to move into second place. Toyota has expressed its strategic intent in the form of a global market share objective of 15 percent by 2010, up from 5 percent in 1980 and 10 percent in 2003. Starbucks' strategic intent is to make the Starbucks brand the world's most recognized and respected brand.

> **Core Concept**
> A company exhibits **strategic intent** when it relentlessly pursues an ambitious strategic objective, concentrating the full force of its resources and competitive actions on achieving that objective.

Ambitious companies that establish exceptionally bold strategic objectives and have an unshakable commitment to achieving them almost invariably begin with strategic intents that are out of proportion to their immediate capabilities and market grasp. But they pursue their strategic target relentlessly, sometimes even obsessively. They rally the organization around efforts to make the strategic intent a reality. They go all out to marshal the resources and capabilities to close in on their strategic target (which is often global market leadership) as rapidly as they can. They craft potent offensive strategies calculated to throw rivals off-balance, put them on the defensive, and force them into an ongoing game of catch-up. They deliberately try to alter the market contest and tilt the rules for competing in their favor. As a consequence, capably managed up-and-coming enterprises with strategic intents exceeding their present reach and resources are a force to be reckoned with, often proving to be more formidable competitors over time than larger, cash-rich rivals that have modest strategic objectives and market ambitions.

The Need for Objectives at All Organizational Levels   Objective setting should not stop with top management's establishing of companywide performance targets. Company objectives need to be broken down into performance targets for each of the organization's separate businesses, product lines, functional departments, and individual work units. Company performance can't reach full potential unless each organizational unit sets and pursues performance targets that contribute directly to the desired companywide outcomes and results. Objective setting is thus a top-down process that must extend to the lowest organizational levels. And it means that each organizational unit must take care to set performance targets that support—rather than conflict with or negate—the achievement of companywide strategic and financial objectives.

The ideal situation is a team effort in which each organizational unit strives to produce results in its area of responsibility that contribute to the achievement of the company's performance targets and strategic vision. Such consistency signals that organizational units know their strategic role and are on board in helping the company move down the chosen strategic path and produce the desired results.

Objective Setting Needs to Be Top-Down Rather than Bottom-Up   To appreciate why a company's objective-setting process needs to be more top-down than bottom-up, consider the following example. Suppose the senior executives of a diversified corporation establish a corporate profit objective of $500 million for next year. Suppose further that, after discussion between corporate management and the general managers of the firm's five different businesses, each business is given a stretch profit objective of $100 million by year-end (i.e., if the five business divisions contribute $100 million each in profit, the corporation can reach its $500 million profit objective). A concrete result has thus been agreed on and translated into measurable action commitments at two levels in the managerial hierarchy. Next, suppose the general manager of business unit A, after some analysis and discussion with functional area managers, concludes that reaching the $100 million profit objective will require selling 1 million units at an average price of $500 and producing them at an average cost of $400 (a $100 profit margin times 1 million units equals $100 million profit). Consequently, the general manager and the manufacturing manager settle on a production objective of 1 million units at a unit cost of $400; and the general manager and the marketing manager agree on a sales objective of 1 million units and a target selling price of $500. In turn, the marketing manager, after consultation with regional sales personnel, breaks the sales objective of 1 million units into unit sales targets for each sales territory, each item in the product line, and each salesperson. It is logical for organizationwide objectives and strategy to be established first so they can guide objective setting and strategy making at lower levels.

A top-down process of setting companywide performance targets first and then insisting that the financial and strategic performance targets established for business units, divisions, functional departments, and operating units be directly connected to the achievement of company objectives has two powerful advantages: One, it helps produce *cohesion* among the objectives and strategies of different parts of the organization. Two, it helps *unify internal efforts* to move the company along the chosen strategic path. If top management, desirous of involving many organization members, allows objective setting to start at the bottom levels of an organization without the benefit of companywide performance targets as a guide, then lower-level organizational units have no basis for connecting their performance targets to the company's. Bottom-up objective setting, with little or no guidance from above, nearly always signals an absence of strategic leadership on the part of senior executives.

CRAFTING A STRATEGY: PHASE 3 OF THE STRATEGY-MAKING, STRATEGY-EXECUTING PROCESS

The task of crafting a strategy entails answering a series of hows: *how* to grow the business, *how* to please customers, *how* to outcompete rivals, *how* to respond to changing market conditions, *how* to manage each functional piece of the business and develop needed competencies and capabilities, *how* to achieve strategic and financial objectives. It also means exercising astute entrepreneurship in choosing among the various strategic alternatives—proactively searching for opportunities to do new things or to do existing things in new or better ways.[12] The faster a company's business environment is changing, the more critical the need for its managers to be good entrepreneurs in diagnosing the direction and force of the changes under way and in responding with timely adjustments in strategy. Strategy makers have to pay attention to early warnings of future change and be willing to experiment with dare-to-be-different ways to alter their market position in preparing for new market conditions. When obstacles unexpectedly appear in a company's path, it is up to management to adapt rapidly and innovatively. *Masterful strategies come partly (maybe mostly) by doing things differently from competitors where it counts—outinnovating them, being more efficient, being more imaginative, adapting faster—rather than running with the herd.* Good strategy making is therefore inseparable from good business entrepreneurship. One cannot exist without the other.

Who Participates in Crafting a Company's Strategy?

A company's senior executives obviously have important strategy-making roles. The chief executive officer (CEO) wears the mantles of chief direction setter, chief objective setter, chief strategy maker, and chief strategy implementer for the total enterprise. Ultimate responsibility for *leading* the strategy-making, strategy-executing process rests with the CEO. In some enterprises the CEO functions as strategic visionary and chief architect of strategy, personally deciding what the key elements of the company's strategy will be, although others may well assist with data gathering and analysis, and the CEO may seek the advice of other senior managers and key employees in fashioning an overall strategy and deciding on important strategic moves. A CEO-centered approach to strategy development is characteristic of small owner-managed companies and sometimes large corporations that have been founded by the present CEO or that have CEOs with strong strategic leadership skills. Meg Whitman at eBay, Andrea Jung at Avon, Jeffrey Immelt at General Electric, and Howard Schultz at Starbucks are prominent examples of corporate CEOs who have wielded a heavy hand in shaping their company's strategy.

In most companies, however, strategy is the product of more than just the CEO's handiwork. Typically, other senior executives—business unit heads, the chief financial officer, and vice presidents for production, marketing, human resources, and other functional departments—have influential strategy-making roles and help fashion the chief strategy components. Normally, a company's chief financial officer (CFO) is in charge of devising and implementing an appropriate financial strategy; the production vice president takes the lead in developing the company's production strategy; the marketing vice president orchestrates sales and marketing strategy; a brand manager is in charge of the strategy for a particular brand in the company's product lineup; and so on.

But even here it is a mistake to view strategy making as a *top* management function, the exclusive province of owner-entrepreneurs, CEOs, and other senior executives. The more that a company's operations cut across different products, industries, and geographical areas, the more that headquarters executives have little option but to delegate considerable strategy-making authority to down-the-line managers in charge of particular subsidiaries, divisions, product lines, geographic sales offices, distribution centers, and plants. On-the-scene managers with authority over specific operating units are in the best position to evaluate the local situation in which the strategic choices must be made and can be expected to have detailed familiarity with local market and competitive conditions, customer requirements and expectations, and all the other aspects surrounding the strategic issues and choices in their arena of authority. This gives them an edge over headquarters executives in keeping the local aspects of the company's strategy responsive to local market and competitive conditions.

Take a company like Toshiba, a $43 billion corporation with 300 subsidiaries, thousands of products, and operations extending across the world. While top-level Toshiba executives may well be personally involved in shaping Toshiba's *overall* strategy and fashioning *important* strategic moves, it doesn't follow that a few senior executives at Toshiba headquarters have either the expertise or a sufficiently detailed understanding of all the relevant factors to wisely craft all the strategic initiatives taken for 300 subsidiaries and thousands of products. They simply cannot know enough about the situation in every Toshiba organizational unit to decide upon every strategy detail and direct every strategic move made in Toshiba's worldwide organization. Rather, it takes involvement on the part of Toshiba's whole management team—top executives, subsidiary heads, division heads, and key managers in such geographic units as sales offices, distribution centers, and plants—to craft the thousands of strategic initiatives that end up comprising the whole of Toshiba's strategy. The same can be said for a company like General Electric, which employs 300,000 people in businesses ranging from jet engines to plastics, power generation equipment to appliances, medical equipment to TV broadcasting, and locomotives to financial services (among many others) and that sells to customers in over 100 countries.

While managers farther down in the managerial hierarchy obviously have a narrower, more specific strategy-making role than managers closer to the top, the important understanding here is that in most of today's companies *every company manager typically has a strategy-making role—ranging from minor to major—for the area he or she heads.* Hence, any notion that an organization's strategists are at the top of the management hierarchy and that midlevel and frontline personnel merely carry out the strategic directives of senior managers needs to be cast aside. In companies with wide-ranging operations, it is far more accurate to view strategy making as a *collaborative or team effort* involving managers (and sometimes key employees) down through the whole organizational hierarchy.

> **Core Concept**
> In most companies, crafting and executing strategy is a team effort in which every manager has a role for the area he or she heads. It is flawed thinking to view crafting and executing strategy as something only high-level managers do.

In fact, the necessity of delegating some strategy-making authority to down-the-line managers has resulted in it being fairly common for key pieces of a company's strategy to originate in a company's middle and lower ranks.[13] Electronic Data Systems conducted a yearlong strategy review involving 2,500 of its 55,000 employees and coordinated by a core of 150 managers and staffers from all over the world.[14] J. M. Smucker, best-known for its jams and jellies, formed a team of 140 employees (7 percent of its 2,000-person workforce) who spent 25 percent of their time over a six-month period looking for ways to rejuvenate the company's growth. Involving teams of people to dissect complex situations and come up with strategic solutions is an often-used component of the strategy-making process because many strategic issues are complex or cut across multiple areas of expertise and operating units, thus calling for the contributions of many disciplinary experts and the collaboration of managers from different parts of the organization. A valuable strength of collaborative strategy-making is that the team of people charged with crafting the strategy can easily include the very people who will also be charged with implementing and executing it. Giving people an influential stake in crafting the strategy they must later help implement and execute not only builds motivation and commitment but also means those people can be held accountable for putting the strategy into place and making it work—the excuse of "It wasn't my idea to do this" won't fly.

The Strategy-Making Role of Corporate Intrapreneurs   In some companies, top management makes a regular practice of encouraging individuals and teams to develop and champion proposals for new product lines and new business ventures. The idea is to unleash the talents and energies of promising "corporate intrapreneurs," letting them try out untested business ideas and giving them the room to pursue new strategic initiatives. Executives judge which proposals merit support, give the chosen intrapreneurs the organizational and budgetary support they need, and let them proceed freely. Thus, important pieces of company strategy can originate with those intrapreneurial individuals and teams who succeed in championing a proposal through the approval stage and then end up being charged with the lead role in launching new products, overseeing the company's entry into new geographic markets, or heading up new business ventures. W. L. Gore and Associates, a privately owned company famous for its Gore-Tex waterproofing film, is an avid and highly successful practitioner of the corporate intrapreneur approach to strategy making. Gore expects all employees to initiate improvements and to display innovativeness. Each employee's intrapreneurial contributions are prime considerations in determining raises, stock option bonuses, and promotions. Gore's commitment to intrapreneurship has produced a stream of product innovations and new strategic initiatives that have kept the company vibrant and growing for nearly two decades.

A Company's Strategy-Making Hierarchy

It thus follows that *a company's overall strategy is a collection of strategic initiatives and actions* devised by managers and key employees up and down the whole organizational hierarchy. The larger and more diverse the operations of an enterprise, the more points of strategic initiative it has and the more managers and employees at more levels of management that have a relevant strategy-making role. Figure 2.2 shows who is generally responsible for devising what pieces of a company's overall strategy.

In diversified, multibusiness companies where the strategies of several different businesses have to be managed, the strategy-making task involves four distinct types or levels of strategy, each of which involves different facets of the company's overall strategy:

1. *Corporate strategy* consists of the kinds of initiatives the company uses to establish business positions in different industries, the approaches corporate executives pursue to boost the combined performance of the set of businesses the company has diversified into, and the means of capturing cross-business synergies and turning them into competitive advantage. Senior corporate executives normally have lead responsibility for devising corporate strategy and for choosing from among whatever recommended actions bubble up from the organization below. Key business-unit heads may also be influential, especially in strategic decisions affecting the businesses they head. Major strategic decisions are usually reviewed and approved by the company's board of directors. We will look deeper into the strategy-making process at diversified companies when we get to Chapter 9.

2. *Business strategy* concerns the actions and the approaches crafted to produce successful performance in one specific line of business. The key focus is crafting responses to changing market circumstances and initiating actions to strengthen market position, build competitive advantage, and develop strong competitive capabilities. Orchestrating the development of business-level strategy is the responsibility of the manager in charge of the business. The business head has at least two other strategy-related roles: (*a*) seeing that lower-level strategies are well conceived, consistent, and adequately matched to the overall business strategy, and (*b*) getting major business-level strategic moves approved by corporate-level officers (and sometimes the board of directors) and keeping them informed of emerging strategic issues. In diversified companies, business-unit heads may have the additional obligation of making sure business-level objectives and strategy conform to corporate-level objectives and strategy themes.

3. *Functional-area strategies* concern the actions, approaches, and practices to be employed in managing particular functions or business processes or key activities within a business. A company's marketing strategy, for example, represents the managerial game plan for running the sales and marketing part of the business. A company's product development strategy represents the managerial game plan for keeping the company's product lineup fresh and in tune with what buyers are looking for. Functional strategies add specifics to the hows of business-level strategy. Plus, they aim at establishing or strengthening a business unit's competencies and capabilities in performing strategy-critical activities so as to enhance the business's market position and standing with customers. The primary role of a functional strategy is to *support* the company's overall business strategy and competitive approach.

    Lead responsibility for functional strategies within a business is normally delegated to the heads of the respective functions, with the general manager of

Figure 2.2   **A Company's Strategy-Making Hierarchy**

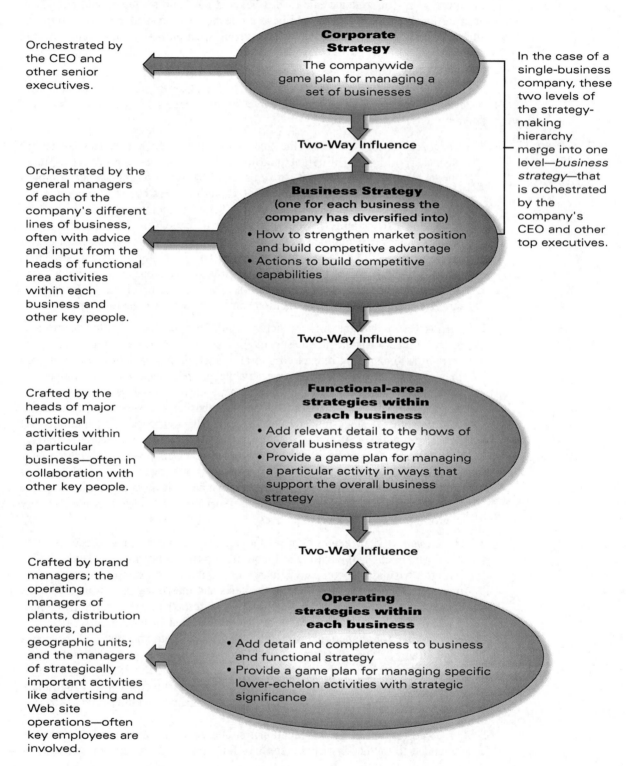

Orchestrated by the CEO and other senior executives.

Corporate Strategy

The companywide game plan for managing a set of businesses

In the case of a single-business company, these two levels of the strategy-making hierarchy merge into one level—*business strategy*—that is orchestrated by the company's CEO and other top executives.

Two-Way Influence

Orchestrated by the general managers of each of the company's different lines of business, often with advice and input from the heads of functional area activities within each business and other key people.

Business Strategy
(one for each business the company has diversified into)

- How to strengthen market position and build competitive advantage
- Actions to build competitive capabilities

Two-Way Influence

Crafted by the heads of major functional activities within a particular business—often in collaboration with other key people.

Functional-area strategies within each business

- Add relevant detail to the hows of overall business strategy
- Provide a game plan for managing a particular activity in ways that support the overall business strategy

Two-Way Influence

Crafted by brand managers; the operating managers of plants, distribution centers, and geographic units; and the managers of strategically important activities like advertising and Web site operations—often key employees are involved.

Operating strategies within each business

- Add detail and completeness to business and functional strategy
- Provide a game plan for managing specific lower-echelon activities with strategic significance

the business having final approval and perhaps even exerting a strong influence over the content of particular pieces of the strategies. To some extent, functional managers have to collaborate and coordinate their strategy-making efforts to avoid uncoordinated or conflicting strategies. For the overall business strategy to have maximum impact, a business's marketing strategy, production strategy, finance strategy, customer service strategy, product development strategy, and human resources strategy should be compatible and mutually reinforcing rather than each serving its own narrower purposes. If inconsistent functional-area strategies are sent up the line for final approval, the business head is responsible for spotting the conflicts and getting them resolved.

4. *Operating strategies* concern the relatively narrow strategic initiatives and approaches for managing key operating units (plants, distribution centers, geographic units) and specific operating activities with strategic significance (advertising campaigns, the management of specific brands, supply chain–related activities, and Web site sales and operations). A plant manager needs a strategy for accomplishing the plant's objectives, carrying out the plant's part of the company's overall manufacturing game plan, and dealing with any strategy-related problems that exist at the plant. A company's advertising manager needs a strategy for getting maximum audience exposure and sales impact from the ad budget. Operating strategies, while of limited scope, add further detail and completeness to functional strategies and to the overall business strategy. Lead responsibility for operating strategies is usually delegated to frontline managers, subject to review and approval by higher-ranking managers.

Even though operating strategy is at the bottom of the strategy-making hierarchy, its importance should not be downplayed. A major plant that fails in its strategy to achieve production volume, unit cost, and quality targets can undercut the achievement of company sales and profit objectives and wreak havoc with strategic efforts to build a quality image with customers. Frontline managers are thus an important part of an organization's strategy-making team because many operating units have strategy-critical performance targets and need to have strategic action plans in place to achieve them. One cannot reliably judge the strategic importance of a given action simply by the strategy level or location within the managerial hierarchy where it is initiated.

In single-business enterprises, the corporate and business levels of strategy making merge into one level—business strategy—because the strategy for the whole company involves only one distinct line of business. Thus, a single-business enterprise has three levels of strategy: business strategy for the company as a whole, functional-area strategies for each main area within the business, and operating strategies undertaken by lower-echelon managers to flesh out strategically significant aspects for the company's business and functional-area strategies. Proprietorships, partnerships, and owner-managed enterprises may have only one or two strategy-making levels since their strategy-making, strategy-executing process can be handled by just a few key people.

Uniting the Strategy-Making Effort

Ideally, the pieces of a company's strategy up and down the strategy hierarchy should be cohesive and mutually reinforcing, fitting together like a jigsaw puzzle. To achieve such unity, the strategizing process requires leadership from the top. It is the responsibility of top executives to provide strategy-making direction and clearly articulate key strategic themes that paint the white lines for lower-level strategy-making efforts. *Mid-level and frontline managers cannot craft unified strategic moves without first understanding the company's long-term direction and knowing the major components of the overall and business strategies that their strategy-making efforts are supposed to support and enhance.* Thus, as a general rule, strategy making must start at the top of the organization and then proceed downward through the hierarchy from the corporate level to the business level and then from the business level to the associated functional and operating levels. Strategy cohesion requires that business-level strategies complement and be compatible with the overall corporate strategy. Likewise, functional and operating strategies have to complement and support the overall business-level strategy of which they are a part. When the strategizing process is mostly top-down, with lower-level strategy-making efforts taking their cues from the higher-level strategy elements they are supposed to complement and support, there's less potential for strategy conflict between different levels. An absence of strong strategic leadership from the top sets the stage for some degree of strategic disunity. The strategic disarray that occurs in an organization when there is weak leadership and too few strategy guidelines coming from top executives is akin to what would happen to a football team's offensive performance if the quarterback decided not to call a play for the team but instead let each player do whatever he/thought would work best at his respective position. In business, as in sports, all the strategy makers in a company are on the same team and the many different pieces of the overall strategy crafted at various organizational levels need to be in sync. *Anything less than a unified collection of strategies weakens the overall strategy and is likely to impair company performance.*

> **Core Concept**
> A company's strategy is at full power only when its many pieces are united.

There are two things that top-level executives can do to drive consistent strategic action down through the organizational hierarchy. One is to effectively communicate the company's vision, objectives, and major strategy components to down-the-line managers and key personnel. The greater the numbers of company personnel who know, understand, and buy into the company's long-term direction and overall strategy, the smaller the risk that organization units will go off in conflicting strategic directions when strategy making is pushed down to frontline levels and many people are given a strategy-making role. The second is to exercise due diligence in reviewing lower-level strategies for consistency and support of higher level strategies. Any strategy conflicts must be addressed and resolved, either by modifying the lower-level strategies with conflicting elements or by adapting the higher-level strategy to accommodate what may be more appealing strategy ideas and initiatives bubbling from below. Thus, the process of synchronizing the strategy initiatives up and down the organizational hierarchy does not necessarily mean that lower-level strategies must be changed whenever conflicts and inconsistencies are spotted. When more attractive strategies ideas originate at lower organizational levels, it makes sense to adapt higher-level strategies to accommodate them.

A Strategic Vision + Objectives + Strategy = A Strategic Plan

Developing a strategic vision and mission, setting objectives, and crafting a strategy are basic direction-setting tasks. They map out where a company is headed, the targeted strategic and financial outcomes, and the competitive moves and internal action approaches to be used in achieving the desired business results. Together, they constitute a **strategic plan** for coping with industry and competitive conditions, the expected actions of the industry's key players, and the challenges and issues that stand as obstacles to the company's success.[15]

> **Core Concept**
> A **strategic plan** lays out the company's future direction, performance targets, and strategy.

In companies that do regular strategy reviews and develop explicit strategic plans, the strategic plan usually ends up as a written document that is circulated to most managers and perhaps selected employees. Near-term performance targets are the part of the strategic plan most often spelled out explicitly and communicated to managers and employees. A number of companies summarize key elements of their strategic plans in the company's annual report to shareholders, in postings on their Web site, or in statements provided to the business media. Other companies, perhaps for reasons of competitive sensitivity, make only vague, general statements about their strategic plans. In small, privately owned companies, it is rare for strategic plans to exist in written form. Small companies' strategic plans tend to reside in the thinking and directives of owners/ executives, with aspects of the plan being revealed in meetings and conversations with company personnel, and the understandings and commitments among managers and key employees about where to head, what to accomplish, and how to proceed.

IMPLEMENTING AND EXECUTING THE STRATEGY: PHASE 4 OF THE STRATEGY-MAKING, STRATEGY-EXECUTING PROCESS

Managing the implementation and execution of strategy is an operations-oriented, make-things-happen activity aimed at performing core business activities in a strategy-supportive manner. It is easily the most demanding and time-consuming part of the strategy management process. Converting strategic plans into actions and results tests a manager's ability to direct organizational change, motivate people, build and strengthen company competencies and competitive capabilities, create and nurture a strategy-supportive work climate, and meet or beat performance targets. Initiatives to put the strategy in place and execute it proficiently have to be launched and managed on many organizational fronts.

Management's action agenda for implementing and executing the chosen strategy emerges from assessing what the company will have to do differently or better, given its particular operating practices and organizational circumstances, to execute the strategy competently and achieve the targeted financial and strategic performance. Each company manager has to think through the answer to "What has to be done in my area to execute my piece of the strategic plan, and what actions should I take to get the process under way?" How much internal change is needed depends on how much of the strategy is new, how far internal practices and competencies deviate from what the strategy requires, and how well the present work climate/culture supports good strategy execution. Depending on the amount of internal change involved, full implementation and proficient execution of company strategy (or important new pieces thereof) can take several months to several years.

In most situations, managing the strategy execution process includes the following principal aspects:

- Staffing the organization with the needed skills and expertise, consciously building and strengthening strategy-supportive competencies and competitive capabilities, and organizing the work effort.
- Allocating ample resources to those activities critical to strategic success.
- Ensuring that policies and procedures facilitate rather than impede effective execution.

- Using best practices to perform core business activities and pushing for continuous improvement. Organizational units have to periodically reassess how things are being done and diligently pursue useful changes and improvements.
- Installing information and operating systems that enable company personnel to better carry out their strategic roles day in and day out.
- Motivating people to pursue the target objectives energetically and, if need be, modifying their duties and job behavior to better fit the requirements of successful strategy execution.
- Tying rewards and incentives directly to the achievement of performance objectives and good strategy execution.
- Creating a company culture and work climate conducive to successful strategy execution.
- Exerting the internal leadership needed to drive implementation forward and keep improving on how the strategy is being executed. When stumbling blocks or weaknesses are encountered, management has to see that they are addressed and rectified in timely and effective fashion.

Good strategy execution requires diligent pursuit of operating excellence. It is a job for a company's whole management team. And success hinges on the skills and cooperation of operating managers who can push needed changes in their organization units and consistently deliver good results. Strategy implementation can be considered successful if things go smoothly enough that the company meets or beats its strategic and financial performance targets and shows good progress in achieving management's strategic vision.

EVALUATING PERFORMANCE AND INITIATING CORRECTIVE ADJUSTMENTS: PHASE 5 OF THE STRATEGY-MAKING, STRATEGY-EXECUTING PROCESS

The fifth phase of the strategy management process—monitoring new external developments, evaluating the company's progress, and making corrective adjustments—is the trigger point for deciding whether to continue or change the company's vision, objectives, strategy, or strategy execution methods. So long as the company's direction and strategy seem well matched to industry and competitive conditions, and performance targets are being met, company executives may well decide to stay the course. Simply fine-tuning the strategic plan and continuing with efforts to improve strategy execution are sufficient.

> **Core Concept**
> A company's vision, objectives, strategy, and approach to strategy execution are never final; managing strategy is an ongoing process, not an every-now-and-then task.

But whenever a company encounters disruptive changes in its environment, questions need to be raised about the appropriateness of its direction and strategy. If a company experiences a downturn in its market position or persistent shortfalls in performance, then company managers are obligated to ferret out the causes—do they relate to poor strategy, poor strategy execution, or both?—and take timely corrective action. A company's direction, objectives, and strategy have to be revisited anytime external or internal conditions warrant. It is to be expected that a company will modify its strategic vision, direction, objectives, and strategy over time.

Likewise, it is not unusual for a company to find that one or more aspects of its strategy implementation and execution are not going as well as intended. Proficient strategy execution is always the product of much organizational learning. It is achieved unevenly—coming quickly in some areas and proving nettlesome in others. It is both normal and desirable to periodically assess strategy execution to determine which aspects are working well and which need improving. Successful strategy execution entails vigilantly searching for ways to improve and then making corrective adjustments whenever and wherever it is useful to do so.

CORPORATE GOVERNANCE: THE ROLE OF THE BOARD OF DIRECTORS IN THE STRATEGY-MAKING, STRATEGY-EXECUTING PROCESS

Although senior managers have *lead responsibility* for crafting and executing a company's strategy, it is the duty of the board of directors to exercise *strong oversight* and see that the five tasks of strategic management are done in a manner that benefits shareholders (in the case of investor-owned enterprises) or stakeholders (in the case of not-for-profit organizations). In watching over management's strategy-making, strategy-executing actions and making sure that executive actions are not only proper but also aligned with the interests of stakeholders, a company's board of directors has four important obligations to fulfill:

1. *Be inquiring critics and oversee the company's direction, strategy, and business approaches.* Board members must ask probing questions and draw on their business acumen to make independent judgments about whether strategy proposals have been adequately analyzed and whether proposed strategic actions appear to have greater promise than alternatives. If executive management is bringing well-supported and reasoned strategy proposals to the board, there's little reason for board members to aggressively challenge or pick apart everything put before them. Asking incisive questions is usually sufficient to test whether the case for management's proposals is compelling. However, when the company's strategy is failing or is plagued with faulty execution, and certainly when there is a precipitous collapse in profitability, board members have a duty to express their concerns about the validity of the strategy and/or operating methods, initiate debate about the company's strategic path, hold one-on-one discussions with key executives and other board members, and perhaps directly intervene as a group to alter the company's executive leadership and, ultimately, its strategy and business approaches.

2. *Evaluate the caliber of senior executives' strategy-making and strategy-executing skills.* The board is always responsible for determining whether the current CEO is doing a good job of strategic leadership (as a basis for awarding salary increases and bonuses and deciding on retention or removal). Boards must also exercise due diligence in evaluating the strategic leadership skills of other senior executives in line to succeed the CEO. When the incumbent CEO steps down or leaves for a position elsewhere, the board must elect a successor, either going with an insider or deciding that a better-qualified outsider is needed to perhaps radically change the company's strategic course.

3. *Institute a compensation plan for top executives that rewards them for actions and results that serve stakeholder interests, and most especially those of shareholders.* A basic principle of corporate governance is that the owners of a corporation delegate operating authority and managerial control to top management in return for compensation. In their role as an *agent* of shareholders, top executives have a

clear and unequivocal duty to make decisions and operate the company in accord with shareholder interests (but this does not mean disregarding the interests of other stakeholders, particularly those of employees, with whom they also have an agency relationship). Most boards of directors have a compensation committee, composed entirely of outside directors, to develop a salary and incentive compensation plan that makes it in the self-interest of executives to operate the business in a manner that benefits the owners; the compensation committee's recommendations are presented to the full board for approval. But in addition to creating compensation plans intended to align executive actions with owner interests, the board of directors must put a halt to self-serving executive perks and privileges that simply line the financial pockets of executives. Numerous media reports have recounted instances in which boards of directors have gone along with opportunistic executive efforts to secure excessive, if not downright obscene, compensation of one kind or another (multimillion-dollar interest-free loans, personal use of corporate aircraft, lucrative severance and retirement packages, outsized stock incentive awards, and so on).

4. *Oversee the company's financial accounting and financial reporting practices.* While top managers, particularly the company's CEO and CFO, are primarily responsible for seeing that the company's financial statements fairly and accurately report the results of the company's operations, it is well established that board members have a fiduciary duty to protect shareholders by exercising oversight of the company's financial practices, ensuring that generally accepted accounting principles (GAAP) are properly used in preparing the company's financial statements, and determining whether proper financial controls are in place to prevent fraud and misuse of funds. Virtually all boards of directors monitor the financial reporting activities by appointing an audit committee, always composed entirely of outside directors. The members of the audit committee have lead responsibility for overseeing the company's financial officers and consulting with both internal and external auditors to ensure accurate financial reporting and adequate financial controls.

The number of prominent companies penalized because of the actions of scurrilous or out-of-control CEOs and CFOs, the growing propensity of disgruntled stockholders to file lawsuits alleging director negligence, and the escalating costs of liability insurance for directors all underscore the responsibility that a board of directors has for overseeing a company's strategy-making, strategy-executing process and ensuring that management actions are proper and responsible. Moreover, holders of large blocks of shares (mutual funds and pension funds), regulatory authorities, and the financial press consistently urge that board members, especially outside directors, be active and diligent in their oversight of company strategy and maintain a tight rein on executive actions.

Every corporation should have a strong, independent board of directors that (1) is well informed about the company's performance, (2) guides and judges the CEO and other top executives, (3) has the courage to curb inappropriate or unduly risky management actions, (4) certifies to shareholders that the CEO is doing what the board expects, (5) provides insight and advice to management, and (6) is intensely involved in debating the pros and cons of key decisions and actions.[14] Boards of directors that lack the backbone to challenge a strong-willed or imperial CEO or that rubber-stamp most anything the CEO recommends without probing inquiry and debate (perhaps because the board is stacked with the CEO's cronies) abdicate their duty to represent and protect shareholder interests. The whole fabric of effective corporate governance is undermined when boards of directors shirk their responsibility to maintain ultimate control over the company's strategic direction, the major elements of its strategy, the business approaches management is using to implement and execute the strategy, executive compensation, and the financial reporting process. Thus, even though lead responsibility for crafting and executing strategy falls to top executives, boards of directors have a very important oversight role in the strategy-making, strategy-executing process.

Key Points

The managerial process of crafting and executing a company's strategy consists of five interrelated and integrated phases:

1. *Developing a strategic vision* of where the company needs to head and what its future product/market/customer/technology focus should be. This managerial step provides long-term direction, infuses the organization with a sense of purposeful action, and communicates management's aspirations to stakeholders.

2. *Setting objectives* to spell out for the company *how much* of *what kind* of performance is expected, and *by when.* The objectives need to require a significant amount of organizational stretch. A balanced scorecard approach for measuring company performance entails setting both *financial objectives* and *strategic objectives.*

3. *Crafting a strategy to achieve the objectives* and move the company along the strategic course that management has charted. Crafting strategy is concerned principally with forming responses to changes under way in the external environment, devising competitive moves and market approaches aimed at producing sustainable competitive advantage, building competitively valuable competencies and capabilities, and uniting the strategic actions initiated in various parts of the company. The more that a company's operations cut across different products, industries, and geographical areas, the more that strategy making becomes a *team effort* involving managers and company personnel at many organizational levels. The total strategy that emerges in such companies is really a collection of strategic actions and business approaches initiated partly by senior company executives, partly by the heads of major business divisions, partly by functional-area managers, and partly by frontline operating managers. The larger and more diverse the operations of an enterprise, the more points of strategic initiative it has and the more managers and employees at more levels of management that have a relevant strategy-making role. A single business enterprise has three levels of strategy—business strategy for the company as a whole, functional-area strategies for each main area within the business, and operating strategies undertaken by lower-echelon managers to flesh out strategically significant aspects for the company's business and functional-area strategies. In diversified, multibusiness companies, the strategy-making task involves four distinct types or levels of strategy: corporate strategy for the company as a whole, business strategy (one for each business the company has diversified into), functional-area strategies within each business, and operating strategies. Typically, the strategy-making task is more top-down than bottom-up, with higher-level strategies serving as the guide for developing lower-level strategies.

4. *Implementing and executing the chosen strategy efficiently and effectively.* Managing the implementation and execution of strategy is an operations-oriented, make-things-happen activity aimed at shaping the performance of core business activities in a strategy-supportive manner. Management's handling of the strategy implementation process can be considered successful if things go smoothly

enough that the company meets or beats its strategic and financial performance targets and shows good progress in achieving management's strategic vision.

5. *Evaluating performance and initiating corrective adjustments* in vision, long-term direction, objectives, strategy, or execution in light of actual experience, changing conditions, new ideas, and new opportunities. This phase of the strategy management process is the trigger point for deciding whether to continue or change the company's vision, objectives, strategy, and/or strategy execution methods.

A company's strategic vision, objectives, and strategy constitute a *strategic plan* for coping with industry and competitive conditions, outcompeting rivals, and addressing the challenges and issues that stand as obstacles to the company's success.

Boards of directors have a duty to shareholders to play a vigilant role in overseeing management's handling of a company's strategy-making, strategy-executing process. A company's board is obligated to (1) critically appraise and ultimately approve strategic action plans; (2) evaluate the strategic leadership skills of the CEO and others in line to succeed the incumbent CEO; (3) institute a compensation plan for top executives that rewards them for actions and results that serve stakeholder interests, most especially those of shareholders; and (4) ensure that the company issues accurate financial reports and has adequate financial controls.

Exercises

1. Go to the Investors section of Heinz's Web site (www.heinz.com) and read the letter to the shareholders in the company's fiscal 2003 annual report. Is the vision for Heinz articulated by Chairman and CEO William R. Johnson sufficiently clear and well defined? Why or why not? Are the company's objectives well stated and appropriate? What about the strategy that Johnson outlines for the company? If you were a shareholder, would you be satisfied with what Johnson has told you about the company's direction, performance targets, and strategy?

2. Consider the following mission statement of the American Association of Retired People (AARP):

AARP Mission Statement

- AARP is a nonprofit, nonpartisan membership organization for people age 50 and over.
- AARP is dedicated to enhancing quality of life for all as we age. We lead positive social change and deliver value to members through information, advocacy and service.
- AARP also provides a wide range of unique benefits, special products, and services for our members. These benefits include AARP Web site at www.aarp.org, "AARP The Magazine," the monthly "AARP Bulletin," and a Spanish-language newspaper, "Segunda Juventud."
- Active in every state, the District of Columbia, Puerto Rico, and the U.S. Virgin Islands, AARP celebrates the attitude that age is just a number and life is what you make it.

Is AARP's mission statement well-crafted? Does it do an adequate job of indicating "who we are, what we do, and why we are here"? Why or why not?

3. How would you rewrite/restate the strategic vision for Caterpillar in Illustration Capsule 2.1 so as to better exemplify the characteristics of effective vision statements presented in Tables 2.2 and 2.3? Visit www.caterpillar.com to get more information about Caterpillar and figure out how a more appropriate strategic vision might be worded.

chapter three

Evaluating a Company's External Environment

Analysis is the critical starting point of strategic thinking.
—Kenichi Ohmae
Consultant and Author

Things are always different—the art is figuring out which differences matter.
—Laszlo Birinyi
Investments Manager

Competitive battles should be seen not as one-shot skirmishes but as a dynamic multiround game of moves and countermoves.
—Anil K. Gupta
Professor

anagers are not prepared to act wisely in steering a company in a different direction or altering its strategy until they have a deep understanding of the pertinent factors surrounding the company's situation. As indicated in the opening paragraph of Chapter 1, one of the three central questions that managers must address in evaluating their company's business prospects is "What's the company's present situation?" Two facets of a company's situation are especially pertinent: (1) the industry and competitive environment in which the company operates and the forces acting to reshape this environment, and (2) the company's own market position and competitiveness—its resources and capabilities, its strengths and weaknesses vis-à-vis rivals, and its windows of opportunity.

Insightful diagnosis of a company's external and internal environment is a prerequisite for managers to succeed in crafting a strategy that is an excellent fit with the company's situation, is capable of building competitive advantage, and holds good prospect for boosting company performance—the three criteria of a winning strategy. As depicted in Figure 3.1, the task of crafting a strategy thus should always begin with an appraisal of the company's external and internal situation (as a basis for developing strategic vision of where the company needs to head), then move toward an evaluation of the most promising alternative strategies and business models, and culminate in choosing a specific strategy.

This chapter presents the concepts and analytical tools for zeroing in on those aspects of a single-business company's external environment that should be considered in making strategic choices. Attention centers on the competitive arena in which a company operates, the drivers of market change, and what rival companies are doing. In Chapter 4 we explore the methods of evaluating a company's internal circumstances and competitiveness.

THE STRATEGICALLY RELEVANT COMPONENTS OF A COMPANY'S EXTERNAL ENVIRONMENT

All companies operate in a "macroenvironment" shaped by influences emanating from the economy at large; population demographics; societal values and lifestyles; governmental legislation and regulation; technological factors; and, closer to home, the

Figure 3.1   **From Thinking Strategically about the Company's Situation to Choosing a Strategy**

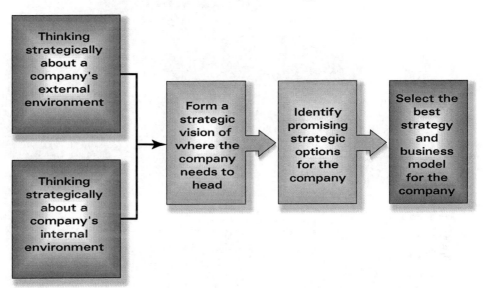

industry and competitive arena in which the company operates (see Figure 3.2). Strictly speaking, a company's macroenvironment includes *all relevant factors and influences* outside the company's boundaries; by relevant, we mean important enough to have a bearing on the decisions the company ultimately makes about its direction, objectives, strategy, and business model. Strategically relevant influences coming from the outer ring of the macroenvironment can sometimes have a high impact on a company's business situation and have a very significant impact on the company's direction and strategy. The strategic opportunities of cigarette producers to grow their business are greatly reduced by antismoking ordinances and the growing cultural stigma attached to smoking. Motor vehicle companies must adapt their strategies (especially as concerns the fuel mileage of their vehicles) to customer concerns about gasoline prices. The demographics of an aging population and longer life expectancies are having a dramatic impact on the business prospects and strategies of health care and prescription drug companies. Companies in most all industries have to craft strategies that are responsive to environmental regulations, growing use of the Internet and broadband technology, and energy prices. Companies in the food-processing, restaurant, sports, and fitness industries have to pay special attention to changes in lifestyles, eating habits, leisure-time preferences, and attitudes toward nutrition and exercise in fashioning their strategies.

Happenings in the outer ring of the macroenvironment may occur rapidly or slowly, with or without advance warning. The impact of outer-ring factors on a company's choice of strategy can range from big to small. But even if the factors in the outer ring of the macroenvironment change slowly or have such a comparatively low impact on a company's situation that only the edges of a company's direction and strategy are affected, there are enough strategically relevant outer-ring trends and events to justify a watchful eye. As company managers scan the external environment, they must be alert for potentially important outer-ring developments, assess their impact and influence, and adapt the company's direction and strategy as needed.

Figure 3.2 **The Components of a Company's Macroenvironment**

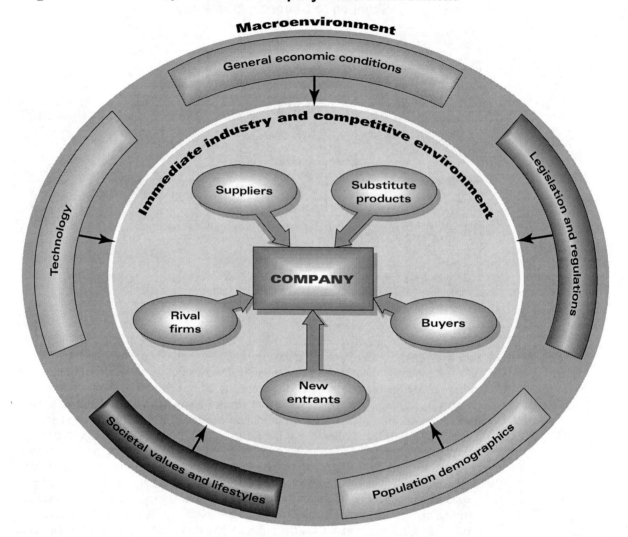

However, the factors and forces in a company's macroenvironment having the *biggest* strategy-shaping impact typically pertain to the company's immediate industry and competitive environment—competitive pressures, the actions of rivals firms, buyer behavior, supplier-related considerations, and so on. Consequently, it is on a company's industry and competitive environment that we concentrate our attention in this chapter.

THINKING STRATEGICALLY ABOUT A COMPANY'S INDUSTRY AND COMPETITIVE ENVIRONMENT

To gain a deep understanding of a company's industry and competitive environment, managers do not need to gather all the information they can find and spend lots of time digesting it. Rather, the task is much more focused. Thinking strategically about a company's industry and competitive environment entails using some well-defined concepts and analytical tools to get clear answers to seven questions:

1.   What are the industry's dominant economic features?
2.   What kinds of competitive forces are industry members facing and how strong is each force?
3.   What forces are driving industry change and what impacts will they have on competitive intensity and industry profitability?
4.   What market positions do industry rivals occupy—who is strongly positioned and who is not?
5.   What strategic moves are rivals likely to make next?
6.   What are the key factors for future competitive success?
7.   Does the outlook for the industry present the company with sufficiently attractive prospects for profitability?

Analysis-based answers to these questions provide managers with the understanding needed to craft a strategy that fits the company's external situation. The remainder of this chapter is devoted to describing the methods of obtaining solid answers to the seven questions and explaining how the nature of a company's industry and competitive environment weighs upon the strategic choices of company managers.

QUESTION 1: WHAT ARE THE INDUSTRY'S DOMINANT ECONOMIC FEATURES?

Because industries differ so significantly, analyzing a company's industry and competitive environment begins with identifying an industry's dominant economic features and forming a picture of what the industry landscape is like. An industry's dominant economic features are defined by such factors as market size and growth rate, the number and sizes of buyers and sellers, the geographic boundaries of the market (which can extend from local to worldwide), the degree to which sellers' products are differentiated, the pace of product innovation, market supply/demand conditions, the pace of technological change, the extent of vertical integration, and the extent to which costs are affected by scale economies (i.e., situations in which large-volume operations result in lower unit costs) and learning/experience curve effects (i.e., situations in which costs decline as a company gains knowledge and experience). Table 3.1 provides a convenient summary of what economic features to look at and the corresponding questions to consider in profiling an industry's landscape.

Getting a handle on an industry's distinguishing economic features not only sets the stage for the analysis to come but also promotes understanding of the kinds of strategic moves that industry members are likely to employ. For example, in industries characterized by one product advance after another, companies must invest in research and development (R&D) and develop strong product innovation capabilities—a strategy of continuous product innovation becomes a condition of survival in such industries as video games, mobile phones, and pharmaceuticals. An industry that has recently passed through the rapid-growth stage and is looking at single-digit percentage increases in buyer demand is likely to be experiencing a competitive shake-out and much stronger strategic emphasis on cost reduction and improved customer service.

In industries like semiconductors, strong *learning/experience curve effects* in manufacturing cause unit costs to decline about 20 percent each time *cumulative* production

Table 3.1 **What to Consider in Identifying an Industry's Dominant Economic Features**

Economic Feature	Questions to Answer
Market size and growth rate	• How big is the industry and how fast is it growing? • What does the industry's position in the life cycle (early development, rapid growth and takeoff, early maturity and slowing growth, saturation and stagnation, decline) reveal about the industry's growth prospects?
Number of rivals	• Is the industry fragmented into many small companies or concentrated and dominated by a few large companies? • Is the industry going through a period of consolidation to a smaller number of competitors?
Scope of competitive rivalry	• Is the geographic area over which most companies compete local, regional, national, multinational, or global? • Is having a presence in the foreign country markets becoming more important to a company's long-term competitive success?
Number of buyers	• Is market demand fragmented among many buyers? • Do some buyers have bargaining power because they purchase in large volume?
Degree of product differentiation	• Are the products of rivals becoming more differentiated or less differentiated? • Are increasingly look-alike products of rivals causing heightened price competition?
Product innovation	• Is the industry characterized by rapid product innovation and short product life cycles? • How important is R&D and product innovation? • Are there opportunities to overtake key rivals by being first-to-market with next-generation products?
Supply/demand conditions	• Is a surplus of capacity pushing prices and profit margins down? • Is the industry overcrowded with too many competitors? • Are short supplies creating a sellers' market?
Pace of technological change	• What role does advancing technology play in this industry? • Are ongoing upgrades of facilities/equipment essential because of rapidly advancing production process technologies? • Do most industry members have or need strong technological capabilities?
Vertical integration	• Do most competitors operate in only one stage of the industry (parts and components production, manufacturing and assembly, distribution, retailing) or do some competitors operate in multiple stages? • Is there any cost or competitive advantage or disadvantage associated with being fully or partially integrated?
Economies of scale	• Is the industry characterized by economies of scale in purchasing, manufacturing, advertising, shipping, or other activities? • Do companies with large-scale operations have an important cost advantage over small-scale firms?
Learning/experience curve effects	• Are certain industry activities characterized by strong learning/experience curve effects ("learning by doing") such that unit costs decline as a company's experience in performing the activity builds? • Do any companies have significant cost advantages because of their learning/experience in performing particular activities?

volume doubles. With a 20 percent experience curve effect, if the first 1 million chips cost $100 each, the unit cost would be $80 (80 percent of $100) by a production volume of 2 million, the unit cost would be $64 (80 percent of $80) by a production volume of 4 million, and so on.[1] The bigger the learning/experience curve effect, the bigger the cost advantage of the company with the largest *cumulative* production volume.

Thus, when an industry is characterized by important learning/experience curve effects (or by economies of scale), industry members are strongly motivated to adopt volume-increasing strategies to capture the resulting cost-saving economies and maintain their competitiveness. Unless small-scale firms succeed in pursuing strategic options that allow them to grow sales sufficiently to remain cost-competitive with larger-volume rivals, they are unlikely to survive. The bigger the learning/experience curve effects and/or scale economies in an industry, the more imperative it becomes for competing sellers to pursue strategies to win additional sales and market share—the company with the biggest sales volume gains sustainable competitive advantage as the low-cost producer.

QUESTION 2: WHAT KINDS OF COMPETITIVE FORCES ARE INDUSTRY MEMBERS FACING?

The character, mix, and subtleties of the competitive forces operating in a company's industry are never the same from one industry to another. Far and away the most powerful and widely used tool for systematically diagnosing the principal competitive pressures in a market and assessing the strength and importance of each is the *five-forces model of competition*.[2] This model, depicted in Figure 3.3, holds that the state of competition in an industry is a composite of competitive pressures operating in five areas of the overall market:

1. Competitive pressures associated with the market maneuvering and jockeying for buyer patronage that goes on among *rival sellers* in the industry.

2. Competitive pressures associated with the threat of *new entrants* into the market.

3. Competitive pressures coming from the attempts of companies in other industries to win buyers over to their own *substitute products*.

4. Competitive pressures stemming from *supplier* bargaining power and supplier–seller collaboration.

5. Competitive pressures stemming from *buyer* bargaining power and seller–buyer collaboration.

The way one uses the five-forces model to determine the nature and strength of competitive pressures in a given industry is to build the picture of competition in three steps:

- *Step 1:* Identify the specific competitive pressures associated with each of the five forces.
- *Step 2:* Evaluate how strong the pressures comprising each of the five forces are (fierce, strong, moderate to normal, or weak).
- *Step 3:* Determine whether the collective strength of the five competitive forces is conducive to earning attractive profits.

Figure 3.3   **The Five-Forces Model of Competition: A Key Analytical Tool**

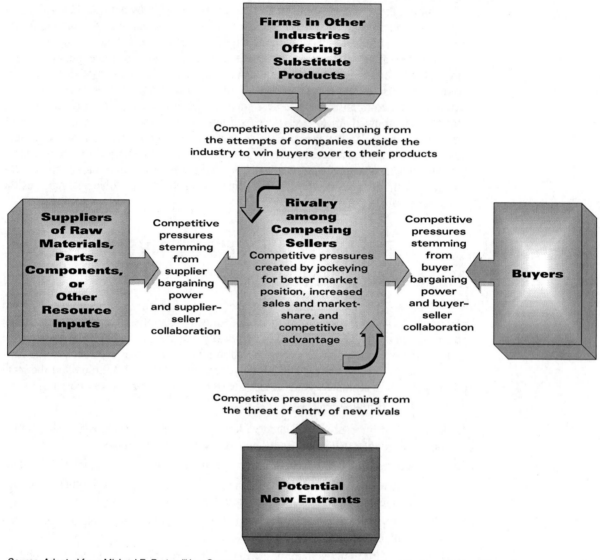

Source: Adapted from Michael E. Porter, "How Competitive Forces Shape Strategy," *Harvard Business Review* 57, no. 2 (March–April 1979), pp. 137–45.

Competitive Pressures Associated with the Jockeying among Rival Sellers

The strongest of the five competitive forces is nearly always the market maneuvering and jockeying for buyer patronage that goes on among rival sellers of a product or service. In effect, *a market is a competitive battlefield* where there's no end to the jockeying for buyer patronage. Rival sellers are prone to employ whatever weapons they

Core Concept

Competitive jockeying among industry rivals is ever changing, as rivals initiate fresh offensive and defensive moves and emphasize first one mix of competitive weapons and then another in efforts to improve their market positions.

have in their business arsenal to improve their market positions, strengthen their market position with buyers, and earn good profits. The challenge is to craft a competitive strategy that, at the very least, allows a company to hold its own against rivals and that, ideally, *produces a competitive edge over rivals.* But competitive contests are ongoing and dynamic. When one firm makes a strategic move that produces good results, its rivals typically respond with offensive or defensive countermoves, shifting their strategic emphasis from one combination of product attributes, marketing tactics, and capabilities to another. This pattern of action and reaction, move and countermove, adjust and readjust produces a continually evolving competitive landscape in which the market battle ebbs and flows, sometimes takes unpredictable twists and turns, and produces winners and losers. But the winners—the current market leaders—have no guarantees of continued leadership; their market success is no more durable than the power of their strategies to fend off the strategies of ambitious challengers. In every industry, the ongoing jockeying of rivals leads to one or another companies gaining or losing momentum in the marketplace according to whether their latest strategic maneuvers succeed or fail.

Figure 3.4 shows a sampling of competitive weapons that firms can deploy in battling rivals and indicates the factors that influence the intensity of their rivalry. A brief discussion of some of the factors that influence the tempo of rivalry among industry competitors is in order:[3]

- *Rivalry intensifies when competing sellers are active in launching fresh actions to boost their market standing and business performance.* One indicator of active rivalry is lively price competition, a condition that puts pressure on industry members to drive costs out of the business and threatens the survival of high-cost companies. Another indicator of active rivalry is rapid introduction of next-generation products—when one or more rivals frequently introduce new or improved products, competitors that lack good product innovation capabilities feel considerable competitive heat to get their own new and improved products into the marketplace quickly. Other indicators of active rivalry among industry members include:

  - Whether industry members are racing to differentiate their products from rivals by offering better performance features or higher quality or improved customer service or a wider product selection.

  - How frequently rivals resort to such marketing tactics as special sales promotions, heavy advertising, rebates, or low-interest-rate financing to drum up additional sales.

  - How actively industry members are pursuing efforts to build stronger dealer networks or establish positions in foreign markets or otherwise expand their distribution capabilities and market presence.

  - How hard companies are striving to gain a market edge over rivals by developing valuable expertise and capabilities that rivals are hard pressed to match.

  Normally, competitive jockeying among rival sellers is active and fairly intense because competing companies are highly motivated to launch whatever fresh actions and creative market maneuvers they can think of to try to strengthen their market positions and business performance.

- *Rivalry intensifies as the number of competitors increases and as competitors become more equal in size and capability.* Rivalry is not as vigorous in microprocessors for PCs, where Advanced Micro Devices (AMD) is one of the few

Figure 3.4 **Weapons for Competing and Factors Affecting the Strength of Rivalry**

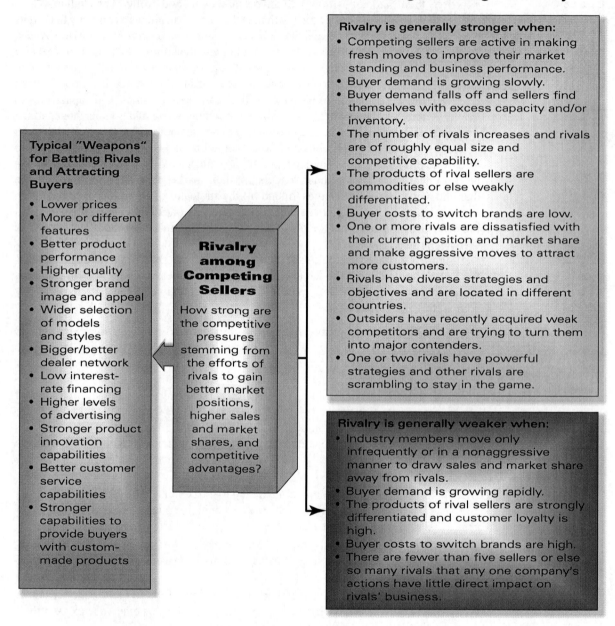

Typical "Weapons" for Battling Rivals and Attracting Buyers

- Lower prices
- More or different features
- Better product performance
- Higher quality
- Stronger brand image and appeal
- Wider selection of models and styles
- Bigger/better dealer network
- Low interest-rate financing
- Higher levels of advertising
- Stronger product innovation capabilities
- Better customer service capabilities
- Stronger capabilities to provide buyers with custom-made products

Rivalry among Competing Sellers

How strong are the competitive pressures stemming from the efforts of rivals to gain better market positions, higher sales and market shares, and competitive advantages?

Rivalry is generally stronger when:
- Competing sellers are active in making fresh moves to improve their market standing and business performance.
- Buyer demand is growing slowly.
- Buyer demand falls off and sellers find themselves with excess capacity and/or inventory.
- The number of rivals increases and rivals are of roughly equal size and competitive capability.
- The products of rival sellers are commodities or else weakly differentiated.
- Buyer costs to switch brands are low.
- One or more rivals are dissatisfied with their current position and market share and make aggressive moves to attract more customers.
- Rivals have diverse strategies and objectives and are located in different countries.
- Outsiders have recently acquired weak competitors and are trying to turn them into major contenders.
- One or two rivals have powerful strategies and other rivals are scrambling to stay in the game.

Rivalry is generally weaker when:
- Industry members move only infrequently or in a nonaggressive manner to draw sales and market share away from rivals.
- Buyer demand is growing rapidly.
- The products of rival sellers are strongly differentiated and customer loyalty is high.
- Buyer costs to switch brands are high.
- There are fewer than five sellers or else so many rivals that any one company's actions have little direct impact on rivals' business.

challengers to Intel, as it is in fast-food restaurants, where numerous sellers are actively jockeying for buyer patronage. Up to a point, the greater the number of competitors, the greater the probability of fresh, creative strategic initiatives. In addition, when rivals are nearly equal in size and capability, they can usually compete on a fairly even footing, making it harder for one or two firms to win commanding market shares and confront weaker market challenges from rivals.

- *Rivalry is usually stronger in slow-growing markets and weaker in fast-growing markets.* Rapidly expanding buyer demand produces enough new business for all industry members to grow. Indeed, in a fast-growing market, a company may find itself stretched just to keep abreast of incoming orders, let alone devote resources to stealing customers away from rivals. But in markets where growth is sluggish or where buyer demand drops off unexpectedly, expansion-minded firms and firms with excess capacity often are quick to cut prices and initiate other sales-increasing tactics, thereby igniting a battle for market share that can result in a shake-out of weak, inefficient firms.

- *Rivalry is usually weaker in industries comprised of so many rivals that the impact of any one company's actions is spread thin across all industry members; likewise, it is often weak when there are fewer than five competitors.* A progressively larger number of competitors can actually begin to weaken head-to-head rivalry once an industry becomes populated with so many rivals that the impact of successful moves by any one company is spread thin across many industry members. To the extent that a company's strategic moves ripple out to have little discernible impact on the businesses of its many rivals, then industry members soon learn that it is not imperative to respond every time one or another rival does something to enhance its market position—an outcome that weakens the intensity of head-to-head battles for market share. Rivalry also *tends* to be weak if an industry consists of just two or three or four sellers. In a market with few rivals, each competitor soon learns that aggressive moves to grow its sales and market share can have immediate adverse impact on rivals' businesses, almost certainly provoking vigorous retaliation and risking an all-out battle for market share that is likely to lower the profits of all concerned. Companies that have a few strong rivals thus come to understand the merits of *restrained* efforts to wrest sales and market share from competitors as opposed to undertaking hard-hitting offensives that escalate into a profit-eroding arms-race or price war. However, some caution must be exercised in concluding that rivalry is weak just because there are only a few competitors. Thus, although occasional warfare can break out (the fierceness of the current battle between Red Hat and Microsoft and the decades-long war between Coca-Cola and Pepsi are prime examples), competition among the few normally produces a live-and-let-live approach to competing because rivals see the merits of restrained efforts to wrest sales and market share from competitors as opposed to undertaking hard-hitting offensives that escalate into a profit-eroding arms race or price war.

- *Rivalry increases when buyer demand falls off and sellers find themselves with excess capacity and/or inventory.* Excess supply conditions create a "buyers' market," putting added competitive pressure on industry rivals to scramble for profitable sales levels (often by price discounting).

- *Rivalry increases as it becomes less costly for buyers to switch brands.* The less expensive it is for buyers to switch their purchases from the seller of one brand to the s eller of another brand, the easier it is for sellers to steal customers away from rivals. But the higher the costs buyers incur to switch brands, the less prone they are to brand switching. Even if consumers view one or more rival brands as more attractive, they may not be inclined to switch because of the added time and inconvenience or the psychological costs of abandoning a familiar brand. Distributors and retailers may not switch to the brands of rival manufacturers because they are hesitant to sever long-standing supplier relationships, incur any technical support costs or retraining expenses in making the switchover, go to the trouble of testing the quality and reliability of the rival brand, or devote resources to marketing the new brand (especially if the brand is lesser known).

Apple Computer, for example, has been unable to convince PC users to switch from Windows-based PCs because of the time burdens and inconvenience associated with learning Apple's operating system and because so many Windows-based applications will not run on a MacIntosh due to operating system incompatibility. Consequently, unless buyers are dissatisfied with the brand they are presently purchasing, high switching costs can significantly weaken the rivalry among competing sellers.

- *Rivalry increases as the products of rival sellers become more standardized and diminishes as the products of industry rivals become more strongly differentiated.* When the offerings of rivals are identical or weakly differentiated, buyers have less reason to be brand-loyal—a condition that makes it easier for rivals to convince buyers to switch to their offering. And since the brands of different sellers have comparable attributes, buyers can shop the market for the best deal and switch brands at will. In contrast, strongly differentiated product offerings among rivals breed high brand loyalty on the part of buyers—because many buyers view the attributes of certain brands as better suited to their needs. Strong brand attachments make it tougher for sellers to draw customers away from rivals. Unless meaningful numbers of buyers are open to considering new or different product attributes being offered by rivals, the high degrees of brand loyalty that accompany strong product differentiation work against fierce rivalry among competing sellers. *The degree of product differentiation also affects switching costs.* When the offerings of rivals are identical or weakly differentiated, it is usually easy and inexpensive for buyers to switch their purchases from one seller to another. Strongly differentiated products raise the probability that buyers will find it costly to switch brands.

- *Rivalry is more intense when industry conditions tempt competitors to use price cuts or other competitive weapons to boost unit volume.* When a product is perishable, seasonal, or costly to hold in inventory, competitive pressures build quickly anytime one or more firms decide to cut prices and dump supplies on the market. Likewise, whenever fixed costs account for a large fraction of total cost, such that unit costs tend to be lowest at or near full capacity, then firms come under significant pressure to cut prices or otherwise try to boost sales whenever they are operating below full capacity. Unused capacity imposes a significant cost-increasing penalty because there are fewer units over which to spread fixed costs. The pressure of high fixed costs can push rival firms into price concessions, special discounts, rebates, low-interest-rate financing, and other volume-boosting tactics.

- *Rivalry increases when one or more competitors become dissatisfied with their market position and launch moves to bolster their standing at the expense of rivals.* Firms that are losing ground or in financial trouble often pursue aggressive (or perhaps desperate) turnaround strategies that can involve price discounts, more advertising, acquisition of or merger with other rivals, or new product introductions—such strategies can turn competitive pressures up a notch.

- *Rivalry becomes more volatile and unpredictable as the diversity of competitors increases in terms of visions, strategic intents, objectives, strategies, resources, and countries of origin.* A diverse group of sellers often contains one or more mavericks willing to try novel or high-risk or rule-breaking market approaches, thus generating a livelier and less predictable competitive environment. Globally competitive markets often contain rivals with different views about where the industry is headed and a willingness to employ perhaps radically different competitive approaches. Attempts by cross-border rivals to gain stronger footholds in each other's domestic markets usually boost the intensity of rivalry, especially when the aggressors have lower costs or products with more attractive features.

- *Rivalry increases when strong companies outside the industry acquire weak firms in the industry and launch aggressive, well-funded moves to transform their newly acquired competitors into major market contenders.* A concerted effort to turn a weak rival into a market leader nearly always entails launching well-financed strategic initiatives to dramatically improve the competitor's product offering, excite buyer interest, and win a much bigger market share—actions that, if successful, put added pressure on rivals to counter with fresh strategic moves of their own.

- *A powerful, successful competitive strategy employed by one company greatly intensifies the competitive pressures on its rivals to develop effective strategic responses or be relegated to also-ran status.*

Rivalry can be characterized as *cutthroat* or *brutal* when competitors engage in protracted price wars or habitually employ other aggressive tactics that are mutually destructive to profitability. Rivalry can be considered *fierce* to *strong* when the battle for market share is so vigorous that the profit margins of most industry members are squeezed to bare-bones levels. Rivalry can be characterized as *moderate* or *normal* when the maneuvering among industry members, while lively and healthy, still allows most industry members to earn acceptable profits. Rivalry is *weak* when most companies in the industry are relatively well satisfied with their sales growth and market shares, rarely undertake offensives to steal customers away from one another, and have comparatively attractive earnings and returns on investment.

Competitive Pressures Associated with the Threat of New Entrants

Several factors determine whether the threat of new companies entering the marketplace poses significant competitive pressure (see Figure 3.5). One factor relates to the size of the pool of likely entry candidates and the resources at their command. As a rule, the bigger the pool of entry candidates, the stronger the threat of potential entry. This is especially true when some of the likely entry candidates have ample resources and the potential to become formidable contenders for market leadership. Frequently, the strongest competitive pressures associated with potential entry come not from outsiders, but from current industry participants looking for growth opportunities. *Existing industry members are often strong candidates for entering market segments or geographic areas where they currently do not have a market presence.* Companies already well established in certain product categories or geographic areas often possess the resources, competencies, and competitive capabilities to hurdle the barriers of entering a different market segment or new geographic area.

A second factor concerns whether the likely entry candidates face high or low entry barriers. High barriers reduce the competitive threat of potential entry, while low barriers make entry more likely, especially if the industry is growing and offers attractive profit opportunities. The most widely encountered barriers that entry candidates must hurdle include:[4]

- *The presence of sizable economies of scale in production or other areas of operation*—When incumbent companies enjoy cost advantages associated with

Figure 3.5   **Factors Affecting the Threat of Entry**

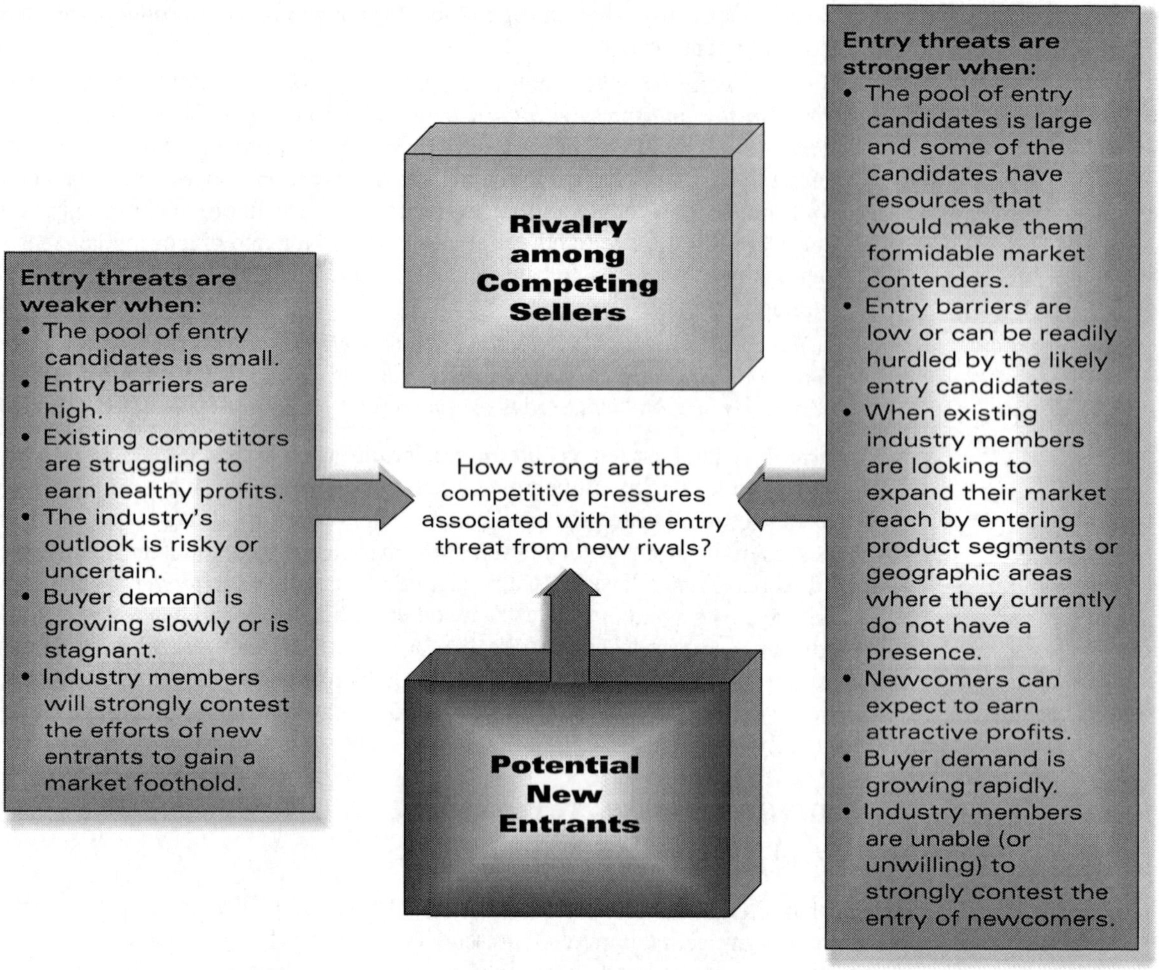

Entry threats are weaker when:
- The pool of entry candidates is small.
- Entry barriers are high.
- Existing competitors are struggling to earn healthy profits.
- The industry's outlook is risky or uncertain.
- Buyer demand is growing slowly or is stagnant.
- Industry members will strongly contest the efforts of new entrants to gain a market foothold.

Rivalry among Competing Sellers

How strong are the competitive pressures associated with the entry threat from new rivals?

Potential New Entrants

Entry threats are stronger when:
- The pool of entry candidates is large and some of the candidates have resources that would make them formidable market contenders.
- Entry barriers are low or can be readily hurdled by the likely entry candidates.
- When existing industry members are looking to expand their market reach by entering product segments or geographic areas where they currently do not have a presence.
- Newcomers can expect to earn attractive profits.
- Buyer demand is growing rapidly.
- Industry members are unable (or unwilling) to strongly contest the entry of newcomers.

large-scale operation, outsiders must either enter on a large scale (a costly and perhaps risky move) or accept a cost disadvantage and consequently lower profitability. Trying to overcome the disadvantages of small size by entering on a large scale at the outset can result in long-term overcapacity problems for the new entrant (until sales volume builds up), and it can so threaten the market shares of existing firms that they launch strong defensive maneuvers (price cuts, increased advertising and sales promotion, and similar blocking actions) to maintain their positions and make things hard on a newcomer.

- *Cost and resource disadvantages not related to scale of operation*—Aside from enjoying economies of scale, there are other reasons why existing firms may have low unit costs that are hard to replicate by newcomers. Industry incumbents can have cost advantages that stem from learning/experience curve effects, the possession of key patents or proprietary technology, partnerships with the best and cheapest suppliers of raw materials and components, favorable locations, and low fixed costs (because they have older facilities that have been mostly depreciated).

- *Strong brand preferences and high degrees of customer loyalty*—The stronger the attachment of buyers to established brands, the harder it is for a newcomer to break into the marketplace. In such cases, a new entrant must have the financial resources to spend enough on advertising and sales promotion to overcome customer loyalties and build its own clientele. Establishing brand recognition and building customer loyalty can be a slow and costly process. In addition, if it is difficult or costly for a customer to switch to a new brand, a new entrant must persuade buyers that its brand is worth the switching costs. To overcome switching-cost barriers, new entrants may have to offer buyers a discounted price or an extra margin of quality or service. All this can mean lower expected profit margins for new entrants, which increases the risk to start-up companies dependent on sizable early profits to support their new investments.

- *High capital requirements*—The larger the total dollar investment needed to enter the market successfully, the more limited the pool of potential entrants. The most obvious capital requirements for new entrants relate to manufacturing facilities and equipment, introductory advertising and sales promotion campaigns, working capital to finance inventories and customer credit, and sufficient cash to cover start-up costs.

- *The difficulties of building a network of distributors or retailers and securing adequate space on retailers' shelves*—A potential entrant can face numerous distribution channel challenges. Wholesale distributors may be reluctant to take on a product that lacks buyer recognition. Retailers have to be recruited and convinced to give a new brand ample display space and an adequate trial period. When existing sellers have strong, well-functioning distributor or retailer networks, a newcomer has an uphill struggle in squeezing its way in. Potential entrants sometimes have to "buy" their way into wholesale or retail channels by cutting their prices to provide dealers and distributors with higher markups and profit margins or by giving them big advertising and promotional allowances. As a consequence, a potential entrant's own profits may be squeezed unless and until its product gains enough consumer acceptance that distributors and retailers are anxious to carry it.

- *Restrictive regulatory policies*—Government agencies can limit or even bar entry by requiring licenses and permits. Regulated industries like cable TV, telecommunications, electric and gas utilities, radio and television broadcasting, liquor retailing, and railroads entail government-controlled entry. In international markets, host governments commonly limit foreign entry and must approve all foreign investment applications. Stringent government-mandated safety regulations and environmental pollution standards are entry barriers because they raise entry costs.

- *Tariffs and international trade restrictions*—National governments commonly use tariffs and trade restrictions (antidumping rules, local content requirements, quotas, etc.) to raise entry barriers for foreign firms and protect domestic producers from outside competition.

- *The ability and inclination of industry incumbents to launch vigorous initiatives to block a newcomer's successful entry*—Even if a potential entrant has or can acquire the needed competencies and resources to attempt entry, it must still worry about the reaction of existing firms.[5] Sometimes, there's little that incumbents can do to throw obstacles in an entrant's path—for instance, existing restaurants have little in their arsenal to discourage a new restaurant from opening or to dissuade people from trying the new restaurant. But there are times when incumbents do all they can to make it difficult for a new entrant, using price cuts, increased advertising, product improvements, and whatever else they can think of to prevent the entrant from building a clientele. Cable TV companies vigorously fight the entry of satellite TV companies; Sony and Nintendo have mounted strong defenses to thwart Microsoft's entry in videogames with its Xbox; existing hotels try to combat the opening of new hotels with loyalty programs, renovations of their own, the addition of new services, and so on. A potential entrant can have second thoughts when financially strong incumbent firms send clear signals that they will give newcomers a hard time.

Whether an industry's entry barriers ought to be considered high or low depends on the resources and competencies possessed by the pool of potential entrants. Companies with sizable financial resources, proven competitive capabilities, and a respected brand name may be able to hurdle an industry's entry barriers rather easily. Small start-up enterprises may find the same entry barriers insurmountable. Thus, how hard it will be for potential entrants to compete on a level playing field is always relative to the financial resources and competitive capabilities of likely entrants. For example, when Honda opted to enter the U.S. lawn-mower market in competition against Toro, Snapper, Craftsman, John Deere, and others, it was easily able to hurdle entry barriers that would have been formidable to other newcomers because it had long-standing expertise in gasoline engines and because its well-known reputation for quality and durability gave it instant credibility with shoppers looking to buy a new lawn mower. Honda had to spend relatively little on advertising to attract buyers and gain a market foothold, distributors and dealers were quite willing to handle the Honda lawn-mower line, and Honda had ample capital to build a U.S. assembly plant.

In evaluating whether the threat of additional entry is strong or weak, company managers must look at (1) how formidable the entry barriers are for each type of potential entrant—start-up enterprises, specific candidate companies in other industries, and current industry participants looking to expand their market reach—and (2) how attractive the growth and profit prospects are for new entrants. Rapidly growing market demand and high potential profits act as magnets, motivating potential entrants to commit the resources needed to hurdle entry barriers.[6] When profits are sufficiently attractive, entry barriers are unlikely to be an effective entry deterrent. At most, they limit the pool of candidate entrants to enterprises with the requisite competencies and resources and with the creativity to fashion a strategy for competing with incumbent firms.

Hence, *the best test of whether potential entry is a strong or weak competitive force in the marketplace is to ask if the industry's growth and profit prospects are strongly attractive to potential entry candidates.* When the answer is no, potential entry is a weak competitive force. When the answer is yes and there are entry candidates with sufficient expertise and resources, then potential entry adds significantly to competitive pressures in the marketplace. The stronger the threat of entry, the more that incumbent firms are driven to seek ways to fortify their positions against newcomers, pursuing strategic moves not only to protect their market shares but also to make entry more costly or difficult.

One additional point: *The threat of entry changes as the industry's prospects grow brighter or dimmer and as entry barriers rise or fall.* For example, in the pharmaceutical industry the expiration of a key patent on a widely prescribed drug virtually guarantees that one or more drug makers will enter with generic offerings of their own. Growing use of the Internet for shopping is making it much easier for Web-based retailers to enter into competition

> High entry barriers and weak entry threats today do not always translate into high entry barriers and weak entry threats tomorrow.

against such well-known retail chains as Sears, Circuit City, and Barnes and Noble. In international markets, entry barriers for foreign-based firms fall as tariffs are lowered, as host governments open up their domestic markets to outsiders, as domestic wholesalers and dealers seek out lower-cost foreign-made goods, and as domestic buyers become more willing to purchase foreign brands.

Competitive Pressures from the Sellers of Substitute Products

Companies in one industry come under competitive pressure from the actions of companies in a closely adjoining industry whenever buyers view the products of the two industries as good substitutes. For instance, the producers of sugar experience competitive pressures from the sales and marketing efforts of the makers of artificial sweeteners. Similarly, the producers of eyeglasses and contact lenses are currently facing mounting competitive pressures from growing consumer interest in corrective laser surgery. Newspapers are feeling the competitive force of the general public turning to cable news channels for late-breaking news and using Internet sources to get information about sports results, stock quotes, and job opportunities. The makers of videotapes and VCRs have watched demand evaporate as more and more consumers have been attracted to substitute use of DVDs and DVD recorders/players. Traditional providers of telephone service like BellSouth, AT&T, Verizon, and Qwest are feeling enormous competitive pressure from cell phone providers, as more and more consumers find cell phones preferable to landline phones.

Just how strong the competitive pressures are from the sellers of substitute products depends on three factors:

1. *Whether substitutes are readily available and attractively priced.* The presence of readily available and attractively priced substitutes creates competitive pressure by placing a ceiling on the prices industry members can charge without giving customers an incentive to switch to substitutes and risking sales erosion.[7] This price ceiling, at the same time, puts a lid on the profits that industry members can earn unless they find ways to cut costs. When substitutes are cheaper than an industry's product, industry members come under heavy competitive pressure to reduce their prices and find ways to absorb the price cuts with cost reductions.

2. *Whether buyers view the substitutes as being comparable or better in terms of quality, performance, and other relevant attributes.* The availability of substitutes inevitably invites customers to compare performance, features, ease of use, and other attributes as well as price. For example, ski boat manufacturers are experiencing strong competition from personal water-ski craft because water sports enthusiasts see personal water skis as fun to ride and less expensive. The users of paper cartons constantly weigh the performance trade-offs with plastic containers and metal cans. Camera users consider the convenience and performance trade-offs when deciding whether to substitute a digital camera for a film-based camera. Competition from good-performing substitutes unleashes competitive pressures on industry participants to incorporate new performance features and attributes that makes their product offerings more competitive.

3. *Whether the costs that buyers incur in switching to the substitutes are high or low.* High switching costs deter switching to substitutes, while low switching costs make it easier for the sellers of attractive substitutes to lure buyers to their offering.[8] Typical switching costs include the time and inconvenience that may be involved, the costs of additional equipment, the time and cost in testing the quality

Figure 3.6 **Factors Affecting Competition from Substitute Products**

Firms in Other Industries Offering Substitute Products

Competitive pressures from substitutes are weaker when:
- Good substitutes are not readily available or don't exist.
- Substitutes are higher priced relative to the performance they deliver.
- End users have high costs in switching to substitutes.

How strong are competitive pressures coming from the attempts of companies outside the industry to win buyers over to their products?

Competitive pressures from substitutes are stronger when:
- Good substitutes are readily available or new ones are emerging.
- Substitutes are attractively priced.
- Substitutes have comparable or better performance features.
- End users have low costs in switching to substitutes.
- End users grow more comfortable with using substitutes

Rivalry among Competing Sellers

Signs That Competition from Substitutes Is Strong
- Sales of substitutes are growing faster than sales of the industry being analyzed (an indication that the sellers of substitutes are drawing customers away from the industry in question).
- Producers of substitutes are moving to add new capacity.
- Profits of the producers of substitutes are on the rise.

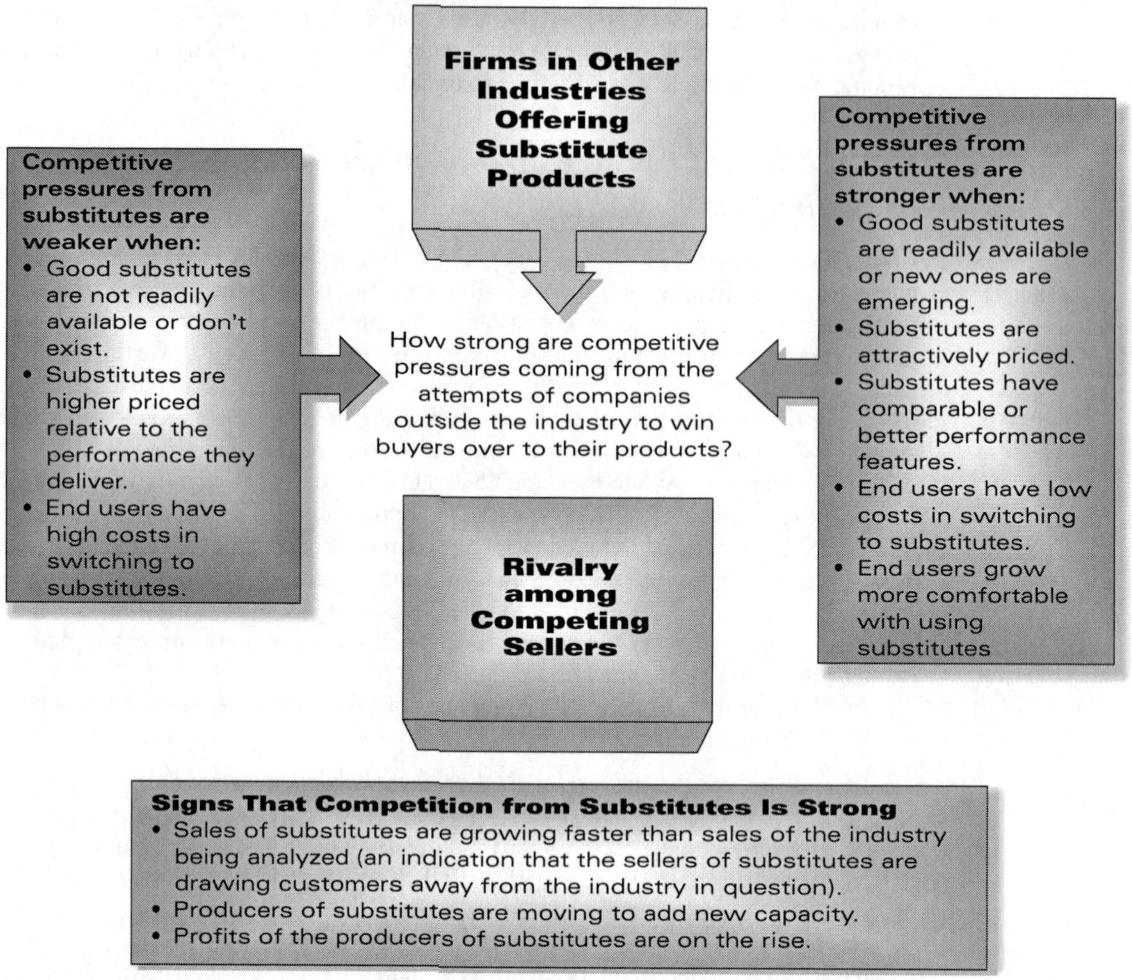

and reliability of the substitute, the psychological costs of severing old supplier relationships and establishing new ones, payments for technical help in making the changeover, and employee retraining costs. High switching costs can materially weaken the competitive pressures that industry members experience from substitutes unless the sellers of substitutes are successful in offsetting the high switching costs with enticing price discounts or additional performance enhancements.

Figure 3.6 summarizes the conditions that determine whether the competitive pressures from substitute products are strong, moderate, or weak.

As a rule, the lower the price of substitutes, the higher their quality and performance, and the lower the user's switching costs, the more intense the competitive pressures posed by substitute products. Other market indicators of the competitive strength of substitute products include (1) whether the sales of substitutes are growing faster than the sales of the industry being analyzed (a sign that the sellers of substitutes may be drawing customers away from the industry in question), (2) whether the producers of substitutes are moving to add new capacity, and (3) whether the profits of the producers of substitutes are on the rise.

Competitive Pressures Stemming from Supplier Bargaining Power and Supplier–Seller Collaboration

Whether supplier–seller relationships represent a weak or strong competitive force depends on (1) whether the major suppliers can exercise sufficient bargaining power to influence the terms and conditions of supply in their favor, and (2) the nature and extent of supplier–seller collaboration in the industry.

How Supplier Bargaining Power Can Create Competitive Pressures

Whenever the major suppliers to an industry have considerable leverage in determining the terms and conditions of the item they are supplying, then they are in a position to exert competitive pressure on one or more rival sellers. For instance, Microsoft and Intel, both of which supply personal computer (PC) makers with products that most PC users consider essential, are known for using their dominant market status not only to charge PC makers premium prices but also to leverage PC makers in other ways. Microsoft pressures PC makers to load only Microsoft products on the PCs they ship and to position the icons for Microsoft software prominently on the screens of new computers that come with factory-loaded software. Intel pushes greater use of Intel microprocessors in PCs by granting PC makers sizable advertising allowances on PC models equipped with "Intel Inside" stickers; it also tends to give PC makers that use the biggest percentages of Intel chips in their PC models top priority in filling orders for newly introduced Intel chips. Being on Intel's list of preferred customers helps a PC maker get an allocation of the first production runs of Intel's latest and greatest chips and thus get new PC models equipped with these chips to market ahead of rivals who are heavier users of chips made by Intel's rivals. The ability of Microsoft and Intel to pressure PC makers for preferential treatment of one kind or another in turn affects competition among rival PC makers.

Several other instances of supplier bargaining power are worth citing. Small-scale retailers must often contend with the power of manufacturers whose products enjoy prestigious and well-respected brand names; when a manufacturer knows that a retailer needs to stock the manufacturer's product because consumers expect to find the product on the shelves of retail stores where they shop, the manufacturer usually has some degree of pricing power and can also push hard for favorable shelf displays. Motor vehicle manufacturers typically exert considerable power over the terms and conditions with which they supply new vehicles to their independent automobile dealerships. The operators of franchised units of such chains as McDonald's, Dunkin' Donuts, Pizza Hut, Sylvan Learning Centers, and Hampton Inns must frequently agree not only to source some of their supplies from the franchisor at prices and terms favorable to that franchisor but also to operate their facilities in a manner largely dictated by the franchisor.

Strong supplier bargaining power is a competitive factor in industries where unions have been able to organize the workforces of some industry members but not others; those industry members that must negotiate wages, fringe benefits, and working conditions with powerful unions (which control the supply of labor) often find themselves with higher labor costs than their competitors with nonunion labor forces. The bigger the gap between union and nonunion labor costs in an industry, the more that unionized industry members must scramble to find ways to relieve the competitive pressure associated with their disadvantage on labor costs. High labor costs are proving a huge competitive liability to unionized supermarket chains like Kroger and Safeway in trying to combat the market share gains being made by Wal-Mart in supermarket retailing—Wal-Mart has a nonunion workforce, and the prices for supermarket items at its Supercenters tend to run 5 to 20 percent lower than those at unionized supermarket chains.

The factors that determine whether any of the suppliers to an industry are in a position to exert substantial bargaining power or leverage are fairly clear-cut:[9]

- *Whether the item being supplied is a commodity that is readily available from many suppliers at the going market price.* Suppliers have little or no bargaining power or leverage whenever industry members have the ability to source their requirements at competitive prices from any of several alternative and eager suppliers, perhaps dividing their purchases among two or more suppliers to promote lively competition for orders. The suppliers of commodity items have market power only when supplies become quite tight and industry members are so eager to secure what they need that they agree to terms more favorable to suppliers.

- *Whether a few large suppliers are the primary sources of a particular item.* The leading suppliers may well have pricing leverage unless they are plagued with excess capacity and are scrambling to secure additional orders for their products. Major suppliers with good reputations and strong demand for the items they supply are harder to wring concessions from than struggling suppliers striving to broaden their customer base or more fully utilize their production capacity.

- *Whether it is difficult or costly for industry members to switch their purchases from one supplier to another or to switch to attractive substitute inputs.* High switching costs signal strong bargaining power on the part of suppliers, whereas low switching costs and ready availability of good substitute inputs signal weak bargaining power. Soft-drink bottlers, for example, can counter the bargaining power of aluminum can suppliers by shifting or threatening to shift to greater use of plastic containers and introducing more attractive plastic container designs.

- *Whether certain needed inputs are in short supply.* Suppliers of items in short supply have some degree of pricing power, whereas a surge in the availability of particular items greatly weakens supplier pricing power and bargaining leverage.

- *Whether certain suppliers provide a differentiated input that enhances the performance or quality of the industry's product.* The more valuable that a particular input is in terms of enhancing the performance or quality of the products of industry members or of improving the efficiency of their production processes, the more bargaining leverage its suppliers are likely to possess.

- *Whether certain suppliers provide equipment or services that deliver valuable cost-saving efficiencies to industry members in operating their production processes.* Suppliers who provide cost-saving equipment or other valuable or necessary production-related services are likely to possess bargaining leverage. Industry members that do not source from such suppliers may find themselves at a cost disadvantage and thus under competitive pressure to do so (on terms that are favorable to the suppliers).

- *Whether suppliers provide an item that accounts for a sizable fraction of the costs of the industry's product.* The bigger the cost of a particular part or component, the more opportunity for the pattern of competition in the marketplace to be affected by the actions of suppliers to raise or lower their prices.

- *Whether industry members are major customers of suppliers.* As a rule, suppliers have less bargaining leverage when their sales to members of this one industry constitute a big percentage of their total sales. In such cases, the well-being of suppliers is closely tied to the well-being of their major customers.

Suppliers then have a big incentive to protect and enhance their customers' competitiveness via reasonable prices, exceptional quality, and ongoing advances in the technology of the items supplied.

- *Whether it makes good economic sense for industry members to integrate backward and self-manufacture items they have been buying from suppliers.* The make-or-buy issue generally boils down to whether suppliers who specialize in the production of a particular part or component and make them in volume for many different customers have the expertise and scale economies to supply as good or better component at a lower cost than industry members could achieve via self-manufacture. Frequently, it is difficult for industry members to self-manufacture parts and components more economically than they can obtain them from suppliers who specialize in making such items. For instance, most producers of outdoor power equipment (lawn mowers, rotary tillers, leaf blowers, etc.) find it cheaper to source the small engines they need from outside manufacturers who specialize in small-engine manufacture rather than make their own engines because the quantity of engines they need is too small to justify the investment in manufacturing facilities, master the production process, and capture scale economies. Specialists in small-engine manufacture, by supplying many kinds of engines to the whole power equipment industry, can obtain a big enough sales volume to fully realize scale economies, become proficient in all the manufacturing techniques, and keep costs low. As a rule, suppliers are safe from the threat of self-manufacture by their customers *until* the volume of parts a customer needs becomes large enough for the customer to justify backward integration into self-manufacture of the component. Suppliers also gain bargaining power when they have the resources and profit incentive to integrate forward into the business of the customers they are supplying and thus become a strong rival.

Figure 3.7 summarizes the conditions that tend to make supplier bargaining power strong or weak.

How Seller–Supplier Partnerships Can Create Competitive Pressures

In more and more industries, sellers are forging strategic partnerships with select suppliers in efforts to (1) reduce inventory and logistics costs (e.g., through just-in-time deliveries), (2) speed the availability of next-generation components, (3) enhance the quality of the parts and components being supplied and reduce defect rates, and (4) squeeze out important cost savings for both themselves and their suppliers. Numerous Internet technology applications are now available that permit real-time data sharing, eliminate paperwork, and produce cost savings all along the supply chain. The many benefits of effective seller–supplier collaboration can translate into competitive advantage for industry members that do the best job of managing supply chain relationships.

Dell Computer has used strategic partnering with key suppliers as a major element in its strategy to be the world's lowest-cost supplier of branded PCs, servers, and workstations. Because Dell has managed its supply chain relationships in ways that contribute to a low-cost, high-quality competitive edge in components supply, it has put enormous pressure on its PC rivals to try to imitate its supply chain management practices. Effective partnerships with suppliers on the part of one or more industry members can thus become a major source of competitive pressure for rival firms.

The more opportunities that exist for win–win efforts between a company and its suppliers, the less their relationship is characterized by who has the upper hand in

Figure 3.7   **Factors Affecting the Bargaining Power of Suppliers**

Supplier bargaining power is stronger when:
- Industry members incurs high costs in switching their purchases to alternative suppliers.
- Needed inputs are in short supply (which gives suppliers more leverage in setting prices).
- A supplier has a differentiated input that enhances the quality or performance of sellers' products or is a valuable or critical part of sellers' production process.
- There are only a few suppliers of a particular input.
- Some suppliers threaten to integrate forward into the business of industry members and perhaps become a powerful rival.

Supplier bargaining power is weaker when:
- The item being supplied is a commodity that is readily available from many suppliers at the going market price.
- Seller switching costs to alternative suppliers are low.
- Good substitute inputs exist or new ones emerge.
- There is a surge in the availability of supplies (thus greatly weakening supplier pricing power).
- Industry members account for a big fraction of suppliers' total sales and continued high volume purchases are important to the well-being of suppliers.
- Industry members are a threat to integrate backward into the business of suppliers and to self-manufacture their own requirements.
- Seller collaboration or partnering with selected suppliers provides attractive win–win opportunities.

bargaining with the other. Collaborative partnerships between a company and a supplier tend to last so long as the relationship is producing valuable benefits for both parties. Only if a supply partner is falling behind alternative suppliers is a company likely to switch suppliers and incur the costs and trouble of building close working ties with a different supplier.

Competitive Pressures Stemming from Buyer Bargaining Power and Seller–Buyer Collaboration

Whether seller–buyer relationships represent a weak or strong competitive force depends on (1) whether some or many buyers have sufficient bargaining leverage to obtain price concessions and other favorable terms and conditions of sale, and (2) the extent and competitive importance of seller–buyer strategic partnerships in the industry.

How Buyer Bargaining Power Can Create Competitive Pressures   As with suppliers, the leverage that certain types of buyers have in negotiating favorable terms can range from weak to strong. Individual consumers, for example, rarely have much bargaining power in negotiating price concessions or other favorable terms with sellers; the primary exceptions involve situations in which price haggling is customary, such as the purchase of new and used motor vehicles, homes, and certain big-ticket items like luxury watches, jewelry, and pleasure boats. For most consumer goods and services, individual buyers have no bargaining leverage—their option is to pay the seller's posted price or take their business elsewhere.

In contrast, large retail chains like Wal-Mart, Best Buy, Staples, and Home Depot typically have considerable negotiating leverage in purchasing products from manufacturers because of manufacturers' need for broad retail exposure and the most appealing shelf locations. Retailers may stock two or three competing brands of a product but rarely all competing brands, so competition among rival manufacturers for visibility on the shelves of popular multistore retailers gives such retailers significant bargaining strength. Major supermarket chains like Kroger, Safeway, and Royal Ahold, which provide access to millions of grocery shoppers, have sufficient bargaining power to demand promotional allowances and lump-sum payments (called slotting fees) from food products manufacturers in return for stocking certain brands or putting them in the best shelf locations. Motor vehicle manufacturers have strong bargaining power in negotiating to buy original equipment tires from Goodyear, Michelin, Bridgestone/Firestone, Continental, and Pirelli not only because they buy in large quantities but also because tire makers believe they gain an advantage in supplying replacement tires to vehicle owners if their tire brand is original equipment on the vehicle. "Prestige" buyers have a degree of clout in negotiating with sellers because a seller's reputation is enhanced by having prestige buyers on its customer list.

Even if buyers do not purchase in large quantities or offer a seller important market exposure or prestige, they gain a degree of bargaining leverage in the following circumstances:[10]

- *If buyers' costs of switching to competing brands or substitutes are relatively low*—Buyers who can readily switch brands or source from several sellers have more negotiating leverage than buyers who have high switching costs. When the products of rival sellers are virtually identical, it is relatively easy for buyers to switch from seller to seller at little or no cost and anxious sellers may be willing to make concessions to win or retain a buyer's business.

- *If the number of buyers is small or if a customer is particularly important to a seller*—The smaller the number of buyers, the less easy it is for sellers to find alternative buyers when a customer is lost to a competitor. The prospect of losing a customer not easily replaced often makes a seller more willing to grant concessions of one kind or another.

- *If buyer demand is weak and sellers are scrambling to secure additional sales of their products*—Weak or declining demand creates a "buyers' market"; conversely, strong or rapidly growing demand creates a "sellers' market" and shifts bargaining power to sellers.

- *If buyers are well informed about sellers' products, prices, and costs*—The more information buyers have, the better bargaining position they are in. The mushrooming availability of product information on the Internet is giving added bargaining power to individuals. Buyers can easily use the Internet to compare prices and features of vacation packages, shop for the best interest rates on mortgages and loans, and find the best prices on big-ticket items such as digital cameras. Bargain-hunting individuals can shop around for the best deal on the Internet and use that information to negotiate a better deal from local retailers; this method is becoming commonplace in buying new and used motor vehicles. Further, the Internet has created opportunities for manufacturers, wholesalers, retailers, and sometimes individuals to join online buying groups to pool their purchasing power and approach vendors for better terms than could be gotten individually. A multinational manufacturer's geographically scattered purchasing groups can use Internet technology to pool their orders with parts and components suppliers and bargain for volume discounts. Purchasing agents at some companies are banding together at third-party Web sites to pool corporate purchases to get better deals or special treatment.

- *If buyers pose a credible threat of integrating backward into the business of sellers*—Companies like Anheuser-Busch, Coors, and Heinz have integrated backward into metal can manufacturing to gain bargaining power in obtaining the balance of their can requirements from otherwise powerful metal can manufacturers. Retailers gain bargaining power by stocking and promoting their own private-label brands alongside manufacturers' name brands. Wal-Mart, for example, has elected to compete against Procter & Gamble (P&G), its biggest supplier, with its own brand of laundry detergent, called Sam's American Choice, which is priced 25 to 30 percent lower than P&G's Tide.

- *If buyers have discretion in whether and when they purchase the product*—Many consumers, if they are unhappy with the present deals offered on major appliances or hot tubs or home entertainment centers, may be in a position to delay purchase until prices and financing terms improve. If business customers are not happy with the prices or security features of bill-payment software systems, they can either delay purchase until next-generation products become available or attempt to develop their own software in-house. If college students believe that the prices of new textbooks are too high, they can purchase used copies.

Figure 3.8 highlights the factors causing buyer bargaining power to be strong or weak.

A final point to keep in mind is that *not all buyers of an industry's product have equal degrees of bargaining power with sellers*, and some may be less sensitive than others to price, quality, or service differences. For example, independent tire retailers have less bargaining power in purchasing tires than do Honda, Ford, and DaimlerChrysler (which buy in much larger quantities), and they are also less sensitive to quality. Motor vehicle manufacturers are very particular about tire quality and tire performance because of the effects on vehicle performance, and they drive a hard bargain with tire manufacturers on both price and quality. Apparel manufacturers confront significant bargaining power when selling to big retailers like JCPenney, Macy's, or L. L. Bean but they can command much better prices selling to small owner-managed apparel boutiques.

How Seller–Buyer Partnerships Can Create Competitive Pressures Partnerships between sellers and buyers are an increasingly important element of the competitive picture in *business-to-business relationships* (as opposed to business-to-consumer relationships). Many sellers that provide items to business customers have found it in their mutual interest to collaborate closely on such matters as just-in-time deliveries, order processing, electronic invoice payments, and data sharing. Wal-Mart, for example, provides the manufacturers with which it does business (like Procter & Gamble) with daily sales at each of its stores so that the manufacturers can maintain sufficient inventories at Wal-Mart's distribution centers to keep the shelves at each Wal-Mart store amply stocked. Dell has partnered with its largest PC customers to create

Figure 3.8   **Factors Affecting the Bargaining Power of Buyers**

Buyer bargaining power is stronger when:
- Buyer switching costs to competing brands or substitute products are low.
- Buyers are large and can demand concessions when purchasing large quantities.
- Large-volume purchases by buyers are important to sellers.
- Buyer demand is weak or declining.
- There are only a few buyers—so that each one's business is important to sellers.
- Identity of buyer adds prestige to the seller's list of customers.
- Quantity and quality of information available to buyers improves.
- Buyers have the ability to postpone purchases until later if they do not like the present deals being offered by sellers.
- Some buyers are a threat to integrate backward into the business of sellers and become an important competitor.

Buyer bargaining power is weaker when:
- Buyers purchase the item infrequently or in small quantities.
- Buyer switching costs to competing brands are high.
- There is a surge in buyer demand that creates a "sellers' market."
- A seller's brand reputation is important to a buyer.
- A particular seller's product delivers quality or performance that is very important to buyer and that is not matched in other brands.
- Buyer collaboration or partnering with selected sellers provides attractive win–win opportunities.

online systems for over 50,000 corporate customers, providing their employees with information on approved product configurations, global pricing, paperless purchase orders, real-time order tracking, invoicing, purchasing history, and other efficiency tools. Dell loads a customer's software at the factory and installs asset tags so that customer setup time is minimal; it also helps customers upgrade their PC systems to next-generation hardware and software. Dell's partnerships with its corporate customers have put significant competitive pressure on other PC makers.

Is the Collective Strength of the Five Competitive Forces Conducive to Good Profitability?

Scrutinizing each of the five competitive forces one by one provides a powerful diagnosis of what competition is like in a given market. Once the strategist has gained an understanding of the specific competitive pressures comprising each force and determined whether these pressures constitute a strong, moderate, or weak competitive force, the next step is to evaluate the collective strength of the five forces and determine whether the state of competition is conducive to good profitability. Is the collective impact of the five competitive forces stronger than "normal"? Are some of the competitive forces sufficiently strong to undermine industry profitability? Can companies in this industry reasonably expect to earn decent profits in light of the prevailing competitive forces?

Is the Industry Competitively Attractive or Unattractive?   *As a rule, the stronger the collective impact of the five competitive forces, the lower the combined profitability of industry participants.* The most extreme case of a competitively unattractive industry is when all five forces are producing strong competitive pressures: Rivalry among sellers is vigorous, low entry barriers allow new rivals to gain a market foothold, competition from substitutes is intense, and both suppliers and customers are able to exercise considerable bargaining leverage. Fierce to strong competitive pressures coming from all five directions nearly always drive industry profitability to unacceptably low levels, frequently producing losses for many industry members and forcing some out of business. But an industry can be competitively unattractive even when not all five competitive forces are strong. Intense competitive pressures from just two or three of the five forces may suffice to destroy the conditions for good profitability and prompt some companies to exit the business. The manufacture of disk drives, for example, is brutally competitive; IBM recently announced the sale of its disk drive business to Hitachi, taking a loss of over $2 billion on its exit from the business. Especially intense competitive conditions seem to be the norm in tire manufacturing and apparel, two industries where profit margins have historically been thin.

> The stronger the forces of competition, the harder it becomes for industry members to earn attractive profits.

In contrast, when the collective impact of the five competitive forces is moderate to weak, an industry is competitively attractive in the sense that industry members can reasonably expect to earn good profits and a nice return on investment. The ideal competitive environment for earning superior profits is one in which both suppliers and customers are in weak bargaining positions, there are no good substitutes, high barriers block further entry, and rivalry among present sellers generates only moderate competitive pressures. Weak competition is the best of all possible worlds for also-ran companies because even they can usually eke out a decent profit—if a company can't make a decent profit when competition is weak, then its business outlook is indeed grim.

In most industries, the collective strength of the five competitive forces is somewhere near the middle of the two extremes of very intense and very weak, typically ranging from slightly stronger than normal to slightly weaker than normal and typically allowing well-managed companies with sound strategies to earn attractive profits.

Matching Company Strategy to Competitive Conditions   Working through the five-forces model step by step not only aids strategy makers in assessing whether the intensity of competition allows good profitability but also promotes sound strategic thinking about how to better match company strategy to the specific competitive character of the marketplace. Effectively matching a company's strategy to prevailing competitive conditions has two aspects:

> A company's strategy is increasingly effective the more it provides some insulation from competitive pressures and shifts the competitive battle in the company's favor.

1. Pursuing avenues that shield the firm from as many of the different competitive pressures as possible.
2. Initiating actions calculated to produce sustainable competitive advantage, thereby shifting competition in the company's favor, putting added competitive pressure on rivals, and perhaps even defining the business model for the industry.

But making headway on these two fronts first requires identifying competitive pressures, gauging the relative strength of each of the five competitive forces, and gaining a deep enough understanding of the state of competition in the industry to know which strategy buttons to push.

QUESTION 3: WHAT FACTORS ARE DRIVING INDUSTRY CHANGE AND WHAT IMPACTS WILL THEY HAVE?

An industry's present conditions don't necessarily reveal much about the strategically relevant ways in which the industry environment is changing. All industries are characterized by trends and new developments that gradually or speedily produce changes important enough to require a strategic response from participating firms. A popular hypothesis states that industries go through a life cycle of takeoff, rapid growth, early maturity and slowing growth, market saturation, and stagnation or decline. This hypothesis helps explain industry change—but it is far from complete.[11] There are more causes of industry change than an industry's normal progression through the life cycle—these need to be identified and their impacts understood.

The Concept of Driving Forces

Core Concept
Industry conditions change because important forces are *driving* industry participants (competitors, customers, or suppliers) to alter their actions; the **driving forces** in an industry are the *major underlying causes* of changing industry and competitive conditions—they have the biggest influence on how the industry landscape will be altered. Some driving forces originate in the outer ring of macroenvironment and some originate from the inner ring.

While it is important to track where an industry is in the life cycle, there's more analytical value in identifying the other factors that may be even stronger drivers of industry and competitive change. The point to be made here is that industry and competitive conditions change because forces are enticing or pressuring certain industry participants (competitors, customers, suppliers) to alter their actions in important ways.[12] The most powerful of the change agents are called **driving forces** because they have the biggest influences in reshaping the industry landscape and altering competitive conditions. Some driving forces originate in the outer ring of the company's macroenvironment (see Figure 3.2), but most originate in the company's more immediate industry and competitive environment.

Driving-forces analysis has three steps: (1) identifying what the driving forces are; (2) assessing whether the drivers of change are, on the whole, acting to make the industry more or less attractive; and (3) determining what strategy changes are needed to prepare for the impacts of the driving forces. All three steps merit further discussion.

Identifying an Industry's Driving Forces

Many developments can affect an industry powerfully enough to qualify as driving forces. Some drivers of change are unique and specific to a particular industry situation, but most drivers of industry and competitive change fall into one of the following categories:[13]

- *Emerging new Internet capabilities and applications*—Since the late 1990s, the Internet has woven its way into everyday business operations and the social fabric of life all across the world. Mushrooming Internet use, growing acceptance of Internet shopping, the emergence of high-speed Internet service and Voice over Internet Protocol (VoIP) technology, and an ever-growing series of Internet applications and capabilities have been major drivers of change in industry after industry. Companies are increasingly using online technology (1) to collaborate closely with suppliers and streamline their supply chains and (2) to revamp internal operations and squeeze out cost savings. Manufacturers can use their Web sites to access customers directly rather than distribute exclusively through traditional wholesale and retail channels. Businesses of all types can use Web stores to extend their geographic reach and vie for sales in areas where they formerly did not have a presence. The ability of companies to reach consumers via the Internet increases the number of rivals a company faces and often escalates rivalry by pitting pure online sellers against combination brick-and-click sellers against pure brick-and-mortar sellers. The Internet gives buyers unprecedented ability to research the product offerings of competitors and shop the market for the best value. Mounting ability of consumers to download music from the Internet via either file sharing or online music retailers has profoundly and reshaped the music industry and the business of traditional brick-and-mortar music retailers. Widespread use of e-mail has forever eroded the business of providing fax services and the first-class mail delivery revenues of government postal services worldwide. Videoconferencing via the Internet can erode the demand for business travel. Online course offerings at universities have the potential to revolutionize higher education. The Internet of the future will feature faster speeds, dazzling applications, and over a billion connected gadgets performing an array of functions, thus driving further industry and competitive changes. But Internet-related impacts vary from industry to industry. The challenges here are to assess precisely how emerging Internet developments are altering a particular industry's landscape and to factor these impacts into the strategy-making equation.

- *Increasing globalization*—Competition begins to shift from primarily a regional or national focus to an international or global focus when industry members begin seeking out customers in foreign markets or when production activities begin to migrate to countries where costs are lowest. Globalization of competition really starts to take hold when one or more ambitious companies precipitate a race for worldwide market leadership by launching initiatives to expand into more and more country markets. Globalization can also be precipitated by the blossoming of consumer demand in more and more countries and by the actions of government officials in many countries to reduce trade barriers or open up once-closed markets to foreign competitors, as is occurring in many parts of Europe, Latin America, and Asia. Significant differences in labor costs among countries give manufacturers a strong incentive to locate plants for labor-intensive products in low-wage countries and use these plants to supply market demand across the world. Wages in China, India, Singapore, Mexico, and Brazil, for example, are about one-fourth those in the United States, Germany, and Japan. The forces of globalization are sometimes such a strong driver that companies find it highly advantageous, if not necessary, to spread their operating reach into more and more country markets. Globalization is very much a driver of industry change in such industries as credit cards, cell phones, digital cameras, golf and ski equipment, motor vehicles, steel, petroleum, personal computers, video games, public accounting, and textbook publishing.

- *Changes in an industry's long-term growth rate*—Shifts in industry growth up or down are a driving force for industry change, affecting the balance between

74

industry supply and buyer demand, entry and exit, and the character and strength of competition. An upsurge in buyer demand triggers a race among established firms and newcomers to capture the new sales opportunities; ambitious companies with trailing market shares may see the upturn in demand as a golden opportunity to launch offensive strategies to broaden their customer base and move up several notches in the industry standings. A slowdown in the rate at which demand is growing nearly always portends mounting rivalry and increased efforts by some firms to maintain their high rates of growth by taking sales and market share away from rivals. If industry sales suddenly turn flat or begin to shrink after years of rising at double-digit levels, competition is certain to intensify as industry members scramble for the available business and as mergers and acquisitions result in industry consolidation to a smaller number of competitively stronger participants. Stagnating sales usually prompt both competitively weak and growth-oriented companies to sell their business operations to those industry members who elect to stick it out; as demand for the industry's product continues to shrink, the remaining industry members may be forced to close inefficient plants and retrench to a smaller production base—all of which results in a much-changed competitive landscape.

- *Changes in who buys the product and how they use it*—Shifts in buyer demographics and new ways of using the product can alter the state of competition by opening the way to market an industry's product through a different mix of dealers and retail outlets; prompting producers to broaden or narrow their product lines; bringing different sales and promotion approaches into play; and forcing adjustments in customer service offerings (credit, technical assistance, maintenance, and repair). The mushrooming popularity of downloading music from the Internet, storing music files on PC hard drives, and burning custom discs has forced recording companies to reexamine their distribution strategies and raised questions about the future of traditional retail music stores; at the same time, it has stimulated sales of disc burners and blank discs. Longer life expectancies and growing percentages of relatively well-to-do retirees are driving changes in such industries as health care, prescription drugs, recreational living, and vacation travel. The growing percentage of households with PCs and Internet access is opening opportunities for banks to expand their electronic bill-payment services and for retailers to move more of their customer services online.

- *Product innovation*—Competition in an industry is always affected by rivals racing to be first to introduce one new product or product enhancement after another. An ongoing stream of product innovations tends to alter the pattern of competition in an industry by attracting more first-time buyers, rejuvenating industry growth, and/or creating wider or narrower product differentiation among rival sellers. Successful new product introductions strengthen the market positions of the innovating companies, usually at the expense of companies that stick with their old products or are slow to follow with their own versions of the new product. Product innovation has been a key driving force in such industries as digital cameras, golf clubs, video games, toys, and prescription drugs.

- *Technological change and manufacturing process innovation*—Advances in technology can dramatically alter an industry's landscape, making it possible to produce new and better products at lower cost and opening up whole new industry frontiers. For instance, Voice over Internet Protocol (VoIP) technology has spawned low-cost, Internet-based phone networks that are stealing large numbers of customers away from traditional telephone companies worldwide (whose higher cost technology depends on hardwired connections via overhead and underground telephone lines). Flat-screen technology for PC monitors is killing the demand for conventional cathode ray tube (CRT) monitors. Liquid crystal display (LCD), plasma screen technology, and high-definition technology are precipitating a revolution in the television industry and driving use of cathode ray technology (CRT) into the background. MP3 technology is transforming how people listen to music. Digital technology is driving huge changes in the camera and film industries. Satellite radio technology is allowing satellite radio companies with their largely commercial-free programming to draw millions of listeners away from traditional radio stations whose revenue streams from commercials are dependent on audience size. Technological developments can also produce competitively significant changes in capital requirements, minimum efficient plant sizes, distribution channels and logistics, and learning/experience curve effects. In the steel industry, ongoing advances in electric arc minimill technology (which involve recycling scrap steel to make new products) have allowed steelmakers with state-of-the-art minimills to gradually expand into the production of more and more steel products, steadily taking sales and market share from higher-cost integrated producers (which make steel from scratch using iron ore, coke, and traditional blast furnace technology). Nucor Corporation, the leader of the minimill technology revolution in the United States, began operations in 1970 and has ridden the wave of technological advances in minimill technology to become the biggest U.S. steel producer (as of 2004) and rank among the lowest-cost producers in the world. In a space of 30 years, advances in minimill technology have changed the face of the steel industry worldwide.

- *Marketing innovation*—When firms are successful in introducing new ways to *market* their products, they can spark a burst of buyer interest, widen industry demand, increase product differentiation, and lower unit costs—any or all of which can alter the competitive positions of rival firms and force strategy revisions. Online marketing is shaking up competition in electronics (where there are dozens of online electronics retailers, often with deep-discount prices) and office supplies (where Office Depot, Staples, and Office Max are using their Web sites to market office supplies to corporations, small businesses, schools and universities, and government agencies). Increasing numbers of music artists are marketing their recordings at their own Web sites rather than entering into contracts with recording studios that distribute through online and brick-and-mortar music retailers.

- *Entry or exit of major firms*—The entry of one or more foreign companies into a geographic market once dominated by domestic firms nearly always shakes up competitive conditions. Likewise, when an established domestic firm from another industry attempts entry either by acquisition or by launching its own start-up venture, it usually applies its skills and resources in some innovative fashion that pushes competition in new directions. Entry by a major firm thus often produces a new ball game, not only with new key players but also with new rules for competing. Similarly, exit of a major firm changes the competitive structure by reducing the number of market leaders (perhaps increasing the dominance of the leaders who remain) and causing a rush to capture the exiting firm's customers.

- *Diffusion of technical know-how across more companies and more countries*— As knowledge about how to perform a particular activity or execute a particular manufacturing technology spreads, the competitive advantage held by firms originally possessing this know-how erodes. Knowledge diffusion can occur through scientific journals, trade publications, on-site plant tours, word of mouth among suppliers and customers, employee migration, and Internet sources. It can also occur when those possessing technological knowledge license others to use that knowledge for a royalty fee or team up with a company interested in turning the technology into a new business venture. Quite often, technological know-how can be acquired by simply buying a company that has the wanted skills, patents, or manufacturing capabilities. In recent years, *rapid technology transfer across national boundaries has been a prime factor in causing industries to become more globally competitive.* As companies worldwide gain access to valuable technical know-how, they upgrade their manufacturing capabilities in a long-term effort to compete head-on with established companies. Cross-border technology transfer has made the once domestic industries of automobiles, tires, consumer electronics, telecommunications, computers, and others increasingly global.

- *Changes in cost and efficiency*—Widening or shrinking differences in the costs among key competitors tend to dramatically alter the state of competition. The low cost of fax and e-mail transmission has put mounting competitive pressure on the relatively inefficient and high-cost operations of the U.S. Postal Service—sending a one-page fax is cheaper and far quicker than sending a first-class letter; sending e-mail is faster and cheaper still. In the steel industry, the lower costs of companies using electric-arc furnaces to recycle scrap steel into new steel products has forced traditional manufacturers that produce steel from iron ore using blast furnace technology to overhaul their plants and to withdraw totally from making those steel products where they could no longer be cost competitive. Shrinking cost differences in producing multifeatured mobile phones is turning the mobile phone market into a commodity business and causing more buyers to base their purchase decisions on price.

- *Growing buyer preferences for differentiated products instead of a commodity product (or for a more standardized product instead of strongly differentiated products)*—When buyer tastes and preferences start to diverge, sellers can win a loyal following with product offerings that stand apart from those of rival sellers. In recent years, beer drinkers have grown less loyal to a single brand and have begun to drink a variety of domestic and foreign beers; as a consequence, beer manufacturers have introduced a host of new brands and malt beverages with different tastes and flavors. Buyer preferences for motor vehicles are becoming increasingly diverse, with few models generating sales of more than 250,000 units annually. When a shift from standardized to differentiated products occurs, the driver of change is the contest among rivals to cleverly outdifferentiate one another.

  However, buyers sometimes decide that a standardized, budget-priced product suits their requirements as well as or better than a premium-priced product with lots of snappy features and personalized services. Online brokers, for example, have used the lure of cheap commissions to attract many investors willing to place their own buy–sell orders via the Internet; growing acceptance of online trading has put significant competitive pressures on full-service brokers whose business model has always revolved around convincing clients of the value of asking for personalized advice from professional brokers and paying their high commission fees to make trades. Pronounced shifts toward greater product standardization usually spawn lively price competition and force rival sellers to drive down their costs to maintain profitability. The lesson here is that competition is driven partly by whether the market forces in motion are acting to increase or decrease product differentiation.

- *Reductions in uncertainty and business risk*—An emerging industry is typically characterized by much uncertainty over potential market size, how much time and money will be needed to surmount technological problems, and what distribution channels and buyer segments to emphasize. Emerging industries tend to attract only risk-taking entrepreneurial companies. Over time, however, if the business model of industry pioneers proves profitable and market demand for the product appears durable, more conservative firms are usually enticed to enter the market. Often, these later entrants are large, financially strong firms looking to invest in attractive growth industries.

  Lower business risks and less industry uncertainty also affect competition in international markets. In the early stages of a company's entry into foreign markets, conservatism prevails and firms limit their downside exposure by using less risky strategies like exporting, licensing, joint marketing agreements, or joint ventures with local companies to accomplish entry. Then, as experience accumulates and perceived risk levels decline, companies move more boldly and more independently, making acquisitions, constructing their own plants, putting in their own sales and marketing capabilities to build strong competitive positions in each country market, and beginning to link the strategies in each country to create a more globalized strategy.

- *Regulatory influences and government policy changes*—Government regulatory actions can often force significant changes in industry practices and strategic approaches. Deregulation has proved to be a potent pro-competitive force in the airline, banking, natural gas, telecommunications, and electric utility industries. Government efforts to reform Medicare and health insurance have become potent driving forces in the health care industry. In international markets, host governments can drive competitive changes by opening their domestic markets to foreign participation or closing them to protect domestic companies. Note that this driving force is spawned by forces in a company's macroenvironment.

- *Changing societal concerns, attitudes, and lifestyles*—Emerging social issues and changing attitudes and lifestyles can be powerful instigators of industry change. Growing antismoking sentiment has emerged as a major driver of change in the tobacco industry; concerns about terrorism are having a big impact on the travel industry. Consumer concerns about salt, sugar, chemical additives, saturated fat, cholesterol, carbohydrates, and nutritional value have forced food producers to revamp food-processing techniques, redirect R&D efforts into the use of healthier ingredients, and compete in developing nutritious, good-tasting products. Safety concerns have driven product design changes in the automobile, toy, and outdoor power equipment industries, to mention a few. Increased interest in physical fitness has spawned new industries in exercise equipment, biking, outdoor apparel, sports gyms and recreation centers, vitamin and nutrition supplements, and medically supervised diet programs. Social concerns about air and water pollution have forced industries to incorporate expenditures for controlling pollution into their cost structures. Shifting societal concerns, attitudes, and lifestyles alter the pattern of competition, usually favoring those

Table 3.2   **The Most Common Driving Forces**

1. Emerging new Internet capabilities and applications
2. Increasing globalization
3. Changes in an industry's long-term growth rate
4. Changes in who buys the product and how they use it
5. Product innovation
6. Technological change and manufacturing process innovation
7. Marketing innovation
8. Entry or exit of major firms
9. Diffusion of technical know-how across more companies and more countries
10. Changes in cost and efficiency
11. Growing buyer preferences for differentiated products instead of a commodity product (or for a more standardized product instead of strongly differentiated products)
12. Reductions in uncertainty and business risk
13. Regulatory influences and government policy changes
14. Changing societal concerns, attitudes, and lifestyles

players that respond quickly and creatively with products targeted to the new trends and conditions. As with the preceding driving force, this driving force springs from factors at work in a company's macroenvironment.

Table 3.2 lists these 14 most common driving forces.

That there are so many different potential driving forces explains why it is too simplistic to view industry change only in terms of moving through the different stages in an industry's life cycle and why a full understanding of all types of change drivers is a fundamental part of industry analysis. However, while many forces of change may be at work in a given industry, no more than three or four are likely to be true driving forces powerful enough to qualify as the *major determinants* of why and how the industry is changing. Thus company strategists must resist the temptation to label every change they see as a driving force; the analytical task is to evaluate the forces of industry and competitive change carefully enough to separate major factors from minor ones.

Assessing the Impact of the Driving Forces

> An important part of driving-forces analysis is to determine whether the collective impact of the driving forces will be to increase or decrease market demand, make competition more or less intense, and lead to higher or lower industry profitability.

Just identifying the driving forces is not sufficient, however. The second, and more important, step in driving-forces analysis is to determine whether the prevailing driving forces are, on the whole, acting to make the industry environment more or less attractive. Answers to three questions are needed here:

1. Are the driving forces collectively acting to cause demand for the industry's product to increase or decrease?
2. Are the driving forces acting to make competition more or less intense?
3. Will the combined impacts of the driving forces lead to higher or lower industry profitability?

Getting a handle on the collective impact of the driving forces usually requires looking at the likely effects of each force separately, since the driving forces may not all be pushing change in the same direction. For example, two driving forces may be acting to spur demand for the industry's product while one driving force may be working to curtail demand. Whether the net effect on industry demand is up or down hinges on which driving forces are the more powerful. The analyst's objective here is to get a good grip on what external factors are shaping industry change and what difference these factors will make.

Developing a Strategy That Takes the Impacts of the Driving Forces into Account

The third step of driving-forces analysis—where the real payoff for strategy making comes—is for managers to draw some conclusions about what strategy adjustments will be needed to deal with the impacts of the driving forces. The real value of doing driving-forces analysis is to gain better understanding of what strategy adjustments will be needed to cope with the drivers of industry change and the impacts they are likely to have on market demand, competitive intensity, and industry profitability. In short, the strategy-making challenge that flows from driving-forces analysis is what to do to prepare for the industry and competitive changes being wrought by the driving forces. Indeed, without understanding the forces driving industry change and the impacts these forces will have on the character of the industry environment and on the company's business over the next one to three years, managers are ill-prepared to craft a strategy tightly matched to emerging conditions. Similarly, if managers are uncertain about the implications of one or more driving forces, or if their views are incomplete or off base, it's difficult for them to craft a strategy that is responsive to the driving forces and their consequences for the industry. So driving-forces analysis is not something to take lightly; it has practical value and is basic to the task of thinking strategically about where the industry is headed and how to prepare for the changes ahead.

> Driving-forces analysis, when done properly, pushes company managers to think about what's around the corner and what the company needs to be doing to get ready for it.

> The real payoff of driving-forces analysis is to help managers understand what strategy changes are needed to prepare for the impacts of the driving forces.

QUESTION 4: WHAT MARKET POSITIONS DO RIVALS OCCUPY—WHO IS STRONGLY POSITIONED AND WHO IS NOT?

Since competing companies commonly sell in different price/quality ranges, emphasize different distribution channels, incorporate product features that appeal to different types of buyers, have different geographic coverage, and so on, it stands to reason that some companies enjoy stronger or more attractive market positions than other companies. Understanding which companies are strongly positioned and which are weakly positioned is an integral part of analyzing an industry's competitive structure. The best technique for revealing the market positions of industry competitors is **strategic group mapping**.[14] This analytical tool is useful for comparing the market positions of each firm separately or for grouping them into like positions when an industry has so many competitors that it is not practical to examine each one in depth.

> **Core Concept**
> **Strategic group mapping** is a technique for displaying the different market or competitive positions that rival firms occupy in the industry.

Using Strategic Group Maps to Assess the Market Positions of Key Competitors

A **strategic group** consists of those industry members with similar competitive approaches and positions in the market.[15] Companies in the same strategic group can resemble one another in any of several ways: They may have comparable product-line breadth, sell in the same price/quality range, emphasize the same distribution channels, use essentially

> **Core Concept**
> A ***strategic group*** is a cluster of industry rivals that have similar competitive approaches and market positions.

the same product attributes to appeal to similar types of buyers, depend on identical technological approaches, or offer buyers similar services and technical assistance.[16] An industry contains only one strategic group when all sellers pursue essentially identical strategies and have comparable market positions. At the other extreme, an industry may contain as many strategic groups as there are competitors when each rival pursues a distinctively different competitive approach and occupies a substantially different market position.

The procedure for constructing a *strategic group map* is straightforward:

- Identify the competitive characteristics that differentiate firms in the industry. Typical variables are price/quality range (high, medium, low); geographic coverage (local, regional, national, global); degree of vertical integration (none, partial, full); product-line breadth (wide, narrow); use of distribution channels (one, some, all); and degree of service offered (no-frills, limited, full).
- Plot the firms on a two-variable map using pairs of these differentiating characteristics.
- Assign firms that fall in about the same strategy space to the same strategic group.
- Draw circles around each strategic group, making the circles proportional to the size of the group's share of total industry sales revenues.

This produces a two-dimensional diagram like the one for the retailing industry in Illustration Capsule 3.1.

Several guidelines need to be observed in mapping the positions of strategic groups in the industry's overall strategy space.[17] First, the two variables selected as axes for the map should *not* be highly correlated; if they are, the circles on the map will fall along a diagonal and strategy makers will learn nothing more about the relative positions of competitors than they would by considering just one of the variables. For instance, if companies with broad product lines use multiple distribution channels while companies with narrow lines use a single distribution channel, then looking at broad versus narrow product lines reveals just as much about who is positioned where as looking at single versus multiple distribution channels; that is, one of the variables is redundant. Second, the variables chosen as axes for the map should expose big differences in how rivals position themselves to compete in the marketplace. This, of course, means analysts must identify the characteristics that differentiate rival firms and use these differences as variables for the axes and as the basis for deciding which firm belongs in which strategic group. Third, the variables used as axes don't have to be either quantitative or continuous; rather, they can be discrete variables or defined in terms of distinct classes and combinations. Fourth, drawing the sizes of the circles on the map proportional to the combined sales of the firms in each strategic group allows the map to reflect the relative sizes of each strategic group. Fifth, if more than two good competitive variables can be used as axes for the map, several maps can be drawn to give different exposures to the competitive positioning relationships present

Illustration Capsule 3.1

Comparative Market Positions of Selected Retail Chains: A Strategic Group Map Application

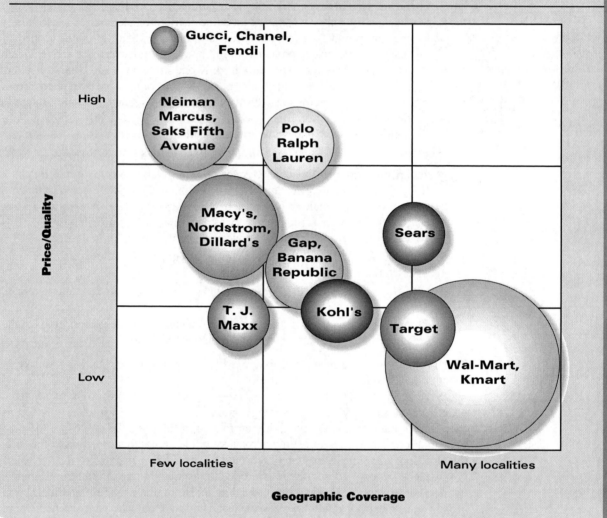

Note: Circles are drawn roughly proportional to the sizes of the chains, based on revenues.

in the industry's structure. Because there is not necessarily one best map for portraying how competing firms are positioned in the market, it is advisable to experiment with different pairs of competitive variables.

What Can Be Learned from Strategic Group Maps?

Strategic group maps are revealing in several respects. The most important has to do with which rivals are similarly positioned and are thus close rivals and which are distant rivals. Generally speaking, *the closer strategic groups are to each other on the*

Strategic group maps reveal which companies are close competitors and which are distant competitors.

map, the stronger the cross-group competitive rivalry tends to be. Although firms in the same strategic group are the closest rivals, the next closest rivals are in the immediately adjacent groups.[18] Often, firms in strategic groups that are far apart on the map hardly compete at all. For instance, Wal-Mart's clientele, merchandise selection, and pricing points are much too different to justify calling them close competitors of Neiman Marcus or Saks Fifth Avenue in retailing. For the same reason, Timex is not a meaningful competitive rival of Rolex, and Subaru is not a close competitor of Lincoln or Mercedes-Benz.

The second thing to be gleaned from strategic group mapping is that *not all positions on the map are equally attractive.* Two reasons account for why some positions can be more attractive than others:

1. *Prevailing competitive pressures and industry driving forces favor some strategic groups and hurt others.*[19] Discerning which strategic groups are advantaged and disadvantaged requires scrutinizing the map in light of what has also been learned from the prior analysis of competitive forces and driving forces. Quite often the strength of competition varies from group to group—there's little reason to believe that all firms in an industry feel the same degrees of competitive pressure, since their strategies and market positions may well differ in important respects. For instance, the competitive battle among Wal-Mart, Target, and Sears/Kmart (Kmart acquired Sears in 2005) is more intense (with consequently smaller profit margins) than the rivalry among Gucci, Chanel, Fendi, and other high-end fashion retailers. Likewise, industry driving forces may be acting to grow the demand for the products of firms in some strategic groups and shrink the demand for the products of firms in other strategic groups—as is the case in the radio broadcasting industry where satellite radio firms like XM and Sirius stand to gain market ground at the expense of commercial-based radio broadcasters due to the impacts of such driving forces as technological advances in satellite broadcasting, growing buyer preferences for more diverse radio programming, and product innovation in satellite radio devices. Firms in strategic groups that are being adversely impacted by intense competitive pressures or driving forces may try to shift to a more favorably situated group. But shifting to a different position on the map can prove difficult when entry barriers for the target strategic group are high. Moreover, attempts to enter a new strategic group nearly always increase competitive pressures in the target strategic group. If certain firms are known to be trying to change their competitive positions on the map, then attaching arrows to the circles showing the targeted direction helps clarify the picture of competitive maneuvering among rivals.

Core Concept
Not all positions on a strategic group map are equally attractive.

2. *The profit potential of different strategic groups varies due to the strengths and weaknesses in each group's market position.* The profit prospects of firms in different strategic groups can vary from good to ho-hum to poor because of differing growth rates for the principal buyer segments served by each group, differing degrees of competitive rivalry within strategic groups, differing degrees of exposure to competition from substitute products outside the industry, and differing degrees of supplier or customer bargaining power from group to group.

Thus, part of strategic group map analysis always entails drawing conclusions about where on the map is the "best" place to be and why. Which companies/strategic groups are destined to prosper because of their positions? Which companies/strategic groups seem destined to struggle because of their positions? What accounts for why some parts of the map are better than others?

QUESTION 5: WHAT STRATEGIC MOVES ARE RIVALS LIKELY TO MAKE NEXT?

Unless a company pays attention to what competitors are doing and knows their strengths and weaknesses, it ends up flying blind into competitive battle. As in sports, scouting the opposition is essential. *Competitive intelligence* about rivals' strategies, their latest actions and announcements, their resource strengths and weaknesses, the efforts being made to improve their situation, and the thinking and leadership styles of their executives is valuable for predicting or anticipating the strategic moves competitors are likely to make next in the marketplace. Having good information to predict the strategic direction and likely moves of key competitors allows a company to prepare defensive countermoves, to craft its own strategic moves with some confidence about what market maneuvers to expect from rivals, and to exploit any openings that arise from competitors' missteps or strategy flaws.

> Good scouting reports on rivals provide a valuable assist in anticipating what moves rivals are likely to make next and outmaneuvering them in the marketplace.

Identifying Competitors' Strategies and Resource Strengths and Weaknesses

Keeping close tabs on a com.petitor's strategy entails monitoring what the rival is doing in the marketplace, what its management is saying in company press releases, information posted on the company's Web site (especially press releases and the presentations management has recently made to securities analysts), and such public documents as annual reports and 10-K filings, articles in the business media, and the reports of securities analysts. (Figure 1.1 in Chapter 1 indicates what to look for in identifying a company's strategy.) Company personnel may be able to pick up useful information from a rival's exhibits at trade shows and from conversations with a rival's customers, suppliers, and former employees.[20] Many companies have a competitive intelligence unit that sifts through the available information to construct up-to-date strategic profiles of rivals—their current strategies, resource strengths and competitive capabilities, competitive shortcomings, press releases, and recent executive pronouncements. Such profiles are typically updated regularly and made available to managers and other key personnel.

Those who gather competitive intelligence on rivals, however, can sometimes cross the fine line between honest inquiry and unethical or even illegal behavior. For example, calling rivals to get information about prices, the dates of new product introductions, or wage and salary levels is legal, but misrepresenting one's company affiliation during such calls is unethical. Pumping rivals' representatives at trade shows is ethical only if one wears a name tag with accurate company affiliation indicated. Avon Products at one point secured information about its biggest rival, Mary Kay Cosmetics (MKC), by having its personnel search through the garbage bins outside MKC's headquarters.[21] When MKC officials learned of the action and sued, Avon claimed it did nothing illegal, since a 1988 Supreme Court case had ruled that trash left on public property (in this case, a sidewalk) was anyone's for the taking. Avon even produced a videotape of its removal of the trash at the MKC site. Avon won the lawsuit—but Avon's action, while legal, scarcely qualifies as ethical.

In sizing up competitors, it makes sense for company strategists to make three assessments:

1. Which competitor has the best strategy? Which competitors appear to have flawed or weak strategies?

2. Which competitors are poised to gain market share, and which ones seem destined to lose ground?

3. Which competitors are likely to rank among the industry leaders five years from now? Do one or more up-and-coming competitors have powerful strategies and sufficient resource capabilities to overtake the current industry leader?

The industry's *current* major players are generally easy to identify, but some of the leaders may be plagued with weaknesses that are causing them to lose ground; other notable rivals may lack the resources and capabilities to remain strong contenders given the superior strategies and capabilities of up-and-coming companies. In evaluating which competitors are favorably or unfavorably positioned to gain market ground, company strategists need to focus on why there is potential for some rivals to do better or worse than other rivals. Usually, a competitor's prospects are a function of whether it is in a strategic group that is being favored or hurt by competitive pressures and driving forces, whether its strategy has resulted in competitive advantage or disadvantage, and whether its resources and capabilities are well suited for competing on the road ahead.

> Today's market leaders don't automatically become tomorrow's.

Predicting Competitors' Next Moves

Predicting the next strategic moves of competitors is the hardest yet most useful part of competitor analysis. Good clues about what actions a specific company is likely to undertake can often be gleaned from how well it is faring in the marketplace, the problems or weaknesses it needs to address, and how much pressure it is under to improve its financial performance. Content rivals are likely to continue their present strategy with only minor fine-tuning. Ailing rivals can be performing so poorly that fresh strategic moves are virtually certain. Ambitious rivals looking to move up in the industry ranks are strong candidates for launching new strategic offensives to pursue emerging market opportunities and exploit the vulnerabilities of weaker rivals.

Since the moves a competitor is likely to make are generally predicated on the views their executives have about the industry's future and their beliefs about their firm's situation, it makes sense to closely scrutinize the public pronouncements of rival company executives about where the industry is headed and what it will take to be successful, what they are saying about their firm's situation, information from the grapevine about what they are doing, and their past actions and leadership styles. Other considerations in trying to predict what strategic moves rivals are likely to make next include the following:

- Which rivals badly need to increase their unit sales and market share? What strategic options are they most likely to pursue: lowering prices, adding new models and styles, expanding their dealer networks, entering additional geographic markets, boosting advertising to build better brand-name awareness, acquiring a weaker competitor, or placing more emphasis on direct sales via their Web site?

- Which rivals have a strong incentive, along with the resources, to make major strategic changes, perhaps moving to a different position on the strategic group map? Which rivals are probably locked in to pursuing the same basic strategy with only minor adjustments?

- Which rivals are good candidates to be acquired? Which rivals may be looking to make an acquisition and are financially able to do so?

- Which rivals are likely to enter new geographic markets?
- Which rivals are strong candidates to expand their product offerings and enter new product segments where they do not currently have a presence?

To succeed in predicting a competitor's next moves, company strategists need to have a good feel for each rival's situation, how its managers think, and what the rival's best strategic options are. Doing the necessary detective work can be tedious and time-consuming, but scouting competitors well enough to anticipate their next moves allows managers to prepare effective countermoves (perhaps even beat a rival to the punch) and to take rivals' probable actions into account in crafting their own best course of action.

> Managers who fail to study competitors closely risk being caught napping when rivals make fresh and perhaps bold strategic moves.

QUESTION 6: WHAT ARE THE KEY FACTORS FOR FUTURE COMPETITIVE SUCCESS?

An industry's **key success factors (KSFs)** are those competitive factors that most affect industry members' ability to prosper in the marketplace—the particular strategy elements, product attributes, resources, competencies, competitive capabilities, and market achievements that spell the difference between being a strong competitor and a weak competitor—and sometimes between profit and loss. KSFs by their very nature are so important to future competitive success that *all firms* in the industry must pay close attention to them or risk becoming an industry also-ran. To indicate the significance of KSFs another way, how well a company's product offering, resources, and capabilities measure up against an industry's KSFs determines just how financially and competitively successful that company will be. Identifying KSFs, in light of the prevailing and anticipated industry and competitive conditions, is therefore always a top-priority analytical and strategy-making consideration. Company strategists need to understand the industry landscape well enough to separate the factors most important to competitive success from those that are less important.

> **Core Concept**
> **Key success factors** are the product attributes, competencies, competitive capabilities, and market achievements with the greatest impact on future competitive success in the marketplace.

In the beer industry, the KSFs are full utilization of brewing capacity (to keep manufacturing costs low), a strong network of wholesale distributors (to get the company's brand stocked and favorably displayed in retail outlets where beer is sold), and clever advertising (to induce beer drinkers to buy the company's brand and thereby pull beer sales through the established wholesale/retail channels). In apparel manufacturing, the KSFs are appealing designs and color combinations (to create buyer interest) and low-cost manufacturing efficiency (to permit attractive retail pricing and ample profit margins). In tin and aluminum cans, because the cost of shipping empty cans is substantial, one of the keys is having can-manufacturing facilities located close to end-use customers. Key success factors thus vary from industry to industry, and even from time to time within the same industry, as driving forces and competitive conditions change. Table 3.3 lists the most common types of industry key success factors.

An industry's key success factors can usually be deduced from what was learned from the previously described analysis of the industry and competitive environment. Which factors are most important to future competitive success flow directly from the industry's dominant characteristics, what competition is like, the impacts of the driving forces, the comparative market positions of industry members, and the likely

Table 3.3   **Common Types of Industry Key Success Factors**

Technology-related KSFs	• Expertise in a particular technology or in scientific research (important in pharmaceuticals, Internet applications, mobile communications, and most high-tech industries) • Proven ability to improve production processes (important in industries where advancing technology opens the way for higher manufacturing efficiency and lower production costs)
Manufacturing-related KSFs	• Ability to achieve scale economies and/or capture learning/experience curve effects (important to achieving low production costs) • Quality control know-how (important in industries where customers insist on product reliability) • High utilization of fixed assets (important in capital-intensive, high-fixed-cost industries) • Access to attractive supplies of skilled labor • High labor productivity (important for items with high labor content) • Low-cost product design and engineering (reduces manufacturing costs) • Ability to manufacture or assemble products that are customized to buyer specifications
Distribution-related KSFs	• A strong network of wholesale distributors/dealers • Strong direct sales capabilities via the Internet and/or having company-owned retail outlets • Ability to secure favorable display space on retailer shelves
Marketing-related KSFs	• Breadth of product line and product selection • A well-known and well-respected brand name • Fast, accurate technical assistance • Courteous, personalized customer service • Accurate filling of buyer orders (few back orders or mistakes) • Customer guarantees and warranties (important in mail-order and online retailing, big-ticket purchases, new product introductions) • Clever advertising
Skills and capability-related KSFs	• A talented workforce (important in professional services like accounting and investment banking) • National or global distribution capabilities • Product innovation capabilities (important in industries where rivals are racing to be first-to-market with new product attributes or performance features) • Design expertise (important in fashion and apparel industries) • Short delivery time capability • Supply chain management capabilities • Strong e-commerce capabilities—a user-friendly Web site and/or skills in using Internet technology applications to streamline internal operations
Other types of KSFs	• Overall low costs (not just in manufacturing) so as to be able to meet customer expectations of low price • Convenient locations (important in many retailing businesses) • Ability to provide fast, convenient after-the-sale repairs and service • A strong balance sheet and access to financial capital (important in newly emerging industries with high degrees of business risk and in capital-intensive industries) • Patent protection

next moves of key rivals. In addition, the answers to three questions help identify an industry's key success factors:

1. On what basis do buyers of the industry's product choose between the competing brands of sellers? That is, what product attributes are crucial?
2. Given the nature of competitive rivalry and the competitive forces prevailing in the marketplace, what resources and competitive capabilities does a company need to have to be competitively successful?
3. What shortcomings are almost certain to put a company at a significant competitive disadvantage?

Only rarely are there more than five or six key factors for future competitive success. And even among these, two or three usually outrank the others in importance. Managers should therefore bear in mind the purpose of identifying key success factors—to determine which factors are most important to future competitive success—and resist the temptation to label a factor that has only minor importance a KSF. To compile a list of every factor that matters even a little bit defeats the purpose of concentrating management attention on the factors truly critical to long-term competitive success.

Correctly diagnosing an industry's KSFs raises a company's chances of crafting a sound strategy. The goal of company strategists should be to design a strategy aimed at stacking up well on all of the industry's future KSFs and trying to be *distinctively better* than rivals on one (or possibly two) of the KSFs. Indeed, companies that stand out or excel on a particular KSF are likely to enjoy a stronger market position—*being distinctively better than rivals on one or two key success factors tends to translate into competitive advantage.* Hence, using the industry's KSFs as *cornerstones* for the company's strategy and trying to gain sustainable competitive advantage by excelling at one particular KSF is a fruitful competitive strategy approach.[22]

> **Core Concept**
> A sound strategy incorporates the intent to stack up well on all of the industry's key success factors and to excel on one or two KSFs.

QUESTION 7: DOES THE OUTLOOK FOR THE INDUSTRY PRESENT THE COMPANY WITH AN ATTRACTIVE OPPORTUNITY?

The final step in evaluating the industry and competitive environment is to use the preceding analysis to decide whether the outlook for the industry presents the company with a sufficiently attractive business opportunity. The important factors on which to base such a conclusion include:

- The industry's growth potential.
- Whether powerful competitive forces are squeezing industry profitability to subpar levels and whether competition appears destined to grow stronger or weaker.
- Whether industry profitability will be favorably or unfavorably affected by the prevailing driving forces.
- The degrees of risk and uncertainty in the industry's future.
- Whether the industry as a whole confronts severe problems—regulatory or environmental issues, stagnating buyer demand, industry overcapacity, mounting competition, and so on.

- The company's competitive position in the industry vis-à-vis rivals. (Being a well-entrenched leader or strongly positioned contender in a lackluster industry may present adequate opportunity for good profitability; however, having to fight a steep uphill battle against much stronger rivals may hold little promise of eventual market success or good return on shareholder investment, even though the industry environment is attractive.)

- The company's potential to capitalize on the vulnerabilities of weaker rivals, perhaps converting a relatively unattractive *industry* situation into a potentially rewarding *company* opportunity.

- Whether the company has sufficient competitive strength to defend against or counteract the factors that make the industry unattractive.

- Whether continued participation in this industry adds importantly to the firm's ability to be successful in other industries in which it may have business interests.

Core Concept
The degree to which an industry is attractive or unattractive is not the same for all industry participants and all potential entrants; the attractiveness of the opportunities an industry presents depends heavily on whether a company has the resource strengths and competitive capabilities to capture them.

As a general proposition, *if an industry's overall profit prospects are above average, the industry environment is basically attractive; if industry profit prospects are below average, conditions are unattractive.* However, it is a mistake to think of a particular industry as being equally attractive or unattractive to all industry participants and all potential entrants. Attractiveness is relative, not absolute, and conclusions one way or the other have to be drawn from the perspective of a particular company. Industries attractive to insiders may be unattractive to outsiders. Companies on the outside may look at an industry's environment and conclude that it is an unattractive business for them to get into, given the prevailing entry barriers, the difficulty of challenging current market leaders with their particular resources and competencies, and the opportunities they have elsewhere. Industry environments unattractive to weak competitors may be attractive to strong competitors. A favorably positioned company may survey a business environment and see a host of opportunities that weak competitors cannot capture.

When a company decides an industry is fundamentally attractive and presents good opportunities, a strong case can be made that it should invest aggressively to capture the opportunities it sees and to improve its long-term competitive position in the business. When a strong competitor concludes an industry is relatively unattractive and lacking in opportunity, it may elect to simply protect its present position, investing cautiously if at all and looking for opportunities in other industries. A competitively weak company in an unattractive industry may see its best option as finding a buyer, perhaps a rival, to acquire its business.

Key Points

Thinking strategically about a company's external situation involves probing for answers to the following seven questions:

1. *What are the industry's dominant economic features?* Industries differ significantly on such factors as market size and growth rate, the number and relative sizes of both buyers and sellers, the geographic scope of competitive rivalry, the degree of product differentiation, the speed of product innovation, demand–supply conditions, the extent of vertical integration, and the extent of scale economies and learning-curve effects. In addition to setting the stage for the analysis to come,

identifying an industry's economic features also promotes understanding of the kinds of strategic moves that industry members are likely to employ.

2. *What kinds of competitive forces are industry members facing, and how strong is each force?* The strength of competition is a composite of five forces: (1) competitive pressures stemming from the competitive jockeying and market maneuvering among industry rivals, (2) competitive pressures associated with the market inroads being made by the sellers of substitutes, (3) competitive pressures associated with the threat of new entrants into the market, (4) competitive pressures stemming from supplier bargaining power and supplier–seller collaboration, and (5) competitive pressures stemming from buyer bargaining power and seller–buyer collaboration. The nature and strength of the competitive pressures associated with these five forces have to be examined force by force to identify the specific competitive pressures they each comprise and to decide whether these pressures constitute a strong or weak competitive force. The next step in competition analysis is to evaluate the collective strength of the five forces and determine whether the state of competition is conducive to good profitability. Working through the five-forces model step by step not only aids strategy makers in assessing whether the intensity of competition allows good profitability but also promotes sound strategic thinking about how to better match company strategy to the specific competitive character of the marketplace. Effectively matching a company's strategy to the particular competitive pressures and competitive conditions that exist has two aspects: (1) pursuing avenues that shield the firm from as many of the prevailing competitive pressures as possible, and (2) initiating actions calculated to produce sustainable competitive advantage, thereby shifting competition in the company's favor, putting added competitive pressure on rivals, and perhaps even defining the business model for the industry.

3. *What factors are driving industry change and what impact will they have on competitive intensity and industry profitability?* Industry and competitive conditions change because forces are in motion that create incentives or pressures for change. The first phase is to identify the forces that are driving change in the industry; the most common driving forces include the Internet and Internet technology applications, globalization of competition in the industry, changes in the long-term industry growth rate, changes in buyer composition, product innovation, entry or exit of major firms, changes in cost and efficiency, changing buyer preferences for standardized versus differentiated products or services, regulatory influences and government policy changes, changing societal and lifestyle factors, and reductions in uncertainty and business risk. The second phase of driving-forces analysis is to determine whether the driving forces, taken together, are acting to make the industry environment more or less attractive. Are the driving forces causing demand for the industry's product to increase or decrease? Are the driving forces acting to make competition more or less intense? Will the driving forces lead to higher or lower industry profitability?

4. *What market positions do industry rivals occupy—who is strongly positioned and who is not?* Strategic group mapping is a valuable tool for understanding the similarities, differences, strengths, and weaknesses inherent in the market positions of rival companies. Rivals in the same or nearby strategic groups are close competitors, whereas companies in distant strategic groups usually pose little or no immediate threat. The lesson of strategic group mapping is that some positions on the map are more favorable than others. The profit potential of different strategic groups varies due to strengths and weaknesses in each group's market

position. Often, industry driving forces and competitive pressures favor some strategic groups and hurt others.

5. *What strategic moves are rivals likely to make next?* This analytical step involves identifying competitors' strategies, deciding which rivals are likely to be strong contenders and which are likely to be weak, evaluating rivals' competitive options, and predicting their next moves. Scouting competitors well enough to anticipate their actions can help a company prepare effective countermoves (perhaps even beating a rival to the punch) and allows managers to take rivals' probable actions into account in designing their own company's best course of action. Managers who fail to study competitors risk being caught unprepared by the strategic moves of rivals.

6. *What are the key factors for future competitive success?* An industry's key success factors (KSFs) are the particular strategy elements, product attributes, competitive capabilities, and business outcomes that spell the difference between being a strong competitor and a weak competitor—and sometimes between profit and loss. KSFs by their very nature are so important to competitive success that *all firms* in the industry must pay close attention to them or risk becoming an industry also-ran. Correctly diagnosing an industry's KSFs raises a company's chances of crafting a sound strategy. The goal of company strategists should be to design a strategy aimed at stacking up well on all of the industry KSFs and trying to be *distinctively better* than rivals on one (or possibly two) of the KSFs. Indeed, using the industry's KSFs as *cornerstones* for the company's strategy and trying to gain sustainable competitive advantage by excelling at one particular KSF is a fruitful competitive strategy approach.

7. *Does the outlook for the industry present the company with sufficiently attractive prospects for profitability?* If an industry's overall profit prospects are above average, the industry environment is basically attractive; if industry profit prospects are below average, conditions are unattractive. Conclusions regarding industry attractive are a major driver of company strategy. When a company decides an industry is fundamentally attractive and presents good opportunities, a strong case can be made that it should invest aggressively to capture the opportunities it sees and to improve its long-term competitive position in the business. When a strong competitor concludes an industry is relatively unattractive and lacking in opportunity, it may elect to simply protect its present position, investing cautiously if at all and looking for opportunities in other industries. A competitively weak company in an unattractive industry may see its best option as finding a buyer, perhaps a rival, to acquire its business. On occasion, an industry that is unattractive overall is still very attractive to a favorably situated company with the skills and resources to take business away from weaker rivals.

A competently conducted industry and competitive analysis generally tells a clear, easily understood story about the company's external environment. Different analysts can have varying judgments about competitive intensity, the impacts of driving forces, how industry conditions will evolve, how good the outlook is for industry profitability, and the degree to which the industry environment offers the company an attractive business opportunity. However, while no method can guarantee that all analysts will come to identical conclusions about the state of industry and competitive conditions and an industry's future outlook, this doesn't justify shortcutting hardnosed strategic analysis and relying instead on opinion and casual observation. Managers become better strategists when they know what questions to pose and what tools to use. This is why this chapter has concentrated on suggesting the right questions to ask, explaining concepts and analytical approaches, and indicating the kinds of things to look for. There's no substitute for doing cutting edge strategic thinking about a company's external situation—anything less weakens managers' ability to craft strategies that are well matched to industry and competitive conditions.

Exercises

1. As the owner of a fast-food enterprise seeking a loan from a bank to finance the construction and operation of three new store locations, you have been asked to provide the loan officer with a brief analysis of the competitive environment in fast food. Draw a five-forces diagram for the fast-food industry, and briefly discuss the nature and strength of each of the five competitive forces in fast food. Do whatever Internet research is required to expand your understanding of competition in the fast-food industry and do a competent five-forces analysis.

2. Based on the strategic group map in Illustration Capsule 3.1: Who are Polo Ralph Lauren's closest competitors? Between which two strategic groups is competition the strongest? Why do you think no retailers are positioned in the upper right-hand corner of the map? Which company/strategic group faces the weakest competition from the members of other strategic groups?

3. With regard to the ice cream industry, which of the following factors might qualify as possible driving forces capable of causing fundamental change in the industry's structure and competitive environment?

   a. Increasing sales of frozen yogurt and frozen sorbets.

   b. The potential for additional makers of ice cream to enter the market.

   c. Growing consumer interest in low-calorie/low-fat/low-carb/sugar-free dessert alternatives.

   d. A slowdown in consumer purchases of ice cream products.

   e. Rising prices for milk, sugar, and other ice cream ingredients.

   f. A decision by Häagen-Dazs to increase its prices by 10 percent.

   g. A decision by Ben & Jerry's to add five new flavors to its product line.

Evaluating a Company's Resources and Competitive Position

Before executives can chart a new strategy, they must reach common understanding of the company's current position.

—W. Chan Kim and Rene Mauborgne

The real question isn't how well you're doing today against your own history, but how you're doing against your competitors.

—Donald Kress

Organizations succeed in a competitive marketplace over the long run because they can do certain things their customers value better than can their competitors.

—Robert Hayes, Gary Pisano, and David Upton

Only firms who are able to continually build new strategic assets faster and cheaper than their competitors will earn superior returns over the long term.

—C. C. Markides and P. J. Williamson

In Chapter 3 we described how to use the tools of industry and competitive analysis to assess a company's external environment and lay the groundwork for matching a company's strategy to its external situation. In this chapter we discuss the techniques of evaluating a company's resource capabilities, relative cost position, and competitive strength vis-á-vis its rivals. The analytical spotlight will be trained on five questions:

1. How well is the company's present strategy working?
2. What are the company's resource strengths and weaknesses, and its external opportunities and threats?
3. Are the company's prices and costs competitive?
4. Is the company competitively stronger or weaker than key rivals?
5. What strategic issues and problems merit front-burner managerial attention?

We will describe four analytical tools that should be used to probe for answers to these questions—SWOT analysis, value chain analysis, benchmarking, and competitive strength assessment. All four are valuable techniques for revealing a company's competitiveness and for helping company managers match their strategy to the company's own particular circumstances.

QUESTION 1: HOW WELL IS THE COMPANY'S PRESENT STRATEGY WORKING?

In evaluating how well a company's present strategy is working, a manager has to start with what the strategy is. Figure 4.1 shows the key components of a single-business company's strategy. The first thing to pin down is the company's competitive approach. Is the company striving to be a low-cost leader *or* stressing ways to differentiate its product offering from rivals? Is it concentrating its efforts on serving a broad spectrum of customers *or* a narrow market niche? Another strategy-defining consideration is the firm's competitive scope within the industry—what its geographic market coverage is and whether it operates in just a single stage of the industry's production/distribution chain or is vertically integrated across several stages. Another good indication of the company's strategy is whether the company has made moves recently to improve its competitive position and performance—for instance, by cutting prices, improving design, stepping up advertising, entering a new geographic market (domestic or foreign),

Figure 4.1 **Identifying the Components of a Single-Business Company's Strategy**

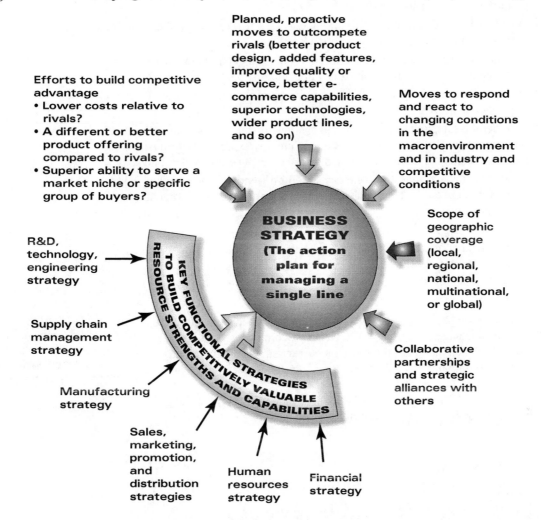

or merging with a competitor. The company's functional strategies in R&D, production, marketing, finance, human resources, information technology, and so on further characterize company strategy.

While there's merit in evaluating the strategy from a *qualitative* standpoint (its completeness, internal consistency, rationale, and relevance), the best *quantitative* evidence of how well a company's strategy is working comes from its results. The two best empirical indicators are (1) whether the company is achieving its stated financial and strategic objectives, and (2) whether the company is an above-average industry performer. Persistent shortfalls in meeting company performance targets and weak performance relative to rivals are reliable warning signs that the company suffers from poor strategy making, less-than-competent strategy execution, or both. Other indicators of how well a company's strategy is working include:

- Whether the firm's sales are growing faster, slower, or about the same pace as the market as a whole, thus resulting in a rising, eroding, or stable market share.

- Whether the company is acquiring new customers at an attractive rate as well as retaining existing customers.
- Whether the firm's profit margins are increasing or decreasing and how well its margins compare to rival firms' margins.
- Trends in the firm's net profits and return on investment and how these compare to the same trends for other companies in the industry.
- Whether the company's overall financial strength and credit rating are improving or on the decline.
- Whether the company can demonstrate continuous improvement in such internal performance measures as days of inventory, employee productivity, unit cost, defect rate, scrap rate, misfilled orders, delivery times, warranty costs, and so on.
- How shareholders view the company based on trends in the company's stock price and shareholder value (relative to the stock price trends at other companies in the industry).
- The firm's image and reputation with its customers.
- How well the company stacks up against rivals on technology, product innovation, customer service, product quality, delivery time, price, getting newly developed products to market quickly, and other relevant factors on which buyers base their choice of brands.

The stronger a company's current overall performance, the less likely the need for radical changes in strategy. The weaker a company's financial performance and market standing, the more its current strategy must be questioned. Weak performance is almost always a sign of weak strategy, weak execution, or both.

Table 4.1 provides a compilation of the financial ratios most commonly used to evaluate a company's financial performance and balance sheet strength.

> The stronger a company's financial performance and market position, the more likely it has a well-conceived, well-executed strategy.

QUESTION 2: WHAT ARE THE COMPANY'S RESOURCE STRENGTHS AND WEAKNESSES AND ITS EXTERNAL OPPORTUNITIES AND THREATS?

Appraising a company's resource strengths and weaknesses and its external opportunities and threats, commonly known as **SWOT analysis,** provides a good overview of whether the company's overall situation is fundamentally healthy or unhealthy. Just as important, a first-rate SWOT analysis provides the basis for crafting a strategy that capitalizes on the company's resources, aims squarely at capturing the company's best opportunities, and defends against the threats to its well-being.

> **Core Concept**
> **SWOT analysis** is a simple but powerful tool for sizing up a company's resource capabilities and deficiencies, its market opportunities, and the external threats to its future well-being.

Identifying Company Resource Strengths and Competitive Capabilities

A *resource strength* is something a company is good at doing or an attribute that enhances its competitiveness in the marketplace. Resource strengths can take any of several forms:

Table 4.1   **Key Financial Ratios: How to Calculate Them and What They Mean**

Ratio	How Calculated	What It Shows
Profitability ratios		
1. Gross profit margin	$\dfrac{\text{Sales} - \text{cost of goods sold}}{\text{Sales}}$	Shows the percentage of revenues available to cover operating expenses and yield a profit. Higher is better, and the trend should be upward.
2. Operating profit margin (or return on sales)	$\dfrac{\text{Sales} - \text{Operating expenses}}{\text{Sales}}$ or $\dfrac{\text{Operating income}}{\text{Sales}}$	Shows the profitability of current operations without regard to interest charges and income taxes. Higher is better, and the trend should be upward.
3. Net profit margin (or net return on sales)	$\dfrac{\text{Profits after taxes}}{\text{Sales}}$	Shows after-tax profits per dollar of sales. Higher is better, and the trend should be upward.
4. Return on total assets	$\dfrac{\text{Profits after taxes} + \text{Interest}}{\text{Total assets}}$	A measure of the return on total investment in the enterprise. Interest is added to after-tax profits to form the numerator since total assets are financed by creditors as well as by stockholders. Higher is better, and the trend should be upward.
5. Return on stockholders' equity	$\dfrac{\text{Profits after taxes}}{\text{Total stockholders' equity}}$	Shows the return stockholders are earning on their investment in the enterprise. A return in the 12–15 percent range is average, and the trend should be upward.
6. Earnings per share	$\dfrac{\text{Profits after taxes}}{\text{Number of shares of common stock outstanding}}$	Shows the earnings for each share of common stock outstanding. The trend should be upward, and the bigger the annual percentage gains, the better.
Liquidity ratios		
1. Current ratio	$\dfrac{\text{Current assets}}{\text{Current liabilities}}$	Shows a firm's ability to pay current liabilities using assets that can be converted to cash in the near term. Ratio should definitely be higher than 1.0; ratios of 2 or higher are better still.
2. Quick ratio (or acid-test ratio)	$\dfrac{\text{Current assets} - \text{Inventory}}{\text{Current liabilities}}$	Shows a firm's ability to pay current liabilities without relying on the sale of its inventories.
3. Working capital	Current assets − Current liabilities	Bigger amounts are better because the company has more internal funds available to (1) pay its current liabilities on a timely basis and (2) finance inventory expansion, additional accounts receivable, and a larger base of operations without resorting to borrowing or raising more equity capital.
Leverage ratios		
1. Debt-to-assets ratio	$\dfrac{\text{Total debt}}{\text{Total assets}}$	Measures the extent to which borrowed funds have been used to finance the firm's operations. Low fractions or ratios are better—high fractions indicate overuse of debt and greater risk of bankruptcy.

(Continued)

Table 4.1   **Continued**

Ratio	How Calculated	What It Shows
2. Debt-to-equity ratio	$\dfrac{\text{Total debt}}{\text{Total stockholders' equity}}$	Should usually be less than 1.0. High ratios (especially above 1.0) signal excessive debt, lower creditworthiness, and weaker balance sheet strength.
3. Long-term debt-to-equity ratio	$\dfrac{\text{Long-term debt}}{\text{Total stockholders' equity}}$	Shows the balance between debt and equity in the firm's *long-term* capital structure. Low ratios indicate greater capacity to borrow additional funds if needed.
4. Times-interest-earned (or coverage) ratio	$\dfrac{\text{Operating income}}{\text{Interest expenses}}$	Measures the ability to pay annual interest charges. Lenders usually insist on a minimum ratio of 2.0, but ratios above 3.0 signal better creditworthiness.
Activity ratios		
1. Days of inventory	$\dfrac{\text{Sales} \div 365}{\text{Inventory}}$	Measures inventory management efficiency. Fewer days of inventory are usually better.
2. Inventory turnover	$\dfrac{\text{Sales}}{\text{Inventory}}$	Measures the number of inventory turns per year. Higher is better.
3. Average collection period	$\dfrac{\text{Accounts receivable}}{\text{Total sales} \div 365}$ or $\dfrac{\text{Accounts receivable}}{\text{Average daily sales}}$	Indicates the average length of time the firm must wait after making a sale to receive cash payment. A shorter collection time is better.
Other important measures of financial performance		
1. Dividend yield on common stock	$\dfrac{\text{Annual dividends per share}}{\text{Current market price per share}}$	A measure of the return that shareholders receive in the form of dividends. A "typical" dividend yield in 2–3%. The dividend yield for fast-growth companies in often below 1% (may be even 0); the dividend yield for slow-growth companies can run 4–5%.
2. Price/earnings ratio	$\dfrac{\text{Current market price per share}}{\text{Earnings per share}}$	P/E ratios above 20 indicate strong investor confidence in a firm's outlook and earnings growth; firms whose future earnings are at risk or likely to grow slowly typically have ratios below 12.
3. Dividend payout ratio	$\dfrac{\text{Annual dividends per share}}{\text{Earnings per share}}$	Indicates the percentage of after-tax profits paid out as dividends.
4. Internal cash flow	After tax profits + Depreciation	A quick and rough estimate of the cash a company's business is generating after payment of operating expenses, interest, and taxes. Such amounts can be used for dividend payments or funding capital expenditures.

- *A skill, specialized expertise, or competitively important capability*—skills in low-cost operations, technological expertise, expertise in defect-free manufacture, proven capabilities in developing and introducing innovative products, cutting-edge supply chain management capabilities, expertise in getting new products to market quickly, strong e-commerce expertise, expertise in providing consistently good customer service, excellent mass merchandising skills, or unique advertising and promotional talents.

- *Valuable physical assets*—state-of-the-art plants and equipment, attractive real estate locations, worldwide distribution facilities, or ownership of valuable natural resource deposits.

- *Valuable human assets and intellectual capital*—an experienced and capable workforce, talented employees in key areas, cutting-edge knowledge in technology or other important areas of the business, collective learning embedded in the organization and built up over time, or proven managerial know-how.[1]

- *Valuable organizational assets*—proven quality control systems, proprietary technology, key patents, state-of-the-art systems for doing business via the Internet, ownership of important natural resources, a cadre of highly trained customer service representatives, a strong network of distributors or retail dealers, sizable amounts of cash and marketable securities, a strong balance sheet and credit rating (thus giving the company access to additional financial capital), or a comprehensive list of customers' e-mail addresses.

- *Valuable intangible assets*—a powerful or well-known brand name, a reputation for technological leadership, or strong buyer loyalty and goodwill.

- *An achievement or attribute that puts the company in a position of market advantage*—low overall costs relative to competitors, market share leadership, a superior product, a wider product line than rivals, wide geographic coverage, or award-winning customer service.

- *Competitively valuable alliances or cooperative ventures*—fruitful partnerships with suppliers that reduce costs and/or enhance product quality and performance; alliances or joint ventures that provide access to valuable technologies, specialized know-how, or geographic markets.

Core Concept

A company's resource strengths represent *competitive assets* and are big determinants of its competitiveness and ability to succeed in the marketplace.

A company's resource strengths represent its endowment of *competitive assets*. The caliber of a firm's resource strengths is a big determinant of its competitiveness—whether it has the wherewithal to be a strong competitor in the marketplace or whether its capabilities and competitive strengths are modest, thus relegating it to a trailing position in the industry.[2] Plainly, a company's resource strengths may or may not enable it to improve its competitive position and financial performance.

Assessing a Company's Competencies and Capabilities—What Activities Does It Perform Well?   One of the most important aspects of appraising a company's resource strengths has to do with its competence level in performing key pieces of its business—such as supply chain management, research and development (R&D), production, distribution, sales and marketing, and customer service. Which activities does it perform especially well? And are there any activities it performs better than rivals? A company's proficiency in conducting different facets of its operations can range from merely a competence in performing an activity to a core competence to a distinctive competence:

1.   A **competence** is something an organization is good at doing. It is nearly always the product of experience, representing an accumulation of learning and the buildup

of proficiency in performing an internal activity. Usually a company competence originates with deliberate efforts to develop the organizational ability to do something, however imperfectly or inefficiently. Such efforts involve selecting people with the requisite knowledge and skills, upgrading or expanding individual abilities as needed, and then molding the efforts and work products of individuals into a cooperative group effort to create organizational ability. Then, as experience builds, such that the company gains proficiency in performing the activity consistently well and at an acceptable cost, the ability evolves into a true competence and company capability. Some competencies relate to fairly specific skills and expertise (like just-in-time inventory control or low-cost manufacturing efficiency or picking locations for new stores or designing an unusually appealing and user-friendly Web site); they spring from proficiency in a single discipline or function and may be performed in a single department or organizational unit. Other competencies, however, are inherently multidisciplinary and cross-functional—they are the result of effective collaboration among people with different expertise working in different organizational units. A competence in continuous product innovation, for example, comes from teaming the efforts of people and groups with expertise in market research, new product R&D, design and engineering, cost-effective manufacturing, and market testing.

> **Core Concept**
> A **competence** is an activity that a company has learned to perform well.

2. A **core competence** is a proficiently performed internal activity that is *central* to a company's strategy and competitiveness. A core competence is a more valuable resource strength than a competence because of the well-performed activity's core role in the company's strategy and the contribution it makes to the company's success in the marketplace. A core competence can relate to any of several aspects of a company's business: expertise in integrating multiple technologies to create families of new products, know-how in creating and operating systems for cost-efficient supply chain management, the capability to speed new or next-generation products to market, good after-sale service capabilities, skills in manufacturing a high-quality product at a low cost, or the capability to fill customer orders accurately and swiftly. A company may have more than one core competence in its resource portfolio, but rare is the company that can legitimately claim more than two or three core competencies. Most often, *a core competence is knowledge-based, residing in people and in a company's intellectual capital and not in its assets on the balance sheet.* Moreover, a core competence is more likely to be grounded in cross-department combinations of knowledge and expertise rather than being the product of a single department or work group. 3M Corporation has a core competence in product innovation—its record of introducing new products goes back several decades and new product introduction is central to 3M's strategy of growing its business. Ben & Jerry's Homemade, a subsidiary of Unilever, has a core competence in creating unusual flavors of ice cream and marketing them with catchy names like Chunky Monkey, Wavy Gravy, Chubby Hubby, The Gobfather, Dublin Mudslide, and Marsha Marsha Marshmallow.

> **Core Concept**
> A **core competence** is a *competitively important* activity that a company performs better than other internal activities.

3. A **distinctive competence** is a competitively valuable activity that a company *performs better than its rivals.* A distinctive competence thus signifies even greater proficiency than a core competence. But what is especially important about a distinctive competence is that the company enjoys *competitive superiority*

in performing that activity—a distinctive competence represents a level of proficiency that rivals do not have. Because a distinctive competence represents uniquely strong capability relative to rival companies, it qualifies as a *competitively superior resource strength* with competitive advantage potential. This is particularly true when the distinctive competence enables a company to deliver standout value to customers (in the form of lower costs and prices or better product performance or superior service). Toyota has worked diligently over several decades to establish a distinctive competence in low-cost, high-quality manufacturing of motor vehicles; its "lean production" system is far superior to that of any other automaker's, and the company is pushing the boundaries of its production advantage with a new type of assembly line—called the Global Body line—that costs 50 percent less to install and can be changed to accommodate a new model for 70 percent less than its previous production system.[3] Starbucks' distinctive competence in innovative coffee drinks and store ambience has propelled it to the forefront among coffee retailers.

The conceptual differences between a competence, a core competence, and a distinctive competence draw attention to the fact that a company's resource strengths and competitive capabilities are not all equal.[4] Some competencies and competitive capabilities merely enable market survival because most rivals have them—indeed, not having a competence or capability that rivals have can result in competitive disadvantage. If an apparel company does not have the competence to produce its apparel items cost-efficiently, it is unlikely to survive given the intensely price-competitive nature of the apparel industry. Every Web retailer requires a basic competence in designing an appealing and user-friendly Web site.

Core competencies are *competitively* more important resource strengths than competencies because they add power to the company's strategy and have a bigger positive impact on its market position and profitability. Distinctive competencies are even more competitively important. A distinctive competence is a competitively potent resource strength for three reasons: (1) it gives a company competitively valuable capability that is unmatched by rivals, (2) it has potential for being the cornerstone of the company's strategy, and (3) it can produce a competitive edge in the marketplace since it represents a level of proficiency that is superior to rivals. It is always easier for a company to build competitive advantage when it has a distinctive competence in performing an activity important to market success, when rival companies do not have offsetting competencies, and when it is costly and time-consuming for rivals to imitate the competence. A distinctive competence is thus potentially the mainspring of a company's success—unless it is trumped by more powerful resources possessed by rivals.

What Is the Competitive Power of a Resource Strength?   It is not enough to simply compile a list of a company's resource strengths and competitive capabilities. What is most telling about a company's resource strengths, individually and collectively, is how powerful they are in the marketplace. The competitive power of a resource strength is measured by how many of the following four tests it can pass:[5]

1.   Is the resource strength hard to copy? The more difficult and more expensive it is to imitate a company's resource strength, the greater its potential competitive value. Resources tend to be difficult to copy when they are unique (a fantastic real estate location, patent protection), when they must be built over time in ways that are difficult to imitate (a brand name, mastery of a technology), and when they carry big capital requirements (a cost-effective plant to manufacture cutting-edge microprocessors). Wal-Mart's competitors have failed miserably in their attempts over the past two decades to match Wal-Mart's super-efficient state-of-the-art distribution capabilities. Hard-to-copy strengths and capabilities are valuable competitive assets, adding to a company's market strength and contributing to sustained profitability.

2. *Is the resource strength durable—does it have staying power?* The longer the competitive value of a resource lasts, the greater its value. Some resources lose their clout in the marketplace quickly because of the rapid speeds at which technologies or industry conditions are moving. The value of Eastman Kodak's resources in film and film processing is rapidly being undercut by the growing popularity of digital cameras. The investments that commercial banks have made in branch offices is a rapidly depreciating asset because of growing use of direct deposits, debit cards, automated teller machines, and telephone and Internet banking options.

3. *Is the resource really competitively superior?* Companies have to guard against pridefully believing that their core competencies are distinctive competencies or that their brand name is more powerful than the brand names of rivals. Who can really say whether Coca-Cola's consumer marketing prowess is better than Pepsi-Cola's or whether the Mercedes-Benz brand name is more powerful than that of BMW or Lexus? Although many retailers claim to be quite proficient in product selection and in-store merchandising, a number run into trouble in the marketplace because they encounter rivals whose competencies in product selection and in-store merchandising are better than theirs. Apple's operating system for its MacIntosh PCs is by most accounts a world beater (compared to Windows XP), but Apple has failed miserably in converting its resource strength in operating system design into competitive success in the global PC market—it is an also-ran with a paltry 2–3 percent market share worldwide.

4. *Can the resource strength be trumped by the different resource strengths and competitive capabilities of rivals?* Many commercial airlines have invested heavily in developing the resources and capabilities to offer passengers safe, reliable flights at convenient times, along with an array of in-flight amenities. However, Southwest Airlines and JetBlue in the United States and Ryanair and easyJet in Europe have been quite successful deploying their resources in ways that enable them to provide commercial air services at radically lower fares. Amazon.com's strengths in online retailing of books have put a big dent in the business prospects of brick-and-mortar bookstores. Whole Foods Market has a resource lineup that enables it to merchandise a dazzling array of natural and organic food products in a supermarket setting, thus putting strong competitive pressure on Kroger, Safeway, Albertson's, and other prominent supermarket chains. The prestigious brand names of Cadillac and Lincoln have faded because Mercedes, BMW, Audi, and Lexus have used their resources to design, produce, and market more appealing luxury vehicles.

The vast majority of companies are not well endowed with standout resource strengths, much less with one or more competitively superior resources (or distinctive competencies) capable of passing all four tests with high marks. Most firms have a mixed bag of resources—one or two quite valuable, some good, many satisfactory to mediocre.

Companies in the top tier of their industry may have as many as two core competencies in their resource strength lineup. But only a few companies, usually the strongest industry leaders or up-and-coming challengers, have a resource strength that truly qualifies as a distinctive competence. Even so, a company can still marshal the resource strengths to be competitively successful without having a competitively superior resource or distinctive competence. A company can achieve considerable competitive vitality,

<table>
<tr><td>

Core Concept

A company's ability to succeed in the marketplace hinges to a considerable extent on the competitive power of its resources—the set of competencies, capabilities, and competitive assets at its command.

</td><td>

maybe even competitive advantage, from a collection of good-to-adequate resource strengths that collectively give it competitive power in the marketplace. A number of fast-food chains—for example, Wendy's, Taco Bell, and Subway—have achieved a respectable market position competing against McDonald's with satisfactory sets of resource strengths and no apparent distinctive competence. The same can be said for Lowe's, which competes against industry leader Home Depot, and such regional banks as Compass, State Street, Keybank, PNC, BB&T, and AmSouth, which increasingly find themselves in competition with the top five U.S. banks—JPMorgan Chase,

</td></tr>
</table>

Bank of America, Citibank, Wachovia, and Wells Fargo.

Identifying Company Resource Weaknesses and Competitive Deficiencies

A *resource weakness,* or *competitive deficiency,* is something a company lacks or does poorly (in comparison to others) or a condition that puts it at a disadvantage in the marketplace. A company's resource weaknesses can relate to (1) inferior or unproven skills, expertise, or intellectual capital in competitively important areas of the business; (2) deficiencies in competitively important physical, organizational, or intangi-

<table>
<tr><td>

Core Concept

A company's resource strengths represent competitive assets; its resource weaknesses represent competitive liabilities.

</td><td>

ble assets; or (3) missing or competitively inferior capabilities in key areas. *Internal weaknesses are thus shortcomings in a company's complement of resources and represent competitive liabilities.* Nearly all companies have competitive liabilities of one kind or another. Whether a company's resource weaknesses make it competitively vulnerable depends on how much they matter in the marketplace and whether they are offset by the company's resource strengths.

</td></tr>
</table>

Table 4.2 lists the kinds of factors to consider in compiling a company's resource strengths and weaknesses. Sizing up a company's complement of resource capabilities and deficiencies is akin to constructing a *strategic balance sheet,* where resource strengths represent *competitive assets* and resource weaknesses represent *competitive liabilities.* Obviously, the ideal condition is for the company's competitive assets to outweigh its competitive liabilities by an ample margin—a 50–50 balance is definitely not the desired condition!

Identifying a Company's Market Opportunities

Market opportunity is a big factor in shaping a company's strategy. Indeed, managers can't properly tailor strategy to the company's situation without first identifying its market opportunities and appraising the growth and profit potential each one holds. Depending on the prevailing circumstances, a company's opportunities can be plentiful or scarce, fleeting or lasting, and can range from wildly attractive (an absolute "must" to pursue) to marginally interesting (because the growth and profit potential are questionable) to unsuitable (because there's not a good match with the company's

Table 4.2   **What to Look for in Identifying a Company's Strengths, Weaknesses, Opportunities, and Threats**

Potential Resource Strengths and Competitive Capabilities	Potential Resource Weaknesses and Competitive Deficiencies
• A powerful strategy • Core competencies in _____ • A distinctive competence in _____ • A product that is strongly differentiated from those of rivals • Competencies and capabilities that are well matched to industry key success factors • A strong financial condition; ample financial resources to grow the business • Strong brand-name image/company reputation • An attractive customer base • Economy of scale and/or learning/experience curve advantages over rivals • Proprietary technology/superior technological skills/important patents • Superior intellectual capital relative to key rivals • Cost advantages over rivals • Strong advertising and promotion • Product innovation capabilities • Proven capabilities in improving production processes • Good supply chain management capabilities • Good customer service capabilities • Better product quality relative to rivals • Wide geographic coverage and/or strong global distribution capability • Alliances/joint ventures with other firms that provide access to valuable technology, competencies, and/or attractive geographic markets	• No clear strategic direction • Resources that are not well matched to industry key success factors • No well-developed or proven core competencies • A weak balance sheet; burdened with too much debt • Higher overall unit costs relative to key competitors • Weak or unproven product innovation capabilities • A product/service with ho-hum attributes or features inferior to those of rivals • Too narrow a product line relative to rivals • Weak brand image or reputation • Weaker dealer network than key rivals and/or lack of adequate global distribution capability • Behind on product quality, R&D, and/or technological know-how • In the wrong strategic group • Losing market share because . . . • Lack of management depth • Inferior intellectual capital relative to leading rivals • Subpar profitability because . . . • Plagued with internal operating problems or obsolete facilities • Behind rivals in e-commerce capabilities • Short on financial resources to grow the business and pursue promising initiatives • Too much underutilized plant capacity
Potential Market Opportunities	**Potential External Threats to a Company's Future Prospects**
• Openings to win market share from rivals • Sharply rising buyer demand for the industry's product • Serving additional customer groups or market segments • Expanding into new geographic markets • Expanding the company's product line to meet a broader range of customer needs • Using existing company skills or technological know-how to enter new product lines or new businesses • Online sales • Integrating forward or backward • Falling trade barriers in attractive foreign markets • Acquiring rival firms or companies with attractive technological expertise or capabilities • Entering into alliances or joint ventures to expand the firm's market coverage or boost its competitive capability • Openings to exploit emerging new technologies	• Increasing intensity of competition among industry rivals—may squeeze profit margins • Slowdowns in market growth • Likely entry of potent new competitors • Loss of sales to substitute products • Growing bargaining power of customers or suppliers • A shift in buyer needs and tastes away from the industry's product • Adverse demographic changes that threaten to curtail demand for the industry's product • Vulnerability to unfavorable industry driving forces • Restrictive trade policies on the part of foreign governments • Costly new regulatory requirements

resource strengths and capabilities). A checklist of potential market opportunities is included in Table 4.2.

While stunningly big or "golden" opportunities appear fairly frequently in volatile, fast-changing markets (typically due to important technological developments or rapidly shifting consumer preferences), they are nonetheless hard to see before most all companies in the industry identify them. The more volatile and thus unpredictable market conditions are, the more limited a company's ability to do market reconnaissance and spot important opportunities much ahead of rivals—there are simply too many variables in play for managers to peer into the fog of the future, identify one or more upcoming opportunities, and get a jump on rivals in pursuing it.[6] In mature markets, unusually attractive market opportunities emerge sporadically, often after long periods of relative calm—but future market conditions may be less foggy, thus facilitating good market reconnaissance and making emerging opportunities easier for industry members to detect. But in both volatile and stable markets, the rise of a golden opportunity is almost never under the control of a single company or manufactured by company executives—rather, it springs from the simultaneous alignment of several external factors. For instance, in China the recent upsurge in demand for motor vehicles was spawned by a convergence of many factors—increased disposable income, rising middle-class aspirations, a major road-building program by the government, the demise of employer-provided housing, and easy credit.[7] But golden opportunities are nearly always seized rapidly—and the companies that seize them are usually those that have been actively waiting, staying alert with diligent market reconnaissance, and preparing themselves to capitalize on shifting market conditions by patiently assembling an arsenal of competitively valuable resources—talented personnel, technical know-how, strategic partnerships, and a war chest of cash to finance aggressive action when the time comes.[8]

A company is well advised to pass on a particular market opportunity unless it has or can acquire the resources to capture it.

In evaluating a company's market opportunities and ranking their attractiveness, managers have to guard against viewing every *industry* opportunity as a *company* opportunity. Not every company is equipped with the resources to successfully pursue each opportunity that exists in its industry. Some companies are more capable of going after particular opportunities than others, and a few companies may be hopelessly outclassed. *The market opportunities most relevant to a company are those that match up well with the company's financial and organizational resource capabilities, offer the best growth and profitability, and present the most potential for competitive advantage.*

Identifying the External Threats to a Company's Future Profitability

Often, certain factors in a company's external environment pose *threats* to its profitability and competitive well-being. Threats can stem from the emergence of cheaper or better technologies, rivals' introduction of new or improved products, the entry of lower-cost foreign competitors into a company's market stronghold, new regulations that are more burdensome to a company than to its competitors, vulnerability to a rise in interest rates, the potential of a hostile takeover, unfavorable demographic shifts, adverse changes in foreign exchange rates, political upheaval in a foreign country where the company has facilities, and the like. A list of potential threats to a company's future profitability and market position is shown in Table 4.2.

External threats may pose no more than a moderate degree of adversity (all companies confront some threatening elements in the course of doing business), or they may be so imposing as to make a company's situation and outlook quite tenuous. On rare occasions, market shocks can give birth to a *sudden-death* threat that throws a company into an immediate crisis and battle to survive. Many of the world's major airlines have been plunged into unprecedented financial crisis by the perfect storm of the September 11, 2001, terrorist attacks, rising prices for jet fuel, mounting competition from low-fare carriers, shifting traveler preferences for low fares as opposed to lots of in-flight amenities, and out-of-control labor costs. It is management's job to identify the threats to the company's future prospects and to evaluate what strategic actions can be taken to neutralize or lessen their impact.

What Do the SWOT Listings Reveal?

SWOT analysis involves more than making four lists. The two most important parts of SWOT analysis are *drawing conclusions* from the SWOT listings about the company's overall situation, and *translating these conclusions into strategic actions* to better match the company's strategy to its resource strengths and market opportunities, to correct the important weaknesses, and to defend against external threats. Figure 4.2 shows the three steps of SWOT analysis.

Just what story the SWOT listings tell about the company's overall situation is often revealed in the answers to the following sets of questions:

> Simply making lists of a company's strengths, weaknesses, opportunities, and threats is not enough; the payoff from SWOT analysis comes from the conclusions about a company's situation and the implications for strategy improvement that flow from the four lists.

- Does the company have an attractive set of resource strengths? Does it have any strong core competencies or a distinctive competence? Are the company's strengths and capabilities well matched to the industry key success factors? Do they add adequate power to the company's strategy, or are more or different strengths needed? Will the company's current strengths and capabilities matter in the future?

- How serious are the company's weaknesses and competitive deficiencies? Are they mostly inconsequential and readily correctable, or could one or more prove fatal if not remedied soon? Are some of the company's weaknesses in areas that relate to the industry's key success factors? Are there any weaknesses that if uncorrected, would keep the company from pursuing an otherwise attractive opportunity? Does the company have important resource gaps that need to be filled for it to move up in the industry rankings and/or boost its profitability?

- Do the company's resource strengths and competitive capabilities (its competitive assets) outweigh its resource weaknesses and competitive deficiencies (its competitive liabilities) by an attractive margin?

- Does the company have attractive market opportunities that are well suited to its resource strengths and competitive capabilities? Does the company lack the resources and capabilities to pursue any of the most attractive opportunities?

- Are the threats alarming, or are they something the company appears able to deal with and defend against?

Figure 4.2   **The Three Steps of SWOT Analysis: Identify, Draw Conclusions, Translate into Strategic Action**

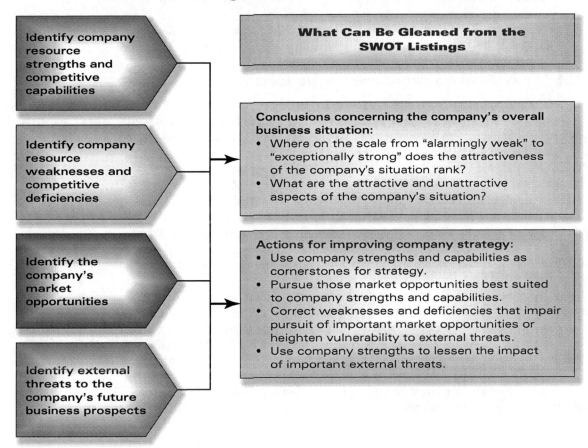

- All things considered, how strong is the company's overall situation? Where on a scale of 1 to 10 (1 being alarmingly weak and 10 exceptionally strong) should the firm's position and overall situation be ranked? What aspects of the company's situation are particularly attractive? What aspects are of the most concern?

The final piece of SWOT analysis is to translate the diagnosis of the company's situation into actions for improving the company's strategy and business prospects. The following questions point to implications the SWOT listings have for strategic action:

- Which competitive capabilities need to be strengthened immediately, so as to add greater power to the company's strategy and boost sales and profitability? Do new types of competitive capabilities need to be put in place to help the company better respond to emerging industry and competitive conditions? Which resources and capabilities need to be given greater emphasis, and which merit less emphasis? Should the company emphasize leveraging its existing resource strengths and capabilities, or does it need to create new resource strengths and capabilities?

- What actions should be taken to reduce the company's competitive liabilities? Which weaknesses or competitive deficiencies are in urgent need of correction?

- Which market opportunities should be top priority in future strategic initiatives (because they are good fits with the company's resource strengths and competitive capabilities, present attractive growth and profit prospects, and/or offer the best potential for securing competitive advantage)? Which opportunities should be ignored, at least for the time being (because they offer less growth potential or are not suited to the company's resources and capabilities)?

- What should the company be doing to guard against the threats to its well-being?

A company's resource strengths should generally form the cornerstones of strategy because they represent the company's best chance for market success.[9] As a rule, strategies that place heavy demands on areas where the company is weakest or has unproven ability are suspect and should be avoided. If a company doesn't have the resources and competitive capabilities around which to craft an attractive strategy, managers need to take decisive remedial action either to upgrade existing organizational resources and capabilities and add others as needed or to acquire them through partnerships or strategic alliances with firms possessing the needed expertise. Plainly, managers have to look toward correcting competitive weaknesses that make the company vulnerable, hold down profitability, or disqualify it from pursuing an attractive opportunity.

At the same time, sound strategy making requires sifting through the available market opportunities and aiming strategy at capturing those that are most attractive and suited to the company's circumstances. Rarely does a company have the resource depth to pursue all available market opportunities simultaneously without spreading itself too thin. How much attention to devote to defending against external threats to the company's market position and future performance hinges on how vulnerable the company is, whether there are attractive defensive moves that can be taken to lessen their impact, and whether the costs of undertaking such moves represent the best use of company resources.

QUESTION 3: ARE THE COMPANY'S PRICES AND COSTS COMPETITIVE?

Company managers are often stunned when a competitor cuts its price to "unbelievably low" levels or when a new market entrant comes on strong with a very low price. The competitor may not, however, be "dumping" (an economic term for selling at prices that are below cost), buying its way into the market with a super-low price, or waging a desperate move to gain sales—it may simply have substantially lower costs. One of the most telling signs of whether a company's business position is strong or precarious is whether its prices and costs are competitive with industry rivals. For a company to compete successfully, its costs must be *in line* with those of close rivals.

> The higher a company's costs are above those of close rivals, the more competitively vulnerable it becomes.

Price–cost comparisons are especially critical in a commodity-product industry where the value provided to buyers is the same from seller to seller, price competition is typically the ruling market force, and low-cost companies have the upper hand. But even in industries where products are differentiated and competition centers on the different attributes of competing brands as much as on price, rival companies have to keep their costs in line and make sure that any added costs they incur, and any price premiums they charge, create ample value that buyers are willing to pay extra for.

While some cost disparity is justified so long as the products or services of closely competing companies are sufficiently differentiated, a high-cost firm's market position becomes increasingly vulnerable the more its costs exceed those of close rivals.

Two analytical tools are particularly useful in determining whether a company's prices and costs are competitive: value chain analysis and benchmarking.

The Concept of a Company Value Chain

Core Concept
A company's *value chain* identifies the primary activities that create customer value and the related support activities.

Every company's business consists of a collection of activities undertaken in the course of designing, producing, marketing, delivering, and supporting its product or service. All of the various activities that a company performs internally combine to form a **value chain**—so called because the underlying intent of a company's activities is to do things that ultimately *create value for buyers*. A company's value chain also includes an allowance for profit because a markup over the cost of performing the firm's value-creating activities is customarily part of the price (or total cost) borne by buyers—unless an enterprise succeeds in creating and delivering sufficient value to buyers to produce an attractive profit, it can't survive for long.

As shown in Figure 4.3, a company's value chain consists of two broad categories of activities: the *primary activities* that are foremost in creating value for customers and the requisite *support activities* that facilitate and enhance the performance of the primary activities.[10] For example, the primary value-creating activities for a maker of bakery goods include supply chain management, recipe development and testing, mixing and baking, packaging, sales and marketing, and distribution; related support activities include quality control, human resource management, and administration. A wholesaler's primary activities and costs deal with merchandise selection and purchasing, inbound shipping and warehousing from suppliers, and outbound distribution to retail customers. The primary activities for a department store retailer include merchandise selection and buying, store layout and product display, advertising, and customer service; its support activities include site selection, hiring and training, and store maintenance, plus the usual assortment of administrative activities. A hotel chain's primary activities and costs are in site selection and construction, reservations, operation of its hotel properties (check-in and check-out, maintenance and housekeeping, dining and room service, and conventions and meetings), and managing its lineup of hotel locations; principal support activities include accounting, hiring and training hotel staff, advertising, building a brand and reputation, and general administration. Supply chain management is a crucial activity for Nissan and Amazon.com but is not a value chain component at Google or a TV and radio broadcasting company. Sales and marketing are dominant activities at Procter & Gamble and Sony but have minor roles at oil drilling companies and natural gas pipeline companies. Delivery to buyers is a crucial activity at Domino's Pizza but comparatively insignificant at Starbucks. Thus, what constitutes a primary or secondary activity varies according to the specific nature of a company's business, meaning that you should view the listing of the primary and support activities in Figure 4.3 as illustrative rather than definitive.

A Company's Primary and Support Activities Identify the Major Components of Its Cost Structure   Segregating a company's operations into different types of primary and support activities is the first step in understanding its cost structure. Each activity in the value chain gives rise to costs and ties up assets.

Figure 4.3   **A Representative Company Value Chain**

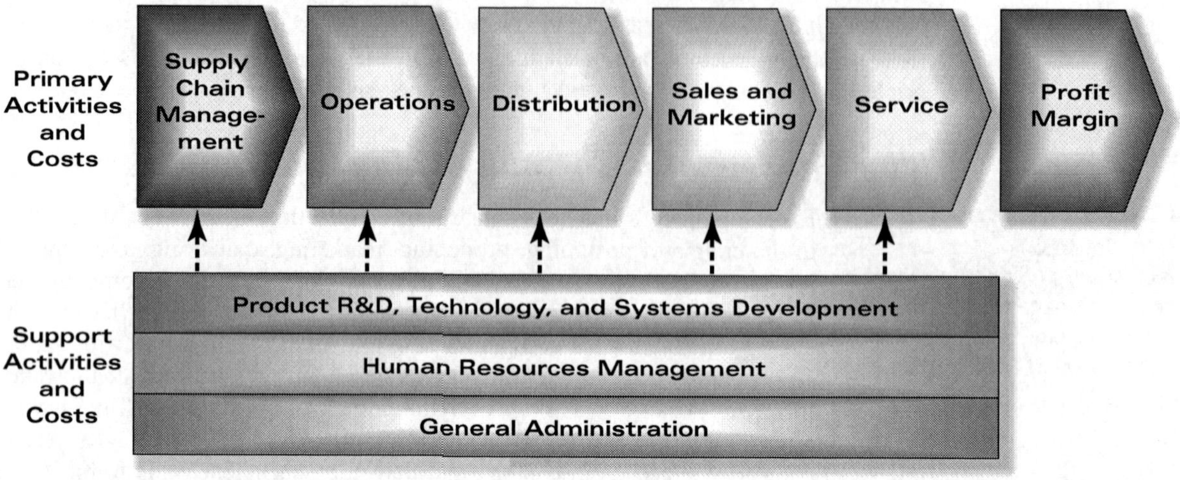

PRIMARY ACTIVITIES
- **Supply chain management**—activities, costs, and assets associated with purchasing fuel, energy, raw materials, parts and components, merchandise, and consumable items from vendors; receiving, storing, and disseminating inputs from suppliers; inspection; and inventory management.

- **Operations**—activities, costs, and assets associated with converting inputs into final product from (production, assembly, packaging, equipment maintenance, facilities, operations, quality assurance, environmental protection).

- **Distribution**—activities, costs, and assets dealing with physically distributing the product to buyers (finished goods warehousing, order processing, order picking and packing, shipping, delivery vehicle operations, establishing and maintaining a network of dealers and distributors).

- **Sales and marketing**—activities, costs, and assets related to sales force efforts, advertising and promotion, market research and planning, and dealer/distributor support.

- **Service**—activities, costs, and assets associated with providing assistance to buyers, such as installation, spare parts delivery, maintenance and repair, technical assistance, buyer inquiries, and complaints.

SUPPORT ACTIVITIES
- **Product R&D, technology, and systems development**—activities, costs, and assets relating to product R&D, process R&D, process design improvement, equipment design, computer software development, telecommunications systems, computer-assisted design and engineering, database capabilities, and development of computerized support systems.

- **Human resources management**—activities, costs, and assets associated with the recruitment, hiring, training, development, and compensation of all types of personnel; labor relations activities; and development of knowledge-based skills and core competencies.

- **General administration**—activities, costs, and assets relating to general management, accounting and finance, legal and regulatory affairs, safety and security, management information systems, forming strategic alliances and collaborating with strategic partners, and other overhead functions.

Source: Based on the discussion in Michael E. Porter, *Competitive Advantage* (New York: Free Press, 1985), pp. 37–43.

Assigning the company's operating costs and assets to each individual activity in the chain provides cost estimates and capital requirements—a process that accountants call activity-based cost accounting. Quite often, there are links between activities such that the manner in which one activity is done can affect the costs of performing other activities. For instance, how a product is designed has a huge impact on the number of different parts and components, their respective manufacturing costs, and the expense of assembling the various parts and components into a finished product.

The combined costs of all the various activities in a company's value chain define the company's internal cost structure. Further, the cost of each activity contributes to whether the company's overall cost position relative to rivals is favorable or unfavorable. The tasks of value chain analysis and benchmarking are to develop the data for comparing a company's costs activity-by-activity against the costs of key rivals and to learn which internal activities are a source of cost advantage or disadvantage. A company's relative cost position is a function of how the overall costs of the activities it performs in conducting business compare to the overall costs of the activities performed by rivals.

Why the Value Chains of Rival Companies Often Differ

A company's value chain and the manner in which it performs each activity reflect the evolution of its own particular business and internal operations, its strategy, the approaches it is using to execute its strategy, and the underlying economics of the activities themselves.[11] Because these factors differ from company to company, the value chains of rival companies sometimes differ substantially—a condition that complicates the task of assessing rivals' relative cost positions. For instance, music retailers like Blockbuster and Musicland, which purchase CDs from recording studios and wholesale distributors and sell them in their own retail store locations, have value chains and cost structures different from those of rival online music stores like Apple's iTunes and Musicmatch, which sell downloadable music files directly to music shoppers. Competing companies may differ in their degrees of vertical integration. The operations component of the value chain for a manufacturer that *makes* all of its own parts and assembles them into a finished product differs from the operations component of a rival producer that *buys* the needed parts from outside suppliers and performs assembly operations only. Likewise, there is legitimate reason to expect value chain and cost differences between a company that is pursuing a low-cost/low-price strategy and a rival that is positioned on the high end of the market. The costs of certain activities along the low-cost company's value chain should indeed be relatively low, whereas the high-end firm may understandably be spending relatively more to perform those activities that create the added quality and extra features of its products.

Moreover, cost and price differences among rival companies can have their origins in activities performed by suppliers or by distribution channel allies involved in getting the product to end users. Suppliers or wholesale/retail dealers may have excessively high cost structures or profit margins that jeopardize a company's cost-competitiveness even though its costs for internally performed activities are competitive. For example, when determining Michelin's cost-competitiveness vis-à-vis Goodyear and Bridgestone in supplying replacement tires to vehicle owners, we have to look at more than whether Michelin's tire manufacturing costs are above or below Goodyear's and Bridgestone's. Let's say that a motor vehicle owner looking for a new set of tires has to pay $400 for a set of Michelin tires and only $350 for a set of Goodyear or Bridgestone tires. Michelin's $50 price disadvantage can stem not only from higher manufacturing costs (reflecting, perhaps, the added costs of Michelin's strategic efforts to build a better-quality tire with more performance features) but also from (1) differences in what the three tire makers pay their suppliers for materials and tire-making components, and (2) differences in the operating efficiencies, costs, and markups of Michelin's wholesale–retail dealer outlets versus those of Goodyear and Bridgestone.

The Value Chain System for an Entire Industry

As the tire industry example makes clear, a company's value chain is embedded in a larger system of activities that includes the value chains of its suppliers and the value chains of whatever distribution channel allies it uses in getting its product or service to end users.[12] Suppliers' value chains are relevant because suppliers perform activities and incur costs in creating and delivering the purchased inputs used in a company's own value-creating activities. The costs, performance features, and quality of these inputs influence a company's own costs and product differentiation capabilities. Anything a company can do to help its suppliers' drive down the costs of their value chain activities or improve the quality and performance of the items being supplied can enhance its own competitiveness—a powerful reason for working collaboratively with suppliers in managing supply chain activities.[13]

The value chains of forward channel partners and/or the customers to whom a company sells are relevant because (1) the costs and margins of a company's distributors and retail dealers are part of the price the ultimate consumer pays, and (2) the activities that distribution allies perform affect customer satisfaction. For these reasons, companies normally work closely with their forward channel allies (who are their direct customers) to perform value chain activities in mutually beneficial ways. For instance, motor vehicle manufacturers work closely with their local automobile dealers to keep the retail prices of their vehicles competitive with rivals' models and to ensure that owners are satisfied with dealers' repair and maintenance services. Some aluminum can producers have constructed plants next to beer breweries and deliver cans on overhead conveyors directly to the breweries' can-filling lines; this has resulted in significant savings in production scheduling, shipping, and inventory costs for both container producers and breweries.[14] Many automotive parts suppliers have built plants near the auto assembly plants they supply to facilitate just-in-time deliveries, reduce warehousing and shipping costs, and promote close collaboration on parts design and production scheduling. Irrigation equipment companies, suppliers of grape-harvesting and winemaking equipment, and firms making barrels, wine bottles, caps, corks, and labels all have facilities in the California wine country to be close to the nearly 700 winemakers they supply.[15] The lesson here is that a company's value chain activities are often closely linked to the value chains of their suppliers and the forward allies or customers to whom they sell.

As a consequence, *accurately assessing a company's competitiveness from the perspective of the consumers who ultimately use its products or services thus requires that company managers understand an industry's entire value chain system for delivering a product or service to customers, not just the company's own value chain.* A typical industry value chain that incorporates the value chains of suppliers and forward channel allies (if any) is shown in Figure 4.4. However, industry value chains

> A company's cost-competitiveness depends not only on the costs of internally performed activities (its own value chain) but also on costs in the value chains of its suppliers and forward channel allies.

Figure 4.4   **Representative Value Chain for an Entire Industry**

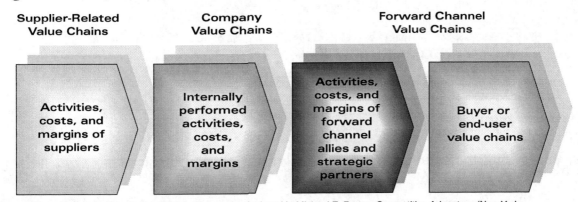

Supplier-Related Value Chains

Activities, costs, and margins of suppliers

Company Value Chains

Internally performed activities, costs, and margins

Forward Channel Value Chains

Activities, costs, and margins of forward channel allies and strategic partners

Buyer or end-user value chains

Source: Based in part on the single-industry value chain displayed in Michael E. Porter, *Competitive Advantage* (New York: Free Press, 1985), p. 35.

vary significantly by industry. The primary value chain activities in the pulp and paper industry (timber farming, logging, pulp mills, and papermaking) differ from the primary value chain activities in the home appliance industry (parts and components manufacture, assembly, wholesale distribution, retail sales). The value chain for the soft-drink industry (processing of basic ingredients and syrup manufacture, bottling and can filling, wholesale distribution, advertising, and retail merchandising) differs from that for the computer software industry (programming, disk loading, marketing, distribution). Producers of bathroom and kitchen faucets depend heavily on the activities of wholesale distributors and building supply retailers in winning sales to homebuilders and do-it-yourselfers, but producers of papermaking machines internalize their distribution activities by selling directly to the operators of paper plants. Illustration Capsule 4.1 shows representative costs for various activities performed by the producers and marketers of music CDs.

Activity-Based Costing: A Tool for Assessing a Company's Cost Competitiveness

Once the company has identified its major value chain activities, the next step in evaluating its cost competitiveness involves determining the costs of performing specific value chain activities, using what accountants call activity-based costing.[16] Traditional accounting identifies costs according to broad categories of expenses—wages and salaries, employee benefits, supplies, maintenance, utilities, travel, depreciation, R&D, interest, general administration, and so on. But activity-based cost accounting involves establishing expense categories for specific value chain activities and assigning costs to the activity responsible for creating the cost. An illustrative example is shown in Table 4.3. Perhaps 25 percent of the companies that have explored the feasibility of activity-based costing have adopted this accounting approach.

Illustration Capsule 4.1

Estimated Value Chain Costs for Recording and Distributing Music CDs through Traditional Music Retailers

The following table presents the representative costs and markups associated with producing and distributing a music CD retailing for $15 in music stores (as opposed to Internet sources).

Value Chain Activities and Costs in Producing and Distributing a CD		
1. Record company direct production costs:		$2.40
Artists and repertoire	$0.75	
Pressing of CD and packaging	1.65	
2. Royalties		0.99
3. Record company marketing expenses		1.50
4. Record company overhead		1.50
5. Total record company costs		6.39
6. Record company's operating profit		1.86
7. Record company's selling price to distributor/wholesaler		8.25
8. Average wholesale distributor markup to cover distribution activities and profit margins		1.50
9. Average wholesale price charged to retailer		9.75
10. Average retail markup over wholesale cost		5.25
11. Average price to consumer at retail		$15.00

Source: Developed from information in "Fight the Power," a case study prepared by Adrian Aleyne, Babson College, 1999.

The degree to which a company's costs should be disaggregated into specific activities depends on how valuable it is to develop cross-company cost comparisons for narrowly defined activities as opposed to broadly defined activities. Generally speaking, cost estimates are needed at least for each broad category of primary and secondary activities, but finer classifications may be needed if a company discovers that it has a cost disadvantage vis-à-vis rivals and wants to pin down the exact source or activity causing the cost disadvantage. It can also be necessary to develop cost estimates for activities performed in the competitively relevant portions of suppliers' and customers' value chains—which requires going to outside sources for reliable cost information.

Once a company has developed good cost estimates for each of the major activities in its value chain, and perhaps has cost estimates for subactivities within each primary/ secondary value chain activity, then it is ready to see how its costs for these activities compare with the costs of rival firms. This is where benchmarking comes in.

Table 4.3   **The Difference between Traditional Cost Accounting and Activity-Based Cost Accounting: A Supply Chain Activity Example**

Traditional Cost Accounting Categories for Supply Chain Activities		Cost of Performing Specific Supply Chain Activities Using Activity-Based Cost Accounting	
Wages and salaries	$450,000	Evaluate supplier capabilities	$150,000
Employee benefits	95,000	Process purchase orders	92,000
Supplies	21,500	Collaborate with suppliers on just-in-time deliveries	180,000
Travel	12,250		
Depreciation	19,000	Share data with suppliers	69,000
Other fixed charges (office space, utilities)	112,000	Check quality of items purchased	94,000
Miscellaneous operating expenses	40,250	Check incoming deliveries against purchase orders	50,000
	$750,000	Resolve disputes	15,000
		Conduct internal administration	100,000
			$750,000

Source: Developed from information in Terence P. Par, "A New Tool for Managing Costs," *Fortune,* June 14, 1993, pp. 124–29.

Benchmarking: A Tool for Assessing Whether a Company's Value Chain Costs Are in Line

Core Concept

Benchmarking is a potent tool for learning which companies are best at performing particular activities and then using their techniques (or "best practices") to improve the cost and effectiveness of a company's own internal activities.

Many companies today are **benchmarking** their costs of performing a given activity against competitors' costs (and/or against the costs of a noncompetitor that efficiently and effectively performs much the same activity in another industry). *Benchmarking is a tool that allows a company to determine whether its performance of a particular function or activity represents the "best practice" when both cost and effectiveness are taken into account.*

Benchmarking entails comparing how different companies perform various value chain activities—how materials are purchased, how suppliers are paid, how inventories are managed, how products are assembled, how fast the company can get new products to market, how the quality control function is performed, how customer orders are filled and shipped, how employees are trained, how payrolls are processed, and how maintenance is performed—and then making cross-company comparisons of the costs of these activities.[17] The objectives of benchmarking are to identify the best practices in performing an activity, to learn how other companies have actually achieved lower costs or better results in performing benchmarked activities, and to take action to improve a company's competitiveness whenever benchmarking reveals that its costs and results of performing an activity are not on a par with what other companies (either competitors or noncompetitors) have achieved.

Xerox became one of the first companies to use benchmarking when, in 1979, Japanese manufacturers began selling midsize copiers in the United States for $9,600 each—less than Xerox's production costs.[18] Xerox management suspected its Japanese competitors were dumping, but it sent a team of line managers to Japan, including the head of manufacturing, to study competitors' business processes and costs. With the aid of Xerox's joint venture partner in Japan, Fuji-Xerox, which knew the competitors well, the team found that Xerox's costs were excessive due to gross inefficiencies in the company's manufacturing processes and business practices. The findings triggered a major internal effort at Xerox to become cost-competitive and prompted Xerox to begin benchmarking 67 of its key work processes against companies identified as employing the best practices. Xerox quickly decided not to restrict its benchmarking efforts to its office equipment rivals but to extend them to any company regarded as world class in performing *any activity* relevant to Xerox's business. Other companies quickly picked up on Xerox's approach. Toyota managers got their idea for just-in-time inventory deliveries by studying how U.S. supermarkets replenished their shelves. Southwest Airlines reduced the turnaround time of its aircraft at each scheduled stop by studying pit crews on the auto racing circuit. Over 80 percent of Fortune 500 companies reportedly use benchmarking for comparing themselves against rivals on cost and other competitively important measures.

The tough part of benchmarking is not whether to do it, but rather how to gain access to information about other companies' practices and costs. Sometimes benchmarking can be accomplished by collecting information from published reports, trade groups, and industry research firms and by talking to knowledgeable industry analysts, customers, and suppliers. Sometimes field trips to the facilities of competing or noncompeting companies can be arranged to observe how things are done, ask questions, compare practices and processes, and perhaps exchange data on productivity, staffing levels, time requirements, and other cost components—but the problem here is that such companies, even if they agree to host facilities tours and answer questions, are unlikely to share competitively sensitive cost information. Furthermore, comparing one company's costs to another's costs may not involve comparing apples to apples if the two companies employ different cost accounting principles to calculate the costs of particular activities.

> Benchmarking the costs of company activities against rivals provides hard evidence of whether a company is cost-competitive.

However, a third and fairly reliable source of benchmarking information has emerged. The explosive interest of companies in benchmarking costs and identifying best practices has prompted consulting organizations (e.g., Accenture, A. T. Kearney, Benchnet—The Benchmarking Exchange, Towers Perrin, and Best Practices) and several councils and associations (e.g., the American Productivity and Quality Center, the Qualserve Benchmarking Clearinghouse, and the Strategic Planning Institute's Council on Benchmarking) to gather benchmarking data, distribute information about best practices, and provide comparative cost data without identifying the names of particular companies. Having an independent group gather the information and report it in a manner that disguises the names of individual companies avoid having the disclosure of competitively sensitive data and lessens the potential for unethical behavior on the part of company personnel in gathering their own data about competitors.Illustration Capsule 4.2 presents a widely recommended code of conduct for engaging in benchmarking that is intended to help companies avoid any improprieties in gathering and using benchmarking data.

Strategic Options for Remedying a Cost Disadvantage

Value chain analysis and benchmarking can reveal a great deal about a firm's cost competitiveness. Examining the costs of a company's own value chain activities and comparing them to rivals' indicates who has how much of a cost advantage or

Illustration Capsule 4.2
Benchmarking and Ethical Conduct

Because discussions between benchmarking partners can involve competitively sensitive data, conceivably raising questions about possible restraint of trade or improper business conduct, many benchmarking organizations urge all individuals and organizations involved in benchmarking to abide by a code of conduct grounded in ethical business behavior. Among the most widely used codes of conduct is the one developed by the American Productivity and Quality Center and advocated by the Qualserve Benchmarking Clearinghouse; it is based on the following principles and guidelines:

- Avoid discussions or actions that could lead to or imply an interest in restraint of trade, market and/or customer allocation schemes, price fixing, dealing arrangements, bid rigging, or bribery. Don't discuss costs with competitors if costs are an element of pricing.

- Refrain from the acquisition of trade secrets from another by any means that could be interpreted as improper including the breach or inducement of a breach of any duty to maintain secrecy. Do not disclose or use any trade secret that may have been obtained through improper means or that was disclosed by another in violation of duty to maintain its secrecy or limit its use.

- Be willing to provide the same type and level of information that you request from your benchmarking partner to your benchmarking partner.

- Communicate fully and early in the relationship to clarify expectations, avoid misunderstanding, and establish mutual interest in the benchmarking exchange.

- Be honest and complete.

- Treat benchmarking interchange as confidential to the individuals and companies involved. Information must not be communicated outside the partnering organizations without the prior consent of the benchmarking partner who shared the information.

- Use information obtained through benchmarking only for purposes stated to the benchmarking partner.

- The use or communication of a benchmarking partner's name with the data obtained or practices observed requires the prior permission of that partner.

- Respect the corporate culture of partner companies and work within mutually agreed-on procedures.

- Use benchmarking contacts designated by the partner company, if that is the company's preferred procedure.

- Obtain mutual agreement with the designated benchmarking contact on any hand-off of communication or responsibility to other parties.

- Make the most of your benchmarking partner's time by being fully prepared for each exchange.

- Help your benchmarking partners prepare by providing them with a questionnaire and agenda prior to benchmarking visits.

- Follow through with each commitment made to your benchmarking partner in a timely manner.

- Understand how your benchmarking partner would like to have the information he or she provides handled and used, and handle and use it in that manner.

Note: Identification of firms, organizations, and contacts visited is prohibited without advance approval from the organization.

Sources: The American Productivity and Quality Center, www.apqc.org, and the Qualserve Benchmarking Clearinghouse, www.awwa.org (accessed September 14, 2005).

disadvantage and which cost components are responsible. Such information is vital in strategic actions to eliminate a cost disadvantage or create a cost advantage. One of the fundamental insights of value chain analysis and benchmarking is that *a company's competitiveness on cost depends on how efficiently it manages its value chain activities relative to how well competitors manage theirs.*[19] There are three main areas in a company's overall value chain where important differences in the costs of competing firms can occur: a company's own activity segments, suppliers' part of the industry value chain, and the forward channel portion of the industry chain.

Remedying an Internal Cost Disadvantage   When a company's cost disadvantage stems from performing internal value chain activities at a higher cost than key rivals, then managers can pursue any of several strategic approaches to restore cost parity:[20]

1. Implement the use of best practices throughout the company, particularly for high-cost activities.

2. Try to eliminate some cost-producing activities altogether by revamping the value chain. Examples include cutting out low-value-added activities or bypassing the value chains and associated costs of distribution allies and marketing directly to end users. Dell has used this approach in PCs, and airlines have begun bypassing travel agents by getting passengers to purchase their tickets directly at airline Web sites.

3. Relocate high-cost activities (such as manufacturing) to geographic areas—such as China, Latin America, or Eastern Europe—where they can be performed more cheaply.

4. See if certain internally performed activities can be outsourced from vendors or performed by contractors more cheaply than they can be done in-house.

5. Invest in productivity-enhancing, cost-saving technological improvements (robotics, flexible manufacturing techniques, state-of-the-art electronic networking).

6. Find ways to detour around the activities or items where costs are high—computer chip makers regularly design around the patents held by others to avoid paying royalties; automakers have substituted lower-cost plastic and rubber for metal at many exterior body locations.

7. Redesign the product and/or some of its components to facilitate speedier and more economical manufacture or assembly.

8. Try to make up the internal cost disadvantage by reducing costs in the supplier or forward channel portions of the industry value chain—usually a last resort.

Remedying a Supplier-Related Cost Disadvantage   Supplier-related cost disadvantages can be attacked by pressuring suppliers for lower prices, switching to lower-priced substitute inputs, and collaborating closely with suppliers to identify mutual cost-saving opportunities.[21] For example, just-in-time deliveries from suppliers can lower a company's inventory and internal logistics costs and may also allow its suppliers to economize on their warehousing, shipping, and production scheduling costs—a win–win outcome for both. In a few instances, companies may find that it is cheaper to integrate backward into the business of high-cost suppliers and make the item in-house instead of buying it from outsiders. If a company strikes out in wringing savings out of its high-cost supply chain activities, then it must resort to finding cost savings either in-house or in the forward channel portion of the industry value chain to offset its supplier-related cost disadvantage.

Remedying a Cost Disadvantage Associated with Activities Performed by Forward Channel Allies   There are three main ways to combat a cost disadvantage in the forward portion of the industry value chain:

1. Pressure dealer-distributors and other forward channel allies to reduce their costs and markups so as to make the final price to buyers more competitive with the prices of rivals.

2. Work closely with forward channel allies to identify win–win opportunities to reduce costs. For example, a chocolate manufacturer learned that by shipping its bulk chocolate in liquid form in tank cars instead of 10-pound molded bars, it could not only save its candy bar manufacturing customers the costs associated with unpacking and melting but also eliminate its own costs of molding bars and packing them.

3. Change to a more economical distribution strategy, including switching to cheaper distribution channels (perhaps direct sales via the Internet) or perhaps integrating forward into company-owned retail outlets.

If these efforts fail, the company can either try to live with the cost disadvantage or pursue cost-cutting earlier in the value chain system.

Translating Proficient Performance of Value Chain Activities into Competitive Advantage

Performing value chain activities in ways that give a company the capabilities to either outmatch the competencies and capabilities of rivals or else beat them on costs are two good ways to secure competitive advantage.

A company that does a *first-rate job* of managing its value chain activities *relative to competitors* stands a good chance of achieving sustainable competitive advantage. As shown in Figure 4.5, outmanaging rivals in performing value chain activities can be accomplished in either or both of two ways: (1) by astutely developing core competencies and maybe a distinctive competence that rivals don't have or can't quite match and that are instrumental in helping it deliver attractive value to customers, and/or (2) by simply doing an overall better job than rivals of lowering its combined costs of performing all the various value chain activities, such that it ends up with a low-cost advantage over rivals.

The first of these two approaches begins with management efforts to build more organizational expertise in performing certain competitively important value chain activities, deliberately striving to develop competencies and capabilities that add power to its strategy and competitiveness. If management begins to make selected competencies and capabilities cornerstones of its strategy and continues to invest resources in building greater and greater proficiency in performing them, then over time one (or maybe several) of the targeted competencies/capabilities may rise to the level of a core competence. Later, following additional organizational learning and investments in gaining still greater proficiency, a core competence could evolve into a distinctive competence, giving the company superiority over rivals in performing an important value chain activity. Such superiority, if it gives the company significant competitive clout in the marketplace, can produce an attractive competitive edge over rivals and, more important, prove difficult for rivals to match or offset with competencies and capabilities of their own making. As a general rule, it is substantially harder for rivals to achieve best-in-industry proficiency in performing a key value chain activity than it is for them to clone the features and attributes of a hot-selling product or service.[22] This is especially true when a company with a distinctive competence avoids becoming complacent and works diligently to maintain its industry-leading expertise and capability. GlaxoSmithKline, one of the world's most competitively capable pharmaceutical companies, has built its business position around expert performance of a few competitively crucial activities: extensive R&D to achieve first discovery of new drugs, a carefully constructed approach to patenting, skill in gaining rapid and thorough clinical clearance through regulatory bodies, and unusually strong distribution and sales-force

Figure 4.5 **Translating Company Performance of Value Chain Activities into Competitive Advantage**

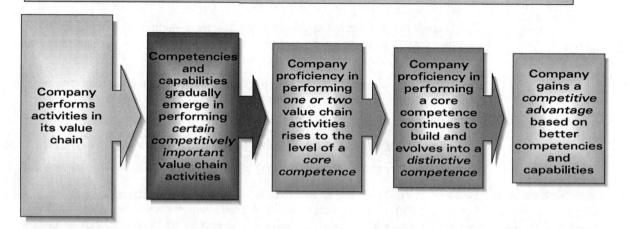

Option 1: Beat rivals in performing value chain activities more proficiently

Company performs activities in its value chain → Competencies and capabilities gradually emerge in performing *certain competitively important* value chain activities → Company proficiency in performing *one or two* value chain activities rises to the level of a *core competence* → Company proficiency in performing a core competence continues to build and evolves into a *distinctive competence* → Company gains a *competitive advantage* based on better competencies and capabilities

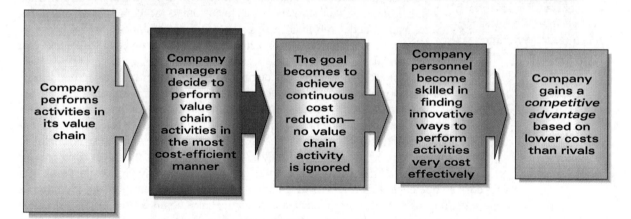

Option 2: Beat rivals in performing value chain activities more cheaply

Company performs activities in its value chain → Company managers decide to perform value chain activities in the most cost-efficient manner → The goal becomes to achieve continuous cost reduction—no value chain activity is ignored → Company personnel become skilled in finding innovative ways to perform activities very cost effectively → Company gains a *competitive advantage* based on lower costs than rivals

capabilities.[23] FedEx's astute management of its value chain has produced unmatched competencies and capabilities in overnight package delivery.

The second approach to building competitive advantage entails determined management efforts to be cost-efficient in performing value chain activities. Such efforts have to be ongoing and persistent, and they have to involve each and every value chain activity. The goal must be continuous cost reduction, not a one-time or on-again/off-again effort. Companies whose managers are truly committed to low-cost performance of value chain activities and succeed in engaging company personnel to discover innovative ways to drive costs out of the business have a real chance of gaining a durable low-cost edge over rivals. It is not as easy as it seems to imitate a company's low-cost practices. Companies like Wal-Mart, Dell, Nucor Steel, Southwest Airlines,

Toyota, and French discount retailer Carrefour have been highly successful in managing their values chains in a low-cost manner.

QUESTION 4: IS THE COMPANY COMPETITIVELY STRONGER OR WEAKER THAN KEY RIVALS?

Using value chain analysis and benchmarking to determine a company's competitiveness on price is necessary but not sufficient. A more comprehensive assessment needs to be made of the company's overall competitive strength. The answers to two questions are of particular interest: First, how does the company rank relative to competitors on each of the important factors that determine market success? Second, all things considered, does the company have a net competitive advantage or disadvantage versus major competitors?

An easy-to-use method for answering the two questions posed above involves developing quantitative strength ratings for the company and its key competitors on each industry key success factor and each competitively pivotal resource capability. Much of the information needed for doing a competitive strength assessment comes from previous analyses. Industry and competitive analysis reveals the key success factors and competitive capabilities that separate industry winners from losers. Benchmarking data and scouting key competitors provide a basis for judging the competitive strength of rivals on such factors as cost, key product attributes, customer service, image and reputation, financial strength, technological skills, distribution capability, and other competitively important resources and capabilities. SWOT analysis reveals how the company in question stacks up on these same strength measures.

Step 1 in doing a competitive strength assessment is to make a list of the industry's key success factors and most telling measures of competitive strength or weakness (6 to 10 measures usually suffice). Step 2 is to rate the firm and its rivals on each factor. Numerical rating scales (e.g., from 1 to 10) are best to use, although ratings of stronger (+), weaker (−), and about equal (=) may be appropriate when information is scanty and assigning numerical scores conveys false precision. Step 3 is to sum the strength ratings on each factor to get an overall measure of competitive strength for each company being rated. Step 4 is to use the overall strength ratings to draw conclusions about the size and extent of the company's net competitive advantage or disadvantage and to take specific note of areas of strength and weakness.

Table 4.5 provides two examples of competitive strength assessment, using the hypothetical ABC Company against four rivals. The first example employs an *unweighted rating system*. With unweighted ratings, each key success factor/competitive strength measure is assumed to be equally important (a rather dubious assumption). Whichever company has the highest strength rating on a given measure has an implied competitive edge on that factor; the size of its edge is mirrored in the margin of difference between its rating and the ratings assigned to rivals—a rating of 9 for one company versus ratings of 5, 4, and 3, respectively, for three other companies indicates a bigger advantage than a rating of 9 versus ratings of 8, 7, and 6. Summing a company's ratings on all the measures produces an overall strength rating. The higher a company's overall strength rating, the stronger its overall competitiveness versus rivals. The bigger the difference between a company's overall rating and the scores of *lower-rated* rivals, the greater its implied *net competitive advantage.* Conversely, the bigger the difference between a company's overall rating and the scores of *higher-rated* rivals, the greater its implied

Table 4.5 Illustrations of Unweighted and Weighted Competitive Strength Assessments

A. An Unweighted Competitive Strength Assessment

Key Success Factor/Strength Measure	Strength Rating (Scale: 1 = Very weak; 10 = Very strong)				
	ABC Co.	Rival 1	Rival 2	Rival 3	Rival 4
Quality/product performance	8	5	10	1	6
Reputation/image	8	7	10	1	6
Manufacturing capability	2	10	4	5	1
Technological skills	10	1	7	3	8
Dealer network/distribution capability	9	4	10	5	1
New product innovation capability	9	4	10	5	1
Financial resources	5	10	7	3	1
Relative cost position	5	10	3	1	4
Customer service capabilities	5	7	10	1	4
Unweighted overall strength rating	**61**	**58**	**71**	**25**	**32**

B. A Weighted Competitive Strength Assessment
(Rating Scale: 1 = Very weak; 10 = Very strong)

Key Success Factor/Strength Measure	Importance Weight	ABC Co.		Rival 1		Rival 2		Rival 3		Rival 4	
		Strength Rating	Score	Strength Rating	Score	Strength Rating	Score	Strength Rating	Score	Strength Rating	Score
Quality/product performance	0.10	8	0.80	5	0.50	10	1.00	1	0.10	6	0.60
Reputation/image	0.10	8	0.80	7	0.70	10	1.00	1	0.10	6	0.60
Manufacturing capability	0.10	2	0.20	10	1.00	4	0.40	5	0.50	1	0.10
Technological skills	0.05	10	0.50	1	0.05	7	0.35	3	0.15	8	0.40
Dealer network/distribution capability	0.05	9	0.45	4	0.20	10	0.50	5	0.25	1	0.05
New product innovation capability	0.05	9	0.45	4	0.20	10	0.50	5	0.25	1	0.05
Financial resources	0.10	5	0.50	10	1.00	7	0.70	3	0.30	1	0.10
Relative cost position	0.30	5	1.50	10	3.00	3	0.95	1	0.30	4	1.20
Customer service capabilities	0.15	5	0.75	7	1.05	10	1.50	1	0.15	4	0.60
Sum of importance weights	1.00										
Weighted overall strength rating		61	**5.95**	58	**7.70**	71	**6.85**	25	**2.10**	32	**3.70**

net competitive disadvantage. Thus, ABC's total score of 61 (see the top half of Table 4.5) signals a much greater net competitive advantage over Rival 4 (with a score of 32) than over Rival 1 (with a score of 58) but indicates a moderate net competitive disadvantage against Rival 2 (with an overall score of 71).

However, a better method is a *weighted rating system* (shown in the bottom half of Table 4.5) because the different measures of competitive strength are unlikely to be equally important. In an industry where the products/services of rivals are virtually identical, for instance, having low unit costs relative to rivals is nearly always the most important determinant of competitive strength. In an industry with strong product differentiation, the most significant measures of competitive strength may be brand awareness, amount of advertising, product attractiveness, and distribution capability. In a weighted rating system each measure of competitive strength is assigned a weight based on its perceived importance in shaping competitive success. A weight could be as high as 0.75 (maybe even higher) in situations where one particular competitive variable is overwhelmingly decisive, or a weight could be as low as 0.20 when two or three strength measures are more important than the rest. Lesser competitive strength indicators can carry weights of 0.05 or 0.10. No matter whether the differences between the importance weights are big or little, *the sum of the weights must equal 1.0.*

> A weighted competitive strength analysis is conceptually stronger than an unweighted analysis because of the inherent weakness in assuming that all the strength measures are equally important.

Weighted strength ratings are calculated by rating each competitor on each strength measure (using the 1 to 10 rating scale) and multiplying the assigned rating by the assigned weight (a rating of 4 times a weight of 0.20 gives a weighted rating, or score, of 0.80). Again, the company with the highest rating on a given measure has an implied competitive edge on that measure, with the size of its edge reflected in the difference between its rating and rivals' ratings. The weight attached to the measure indicates how important the edge is. Summing a company's weighted strength ratings for all the measures yields an overall strength rating. Comparisons of the weighted overall strength scores indicate which competitors are in the strongest and weakest competitive positions and who has how big a net competitive advantage over whom.

Note in Table 4.5 that the unweighted and weighted rating schemes produce different orderings of the companies. In the weighted system, ABC Company drops from second to third in strength, and Rival 1 jumps from third to first because of its high strength ratings on the two most important factors. Weighting the importance of the strength measures can thus make a significant difference in the outcome of the assessment.

Interpreting the Competitive Strength Assessments

> High competitive strength ratings signal a strong competitive position and possession of competitive advantage; low ratings signal a weak position and competitive disadvantage.

Competitive strength assessments provide useful conclusions about a company's competitive situation. The ratings show how a company compares against rivals, factor by factor or capability by capability, thus revealing where it is strongest and weakest, and against whom. Moreover, the overall competitive strength scores indicate how all the different factors add up—whether the company is at a net competitive advantage or disadvantage against each rival. The firm with the largest overall competitive strength rating enjoys the strongest competitive position, with the size of its net competitive advantage reflected by how much its score exceeds the scores of rivals.

In addition, the strength ratings provide guidelines for designing wise offensive and defensive strategies. For example, consider the ratings and weighted scores in the bottom half of Table 4.5. If ABC Company wants to go on the offensive to win additional sales and market share, such an offensive probably needs to be aimed directly at winning customers away from Rivals 3 and 4 (which have lower overall strength scores) rather than Rivals 1 and 2 (which have higher overall strength scores). Moreover, while ABC has high ratings for quality/product performance (an 8 rating), reputation/image (an 8 rating), technological skills (a 10 rating), dealer network/distribution capability (a 9 rating), and new product innovation capability (a 9 rating), these strength measures have low importance weights—meaning that ABC has strengths in areas that don't translate into much competitive clout in the marketplace. Even so, it outclasses Rival 3 in all five areas, plus it enjoys lower costs than Rival 3: On relative cost position ABC has a 5 rating versus a 1 rating for Rival 3—and relative cost position carries the highest importance weight of all the strength measures. ABC also has greater competitive strength than Rival 3 as concerns customer service capabilities (which carries the second-highest importance weight). Hence, because ABC's strengths are in the very areas where Rival 3 is weak, ABC is in good position to attack Rival 3—it may well be able to persuade a number of Rival 3's customers to switch their purchases over to ABC's product.

But in mounting an offensive to win customers away from Rival 3, ABC should note that Rival 1 has an excellent relative cost position—its rating of 10, combined with the importance weight of 0.30 for relative cost, means that Rival 1 has meaningfully lower costs in an industry where low costs are competitively important. Rival 1 is thus strongly positioned to retaliate against ABC with lower prices if ABC's strategy offensive ends up drawing customers away from Rival 1. Moreover, Rival 1's very strong relative cost position vis-à-vis all the other companies arms it with the ability to use its lower-cost advantage to underprice all of its rivals and gain sales and market share at their expense. If ABC wants to defend against its vulnerability to potential price cutting by Rival 1, then it needs to aim a portion of its strategy at lowering its costs.

> A company's competitive strength scores pinpoint its strengths and weaknesses against rivals and point directly to the kinds of offensive/defensive actions it can use to exploit its competitive strengths and reduce its competitive vulnerabilities.

The point here is that a competitively astute company should use the strength assessment in deciding what strategic moves to make—which strengths to exploit in winning business away from rivals and which competitive weaknesses to try to correct. When a company has important competitive strengths in areas where one or more rivals are weak, it makes sense to consider offensive moves to exploit rivals' competitive weaknesses. When a company has important competitive weaknesses in areas where one or more rivals are strong, it makes sense to consider defensive moves to curtail its vulnerability.

QUESTION 5: WHAT STRATEGIC ISSUES AND PROBLEMS MERIT FRONT-BURNER MANAGERIAL ATTENTION?

The final and most important analytical step is to zero in on exactly what strategic issues that company managers need to address—and resolve—for the company to be more financially and competitively successful in the years ahead. This step involves drawing on the results of both industry and competitive analysis and the evaluations of the company's own competitiveness. The task here is to get a clear fix on exactly what strategic and competitive challenges confront the company, which of the company's competitive shortcomings need fixing, what obstacles stand in the way of improving the company's competitive position in the marketplace, and what specific problems

Zeroing in on the strategic issues a company faces and compiling a "worry list" of problems and roadblocks creates a strategic agenda of problems that merit prompt managerial attention.

merit front-burner attention by company managers. *Pinpointing the precise things that management needs to worry about sets the agenda for deciding what actions to take next to improve the company's performance and business outlook.*

The "worry list" of issues and problems that have to be wrestled with can include such things as *how* to stave off market challenges from new foreign competitors, *how* to combat the price discounting of rivals, *how* to reduce the company's high costs and pave the way for price reductions, *how* to sustain the company's present rate of growth in light of slowing buyer demand, *whether* to expand the company's product line, *whether* to correct the company's competitive deficiencies by acquiring a rival company with the missing strengths, *whether* to expand into foreign markets rapidly or cautiously, *whether* to reposition the company and move to a different strategic group, *what to do* about growing buyer interest in substitute products, and *what to do* to combat the aging demographics of the company's customer base. The worry list thus always centers on such concerns as "how to . . .," "what to do about . . .," and "whether to . . ."—the purpose of the worry list is to identify the specific issues/problems that management needs to address, not to figure out what specific actions to take. Deciding what to do—which strategic actions to take and which strategic moves to make—comes later (when it is time to craft the strategy and choose from among the various strategic alternatives).

Actually deciding upon a strategy and what specific actions to take is what comes *after* developing the list of strategic issues and problems that merit front-burner management attention.

If the items on the worry list are relatively minor—which suggests the company's strategy is mostly on track and reasonably well matched to the company's overall situation—then company managers seldom need to go much beyond fine-tuning of the present strategy. If, however, the issues and problems confronting the company are serious and indicate the present strategy is not well suited for the road ahead, the task of crafting a better strategy has got to go to the top of management's action agenda.

A good strategy must contain ways to deal with all the strategic issues and obstacles that stand in the way of the company's financial and competitive success in the years ahead.

Key Points

There are five key questions to consider in analyzing a company's own particular competitive circumstances and its competitive position vis-à-vis key rivals:

1. *How well is the present strategy working?* This involves evaluating the strategy from a qualitative standpoint (completeness, internal consistency, rationale, and suitability to the situation) and also from a quantitative standpoint (the strategic and financial results the strategy is producing). The stronger a company's current overall performance, the less likely the need for radical strategy changes. The weaker a company's performance and/or the faster the changes in its external situation (which can be gleaned from industry and competitive analysis), the more its current strategy must be questioned.

2. *What are the company's resource strengths and weaknesses, and its external opportunities and threats?* A SWOT analysis provides an overview of a firm's situation and is an essential component of crafting a strategy tightly matched to the company's situation. The two most important parts of SWOT analysis are (*a*) drawing conclusions about what story the compilation of strengths, weaknesses, opportunities, and threats tells about the company's overall situation, and

(*b*) acting on those conclusions to better match the company's strategy, to its resource strengths and market opportunities, to correct the important weaknesses, and to defend against external threats. A company's resource strengths, competencies, and competitive capabilities are strategically relevant because they are the most logical and appealing building blocks for strategy; resource weaknesses are important because they may represent vulnerabilities that need correction. External opportunities and threats come into play because a good strategy necessarily aims at capturing a company's most attractive opportunities and at defending against threats to its well-being.

3. *Are the company's prices and costs competitive?* One telling sign of whether a company's situation is strong or precarious is whether its prices and costs are competitive with those of industry rivals. Value chain analysis and benchmarking are essential tools in determining whether the company is performing particular functions and activities cost-effectively, learning whether its costs are in line with competitors, and deciding which internal activities and business processes need to be scrutinized for improvement. Value chain analysis teaches that how competently a company manages its value chain activities relative to rivals is a key to building a competitive advantage based on either better competencies and competitive capabilities or lower costs than rivals.

4. *Is the company competitively stronger or weaker than key rivals?* The key appraisals here involve how the company matches up against key rivals on industry key success factors and other chief determinants of competitive success and whether and why the company has a competitive advantage or disadvantage. Quantitative competitive strength assessments, using the method presented in Table 4.5, indicate where a company is competitively strong and weak, and provide insight into the company's ability to defend or enhance its market position. As a rule a company's competitive strategy should be built around its competitive strengths and should aim at shoring up areas where it is competitively vulnerable. When a company has important competitive strengths in areas where one or more rivals are weak, it makes sense to consider offensive moves to exploit rivals' competitive weaknesses. When a company has important competitive weaknesses in areas where one or more rivals are strong, it makes sense to consider defensive moves to curtail its vulnerability.

5. *What strategic issues and problems merit front-burner managerial attention?* This analytical step zeros in on the strategic issues and problems that stand in the way of the company's success. It involves using the results of both industry and competitive analysis and company situation analysis to identify a "worry list" of issues to be resolved for the company to be financially and competitively successful in the years ahead. The worry list always centers on such concerns as "how to . . .," "what to do about . . .," and "whether to . . ."—the purpose of the worry list is to identify the specific issues/problems that management needs to address. Actually deciding upon a strategy and what specific actions to take is what comes after the list of strategic issues and problems that merit front-burner management attention is developed.

Good company situation analysis, like good industry and competitive analysis, is a valuable precondition for good strategy making. A competently done evaluation of a company's resource capabilities and competitive strengths exposes strong and weak points in the present strategy and how attractive or unattractive the company's competitive position is and why. Managers need such understanding to craft a strategy that is well suited to the company's competitive circumstances.

Exercises

1. Review the information in Illustration Capsule 4.1 concerning the costs of the different value chain activities associated with recording and distributing music CDs through traditional brick-and-mortar retail outlets. Then answer the following questions:

   a. Does the growing popularity of downloading music from the Internet give rise to a new music industry value chain that differs considerably from the traditional value chain? Explain why or why not.

   b. What costs are cut out of the traditional value chain or bypassed when *online music retailers* (Apple, Sony, Microsoft, Musicmatch, Napster, Cdigix, and others) sell songs directly to online buyers? (Note: In 2005, online music stores were selling download-only titles for $0.79 to $0.99 per song and $9.99 for most albums.)

   c. What costs would be cut out of the traditional value chain or bypassed in the event that *recording studios* sell downloadable files of artists' recordings directly to online buyers?

   d. What happens to the traditional value chain if more and more music lovers use peer-to-peer file-sharing software to download music from the Internet to play music on their PCs or MP3 players or make their own CDs? (Note: It was estimated that, in 2004, about 1 billion songs were available for online trading and file sharing via such programs as Kazaa, Grokster, Shareaza, BitTorrent, and eDonkey, despite the fact that some 4,000 people had been sued by the Recording Industry Association of America for pirating copyrighted music via peer-to-peer file sharing.)

2. Using the information in Table 4.1 and the following financial statement information for Avon Products, calculate the following ratios for Avon for both 2003 and 2004:

   a. Gross profit margin.

   b. Operating profit margin.

   c. Net profit margin.

   d. Return on total assets.

   e. Return on stockholders' equity.

   f. Debt-to-equity ratio.

   g. Times-interest-earned.

   h. Days of inventory.

   i. Inventory turnover ratio.

   j. Average collection period.

   Based on these ratios, did Avon's financial performance improve, weaken, or remain about the same from 2003 to 2004?

Avon Products Inc., Consolidated Statements of Income
(in millions, except per share data)

	Years Ended December 31	
	2004	2003
Net sales	$7,656.2	$6,773.7
Other revenue	91.6	71.4
Total revenue	7,747.8	6,845.1
Costs, expenses and other:		
Cost of sales	2,911.7	2,611.8
Marketing, distribution and administrative expenses	3,610.3	3,194.4
Special charges, net	(3.2)	(3.9)
Operating profit	1,229.0	1,042.8
Interest expense	33.8	33.3
Interest income	(20.6)	(12.6)
Other expense (income), net	28.3	28.6
Total other expenses	41.5	49.3
Income before taxes and minority interest	1,187.5	993.5
Income taxes	330.6	318.9
Income before minority interest	856.9	674.6
Minority interest	(10.8)	(9.8)
Net income	$ 846.1	$ 664.8
Earnings per share:		
Basic	$ 1.79	$ 1.41
Diluted	$ 1.77	$ 1.39
Weighted-average shares outstanding (in millions):		
Basic	472.35	471.08
Diluted	477.96	483.13

Avon Products Inc. Consolidated Balance Sheets (in millions)

	December 31	
	2004	2003
Current assets		
Cash, including cash equivalents of $401.2 and $373.8	$ 769.6	$ 694.0
Accounts receivable (less allowances of $101.0 and $81.1)	599.1	553.2
Inventories	740.5	653.4
Prepaid expenses and other	397.2	325.5
Total current assets	$2,506.4	$2,226.1
Property, plant and equipment, at cost:		
Land	$ 61.7	$ 58.6
Buildings and improvements	886.8	765.9
Equipment	1,006.7	904.4
	1,955.2	1,728.9
Less accumulated depreciation	(940.4)	(873.3)
	1,014.8	855.6
Other assets	626.9	499.9
Total assets	$4,148.1	$3,581.6
Liabilities and shareholders' equity		
Current liabilities		
Debt maturing within one year	$ 51.7	$ 244.1
Accounts payable	490.1	400.1
Accrued compensation	164.5	149.5
Other accrued liabilities	360.1	332.6
Sales and taxes other than income	154.4	139.5
Income taxes	304.7	341.2
Total current liabilities	$1,525.5	$1,607.0
Long-term debt	$ 866.3	$ 877.7
Employee benefit plans	620.6	502.1
Deferred income taxes	12.1	50.6
Other liabilities (including minority interest of $42.5 and $46.0)	173.4	172.9
Total liabilities	$3,197.9	$3,210.3

(*Continued*)

	December 31	
	2004	2003
Shareholders' equity		
Common stock, par value $.25—authorized 1,500 shares; issued 728.61 and 722.25 shares	182.2	90.3
Additional paid-in capital	1,356.8	1,188.4
Retained earnings	2,693.5	2,202.4
Accumulated other comprehensive loss	(679.5)	(729.4)
Treasury stock, at cost—257.08 and 251.66 shares	(2,602.8)	(2,380.4)
Total shareholders' equity	950.2	371.3
Total liabilities and shareholders' equity	$4,148.1	$3,581.6

Source: Avon Products Inc., 2004 10-K

chapter five

The Five Generic Competitive Strategies

Which One to Employ?

Competitive strategy is about being different. It means deliberately choosing to perform activities differently or to perform different activities than rivals to deliver a unique mix of value.

—Michael E. Porter

Strategy . . . is about first analyzing and then experimenting, trying, learning, and experimenting some more.

—Ian C. McMillan and Rita Gunther McGrath

Winners in business play rough and don't apologize for it. The nicest part of playing hardball is watching your competitors squirm.

—George Stalk Jr. and Rob Lachenauer

The essence of strategy lies in creating tomorrow's competitive advantages faster than competitors mimic the ones you possess today.

—Gary Hamel and C. K. Prahalad

This chapter describes the *five basic competitive strategy options*—which of the five to employ is a company's first and foremost choice in crafting an overall strategy and beginning its quest for competitive advantage. A company's **competitive strategy** deals exclusively with the specifics of management's game plan for competing successfully—its specific efforts to please customers, its offensive and defensive moves to counter the maneuvers of rivals, its responses to whatever market conditions prevail at the moment, its initiatives to strengthen its market position, and its approach to securing a competitive advantage vis-à-vis rivals. Companies the world over are imaginative in conceiving competitive strategies to win customer favor. At most companies the aim, quite simply, is to do a significantly better job than rivals of providing what buyers are looking for and thereby secure an upper hand in the marketplace.

A company achieves competitive advantage whenever it has some type of edge over rivals in attracting buyers and coping with competitive forces. There are many routes to competitive advantage, but they all involve giving buyers what they perceive as superior value compared to the offerings of rival sellers. Superior value can mean a good product at a lower price; a superior product that is worth paying more for; or a best-value offering that represents an attractive combination of price, features, quality, service, and other appealing attributes. Delivering superior value—whatever form it takes—nearly always requires performing value chain activities differently than rivals and building competencies and resource capabilities that are not readily matched.

> **Core Concept**
> A **competitive strategy** concerns the specifics of management's game plan for competing successfully and securing a competitive advantage over rivals.

> **Core Concept**
> The objective of competitive strategy is to knock the socks off rival companies by doing a better job of satisfying buyer needs and preferences.

THE FIVE GENERIC COMPETITIVE STRATEGIES

There are countless variations in the competitive strategies that companies employ, mainly because each company's strategic approach entails custom-designed actions to fit its own circumstances and industry environment. The custom-tailored nature of each company's strategy makes the chances remote that any two companies—even companies in the same industry—will employ strategies that are exactly alike in every detail. Managers at different companies always have a slightly different spin on future market conditions and how to best align their company's strategy with these conditions; moreover, they have different notions of how they intend to outmaneuver rivals and what strategic options make the most sense for their particular company. However, when one strips away the details to get at the real substance, the biggest and most important differences among competitive strategies boil down to (1) whether a company's market target is broad or narrow, and (2) whether the company is pursuing a competitive advantage linked to low costs or product differentiation. Five distinct competitive strategy approaches stand out:[1]

1. *A low-cost provider strategy*—striving to achieve lower overall costs than rivals and appealing to a broad spectrum of customers, usually by underpricing rivals.

2. *A broad differentiation strategy*—seeking to differentiate the company's product offering from rivals' in ways that will appeal to a broad spectrum of buyers.

3. *A best-cost provider strategy*—giving customers more value for their money by incorporating good-to-excellent product attributes at a lower cost than rivals; the target is to have the lowest (best) costs and prices compared to rivals offering products with comparable attributes.

Figure 5.1   **The Five Generic Competitive Strategies: Each Stakes Out a Different Market Position**

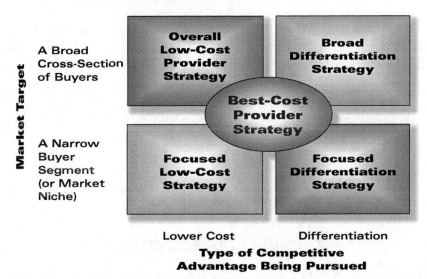

Source: This is an author-expanded version of a three-strategy classification discussed in Michael E. Porter, *Competitive Strategy: Techniques for Analyzing Industries and Competitors* (New York: Free Press, 1980), pp. 35–40.

133

4. *A focused (or market niche) strategy based on low costs*—concentrating on a narrow buyer segment and outcompeting rivals by having lower costs than rivals and thus being able to serve niche members at a lower price.

5. *A focused (or market niche) strategy based on differentiation*—concentrating on a narrow buyer segment and outcompeting rivals by offering niche members customized attributes that meet their tastes and requirements better than rivals' products.

Each of these five generic competitive approaches stakes out a different market position, as shown in Figure 5.1. Each involves distinctively different approaches to competing and operating the business. The remainder of this chapter explores the ins and outs of the five generic competitive strategies and how they differ.

LOW-COST PROVIDER STRATEGIES

Striving to be the industry's overall low-cost provider is a powerful competitive approach in markets with many price-sensitive buyers. A company achieves low-cost leadership when it becomes the industry's lowest-cost provider rather than just being one of perhaps several competitors with comparatively low costs. A low-cost provider's strategic target is meaningfully lower costs than rivals—but not necessarily the absolutely lowest possible cost. In striving for a cost advantage over rivals, managers must take care to include features and services that buyers consider essential—*a product offering that is too frills-free sabotages the attractiveness of the company's product and can turn buyers off even if it is priced lower than competing products.* For maximum effectiveness, companies employing a low-cost provider strategy need to achieve their cost advantage in ways difficult for rivals to copy or match. If rivals find it relatively easy or inexpensive to imitate the leader's low-cost methods, then the leader's advantage will be too short-lived to yield a valuable edge in the marketplace.

> **Core Concept**
> A low-cost leader's basis for competitive advantage is lower overall costs than competitors. Successful low-cost leaders are exceptionally good at finding ways to drive costs out of their businesses.

A company has two options for translating a low-cost advantage over rivals into attractive profit performance. Option 1 is to use the lower-cost edge to underprice competitors and attract price-sensitive buyers in great enough numbers to increase total profits. The trick to profitably underpricing rivals is either to keep the size of the price cut smaller than the size of the firm's cost advantage (thus reaping the benefits of both a bigger profit margin per unit sold and the added profits on incremental sales) or to generate enough added volume to increase total profits despite thinner profit margins (larger volume can make up for smaller margins provided the underpricing of rivals brings in enough extra sales). Option 2 is to maintain the present price, be content with the present market share, and use the lower-cost edge to earn a higher profit margin on each unit sold, thereby raising the firm's total profits and overall return on investment.

Illustration Capsule 5.1 describes Nucor Corporation's strategy for gaining low-cost leadership in manufacturing a variety of steel products.

The Two Major Avenues for Achieving a Cost Advantage

To achieve a low-cost edge over rivals, a firm's cumulative costs across its overall value chain must be lower than competitors' cumulative costs—and the means of achieving

Illustration Capsule 5.1

Nucor Corporation's Low-Cost Provider Strategy

Nucor Corporation is the world's leading minimill producer of such steel products as carbon and alloy steel bars, beams, sheet, and plate; steel joists and joist girders; steel deck; cold finished steel; steel fasteners; metal building systems; and light gauge steel framing. In 2004, it had close to $10 billion in sales, 9,000 employees, and annual production capacity of nearly 22 million tons, making it the largest steel producer in the United States and one of the 10 largest in the world. The company has pursued a strategy that has made it among the world's lowest-cost producers of steel and has allowed the company to consistently outperform its rivals in terms of financial and market performance.

Nucor's low-cost strategy aims to give it a cost and pricing advantage in the commodity-like steel industry and leaves no part of the company's value chain neglected. The key elements of the strategy include the following:

- Using electric arc furnaces where scrap steel and directly reduced iron ore are melted and then sent to a continuous caster and rolling mill to be shaped into steel products, thereby eliminating an assortment of production processes from the value chain used by traditional integrated steel mills. Nucor's minimill value chain makes the use of coal, coke, and iron ore unnecessary; cuts investment in facilities and equipment (eliminating coke ovens, blast furnaces, basic oxygen furnaces, and ingot casters); and requires fewer employees than integrated mills.

- Striving hard for continuous improvement in the efficiency of its plants and frequently investing in state-of-the-art equipment to reduce unit costs. Nucor is known for its technological leadership and its aggressive pursuit of production process innovation.

- Carefully selecting plant sites to minimize inbound and outbound shipping costs and to take advantage of low rates for electricity (electric arc furnaces are heavy users of electricity). Nucor tends to avoid locating new plants in geographic areas where labor unions are a strong influence.

- Hiring a nonunion workforce that uses team-based incentive compensation systems (often opposed by unions). Operating and maintenance employees and supervisors are paid weekly bonuses based on the productivity of their work group. The size of the bonus is based on the capabilities of the equipment employed and ranges from 80 percent to 150 percent of an employee's base pay; no bonus is paid if the equipment is not operating. Nucor's compensation program has boosted the company's labor productivity to levels nearly double the industry average while rewarding productive employees with annual compensation packages that exceed what their union counterparts earn by as much as 20 percent. Nucor has been able to attract and retain highly talented, productive, and dedicated employees. In addition, the company's healthy culture and results-oriented self-managed work teams allow the company to employ fewer supervisors than what would be needed with an hourly union workforce.

- Heavily emphasizing consistent product quality and has rigorous quality systems.

- Minimizing general and administrative expenses by maintaining a lean staff at corporate headquarters (fewer than 125 employees) and allowing only four levels of management between the CEO and production workers. Headquarters offices are modestly furnished and located in an inexpensive building. The company minimizes reports, paperwork, and meetings to keep managers focused on value-adding activities. Nucor is noted not only for its streamlined organizational structure but also for its frugality in travel and entertainment expenses—the company's top managers set the example by flying coach class, avoiding pricey hotels, and refraining from taking customers out for expensive dinners.

In 2001–2003, when many U.S. producers of steel products were in dire economic straits because of weak demand for steel and deep price discounting by foreign rivals, Nucor began acquiring state-of-the-art steelmaking facilities from bankrupt or nearly bankrupt rivals at bargain-basement prices, often at 20 to 25 percent of what it cost to construct the facilities. This has given Nucor much lower depreciation costs than rivals having comparable plants.

Nucor management's outstanding execution of its low-cost strategy and its commitment to drive down costs throughout its value chain has allowed it to compete aggressively on price, earn higher profit margins than rivals, and grow its business at a considerably faster rate than its integrated steel mill rivals.

Source: Company annual reports, news releases, and Web site.

the cost advantage must be durable. There are two ways to accomplish this:[2]

1. Do a better job than rivals of performing value chain activities more cost-effectively.

2. Revamp the firm's overall value chain to eliminate or bypass some cost-producing activities.

Let's look at each of the two approaches to securing a cost advantage.

Cost-Efficient Management of Value Chain Activities For a company to do a more cost-efficient job of managing its value chain than rivals, managers must launch a concerted, ongoing effort to ferret out cost-saving opportunities in every part of the value chain. No activity can escape cost-saving scrutiny, and all company personnel must be expected to use their talents and ingenuity to come up with innovative and effective ways to keep costs down. All avenues for performing value chain activities at a lower cost than rivals have to be explored. Attempts to outmanage rivals on cost commonly involve such actions as:

1. *Striving to capture all available economies of scale.* Economies of scale stem from an ability to lower unit costs by increasing the scale of operation—there are many occasions when a large plant is more economical to operate than a small or medium-size plant or when a large distribution warehouse is more cost efficient than a small warehouse. Often, manufacturing economies can be achieved by using common parts and components in different models and/or by cutting back on the number of models offered (especially slow-selling ones) and then scheduling longer production runs for fewer models. In global industries, making separate products for each country market instead of selling a mostly standard product worldwide tends to boost unit costs because of lost time in model changeover, shorter production runs, and inability to reach the most economic scale of production for each country model.

2. *Taking full advantage of learning/experience curve effects.* The cost of performing an activity can decline over time as the learning and experience of company personnel builds. Learning/experience curve economies can stem from debugging and mastering newly introduced technologies, using the experiences and suggestions of workers to install more efficient plant layouts and assembly procedures, and the added speed and effectiveness that accrues from repeatedly picking sites for and building new plants, retail outlets, or distribution centers. Aggressively managed low-cost providers pay diligent attention to capturing the benefits of learning and experience and to keeping these benefits proprietary to whatever extent possible.

3. *Trying to operate facilities at full capacity.* Whether a company is able to operate at or near full capacity has a big impact on units costs when its value chain contains activities associated with substantial fixed costs. Higher rates of capacity utilization allow depreciation and other fixed costs to be spread over a larger unit volume, thereby lowering fixed costs per unit. The more capital-intensive the business, or the higher the percentage of fixed costs as a percentage of total costs, the more important that full-capacity operation becomes because there's such a stiff unit-cost penalty for underutilizing existing capacity. In such cases, finding ways to operate close to full capacity year-round can be an important source of cost advantage.

4. *Pursuing efforts to boost sales volumes and thus spread such costs as R&D, advertising, and selling and administrative costs out over more units.* The more units

a company sells, the more it lowers its unit costs for R&D, sales and marketing, and administrative overhead.

5. *Improving supply chain efficiency.* Many companies pursue cost reduction by partnering with suppliers to streamline the ordering and purchasing process via online systems, reduce inventory carrying costs via just-in-time inventory practices, economize on shipping and materials handling, and ferret out other cost-saving opportunities. A company with a core competence (or better still a distinctive competence) in cost-efficient supply chain management can sometimes achieve a sizable cost advantage over less adept rivals.

6. *Substituting the use of low-cost for high-cost raw materials or component parts.* If the costs of raw materials and parts are too high, a company can either substitute the use of lower-cost items or maybe even design the high-cost components out of the product altogether.

7. *Using online systems and sophisticated software to achieve operating efficiencies.* Data sharing, starting with customer orders and going all the way back to components production, coupled with the use of enterprise resource planning (ERP) and manufacturing execution system (MES) software, can make custom manufacturing just as cheap as mass production—and sometimes cheaper. Online systems and software can also greatly reduce production times and labor costs. Lexmark used ERP and MES software to cut its production time for inkjet printers from four hours to 24 minutes. Southwest Airlines uses proprietary software to schedule flights and assign flight crews cost-effectively.

8. *Adopting labor-saving operating methods.* Examples of ways for a company to economize on labor costs include the following: installing labor-saving technology, shifting production from geographic areas where labor costs are high to geographic areas where labor costs are low, avoiding the use of union labor where possible (because of work rules that can stifle productivity and because of union demands for above-market pay scales and costly fringe benefits), and using incentive compensation systems that promote high labor productivity.

9. *Using the company's bargaining power vis-à-vis suppliers to gain concessions.* Many large enterprises (e.g., Wal-Mart, Home Depot, the world's major motor vehicle producers) have used their bargaining clout in purchasing large volumes to wrangle good prices on their purchases from suppliers. Having greater buying power than rivals can be an important source of cost advantage.

10. *Being alert to the cost advantages of outsourcing and vertical integration.* Outsourcing the performance of certain value chain activities can be more economical than performing them in-house if outside specialists, by virtue of their expertise and volume, can perform the activities at lower cost. Indeed, outsourcing has in recent years become a widely used cost-reduction approach. However, there can be times when integrating the activities of either suppliers or distribution channel allies can allow an enterprise to detour suppliers or buyers who have an adverse impact on costs because of their considerable bargaining power.

In addition to the above means of achieving lower costs than rivals, managers can also achieve important cost savings by deliberately opting for an inherently economical strategy keyed to a frills-free product offering. For instance, a company can bolster its attempts to open up a durable cost advantage over rivals by:

- Having lower specifications for purchased materials, parts, and components than rivals do. Thus, a maker of personal computers (PCs) can use the cheapest hard drives, microprocessors, monitors, DVD drives, and other components it can find so as to end up with lower production costs than rival PC makers.

- Distributing the company's product only through low-cost distribution channels and avoiding high-cost distribution channels.
- Choosing to use the most economical method for delivering customer orders (even if it results in longer delivery times).

These strategy-related means of keeping costs low don't really involve "outmanaging" rivals, but they can nonetheless contribute materially to becoming the industry's low-cost leader.

Revamping the Value Chain to Curb or Eliminate Unnecessary Activities

Dramatic cost advantages can emerge from finding innovative ways to cut back on or entirely bypass certain cost-producing value chain activities. There are six primary ways companies can achieve a cost advantage by reconfiguring their value chains:

1. *Cutting out distributors and dealers by selling directly to customers.* Selling directly and bypassing the activities and costs of distributors or dealers can involve (1) having the company's own direct sales force (which adds the costs of maintaining and supporting a sales force but may well be cheaper than accessing customers through distributors or dealers) and/or (2) conducting sales operations at the company's Web site (Web site operations may be substantially cheaper than distributor or dealer channels). Costs in the wholesale/retail portions of the value chain frequently represent 35–50 percent of the price final consumers pay. There are several prominent examples in which companies have instituted a sell-direct approach to cutting costs out of the value chain. Software developers allow customers to download new programs directly from the Internet, eliminating the costs of producing and packaging CDs and cutting out the host of activities, costs, and markups associated with shipping and distributing software through wholesale and retail channels. By cutting all these costs and activities out of the value chain, software developers have the pricing room to boost their profit margins and still sell their products below levels that retailers would have to charge. The major airlines now sell most of their tickets directly to passengers via their Web sites, ticket counter agents, and telephone reservation systems, allowing them to save hundreds of millions of dollars in commissions once paid to travel agents.

2. *Replacing certain value chain activities with faster and cheaper online technology.* In recent years the Internet and Internet technology applications have become powerful and pervasive tools for conducting business and reengineering company and industry value chains. For instance, Internet technology has revolutionized supply chain management, turning many time-consuming and labor-intensive activities into paperless transactions performed instantaneously. Company procurement personnel can—with only a few mouse clicks—check materials inventories against incoming customer orders, check suppliers' stocks, check the latest prices for parts and components at auction and e-sourcing Web sites, and check FedEx delivery schedules. Various e-procurement software packages streamline the purchasing process by eliminating paper documents such as requests for quotations, purchase orders, order acceptances, and shipping notices. There's software that permits the relevant details of incoming customer orders to be instantly shared with the suppliers of needed parts and components. All this facilitates

just-in-time deliveries of parts and components and matching the production of parts and components to assembly plant requirements and production schedules, cutting out unnecessary activities and producing savings for both suppliers and manufacturers. Retailers can install online systems that relay data from cash register sales at the check-out counter back to manufacturers and their suppliers. Manufacturers can use online systems to collaborate closely with parts and components suppliers in designing new products and shortening the time it takes to get them into production. Online systems allow warranty claims and product performance problems involving supplier components to be instantly relayed to the relevant suppliers so that corrections can be expedited. Online systems have the further effect of breaking down corporate bureaucracies and reducing overhead costs. The whole back-office data management process (order processing, invoicing, customer accounting, and other kinds of transaction costs) can be handled fast, accurately, and with less paperwork and fewer personnel.

3. *Streamlining operations by eliminating low-value-added or unnecessary work steps and activities.* Examples include using computer-assisted design techniques, standardizing parts and components across models and styles, having suppliers collaborate to combine parts and components into modules so that products can be assembled in fewer steps, and shifting to an easy-to-manufacture product design. At Wal-Mart, some items supplied by manufacturers are delivered directly to retail stores rather than being routed through Wal-Mart's distribution centers and delivered by Wal-Mart trucks; in other instances, Wal-Mart unloads incoming shipments from manufacturers' trucks arriving at its distribution centers directly onto outgoing Wal-Mart trucks headed to particular stores without ever moving the goods into the distribution center. Many supermarket chains have greatly reduced in-store meat butchering and cutting activities by shifting to meats that are cut and packaged at the meat-packing plant and then delivered to their stores in ready-to-sell form.

4. *Relocating facilities so as to curb the need for shipping and handling activities.* Having suppliers locate facilities adjacent to the company's plant or locating the company's plants or warehouses near customers can help curb or eliminate shipping and handling costs.

5. *Offering a frills-free product.* Deliberately restricting a company's product offering to the essentials can help the company cut costs associated with snazzy attributes and a full lineup of options and extras. Activities and costs can also be eliminated by incorporating fewer performance and quality features into the product and by offering buyers fewer services. Stripping extras like first-class sections, meals, and reserved seating is a favorite technique of budget airlines like Southwest, Ryanair (Europe), easyJet (Europe), and Gol (Brazil).

6. *Offering a limited product line as opposed to a full product line.* Pruning slow-selling items from the product lineup and being content to meet the needs of most buyers rather than all buyers can eliminate activities and costs associated with numerous product versions and wide selection.

Illustration Capsule 5.2 describes how Wal-Mart has managed its value chain in the retail grocery portion of its business to achieve a dramatic cost advantage over rival supermarket chains and become the world's biggest grocery retailer.

Examples of Companies That Revamped Their Value Chains to Reduce
Costs   Iowa Beef Packers (IBP), now a subsidiary of Tyson Foods, pioneered the

Ilustration Capsule 5.2

How Wal-Mart Managed Its Value Chain to Achieve a Huge Low-Cost Advantage over Rival Supermarket Chains

Wal-Mart has achieved a very substantial cost and pricing advantage over rival supermarket chains both by revamping portions of the grocery retailing value chain and by out-managing its rivals in efficiently performing various value chain activities. Its cost advantage stems from a series of initiatives and practices:

- Instituting extensive information sharing with vendors via online systems that relay sales at its checkout counters directly to suppliers of the items, thereby providing suppliers with real-time information on customer demand and preferences (creating an estimated 6 percent cost advantage). It is standard practice at Wal-Mart to collaborate extensively with vendors on all aspects of the purchasing and store delivery process to squeeze out mutually beneficial cost savings. Procter & Gamble, Wal-Mart's biggest supplier, went so far as to integrate its enterprise resource planning (ERP) system with Wal-Mart's.

- Pursuing global procurement of some items and centralizing most purchasing activities so as to leverage the company's buying power (creating an estimated 2.5 percent cost advantage).

- Investing in state-of-the-art automation at its distribution centers, efficiently operating a truck fleet that

makes daily deliveries to Wal-Mart's stores, and putting assorted other cost-saving practices into place at its headquarters, distribution centers, and stores (resulting in an estimated 4 percent cost advantage).

- Striving to optimize the product mix and achieve greater sales turnover (resulting in about a 2 percent cost advantage).

- Installing security systems and store operating procedures that lower shrinkage rates (producing a cost advantage of about 0.5 percent).

- Negotiating preferred real estate rental and leasing rates with real estate developers and owners of its store sites (yielding a cost advantage of 2 percent).

- Managing and compensating its workforce in a manner that produces lower labor costs (yielding an estimated 5 percent cost advantage)

Altogether, these value chain initiatives give Wal-Mart an approximately 22 percent cost advantage over Kroger, Safeway, and other leading supermarket chains. With such a sizable cost advantage, Wal-Mart has been able to under-price its rivals and become the world's leading supermarket retailer in little more than a decade.

Source: Developed by the authors from information at www.wal-mart.com (accessed September 15, 2004) and in Marco Iansiti and Roy Levien, "Strategy as Ecology," *Harvard Business Review* 82, no. 3 (March 2004), p. 70.

development of a cheaper value chain system in the beef-packing industry.[3] The traditional cost chain involved raising cattle on scattered farms and ranches; shipping them live to labor-intensive, unionized slaughtering plants; and then transporting whole sides of beef to grocery retailers whose butcher departments cut them into smaller pieces and packaged them for sale to grocery shoppers. IBP revamped the traditional chain with a radically different strategy: It built large automated plants employing nonunion workers near cattle supplies. Near the plants it arranged to set up large feed lots (or holding pens) where cattle were fed grain for a short time to fatten them up prior to slaughter. The meat was butchered at the processing plant into small, high-yield cuts. Some of the trimmed and boned cuts were vacuum-sealed in plastic casings for further butchering in supermarket meat departments, but others were trimmed and/or boned, put in plastic-sealed ready-to-sell trays, boxed, and shipped to retailers. IBP's strategy was to increase the volume of prepackaged, "case-ready" cuts that retail grocers could unpack from boxes and place directly into the meat case. In addition, IBP provided meat retailers with individually wrapped quick-frozen steaks, as well as precooked roasts, beef tip, and meatloaf selections that could be prepared in a matter of minutes. Iowa Beef's inbound cattle transportation expenses, traditionally a major cost item, were cut significantly by avoiding the weight losses that occurred when live animals were shipped long distances just prior to slaughter. Sizable major outbound shipping cost savings were achieved by not having to ship whole sides of beef, which had a high waste factor. Meat retailers had to do far less butchering to stock their meat cases. IBP value chain revamping was so successful that the company became the largest U.S. meatpacker.

Southwest Airlines has reconfigured the traditional value chain of commercial airlines to lower costs and thereby offer dramatically lower fares to passengers. Its mastery of fast turnarounds at the gates (about 25 minutes versus 45 minutes for rivals) allows its planes to fly more hours per day. This translates into being able to schedule more flights per day with fewer aircraft, allowing Southwest to generate more revenue per plane on average than rivals. Southwest does not offer in-flight meals, assigned seating, baggage transfer to connecting airlines, or first-class seating and service, thereby eliminating all the cost-producing activities associated with these features. The company's fast, user-friendly online reservation system facilitates e-ticketing and reduces staffing requirements at telephone reservation centers and airport counters. Its use of automated check-in equipment reduces staffing requirements for terminal check-in.

Dell has created the best, most cost-efficient value chain in the global personal computer industry. Whereas Dell's major rivals (Hewlett-Packard, Lenovo, Sony, and Toshiba) produce their models in volume and sell them through independent resellers and retailers, Dell has elected to market directly to PC users, building its PCs to customer specifications as orders come in and shipping them to customers within a few days of receiving the order. Dell's value chain approach has proved cost-effective in coping with the PC industry's blink-of-an-eye product life cycle. The build-to-order strategy enables the company to avoid misjudging buyer demand for its various models and being saddled with quickly obsolete excess components and finished-goods inventories—all parts and components are obtained on a just-in-time basis from vendors, many of which deliver their items to Dell assembly plants several times a day in volumes matched to the Dell's daily assembly schedule. Also, Dell's sell-direct strategy slices reseller/retailer costs and margins out of the value chain (although some of these savings are offset by the cost of Dell's direct marketing and customer support activities—functions that would otherwise be performed by resellers and retailers). Partnerships with suppliers that facilitate just-in-time deliveries of components and minimize Dell's inventory costs, coupled with Dell's extensive use of e-commerce technologies further reduce Dell's costs. Dell's value chain approach is widely considered to have made it the global low-cost leader in the PC industry.

The Keys to Success in Achieving Low-Cost Leadership

To succeed with a low-cost-provider strategy, company managers have to scrutinize each cost-creating activity and determine what factors cause costs to be high or low. Then they have to use this knowledge to keep the unit costs of each activity low, exhaustively pursuing cost efficiencies throughout the value chain. They have to be proactive in restructuring the value chain to eliminate nonessential work steps and low-value activities. Normally, low-cost producers work diligently to create cost-conscious corporate cultures that feature broad employee participation in continuous cost improvement efforts and limited perks and frills for executives. They strive to operate with exceptionally small corporate staffs to keep administrative costs to a minimum.

Many successful low-cost leaders also use benchmarking to keep close tabs on how their costs compare with rivals and firms performing comparable activities in other industries.

But while low-cost providers are champions of frugality, they are usually aggressive in investing in resources and capabilities that promise to drive costs out of the business. Wal-Mart, one of the foremost practitioners of low-cost leadership, employs state-of-the-art technology throughout its operations—its distribution facilities are an automated showcase, it uses online systems to order goods from suppliers and manage inventories, it equips its stores with cutting-edge sales-tracking and check-out systems, and it sends daily point-of-sale data to 4,000 vendors. Wal-Mart's information and communications systems and capabilities are more sophisticated than those of virtually any other retail chain in the world.

> Success in achieving a low-cost edge over rivals comes from outmanaging rivals in figuring out how to perform value chain activities most cost effectively and eliminating or curbing non essential value chain activities

Other companies noted for their successful use of low-cost provider strategies include Lincoln Electric in arc welding equipment, Briggs & Stratton in small gasoline engines, Bic in ballpoint pens, Black & Decker in power tools, Stride Rite in footwear, Beaird-Poulan in chain saws, and General Electric and Whirlpool in major home appliances.

When a Low-Cost Provider Strategy Works Best

A competitive strategy predicated on low-cost leadership is particularly powerful when:

1. *Price competition among rival sellers is especially vigorous*—Low-cost providers are in the best position to compete offensively on the basis of price, to use the appeal of lower price to grab sales (and market share) from rivals, to win the business of price-sensitive buyers, to remain profitable in the face of strong price competition, and to survive price wars.

2. *The products of rival sellers are essentially identical and supplies are readily available from any of several eager sellers*—Commodity-like products and/or ample supplies set the stage for lively price competition; in such markets, it is less efficient, higher-cost companies whose profits get squeezed the most.

3. *There are few ways to achieve product differentiation that have value to buyers*—When the differences between brands do not matter much to buyers, buyers are nearly always very sensitive to price differences and shop the market for the best price.

4. *Most buyers use the product in the same ways*—With common user requirements, a standardized product can satisfy the needs of buyers, in which case low selling price, not features or quality, becomes the dominant factor in causing buyers to choose one seller's product over another's.

5. *Buyers incur low costs in switching their purchases from one seller to another*—Low switching costs give buyers the flexibility to shift purchases to lower-priced sellers having equally good products or to attractively priced substitute products. A low-cost leader is well positioned to use low price to induce its customers not to switch to rival brands or substitutes.

6. *Buyers are large and have significant power to bargain down prices*—Low-cost providers have partial profit-margin protection in bargaining with high-volume buyers, since powerful buyers are rarely able to bargain price down past the survival level of the next most cost-efficient seller.

7. *Industry newcomers use introductory low prices to attract buyers and build a customer base*—The low-cost leader can use price cuts of its own to make it harder

A low-cost provider is in the best position to win the business of price-sensitive buyers, set the floor on market price, and still earn a profit.

for a new rival to win customers; the pricing power of the low-cost provider acts as a barrier for new entrants.

As a rule, the more price-sensitive buyers are, the more appealing a low-cost strategy becomes. A low-cost company's ability to set the industry's price floor and still earn a profit erects protective barriers around its market position.

The Pitfalls of a Low-Cost Provider Strategy

Perhaps the biggest pitfall of a low-cost provider strategy is getting carried away with overly aggressive price cutting and ending up with lower, rather than higher, profitability. A low-cost/low-price advantage results in superior profitability only if (1) prices are cut by less than the size of the cost advantage or (2) the added gains in unit sales are large enough to bring in a bigger total profit despite lower margins per unit sold. A company with a 5 percent cost advantage cannot cut prices 20 percent, end up with a volume gain of only 10 percent, and still expect to earn higher profits!

A second big pitfall is not emphasizing avenues of cost advantage that can be kept proprietary or that relegate rivals to playing catch-up. The value of a cost advantage depends on its sustainability. Sustainability, in turn, hinges on whether the company achieves its cost advantage in ways difficult for rivals to copy or match.

A low-cost provider's product offering must always contain enough attributes to be attractive to prospective buyers—low price, by itself, is not always appealing to buyers.

A third pitfall is becoming too fixated on cost reduction. Low cost cannot be pursued so zealously that a firm's offering ends up being too features-poor to generate buyer appeal. Furthermore, a company driving hard to push its costs down has to guard against misreading or ignoring increased buyer interest in added features or service, declining buyer sensitivity to price, or new developments that start to alter how buyers use the product. A low-cost zealot risks losing market ground if buyers start opting for more upscale or features-rich products.

Even if these mistakes are avoided, a low-cost competitive approach still carries risk. Cost-saving technological breakthroughs or the emergence of still-lower-cost value chain models can nullify a low-cost leader's hard-won position. The current leader may have difficulty in shifting quickly to the new technologies or value chain approaches because heavy investments lock it in (at least temporarily) to its present value chain approach.

BROAD DIFFERENTIATION STRATEGIES

Core Concept
The essence of a broad differentiation strategy is to be unique in ways that are valuable to a wide range of customers.

Differentiation strategies are attractive whenever buyers' needs and preferences are too diverse to be fully satisfied by a standardized product or by sellers with identical capabilities. A company attempting to succeed through differentiation must study buyers' needs and behavior carefully to learn what buyers consider important, what they think has value, and what they are willing to pay for. Then the company has to incorporate buyer-desired attributes into its product or service offering that will clearly set it apart from rivals. Competitive advantage results once a sufficient number of buyers become strongly attached to the differentiated attributes.

Successful differentiation allows a firm to:

- Command a premium price for its product, and/or
- Increase unit sales (because additional buyers are won over by the differentiating features), and/or

- Gain buyer loyalty to its brand (because some buyers are strongly attracted to the differentiating features and bond with the company and its products).

Differentiation enhances profitability whenever the extra price the product commands outweighs the added costs of achieving the differentiation. Company differentiation strategies fail when buyers don't value the brand's uniqueness and when a company's approach to differentiation is easily copied or matched by its rivals.

Types of Differentiation Themes

Companies can pursue differentiation from many angles: a unique taste (Dr Pepper, Listerine); multiple features (Microsoft Windows, Microsoft Office); wide selection and one-stop shopping (Home Depot, Amazon.com); superior service (FedEx); spare parts availability (Caterpillar); engineering design and performance (Mercedes, BMW); prestige and distinctiveness (Rolex); product reliability (Johnson & Johnson in baby products); quality manufacture (Karastan in carpets, Michelin in tires, Toyota and Honda in automobiles); technological leadership (3M Corporation in bonding and coating products); a full range of services (Charles Schwab in stock brokerage); a complete line of products (Campbell's soups); and top-of-the-line image and reputation (Ralph Lauren and Starbucks).

The most appealing approaches to differentiation are those that are hard or expensive for rivals to duplicate. Indeed, resourceful competitors can, in time, clone almost any product or feature or attribute. If Coca-Cola introduces a vanilla-flavored soft drink, so can Pepsi; if Ford offers a 50,000-mile bumper-to-bumper warranty on its new vehicles, so can Volkswagen and Nissan. If Nokia introduces cell phones with cameras and Internet capability, so can Motorola and Samsung. As a rule, differentiation yields a longer-lasting and more profitable competitive edge when it is based on product innovation, technical superiority, product quality and reliability, comprehensive customer service, and unique competitive capabilities. Such differentiating attributes tend to be tough for rivals to copy or offset profitably, and buyers widely perceive them as having value.

> Easy-to-copy differentiating features cannot produce sustainable competitive advantage; differentiation based on competencies and capabilities tend to be more sustainable.

Where along the Value Chain to Create the Differentiating Attributes

Differentiation is not something hatched in marketing and advertising departments, nor is it limited to the catchalls of quality and service. Differentiation opportunities can exist in activities all along an industry's value chain; possibilities include the following:

- *Supply chain activities* that ultimately spill over to affect the performance or quality of the company's end product. Starbucks gets high ratings on its coffees partly because it has very strict specifications on the coffee beans purchased from suppliers.
- *Product R&D activities* that aim at improved product designs and performance features, expanded end uses and applications, more frequent first-on-the-market victories, wider product variety and selection, added user safety, greater recycling capability, or enhanced environmental protection.
- *Production R&D and technology-related activities* that permit custom-order manufacture at an efficient cost; make production methods safer for the

environment; or improve product quality, reliability, and appearance. Many manufacturers have developed flexible manufacturing systems that allow different models and product versions to be made on the same assembly line. Being able to provide buyers with made-to-order products can be a potent differentiating capability.

- *Manufacturing activities* that reduce product defects, prevent premature product failure, extend product life, allow better warranty coverages, improve economy of use, result in more end-user convenience, or enhance product appearance. The quality edge enjoyed by Japanese automakers stems partly from their distinctive competence in performing assembly-line activities.

- *Distribution and shipping activities* that allow for fewer warehouse and on-the-shelf stockouts, quicker delivery to customers, more accurate order filling, and/or lower shipping costs.

- *Marketing, sales, and customer service activities* that result in superior technical assistance to buyers, faster maintenance and repair services, more and better product information provided to customers, more and better training materials for end users, better credit terms, quicker order processing, or greater customer convenience.

Managers need keen understanding of the sources of differentiation and the activities that drive uniqueness to evaluate various differentiation approaches and design durable ways to set their product offering apart from those of rival brands.

The Four Best Routes to Competitive Advantage via a Broad Differentiation Strategy

While it is easy enough to grasp that a successful differentiation strategy must entail creating buyer value in ways unmatched by rivals, the big issue in crafting a differentiation strategy is which of four basic routes to take in delivering unique buyer value via a broad differentiation strategy. Usually, building a sustainable competitive advantage via differentiation involves pursuing one of four basic routes to delivering superior value to buyers.

One route is to *incorporate product attributes and user features that lower the buyer's overall costs of using the company's product.* Making a company's product more economical for a buyer to use can be done by reducing the buyer's raw materials waste (providing cut-to-size components), reducing a buyer's inventory requirements (providing just-in-time deliveries), increasing maintenance intervals and product reliability so as to lower a buyer's repair and maintenance costs, using online systems to reduce a buyer's procurement and order processing costs, and providing free technical support. Rising costs for gasoline have dramatically spurred the efforts of motor vehicle manufacturers worldwide to introduce models with better fuel economy and reduce operating costs for motor vehicle owners.

A second route is to *incorporate features that raise product performance.*[4] This can be accomplished with attributes that provide buyers greater reliability, ease of use, convenience, or durability. Other performance-enhancing options include making the company's product or service cleaner, safer, quieter, or more maintenance-free than rival brands. Cell phone manufacturrs are in a race to introduce next-generation phones with trendsetting features and options.

A third route to a differentiation-based competitive advantage is to *incorporate features that enhance buyer satisfaction in noneconomic or intangible ways*. Goodyear's Aquatread tire design appeals to safety-conscious motorists wary of slick roads. Rolls Royce, Ralph Lauren, Gucci, Tiffany, Cartier, and Rolex have differentiation-based competitive advantages linked to buyer desires for status, image, prestige, upscale fashion, superior craftsmanship, and the finer things in life. L. L. Bean makes its mail-order customers feel secure in their purchases by providing an unconditional guarantee with no time limit: "All of our products are guaranteed to give 100 percent satisfaction in every way. Return anything purchased from us at any time if it proves otherwise. We will replace it, refund your purchase price, or credit your credit card, as you wish."

The fourth route is to *deliver value to customers by differentiating on the basis of competencies and competitive capabilities that rivals don't have or can't afford to match*.[5] The importance of cultivating competencies and capabilities that add power to a company's resource strengths and competitiveness comes into play here. Core and/or distinctive competencies not only enhance a company's ability to compete successfully in the marketplace but can also be unique in delivering value to buyers. There are numerous examples of companies that have differentiated themselves on the basis of capabilities. Because Fox News and CNN have the capability to devote more air time to breaking news stories and get reporters on the scene very quickly compared to the major networks, many viewers turn to the cable networks when a major news event occurs. Microsoft has stronger capabilities to design, create, distribute, and advertise an array of software products for PC applications than any of its rivals. Avon and Mary Kay Cosmetics have differentiated themselves from other cosmetics and personal care companies by assembling a sales force numbering in the hundreds of thousands that gives them direct sales capability—their sales associates can demonstrate products to interested buyers, take their orders on the spot, and deliver the items to buyers' homes. Japanese automakers have the capability to satisfy changing consumer preferences for one vehicle style versus another because they can bring new models to market faster than American and European automakers.

> **Core Concept**
> A differentiator's basis for competitive advantage is either a product/service offering whose attributes differ significantly from the offerings of rivals or a set of capabilities for delivering customer value that rivals don't have.

The Importance of Perceived Value and Signaling Value

Buyers seldom pay for value they don't perceive, no matter how real the unique extras may be.[6] Thus, the price premium commanded by a differentiation strategy reflects *the value actually delivered* to the buyer and *the value perceived* by the buyer (even if not actually delivered). Actual and perceived value can differ whenever buyers have trouble assessing what their experience with the product will be. Incomplete knowledge on the part of buyers often causes them to judge value based on such signals as price (where price connotes quality), attractive packaging, extensive ad campaigns (i.e., how well-known the product is), ad content and image, the quality of brochures and sales presentations, the seller's facilities, the seller's list of customers, the firm's market share, the length of time the firm has been in business, and the professionalism, appearance, and personality of the seller's employees. Such signals of value may be as important as actual value (1) when the nature of differentiation is subjective or hard to quantify, (2) when buyers are making a first-time purchase, (3) when repurchase is infrequent, and (4) when buyers are unsophisticated.

When a Differentiation Strategy Works Best

Differentiation strategies tend to work best in market circumstances where:

- *Buyer needs and uses of the product are diverse*—Diverse buyer preferences present competitors with a bigger window of opportunity to do things differently and set themselves apart with product attributes that appeal to particular buyers. For instance, the diversity of consumer preferences for menu selection, ambience, pricing, and customer service gives restaurants exceptionally wide latitude in creating a differentiated product offering. Other companies having many ways to strongly differentiate themselves from rivals include the publishers of magazines, the makers of motor vehicles, and the manufacturers of cabinetry and countertops.

- *There are many ways to differentiate the product or service and many buyers perceive these differences as having value*—There is plenty of room for retail apparel competitors to stock different styles and quality of apparel merchandise but very little room for the makers of paper clips, copier paper, or sugar to set their products apart. Likewise, the sellers of different brands of gasoline or orange juice have little differentiation opportunity compared to the sellers of high-definition TVs, patio furniture, or breakfast cereal. Unless different buyers have distinguishably different preferences for certain features and product attributes, profitable differentiation opportunities are very restricted.

- *Few rival firms are following a similar differentiation approach*—The best differentiation approaches involve trying to appeal to buyers on the basis of attributes that rivals are not emphasizing. A differentiator encounters less head-to-head rivalry when it goes its own separate way in creating uniqueness and does not try to outdifferentiate rivals on the very same attributes—when many rivals are all claiming "Ours tastes better than theirs" or "Ours gets your clothes cleaner than theirs," the most likely result is weak brand differentiation and "strategy overcrowding"—a situation in which competitors end up chasing the same buyers with very similar product offerings.

- *Technological change is fast-paced and competition revolves around rapidly evolving product features*—Rapid product innovation and frequent introductions of next-version products not only provide space for companies to pursue separate differentiating paths but also heighten buyer interest. In video game hardware and video games, golf equipment, PCs, cell phones, and MP3 players, competitors are locked into an ongoing battle to set themselves apart by introducing the best next-generation products—companies that fail to come up with new and improved products and distinctive performance features quickly lose out in the marketplace. In network TV broadcasting in the United States, NBC, ABC, CBS, Fox, and several others are always scrambling to develop a lineup of TV shows that will win higher audience ratings and pave the way for charging higher advertising rates and boosting ad revenues.

The Pitfalls of a Differentiation Strategy

Differentiation strategies can fail for any of several reasons. *A differentiation strategy is always doomed when competitors are able to quickly copy most or all of the appealing product attributes a company comes up with.* Rapid imitation means that no rival achieves differentiation, since whenever one firm introduces some aspect of uniqueness that strikes the fancy of buyers, fast-following copycats quickly reestablish similarity. This is why a firm must search out sources of uniqueness that are time-consuming or burdensome for rivals to match if it hopes to use differentiation to win a competitive edge over rivals.

> **Core Concept**
> Any differentiating feature that works well is a magnet for imitators.

A second pitfall is that the company's differentiation strategy produces a ho-hum market reception because buyers see little value in the unique attributes of a company's product. Thus, even if a company sets the attributes of its brand apart from the brands of rivals, its strategy can fail because of trying to differentiate on the basis of something that does not deliver adequate value to buyers (such as lowering a buyer's cost to use the product or enhancing a buyer's well-being). Anytime many potential buyers look at a company's differentiated product offering and conclude "So what?" the company's differentiation strategy is in deep trouble—buyers will likely decide the product is not worth the extra price, and sales will be disappointingly low.

The third big pitfall of a differentiation strategy is overspending on efforts to differentiate the company's product offering, thus eroding profitability. Company efforts to achieve differentiation nearly always raise costs. The trick to profitable differentiation is either to keep the costs of achieving differentiation below the price premium the differentiating attributes can command in the marketplace (thus increasing the profit margin per unit sold) or to offset thinner profit margins per unit by selling enough additional units to increase total profits. If a company goes overboard in pursuing costly differentiation efforts and then unexpectedly discovers that buyers are unwilling to pay a sufficient price premium to cover the added costs of differentiation, it ends up saddled with unacceptably thin profit margins or even losses. The need to contain differentiation costs is why many companies add little touches of differentiation that add to buyer satisfaction but are inexpensive to institute. Upscale restaurants often provide valet parking. Ski resorts provide skiers with complimentary coffee or hot apple cider at the base of the lifts in the morning and late afternoon. FedEx, UPS, and many catalog and online retailers have installed software capabilities that allow customers to track packages in transit. Some hotels and motels provide free continental breakfasts, exercise facilities, and in-room coffeemaking amenities. Publishers are using their Web sites to deliver supplementary educational materials to the buyers of their textbooks. Laundry detergent and soap manufacturers add pleasing scents to their products.

Other common pitfalls and mistakes in crafting a differentiation strategy include:[7]

- *Overdifferentiating so that product quality or service levels exceed buyers' needs.* Even if buyers like the differentiating extras, they may not find them sufficiently valuable for their purposes to pay extra to get them. Many shoppers shy away from buying top-of-the-line items because they have no particular interest in all the bells and whistles; for them, a less deluxe model or style makes better economic sense.

- *Trying to charge too high a price premium.* Even if buyers view certain extras or deluxe features as nice to have, they may still conclude that the added cost is excessive relative to the value they deliver. A differentiator must guard against turning off would-be buyers with what is perceived as price gouging. Normally, the bigger the price premium for the differentiating extras, the harder it is to keep buyers from switching to the lower-priced offerings of competitors.

- *Being timid and not striving to open up meaningful gaps in quality or service or performance features vis-à-vis the products of rivals.* Tiny differences between rivals' product offerings may not be visible or important to buyers. If a company wants to generate the fiercely loyal customer following needed to earn superior profits and open up a differentiation-based competitive advantage over rivals, then its strategy must result in strong rather than weak product differentiation. In markets where differentiators do no better than achieve weak product differentiation (because the attributes of rival brands are fairly similar in the minds of many buyers), customer loyalty to any one brand is weak, the costs of buyers to switch to rival brands are fairly low, and no one company has enough of a market edge that it can get by with charging a price premium over rival brands.

A low-cost provider strategy can defeat a differentiation strategy when buyers are satisfied with a basic product and don't think extra attributes are worth a higher price.

BEST-COST PROVIDER STRATEGIES

Core Concept
The competitive advantage of a best-cost provider is lower costs than rivals in incorporating upscale attributes, putting the company in a position to underprice rivals whose products have similar upscale attributes.

Best-cost provider strategies aim at giving customers *more value for the money.* The objective is to deliver superior value to buyers by satisfying their expectations on key quality/features/performance/service attributes and beating their expectations on price (given what rivals are charging for much the same attributes). *A company achieves best-cost status from an ability to incorporate attractive or upscale attributes at a lower cost than rivals.* The attractive attributes can take the form of appealing features, good-to-excellent product performance or quality, or attractive customer service. When a company has the resource strengths and competitive capabilities to incorporate these upscale attributes into its product offering *at a lower cost than rivals,* it enjoys best-cost status—it is the low-cost provider *of an upscale product.*

Being a best-cost provider is different from being a low-cost provider because the additional upscale features entail additional costs (that a low-cost provider can avoid by offering buyers a basic product with few frills). As Figure 5.1 indicates, best-cost provider strategies stake out a middle ground between pursuing a low-cost advantage and a differentiation advantage and between appealing to the broad market as a whole and a narrow market niche. From a competitive positioning standpoint, best-cost strategies are thus a *hybrid,* balancing a strategic emphasis on low cost against a strategic emphasis on differentiation (upscale features delivered at a price that constitutes superior value).

The competitive advantage of a best-cost provider is its capability to include upscale attributes at a lower cost than rivals whose products have comparable attributes. A best-cost provider can use its low-cost advantage to underprice rivals whose products have similar upscale attributes—it is usually not difficult to entice customers away from rivals charging a higher price for an item with highly comparable features, quality, performance, and/or customer service attributes. To achieve competitive advantage with a best-cost provider strategy, it is critical that a company have the resources and capabilities to incorporate upscale attributes at a lower cost than rivals. In other words, it must be able to (1) incorporate attractive features at a lower cost than rivals whose products have similar features, (2) manufacture a good-to-excellent quality product at a lower cost than rivals with good-to-excellent product quality, (3) develop a product that delivers good-to-excellent performance at a lower cost than rivals whose products also entail good-to-excellent performance, or (4) provide attractive customer service at a lower cost than rivals who provide comparably attractive customer service.

What makes a best-cost provider strategy so appealing is being able to incorporate upscale attributes at a lower cost than rivals and then using the company's low-cost advantage to underprice rivals whose products have similar upscale attributes.

The target market for a best-cost provider is value-conscious buyers—buyers that are looking for appealing extras at an appealingly low price. Value-hunting buyers (as distinct from buyers looking only for bargain-basement prices) often constitute a very sizable part of the overall market. Normally, value-conscious buyers are willing to pay a fair price for extra features, but they shy away from paying top dollar for items havingall the bells and whistles. It is the desire to cater to *value-conscious buyers* as opposed to *budget-conscious buyers* that sets a best-cost provider apart from a low-cost provider—the two strategies aim at distinguishably different market targets.

When a Best-Cost Provider Strategy Works Best

A best-cost provider strategy works best in markets where buyer diversity makes product differentiation the norm and where many buyers are also sensitive to price and value. This is because a best-cost provider can position itself near the middle of the market with either a medium-quality product at a below-average price or a high-quality product at an average or slightly higher price. Often, substantial numbers of buyers prefer midrange products rather than the cheap, basic products of low-cost producers or the expensive products of top-of-the-line differentiators. But unless a company has the resources, know-how, and capabilities to incorporate upscale product or service attributes at a lower cost than rivals, adopting a best-cost strategy is ill advised—a winning strategy must always be matched to a company's resource strengths and capabilities.

Illustration Capsule 5.3 describes how Toyota has applied the principles of a best-cost provider strategy in producing and marketing its Lexus brand.

The Big Risk of a Best-Cost Provider Strategy

A company's biggest vulnerability in employing a best-cost provider strategy is getting squeezed between the strategies of firms using low-cost and high-end differentiation strategies. Low-cost providers may be able to siphon customers away with the appeal of a lower price (despite their less appealing product attributes). High-end differentiators may be able to steal customers away with the appeal of better product attributes (even though their products carry a higher price tag). Thus, to be successful, a best-cost provider must offer buyers *significantly* better product attributes in order to justify a price above what low-cost leaders are charging. Likewise, it has to achieve *significantly* lower costs in providing upscale features so that it can outcompete high-end differentiators on the basis of a *significantly* lower price.

FOCUSED (OR MARKET NICHE) STRATEGIES

What sets focused strategies apart from low-cost leadership or broad differentiation strategies is concentrated attention on a narrow piece of the total market. The target segment, or niche, can be defined by geographic uniqueness, by specialized requirements in using the product, or by special product attributes that appeal only to niche members. Community Coffee, the largest family-owned specialty coffee retailer in the United States, is a company that focused on a geographic market niche; despite having a national market share of only 1.1 percent, Community has won a 50 percent share of the coffee business in supermarkets in southern Louisiana in competition

Illustration Capsule 5.3
Toyota's Best-Cost Producer Strategy for Its Lexus Line

Toyota Motor Company is widely regarded as a low-cost producer among the world's motor vehicle manufacturers. Despite its emphasis on product quality, Toyota has achieved low-cost leadership because it has developed considerable skills in efficient supply chain management and low-cost assembly capabilities, and because its models are positioned in the low-to-medium end of the price spectrum, where high production volumes are conducive to low unit costs. But when Toyota decided to introduce its new Lexus models to compete in the luxury-car market, it employed a classic best-cost provider strategy. Toyota took the following four steps in crafting and implementing its Lexus strategy:

- Designing an array of high-performance characteristics and upscale features into the Lexus models so as to make them comparable in performance and luxury to other high-end models and attractive to Mercedes, BMW, Audi, Jaguar, Cadillac, and Lincoln buyers.

- Transferring its capabilities in making high-quality Toyota models at low cost to making premium-quality Lexus models at costs below other luxury-car makers. Toyota's supply chain capabilities and low-cost assembly know-how allowed it to incorporate high-tech performance features and upscale quality into Lexus models at substantially less cost than comparable Mercedes and BMW models.

- Using its relatively lower manufacturing costs to underprice comparable Mercedes and BMW models. Toyota believed that with its cost advantage it could price attractively equipped Lexus cars low enough to draw price-conscious buyers away from Mercedes and BMW and perhaps induce dissatisfied Lincoln and Cadillac owners to switch to a Lexus. Lexus's pricing advantage over Mercedes and BMW was sometimes quite significant. For example, in 2006 the Lexus RX 330, a midsized SUV, carried a sticker price in the $36,000–$45,000 range (depending on how it was equipped), whereas variously equipped Mercedes M-class SUVs had price tags in the $50,000–$65,000 range and a BMW X5 SUV could range anywhere from $42,000 to $70,000, depending on the optional equipment chosen.

- Establishing a new network of Lexus dealers, separate from Toyota dealers, dedicated to providing a level of personalized, attentive customer service unmatched in the industry.

Lexus models have consistently ranked first in the widely watched J. D. Power & Associates quality survey, and the prices of Lexus models are typically several thousand dollars below those of comparable Mercedes and BMW models—clear signals that Toyota has succeeded in becoming a best-cost producer with its Lexus brand.

---

against Starbucks, Folger's, Maxwell House, and asserted specialty coffee retailers. Community Coffee's geographic version of a focus strategy has allowed it to capture sales in excess of $100 million annually by catering to the tastes of coffee drinkers across an 11-state region. Examples of firms that concentrate on a well-defined market niche keyed to a particular product or buyer segment include Animal Planet and the History Channel (in cable TV); Google (in Internet search engines); Porsche (in sports cars); Cannondale (in top-of-the-line mountain bikes); Domino's Pizza (in pizza delivery); Enterprise Rent-a-Car (a specialist in providing rental cars to repair garage customers); Bandag (a specialist in truck tire recapping that promotes its recaps aggressively at over 1,000 truck stops), CGA Inc. (a specialist in providing insurance to cover the cost of lucrative hole-in-one prizes at golf tournaments); Match.com (the world's largest online dating service); and Avid Technology (the world leader in digital technology products to create 3D animation and to edit films, videos, TV broadcasts, video games, and audio recordings). Microbreweries, local bakeries, bed-and-breakfast inns, and local owner-managed retail boutiques are all good examples of enterprises that have scaled their operations to serve narrow or local customer segments.

A Focused Low-Cost Strategy

A focused strategy based on low cost aims at securing a competitive advantage by serving buyers in the target market niche at a lower cost and lower price than rival competitors. This strategy has considerable attraction when a firm can lower costs significantly by limiting its customer base to a well-defined buyer segment. The avenues to achieving a cost advantage over rivals also serving the target market niche are the same as for low-cost leadership—outmanage rivals in keeping the costs of value chain activities contained to a bare minimum and search for innovative ways to reconfigure the firm's value chain and bypass or reduce certain value chain activities. The only real difference between a low-cost provider strategy and a focused low-cost strategy is the size of the buyer group that a company is trying to appeal to—the former involves a product offering that appeals broadly to most all buyer groups and market segments whereas the latter at just meeting the needs of buyers in a narrow market segment.

Focused low-cost strategies are fairly common. Producers of private-label goods are able to achieve low costs in product development, marketing, distribution, and advertising by concentrating on making generic items imitative of name-brand merchandise and selling directly to retail chains wanting a basic house brand to sell to price-sensitive shoppers. Several small printer-supply manufacturers have begun making low-cost clones of the premium-priced replacement ink and toner cartridges sold by Hewlett-Packard, Lexmark, Canon, and Epson; the clone manufacturers dissect the cartridges of the name-brand companies and then reengineer a similar version that won't violate patents. The components for remanufactured replacement cartridges are aquired from various outside sources, and the clones are then marketed at prices as much as 50 percent below the name-brand cartridges. Cartridge remanufacturers have been lured to focus on this market because replacement cartridges constitute a multibillion-dollar business with considerable profit potential given their low costs and the premium pricing of the name-brand companies. Illustration Capsule 5.4 describes how Motel 6 has kept its costs low in catering to budget-conscious travelers.

A Focused Differentiation Strategy

A focused strategy keyed to differentiation aims at securing a competitive advantage with a product offering carefully designed to appeal to the unique preferences and needs of a narrow, well-defined group of buyers (as opposed to a broad differentiation strategy aimed at many buyer groups and market segments). Successful use of a focused differentiation strategy depends on the existence of a buyer segment that is looking for special product attributes or seller capabilities and on a firm's ability to stand apart from rivals competing in the same target market niche.

Companies like Godiva Chocolates, Chanel, Gucci, Rolls-Royce, Häagen-Dazs, and W. L. Gore (the maker of Gore-Tex) employ successful differentiation-based focused strategies targeted at upscale buyers wanting products and services with world-class attributes. Indeed, most markets contain a buyer segment willing to pay a big price premium for the very finest items available, thus opening the strategic window for some competitors to pursue differentiation-based focused strategies aimed at the very top of the market pyramid. Another successful focused differentiator is Trader Joe's, a 150-store East and West Coast "fashion food retailer" that is a combination gourmet deli and grocery warehouse.[8] Customers shop Trader Joe's as much for entertainment as for conventional grocery items—the store stocks out-of-the-ordinary culinary treats like raspberry salsa, salmon burgers, and jasmine fried rice,

Illustration Capsule 5.4

Motel 6's Focused Low-Cost Strategy

Motel 6 caters to price-conscious travelers who want a clean, no-frills place to spend the night. To be a low-cost provider of overnight lodging, Motel 6 (1) selects relatively inexpensive sites on which to construct its units (usually near interstate exits and high-traffic locations but far enough away to avoid paying prime site prices); (2) builds only basic facilities (no restaurant or bar and only rarely a swimming pool); (3) relies on standard architectural designs that incorporate inexpensive materials and low-cost construction techniques; and (4) provides simple room furnishings and decorations. These approaches lower both investment costs and operating costs. Without restaurants,

bars, and all kinds of guest services, a Motel 6 unit can be operated with just front-desk personnel, room cleanup crews, and skeleton building-and-grounds maintenance.

To promote the Motel 6 concept with travelers who have simple overnight requirements, the chain uses unique, recognizable radio ads done by nationally syndicated radio personality Tom Bodett; the ads describe Motel 6's clean rooms, no-frills facilities, friendly atmosphere, and dependably low rates (usually under $40 a night).

Motel 6's basis for competitive advantage is lower costs than competitors in providing basic, economical overnight accommodations to price-constrained travelers.

as well as the standard goods normally found in supermarkets. What sets Trader Joe's apart is not just its unique combination of food novelties and competitively priced grocery items but also its capability to turn an otherwise mundane grocery excursion into a whimsical treasure hunt that is just plain fun.

Illustration Capsule 5.5 describes Progressive Insurance's focused differentiation strategy.

When a Focused Low-Cost or Focused Differentiation Strategy Is Attractive

A focused strategy aimed at securing a competitive edge based on either low cost or differentiation becomes increasingly attractive as more of the following conditions are met:

- The target market niche is big enough to be profitable and offers good growth potential.
- Industry leaders do not see that having a presence in the niche is crucial to their own success—in which case focusers can often escape battling head-to-head against some of the industry's biggest and strongest competitors.
- It is costly or difficult for multisegment competitors to put capabilities in place to meet the specialized needs of buyers comprising the target market niche and at the same time satisfy the expectations of their mainstream customers.
- The industry has many different niches and segments, thereby allowing a focuser to pick a competitively attractive niche suited to its resource strengths and capabilities. Also, with more niches, there is more room for focusers to avoid each other in competing for the same customers.

Illustration Capsule 5.5
Progressive Insurance's Focused Differentiation Strategy in Auto Insurance

Progressive Insurance has fashioned a strategy in auto insurance focused on people with a record of traffic violations who drive high-performance cars, drivers with accident histories, motorcyclists, teenagers, and other so-called high-risk categories of drivers that most auto insurance companies steer away from. Progressive discovered that some of these high-risk drivers are affluent and pressed for time, making them less sensitive to paying premium rates for their car insurance. Management learned that it could charge such drivers high enough premiums to cover the added risks, plus it differentiated Progressive from other insurers by expediting the process of obtaining insurance and decreasing the annoyance that such drivers faced in obtaining insurance coverage. Progressive pioneered the low-cost direct sales model of allowing customers to purchase insurance online and over the phone.

Progressive also studied the market segments for insurance carefully enough to discover that some motorcycle owners were not especially risky (middle-aged suburbanites who sometimes commuted to work or used their motorcycles mainly for recreational trips with their friends). Progressive's strategy allowed it to become a leader in the market for luxury-car insurance for customers who appreciated Progressive's streamlined approach to doing business.

In further differentiating and promoting Progressive policies, management created teams of roving claims adjusters who would arrive at accident scenes to assess claims and issue checks for repairs on the spot. Progressive introduced 24-hour claims reporting, now an industry standard. In addition, it developed a sophisticated pricing system so that it could quickly and accurately assess each customer's risk and weed out unprofitable customers.

By being creative and excelling at the nuts and bolts of its business, Progressive has won a 7 percent share of the $150 billion market for auto insurance and has the highest underwriting margins in the auto-insurance industry.

Sources: www.progressiveinsurance.com; Ian C. McMillan, Alexander van Putten, and Rita Gunther McGrath, "Global Gamesmanship," *Harvard Business Review* 81, no. 5 (May 2003), p. 68; and *Fortune,* May 16, 2005, p. 34.

- Few, if any, other rivals are attempting to specialize in the same target segment—a condition that reduces the risk of segment overcrowding.
- The focuser has a reservoir of customer goodwill and loyalty (accumulated from having catered to the specialized needs and preferences of niche members over many years) that it can draw on to help stave off ambitious challengers looking to horn in on its business.

The advantages of focusing a company's entire competitive effort on a single market niche are considerable, especially for smaller and medium-sized companies that may lack the breadth and depth of resources to tackle going after a broad customer base with a "something for everyone" lineup of models, styles, and product selection. eBay has made a huge name for itself and very attractive profits for shareholders by focusing its attention on online auctions—at one time a very small niche in the overall auction business that eBay's focus strategy turned into the dominant piece of the global auction industry. Google has capitalized on its specialized expertise in Internet search engines to become one of the most spectacular growth companies of the past 10 years. Two hippie entrepreneurs, Ben Cohen and Jerry Greenfield, built Ben & Jerry's Homemade into an impressive business by focusing their energies and resources solely on the superpremium segment of the ice cream market.

The Risks of a Focused Low-Cost or Focused Differentiation Strategy

Focusing carries several risks. One is the chance that competitors will find effective ways to match the focused firm's capabilities in serving the target niche—perhaps by coming up with products or brands specifically designed to appeal to buyers in the target niche or by developing expertise and capabilities that offset the focuser's strengths. In the lodging business, large chains like Marriott and Hilton have launched multibrand strategies that allow them to compete effectively in several lodging segments simultaneously. Marriott has flagship hotels with a full complement of services and amenities that allow it to attract travelers and vacationers going to major resorts, it has J. W. Marriot hotels usually located in downtown metropolitan areas that cater to business travelers; the Courtyard by Marriott brand is for business travelers looking for moderately priced lodging; Marriott Residence Inns are designed as a home away from home for travelers staying five or more nights; and the 530 Fairfield Inn locations cater to travelers looking for quality lodging at an affordable price. Similarly, Hilton has a lineup of brands (Conrad Hotels, Doubletree Hotels, Embassy Suite Hotels, Hampton Inns, Hilton Hotels, Hilton Garden Inns, and Homewood Suites) that enable it to operate in multiple segments and compete head-to-head against lodging chains that operate only in a single segment. Multibrand strategies are attractive to large companies like Marriott and Hilton precisely because they enable a company to enter a market niche and siphon business away from companies that employ a focus strategy.

A second risk of employing a focus strategy is the potential for the preferences and needs of niche members to shift over time toward the product attributes desired by the majority of buyers. An erosion of the differences across buyer segments lowers entry barriers into a focuser's market niche and provides an open invitation for rivals in adjacent segments to begin competing for the focuser's customers. A third risk is that the segment may become so attractive it is soon inundated with competitors, intensifying rivalry and splintering segment profits.

THE CONTRASTING FEATURES OF THE FIVE GENERIC COMPETITIVE STRATEGIES: A SUMMARY

Deciding which generic competitive strategy should serve as the framework for hanging the rest of the company's strategy is not a trivial matter. Each of the five generic competitive strategies positions the company differently in its market and competitive environment. Each establishes a central theme for how the company will endeavor to outcompete rivals. Each creates some boundaries or guidelines for maneuvering as market circumstances unfold and as ideas for improving the strategy are debated. Each points to different ways of experimenting and tinkering with the basic strategy—for example, employing a low-cost leadership strategy means experimenting with ways that costs can be cut and value chain activities can be streamlined, whereas a broad differentiation strategy means exploring ways to add new differentiating features or to perform value chain activities differently if the result is to add value for customers in ways they are willing to pay for. Each entails differences in terms of product line, production emphasis, marketing emphasis, and means of sustaining the strategy—as shown in Table 5.1.

Table 5.1 **Distinguishing Features of the Five Generic Competitive Strategies**

	Low-Cost Provider	Broad Differentiation	Best-Cost Provider	Focused Low-Cost Provider	Focused Differentiation
Strategic target	• A broad cross-section of the market	• A broad cross-section of the market	• Value-conscious buyers	• A narrow market niche where buyer needs and preferences are distinctively different	• A narrow market niche where buyer needs and preferences are distinctively different
Basis of competitive advantage	• Lower overall costs than competitors	• Ability to offer buyers something attractively different from competitors	• Ability to give customers more value for the money	• Lower overall cost than rivals in serving niche members	• Attributes that appeal specifically to niche members
Product line	• A good basic product with few frills (acceptable quality and limited selection)	• Many product variations, wide selection; emphasis on differentiating features	• Items with appealing attributes; assorted upscale features	• Features and attributes tailored to the tastes and requirements of niche members	• Features and attributes tailored to the tastes and requirements of niche members
Production emphasis	• A continuous search for cost reduction without sacrificing acceptable quality and essential features	• Build in whatever differentiating features buyers are willing to pay for; strive for product superiority	• Build in upscale features and appealing attributes at lower cost than rivals	• A continuous search for cost reduction while incorporating features and attributes matched to niche member preferences	• Custom-made products that match the tastes and requirements of niche members
Marketing emphasis	• Try to make a virtue out of product features that lead to low cost	• Tout differentiating features • Charge a premium price to cover the extra costs of differentiating features	• Tout delivery of best value • Either deliver comparable features at a lower price than rivals or else match rivals on prices and provide better features	• Communicate attractive features of a budget-priced product offering that fits niche buyers' expectations	• Communicate how product offering does the best job of meeting niche buyers' expectations
Keys to sustaining the strategy	• Economical prices/good value • Strive to manage costs down, year after year, in every area of the business	• Stress constant innovation to stay ahead of imitative competitors • Concentrate on a few key differentiating features	• Unique expertise in simultaneously managing costs down while incorporating upscale features and attributes	• Stay committed to serving the niche at lowest overall cost; don't blur the firm's image by entering other market segments or adding other products to widen market appeal	• Stay committed to serving the niche better than rivals; don't blur the firm's image by entering other market segments or adding other products to widen market appeal

Thus, a choice of which generic strategy to employ spills over to affect several aspects of how the business will be operated and the manner in which value chain activities must be managed. Deciding which generic strategy to employ is perhaps the most important strategic commitment a company makes—it tends to drive the rest of the strategic actions a company decides to undertake.

One of the big dangers in crafting a competitive strategy is that managers, torn between the pros and cons of the various generic strategies, will opt for *stuck-in-the-middle strategies* that represent compromises between lower costs and greater differentiation and between broad and narrow market appeal. Compromise or middle-ground strategies rarely produce sustainable competitive advantage or a distinctive competitive position—a well-executed best-cost producer strategy is the only compromise between low cost and differentiation that succeeds. Usually, companies with compromise strategies end up with a middle-of-the-pack industry ranking—they have average costs, some but not a lot of product differentiation relative to rivals, an average image and reputation, and little prospect of industry leadership. Having a competitive edge over rivals is the single most dependable contributor to above-average company profitability. Hence, only if a company makes a strong and unwavering commitment to one of the five generic competitive strategies does it stand much chance of achieving sustainable competitive advantage that such strategies can deliver if properly executed.

Key Points

Early in the process of crafting a strategy company managers have to decide which of the five basic competitive strategies to employ—overall low-cost, broad differentiation, best-cost, focused low-cost, or focused differentiation.

In employing a low-cost provider strategy and trying to achieve a low-cost advantage over rivals, a company must do a better job than rivals of cost-effectively managing value chain activities and/or find innovative ways to eliminate or bypass cost-producing activities. Low-cost provider strategies work particularly well when the products of rival sellers are virtually identical or very weakly differentiated and supplies are readily available from eager sellers, when there are not many ways to differentiate that have value to buyers, when many buyers are price sensitive and shop the market for the lowest price, and when buyer switching costs are low.

Broad differentiation strategies seek to produce a competitive edge by incorporating attributes and features that set a company's product/service offering apart from rivals in ways that buyers consider valuable and worth paying for. Successful differentiation allows a firm to (1) command a premium price for its product, (2) increase unit sales (because additional buyers are won over by the differentiating features), and/or (3) gain buyer loyalty to its brand (because some buyers are strongly attracted to the differentiating features and bond with the company and its products). Differentiation strategies work best in markets with diverse buyer preferences where there are big windows of opportunity to strongly differentiate a company's product offering from those of rival brands, in situations where few other rivals are pursuing a similar differentiation approach, and in circumstances where companies are racing to bring out the most appealing next-generation product. A differentiation strategy is doomed when competitors are able to quickly copy most or all of the appealing product attributes a company comes up with, when a company's differentiation efforts meet with a ho-hum or so what market reception, or when a company erodes profitability by overspending on efforts to differentiate its product offering.

Best-cost provider strategies combine a strategic emphasis on low cost with a strategic emphasis on more than minimal quality, service, features, or performance. The aim is to create competitive advantage by giving buyers more value for the money—an approach that entails matching close rivals on key quality/service/features/performance attributes and beating them on the costs of incorporating such attributes into the product or service. A best-cost provider strategy works best in markets where buyer diversity makes product differentiation the norm and where many buyers are also sensitive to price and value.

A focus strategy delivers competitive advantage either by achieving lower costs than rivals in serving buyers comprising the target market niche or by developing specialized ability to offer niche buyers an appealingly differentiated offering than meets their needs better than rival brands. A focused strategy based on either low cost or differentiation becomes increasingly attractive when the target market niche is big enough to be profitable and offers good growth potential, when it is costly or difficult for multi-segment competitors to put capabilities in place to meet the specialized needs of the target market niche and at the same time satisfy the expectations of their mainstream customers, when there are one or more niches that present a good match with a focuser's resource strengths and capabilities, and when few other rivals are attempting to specialize in the same target segment.

Deciding which generic strategy to employ is perhaps the most important strategic commitment a company makes—it tends to drive the rest of the strategic actions a company decides to undertake and it sets the whole tone for the pursuit of a competitive advantage over rivals.

Exercises

1. Go to www.google.com and do a search for "low-cost producer." See if you can identify five companies that are pursuing a low-cost strategy in their respective industries.

2. Using the advanced search function at www.google.com, enter "best-cost producer" in the exact-phrase box and see if you can locate three companies that indicate they are employing a best-cost producer strategy.

3. Go to BMW's Web site (www.bmw.com) click on the link for BMW Group. The site you find provides an overview of the company's key functional areas, including R&D and production activities. Explore each of the links on the Research & Development page—People & Networks, Innovation & Technology, and Mobility & Traffic—to better understand the company's approach. Also review the statements under Production focusing on vehicle production and sustainable production. How do these activities contribute to BMW's differentiation strategy and the unique position in the auto industry that BMW has achieved?

4. Which of the five generic competitive strategies do you think the following companies are employing (do whatever research at the various company Web sites might be needed to arrive at and support your answer):
   a. The Saturn division of General Motors
   b. Abercrombie & Fitch
   c. Amazon.com
   d. Home Depot
   e. Mary Kay Cosmetics
   f. *USA Today*

chapter seven

Competing in Foreign Markets

You have no choice but to operate in a world shaped by globalization and the information revolution. There are two options: Adapt or die.

—Andrew S. Grove
Former Chairman, Intel Corporation

You do not choose to become global. The market chooses for you; it forces your hand.

—Alain Gomez
CEO, Thomson SA

[I]ndustries actually vary a great deal in the pressures they put on a company to sell internationally.

—Niraj Dawar and Tony Frost
Professors, Richard Ivey School of Business

Any company that aspires to industry leadership in the 21st century must think in terms of global, not domestic, market leadership. The world economy is globalizing at an accelerating pace as countries previously closed to foreign companies open up their markets, as the Internet shrinks the importance of geographic distance, and as ambitious growth-minded companies race to build stronger competitive positions in the markets of more and more countries. Companies in industries that are already globally competitive or in the process of becoming so are under the gun to come up with a strategy for competing successfully in foreign markets.

This chapter focuses on strategy options for expanding beyond domestic boundaries and competing in the markets of either a few or a great many countries. The spotlight will be on four strategic issues unique to competing multinationally:

1. Whether to customize the company's offerings in each different country market to match the tastes and preferences of local buyers or to offer a mostly standardized product worldwide.

2. Whether to employ essentially the same basic competitive strategy in all countries or modify the strategy country by country.

3. Where to locate the company's production facilities, distribution centers, and customer service operations so as to realize the greatest location advantages.

4. How to efficiently transfer the company's resource strengths and capabilities from one country to another in an effort to secure competitive advantage.

In the process of exploring these issues, we will introduce a number of core concepts—multicountry competition, global competition, profit sanctuaries, and cross-market subsidization. The chapter includes sections on cross-country differences in cultural, demographic, and market conditions; strategy options for entering and competing in foreign markets; the growing role of alliances with foreign partners; the importance of locating operations in the most advantageous countries; and the special circumstances of competing in such emerging markets as China, India, Brazil, Russia, and Eastern Europe.

WHY COMPANIES EXPAND INTO FOREIGN MARKETS

A company may opt to expand outside its domestic market for any of four major reasons:

1. *To gain access to new customers*—Expanding into foreign markets offers potential for increased revenues, profits, and long-term growth and becomes an especially attractive option when a company's home markets are mature. Firms like Cisco Systems, Dell, Sony, Nokia, Avon, and Toyota, which are racing for global leadership in their respective industries, are moving rapidly and aggressively to extend their market reach into all corners of the world.

2. *To achieve lower costs and enhance the firm's competitiveness*—Many companies are driven to sell in more than one country because domestic sales volume is not large enough to fully capture manufacturing economies of scale or learning/experience curve effects and thereby substantially improve the firm's cost-competitiveness. The relatively small size of country markets in Europe explains why companies like Michelin, BMW, and Nestlé long ago began selling their products all across Europe and then moved into markets in North America and Latin America.

3. *To capitalize on its core competencies*—A company may be able to leverage its competencies and capabilities into a position of competitive advantage in foreign markets as well as just domestic markets. Nokia's competencies and capabilities in mobile phones have propelled it to global market leadership in the wireless telecommunications business. Wal-Mart is capitalizing on its considerable expertise in discount retailing to expand into China, Latin America, and parts of Europe—Wal-Mart executives believe the company has tremendous growth opportunities in China.

4. *To spread its business risk across a wider market base*—A company spreads business risk by operating in a number of different foreign countries rather than depending entirely on operations in its domestic market. Thus, if the economies of certain Asian countries turn down for a period of time, a company with operations across much of the world may be sustained by buoyant sales in Latin America or Europe.

In a few cases, companies in industries based on natural resources (e.g., oil and gas, minerals, rubber, and lumber) often find it necessary to operate in the international arena because attractive raw material supplies are located in foreign countries.

The Difference Between Competing Internationally and Competing Globally

Typically, a company will start to compete internationally by entering just one or maybe a select few foreign markets. Competing on a truly global scale comes later, after the company has established operations on several continents and is racing against rivals for global market leadership. Thus, there is a meaningful distinction between the competitive scope of a company that operates in a few foreign countries (with perhaps modest ambitions to enter several more country markets) and a company that markets its products in 50 to 100 countries and is expanding its operations into additional country markets annually. The former is most accurately termed an *international competitor,* whereas the latter qualifies as a *global competitor.* In the discussion that follows, we'll continue to make a distinction between strategies for competing internationally and strategies for competing globally.

CROSS-COUNTRY DIFFERENCES IN CULTURAL, DEMOGRAPHIC, AND MARKET CONDITIONS

Regardless of a company's motivation for expanding outside its domestic markets, the strategies it uses to compete in foreign markets must be situation-driven. Cultural, demographic, and market conditions vary significantly among the countries of the world.[1] Cultures and lifestyles are the most obvious areas in which countries differ; market demographics and income levels are close behind. Consumers in Spain do not have the same tastes, preferences, and buying habits as consumers in Norway; buyers differ yet again in Greece, Chile, New Zealand, and Taiwan. Less than 20 percent of the populations of Brazil, India, and China have annual purchasing power equivalent to $25,000. Middle-class consumers represent a much smaller portion of the population in these and other emerging countries than in North America, Japan, and much of Western Europe—China's middle class numbers about 125 million out of a population of 1.3 billion.[2]

Sometimes product designs suitable in one country are inappropriate in another—for example, in the United States electrical devices run on 110-volt systems, but in some European countries the standard is a 240-volt system, necessitating the use of different electrical designs and components. In France consumers prefer top-loading washing machines, while in most other European countries consumers prefer front-loading machines. Northern Europeans want large refrigerators because they tend to shop once a week in supermarkets; southern Europeans can get by on small refrigerators because they shop daily. In parts of Asia refrigerators are a status symbol and may be placed in the living room, leading to preferences for stylish designs and colors—in India bright blue and red are popular colors. In other Asian countries household space is constrained and many refrigerators are only four feet high so that the top can be used for storage. In Hong Kong the preference is for compact European-style appliances, but in Taiwan large American-style appliances are more popular. In Italy, most people use automatic washing machines but prefer to hang the clothes out to dry on a clothesline—there is a strongly entrenched tradition and cultural belief that sun-dried clothes are fresher, which virtually shuts down any opportunities for appliance makers to market clothes dryers in Italy. In China, many parents are reluctant to purchase personal computers (PCs) even when they can afford them because of concerns that their children will be distracted from their schoolwork by surfing the Web, playing PC-based video games, and downloading and listening to pop music.

Similarly, market growth varies from country to country. In emerging markets like India, China, Brazil, and Malaysia, market growth potential is far higher than in the more mature economies of Britain, Denmark, Canada, and Japan. In automobiles, for example, the potential for market growth is explosive in China, where 2005 sales of new vehicles amounted to less than 5 million in a country with 1.3 billion people. In India there are efficient, well-developed national channels for distributing trucks, scooters, farm equipment, groceries, personal care items, and other packaged products to the country's 3 million retailers, whereas in China distribution is primarily local and there is no national network for distributing most products. The marketplace is intensely competitive in some countries and only moderately contested in others. Industry driving forces may be one thing in Spain, quite another in Canada, and different yet again in Turkey or Argentina or South Korea.

One of the biggest concerns of companies competing in foreign markets is whether to customize their offerings in each different country market to match the tastes and preferences of local buyers or whether to offer a mostly standardized product worldwide. While making products that are closely matched to local tastes makes them more appealing to local buyers, customizing a company's products country by country may have the effect of raising production and distribution costs due to the greater variety of designs and components, shorter production runs, and the complications of added inventory handling and distribution logistics. Greater standardization of a global company's product offering, however, can lead to scale economies and experience/learning curve effects, thus contributing to the achievement of a low-cost advantage. *The tension between the market pressures to localize a company's product offerings country by country and the competitive pressures to lower costs is one of the big strategic issues that participants in foreign markets have to resolve.*

Aside from the basic cultural and market differences among countries, a company also has to pay special attention to location advantages that stem from country-to-country variations in manufacturing and distribution costs, the risks of adverse shifts in exchange rates, and the economic and political demands of host governments.

Gaining Competitive Advantage Based on Where Activities Are Located

Differences in wage rates, worker productivity, inflation rates, energy costs, tax rates, government regulations, and the like create sizable variations in manufacturing costs from country to country. Plants in some countries have major manufacturing cost advantages because of lower input costs (especially labor), relaxed government regulations, the proximity of suppliers, or unique natural resources. In such cases, the low-cost countries become principal production sites, with most of the output being exported to markets in other parts of the world. Companies that build production facilities in low-cost countries (or that source their products from contract manufacturers in these countries) have a competitive advantage over rivals with plants in countries where costs are higher. The competitive role of low manufacturing costs is most evident in low-wage countries like China, India, Pakistan, Cambodia, Vietnam, Mexico, Brazil, Guatemala, the Philippines, and several countries in Africa that have become production havens for manufactured goods with high labor content (especially textiles and apparel). Labor costs in China averaged about $0.70 an hour in 2004–2005 versus about $1.50 in Russia, $4.60 in Hungary, $4.90 in Portugal, $16.50 in Canada, $21.00 in the United States, $23.00 in Norway, and $25.00 in Germany.[3] China is fast becoming the manufacturing capital of the world—virtually all of the world's major manufacturing companies now have facilities in China, and China attracted more foreign direct investment in 2002 and 2003 than any other country in the world. Likewise, concerns about short delivery times and low shipping costs make some countries better locations than others for establishing distribution centers.

The quality of a country's business environment also offers locational advantages—the governments of some countries are anxious to attract foreign investments and go all out to create a business climate that outsiders will view as favorable. A good example is Ireland, which has one of the world's most pro-business environments. Ireland offers companies very low corporate tax rates, has a government that is responsive to the needs of industry, and aggressively recruits high-tech manufacturing facilities and multinational companies. Such policies were a significant force in making Ireland the most dynamic, fastest-growing nation in Europe during the 1990s. Ireland's policies were a major factor in Intel's decision to choose Leixlip, County Kildare, as the site for a $2.5 billion chip manufacturing plant that employs over 4,000 people. Another locational advantage is the clustering of suppliers of components and capital equipment; infrastructure suppliers (universities, vocational training providers, research enterprises); trade associations; and makers of complementary products in a geographic area—such clustering can be an important source of cost savings in addition to facilitating close collaboration with key suppliers.

The Risks of Adverse Exchange Rate Shifts

The volatility of exchange rates greatly complicates the issue of geographic cost advantages. Currency exchange rates often move up or down 20 to 40 percent annually. Changes of this magnitude can either totally wipe out a country's low-cost advantage or transform a former high-cost location into a competitive-cost location. For instance, in the mid-1980s, when the dollar was strong relative to the Japanese yen (meaning that $1 would purchase, say, 125 yen as opposed to only 100 yen), Japanese heavy-equipment maker Komatsu was able to undercut U.S.-based Caterpillar's prices by as much as 25 percent, causing Caterpillar to lose sales and market share. But starting in 1985, when exchange rates began to shift and the dollar grew steadily weaker against the yen (meaning that $1 was worth fewer and fewer yen, and that a Komatsu product made in Japan at a cost of 20 million yen translated into costs of many more dollars than before), Komatsu had to raise its prices to U.S. buyers six times over two years. With its competitiveness against Komatsu restored because of the weaker dollar and Komatsu's higher prices, Caterpillar regained sales and market share. *The lesson of fluctuating exchange rates is that companies that export goods to foreign countries always gain in competitiveness when the currency of the country in which the goods are manufactured is weak. Exporters are disadvantaged when the currency of the country where goods are being manufactured grows stronger.* Sizable long-term shifts in exchange rates thus shuffle the global cards of which rivals have the upper hand in the marketplace and which countries represent the low-cost manufacturing location.

> **Core Concept**
> Companies with manufacturing facilities in a particular country are more cost-competitive in exporting goods to world markets when the local currency is weak (or declines in value relative to other currencies); their competitiveness erodes when the local currency grows stronger relative to the currencies of the countries to which the locally made goods are being exported.

As a further illustration of the risks associated with fluctuating exchange rates, consider the case of a U.S. company that has located manufacturing facilities in Brazil (where the currency is reals—pronounced *ray-alls*) and that exports most of the Brazilian-made goods to markets in the European Union (where the currency is euros). To keep the numbers simple, assume that the exchange rate is 4 Brazilian reals for 1 euro and that the product being made in Brazil has a manufacturing cost of 4 Brazilian reals (or 1 euro). Now suppose that for some reason the exchange rate shifts from 4 reals per euro to 5 reals per euro (meaning that the real has declined in value and that the euro is stronger). Making the product in Brazil is now more cost-competitive because a Brazilian good costing 4 reals to produce has fallen to only 0.8 euros at the new exchange rate. If, in contrast, the value of the Brazilian real grows stronger in relation to the euro—resulting in an exchange rate of 3 reals to 1 euro—the same good costing 4 reals to produce now has a cost of 1.33 euros. Clearly, the attraction of manufacturing a good in Brazil and selling it in Europe is far greater when the euro is strong (an exchange rate of 1 euro for 5 Brazilian reals) than when the euro is weak and exchanges for only 3 Brazilian reals.

Insofar as U.S.-based manufacturers are concerned, declines in the value of the U.S. dollar against foreign currencies act to reduce or eliminate whatever cost advantage foreign manufacturers might have over U.S. manufacturers and can even prompt foreign companies to establish production plants in the United States. Likewise, a weak euro enhances the cost competitiveness of companies manufacturing goods in Europe for export to foreign markets; a strong euro versus other currencies weakens the cost competitiveness of European plants that manufacture goods for export.

In 2002, when the Brazilian real declined in value by about 25 percent against the dollar, the euro, and several other currencies, the ability of companies with manufacturing plants in Brazil to compete in world markets was greatly enhanced—of course, in the future years this windfall gain in cost advantage might well be eroded by sustained rises in the value of the Brazilian real against these same currencies. Herein lies the risk: *Currency exchange rates are rather unpredictable, swinging first one way and then another way, so the competitiveness of any company's facilities in any country is partly dependent on whether exchange rate changes over time have a favorable or unfavorable cost impact.* Companies producing goods in one country for export abroad always improve their cost competitiveness when the country's currency grows weaker relative to currencies of the countries where the goods are being exported to, and they find their cost competitiveness eroded when the local currency grows stronger. In contrast, domestic companies that are under pressure from lower-cost imported goods become more cost competitive when their currency grows weaker in relation to the currencies of the countries where the imported goods are made—in other words, a U.S. manufacturer views a weaker U.S. dollar as a *favorable exchange rate shift* because such shifts help make its costs more competitive versus those of foreign rivals.

> **Core Concept**
>
> Fluctuating exchange rates pose significant risks to a company's competitiveness in foreign markets. Exporters win when the currency of the country where goods are being manufactured grows weaker, and they lose when the currency grows stronger. Domestic companies under pressure from lower-cost imports are benefited when their government's currency grows weaker in relation to the countries where the imported goods are being made.

Host Governments' Policies

National governments enact all kinds of measures affecting business conditions and the operation of foreign companies in their markets. Host governments may set local content requirements on goods made inside their borders by foreign-based companies, have rules and policies that protect local companies from foreign competition, put restrictions on exports to ensure adequate local supplies, regulate the prices of imported and locally produced goods, enact deliberately burdensome procedures and requirements for imported goods to pass customs inspection, and impose tariffs or quotas on the imports of certain goods—until 2002, when it joined the World Trade Organization, China imposed a 100 percent tariff on motor vehicle imports. The European Union imposes quotas on textile and apparel imports from China, as a measure to protect European producers in southern Europe. India imposed excise taxes on newly purchased motor vehicles in 2005 ranging from 24 to 40 percent—a policy that has significantly dampened the demand for new vehicles in India (though down from as much as 50 percent in prior years). Governments may or may not have burdensome tax structures, stringent environmental regulations, or strictly enforced worker safety standards. Sometimes outsiders face a web of regulations regarding technical standards, product certification, prior approval of capital spending projects, withdrawal of funds from the country, and required minority (sometimes majority) ownership of foreign company operations by local companies or investors. A few governments may be hostile to or suspicious of foreign companies operating within their borders. Some governments provide subsidies and low-interest loans to domestic companies to help them compete against foreign-based companies. Other governments, anxious to obtain new plants and jobs, offer foreign companies a helping hand in the form of subsidies, privileged market access, and technical assistance. All of these possibilities explain why the managers of companies opting to compete in foreign markets have to take a close look at a country's politics and policies toward business in general, and foreign companies in particular, in deciding which country markets to participate in and which ones to avoid.

THE CONCEPTS OF MULTICOUNTRY COMPETITION AND GLOBAL COMPETITION

There are important differences in the patterns of international competition from industry to industry.[4] At one extreme is **multicountry competition,** in which there's so much cross-country variation in market conditions and in the companies contending for leadership that the market contest among rivals in one country is not closely connected to the market contests in other countries. The standout features of multicountry competition are that (1) buyers in different countries are attracted to different product attributes, (2) sellers vary from country to country, and (3) industry conditions and competitive forces in each national market differ in important respects. Take the banking industry in Italy, Brazil, and Japan as an example—the requirements and expectations of banking customers vary among the three countries, the lead banking competitors in Italy differ from those in Brazil or in Japan, and the competitive battle going on among the leading banks in Italy is unrelated to the rivalry taking place in Brazil or Japan. Thus, with multicountry competition, rival firms battle for national championships, and winning in one country does not necessarily signal the ability to fare well in other countries. In multicountry competition, the power of a company's strategy and resource capabilities in one country may not enhance its competitiveness to the same degree in other countries where it operates. Moreover, any competitive advantage a company secures in one country is largely confined to that country; the spillover effects to other countries are minimal to nonexistent. Industries characterized by multicountry competition include radio and TV broadcasting, consumer banking, life insurance, apparel, metals fabrication, many types of food products (coffee, cereals, breads, canned goods, frozen foods), and retailing.

> **Core Concept**
> *Multicountry competition* exists when competition in one national market is not closely connected to competition in another national market—there is no global or world market, just a collection of self-contained country markets.

At the other extreme is **global competition,** in which prices and competitive conditions across country markets are strongly linked and the term *global market* has true meaning. In a globally competitive industry, much the same group of rival companies competes in many different countries, but especially so in countries where sales volumes are large and where having a competitive presence is strategically important to building a strong global position in the industry. Thus, a company's competitive position in one country both affects and is affected by its position in other countries. In global competition, a firm's overall competitive advantage grows out of its entire worldwide operations; the competitive advantage it creates at its home base is supplemented by advantages growing out of its operations in other countries (having plants in low-wage countries, being able to transfer expertise from country to country, having the capability to serve customers who also have multinational operations, and brand-name recognition in many parts of the world). Rival firms in globally competitive industries vie for worldwide leadership. Global competition exists in motor vehicles, television sets, tires, mobile phones, personal computers, copiers, watches, digital cameras, bicycles, and commercial aircraft.

> **Core Concept**
> *Global competition* exists when competitive conditions across national markets are linked strongly enough to form a true international market and when leading competitors compete head to head in many different countries.

An industry can have segments that are globally competitive and segments in which competition is country by country.[5] In the hotel/motel industry, for example, the low- and medium-priced segments are characterized by multicountry competition—competitors serve travelers mainly within the same country. In the business and luxury segments, however, competition is more globalized. Companies like Nikki, Marriott, Sheraton, and Hilton have hotels at many international locations, use worldwide reservation systems, and establish common quality and service standards to gain marketing advantages in serving businesspeople and other travelers who make frequent international trips. In lubricants, the marine engine segment is globally competitive—ships move from port to port and require the same oil everywhere they stop. Brand reputations in marine lubricants have a global scope, and successful marine engine lubricant producers (Exxon Mobil, BP Amoco, and Shell) operate globally. In automotive motor oil, however, multicountry competition dominates—countries have different weather conditions and driving patterns, production of motor oil is subject to limited scale economies, shipping costs are high, and retail distribution channels differ markedly from country to country. Thus, domestic firms—like Quaker State and Pennzoil in the United States and Castrol in Great Britain—can be leaders in their home markets without competing globally.

It is also important to recognize that an industry can be in transition from multicountry competition to global competition. In a number of today's industries—beer and major home appliances are prime examples—leading domestic competitors have begun expanding into more and more foreign markets, often acquiring local companies or brands and integrating them into their operations. As some industry members start to build global brands and a global presence, other industry members find themselves pressured to follow the same strategic path—especially if establishing multinational operations results in important scale economies and a powerhouse brand name. As the industry consolidates to fewer players, such that many of the same companies find themselves in head-to-head competition in more and more country markets, global competition begins to replace multicountry competition.

At the same time, consumer tastes in a number of important product categories are converging across the world. Less diversity of tastes and preferences opens the way for companies to create global brands and sell essentially the same products in most all countries of the world. Even in industries where consumer tastes remain fairly diverse, companies are learning to use "custom mass production" to economically create different versions of a product and thereby satisfy the tastes of people in different countries.

In addition to taking the obvious cultural and political differences between countries into account, a company has to shape its strategic approach to competing in foreign markets according to whether its industry is characterized by multicountry competition, global competition, or a transition from one to the other.

STRATEGY OPTIONS FOR ENTERING AND COMPETING IN FOREIGN MARKETS

There are a host of generic strategic options for a company that decides to expand outside its domestic market and compete internationally or globally:

1. *Maintain a national (one-country) production base and export goods to foreign markets,* using either company-owned or foreign-controlled forward distribution channels.

2. *License foreign firms to use the company's technology or to produce and distribute the company's products.*

3. *Employ a franchising strategy.*

4. *Follow a multicountry strategy,* varying the company's strategic approach (perhaps a little, perhaps a lot) from country to country in accordance with local conditions and differing buyer tastes and preferences.

5. *Follow a global strategy,* using essentially the same competitive strategy approach in all country markets where the company has a presence.

6. *Use strategic alliances or joint ventures with foreign companies as the primary vehicle for entering foreign markets* and perhaps also using them as an ongoing strategic arrangement aimed at maintaining or strengthening its competitiveness.

The following sections discuss the first five options in more detail; the sixth option is discussed in a separate section later in the chapter.

Export Strategies

Using domestic plants as a production base for exporting goods to foreign markets is an excellent initial strategy for pursuing international sales. It is a conservative way to test the international waters. The amount of capital needed to begin exporting is often quite minimal; existing production capacity may well be sufficient to make goods for export. With an export strategy, a manufacturer can limit its involvement in foreign markets by contracting with foreign wholesalers experienced in importing to handle the entire distribution and marketing function in their countries or regions of the world. If it is more advantageous to maintain control over these functions, however, a manufacturer can establish its own distribution and sales organizations in some or all of the target foreign markets. Either way, a home-based production and export strategy helps the firm minimize its direct investments in foreign countries. Such strategies are commonly favored by Chinese, Korean, and Italian companies—products are designed and manufactured at home and then distributed through local channels in the importing countries; the primary functions performed abroad relate chiefly to establishing a network of distributors and perhaps conducting sales promotion and brand awareness activities.

Whether an export strategy can be pursued successfully over the long run hinges on the relative cost competitiveness of the home-country production base. In some industries, firms gain additional scale economies and experience/learning curve benefits from centralizing production in one or several giant plants whose output capability exceeds demand in any one country market; obviously, a company must export to capture such economies. However, an export strategy is vulnerable when (1) manufacturing costs in the home country are substantially higher than in foreign countries where rivals have plants, (2) the costs of shipping the product to distant foreign markets are relatively high, or (3) adverse shifts occur in currency exchange rates. Unless an exporter can both keep its production and shipping costs competitive with rivals and successfully hedge against unfavorable changes in currency exchange rates, its success will be limited.

Licensing Strategies

Licensing makes sense when a firm with valuable technical know-how or a unique patented product has neither the internal organizational capability nor the resources to enter foreign markets. Licensing also has the advantage of avoiding the risks of committing resources to country markets that are unfamiliar, politically volatile, economically unstable, or otherwise risky. By licensing the technology or the production rights to foreign-based firms, the firm does not have to bear the costs and risks of entering foreign markets on its own, yet it is able to generate income from royalties. The big disadvantage of licensing is the risk of providing valuable technological know-how to foreign companies and thereby losing some degree of control over its use; monitoring licensees and safeguarding the company's proprietary know-how can prove quite difficult in some circumstances. But if the royalty potential is considerable and the companies to whom the licenses are being granted are both trustworthy and reputable, then licensing can be a very attractive option. Many software and pharmaceutical companies use licensing strategies.

Franchising Strategies

While licensing works well for manufacturers and owners of proprietary technology, franchising is often better suited to the global expansion efforts of service and retailing enterprises. McDonald's, Yum! Brands (the parent of Pizza Hut, KFC, and Taco Bell), The UPS Store, Jani-King International (the world's largest commercial cleaning franchisor), Roto-Rooter, 7-Eleven, and Hilton Hotels have all used franchising to build a presence in foreign markets. Franchising has much the same advantages as licensing. The franchisee bears most of the costs and risks of establishing foreign locations; a franchisor has to expend only the resources to recruit, train, support, and monitor franchisees. The big problem a franchisor faces is maintaining quality control; foreign franchisees do not always exhibit strong commitment to consistency and standardization, especially when the local culture does not stress the same kinds of quality concerns. Another problem that can arise is whether to allow foreign franchisees to make modifications in the franchisor's product offering so as to better satisfy the tastes and expectations of local buyers. Should McDonald's allow its franchised units in Japan to modify Big Macs slightly to suit Japanese tastes? Should the franchised KFC units in China be permitted to substitute spices that appeal to Chinese consumers? Or should the same menu offerings be rigorously and unvaryingly required of all franchisees worldwide?

Localized Multicountry Strategies or a Global Strategy?

The issue of whether to vary the company's competitive approach to fit specific market conditions and buyer preferences in each host country or whether to employ essentially the same strategy in all countries is perhaps the foremost strategic issue that companies must address when they operate in two or more foreign markets. Figure 7.1 shows a company's options for resolving this issue.

Core Concept

A *localized* or *multicountry strategy* is one where a company varies its product offering and competitive approach from country to country in an effort to be responsive to differing buyer preferences and market conditions.

Think-Local, Act-Local Approaches to Strategy Making   The bigger the differences in buyer tastes, cultural traditions, and market conditions in different countries, the stronger the case for a think-local, act-local approach to strategy-making, in which a company tailors its product offerings and perhaps its basic competitive strategy to fit buyer tastes and market conditions in each country where it opts to compete. The strength of employing a set of *localized* or *multicountry strategies* is that the company's actions and business approaches are deliberately crafted to accommodate the

Figure 7.1   **A Company's Strategic Options for Dealing with Cross-Country Variations in Buyer Preferences and Market Conditions**

Strategic Posturing Options	Ways to Deal with Cross-Country Variations in Buyer Preferences and Market Conditions
Think Local, Act Local	**Employ localized strategies—one for each country market:** ■ Tailor the company's competitive approach and product offering to fit specific market conditions and buyer preferences in each host country. ■ Delegate strategy making to local managers with firsthand knowledge of local conditions.
Think Global, Act Global	**Employ same strategy worldwide:** ■ Pursue *the same basic competitive strategy theme* (low-cost, differentiation, best-cost, or focused) *in all country markets*—a global strategy. ■ Offer the same products worldwide, with only very minor deviations from one country to another when local market conditions so dictate. ■ Utilize the same capabilities, distribution channels, and marketing approaches worldwide. ■ Coordinate strategic actions from central headquarters
Think Global, Act Local	**Employ a combination global-local strategy:** ■ Employ essentially *the same basic competitive strategy theme* (low-cost, differentiation, best-cost, or focused) in *all country markets.* ■ Develop the capability to customize product offerings and sell different product versions in different countries (perhaps even under different brand names). ■ Give local managers the latitude to adapt the global approach as needed to accommodate local buyer preferences and be responsive to local market and competitive conditions.

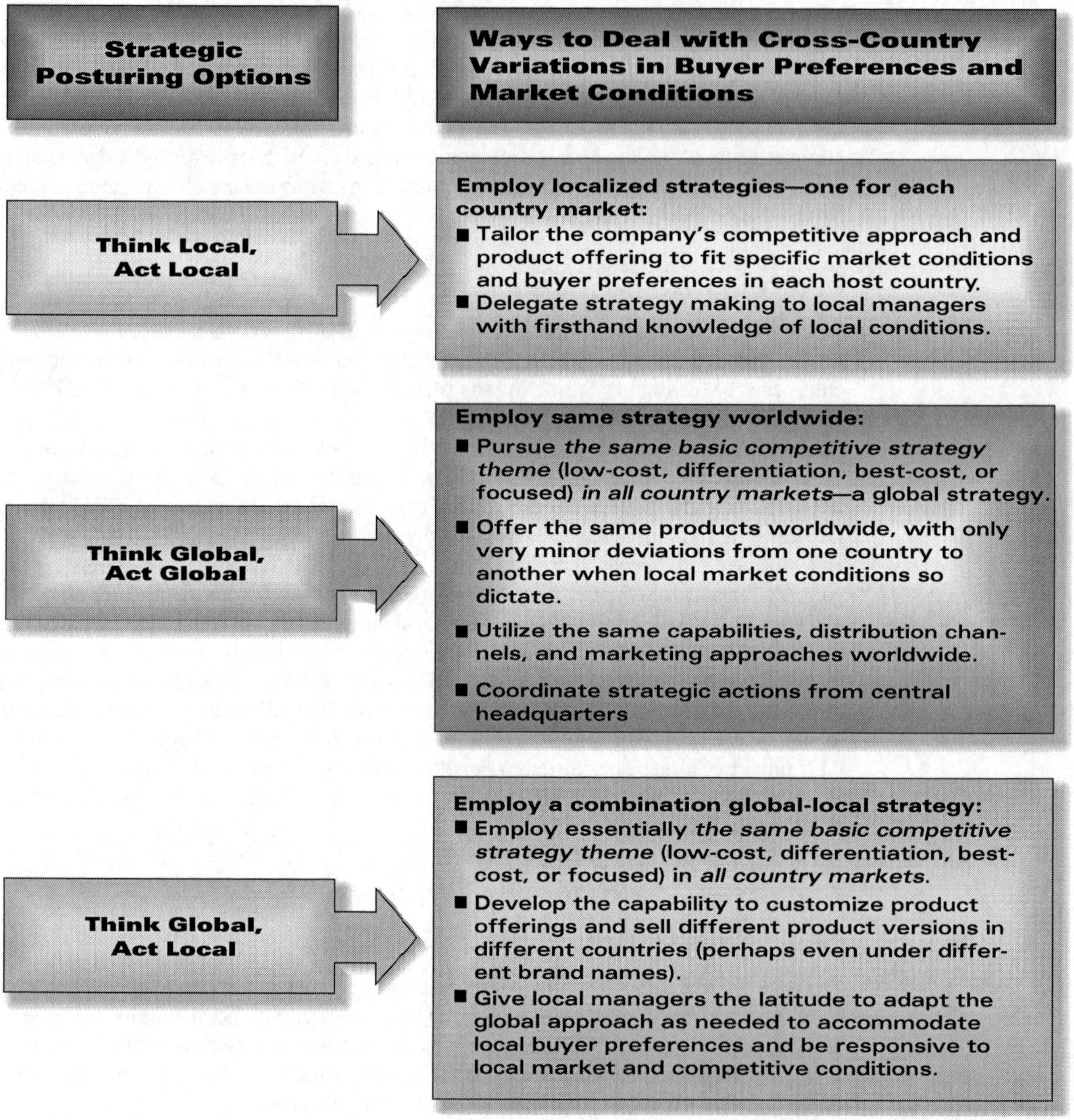

differing tastes and expectations of buyers in each country and to stake out the most attractive market positions vis-à-vis local competitors. A think-local, act-local approach means giving local managers considerable strategy-making latitude. It means having plants produce different product versions for different local markets, and adapting marketing and distribution to fit local customs and cultures. The bigger the country-to-country variations, the more that a company's overall strategy is a collection of its localized country strategies rather than a common or global strategy.

A think-local, act-local approach to strategy making is essential when there are significant country-to-country differences in customer preferences and buying habits, when there are significant cross-country differences in distribution channels and marketing methods, when host governments enact regulations requiring that products sold locally meet strict manufacturing specifications or performance standards, and when the trade restrictions of host governments are so diverse and complicated that they preclude a uniform, coordinated worldwide market approach. With localized strategies, a company often has different product versions for different countries and sometimes sells them under different brand names. Sony markets a different Walkman in Norway than in Sweden to better meet the somewhat different preferences and habits of the users in each market. Castrol, a specialist in oil lubricants, has over 3,000 different formulas of lubricants, many of which have been tailored for different climates, vehicle types and uses, and equipment applications that characterize different country markets. In the food products industry, it is common for companies to vary the ingredients in their products and sell the localized versions under local brand names in order to cater to country-specific tastes and eating preferences. Motor vehicle manufacturers routinely produce smaller, more fuel-efficient vehicles for markets in Europe where roads are often narrower and gasoline prices two or three times higher than they produce for the North American market; the models they manufacture for the Asian market are different yet again. DaimlerChrysler, for example, equips all of the Jeep Grand Cherokees and many of its Mercedes cars sold in Europe with fuel-efficient diesel engines. The Buicks that General Motors sells in China are small compacts, whereas those sold in the United States are large family sedans and SUVs.

However, think-local, act-local strategies have two big drawbacks: They hinder transfer of a company's competencies and resources across country boundaries (since the strategies in different host countries can be grounded in varying competencies and capabilities), and they do not promote building a single, unified competitive advantage—especially one based on low cost. Companies employing highly localized or multicountry strategies face big hurdles in achieving low-cost leadership *unless* they find ways to customize their products and *still* be in position to capture scale economies and experience/learning curve effects. Companies like Dell Computer and Toyota, because they have mass customization production capabilities, can cost effectively adapt their product offerings to local buyer tastes.

Think-Global, Act-Global Approaches to Strategy Making

While multicountry or localized strategies are best suited for industries where multicountry competition dominates and a fairly high degree of local responsiveness is competitively imperative, global strategies are best suited for globally competitive industries. A *global strategy* is one in which the company's approach is predominantly the same in all countries—it sells the same products under the same brand names everywhere, uses much the same distribution channels in all countries, and competes on the basis of the same capabilities and marketing approaches worldwide. Although the company's strategy or product offering may be adapted in very minor ways to accommodate specific situations in a few host countries, the company's fundamental competitive approach (low-cost, differentiation, best-cost, or focused) remains very much intact worldwide, and local managers stick close to the global strategy. A think-global, act-global strategic theme prompts company managers to integrate and coordinate the company's strategic moves worldwide and to expand into most if not all nations where there is significant buyer demand. It puts considerable strategic

Core Concept

A *global strategy* is one where a company employs the same basic competitive approach in all countries where it operates, sells much the same products everywhere, strives to build global brands, and coordinates its actions worldwide.

emphasis on building a *global* brand name and aggressively pursuing opportunities to transfer ideas, new products, and capabilities from one country to another.[6] Indeed, with a think global, act global approach to strategy making, a company's operations in each country can be viewed as experiments that result in learning and in capabilities that may merit transfer to other country markets.

Whenever country-to-country differences are small enough to be accommodated within the framework of a global strategy, a global strategy is preferable to localized strategies because a company can more readily unify its operations and focus on establishing a brand image and reputation that is uniform from country to country. Moreover, with a global strategy a company is better able to focus its full resources on building the resource strengths and capabilities to secure a sustainable low-cost or differentiation-based competitive advantage over both domestic rivals and global rivals racing for world market leadership. Figure 7.2 summarizes the basic differences between a localized or multicountry strategy and a global strategy.

Think-Global, Act-Local Approaches to Strategy Making   Often, a company can accommodate cross-country variations in buyer tastes, local customs, and market conditions with a think-global, act-local approach to developing strategy. This middle-ground approach entails using the same basic competitive theme (low-cost, differentiation, best-cost, or focused) in each country but allowing local mangers the latitude to (1) incorporate whatever country-specific variations in product attributes are needed to best satisfy local buyers and (2) make whatever adjustments in production, distribution, and marketing are needed to be responsive to local market conditions and compete successfully against local rivals. Slightly different product versions sold under the same brand name may suffice to satisfy local tastes, and it may be feasible to accommodate these versions rather economically in the course of designing and manufacturing the company's product offerings. The build-to-order component of Dell's strategy in PCs for example, makes it simple for Dell to be responsive to how buyers in different parts of the world want their PCs equipped. However, Dell has not wavered in its strategy to sell directly to customers rather than through local retailers, even though the majority of buyers in countries such as China are concerned about ordering online and prefer to personally inspect PCs at stores before making a purchase.

As a rule, most companies that operate multinationally endeavor to employ as global a strategy as customer needs and market conditions permit. Philips Electronics, the Netherlands-based electronics and consumer products company, operated successfully with localized strategies for many years but has recently begun moving more toward a unified strategy within the European Union and within North America.[7] Whirlpool has been globalizing its low-cost leadership strategy in home appliances for over 15 years, striving to standardize parts and components and move toward worldwide designs for as many of its appliance products as possible. But it has found it necessary to continue producing significantly different versions of refrigerators, washing machines, and cooking appliances for consumers in different regions of the world because the needs and tastes of local buyers for appliances of different sizes and designs have not converged sufficiently to permit standardization of Whirlpool's product offerings worldwide. General Motors began an initiative in 2004 to insist that its worldwide units share basic parts and work together to design vehicles that can be sold, with modest variations, anywhere around the world; by reducing the types of radios used in its cars and trucks from 270 to 50, it expected to save 40 percent in radio costs.

Illustration Capsule 7.1 on page 209 describes how two companies localize their strategies for competing in country markets across the world.

Figure 7.2   **How a Localized or Multicountry Strategy Differs from a Global Strategy**

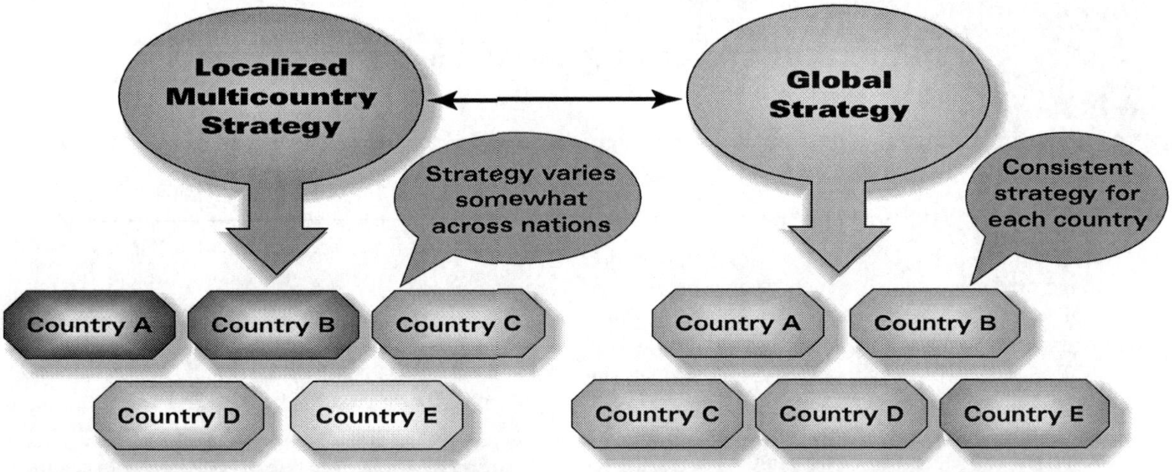

Localized Multicountry Strategy

Strategy varies somewhat across nations

Country A   Country B   Country C

Country D   Country E

- Customize the company's competitive approach as needed to fit market and business circumstances in each host country—strong responsiveness to local conditions.
- Sell different product versions in different countries under different brand names—adapt product attributes to fit buyer tastes and preferences country by country.
- Scatter plants across many host countries, each producing product versions for local markets.
- Preferably use local suppliers (some local sources may be required by host government).
- Adapt marketing and distribution to local customs and culture of each country.
- Transfer competencies and capabilities from country to country where feasible.
- Give country managers fairly wide strategy-making latitude and autonomy over local operations.

Global Strategy

Consistent strategy for each country

Country A   Country B

Country C   Country D   Country E

- Pursue same basic competitive strategy worldwide (low-cost, differentiation, best-cost, focused low-cost, focused differentiation), with minimal responsiveness to local conditions.
- Sell same products under same brand name worldwide; focus efforts on building global brands as opposed to strengthening local/regional brands sold in local/regional markets.
- Locate plants on basis of maximum locational advantage, usually in countries where production costs are lowest but plants may be scattered if shipping costs are high or other locational advantages dominate.
- Use best suppliers from anywhere in world.
- Coordinate marketing and distribution worldwide; make minor adaptation to local countries where needed.
- Compete on basis of same technologies, competencies, and capabilities worldwide; stress rapid transfer of new ideas, products, and capabilities to other countries.
- Coordinate major strategic decisions worldwide; expect local managers to stick close to global strategy.

Illustration Capsule 7.1

Multicountry Strategies at Electronic Arts and Coca-Cola

ELECTRONIC ARTS' MULTICOUNTRY STRATEGY IN VIDEO GAMES

Electronic Arts (EA), the world's largest independent developer and marketer of video games, designs games that are suited to the differing tastes of game players in different countries and also designs games in multiple languages. EA has two major design studios—one in Vancouver, British Columbia, and one in Los Angeles—and smaller design studios in San Francisco, Orlando, London, and Tokyo. This dispersion of design studios helps EA to design games that are specific to different cultures—for example, the London studio took the lead in designing the popular FIFA Soccer game to suit European tastes and to replicate the stadiums, signage, and team rosters; the U.S. studio took the lead in designing games involving NFL football, NBA basketball, and NASCAR racing. No other game software company had EA's ability to localize games or to launch games on multiple platforms in multiple countries in multiple languages. EA's game Harry Potter and the Chamber of Secrets was released simultaneously in 75 countries, in 31 languages, and on seven platforms.

COCA-COLA'S MULTICOUNTRY STRATEGY IN BEVERAGES

Coca-Cola strives to meet the demands of local tastes and cultures, offering 300 brands in some 200 countries. Its network of bottlers and distributors is distinctly local, and the company's products and brands are formulated to cater to local tastes. The ways in which Coca-Cola's local operating units bring products to market, the packaging that is used, and the company's advertising messages are all intended to match the local culture and fit in with local business practices. Many of the ingredients and supplies for Coca-Cola's products are sourced locally.

Sources: Information posted at www.ea.com and www.cocacola.com (accessed September 2004).

THE QUEST FOR COMPETITIVE ADVANTAGE IN FOREIGN MARKETS

There are three important ways in which a firm can gain competitive advantage (or offset domestic disadvantages) by expanding outside its domestic market:[8] One, it can use location to lower costs or achieve greater product differentiation. Two, it can transfer competitively valuable competencies and capabilities from its domestic markets to foreign markets. And three, it can use cross-border coordination in ways that a domestic-only competitor cannot.

Using Location to Build Competitive Advantage

To use location to build competitive advantage, a company must consider two issues: (1) whether to concentrate each activity it performs in a few select countries or to disperse performance of the activity to many nations, and (2) in which countries to locate particular activities.[9]

When to Concentrate Activities in a Few Locations   Companies tend to concentrate their activities in a limited number of locations in the following circumstances:

> Companies that compete multi-nationally can pursue competitive advantage in world markets by locating their value chain activities in whatever nations prove most advantageous.

- *When the costs of manufacturing or other activities are significantly lower in some geographic locations than in others*—For example, much of the world's athletic footwear is manufactured in Asia (China and Korea) because of low labor costs; much of the production of motherboards for PCs is located in Taiwan because of both low costs and the high-caliber technical skills of the Taiwanese labor force.

- *When there are significant scale economies*—The presence of significant economies of scale in components production or final assembly means that a company can gain major cost savings from operating a few superefficient plants as opposed to a host of small plants scattered across the world. Important marketing and distribution economies associated with multinational operations can also yield low-cost leadership. In situations where some competitors are intent on global dominance, being the worldwide low-cost provider is a powerful competitive advantage. Achieving low-cost provider status often requires a company to have the largest worldwide manufacturing share, with production centralized in one or a few world-scale plants in low-cost locations. Some companies even use such plants to manufacture units sold under the brand names of rivals. Manufacturing share (as distinct from brand share or market share) is significant because it provides more certain access to production-related scale economies. Japanese makers of VCRs, microwave ovens, TVs, and DVD players have used their large manufacturing share to establish a low-cost advantage.[10]

- *When there is a steep learning curve associated with performing an activity in a single location*—In some industries experience/learning curve effects in parts manufacture or assembly are so great that a company establishes one or two large plants from which it serves the world market. The key to riding down the learning curve is to concentrate production in a few locations to increase the accumulated volume at a plant (and thus the experience of the plant's workforce) as rapidly as possible.

- *When certain locations have superior resources, allow better coordination of related activities, or offer other valuable advantages*—A research unit or a sophisticated production facility may be situated in a particular nation because of its pool of technically trained personnel. Samsung became a leader in memory chip technology by establishing a major R&D facility in Silicon Valley and transferring the know-how it gained back to headquarters and its plants in South Korea. Where just-in-time inventory practices yield big cost savings and/or where an assembly firm has long-term partnering arrangements with its key suppliers, parts manufacturing plants may be clustered around final assembly plants. An assembly plant may be located in a country in return for the host government's allowing freer import of components from large-scale, centralized parts plants located elsewhere. A customer service center or sales office may be opened in a particular country to help cultivate strong relationships with pivotal customers located nearby.

When to Disperse Activities Across Many Locations   There are several instances when dispersing activities is more advantageous than concentrating them. Buyer-related activities—such as distribution to dealers, sales and advertising, and after-sale service—usually must take place close to buyers. This means physically locating the capability to perform such activities in every country market where a global firm has major customers (unless buyers in several adjoining countries can be served quickly from a nearby central location). For example, firms that make mining and oil-drilling equipment maintain operations in many international locations to support customers' needs for speedy equipment repair and technical assistance. The four biggest public accounting firms have numerous international offices to service the foreign operations of their multinational corporate clients. A global competitor that effectively disperses its buyer-related activities can gain a service-based competitive edge in world markets over rivals whose buyer-related activities are more concentrated—this is one reason the Big Four public accounting firms (PricewaterhouseCoopers, KPMG, Deloitte & Touche, and Ernst & Young) have been so successful relative to regional and national firms. Dispersing activities to many locations is also competitively advantageous when high transportation costs, diseconomies of large size, and trade barriers make it too expensive to operate from a central location. Many companies distribute their products from multiple locations to shorten delivery times to customers. In addition, it is strategically advantageous to disperse activities to hedge against the risks of fluctuating exchange rates; supply interruptions (due to strikes, mechanical failures, and transportation delays); and adverse political developments. Such risks are greater when activities are concentrated in a single location.

The classic reason for locating an activity in a particular country is low cost.[11] Even though multinational and global firms have strong reason to disperse buyer-related activities to many international locations, such activities as materials procurement, parts manufacture, finished goods assembly, technology research, and new product development can frequently be decoupled from buyer locations and performed wherever advantage lies. Components can be made in Mexico; technology research done in Frankfurt; new products developed and tested in Phoenix; and assembly plants located in Spain, Brazil, Taiwan, or South Carolina. Capital can be raised in whatever country it is available on the best terms.

Using Cross-Border Transfers of Competencies and Capabilities to Build Competitive Advantage

One of the best ways for a company with valuable competencies and resource strengths to secure competitive advantage is to use its considerable resource strengths to enter additional country markets. A company whose resource strengths prove particularly potent in competing successfully in newly entered country markets not only grows sales and profits but also may find that its competitiveness is sufficiently enhanced to produce competitive advantage over one or more rivals and contend for global market leadership. Transferring competencies, capabilities, and resource strengths from country to country contributes to the development of broader or deeper competencies and capabilities—ideally helping a company achieve dominating depth in some competitively valuable area. Dominating depth in a competitively valuable capability, resource, or value chain activity is a strong basis for sustainable competitive advantage over other multinational or global competitors, and especially so over domestic-only competitors. A one-country customer base is often too small to support the resource buildup needed to achieve such depth; this is particularly true when the market is just emerging and sophisticated resources have not been required.

Whirlpool, the leading global manufacturer of home appliances, with plants in 14 countries and sales in 170 countries, has used the Internet to create a global information technology platform that allows the company to transfer key product innovations and production processes across regions and brands quickly and effectively. Wal-Mart is slowly but forcefully expanding its operations with a strategy that involves transferring its considerable domestic expertise in distribution and discount retailing to store operations recently established in China, Japan, Latin America, and Europe. Its status as the largest, most resource-deep, and most sophisticated user of distribution/ retailing know-how has served it well in building its foreign sales and profitability. But Wal-Mart is not racing madly to position itself in many foreign markets; rather, it is establishing a strong presence in select country markets and learning how to be successful in these before tackling entry into other countries well-suited to its business model.

However, cross-border resource transfers are not a guaranteed recipe for success. Philips Electronics sells more color TVs and DVD recorders in Europe than any other company does; its biggest technological breakthrough was the compact disc, which it invented in 1982. Philips has worldwide sales of about 38 billion euros, but as of 2005 Philips had lost money for 17 consecutive years in its U.S. consumer electronics business. In the United States, the company's color TVs and DVD recorders (sold under the Magnavox and Philips brands) are slow sellers. Philips notoriously lags in introducing new products into the U.S. market and has been struggling to develop an able sales force that can make inroads with U.S. electronics retailers and change its image as a low-end brand.

Using Cross-Border Coordination to Build Competitive Advantage

Coordinating company activities across different countries contributes to sustainable competitive advantage in several different ways.[12] Multinational and global competitors can choose where and how to challenge rivals. They may decide to retaliate against an aggressive rival in the country market where the rival has its biggest sales volume or its best profit margins in order to reduce the rival's financial resources for competing in other country markets. They may also decide to wage a price-cutting offensive against weak rivals in their home markets, capturing greater market share and subsidizing any short-term losses with profits earned in other country markets.

If a firm learns how to assemble its product more efficiently at, say, its Brazilian plant, the accumulated expertise can be quickly communicated via the Internet to assembly plants in other world locations. Knowledge gained in marketing a company's product in Great Britain can readily be exchanged with company personnel in New Zealand or Australia. A global or multinational manufacturer can shift production from a plant in one country to a plant in another to take advantage of exchange rate fluctuations, to enhance its leverage with host-country governments, and to respond to changing wage rates, components shortages, energy costs, or changes in tariffs and quotas. Production schedules can be coordinated worldwide; shipments can be diverted from one distribution center to another if sales rise unexpectedly in one place and fall in another.

Using online systems, companies can readily gather ideas for new and improved products from customers and company personnel all over the world, permitting informed decisions about what can be standardized and what should be customized. Likewise, online systems enable multinational companies to involve their best design and engineering personnel (wherever they are located) in collectively coming up with next-generation products—it is easy for company personnel in one location to use the Internet to collaborate closely with personnel in other locations in performing all sorts of strategically relevant activities. Efficiencies can also be achieved by shifting workloads from where they are unusually heavy to locations where personnel are underutilized. Whirlpool's efforts to link its product R&D and manufacturing operations in North America, Latin America, Europe, and Asia allowed it to accelerate the discovery of innovative appliance features, coordinate the introduction of these features in the appliance products marketed in different countries, and create a cost-efficient worldwide supply chain. Whirlpool's conscious efforts to integrate and coordinate its various operations around the world have helped it become a low-cost producer and also speed product innovations to market, thereby giving Whirlpool an edge over rivals in designing and rapidly introducing innovative and attractively priced appliances worldwide.

Furthermore, a multinational company that consistently incorporates the same differentiating attributes in its products worldwide has enhanced potential to build a global brand name with significant power in the marketplace. The reputation for quality that Honda established worldwide first in motorcycles and then in automobiles gave it competitive advantage in positioning Honda lawn mowers at the upper end of the U.S. outdoor power equipment market—the Honda name gave the company immediate credibility with U.S. buyers of power equipment and enabled it to become an instant market contender without all the fanfare and cost of a multimillion-dollar ad campaign to build brand awareness.

PROFIT SANCTUARIES, CROSS-MARKET SUBSIDIZATION, AND GLOBAL STRATEGIC OFFENSIVES

Profit sanctuaries are country markets (or geographic regions) in which a company derives substantial profits because of its strong or protected market position. McDonald's serves about 50 million customers daily at nearly 32,000 locations in 119 countries on five continents; not surprisingly, its biggest profit sanctuary is the United States, which generated 61.2 percent of 2004 profits, despite accounting for just 34.2 percent of 2004 revenues. Nike, which markets its products in 160 countries, has two big profit sanctuaries: the United States (where it earned 41.5 percent of its operating profits in 2005) and Europe, the Middle East, and Africa (where it earned 34.8 percent of 2005 operating profits). Discount retailer Carrefour, which has stores across much of Europe plus stores in Asia and the Americas, also has two principal profit sanctuaries; its biggest is in France (which in 2004 accounted for 49.2 percent of revenues and 60.8 percent of earnings before interest and taxes), and its second biggest is Europe outside of France (which in 2004 accounted for 37.3 percent of revenues and 33.1 percent of earnings before interest and taxes). Japan is the chief profit sanctuary for most Japanese companies because trade barriers erected by the Japanese government effectively block foreign companies from competing for a large share of Japanese sales. Protected from the threat of foreign competition in their home market, Japanese companies can safely charge somewhat higher prices to their Japanese customers and thus earn attractively large profits on sales made in Japan. In most cases, a company's biggest and most strategically crucial profit sanctuary is its home market, but international and global companies may also enjoy profit sanctuary status in other nations where they have a strong competitive position, big sales volume, and attractive profit margins. Companies that compete globally are likely to have more profit sanctuaries than companies that compete in just a few country markets; a domestic-only competitor, of course, can have only one profit sanctuary (see Figure 7.3).

Core Concept
Companies with large, protected **profit sanctuaries** have competitive advantage over companies that don't have a protected sanctuary. Companies with multiple profit sanctuaries have a competitive advantage over companies with a single sanctuary.

Figure 7.3   **Profit Sanctuary Potential of Domestic-Only, International, and Global Competitors**

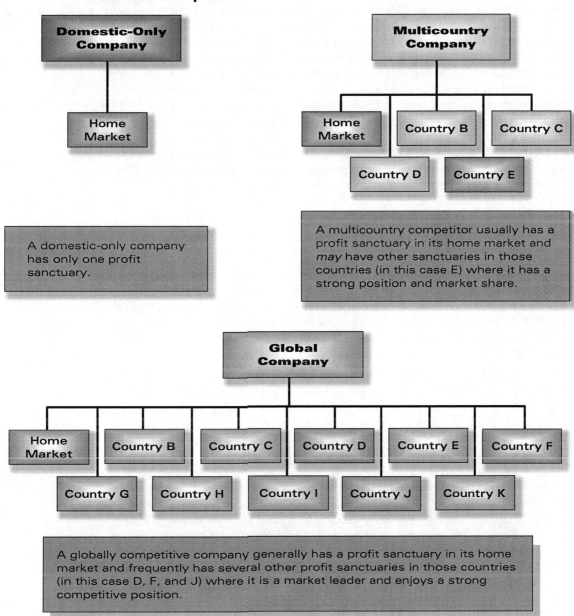

Using Cross-Market Subsidization to Wage a Strategic Offensive

Profit sanctuaries are valuable competitive assets, providing the financial strength to support strategic offensives in selected country markets and fuel a company's race for global market leadership. The added financial capability afforded by multiple profit sanctuaries gives a global or multicountry competitor the financial strength to wage a market offensive against a domestic competitor whose only profit sanctuary is its home market. Consider the case of a purely domestic company in competition with a company that has multiple profit sanctuaries and that is racing for global market leadership. The global company has the flexibility of lowballing its prices in the domestic company's home market and grabbing market share at the domestic company's expense, subsidizing razor-thin margins or even losses with the healthy profits earned in its profit sanctuaries—a practice called **cross-market subsidization.** The global company can adjust the depth of its price cutting to move in and capture market share quickly, or it can shave prices slightly to make gradual market inroads (perhaps over a decade or more) so as not to threaten domestic firms precipitously or trigger protectionist government actions. If the domestic company retaliates with matching price cuts, it exposes its entire revenue and profit base to erosion; its profits can be squeezed substantially and its competitive strength sapped, even if it is the domestic market leader.

> **Core Concept**
> **Cross-market subsidization**—supporting competitive offensives in one market with resources and profits diverted from operations in other markets—is a powerful competitive weapon.

Offensive Strategies Suitable for Competing in Foreign Markets

Companies that compete in multiple foreign markets can, of course, fashion an offensive strategy based on any of the approaches discussed in Chapter 6 (pages 160–193)—these types of offensive strategies are universally applicable and are just as suitable for competing in foreign markets as for domestic markets. But there are three additional types of offensive strategies that are suited to companies competing in foreign markets:[13]

- *Attack a foreign rival's profit sanctuaries.* Launching an offensive in a country market where a rival earns its biggest profits can put the rival on the defensive, forcing it to perhaps spend more on marketing/advertising, trim its prices, boost product innovation efforts, or otherwise undertake actions that raise its costs and erode its profits. If a company's offensive succeeds in eroding a rival's profits in its chief profit sanctuary, the rival's financial resources may be sufficiently weakened to enable the attacker to gain the upper hand and build market momentum. While attacking a rival's profit sanctuary violates the principle of attacking competitor weaknesses instead of competitor strengths, it can nonetheless prove valuable when there is special merit in pursuing actions that cut into a foreign rival's profit margins and force it to defend a market that is important to its competitive well-being. This is especially true when the attacker has important resource strengths and profit sanctuaries of its own that it can draw on to support its offensive.

- *Employ cross-market subsidization to win customers and sales away from select rivals in select country markets.* This can be a particularly attractive offensive strategy for companies that compete in multiple country markets with multiple products (several brands of cigarettes or different brands of food products). Competing in multiple country markets gives a company the luxury of drawing upon the resources, profits, and cash flows derived from particular country markets (especially its profit sanctuaries) to support offensives aimed at winning customers away from select rivals in those country markets that it wants either to enter or to boost its sales and market share. Alternatively, a company whose product lineup consists of different items can shift resources from a product category where it is competitively strong and resource deep (say soft drinks) to add firepower to an offensive in those countries with bright growth prospects in another product category (say bottled water or fruit juices).

- *Dump goods at cut-rate prices in the markets of foreign rivals.* A company is said to be dumping when it sells its goods in foreign markets at prices that are (1) well below the prices at which it normally sells in its home market or (2) well below its full costs per unit. Companies that engage in dumping usually keep their selling prices high enough to cover variable costs per unit, thereby limiting their losses on each unit to some percentage of fixed costs per unit. Dumping can be an appealing offensive strategy in either of two instances. One is when dumping drives down the price so far in the targeted country that domestic firms are quickly put in dire financial straits and end up declaring bankruptcy or being driven out of business—for dumping to pay off in this instance, however, the dumping company needs to have deep enough financial pockets to cover any losses from selling at below-market prices, and the targeted domestic companies need to be financially weak. The second instance in which dumping becomes an attractive strategy is when a company with unused production capacity discovers that it is cheaper to keep producing (as long as the selling prices cover average variable costs per unit) than it is to incur the costs associated with idle plant capacity. By keeping its plants operating at or near capacity, a dumping company not only may be able to cover variable costs and earn a contribution to fixed costs but also may be able to use its below-market prices to draw price-sensitive customers away from foreign rivals, then attentively court these new customers and retain their business when prices later begin a gradual rise back to normal market levels. Thus, dumping may prove useful as a way of entering the market of a particular foreign country and establishing a customer base.

Core Concept

Three strategy offensives that are particularly suitable for competing in foreign markets involve (1) attacking a foreign rival's profit sanctuaries, (2) employing cross-market subsidization, and (3) dumping.

However, dumping strategies run a high risk of host government retaliation on behalf of the adversely affected domestic companies. Indeed, as the trade among nations has mushroomed over the past 10 years, most governments have joined the World Trade Organization (WTO), which promotes fair trade practices among nations and actively polices dumping. The WTO allows member governments to take actions against dumping wherever there is material injury to domestic competitors. In 2002, for example, the U.S. government imposed tariffs of up to 30 percent on selected steel products that Asian and European steel manufacturers were said to be selling at ultra-low prices in the U.S. market. Canada recently investigated charges that companies in Austria, Belgium, France, Germany, Poland and China were dumping supplies of laminate flooring in Canada to the detriment of Canadian producers and concluded that companies in France and China were indeed selling such flooring in Canada at unreasonably low prices.[14] Most all governments can be expected to retaliate against dumping by imposing special tariffs on goods being imported from the countries of the guilty companies. Companies deemed guilty of dumping frequently come under pressure from their government to cease and desist, especially if the tariffs adversely affect innocent companies based in the same country or if the advent of special tariffs raises the specter of a trade war.

A company desirous of employing some type of offensive strategy in foreign markets is well advised to observe the principles for employing offensive strategies in general. For instance, it usually wise to attack foreign rivals on grounds that pit the challenger's competitive strengths against the defender's weaknesses and vulnerabilities. As a rule, trying to steal customers away from foreign rivals with strategies aimed at besting rivals where they are strongest stand a lower chance of succeeding than strategies that attack their competitive weaknesses, especially when the challenger has resource strengths that enable it to exploit rivals' weaknesses and when its attack involves an element of surprise.[15] It nearly always makes good strategic sense to use the challenger's core competencies and best competitive capabilities to spearhead the offensive. Furthermore, strategic offensives in foreign markets should, as a general rule, be predicated on exploiting the challenger's core competencies and best competitive capabilities. The ideal condition for a strategic offensive is when the attacker's resource strengths give it a competitive advantage over the targeted foreign rivals. The only two exceptions to these offensive strategy principles come when a competitively strong company with deep financial pockets sees considerable benefit in attacking a foreign rival's profit sanctuary and/or has the ability to employ cross-market subsidization—both of these offensive strategies can involve attacking a foreign rival's strengths (but they also are grounded in important strengths of the challenger and don't fall into the trap of challenging a competitively strong rival with a strategic offensive based on unproven expertise or inferior technology or a relatively unknown brand name or other resource weaknesses).

STRATEGIC ALLIANCES AND JOINT VENTURES WITH FOREIGN PARTNERS

Strategic alliances, joint ventures, and other cooperative agreements with foreign companies are a favorite and potentially fruitful means for entering a foreign market or strengthening a firm's competitiveness in world markets.[16] Historically, export-minded firms in industrialized nations sought alliances with firms in less-developed countries to import and market their products locally—such arrangements were often necessary to win approval for entry from the host country's government. Both Japanese and American companies are actively forming alliances with European companies to strengthen their ability to compete in the 25-nation European Union (and the five countries that are seeking to become EU members) and to capitalize on the opening up of Eastern European markets. Many U.S. and European companies are allying with Asian companies in their efforts to enter markets in China, India, Malaysia, Thailand, and other Asian countries. Companies in Europe, Latin America, and Asia are using alliances and joint ventures as a means of strengthening their mutual ability to compete across a wider geographical area—for instance, all the countries in the European Union or whole continents or most all country markets where there is sizable demand for the industry's product. Many foreign companies, of course, are particularly interested in strategic partnerships that will strengthen their ability to gain a foothold in the U.S. market.

> Cross-border alliances have proved to be popular and viable vehicles for companies to edge their way into the markets of foreign countries.

However, cooperative arrangements between domestic and foreign companies have strategic appeal for reasons besides gaining better access to attractive country markets.[17] A second big appeal of cross-border alliances is to capture economies of scale in production and/or marketing—cost reduction can be the difference that allows a company to be cost-competitive. By joining forces in producing components, assembling models, and marketing their products, companies can realize cost savings not achievable with their own small volumes. A third motivation for entering into a cross-border alliance is to fill gaps in technical expertise and/or knowledge of local markets (buying habits and product preferences of consumers, local customs, and so on). Allies learn much from one another in performing joint research, sharing technological know-how, studying one another's manufacturing methods, and understanding how to tailor sales and marketing approaches to fit local cultures and traditions. Indeed, one of the win–win benefits of an alliance is to learn from the skills, technological know-how, and capabilities of alliance partners and implant the knowledge and know-how of these partners in personnel throughout the company.

A fourth motivation for cross-border alliances is to share distribution facilities and dealer networks, thus mutually strengthening their access to buyers. A fifth benefit is that cross-border allies can direct their competitive energies more toward mutual rivals and less toward one another; teaming up may help them close the gap on leading companies. A sixth driver of cross-border alliances comes into play when companies desirous of entering a new foreign market conclude that alliances with local companies are an effective way to tap into a partner's local market knowledge and help it establish working relationships with key officials in the host-country government.[18] And, finally, alliances can be a particularly useful way for companies across the world to gain agreement on important technical standards—they have been used to arrive at standards for DVD players, assorted PC devices, Internet-related technologies, high-definition televisions, and mobile phones.

> Cross-border alliances enable a growth-minded company to widen its geographic coverage and strengthen its competitiveness in foreign markets while, at the same time, offering flexibility and allowing a company to retain some degree of autonomy and operating control.

What makes cross-border alliances an attractive strategic means of gaining the above types of benefits (as compared to acquiring or merging with foreign-based companies to gain much the same benefits) is that entering into alliances and strategic partnerships to gain market access and/ or expertise of one kind or another allows a company to preserve its independence (which is not the case with a merger), retain veto power over how the alliance operates, and avoid using perhaps scarce financial resources to fund acquisitions. Furthermore, an alliance offers the flexibility to readily disengage once its purpose has been served or if the benefits prove elusive, whereas an acquisition is more permanent sort of arrangement (although the acquired company can, of course, be divested).[19]

Illustration Capsule 7.2 provides six examples of cross-border strategic alliances.

The Risks of Strategic Alliances with Foreign Partners

Alliances and joint ventures with foreign partners have their pitfalls, however. Cross-border allies typically have to overcome language and cultural barriers and figure out how to deal with diverse (or perhaps conflicting) operating practices. The communication, trust-building, and coordination costs are high in terms of management time.[20] It is not unusual for there to be little personal chemistry among some of the key people on whom success or failure of the alliance depends—the rapport such personnel need to work well together may never emerge. And even if allies are able to develop productive personal relationships, they can still have trouble reaching mutually agreeable ways to deal with key issues or resolve differences. There is a natural tendency for allies to struggle to collaborate effectively in competitively sensitive areas, thus spawning suspicions on both sides about forthright exchanges of information and expertise. Occasionally, the egos of corporate executives can clash—an alliance between Northwest Airlines and KLM Royal Dutch Airlines resulted in a bitter feud among both companies' top officials (who, according to some reports, refused to speak to each other).[21] In addition, there is the thorny problem of getting alliance partners to sort through issues and reach decisions fast enough to stay abreast of rapid advances in technology or fast-changing market conditions.

Illustration Capsule 7.2
Six Examples of Cross-Border Strategic Alliances

1. Two auto firms, Renault of France and Nissan of Japan, formed a broad-ranging global partnership in 1999 and then strengthened and expanded the alliance in 2002. The initial objective was to gain sales for new Nissan vehicles introduced in the European market, but the alliance now extends to full cooperation in all major areas, including the use of common platforms, joint development and use of engines and transmissions, fuel cell research, purchasing and use of common suppliers, and exchange of best practices. When the alliance was formed in 1999, Renault acquired a 36.8 percent ownership stake in Nissan; this was extended to 44.4 percent in 2002 when the alliance was expanded. Also, in 2002, the partners formed a jointly and equally owned strategic management company, named Renault-Nissan, to coordinate cooperative efforts.

2. Intel, the world's largest chip maker, has formed strategic alliances with leading software application providers and computer hardware providers to bring more innovativeness and expertise to the architecture underlying Intel's family of microprocessors and semiconductors. Intel's partners in the effort to enhance Intel's next-generation products include SAP, Oracle, SAS, BEA, IBM, Hewlett-Packard, Dell, Microsoft, Cisco Systems, and Alcatel. One of the alliances between Intel and Cisco involves a collaborative effort in Hong Kong to build next-generation infrastructure for Electronic Product Code/Radio Frequency Identification (EPC/RFID) solutions used to link manufacturers and logistics companies in the Hong Kong region with retailers worldwide. Intel and France-based Alcatel (a leading provider of fixed and mobile broadband access products, marketed in 130 countries) formed an alliance in 2004 to advance the definition, standardization, development, integration, and marketing of WiMAX broadband services solutions. WiMAX was seen as a cost-effective wireless or mobile broadband solution for deployment in both emerging markets and developed countries when, for either economic or technical reasons, it was not feasible to provide urban or rural customers with hardwired DSL broadband access.

3. Verio, a subsidiary of Japan-based NTT Communications and one of the leading global providers of Web hosting services and IP data transport, operates with the philosophy that in today's highly competitive and challenging technology market, companies must gain and share skills, information, and technology with technology leaders across the world. Believing that no company can be all things to all customers in the Web hosting industry, Verio executives have developed an alliance-oriented business model that combines the company's core competencies with the skills and products of best-of-breed, technology partners. Verio's strategic partners include Accenture, Cisco Systems, Microsoft, Sun Microsystems,

Oracle, Arsenal Digital Solutions (a provider of worry-free tape backup, data restore, and data storage services), Internet Security Systems (a provider of firewall and intrusion detection systems), and Mercantec (a developer of storefront and shopping cart software). Verio management believes that its portfolio of strategic alliances allows it to use innovative, best-of-class technologies in providing its customers with fast, efficient, accurate data transport and a complete set of Web hosting services. An independent panel of 12 judges recently selected Verio as the winner of the Best Technology Foresight Award for its efforts in pioneering new technologies.

4. Toyota and First Automotive Works, China's biggest automaker, entered into an alliance in 2002 to make luxury sedans, sport-utility vehicles (SUVs), and minivehicles for the Chinese market. The intent was to make as many as 400,000 vehicles annually by 2010, an amount equal to the number that Volkswagen, the company with the largest share of the Chinese market, was making as of 2002. The alliance envisioned a joint investment of about $1.2 billion. At the time of the announced alliance, Toyota was lagging behind Honda, General Motors, and Volkswagen in setting up production facilities in China. Capturing a bigger share of the Chinese market was seen as crucial to Toyota's success in achieving its strategic objective of having a 15 percent share of the world's automotive market by 2010.

5. Airbus Industrie was formed by an alliance of aerospace companies from Britain, Spain, Germany, and France that included British Aerospace, Daimler-Benz Aerospace, and Aerospatiale. The objective of the alliance was to create a European aircraft company capable of competing with U.S.-based Boeing Corporation. The alliance has proved highly successful, infusing Airbus with the know-how and resources to compete head-to-head with Boeing for world leadership in large commercial aircraft (over 100 passengers).

6. General Motors, DaimlerChrysler, and BMW have entered into an alliance to develop a hybrid gasoline-electric engine that is simpler and less expensive to produce than the hybrid engine technology being pioneered by Toyota. Toyota, the acknowledged world leader in hybrid engines, is endeavoring to establish its design as the industry standard by signing up other automakers to use it. But the technology favored by the General Motors/DaimlerChrysler/BMW alliance is said to be less costly to produce and easier to configure for large trucks and SUVs than Toyota's (although it is also less fuel efficient). Europe's largest automaker, Volkswagen, has allied with Porsche to pursue the development of hybrid engines. Ford Motor and Honda, so far, have elected to go it alone in developing hybrid engine technology.

Sources: Company Web sites and press releases; Yves L. Doz and Gary Hamel, *Alliance Advantage: The Art of Creating Value through Partnering* (Boston, MA: Harvard Business School Press, 1998); and Norihiko Shirouzu and Jathon Sapsford, "As Hybrid Cars Gain Traction, Industry Battles over Designs," *The Wall Street Journal,* October 19, 2005, pp. A1, A9B.

It requires many meetings of many people working in good faith over time to iron out what is to be shared, what is to remain proprietary, and how the cooperative arrangements will work. Often, once the bloom is off the rose, partners discover they have conflicting objectives and strategies, deep differences of opinion about how to proceed, or important differences in corporate values and ethical standards. Tensions build up, working relationships cool, and the hoped-for benefits never materialize.[22]

Even if the alliance becomes a win–win proposition for both parties, there is the danger of becoming overly dependent on foreign partners for essential expertise and competitive capabilities. If a company is aiming for global market leadership and needs to develop capabilities of its own, then at some juncture cross-border merger or acquisition may have to be substituted for cross-border alliances and joint ventures. One of the lessons about cross-border alliances is that they are more effective in helping a company establish a beachhead of new opportunity in world markets than they are in enabling a company to achieve and sustain global market leadership. Global market leaders, while benefiting from alliances, usually must guard against becoming overly dependent on the assistance they get from alliance partners—otherwise, they are not masters of their own destiny.

Strategic alliances are more effective in helping establish a beachhead of new opportunity in world markets than in achieving and sustaining global leadership.

When a Cross-Border Alliance May Be Unnecessary

Experienced multinational companies that market in 50 to 100 or more countries across the world find less need for entering into cross-border alliances than do companies in the early stages of globalizing their operations.[23] Multinational companies make it a point to develop senior managers who understand how "the system" works in different countries; these companies can also avail themselves of local managerial talent and know-how by simply hiring experienced local managers and thereby detouring the hazards of collaborative alliances with local companies. If a multinational enterprise with considerable experience in entering the markets of different countries wants to detour the hazards and hassles of allying with local businesses, it can simply assemble a capable management team consisting of both senior managers with considerable international experience and local managers. The responsibilities of its own in-house managers with international business savvy are (1) to transfer technology, business practices, and the corporate culture into the company's operations in the new country market, and (2) to serve as conduits for the flow of information between the corporate office and local operations. The responsibilities of local managers are (1) to contribute needed understanding of the local market conditions, local buying habits, and local ways of doing business, and (2) in many cases, to head up local operations.

Hence, one cannot automatically presume that a company needs the wisdom and resources of a local partner to guide it through the process of successfully entering the markets of foreign countries. Indeed, experienced multinationals often discover that local partners do not always have adequate local market knowledge—much of the so-called experience of local partners can predate the emergence of current market trends and conditions, and sometimes their operating practices can be archaic.[24]

STRATEGIES THAT FIT THE MARKETS OF EMERGING COUNTRIES

Companies racing for global leadership have to consider competing in emerging markets like China, India, Brazil, Indonesia, and Mexico—countries where the business risks are considerable but where the opportunities for growth are huge, especially as their

Illustration Capsule 7.3

Coca-Cola's Strategy for Growing Its Sales in China and India

In 2004, Coca-Cola developed a strategy to dramatically boost its market penetration in such emerging countries as China and India, where annual growth had recently dropped from about 30 percent in 1994–1998 to 10–12 percent in 2001–2003. Prior to 2003, Coca-Cola had focused its marketing efforts in China and India on making its drinks attractive to status-seeking young people in urbanized areas (cities with populations of 500,000 or more), but as annual sales growth steadily declined in these areas during the 1998–2003 period, Coca-Cola's management decided that the company needed a new, bolder strategy aimed at more rural areas of these countries. It began promoting the sales of 6.5-ounce returnable glass bottles of Coke in smaller cities and outlying towns with populations in the 50,000 to 250,000 range. Returnable bottles (which could be reused about 20 times) were much cheaper than plastic bottles or aluminum cans, and the savings in packaging costs were enough to slash the price of single-serve bottles to one yuan in China and about five rupees in India,

the equivalent in both cases of about 12 cents. Initial results were promising. Despite the fact that annual disposable incomes in these rural areas were often less than $1,000, the one-yuan and five-rupee prices proved attractive. Sales of the small bottles of Coke for one local Coca-Cola distributor in Anning, China, soon accounted for two-thirds of the distributor's total sales; a local distributor in India boosted sales from 9,000 cases in 2002 to 27,000 cases in 2003 and was expecting sales of 45,000 cases in 2004. Coca-Cola management expected that greater emphasis on rural sales would boost its growth rate in Asia to close to 20 percent and help boost worldwide volume growth to the 3–5 percent range as opposed to the paltry 1 percent rate experienced in 2003.

However, Pepsi, which had a market share of about 27 percent in China versus Coca-Cola's 55 percent, was skeptical of Coca-Cola's rural strategy and continued with its all-urban strategy of marketing to consumers in China's 165 cities with populations greater than 1 million people.

Sources: Based on information in Gabriel Kahn and Eric Bellman, "Coke's Big Gamble in Asia: Digging Deeper in China, India," *The Wall Street Journal,* August 11, 2004, pp. A1, A4, plus information at www.cocacola.com (accessed September 20, 2004 and October 6, 2005).

economies develop and living standards climb toward levels in the industrialized world.[25] With the world now comprising more than 6 billion people—fully one-third of whom are in India and China, and hundreds of millions more in other less-developed countries of Asia and in Latin America—a company that aspires to world market leadership (or to sustained rapid growth) cannot ignore the market opportunities or the base of technical and managerial talent such countries offer. For example, in 2003 China's population of 1.3 billion people consumed nearly 33 percent of the world's annual cotton production, 51 percent of the world's pork, 35 percent of all the cigarettes, 31 percent of worldwide coal production, 27 percent of the world's steel production, 19 percent of the aluminum, 23 percent of the TVs, 20 percent of the cell phones, and 18 percent of the washing machines.[26] China is the world's largest consumer of copper, aluminum, and cement and the second largest importer of oil; it is the world's biggest market for mobile phones and the second biggest for PCs, and it is on track to become the second largest market for motor vehicles by 2010.

Illustration Capsule 7.3 describes Coca-Cola's strategy to boost its sales and market share in China.

Tailoring products to fit conditions in an emerging-country market, however, often involves more than making minor product changes and becoming more familiar with local cultures.[27] Ford's attempt to sell a Ford Escort in India at a price of $21,000—a luxury-car price, given that India's best-selling Maruti-Suzuki model sold at the time for $10,000 or less, and that fewer than 10 percent of Indian households have annual purchasing power greater than $20,000—met with a less-than-enthusiastic market response. McDonald's has had to offer vegetable burgers in parts of Asia and to rethink its prices, which are often high by local standards and affordable only by the well-to-do. Kellogg has struggled to introduce its cereals successfully because consumers in many less-developed countries do not eat cereal for breakfast—changing habits is difficult and expensive. In several emerging countries, Coca-Cola has found that advertising its world image does not strike a chord with the local populace in a number of emerging-country markets. Single-serving packages of detergents, shampoos, pickles, cough syrup, and cooking oils are very popular in India because they allow buyers to conserve cash by purchasing only what they need immediately. Thus, many companies find that trying to employ a strategy akin to that used in the markets of developed countries is hazardous.[28] Experimenting with some, perhaps many, local twists is usually necessary to find a strategy combination that works.

Strategy Options

Several strategy options for tailoring a company's strategy to fit the sometimes unusual or challenging circumstances presented in emerging-country markets:

- *Prepare to compete on the basis of low price.* Consumers in emerging markets are often highly focused on price, which can give low-cost local competitors the edge unless a company can find ways to attract buyers with bargain prices as well as better products.[29] For example, when Unilever entered the market for laundry detergents in India, it realized that 80 percent of the population could not afford the brands it was selling to affluent consumers there (or the brands it was selling in wealthier countries). To compete against a low-priced detergent made by a local company, Unilever came up with a low-cost formula that was not harsh to the skin, constructed new low-cost production facilities, packaged the detergent (named Wheel) in single-use amounts so that it could be sold very cheaply, distributed the product to local merchants by handcarts, and crafted an economical marketing campaign that included painted signs on buildings and demonstrations near stores—the new brand quickly captured $100 million in sales and was the number one detergent brand in India in 2004 based on dollar sales. Unilever later replicated the strategy with low-priced packets of shampoos and deodorants in India and in South America with a detergent brand named Ala.

- *Be prepared to modify aspects of the company's business model to accommodate local circumstances (but not so much that the company loses the advantage of global scale and global branding).*[30] For instance when Dell entered China, it discovered that individuals and businesses were not accustomed to placing orders through the Internet (in North America, over 50 percent of Dell's sales in 2002–2005 were online). To adapt, Dell modified its direct sales model to rely more heavily on phone and fax orders and decided to be patient in getting Chinese customers to place Internet orders. Further, because numerous Chinese government departments and state-owned enterprises insisted that hardware vendors make their bids through distributors and systems integrators (as opposed to dealing directly with Dell salespeople as did large enterprises in other countries), Dell opted to use third parties in marketing its products to this buyer segment (although it did sell through its own sales force where it could). But Dell was careful not to abandon those parts of its business model that gave it a competitive edge over rivals. When McDonald's moved into Russia in the 1990s, it was forced to alter its practice of obtaining needed supplies from outside vendors because capable local suppliers were not available; to supply its Russian outlets and stay true to its core principle of serving consistent quality fast food, McDonald's set up its own vertically integrated supply chain (cattle were imported from Holland, russet potatoes were imported from the United States); worked with a select number of Russian bakers for its bread; brought in agricultural specialists from Canada and Europe to improve the management practices of Russian farmers; built its own 100,000-square-foot McComplex to produce hamburgers, French fries, ketchup, mustard, and Big Mac sauce; and set up a trucking fleet to move supplies to restaurants.

- *Try to change the local market to better match the way the company does business elsewhere.*[31] A multinational company often has enough market clout to drive major changes in the way a local country market operates. When Hong Kong–based STAR launched its first satellite TV channel in 1991, it profoundly impacted the TV marketplace in India: The Indian government lost its monopoly on TV broadcasts, several other satellite TV channels aimed at Indian audiences quickly emerged, and the excitement of additional channels triggered a boom in TV manufacturing in India. When Japan's Suzuki entered India in 1981, it triggered a quality revolution among Indian auto parts manufacturers. Local parts and components suppliers teamed up with Suzuki's vendors in Japan and worked with Japanese experts to produce higher-quality products. Over the next two decades, Indian companies became very proficient in making top-notch parts and components for vehicles, won more prizes for quality than companies in any country other than Japan, and broke into the global market as suppliers to many automakers in Asia and other parts of the world.

- *Stay away from those emerging markets where it is impractical or uneconomic to modify the company's business model to accommodate local circumstances.*[32] Home Depot has avoided entry into most Latin American countries because its value proposition of good quality, low prices, and attentive customer service relies on (1) good highways and logistical systems to minimize store inventory costs, (2) employee stock ownership to help motivate store personnel to provide good customer service, and (3) high labor costs for housing construction and home repairs to encourage homeowners to engage in do-it-yourself projects. Relying on these factors in the U.S. market has worked spectacularly for Home Depot, but the company has found that it cannot count on these factors in much of Latin America. Thus, to enter the market in Mexico, Home Depot switched to an acquisition strategy; it has acquired two building supply retailers in Mexico with a total of 40-plus stores. But it has not tried to operate them in the style of its U.S. big-box stores, and it doesn't have retail operations in any other developing nations (although it is exploring entry into China).

Company experiences in entering developing markets like China, India, Russia, and Brazil indicate that profitability seldom comes quickly or easily. Building a market for the company's products can often turn into a long-term process that involves reeducation of consumers, sizable investments in advertising and promotion to alter tastes and buying habits, and upgrades of the local infrastructure (the supplier base, transportation systems, distribution channels, labor markets, and capital markets). In such cases, a company must be patient, work within the system to improve the infrastructure, and lay the foundation for generating sizable revenues and profits once conditions are ripe for market takeoff.

> Profitability in emerging markets rarely comes quickly or easily— new entrants have to adapt their business models and strategies to local conditions and be patient in earning a profit.

Figure 7.4   **Strategy Options for Local Companies in Competing Against Global Companies**

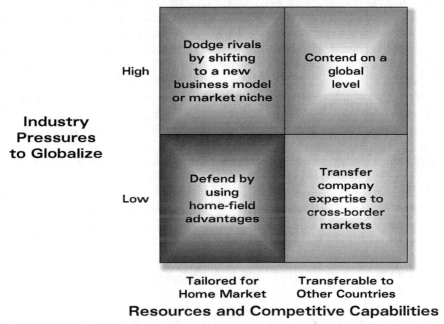

Source: Adapted from Niroj Dawar and Tony Frost, "Competing with Giants: Survival Strategies for Local Companies in Emerging Markets," *Harvard Business Review* 77, no. 1 (January–February 1999), p. 122.

Defending Against Global Giants: Strategies for Local Companies in Emerging Markets

If opportunity-seeking, resource-rich multinational companies are looking to enter emerging markets, what strategy options can local companies use to survive? As it turns out, the prospects for local companies facing global giants are by no means grim. They can employ any of four generic strategic approaches depending on (1) whether their competitive assets are suitable only for the home market or can be transferred abroad, and (2) whether industry pressures to move toward global competition are strong or weak, as shown in Figure 7.4.

Using Home-Field Advantages   When the pressures for competing globally are low and a local firm has competitive strengths well suited to the local market, a good strategy option is to concentrate on the advantages enjoyed in the home market, cater to customers who prefer a local touch, and accept the loss of customers attracted to global brands.[33] A local company may be able to astutely exploit its local orientation— its familiarity with local preferences, its expertise in traditional products, its long-standing customer relationships. In many cases, a local company enjoys a significant cost advantage over global rivals (perhaps because of simpler product design or lower operating and overhead costs), allowing it to compete on the basis of price. Its global competitors often aim their products at upper- and middle-income urban buyers, who tend to be more fashion-conscious, more willing to experiment with new products, and more attracted to global brands.

Another competitive approach is to cater to the local market in ways that pose difficulties for global rivals. A small Middle Eastern cell phone manufacturer competes successfully against industry giants Nokia, Samsung, and Motorola by selling a model designed especially for Muslims—it is loaded with the Koran, alerts people at prayer times, and is equipped with a compass that points them toward Mecca. Several Chinese PC makers have been able to retain customers in competition against global leader Dell because Chinese PC buyers strongly prefer to personally inspect PCs before making a purchase; local PC makers with their extensive retailer networks that allow prospective buyers to check out their offerings in nearby stores have a competitive edge in winning the business of first-time PC buyers vis-à-vis Dell with its build-to-order, sell-direct business strategy (where customers are encouraged to place their orders online or via phone or fax). Bajaj Auto, India's largest producer of scooters, has defended its turf against Honda (which entered the Indian market with local joint venture partner Hero Group to sell scooters, motorcycles, and other vehicles on the basis of its superior technology, quality, and the appeal) by focusing on buyers who wanted low-cost, durable scooters and easy access to maintenance in the countryside. Bajaj designed a rugged, cheap-to-build scooter for India's rough roads, increased its investments in R&D to improve reliability and quality, and created an extensive network of distributors and roadside-mechanic stalls, a strategic approach that allowed it to remain the market leader with a 70–75 percent market share through 2004 despite growing unit sales of Hero Honda motorcycles and scooters.

Transferring the Company's Expertise to Cross-Border Markets   When a company has resource strengths and capabilities suitable for competing in other country markets, launching initiatives to transfer its expertise to cross-border markets becomes a viable strategic option.[34] Televisa, Mexico's largest media company, used its expertise in Spanish culture and linguistics to become the world's most prolific producer of Spanish-language soap operas. Jollibee Foods, a family-owned company with 56 percent of the fast-food business in the Philippines, combated McDonald's entry first by upgrading service and delivery standards and then by using its expertise in seasoning hamburgers with garlic and soy sauce and making noodle and rice meals with fish to open outlets catering to Asian residents in Hong Kong, the Middle East, and California.

Shifting to a New Business Model or Market Niche   When industry pressures to globalize are high, any of the following three options makes the most sense: (1) shift the business to a piece of the industry value chain where the firm's expertise and resources provide competitive advantage, (2) enter into a joint venture with a globally competitive partner, or (3) sell out to (be acquired by) a global entrant into the home market who concludes the company would be a good entry vehicle.[35] When Microsoft entered China, local software developers shifted from cloning Windows products to developing Windows application software customized to the Chinese market. When the Russian PC market opened to IBM, Compaq, and Hewlett-Packard, local Russian PC maker Vist focused on assembling low-cost models, marketing them through exclusive distribution agreements with selected local retailers, and opening company-owned full-service centers in dozens of Russian cities. Vist focused on providing low-cost PCs, giving lengthy warranties, and catering to buyers who felt the need for local service and support. Vist's strategy allowed it to remain the market leader, with a 20 percent share.

An India-based electronics company has been able to carve out a market niche for itself by developing an all-in-one business machine designed especially for India's 1.2 million small shopkeepers that tolerates heat, dust, and power outages and that sells for a modest $180 for the smallest of its three models.[36]

Contending on a Global Level   If a local company in an emerging market has transferable resources and capabilities, it can sometimes launch successful initiatives to meet the pressures for globalization head-on and start to compete on a global level itself.[37] Lenovo, China's biggest PC maker, recently purchased IBM's PC business, moved its headquarters to New York City, put the Lenovo brand on IBM's PCs, and launched initiative to become a global PC maker alongside leaders Dell and Hewlett-Packard. When General Motors (GM) decided to outsource the production of radiator caps for all of its North American vehicles, Sundaram Fasteners of India pursued the opportunity; it purchased one of GM's radiator cap production lines, moved it to India, and became GM's sole supplier of radiator caps in North America—at 5 million units a year. As a participant in GM's supplier network, Sundaram learned about emerging technical standards, built its capabilities, and became one of the first Indian companies to achieve QS 9000 certification, a quality standard that GM now requires for all suppliers. Sundaram's acquired expertise in quality standards enabled it then to pursue opportunities to supply automotive parts in Japan and Europe. Chinese communications equipment maker Huawei has captured a 16 percent share in the global market for Internet routers because its prices are up to 50 percent lower than those of industry leaders like Cisco Systems; Huawei's success in low-priced Internet networking gear has allowed it to expand aggressively outside China, into such country markets as Russia and Brazil, and achieve the number two worldwide market share in broadband networking gear.[38] In 2005 Chinese automakers were laying plans to begin exporting fuel-efficient small cars to the United States and begin the long-term process of competing internationally against the world's leading automakers.

Key Points

Most issues in competitive strategy that apply to domestic companies apply also to companies that compete internationally. But there are four strategic issues unique to competing across national boundaries:

1.   Whether to customize the company's offerings in each different country market to match the tastes and preferences of local buyers or offer a mostly standardized product worldwide.

2.   Whether to employ essentially the same basic competitive strategy in all countries or modify the strategy country by country to fit the specific market conditions and competitive circumstances it encounters.

3.   Where to locate the company's production facilities, distribution centers, and customer service operations so as to realize the greatest locational advantages.

4.   Whether and how to efficiently transfer the company's resource strengths and capabilities from one country to another in an effort to secure competitive advantage.

Multicountry competition refers to situations where competition in one national market is largely independent of competition in another national market—there is no "international market," just a collection of self-contained country (or maybe regional) markets. Global competition exists when competitive conditions across national markets are linked strongly enough to form a true world market and when leading competitors compete head-to-head in many different countries.

In posturing to compete in foreign markets, a company has three basic options: (1) a think-local, act-local approach to crafting a strategy, (2) a think-global, act-global approach to crafting a strategy, and (3) a combination think-global, act-local approach. A think-local, act-local, or multicountry, strategy is appropriate for industries where multicountry competition dominates; a localized approach to strategy making calls for a company to vary its product offering and competitive approach from country to country in order to accommodate differing buyer preferences and market conditions. A think-global, act-global approach (or global strategy) works best in markets that are globally competitive or beginning to globalize; global strategies involve employing the same basic competitive approach (low-cost, differentiation, best-cost, focused) in all country markets and marketing essentially the same products under the same brand names in all countries where the company operates. A think-global, act-local approach can be used when it is feasible for a company to employ essentially the same basic competitive strategy in all markets but still customize its product offering and some aspect of its operations to fit local market circumstances.

Other strategy options for competing in world markets include maintaining a national (one-country) production base and exporting goods to foreign markets, licensing foreign firms to use the company's technology or produce and distribute the company's products, employing a franchising strategy, and using strategic alliances or other collaborative partnerships to enter a foreign market or strengthen a firm's competitiveness in world markets.

Strategic alliances with foreign partners have appeal from several angles: gaining wider access to attractive country markets, allowing capture of economies of scale in production and/or marketing, filling gaps in technical expertise and/or knowledge of local markets, saving on costs by sharing distribution facilities and dealer networks, helping gain agreement on important technical standards, and helping combat the impact of alliances that rivals have formed. Cross-border strategic alliances are fast reshaping competition in world markets, pitting one group of allied global companies against other groups of allied global companies.

There are three ways in which a firm can gain competitive advantage (or offset domestic disadvantages) in global markets. One way involves locating various value chain activities among nations in a manner that lowers costs or achieves greater product differentiation. A second way involves efficient and effective transfer of competitively valuable competencies and capabilities from its domestic markets to foreign markets. A third way draws on a multinational or global competitor's ability to deepen or broaden its resource strengths and capabilities and to coordinate its dispersed activities in ways that a domestic-only competitor cannot.

Profit sanctuaries are country markets in which a company derives substantial profits because of its strong or protected market position. They are valuable competitive assets. A company with multiple profit sanctuaries has the financial strength to support competitive offensives in one market with resources and profits diverted from its operations in other markets—a practice called *cross-market subsidization*. The ability of companies with multiple profit sanctuaries to employ cross-subsidization gives them a powerful offensive weapon and a competitive advantage over companies with a single sanctuary.

Companies racing for global leadership have to consider competing in emerging markets like China, India, Brazil, Indonesia, and Mexico—countries where the business risks are considerable but the opportunities for growth are huge. To succeed in these markets, companies often have to (1) compete on the basis of low price, (2) be prepared to modify aspects of the company's business model to accommodate local circumstances (but not so much that the company loses the advantage of global scale and global branding), and/or (3) try to change the local market to better match the way the company does business elsewhere. Profitability is unlikely to come quickly or easily in emerging markets, typically because of the investments needed to alter buying habits and tastes and/or the need for infrastructure upgrades. And there may be times when a company should simply stay away from certain emerging markets until conditions for entry are better suited to its business model and strategy.

Local companies in emerging country markets can seek to compete against multinational companies by (1) defending on the basis of home-field advantages, (2) transferring their expertise to cross-border markets, (3) dodging large rivals by shifting to a new business model or market niche, or (4) launching initiatives to compete on a global level themselves.

Exercises

1. Go to Caterpillar's Web site (www.caterpillar.com) and search for information about the company's strategy in foreign markets. Is Caterpillar pursuing a global strategy or a localized multicountry strategy? Support your answer.

2. Assume you are in charge of developing the strategy for a multinational company selling products in some 50 different countries around the world. One of the issues you face is whether to employ a multicountry strategy or a global strategy.

    a. If your company's product is personal computers, do you think it would make better strategic sense to employ a multicountry strategy or a global strategy? Why?

    b. If your company's product is dry soup mixes and canned soups, would a multicountry strategy seem to be more advisable than a global strategy? Why?

    c. If your company's product is washing machines, would it seem to make more sense to pursue a multicountry strategy or a global strategy? Why?

    d. If your company's product is basic work tools (hammers, screwdrivers, pliers, wrenches, saws), would a multicountry strategy or a global strategy seem to have more appeal? Why?

3. The Hero Group is among the 10 largest corporations in India, with 19 business segments and annual revenues of $2.75 billion in fiscal 2004–2005. Many of the corporation's business units have used strategic alliances with foreign partners to compete in new product and geographic markets. Review the company's statements concerning its alliances and international business operations at www.herogroup.com and prepare a two-page report that outlines Hero's successful use of international strategic alliances.

4. Using this chapter's discussion of strategies for local companies competing against global rivals and Figure 7.4, develop a strategic approach for a manufacturer or service company in your community that might be forced to compete with a global firm. How might the local company exploit a home-field advantage? Would it make sense for the local company to attempt to transfer its capabilities or expertise to cross-border markets? Or change its business model or market niche? Or join the fight on a global level? Explain.

chapter nine

Diversification

Strategies for Managing a Group of Businesses

To acquire or not to acquire: that is the question.

—Robert J. Terry

Fit between a parent and its businesses is a two-edged sword: a good fit can create value; a bad one can destroy it.

—Andrew Campbell, Michael Goold, and Marcus Alexander

Achieving superior performance through diversification is largely based on relatedness.

—Philippe Very

Make winners out of every business in your company. Don't carry losers.

—Jack Welch
Former CEO, General Electric

We measure each of our businesses against strict criteria: growth, margin, and return-on-capital hurdle rate, and does it have the ability to become number one or two in its industry? We are quite pragmatic. If a business does not contribute to our overall vision, it has to go.

—Richard Wambold
CEO, Pactiv

In this chapter, we move up one level in the strategy-making hierarchy, from strategy making in a single-business enterprise to strategy making in a diversified enterprise. Because a diversified company is a collection of individual businesses, the strategy-making task is more complicated. In a one-business company, managers have to come up with a plan for competing successfully in only a single industry environment—the result is what we labeled in Chapter 2 as *business strategy* (or *business-level strategy*). But in a diversified company, the strategy-making challenge involves assessing multiple industry environments and developing a *set* of business strategies, one for each industry arena in which the diversified company operates. And top executives at a diversified company must still go one step further and devise a company-wide or *corporate strategy* for improving the attractiveness and performance of the company's overall business lineup and for making a rational whole out of its diversified collection of individual businesses.

In most diversified companies, corporate-level executives delegate considerable strategy-making authority to the heads of each business, usually giving them the latitude to craft a business strategy suited to their particular industry and competitive circumstances and holding them accountable for producing good results. But the task of crafting a diversified company's overall or corporate strategy falls squarely in the lap of top-level executives and involves four distinct facets:

1. *Picking new industries to enter and deciding on the means of entry*—The first concerns in diversifying are what new industries to get into and whether to enter by starting a new business from the ground up, acquiring a company already in the target industry, or forming a joint venture or strategic alliance with another company. A company can diversify narrowly into a few industries or broadly into many industries. The choice of whether to enter an industry via a start-up operation; a joint venture; or the acquisition of an established leader, an up-and-coming company, or a troubled company with turnaround potential shapes what position the company will initially stake out for itself.

2. *Initiating actions to boost the combined performance of the businesses the firm has entered*—As positions are created in the chosen industries, corporate strategists typically zero in on ways to strengthen the long-term competitive positions and profits of the businesses the firm has invested in. Corporate parents can help their business subsidiaries by providing financial resources, by supplying missing skills or technological know-how or managerial expertise to better perform key value chain activities, and by providing new avenues for cost reduction. They can also acquire another company in the same industry and merge the two operations into a stronger business, or acquire new businesses that strongly complement existing businesses. Typically, a company will pursue rapid-growth strategies in its most promising businesses, initiate turnaround efforts in weak-performing businesses with potential, and divest businesses that are no longer attractive or that don't fit into management's long-range plans.

3. *Pursuing opportunities to leverage cross-business value chain relationships and strategic fits into competitive advantage*—A company that diversifies into businesses with competitively important value chain matchups (pertaining to technology, supply chain logistics, production, overlapping distribution channels, or common customers) gains competitive advantage potential not open to a company that diversifies into businesses whose value chains are totally unrelated. Capturing this competitive advantage potential requires that corporate strategists spend considerable time trying to capitalize on such cross-business opportunities as transferring skills or technology from one business to another, reducing costs via sharing use of common facilities and resources, and using the company's well-known brand names and distribution muscle to grow the sales of newly acquired products.

4. *Establishing investment priorities and steering corporate resources into the most attractive business units*—A diversified company's different businesses are usually not equally attractive from the standpoint of investing additional funds. It is incumbent on corporate management to (*a*) decide on the priorities for investing capital in the company's different businesses, (*b*) channel resources into areas where earnings potentials are higher and away from areas where they are lower, and (*c*) divest business units that are chronically poor performers or are in an increasingly unattractive industry. Divesting poor performers and businesses in unattractive industries frees up unproductive investments either for redeployment to promising business units or for financing attractive new acquisitions.

The demanding and time-consuming nature of these four tasks explains why corporate executives generally refrain from becoming immersed in the details of crafting and implementing business-level strategies, preferring instead to delegate lead responsibility for business strategy to the heads of each business unit.

In the first portion of this chapter we describe the various means a company can use to become diversified and explore the pros and cons of related versus unrelated diversification strategies. The second part of the chapter looks at how to evaluate the attractiveness of a diversified company's business lineup, decide whether it has a good diversification strategy, and identify ways to improve its future performance. In the chapter's concluding section, we survey the strategic options open to already-diversified companies.

WHEN TO DIVERSIFY

So long as a company has its hands full trying to capitalize on profitable growth opportunities in its present industry, there is no urgency to pursue diversification. The big risk of a single-business company, of course, is having all of the firm's eggs in one industry basket. If demand for the industry's product is eroded by the appearance of alternative technologies, substitute products, or fast-shifting buyer preferences, or if the industry becomes competitively unattractive and unprofitable, then a company's prospects can quickly dim. Consider, for example, what digital cameras have done to erode the revenues of companies dependent on making camera film and doing film processing, what CD and DVD technology have done to business outlook for producers of cassette tapes and 3.5-inch disks, and what cell-phone companies with their no-long-distance-charge plans and marketers of Voice over Internet Protocol (VoIP) are doing to the revenues of such once-dominant long-distance providers as AT&T, British Telecommunications, and NTT in Japan.

Thus, diversifying into new industries always merits strong consideration whenever a single-business company encounters diminishing market opportunities and stagnating sales in its principal business—most landline-based telecommunications companies across the world are quickly diversifying their product offerings to include wireless and VoIP services. But there are four other instances in which a company becomes a prime candidate for diversifying:[1]

1. When it spots opportunities for expanding into industries whose technologies and products complement its present business.

2. When it can leverage existing competencies and capabilities by expanding into businesses where these same resource strengths are key success factors and valuable competitive assets.

3. When diversifying into closely related businesses opens new avenues for reducing costs.

4. When it has a powerful and well-known brand name that can be transferred to the products of other businesses and thereby used as a lever for driving up the sales and profits of such businesses.

The decision to diversify presents wide-open possibilities. A company can diversify into closely related businesses or into totally unrelated businesses. It can diversify its present revenue and earning base to a small extent (such that new businesses account for less than 15 percent of companywide revenues and profits) or to a major extent (such that new businesses produce 30 or more percent of revenues and profits). It can move into one or two large new businesses or a greater number of small ones. It can achieve multibusiness/multi-industry status by acquiring an existing company already in a business/industry it wants to enter, starting up a new business subsidiary from scratch, or forming a joint venture with one or more companies to enter new businesses.

BUILDING SHAREHOLDER VALUE: THE ULTIMATE JUSTIFICATION FOR DIVERSIFYING

Diversification must do more for a company than simply spread its business risk across various industries. In principle, diversification cannot be considered a success unless it results in *added shareholder value*—value that shareholders cannot capture on their own by purchasing stock in companies in different industries or investing in mutual funds so as to spread their investments across several industries.

For there to be reasonable expectations that a company's diversification efforts can produce added value, a move to diversify into a new business must pass three tests:[2]

1. *The industry attractiveness test*—The industry to be entered must be attractive enough to yield consistently good returns on investment. Whether an industry is attractive depends chiefly on the presence of industry and competitive conditions that are conducive to earning as good or better profits and return on investment than the company is earning in its present business(es). It is hard to justify diversifying into an industry where profit expectations are *lower* than in the company's present businesses.

2. *The cost-of-entry test*—The cost to enter the target industry must not be so high as to erode the potential for good profitability. A catch-22 can prevail here, however. The more attractive an industry's prospects are for growth and good long-term profitability, the more expensive it can be to get into. Entry barriers for start-up companies are likely to be high in attractive industries; were barriers low, a rush of new entrants would soon erode the potential for high profitability. And buying a well-positioned company in an appealing industry often entails a high acquisition cost that makes passing the cost-of-entry test less likely. For instance, suppose that the price to purchase a company is $3 million and that the company is earning after-tax profits of $200,000 on an equity investment of $1 million (a 20 percent annual return). Simple arithmetic requires that the profits be tripled if the purchaser (paying $3 million) is to earn the same 20 percent return. Building the acquired firm's earnings from $200,000 to $600,000 annually could take several years—and require additional investment on which the purchaser would also have to earn a 20 percent return. Since the owners of a successful and growing company usually demand a price that reflects their business's profit prospects, it's easy for such an acquisition to fail the cost-of-entry test.

3. *The better-off test*—Diversifying into a new business must offer potential for the company's existing businesses and the new business to perform better together under a single corporate umbrella than they would perform operating as independent, stand-alone businesses. For example, let's say that company A diversifies by purchasing company B in another industry. If A and B's consolidated profits in the years to come prove no greater than what each could have earned on its own, then A's diversification won't provide its shareholders with added value. Company A's shareholders could have achieved the same $1 + 1 = 2$ result by merely purchasing stock in company B. Shareholder value is not created by diversification unless it produces a $1 + 1 = 3$ effect where sister businesses *perform better together* as part of the same firm than they could have performed as independent companies.

> **Core Concept**
> Creating added value for shareholders via diversification requires building a multibusiness company where the whole is greater than the sum of its parts.

Diversification moves that satisfy all three tests have the greatest potential to grow shareholder value over the long term. Diversification moves that can pass only one or two tests are suspect.

STRATEGIES FOR ENTERING NEW BUSINESSES

The means of entering new businesses can take any of three forms: acquisition, internal start-up, or joint ventures with other companies.

Acquisition of an Existing Business

Acquisition is the most popular means of diversifying into another industry. Not only is it quicker than trying to launch a brand-new operation, but it also offers an effective way to hurdle such entry barriers as acquiring technological know-how, establishing supplier relationships, becoming big enough to match rivals' efficiency and unit costs, having to spend large sums on introductory advertising and promotions, and securing adequate distribution. Buying an ongoing operation allows the acquirer to move directly to the task of building a strong market position in the target industry, rather than getting bogged down in going the internal start-up route and trying to develop the knowledge, resources, scale of operation, and market reputation necessary to become an effective competitor within a few years.

The big dilemma an acquisition-minded firm faces is whether to pay a premium price for a successful company or to buy a struggling company at a bargain price.[3] If the buying firm has little knowledge of the industry but ample capital, it is often better off purchasing a capable, strongly positioned firm—unless the price of such an acquisition flunks the cost-of-entry test. However, when the acquirer sees promising ways to transform a weak firm into a strong one and has the resources, the know-how, and the patience to do it, a struggling company can be the better long-term investment.

Internal Start-Up

Achieving diversification through *internal start-up* involves building a new business subsidiary from scratch. This entry option takes longer than the acquisition option and poses some hurdles. A newly formed business unit not only has to overcome entry barriers but also has to invest in new production capacity, develop sources of supply, hire and train employees, build channels of distribution, grow a customer base, and so on. Generally, forming a start-up subsidiary to enter a new business has appeal only when (1) the parent company already has in-house most or all of the skills and resources it needs to piece together a new business and compete effectively; (2) there is ample time to launch the business; (3) internal entry has lower costs than entry via acquisition; (4) the targeted industry is populated with many relatively small firms such that the new start-up does not have to compete head-to-head against larger, more powerful rivals; (5) adding new production capacity will not adversely impact the supply–demand balance in the industry; and (6) incumbent firms are likely to be slow or ineffective in responding to a new entrant's efforts to crack the market.[4]

> The biggest drawbacks to entering an industry by forming an internal start-up are the costs of overcoming entry barriers and the extra time it takes to build a strong and profitable competitive position.

Joint Ventures

Joint ventures entail forming a new corporate entity owned by two or more companies, where the purpose of the joint venture is to pursue a mutually attractive opportunity. The terms and conditions of a joint venture concern joint operation of a mutually owned business, which tends to make the arrangement more definitive and perhaps more durable than a strategic alliance—in a strategic alliance, the arrangement between the partners is one of limited collaboration for a limited purpose and a partner can choose to simply walk away or reduce its commitment at any time.

A joint venture to enter a new business can be useful in at least three types of situations.[5] First, a joint venture is a good vehicle for pursuing an opportunity that is too complex, uneconomical, or risky for one company to pursue alone. Second, joint ventures make sense when the opportunities in a new industry require a broader range of competencies and know-how than a company can marshal. Many of the opportunities in satellite-based telecommunications, biotechnology, and network-based systems that blend hardware, software, and services call for the coordinated development of complementary innovations and tackling an intricate web of financial, technical, political, and regulatory factors simultaneously. In such cases, pooling the resources and competencies of two or more companies is a wiser and less risky way to proceed.

Third, companies sometimes use joint ventures to diversify into a new industry when the diversification move entails having operations in a foreign country—several governments require foreign companies operating within their borders to have a local partner that has minority, if not majority, ownership in the local operations. Aside from fulfilling host government ownership requirements, companies usually seek out a local partner with expertise and other resources that will aid the success of the newly established local operation.

However, as discussed in Chapters 6 and 7, partnering with another company—in either a joint venture or a collaborative alliance—has significant drawbacks due to the potential for conflicting objectives, disagreements over how to best operate the venture, culture clashes, and so on. Joint ventures are generally the least durable of the entry options, usually lasting only until the partners decide to go their own ways.

CHOOSING THE DIVERSIFICATION PATH: RELATED VERSUS UNRELATED BUSINESSES

Core Concept
Related businesses possess competitively valuable cross-business value chain matchups; ***unrelated businesses*** have dissimilar value chains, containing no competitively useful cross-business relationships.

Once a company decides to diversify, its first big strategy decision is whether to diversify into related businesses, unrelated businesses, or some mix of both (see Figure 9.1). *Businesses are said to be related when their value chains possess competitively valuable cross-business relationships that present opportunities for the businesses to perform better under the same corporate umbrella than they could by operating as stand-alone entities.* The big appeal of related diversification is to build shareholder value by leveraging these cross-business relationships into competitive advantage, thus allowing the company as a whole to perform better than just the sum of its individual businesses. *Businesses are said to be unrelated when the activities comprising their respective value chains are so dissimilar that no competitively valuable cross-business relationships are present.*

The next two sections of this chapter explore the ins and outs of related and unrelated diversification.

THE CASE FOR DIVERSIFYING INTO RELATED BUSINESSES

A related diversification strategy involves building the company around businesses whose value chains possess competitively valuable strategic fits, as shown in Figure 9.2. **Strategic fit** exists whenever one or more activities comprising the value chains of different businesses are sufficiently similar as to present opportunities for:[6]

- Transferring competitively valuable expertise, technological know-how, or other capabilities from one business to another.

Figure 9.1 **Strategy Alternatives for a Company Looking to Diversify**

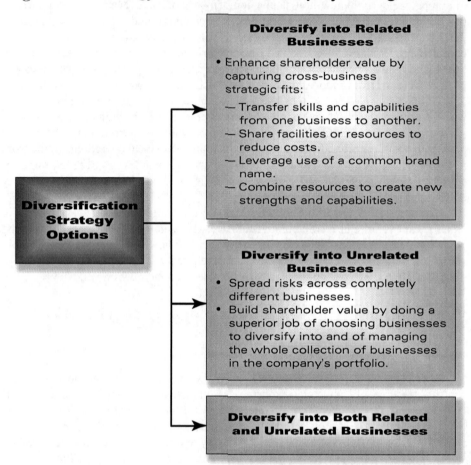

- Combining the related value chain activities of separate businesses into a single operation to achieve lower costs. For instance, it is often feasible to manufacture the products of different businesses in a single plant or use the same warehouses for shipping and distribution or have a single sales force for the products of different businesses (because they are marketed to the same types of customers).
- Exploiting common use of a well-known and potent brand name. For example, Honda's name in motorcycles and automobiles gave it instant credibility and recognition in entering the lawn-mower business, allowing it to achieve a significant market share without spending large sums on advertising to establish a brand identity for its lawn mowers. Canon's reputation in photographic equipment was a competitive asset that facilitated the company's diversification into copying equipment. Sony's name in consumer electronics made it easier and cheaper for Sony to enter the market for video games with its PlayStation console and lineup of PlayStation video games.
- Cross-business collaboration to create competitively valuable resource strengths and capabilities.

Core Concept
Strategic fit exists when the value chains of different businesses present opportunities for cross-business resource transfer, lower costs through combining the performance of related value chain activities, cross-business use of a potent brand name, and cross-business collaboration to build new or stronger competitive capabilities.

Figure 9.2 **Related Businesses Possess Related Value Chain Activities and Competitively Valuable Strategic Fits**

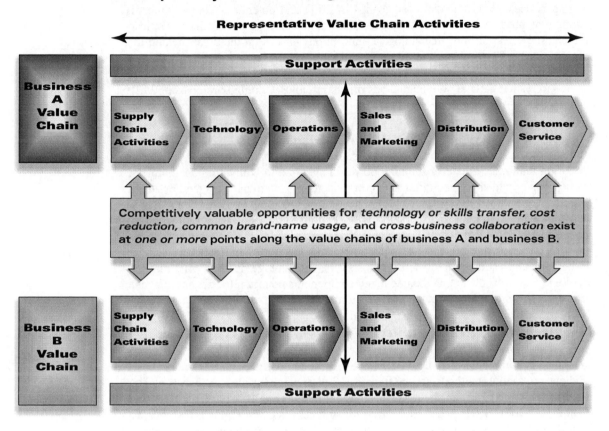

Related diversification thus has strategic appeal from several angles. It allows a firm to reap the competitive advantage benefits of skills transfer, lower costs, a powerful brand name, and/or stronger competitive capabilities and still spread investor risks over a broad business base. Furthermore, the relatedness among the different businesses provides sharper focus for managing diversification and a useful degree of strategic unity across the company's various business activities.

Identifying Cross-Business Strategic Fits along the Value Chain

Cross-business strategic fits can exist anywhere along the value chain—in R&D and technology activities, in supply chain activities and relationships with suppliers, in manufacturing, in sales and marketing, in distribution activities, or in administrative support activities.[7]

Strategic Fits in R&D and Technology Activities   Diversifying into businesses where there is potential for sharing common technology, exploiting the full range of business opportunities associated with a particular technology and its derivatives, or transferring technological know-how from one business to another has considerable appeal. Businesses with technology-sharing benefits can perform better together than apart because of potential cost savings in R&D and potentially shorter times in getting new products to market; also, technological advances in one business can lead to increased sales for both. Technological innovations have been the driver behind the efforts of cable TV companies to diversify into high-speed Internet access (via the use of cable modems) and, further, to explore providing local and long-distance telephone service to residential and commercial customers in either a single wire or using VoIP technology.

Strategic Fits in Supply Chain Activities   Businesses that have supply chain strategic fits can perform better together because of the potential for skills transfer in procuring materials, greater bargaining power in negotiating with common suppliers, the benefits of added collaboration with common supply chain partners, and/or added leverage with shippers in securing volume discounts on incoming parts and components. Dell Computer's strategic partnerships with leading suppliers of microprocessors, motherboards, disk drives, memory chips, flat-panel displays, wireless capabilities, long-life batteries, and other PC-related components have been an important element of the company's strategy to diversify into servers, data storage devices, MP3 players, and LCD TVs—products that include many components common to PCs and that can be sourced from the same strategic partners that provide Dell with PC components.

Manufacturing-Related Strategic Fits   Cross-business strategic fits in manufacturing-related activities can represent an important source of competitive advantage in situations where a diversifier's expertise in quality manufacture and cost-efficient production methods can be transferred to another business. When Emerson Electric diversified into the chain-saw business, it transferred its expertise in low-cost manufacture to its newly acquired Beaird-Poulan business division; the transfer drove Beaird-Poulan's new strategy—to be the low-cost provider of chain-saw products—and fundamentally changed the way Beaird-Poulan chain saws were designed and manufactured. Another benefit of production-related value chain matchups is the ability to consolidate production into a smaller number of plants and significantly reduce overall production costs. When snowmobile maker Bombardier diversified into motorcycles, it was able to set up motorcycle assembly lines in the same manufacturing facility where it was assembling snowmobiles. When Smuckers acquired Procter & Gamble's Jif peanut butter business, it was able to combine the manufacture of its own Smucker's peanut butter products with those of Jif; in addition, it gained greater leverage with vendors in purchasing its peanut supplies.

Distribution-Related Strategic Fits   Businesses with closely related distribution activities can perform better together than apart because of potential cost savings in sharing the same distribution facilities or using many of the same wholesale distributors and retail dealers to access customers. When Sunbeam acquired Mr. Coffee, it was able to consolidate its own distribution centers for small household appliances with those of Mr. Coffee, thereby generating considerable cost savings. Likewise, since Sunbeam products were sold to many of the same retailers as Mr. Coffee products (Wal-Mart, Kmart, Target, department stores, home centers, hardware chains, supermarket chains, and drugstore chains), Sunbeam was able to convince many of the retailers carrying Sunbeam appliances to also take on the Mr. Coffee line and vice versa.

Strategic Fits in Sales and Marketing Activities Various cost-saving opportunities spring from diversifying into businesses with closely related sales and marketing activities. The same distribution centers can be used for warehousing and shipping the products of different businesses. When the products are sold directly to the same customers, sales costs can often be reduced by using a single sales force and avoiding having two different salespeople call on the same customer. The products of related businesses can be promoted at the same Web site, and included in the same media ads and sales brochures. After-sale service and repair organizations for the products of closely related businesses can often be consolidated into a single operation. There may be opportunities to reduce costs by consolidating order processing and billing and using common promotional tie-ins (cents-off couponing, free samples and trial offers, seasonal specials, and the like). When global power-tool maker Black & Decker acquired General Electric's domestic small household appliance business, it was able to use its own global sales force and distribution facilities to sell and distribute the newly acquired GE line of toasters, irons, mixers, and coffeemakers because the types of customers that carried its power tools (discounters like Wal-Mart and Target, home centers, and hardware stores) also stocked small appliances. The economies Black & Decker achieved for both product lines were substantial.

A second category of benefits arises when different businesses use similar sales and marketing approaches; in such cases, there may be competitively valuable opportunities to transfer selling, merchandising, advertising, and product differentiation skills from one business to another. Procter & Gamble's product lineup includes Folgers coffee, Tide laundry detergent, Crest toothpaste, Ivory soap, Charmin toilet tissue, Gillette razors and blades, Duracell batteries, Oral-B toothbrushes, and Head & Shoulders shampoo. All of these have different competitors and different supply chain and production requirements, but they all move through the same wholesale distribution systems, are sold in common retail settings to the same shoppers, are advertised and promoted in much the same ways, and require the same marketing and merchandising skills.

Strategic Fits in Managerial and Administrative Support Activities Often, different businesses require comparable types managerial know-how, thereby allowing know-how in one line of business to be transferred to another. At General Electric (GE), managers who were involved in GE's expansion into Russia were able to expedite entry because of information gained from GE managers involved in expansions into other emerging markets. The lessons GE managers learned in China were passed along to GE managers in Russia, allowing them to anticipate that the Russian government would demand that GE build production capacity in the country rather than enter the market through exporting or licensing. In addition, GE's managers in Russia were better able to develop realistic performance expectations and make tough upfront decisions since experience in China and elsewhere warned them (1) that there would likely be increased short-term costs during the early years of start-up and (2) that if GE committed to the Russian market for the long term and aided the country's economic development it could eventually expect to be given the freedom to pursue profitable penetration of the Russian market.[8]

Likewise, different businesses can often use the same administrative and customer service infrastructure. For instance, an electric utility that diversifies into natural gas, water, appliance sales and repair services, and home security services can use the same customer data network, the same customer call centers and local offices, the same

Illustration Capsule 9.1

Related Diversification at L'Oréal, Johnson & Johnson, PepsiCo, and Darden Restaurants

See if you can identify the value chain relationships that make the businesses of the following companies related in competitively relevant ways. In particular, you should consider whether there are cross-business opportunities for (1) transferring skills/technology, (2) combining related value chain activities to achieve lower costs, (3) leveraging use of a well-respected brand name, and/or (4) establishing cross-business collaboration to create new resource strengths and capabilities.

L'ORÉAL

- Maybelline, Lancôme, Helena Rubenstein, Kiehl's, Garner, and Shu Uemura cosmetics.
- L'Oréal and Soft Sheen/Carson hair care products.
- Redken, Matrix, L'Oréal Professional, and Kerastase Paris professional hair care and skin care products.
- Ralph Lauren and Giorgio Armani fragrances.
- Biotherm skin care products.
- La Roche–Posay and Vichy Laboratories dermocosmetics.

JOHNSON & JOHNSON

- Baby products (powder, shampoo, oil, lotion).
- Band-Aids and other first-aid products.
- Women's health and personal care products (Stayfree, Carefree, Sure & Natural).
- Neutrogena and Aveeno skin care products.

- Nonprescription drugs (Tylenol, Motrin, Pepcid AC, Mylanta, Monistat).
- Prescription drugs.
- Prosthetic and other medical devices.
- Surgical and hospital products.
- Accuvue contact lenses.

PEPSICO

- Soft drinks (Pepsi, Diet Pepsi, Pepsi One, Mountain Dew, Mug, Slice).
- Fruit juices (Tropicana and Dole).
- Sports drinks (Gatorade).
- Other beverages (Aquafina bottled water, SoBe, Lipton ready-to-drink tea, Frappucino—in partnership with Starbucks, international sales of 7UP).
- Snack foods (Fritos, Lay's, Ruffles, Doritos, Tostitos, Santitas, Smart Food, Rold Gold pretzels, Chee-tos, Grandma's cookies, Sun Chips, Cracker Jack, Frito-Lay dips and salsas).
- Cereals, rice, and breakfast products (Quaker oatmeal, Cap'n Crunch, Life, Rice-A-Roni, Quaker rice cakes, Aunt Jemima mixes and syrups, Quaker grits).

DARDEN RESTAURANTS

- Olive Garden restaurant chain (Italian-themed).
- Red Lobster restaurant chain (seafood-themed).
- Bahama Breeze restaurant chain (Caribbean-themed).

Source: Company Web sites, annual reports, and 10-K reports.

billing and customer accounting systems, and the same customer service infrastructure to support all of its products and services.

Illustration Capsule 9.1 lists the businesses of five companies that have pursued a strategy of related diversification.

Strategic Fit, Economies of Scope, and Competitive Advantage

What makes related diversification an attractive strategy is the opportunity to convert cross-business strategic fits into a competitive advantage over business rivals whose operations do not offer comparable strategic-fit benefits. The greater the relatedness among a diversified company's sister businesses, the bigger a company's window for converting strategic fits into competitive advantage via (1) skills transfer, (2) combining related value chain activities to achieve lower costs, (3) leveraging use of a well-respected brand name, and/or (4) cross-business collaboration to create new resource strengths and capabilities.

Economies of Scope: A Path to Competitive Advantage

One of the most important competitive advantages that a related diversification strategy can produce is lower costs than competitors. Related businesses often present opportunities to eliminate or reduce the costs of performing certain value chain activities; such cost savings are termed **economies of scope**—a concept distinct from *economies of scale*. Economies of *scale* are cost savings that accrue directly from a larger-sized operation; for example, unit costs may be lower in a large plant than in a small plant, lower in a large distribution center than in a small one, and lower for large-volume purchases of components than for small-volume purchases. Economies of *scope,* however, stem directly from cost-saving strategic fits along the value chains of related businesses. Such economies are open only to a multibusiness enterprise and are the result of a related diversification strategy that allows sister businesses to share technology, perform R&D together, use common manufacturing or distribution facilities, share a common sales force or distributor/dealer network, use the same established brand name, and/or share the same administrative infrastructure. *The greater the cross-business economies associated with cost-saving strategic fits, the greater the potential for a related diversification strategy to yield a competitive advantage based on lower costs than rivals.*

> **Core Concept**
> *Economies of scope* are cost reductions that flow from operating in multiple businesses; such economies stem directly from strategic fit efficiencies along the value chains of related businesses.

From Competitive Advantage to Added Profitability and Gains in Shareholder Value

The competitive advantage potential that flows from economies of scope and the capture of other strategic-fit benefits is what enables a company pursuing related diversification to achieve $1 + 1 = 3$ financial performance and the hoped-for gains in shareholder value. The strategic and business logic is compelling: Capturing strategic fits along the value chains of its related businesses gives a diversified company a clear path to achieving competitive advantage over undiversified competitors and competitors whose own diversification efforts don't offer equivalent strategic-fit benefits.[9] Such competitive advantage potential provides a company with a dependable basis for earning profits and a return on investment that exceed what the company's businesses could earn as stand-alone enterprises. Converting the competitive advantage potential into greater profitability is what fuels $1 + 1 = 3$ gains in shareholder value—the necessary outcome for satisfying the better-off test and proving the business merit of a company's diversification effort.

> **Core Concept**
> Diversifying into related businesses where competitively valuable strategic fit benefits can be captured puts sister businesses in position to perform better financially as part of the same company than they could have performed as independent enterprises, thus providing a clear avenue for boosting shareholder value.

There are three things to bear in mind here. One, capturing cross-business strategic fits via a strategy of related diversification builds shareholder value in ways that shareholders cannot undertake by simply owning a portfolio of stocks of companies in different industries. Two, the capture of cross-business strategic-fit benefits is possible only via a strategy of related diversification. Three, the benefits of cross-business strategic fits are not automatically realized when a company diversifies into related businesses; *the benefits materialize only after management has successfully pursued internal actions to capture them.*

Figure 9.3   **Unrelated Businesses Have Unrelated Value Chains and No Strategic Fits**

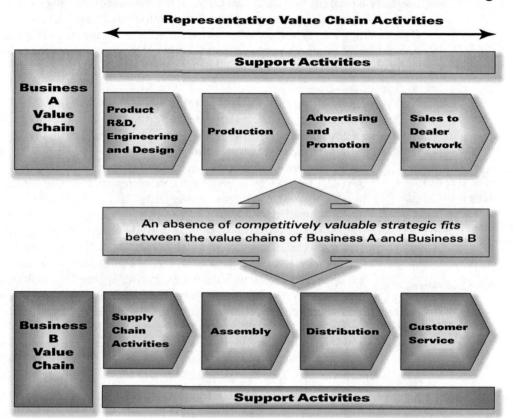

THE CASE FOR DIVERSIFYING INTO UNRELATED BUSINESSES

An unrelated diversification strategy discounts the merits of pursuing cross-business strategic fits and, instead, focuses squarely on entering and operating businesses in industries that allow the company as a whole to grow its revenues and earnings. Companies that pursue a strategy of unrelated diversification generally exhibit a willingness to diversify into *any industry* where senior managers see *opportunity* to realize consistently good financial results—*the basic premise of unrelated diversification is that any company or business that can be acquired on good financial terms and that has satisfactory growth and earnings potential represents a good acquisition and a good business opportunity.* With a strategy of unrelated diversification, the emphasis is on satisfying the attractiveness and cost-of-entry tests and each business's prospects for good financial performance. As indicated in Figure 9.3, there's no deliberate effort to satisfy the better-off test in the sense of diversifying only into businesses having strategic fits with the firm's other businesses.

Thus, with an unrelated diversification strategy, company managers spend much time and effort screening acquisition candidates and evaluating the pros and cons or keeping or divesting existing businesses, using such criteria as:

- Whether the business can meet corporate targets for profitability and return on investment.

- Whether the business is in an industry with attractive growth potential.
- Whether the business is big enough to contribute *significantly* to the parent firm's bottom line.
- Whether the business has burdensome capital requirements (associated with replacing out-of-date plants and equipment, growing the business, and/or providing working capital).
- Whether the business is plagued with chronic union difficulties and labor problems.
- Whether there is industry vulnerability to recession, inflation, high interest rates, tough government regulations concerning product safety or the environment, and other potentially negative factors.

Companies that pursue unrelated diversification nearly always enter new businesses by acquiring an established company rather than by forming a start-up subsidiary within their own corporate structures. The premise of acquisition-minded corporations is that growth by acquisition can deliver enhanced shareholder value through upward-trending corporate revenues and earnings and a stock price that *on average* rises enough year after year to amply reward and please shareholders. Three types of acquisition candidates are usually of particular interest: (1) businesses that have bright growth prospects but are short on investment capital—cash-poor, opportunity-rich businesses are highly coveted acquisition targets for cash-rich companies scouting for good market opportunities; (2) undervalued companies that can be acquired at a bargain price; and (3) struggling companies whose operations can be turned around with the aid of the parent company's financial resources and managerial know-how.

A key issue in unrelated diversification is how wide a net to cast in building a portfolio of unrelated businesses. In other words, should a company pursuing unrelated diversification seek to have few or many unrelated businesses? How much business diversity can corporate executives successfully manage? A reasonable way to resolve the issue of how much diversification comes from answering two questions: "What is the least diversification it will take to achieve acceptable growth and profitability?" and "What is the most diversification that can be managed, given the complexity it adds?"[10] The optimal amount of diversification usually lies between these two extremes.

Illustration Capsule 9.2 lists the businesses of three companies that have pursued unrelated diversification. Such companies are frequently labeled *conglomerates* because their business interests range broadly across diverse industries.

The Merits of an Unrelated Diversification Strategy

A strategy of unrelated diversification has appeal from several angles:

1. Business risk is scattered over a set of truly *diverse* industries. In comparison to related diversification, unrelated diversification more closely approximates *pure* diversification of financial and business risk because the company's investments are spread over businesses whose technologies and value chain activities bear no close relationship and whose markets are largely disconnected.[11]

2. The company's financial resources can be employed to maximum advantage by (*a*) investing in *whatever industries* offer the best profit prospects (as opposed to considering only opportunities in industries with related value chain activities) and (*b*) diverting cash flows from company businesses with lower growth and profit prospects to acquiring and expanding businesses with higher growth and profit potentials.

Illustration Capsule 9.2

Unrelated Diversification at General Electric, United Technologies, American Standard, and Lancaster Colony

The defining characteristic of unrelated diversification is few competitively valuable cross-business relationships. Peruse the business group listings for General Electric, United Technologies, American Standard, and Lancaster Colony and see if you can confirm why these four companies have unrelated diversification strategies.

GENERAL ELECTRIC

- Advanced materials (engineering thermoplastics, silicon-based products and technology platforms, and fused quartz and ceramics)—revenues of $8.3 billion in 2004.
- Commercial and consumer finance (loans, operating leases, financing programs and financial services provided to corporations, retailers, and consumers in 38 countries)—revenues of $39.2 billion in 2004.
- Major appliances, lighting, and integrated industrial equipment, systems and services—revenues of $13.8 billion in 2004.
- Commercial insurance and reinsurance products and services for insurance companies, Fortune 1000 companies, self-insurers, health care providers and other groups—revenues of $23.1 billion in 2004.
- Jet engines for military and civil aircraft, freight and passenger locomotives, motorized systems for mining trucks and drills, and gas turbines for marine and industrial applications—revenues of $15.6 billion in 2004.
- Electric power generation equipment, power transformers, high-voltage breakers, distribution transformers and breakers, capacitors, relays, regulators, substation equipment, metering products—revenues of $17.3 billion in 2004.
- Medical imaging and information technologies, medical diagnostics, patient monitoring systems, disease research, drug discovery and biopharmaceuticals—revenues of $13.5 billion in 2004.
- NBC Universal—owns and operates the NBC television network, a Spanish-language network (Telemundo), several news and entertainment networks (CNBC, MSNBC, Bravo, Sci-Fi Channel, USA Network), Universal Studios, various television production operations, a group of television stations, and theme parks—revenues of $12.9 billion in 2004.
- Chemical treatment programs for water and industrial process systems; precision sensors; security and safety systems for intrusion and fire detection, access and

building control, video surveillance, explosives and drug detection; and real estate services—revenues of $3.4 billion in 2004.
- Equipment services, including Penske truck leasing; operating leases, loans, sales, and asset management services for owners of computer networks, trucks, trailers, railcars, construction equipment, and shipping containers—revenues of $8.5 billion in 2004.

UNITED TECHNOLOGIES

- Pratt & Whitney aircraft engines—2005 revenues of $9.3 billion.
- Carrier heating and air-conditioning equipment—2005 revenues of $12.5 billion.
- Otis elevators and escalators—2005 revenues of $9.6 billion.
- Sikorsky helicopters and Hamilton Sunstrand aerospace systems—2005 revenues of $7.2 billion.
- Chubb fire detection and security systems—2005 revenues of $4.3 billion.

AMERICAN STANDARD

- Trane and American Standard furnaces, heat pumps, and air conditioners—2005 revenues of $6.0 billion.
- American Standard, Ideal Standard, Standard, and Porcher lavatories, toilets, bath tubs, faucets, whirlpool baths, and shower basins—2005 revenues of $2.4 billion.
- Commercial and utility vehicle braking and control systems—2005 revenues of $1.8 billion.

LANCASTER COLONY

- Specialty food products: Cardini, Marzetti, Girard's, and Pheiffer salad dressings; Chatham Village croutons; New York Brand, Sister Schubert, and Mamma Bella frozen breads and rolls; Reames and Aunt Vi's frozen noodles and pastas; Inn Maid and Amish dry egg noodles; and Romanoff caviar—fiscal 2005 revenues of $674 million.
- Candles and glassware: Candle-lite candles; Indiana Glass and Fostoria drinkware and tabletop items; Colony giftware; and Brody floral containers—fiscal 2005 revenues of $234 million.
- Automotive products: Rubber Queen automotive floor mats; Dee Zee aluminum accessories and running boards for light trucks; Protecta truck bed mats; and assorted other truck accessories—fiscal 2005 revenues of $224 million.

Source: Company Web sites, annual reports, and 10-K reports.

3. To the extent that corporate managers are exceptionally astute at spotting bargain-priced companies with big upside profit potential, shareholder wealth can be enhanced by buying distressed businesses at a low price, turning their operations around fairly quickly with infusions of cash and managerial know-how supplied by the parent company, and then riding the crest of the profit increases generated by the newly acquired businesses.

4. Company profitability may prove somewhat more stable over the course of economic upswings and downswings because market conditions in all industries don't move upward or downward simultaneously—in a broadly diversified company, there's a chance that market downtrends in some of the company's businesses will be partially offset by cyclical upswings in its other businesses, thus producing somewhat less earnings volatility. (In actual practice, however, there's no convincing evidence that the consolidated profits of firms with unrelated diversification strategies are more stable or less subject to reversal in periods of recession and economic stress than the profits of firms with related diversification strategies.)

Unrelated diversification certainly merits consideration when a firm is trapped in or overly dependent on an endangered or unattractive industry, especially when it has no competitively valuable resources or capabilities it can transfer to an adjacent industry. A case can also be made for unrelated diversification when a company has a strong preference for spreading business risks widely and not restricting itself to investing in a family of closely related businesses.

Building Shareholder Value via Unrelated Diversification   Given the absence of cross-business strategic fits with which to capture added competitive advantage, the task of building shareholder value via unrelated diversification ultimately hinges on the business acumen of corporate executives. To succeed in using a strategy of unrelated diversification to produce companywide financial results above and beyond what the businesses could generate operating as stand-alone entities, corporate executives must:

- Do a superior job of diversifying into new businesses that can produce consistently good earnings and returns on investment (thereby satisfying the attractiveness test).
- Do an excellent job of negotiating favorable acquisition prices (thereby satisfying the cost-of-entry test).
- Do such a good job overseeing the firm's business subsidiaries and contributing to how they are managed—by providing expert problem-solving skills, creative strategy suggestions, and high caliber decision-making guidance to the heads of the various business subsidiaries—that the subsidiaries perform at a higher level than they would otherwise be able to do through the efforts of the business-unit heads alone (a possible way to satisfy the better-off test).
- Be shrewd in identifying when to shift resources out of businesses with dim profit prospects and into businesses with above-average prospects for growth and profitability.
- Be good at discerning when a business needs to be sold (because it is on the verge of confronting adverse industry and competitive conditions and probable declines in long-term profitability) and also finding buyers who will pay a price higher than the company's net investment in the business (so that the sale of divested businesses will result in capital gains for shareholders rather than capital losses).

To the extent that corporate executives are able to craft and execute a strategy of unrelated diversification that produces enough of the above outcomes to result in a stream of dividends and capital gains for stockholders greater than a $1 + 1 = 2$ outcome, a case can be made that shareholder value has truly been enhanced.

The Drawbacks of Unrelated Diversification

Unrelated diversification strategies have two important negatives that undercut the pluses: demanding managerial requirements and limited competitive advantage potential.

Demanding Managerial Requirements Successfully managing a set of fundamentally different businesses operating in fundamentally different industry and competitive environments is an exceptionally challenging proposition for corporate-level managers. It is difficult because key executives at the corporate level, while perhaps having personally worked in one or two of the company's businesses, rarely have the time and expertise to be sufficiently familiar with all the circumstances surrounding each of the company's businesses to be in a position to give high-caliber guidance to business-level managers. Indeed, the greater the number of businesses a company is in and the more diverse they are, the harder it is for corporate managers to (1) stay abreast of what's happening in each industry and each subsidiary and thus judge whether a particular business has bright prospects or is headed for trouble, (2) know enough about the issues and problems facing each subsidiary to pick business-unit heads having the requisite combination of managerial skills and know-how, (3) be able to tell the difference between those strategic proposals of business-unit managers that are prudent and those that are risky or unlikely to succeed, and (4) know what to do if a business unit stumbles and its results suddenly head downhill.[12]

> **Core Concept**
> The two biggest drawbacks to unrelated diversification are the difficulties of competently managing many different businesses and being without the added source of competitive advantage that cross-business strategic fit provides.

In a company like General Electric (see Illustration Capsule 9.2) or Tyco International (which acquired over 1,000 companies during the 1990–2001 period), corporate executives are constantly scrambling to stay on top of fresh industry developments and the strategic progress and plans of each subsidiary, often depending on briefings by business-level managers for many of the details. As a rule, the more unrelated businesses that a company has diversified into, the more corporate executives are dependent on briefings from business unit heads and "managing by the numbers"—that is, keeping a close track on the financial and operating results of each subsidiary and assuming that the heads of the various subsidiaries have most everything under control so long as the latest key financial and operating measures look good. Managing by the numbers works if the heads of the various business units are quite capable and consistently meet their numbers. But the problem comes when things start to go awry in a business despite the best effort of business-unit managers and corporate management has to get deeply involved in turning around a business it does not know all that much about—as the former chairman of a Fortune 500 company advised, "Never acquire a business you don't know how to run." Because every business tends to encounter rough sledding, a good way to gauge the merits of acquiring a company in an unrelated industry is to ask, "If the business got into trouble, is corporate management likely to know how to bail it out?" When the answer is no (or even a qualified yes or maybe), growth via acquisition into unrelated businesses is a chancy strategy.[13] Just one or two unforeseen declines or big strategic mistakes (misjudging the importance of certain competitive forces or the impact of driving forces or key success factors, encountering unexpected problems in a newly acquired business, or being too optimistic about turning around a struggling subsidiary) can cause a precipitous drop in corporate earnings and crash the parent company's stock price.

Relying solely on the expertise of corporate executives to wisely manage a set of unrelated businesses is *a much weaker foundation for enhancing shareholder value* than is a strategy of related diversification where corporate performance can be boosted by competitively valuable cross-business strategic fits.

Hence, competently overseeing a set of widely diverse businesses can turn out to be much harder than it sounds. In practice, comparatively few companies have proved up to the task. There are far more companies whose corporate executives have failed at delivering consistently good financial results with an unrelated diversification strategy than there are companies with corporate executives who have been successful.[14] It is simply very difficult for corporate executives to achieve $1 + 1 = 3$ gains in shareholder value based on their expertise in (*a*) picking which industries to diversify into and which companies in these industries to acquire, (*b*) shifting resources from low-performing businesses into high-performing businesses, and (*c*) giving high-caliber decision-making guidance to the general managers of their business subsidiaries. The odds are that the result of unrelated diversification will be $1 + 1 = 2$ or less.

Limited Competitive Advantage Potential   The second big negative is that *unrelated diversification offers no potential for competitive advantage beyond what each individual business can generate on its own.* Unlike a related diversification strategy, there are no cross-business strategic fits to draw on for reducing costs, beneficially transferring skills and technology, leveraging use of a powerful brand name, or collaborating to build mutually beneficial competitive capabilities and thereby *adding to any competitive advantage possessed by individual businesses.* Yes, a cash-rich corporate parent pursuing unrelated diversification can provide its subsidiaries with much-needed capital and maybe even the managerial know-how to help resolve problems in particular business units, but otherwise it has little to offer in the way of enhancing the competitive strength of its individual business units. *Without the competitive advantage potential of strategic fits, consolidated performance of an unrelated group of businesses stands to be little or no better than the sum of what the individual business units could achieve if they were independent.*

COMBINATION RELATED–UNRELATED DIVERSIFICATION STRATEGIES

There's nothing to preclude a company from diversifying into both related and unrelated businesses. Indeed, in actual practice the business makeup of diversified companies varies considerably. Some diversified companies are really *dominant-business enterprises*—one major "core" business accounts for 50 to 80 percent of total revenues and a collection of small related or unrelated businesses accounts for the remainder. Some diversified companies are *narrowly diversified* around a few (two to five) related or unrelated businesses. Others are *broadly diversified* around a wide-ranging collection of related businesses, unrelated businesses, or a mixture of both. And a number of multibusiness enterprises have diversified into unrelated areas but have a collection of related businesses within each area—thus giving them a business portfolio consisting of *several unrelated groups of related businesses.* There's ample room for companies to customize their diversification strategies to incorporate elements of both related and unrelated diversification, as may suit their own risk preferences and strategic vision.

Figure 9.4 **Identifying a Diversified Company's Strategy**

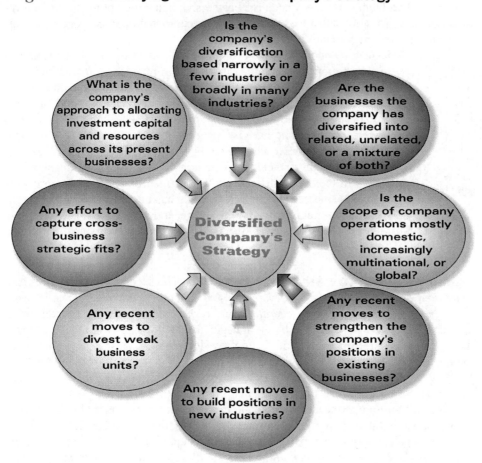

Figure 9.4 indicates what to look for in identifying the main elements of a company's diversification strategy. Having a clear fix on the company's current corporate strategy sets the stage for evaluating how good the strategy is and proposing strategic moves to boost the company's performance.

EVALUATING THE STRATEGY OF A DIVERSIFIED COMPANY

Strategic analysis of diversified companies builds on the concepts and methods used for single-business companies. But there are some additional aspects to consider and a couple of new analytical tools to master. The procedure for evaluating the pluses and minuses of a diversified company's strategy and deciding what actions to take to improve the company's performance involves six steps:

1. Assessing the attractiveness of the industries the company has diversified into, both individually and as a group.
2. Assessing the competitive strength of the company's business units and determining how many are strong contenders in their respective industries.

3. Checking the competitive advantage potential of cross-business strategic fits among the company's various business units.

4. Checking whether the firm's resources fit the requirements of its present business lineup.

5. Ranking the performance prospects of the businesses from best to worst and determining what the corporate parent's priority should be in allocating resources to its various businesses.

6. Crafting new strategic moves to improve overall corporate performance.

The core concepts and analytical techniques underlying each of these steps merit further discussion.

Step 1: Evaluating Industry Attractiveness

A principal consideration in evaluating a diversified company's business makeup and the caliber of its strategy is the attractiveness of the industries in which it has business operations. Answers to several questions are required:

1. *Does each industry the company has diversified into represent a good business for the company to be in?* Ideally, each industry in which the firm operates will pass the attractiveness test.

2. *Which of the company's industries are most attractive and which are least attractive?* Comparing the attractiveness of the industries and ranking them from most to least attractive is a prerequisite to wise allocation of corporate resources across the various businesses.

3. *How appealing is the whole group of industries in which the company has invested?* The answer to this question points to whether the group of industries holds promise for attractive growth and profitability. A company whose revenues and profits come chiefly from businesses in relatively unattractive industries probably needs to look at divesting businesses in unattractive industries and entering industries that qualify as highly attractive.

The more attractive the industries (both individually and as a group) a diversified company is in, the better its prospects for good long-term performance.

Calculating Industry Attractiveness Scores for Each Industry into Which the Company Has Diversified   A simple and reliable analytical tool involves calculating quantitative industry attractiveness scores, which can then be used to gauge each industry's attractiveness, rank the industries from most to least attractive, and make judgments about the attractiveness of all the industries as a group.

The following measures are typically used to gauge an industry's attractiveness:

- *Market size and projected growth rate*—Big industries are more attractive than small industries, and fast-growing industries tend to be more attractive than slow-growing industries, other things being equal.

- *The intensity of competition*—Industries where competitive pressures are relatively weak are more attractive than industries where competitive pressures are strong.

- *Emerging opportunities and threats*—Industries with promising opportunities and minimal threats on the near horizon are more attractive than industries with modest opportunities and imposing threats.

- *The presence of cross-industry strategic fits*—The more the industry's value chain and resource requirements match up well with the value chain activities of other industries in which the company has operations, the more attractive the industry is to a firm pursuing related diversification. However, cross-industry strategic fits may be of no consequence to a company committed to a strategy of unrelated diversification.

- *Resource requirements*—Industries having resource requirements within the company's reach are more attractive than industries where capital and other resource requirements could strain corporate financial resources and organizational capabilities.

- *Seasonal and cyclical factors*—Industries where buyer demand is relatively steady year-round and not unduly vulnerable to economic ups and downs tend to be more attractive than industries where there are wide swings in buyer demand within or across years. However, seasonality may be a plus for a company that is in several seasonal industries, if the seasonal highs in one industry correspond to the lows in another industry, thus helping even out monthly sales levels. Likewise, cyclical market demand in one industry can be attractive if its up-cycle runs counter to the market down-cycles in another industry where the company operates, thus helping reduce revenue and earnings volatility.

- *Social, political, regulatory, and environmental factors*—Industries with significant problems in such areas as consumer health, safety, or environmental pollution or that are subject to intense regulation are less attractive than industries where such problems are not burning issues.

- *Industry profitability*—Industries with healthy profit margins and high rates of return on investment are generally more attractive than industries where profits have historically been low or unstable.

- *Industry uncertainty and business risk*—Industries with less uncertainty on the horizon and lower overall business risk are more attractive than industries whose prospects for one reason or another are quite uncertain, especially when the industry has formidable resource requirements.

After settling on a set of attractiveness measures that suit a diversified company's circumstances, each attractiveness measure is assigned a weight reflecting its relative importance in determining an industry's attractiveness—it is weak methodology to assume that the various attractiveness measures are equally important. The intensity of competition in an industry should nearly always carry a high weight (say, 0.20 to 0.30). Strategic-fit considerations should be assigned a high weight in the case of companies with related diversification strategies; but, for companies with an unrelated diversification strategy, strategic fits with other industries may be given a low weight or even dropped from the list of attractiveness measures altogether. Seasonal and cyclical factors generally are assigned a low weight (or maybe even eliminated from the analysis) unless a company has diversified into industries strongly characterized by seasonal demand and/or heavy vulnerability to cyclical upswings and downswings. The importance weights must add up to 1.0.

Next, each industry is rated on each of the chosen industry attractiveness measures, using a rating scale of 1 to 10 (where a *high* rating signifies *high* attractiveness and a *low* rating signifies *low* attractiveness). *Keep in mind here that the more intensely competitive an industry is, the lower the attractiveness rating for that industry.* Likewise, the higher the capital and resource requirements associated with being in a particular industry, the lower the attractiveness rating. And an industry that is subject

Table 9.1   **Calculating Weighted Industry Attractiveness Scores**

Industry Attractiveness Measure	Importance Weight	Industry A Rating/ Score	Industry B Rating/ Score	Industry C Rating/ Score	Industry D Rating/ Score
Market size and projected growth rate	0.10	8/0.80	5/0.50	7/0.70	3/0.30
Intensity of competition	0.25	8/2.00	7/1.75	3/0.75	2/0.50
Emerging opportunities and threats	0.10	2/0.20	9/0.90	4/0.40	5/0.50
Cross-industry strategic fits	0.20	8/1.60	4/0.80	8/1.60	2/0.40
Resource requirements	0.10	9/0.90	7/0.70	10/1.00	5/0.50
Seasonal and cyclical influences	0.05	9/0.45	8/0.40	10/0.50	5/0.25
Societal, political, regulatory, and environmental factors	0.05	10/1.00	7/0.70	7/0.70	3/0.30
Industry profitability	0.10	5/0.50	10/1.00	3/0.30	3/0.30
Industry uncertainty and business risk	0.05	5/0.25	7/0.35	10/0.50	1/0.05
Sum of the assigned weights	1.00				
Overall industry attractiveness scores		**7.70**	**7.10**	**5.45**	**3.10**

Rating scale: 1 = Very unattractive to company; 10 = Very attractive to company.

to stringent pollution control regulations or that causes societal problems (like cigarettes or alcoholic beverages) should usually be given a low attractiveness rating. Weighted attractiveness scores are then calculated by multiplying the industry's rating on each measure by the corresponding weight. For example, a rating of 8 times a weight of 0.25 gives a weighted attractiveness score of 2.00. The sum of the weighted scores for all the attractiveness measures provides an overall industry attractiveness score. This procedure is illustrated in Table 9.1.

Interpreting the Industry Attractiveness Scores   Industries with a score much below 5.0 probably do not pass the attractiveness test. If a company's industry attractiveness scores are all above 5.0, it is probably fair to conclude that the group of industries the company operates in is attractive as a whole. But the group of industries takes on a decidedly lower degree of attractiveness as the number of industries with scores below 5.0 increases, especially if industries with low scores account for a sizable fraction of the company's revenues.

For a diversified company to be a strong performer, a substantial portion of its revenues and profits must come from business units with relatively high attractiveness scores. It is particularly important that a diversified company's principal businesses be in industries with a good outlook for growth and above-average profitability. Having a big fraction of the company's revenues and profits come from industries with slow growth, low profitability, or intense competition tends to drag overall company performance down. Business units in the least attractive industries are potential candidates for divestiture, unless they are positioned strongly enough to overcome the unattractive aspects of their industry environments or they are a strategically important component of the company's business makeup.

The Difficulties of Calculating Industry Attractiveness Scores   There are two hurdles to calculating industry attractiveness scores. One is deciding on appropriate weights for the industry attractiveness measures. Not only may different analysts have different views about which weights are appropriate for the different attractiveness measures but also different weightings may be appropriate for different companies—based on their strategies, performance targets, and financial circumstances. For instance, placing a low weight on industry resource requirements may be justifiable for a cash-rich company, whereas a high weight may be more appropriate for a financially strapped company. The second hurdle is gaining sufficient command of the industry to assign accurate and objective ratings. Generally, a company can come up with the statistical data needed to compare its industries on such factors as market size, growth rate, seasonal and cyclical influences, and industry profitability. Cross-industry fits and resource requirements are also fairly easy to judge. But the attractiveness measure where judgment weighs most heavily is that of intensity of competition. It is not always easy to conclude whether competition in one industry is stronger or weaker than in another industry because of the different types of competitive influences that prevail and the differences in their relative importance. In the event that the available information is too skimpy to confidently assign a rating value to an industry on a particular attractiveness measure, then it is usually best to use a score of 5, which avoids biasing the overall attractiveness score either up or down.

But despite the hurdles, calculating industry attractiveness scores is a systematic and reasonably reliable method for ranking a diversified company's industries from most to least attractive—numbers like those shown for the four industries in Table 9.1 help pin down the basis for judging which industries are more attractive and to what degree.

Step 2: Evaluating Business-Unit Competitive Strength

The second step in evaluating a diversified company is to appraise how strongly positioned each of its business units are in their respective industry. Doing an appraisal of each business unit's strength and competitive position in its industry not only reveals its chances for industry success but also provides a basis for ranking the units from competitively strongest to competitively weakest and sizing up the competitive strength of all the business units as a group.

Calculating Competitive Strength Scores for Each Business Unit   Quantitative measures of each business unit's competitive strength can be calculated using a procedure similar to that for measuring industry attractiveness. The following factors are using in quantifying the competitive strengths of a diversified company's business subsidiaries:

- *Relative market share*—A business unit's *relative market share* is defined as the ratio of its market share to the market share held by the largest rival firm in the industry, with market share measured in unit volume, not dollars. For instance, if business A has a market-leading share of 40 percent and its largest rival has 30 percent, A's relative market share is 1.33. (Note that only business units that are market share leaders in their respective industries can have relative market shares greater then 1.0.) If business B has a 15 percent market share and B's largest rival has 30 percent, B's relative market share is 0.5. *The further below 1.0 a business unit's relative market share is, the weaker its competitive strength and market position vis-à-vis rivals.* A 10 percent market share, for example, does not signal much competitive strength if the leader's share is 50 percent

> Using relative market share to measure competitive strength is analytically superior to using straight-percentage market share.

(a 0.20 relative market share), but a 10 percent share is actually quite strong if the leader's share is only 12 percent (a 0.83 relative market share)—this is why a company's relative market share is a better measure of competitive strength than a company's market share based on either dollars or unit volume.

- *Costs relative to competitors' costs*—Business units that have low costs relative to key competitors' costs tend to be more strongly positioned in their industries than business units struggling to maintain cost parity with major rivals. Assuming that the prices charged by industry rivals are about the same, there's reason to expect that business units with higher relative market shares have lower unit costs than competitors with lower relative market shares because their greater unit sales volumes offer the possibility of economies from larger-scale operations and the benefits of any experience/learning curve effects. Another indicator of low cost can be a business unit's supply chain management capabilities. The only time when a business unit's competitive strength may not be undermined by having higher costs than rivals is when it has incurred the higher costs to strongly differentiate its product offering and its customers are willing to pay premium prices for the differentiating features.

- *Ability to match or beat rivals on key product attributes*—A company's competitiveness depends in part on being able to satisfy buyer expectations with regard to features, product performance, reliability, service, and other important attributes.

- *Ability to benefit from strategic fits with sister businesses*—Strategic fits with other businesses within the company enhance a business unit's competitive strength and may provide a competitive edge.

- *Ability to exercise bargaining leverage with key suppliers or customers*—Having bargaining leverage signals competitive strength and can be a source of competitive advantage.

- *Caliber of alliances and collaborative partnerships with suppliers and/or buyers*—Well-functioning alliances and partnerships may signal a potential competitive advantage vis-à-vis rivals and thus add to a business's competitive strength. Alliances with key suppliers are often the basis for competitive strength in supply chain management.

- *Brand image and reputation*—A strong brand name is a valuable competitive asset in most industries.

- *Competitively valuable capabilities*—Business units recognized for their technological leadership, product innovation, or marketing prowess are usually strong competitors in their industry. Skills in supply chain management can generate valuable cost or product differentiation advantages. So can unique production capabilities. Sometimes a company's business units gain competitive strength because of their knowledge of customers and markets and/or their proven managerial capabilities. *An important thing to look for here is how well a business unit's competitive assets match industry key success factors.* The more a business unit's resource strengths and competitive capabilities match the industry's key success factors, the stronger its competitive position tends to be.

- *Profitability relative to competitors*—Business units that consistently earn above-average returns on investment and have bigger profit margins than their rivals usually have stronger competitive positions. Moreover, above-average profitability signals competitive advantage, while below-average profitability usually denotes competitive disadvantage.

Table 9.2   **Calculating Weighted Competitive Strength Scores for a Diversified Company's Business Units**

Competitive Strength Measure	Importance Weight	Business A in Industry A Rating/ Score	Business B in Industry B Rating/ Score	Business C in Industry C Rating/ Score	Business D in Industry D Rating/ Score
Relative market share	0.15	10/1.50	1/0.15	6/0.90	2/0.30
Costs relative to competitors' costs	0.20	7/1.40	2/0.40	5/1.00	3/0.60
Ability to match or beat rivals on key product attributes	0.05	9/0.45	4/0.20	8/0.40	4/0.20
Ability to benefit from strategic fits with sister businesses	0.20	8/1.60	4/0.80	8/0.80	2/0.60
Bargaining leverage with suppliers/ buyers; caliber of alliances	0.05	9/0.90	3/0.30	6/0.30	2/0.10
Brand image and reputation	0.10	9/0.90	2/0.20	7/0.70	5/0.50
Competitively valuable capabilities	0.15	7/1.05	2/0.20	5/0.75	3/0.45
Profitability relative to competitors	0.10	5/0.50	1/0.10	4/0.40	4/0.40
Sum of the assigned weights	1.00				
Overall industry attractiveness scores		**8.30**	**2.35**	**5.25**	**3.15**

Rating scale: 1 = Very weak; 10 = Very strong.

After settling on a set of competitive strength measures that are well matched to the circumstances of the various business units, weights indicating each measure's importance need to be assigned. A case can be made for using different weights for different business units whenever the importance of the strength measures differs significantly from business to business, but otherwise it is simpler just to go with a single set of weights and avoid the added complication of multiple weights. As before, the importance weights must add up to 1.0. Each business unit is then rated on each of the chosen strength measures, using a rating scale of 1 to 10 (where a *high* rating signifies competitive *strength* and a *low* rating signifies competitive *weakness*). In the event that the available information is too skimpy to confidently assign a rating value to a business unit on a particular strength measure, then it is usually best to use a score of 5, which avoids biasing the overall score either up or down. Weighted strength ratings are calculated by multiplying the business unit's rating on each strength measure by the assigned weight. For example, a strength score of 6 times a weight of 0.15 gives a weighted strength rating of 0.90. The sum of weighted ratings across all the strength measures provides a quantitative measure of a business unit's overall market strength and competitive standing. Table 9.2 provides sample calculations of competitive strength ratings for four businesses.

Interpreting the Competitive Strength Scores   Business units with competitive strength ratings above 6.7 (on a scale of 1 to 10) are strong market contenders in their industries. Businesses with ratings in the 3.3 to 6.7 range have moderate competitive strength vis-à-vis rivals. Businesses with ratings below 3.3 are in competitively weak market positions. If a diversified company's business units all have competitive strength scores above 5.0, it is fair to conclude that its business units are all fairly strong market contenders in their respective industries. But as the number of business units with scores below 5.0 increases, there's reason to question whether the company can perform well with so many businesses in relatively weak competitive positions. This concern takes on even more importance when business units with low scores account for a sizable fraction of the company's revenues.

Using a Nine-Cell Matrix to Simultaneously Portray Industry Attractiveness and Competitive Strength   The industry attractiveness and competitive strength scores can be used to portray the strategic positions of each business in a diversified company. Industry attractiveness is plotted on the vertical axis, and competitive strength on the horizontal axis. A nine-cell grid emerges from dividing the vertical axis into three regions (high, medium, and low attractiveness) and the horizontal axis into three regions (strong, average, and weak competitive strength). As shown in Figure 9.5, high attractiveness is associated with scores of 6.7 or greater on a rating scale of 1 to 10, medium attractiveness to scores of 3.3 to 6.7, and low attractiveness to scores below 3.3. Likewise, high competitive strength is defined as a score greater than 6.7, average strength as scores of 3.3 to 6.7, and low strength as scores below 3.3. *Each business unit is plotted on the nine-cell matrix according to its overall attractiveness score and strength score, and then shown as a bubble.* The size of each bubble is scaled to what percentage of revenues the business generates relative to total corporate revenues. The bubbles in Figure 9.5 were located on the grid using the four industry attractiveness scores from Table 9.1 and the strength scores for the four business units in Table 9.2.

The locations of the business units on the attractiveness–strength matrix provide valuable guidance in deploying corporate resources to the various business units. In general, *a diversified company's prospects for good overall performance are enhanced by concentrating corporate resources and strategic attention on those business units having the greatest competitive strength and positioned in highly attractive industries*—specifically, businesses in the three cells in the upper left portion of the attractiveness–strength matrix, where industry attractiveness and competitive strength/ market position are both favorable. The general strategic prescription for businesses falling in these three cells (for instance, business A in Figure 9.5) is "grow and build," with businesses in the high–strong cell standing first in line for resource allocations by the corporate parent.

Next in priority come businesses positioned in the three diagonal cells stretching from the lower left to the upper right (businesses B and C in Figure 9.5). Such businesses usually merit medium or intermediate priority in the parent's resource allocation ranking. However, some businesses in the medium-priority diagonal cells may have brighter or dimmer prospects than others. For example, a small business in the upper right cell of the matrix (like business B), despite being in a highly attractive industry, may occupy too weak a competitive position in its industry to justify the investment and resources needed to turn it into a strong market contender and shift its position leftward in the matrix over time. If, however, a business in the upper right cell has attractive opportunities for rapid growth and a good potential for winning a much stronger market position over time, it may merit a high claim on the corporate parent's resource allocation ranking and be given the capital it needs to pursue a grow-and-build strategy–the strategic objective here would be to move the business leftward in the attractiveness–strength matrix over time.

Businesses in the three cells in the lower right corner of the matrix (like business D in Figure 9.5) typically are weak performers and have the lowest claim on corporate resources. Most such businesses are good candidates for being divested (sold to other companies) or else managed in a manner calculated to squeeze out the maximum cash flows from operations—the cash flows from low-performing/low-potential businesses

Figure 9.5   **A Nine-Cell Industry Attractiveness–Competitive Strength Matrix**

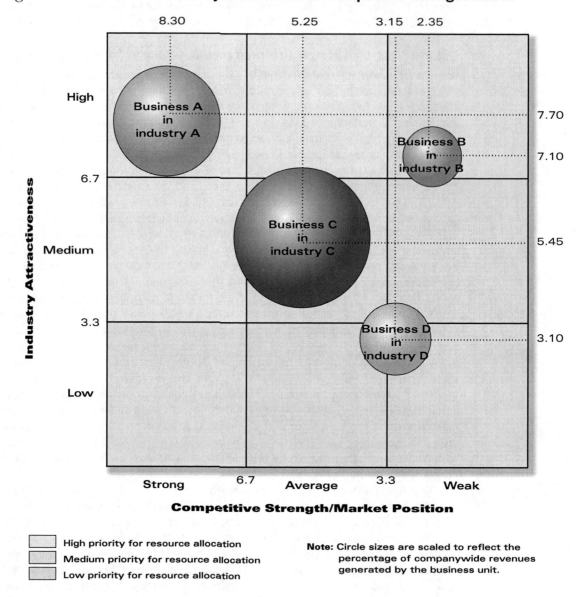

High priority for resource allocation
Medium priority for resource allocation
Low priority for resource allocation

Note: Circle sizes are scaled to reflect the percentage of companywide revenues generated by the business unit.

can then be diverted to financing expansion of business units with greater market opportunities. In exceptional cases where a business located in the three lower right cells is nonetheless fairly profitable (which it might be if it is in the low–average cell) or has the potential for good earnings and return on investment, the business merits retention and the allocation of sufficient resources to achieve better performance.

The nine-cell attractiveness–strength matrix provides clear, strong logic for why a diversified company needs to consider both industry attractiveness and business strength in allocating resources and investment capital to its different businesses. A good case can be made for concentrating resources in those businesses that enjoy higher degrees of attractiveness and competitive strength, being very selective in making investments in businesses with intermediate positions on the grid, and withdrawing resources from businesses that are lower in attractiveness and strength unless they offer exceptional profit or cash flow potential.

Step 3: Checking the Competitive Advantage Potential of Cross-Business Strategic Fits

Core Concept
A company's related diversification strategy derives its power in large part from the presence of competitively valuable strategic fits among its businesses.

While this step can be bypassed for diversified companies whose businesses are all unrelated (since, by design, no strategic fits are present), a high potential for converting strategic fits into competitive advantage is central to concluding just how good a company's related diversification strategy is. Checking the competitive advantage potential of cross-business strategic fits involves searching for and evaluating how much benefit a diversified company can gain from value chain matchups that present (1) opportunities to combine the performance of certain activities, thereby reducing costs and capturing economies of scope; (2) opportunities to transfer skills, technology, or intellectual capital from one business to another, thereby leveraging use of existing resources; (3) opportunities to share use of a well-respected brand name; and (4) opportunities for sister businesses to collaborate in creating valuable new competitive capabilities (such as enhanced supply chain management capabilities, quicker first-to-market capabilities, or greater product innovation capabilities).

Figure 9.6 illustrates the process of comparing the value chains of sister businesses and identifying competitively valuable cross-business strategic fits. *But more than just strategic fit identification is needed. The real test is what competitive value can be generated from these fits.* To what extent can cost savings be realized? How much competitive value will come from cross-business transfer of skills, technology, or intellectual capital? Will transferring a potent brand name to the products of sister businesses grow sales significantly? Will cross-business collaboration to create or strengthen competitive capabilities lead to significant gains in the marketplace or in financial performance? Absent significant strategic fits and dedicated company efforts to capture the benefits, one has to be skeptical about the potential for a diversified company's businesses to perform better together than apart.

Core Concept
The greater the value of cross-business strategic fits in enhancing a company's performance in the marketplace or on the bottom line, the more competitively powerful is its strategy of related diversification.

Step 4: Checking for Resource Fit

Core Concept
Sister businesses possess *resource fit* when they add to a company's overall resource strengths and when a company has adequate resources to support their requirements.

The businesses in a diversified company's lineup need to exhibit good **resource fit.** Resource fit exists when (1) businesses add to a company's overall resource strengths and (2) a company has adequate resources to support its entire group of businesses without spreading itself too thin. One important dimension of resource fit concerns whether a diversified company can generate the internal cash flows sufficient to fund the capital requirements of its businesses, pay its dividends, meet its debt obligations, and otherwise remain financially healthy.

Financial Resource Fits: Cash Cows versus Cash Hogs   Different businesses have different cash flow and investment characteristics. For example, business units in rapidly growing industries are often **cash hogs**—so labeled because the cash flows they are able to generate from internal operations aren't big enough to fund their expansion. To keep pace with rising buyer demand, rapid-growth businesses frequently need sizable annual capital investments—for new facilities and equipment, for

Figure 9.6   **Identifying the Competitive Advantage Potential of Cross-Business Strategic Fits**

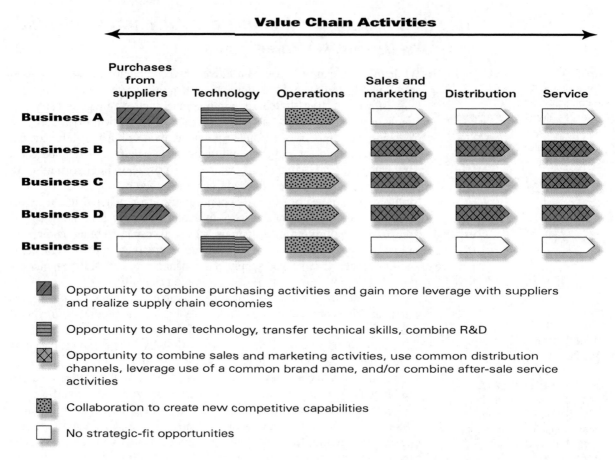

new product development or technology improvements, and for additional working capital to support inventory expansion and a larger base of operations. A business in a fast-growing industry becomes an even bigger cash hog when it has a relatively low market share and is pursuing a strategy to become an industry leader. Because a cash hog's financial resources must be provided by the corporate parent, corporate managers have to decide whether it makes good financial and strategic sense to keep pouring new money into a business that continually needs cash infusions.

In contrast, business units with leading market positions in mature industries may, however, be **cash cows**—businesses that generate substantial cash surpluses over what is needed to adequately fund their operations. Market leaders in slow-growth industries often generate sizable positive cash flows *over and above what is needed for growth and reinvestment* because their industry-leading positions tend to give them the sales volumes and reputation to earn attractive profits and because the slow-growth nature of their industry often entails relatively modest annual investment requirements. Cash cows, though not always attractive from a growth standpoint, are valuable businesses from a financial resource perspective. The surplus cash flows they generate can be used to pay corporate dividends, finance acquisitions, and provide

Core Concept
A *cash hog* generates cash flows that are too small to fully fund its operations and growth; a cash hog requires cash infusions to provide additional working capital and finance new capital investment.

Core Concept

A *cash cow* generates cash flows over and above its internal requirements, thus providing a corporate parent with funds for investing in cash hogs, financing new acquisitions, or paying dividends.

funds for investing in the company's promising cash hogs. It makes good financial and strategic sense for diversified companies to keep cash cows in healthy condition, fortifying and defending their market position so as to preserve their cash-generating capability over the long term and thereby have an ongoing source of financial resources to deploy elsewhere. The cigarette business is one of the world's biggest cash cows. General Electric, whose business lineup is shown in Illustration Capsule 9.2, considers that its advanced materials, equipment services, and appliance and lighting businesses are cash cows.

Viewing a diversified group of businesses as a collection of cash flows and cash requirements (present and future) is a major step forward in understanding what the financial ramifications of diversification are and why having businesses with good financial resource fit is so important. For instance, *a diversified company's businesses exhibit good financial resource fit when the excess cash generated by its cash cows is sufficient to fund the investment requirements of promising cash hogs.* Ideally, investing in promising cash hog businesses over time results in growing the hogs into self-supporting *star businesses* that have strong or market-leading competitive positions in attractive, high-growth markets and high levels of profitability. Star businesses are often the cash cows of the future—when the markets of star businesses begin to mature and their growth slows, their competitive strength should produce self-generated cash flows more than sufficient to cover their investment needs. The "success sequence" is thus cash hog to young star (but perhaps still a cash hog) to self-supporting star to cash cow.

If, however, a cash hog has questionable promise (either because of low industry attractiveness or a weak competitive position), then it becomes a logical candidate for divestiture. Pursuing an aggressive invest-and-expand strategy for a cash hog with an uncertain future seldom makes sense because it requires the corporate parent to keep pumping more capital into the business with only a dim hope of eventually turning the cash hog into a future star and realizing a good return on its investments. Such financially draining businesses fail the resource fit test because they strain the corporate parent's ability to adequately fund its other businesses. Divesting a cash hog is usually the best alternative unless (1) it has valuable strategic fits with other business units or (2) the capital infusions needed from the corporate parent are modest relative to the funds available and there's a decent chance of growing the business into a solid bottom-line contributor yielding a good return on invested capital.

Other Tests of Resource Fit   Aside from cash flow considerations, there are four other factors to consider in determining whether the businesses comprising a diversified company's portfolio exhibit good resource fit:

- *Does the business adequately contribute to achieving companywide performance targets?* A business has good financial fit when it contributes to the achievement of corporate performance objectives (growth in earnings per share, above-average return on investment, recognition as an industry leader, etc.) and when it materially enhances shareholder value via helping drive increases in the company's stock price. A business exhibits poor financial fit if it soaks up a disproportionate share of the company's financial resources, makes subpar or inconsistent bottom-line contributions, is unduly risky and failure would jeopardize the entire enterprise, or remains too small to make a material earnings contribution even though it performs well.

- *Does the company have adequate financial strength to fund its different businesses and maintain a healthy credit rating?* A diversified company's strategy fails the resource fit test when its financial resources are stretched across so many businesses that its credit rating is impaired. Severe financial strain sometimes occurs when a company borrows so heavily to finance new acquisitions that it has to trim way back on capital expenditures for existing businesses and use the big majority of its financial resources to meet interest obligations and to pay down debt. Time Warner, Royal Ahold, and AT&T, for example, have found themselves so financially overextended that they have had to sell off some of their business units to raise the money to pay down burdensome debt obligations and continue to fund essential capital expenditures for the remaining businesses.

- *Does the company have or can it develop the specific resource strengths and competitive capabilities needed to be successful in each of its businesses?*[15] Sometimes the resource strengths a company has accumulated in its core or mainstay business prove to be a poor match with the key success factors and competitive capabilities needed to succeed in one or more businesses it has diversified into. For instance, BTR, a multibusiness company in Great Britain, discovered that the company's resources and managerial skills were quite well suited for parenting industrial manufacturing businesses but not for parenting its distribution businesses (National Tyre Services and Texas-based Summers Group); as a consequence, BTR decided to divest its distribution businesses and focus exclusively on diversifying around small industrial manufacturing.[16] One company with businesses in restaurants and retailing decided that its resource capabilities in site selection, controlling operating costs, management selection and training, and supply chain logistics would enable it to succeed in the hotel business and in property management; but what management missed was that these businesses had some significantly different key success factors—namely, skills in controlling property development costs, maintaining low overheads, product branding (hotels), and ability to recruit a sufficient volume of business to maintain high levels of facility use.[17] Thus, a mismatch between the company's resource strengths and the key success factors in a particular business can be serious enough to warrant divesting an existing business or not acquiring a new business. In contrast, when a company's resources and capabilities are a good match with the key success factors of industries it is not presently in, it makes sense to take a hard look at acquiring companies in these industries and expanding the company's business lineup.

- *Are recently acquired businesses acting to strengthen a company's resource base and competitive capabilities or are they causing its competitive and managerial resources to be stretched too thin?* A diversified company has to guard against overtaxing its resource strengths, a condition that can arise when (1) it goes on an acquisition spree and management is called on to assimilate and oversee many new businesses very quickly or (2) when it lacks sufficient resource depth to do a creditable job of transferring skills and competences from one of its businesses to another (especially, a large acquisition or several lesser ones). The broader the diversification, the greater the concern about whether the company has sufficient managerial depth to cope with the diverse range of operating problems its wide business lineup presents. And the more a company's diversification strategy is tied to transferring its existing know-how or technologies to new businesses, the more it has to develop a big enough and deep enough resource pool to supply these businesses with sufficient capability to create competitive advantage.[18] Otherwise its strengths end up being thinly spread across many businesses and the opportunity for competitive advantage slips through the cracks.

A Cautionary Note About Transferring Resources from One Business to Another   Just because a company has hit a home run in one business doesn't mean it can easily enter a new business with similar resource requirements and hit a second home run.[19] Noted British retailer Marks & Spencer, despite possessing a range of impressive resource capabilities (ability to choose excellent store locations, having a supply chain that gives it both low costs and high merchandise quality, loyal employees, an excellent reputation with consumers, and strong management expertise) that have made it one of Britain's premier retailers for 100 years, has failed repeatedly in its efforts to diversify into department store retailing in the United States. Even though Philip Morris (now named Altria) had built powerful consumer marketing capabilities in its cigarette and beer businesses, it floundered in soft drinks and ended up divesting its acquisition of 7UP after several frustrating years of competing against strongly entrenched and resource-capable rivals like Coca-Cola and PepsiCo. Then in 2002 it decided to divest its Miller Brewing business—despite its long-standing marketing successes in cigarettes and in its Kraft Foods subsidiary—because it was unable to grow Miller's market share in head-to-head competition against the considerable marketing prowess of Anheuser-Busch.

Step 5: Ranking the Performance Prospects of Business Units and Assigning a Priority for Resource Allocation

Once a diversified company's strategy has been evaluated from the perspective of industry attractiveness, competitive strength, strategic fit, and resource fit, the next step is to rank the performance prospects of the businesses from best to worst and determine which businesses merit top priority for resource support and new capital investments by the corporate parent.

The most important considerations in judging business-unit performance are sales growth, profit growth, contribution to company earnings, and return on capital invested in the business. Sometimes cash flow is a big consideration. Information on each business's past performance can be gleaned from a company's financial records. While past performance is not necessarily a good predictor of future performance, it does signal whether a business already has good-to-excellent performance or has problems to overcome.

Furthermore, the industry attractiveness/business strength evaluations provide a solid basis for judging a business's prospects. Normally, strong business units in attractive industries have significantly better prospects than weak businesses in unattractive industries. And, normally, the revenue and earnings outlook for businesses in fast-growing industries is better than for businesses in slow-growing industries—one important exception is when a business in a slow-growing industry has the competitive strength to draw sales and market share away from its rivals and thus achieve much faster growth than the industry as whole. As a rule, the prior analyses, taken together, signal which business units are likely to be strong performers on the road ahead and which are likely to be laggards. And it is a short step from ranking the prospects of business units to drawing conclusions about whether the company as a whole is capable of strong, mediocre, or weak performance in upcoming years.

Figure 9.7   **The Chief Strategic and Financial Options for Allocating a Diversified Company's Financial Resources**

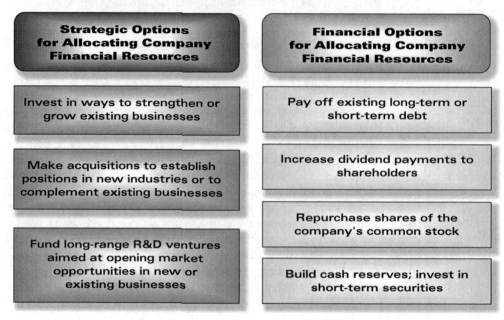

The rankings of future performance generally determine what priority the corporate parent should give to each business in terms of resource allocation. The task here is to decide which business units should have top priority for corporate resource support and new capital investment and which should carry the lowest priority. *Business subsidiaries with the brightest profit and growth prospects and solid strategic and resource fits generally should head the list for corporate resource support.* More specifically, corporate executives need to consider whether and how corporate resources can be used to enhance the competitiveness of particular business units. And they must be diligent in steering resources out of low-opportunity areas and into high-opportunity areas. Divesting marginal businesses is one of the best ways of freeing unproductive assets for redeployment. Surplus funds from cash cows also add to the corporate treasury.

Figure 9.7 shows the chief strategic and financial options for allocating a diversified company's financial resources. Ideally, a company will have enough funds to do what is needed, both strategically and financially. If not, strategic uses of corporate resources should usually take precedence unless there is a compelling reason to strengthen the firm's balance sheet or divert financial resources to pacify shareholders.

Step 6: Crafting New Strategic Moves to Improve Overall Corporate Performance

The diagnosis and conclusions flowing from the five preceding analytical steps set the agenda for crafting strategic moves to improve a diversified company's overall performance. The strategic options boil down to five broad categories of actions:

1. Sticking closely with the existing business lineup and pursuing the opportunities these businesses present.

2. Broadening the company's business scope by making new acquisitions in new industries.

3. Divesting certain businesses and retrenching to a narrower base of business operations.

4. Restructuring the company's business lineup and putting a whole new face on the company's business makeup.

5. Pursuing multinational diversification and striving to globalize the operations of several of the company's business units.

The option of sticking with the current business lineup makes sense when the company's present businesses offer attractive growth opportunities and can be counted on to generate good earnings and cash flows. As long as the company's set of existing businesses puts it in good position for the future and these businesses have good strategic and/or resource fits, then rocking the boat with major changes in the company's business mix is usually unnecessary. Corporate executives can concentrate their attention on getting the best performance from each of its businesses, steering corporate resources into those areas of greatest potential and profitability. The specifics of "what to do" to wring better performance from the present business lineup have to be dictated by each business's circumstances and the preceding analysis of the corporate parent's diversification strategy.

However, in the event that corporate executives are not entirely satisfied with the opportunities they see in the company's present set of businesses and conclude that changes in the company's direction and business makeup are in order, they can opt for any of the four other strategic alternatives listed above. These options are discussed in the following section.

AFTER A COMPANY DIVERSIFIES: THE FOUR MAIN STRATEGY ALTERNATIVES

Diversifying is by no means the final chapter in the evolution of a company's strategy. Once a company has diversified into a collection of related or unrelated businesses and concludes that some overhaul is needed in the company's present lineup and diversification strategy, there are four main strategic paths it can pursue (see Figure 9.8). To more fully understand the strategic issues corporate managers face in the ongoing process of managing a diversified group of businesses, we need to take a brief look at the central thrust of each of the four postdiversification strategy alternatives.

Strategies to Broaden a Diversified Company's Business Base

Diversified companies sometimes find it desirable to build positions in new industries, whether related or unrelated. There are several motivating factors. One is sluggish growth that makes the potential revenue and profit boost of a newly acquired business look attractive. A second is vulnerability to seasonal or recessionary influences or to threats from emerging new technologies. A third is the potential for transferring resources and capabilities to other related or complementary businesses. A fourth is rapidly changing conditions in one or more of a company's core businesses brought on by technological, legislative, or new product innovations that alter buyer requirements and preferences. For instance, the passage of legislation in the United States allowing

Figure 9.8 **A Company's Four Main Strategic Alternatives After It Diversifies**

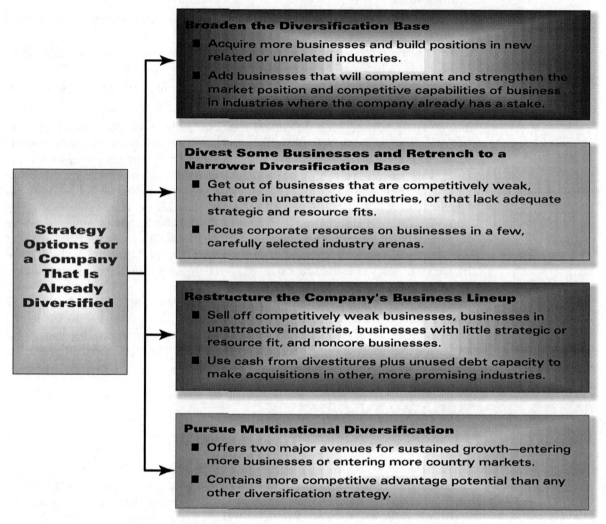

Broaden the Diversification Base
- Acquire more businesses and build positions in new related or unrelated industries.
- Add businesses that will complement and strengthen the market position and competitive capabilities of business in industries where the company already has a stake.

Divest Some Businesses and Retrench to a Narrower Diversification Base
- Get out of businesses that are competitively weak, that are in unattractive industries, or that lack adequate strategic and resource fits.
- Focus corporate resources on businesses in a few, carefully selected industry arenas.

Restructure the Company's Business Lineup
- Sell off competitively weak businesses, businesses in unattractive industries, businesses with little strategic or resource fit, and noncore businesses.
- Use cash from divestitures plus unused debt capacity to make acquisitions in other, more promising industries.

Pursue Multinational Diversification
- Offers two major avenues for sustained growth—entering more businesses or entering more country markets.
- Contains more competitive advantage potential than any other diversification strategy.

Strategy Options for a Company That Is Already Diversified

banks, insurance companies, and stock brokerages to enter each other's businesses spurred a raft of acquisitions and mergers to create full-service financial enterprises capable of meeting the multiple financial needs of customers. Citigroup, already the largest U.S. bank, with a global banking franchise, acquired Salomon Smith Barney to position itself in the investment banking and brokerage business and acquired insurance giant Travelers Group to enable it to offer customers insurance products.

A fifth, and often very important, motivating factor for adding new businesses is to complement and strengthen the market position and competitive capabilities of one or more of its present businesses. Procter & Gamble's recent acquisition of Gillette strengthened and extended P&G's reach into personal care and household products—Gillette's businesses included Oral-B toothbrushes, Gillette razors and razor blades, Duracell batteries, Braun shavers and small appliances (coffeemakers, mixers, hair dryers, and electric toothbrushes), and toiletries (Right Guard, Foamy, Soft & Dry, White Rain, and Dry Idea). Unilever, a leading maker of food and personal care products, expanded its business lineup by acquiring SlimFast, Ben & Jerry's Homemade,

Illustration Capsule 9.3

Managing Diversification at Johnson & Johnson: The Benefits of Cross-Business Strategic Fits

Johnson & Johnson (J&J), once a consumer products company known for its Band-Aid line and its baby care products, has evolved into a $42 billion diversified enterprise consisting of some 200-plus operating companies organized into three divisions: drugs, medical devices and diagnostics, and consumer products. Over the past decade J&J has acquired 56 businesses at a cost of about $30 billion; about 10 to 15 percent of J&J's annual growth in revenues has come from acquisitions. Much of the company's recent growth has been in the pharmaceutical division, which in 2004 accounted for 47 percent of J&J's revenues and 57 percent of its operating profits.

While each of J&J's business units sets its own strategies and operates with its own finance and human resource departments, corporate management strongly encourages cross-business cooperation and collaboration, believing that many of the advances in 21st century medicine will come from applying advances in one discipline to another. J&J had 9,300 scientists working in 40 research labs in 2003, and the frequency of cross-disciplinary collaboration was increasing. One of J&J's new drug-coated stents grew out of a discussion between a drug researcher and a

researcher in the company's stent business. (When stents are inserted to prop open arteries following angioplasty, the drug coating helps prevent infection.) A gene technology database compiled by the company's gene research lab was shared with personnel from the diagnostics division, who developed a test that the drug R&D people could use to predict which patients would most benefit from an experimental cancer therapy. J&J experts in various diseases have been meeting quarterly for the past five years to share information, and top management is setting up cross-disciplinary groups to focus on new treatments for particular diseases. J&J's new liquid Band-Aid product (a liquid coating applied to hard-to-cover places like fingers and knuckles) is based on a material used in a wound-closing product sold by the company's hospital products company.

J&J's corporate management maintains that close collaboration among people in its diagnostics, medical devices, and pharmaceuticals businesses—where numerous cross-business strategic fits exist—gives J&J an edge on competitors, most of whom cannot match the company's breadth and depth of expertise.

Sources: Amy Barrett, "Staying on Top," *BusinessWeek,* May 5, 2003, pp. 60–68, and www.jnj.com (accessed October 19, 2005).

and Bestfoods (whose brands included Knorr's soups, Hellman's mayonnaise, Skippy peanut butter, and Mazola cooking oils). Unilever saw these businesses as giving it more clout in competing against such other diversified food and household products companies as Nestlé, Kraft, Procter & Gamble, Campbell Soup, and General Mills.

Usually, expansion into new businesses is undertaken by acquiring companies already in the target industry. Some companies depend on new acquisitions to drive a major portion of their growth in revenues and earnings, and thus are always on the acquisition trail. Cisco Systems built itself into a worldwide leader in networking systems for the Internet by making 95 technology-based acquisitions during 1993–2005 to extend its market reach from routing and switching into Internet Protocol (IP) telephony, home networking, wireless local-area networking (LAN), storage networking, network security, broadband, and optical and broadband systems. Tyco International, now recovering from charges of looting on the part of several top executives, transformed itself from an obscure company in the early 1990s into a $40 billion global manufacturing enterprise with operations in over 100 countries as of 2005 by making over 1,000 acquisitions; the company's far-flung diversification includes businesses in electronics, electrical components, fire and security systems, health care products, valves, undersea telecommunications systems, plastics, and adhesives. Tyco made over 700 acquisitions of small companies in the 1999–2001 period alone. As a group, Tyco's businesses were cash cows, generating a combined free cash flow in 2005 of around $4.4 billion.

Illustration Capsule 9.3 describes how Johnson & Johnson has used acquisitions to diversify far beyond its well-known Band-Aid and baby care businesses and become a major player in pharmaceuticals, medical devices, and medical diagnostics.

Divestiture Strategies Aimed at Retrenching to a Narrower Diversification Base

A number of diversified firms have had difficulty managing a diverse group of businesses and have elected to get out of some of them. Retrenching to a narrower diversification base is usually undertaken when top management concludes that its diversification strategy has ranged too far afield and that the company can improve long-term performance by concentrating on building stronger positions in a smaller number of core businesses and industries. Hewlett-Packard spun off its testing and measurement businesses into a stand-alone company called Agilent Technologies so that it could better concentrate on its PC, workstation, server, printer and peripherals, and electronics businesses. PepsiCo divested its cash-hog group of restaurant businesses, consisting of KFC, Pizza Hut, Taco Bell, and California Pizza Kitchens, to provide more resources for strengthening its soft-drink business (which was losing market share to Coca-Cola) and growing its more profitable Frito-Lay snack foods business. Kmart divested OfficeMax, Sports Authority, and Borders Bookstores in order to refocus management attention and all of the company's resources on restoring luster to its distressed discount retailing business, which was (and still is) being totally outclassed in the marketplace by Wal-Mart and Target. In 2003–2004, Tyco International began a program to divest itself of some 50 businesses, including its entire undersea fiber-optics telecommunications network and an assortment of businesses in its fire and security division; the initiative also involved consolidating 219 manufacturing, sales, distribution, and other facilities and reducing its workforce of some 260,000 people by 7,200. Lucent Technology's retrenchment strategy is described in Illustration Capsule 9.4.

> Focusing corporate resources on a few core and mostly related businesses avoids the mistake of diversifying so broadly that resources and management attention are stretched too thin.

But there are other important reasons for divesting one or more of a company's present businesses. Sometimes divesting a business has to be considered because market conditions in a once-attractive industry have badly deteriorated. A business can become a prime candidate for divestiture because it lacks adequate strategic or resource fit, because it is a cash hog with questionable long-term potential, or because it is weakly positioned in its industry with little prospect the corporate parent can realize a decent return on its investment in the business. Sometimes a company acquires businesses that, down the road, just do not work out as expected even though management has tried all it can think of to make them profitable—mistakes cannot be completely avoided because it is hard to foresee how getting into a new line of business will actually work out. Subpar performance by some business units is bound to occur, thereby raising questions of whether to divest them or keep them and attempt a turnaround. Other business units, despite adequate financial performance, may not mesh as well with the rest of the firm as was originally thought.

Illustration Capsule 9.4
Lucent Technology's Retrenchment Strategy

At the height of the telecommunications boom in 1999–2000, Lucent Technology was a company with $38.3 billion in revenues and 157,000 employees; it was the biggest maker of telecommunications equipment in the United States and a recognized leader worldwide. The company's strategy was to build positions in a number of blossoming technologies and industry arenas and achieve 20 percent annual revenue growth in each of 11 different business groups. But when customers' orders for new equipment began to evaporate in 2000–2001, Lucent's profits vanished and the once-growing company found itself battling to overcome bloated costs, deep price discounting, and customer defaults on the $7.5 billion in loans Lucent had made to finance their purchases. As it became clear that equipment sales and prices would never return to former levels, Lucent executives concluded that the company had overextended itself trying to do too many things and needed to pare its lineup of businesses.

Alongside efforts to curtail lavish spending at the company's fabled Bell Labs research unit, make deep workforce cutbacks, streamline order-taking and billing systems, shore up the balance sheet, and conserve cash by ending dividend payments, management launched a series of retrenchment initiatives:

- Of the 40 businesses Lucent acquired since 1996, 27 were sold, closed, or spun off.
- Lucent ceased all manufacturing operations, opting to outsource everything.
- It stopped making gear for wireless phone networks based on global system for mobile communication (GSM) technology (the dominant technology used in Europe and much of the world) in order to focus more fully on wireless gear using code division multiple access (CDMA) technology (a technology prevalent in the United States and some developing nations). As of 2004 Lucent had an estimated 45 percent share in the CDMA market and the CDMA gear division was the company's chief revenue and profit producer.
- The wireline and wireless business units were combined to form a single, unified organization called Network Solutions.
- All the remaining businesses were grouped into a unit called Lucent Worldwide Services that was engaged in designing, implementing, integrating, and managing sophisticated voice and data networks for service providers in 45 countries.
- The role of Bell Labs was narrowed to supporting the efforts of both the Network Solutions group and the Worldwide Services group.

Lucent's strategic moves to retrench stemmed a string of 13 straight money-losing quarters. In fiscal 2004 Lucent reported profits of $2 billion from continuing operations (equal to EPS of $0.47 but still far below the levels of $0.93 in 2000 and $1.12 in 1999). In May 2004, Lucent announced its first acquisition in four years, buying a maker of Internet transmission technology for $300 million to help it become a leader in Internet telephony technology. Going into 2006, Lucent was a company with sales of about $9 billion (versus $38 billion in 1999) and a workforce of about 30,000 (versus 157,000 in 1999). The company's stock price, which reached a high of $62 in 1999 before crashing to below $1 in 2002, languished in the $3–$4 range for most of 2004–2005, indicating continuing investor skepticism about Lucent's prospects despite its having retreated to businesses where it was strongest.

Sources: Shawn Young, "Less May Be More," *The Wall Street Journal,* October 23, 2004, p. R10, and www.lucent.com (accessed October 19, 2005).

On occasion, a diversification move that seems sensible from a strategic-fit standpoint turns out to be a poor *cultural fit.*[20] Several pharmaceutical companies had just this experience. When they diversified into cosmetics and perfume, they discovered their personnel had little respect for the "frivolous" nature of such products compared to the far nobler task of developing miracle drugs to cure the ill. The absence of shared values and cultural compatibility between the medical research and chemical-compounding expertise of the pharmaceutical companies and the fashion/marketing orientation of the cosmetics business was the undoing of what otherwise was diversification into businesses with technology-sharing potential, product-development fit, and some overlap in distribution channels.

There's evidence indicating that pruning businesses and narrowing a firm's diversification base improves corporate performance.[21] Corporate parents often end up selling off businesses too late and at too low a price, sacrificing shareholder value.[22] A useful guide to determine whether or when to divest a business subsidiary is to ask, "If we were not in this business today, would we want to get into it now?"[23] When the answer is no or probably not, divestiture should be considered. Another signal that a business should become a divestiture candidate is whether it is worth more to another company than to the present parent; in such cases, shareholders would be well served if the company sells the business and collects a premium price from the buyer for whom the business is a valuable fit.[24]

> Diversified companies need to divest low-performing businesses or businesses that don't fit in order to concentrate on expanding existing businesses and entering new ones where opportunities are more promising.

The Two Options for Divesting a Business: Selling It or Spinning It Off as an Independent Company Selling a business outright to another company is far and away the most frequently used option for divesting a business. But sometimes a business selected for divestiture has ample resource strengths to compete successfully on its own. In such cases, a corporate parent may elect to spin the unwanted business off as a financially and managerially independent company, either by selling shares to the investing public via an initial public offering or by distributing shares in the new company to existing shareholders of the corporate parent. When a corporate parent decides to spin off one of its businesses as a separate company, it must decide whether or not to retain partial ownership. Retaining partial ownership makes sense when the business to be divested has a hot product or technological capabilities that give it good profit prospects. When 3Com elected to divest its PalmPilot business, which investors then saw as having very promising profit potential, it elected to retain a substantial ownership interest so as to provide 3Com shareholders a way of participating in whatever future market success that PalmPilot (now Palm Inc.) might have on its own. In 2001, when Philip Morris (now Altria) became concerned that its popular Kraft Foods subsidiary was suffering because of its affiliation with Philip Morris's cigarette business (antismoking groups were leading a national boycott of Kraft macaroni and cheese, and a Harris poll revealed that about 16 percent of people familiar with Philip Morris had boycotted its products), Philip Morris executives opted to spin Kraft Foods off as an independent public company but retained a controlling ownership interest. R. J. Reynolds Tobacco was also spun off from Nabisco Foods in 1999 in an effort to distance the tobacco operations part of the company from the food operations part. (Nabisco was then acquired by Philip Morris in 2000 and integrated into Kraft Foods.) In 2005, Cendant announced it would split its diversified businesses into four separate publicly traded companies—one for vehicle rental services (which consisted of Avis and Budget car rental companies); one for real estate and mortgage services (which included Century 21, Coldwell Banker, ERA, Sotheby's International Realty, and NRT—a residential real estate brokerage company); one for hospitality and lodging (consisting of such hotels and motel chains as Wyndam, Ramada, Days Inn, Howard Johnson, Travelodge, AmeriHost Inn, and Knights Inn, plus an assortment of time-share resort properties); and one for travel (consisting of various travel agencies, online ticket and vacation travel sites like Orbitz and Cheap Tickets, and vacation rental operations handling some 55,000 villas and condos). Cendant said the reason for the split-up was that shareholders would realize more value from operating the businesses independently—a clear sign that Cendant's diversification strategy had failed to deliver added shareholder value and that the parts were worth more than the whole.

Selling a business outright requires finding a buyer. This can prove hard or easy, depending on the business. As a rule, a company selling a troubled business should not ask, "How can we pawn this business off on someone, and what is the most we can get for it?"[25] Instead, it is wiser to ask, "For what sort of company would this business be a good fit, and under what conditions would it be viewed as a good deal?" Enterprises for which the business is a good fit are likely to pay the highest price. Of course, if a buyer willing to pay an acceptable price cannot be found, then a company must decide whether to keep the business until a buyer appears; spin it off as a separate company; or, in the case of a crisis-ridden business that is losing substantial sums, simply close it down and liquidate the remaining assets. Liquidation is obviously a last resort.

Strategies to Restructure a Company's Business Lineup

Core Concept
Restructuring involves divesting some businesses and acquiring others so as to put a whole new face on the company's business lineup.

Restructuring strategies involve divesting some businesses and acquiring others so as to put a whole new face on the company's business lineup. Performing radical surgery on a company's group of businesses is an appealing strategy alternative when its financial performance is being squeezed or eroded by:

- Too many businesses in slow-growth, declining, low-margin, or otherwise unattractive industries (a condition indicated by the number and size of businesses with industry attractiveness ratings below 5 and located on the bottom half of the attractiveness–strength matrix—see Figure 9.5).
- Too many competitively weak businesses (a condition indicated by the number and size of businesses with competitive strength ratings below 5 and located on the right half of the attractiveness–strength matrix).
- Ongoing declines in the market shares of one or more major business units that are falling prey to more market-savvy competitors.
- An excessive debt burden with interest costs that eat deeply into profitability.
- Ill-chosen acquisitions that haven't lived up to expectations.

Restructuring can also be mandated by the emergence of new technologies that threaten the survival of one or more of a diversified company's important businesses or by the appointment of a new CEO who decides to redirect the company. On occasion, restructuring can be prompted by special circumstances—as when a firm has a unique opportunity to make an acquisition so big and important that it has to sell several existing business units to finance the new acquisition, or when a company needs to sell off some businesses in order to raise the cash for entering a potentially big industry with wave-of-the-future technologies or products.

Candidates for divestiture in a corporate restructuring effort typically include not only weak or up-and-down performers or those in unattractive industries but also business units that lack strategic fit with the businesses to be retained, businesses that are cash hogs or that lack other types of resource fit, and businesses incompatible with the company's revised diversification strategy (even though they may be profitable or in an attractive industry). As businesses are divested, corporate restructuring generally involves aligning the remaining business units into groups with the best strategic fits and then redeploying the cash flows from the divested business to either pay down debt or make new acquisitions to strengthen the parent company's business position in the industries it has chosen to emphasize.[26]

Over the past decade, corporate restructuring has become a popular strategy at many diversified companies, especially those that had diversified broadly into many different industries and lines of business. For instance, one struggling diversified company over a two-year period divested four business units, closed down the operations of four others, and added 25 new lines of business to its portfolio (16 through acquisition and 9 through internal start-up). PerkinElmer used a series of divestitures and new acquisitions to transform itself from a supplier of low-margin services sold to the government agencies into an innovative high-tech company with operations in over 125 countries and businesses in four industry groups—life sciences (drug research and clinical screening), optoelectronics, medical instruments, and fluid control and containment services (for customers in aerospace, power generation, and semiconductors). In 2005, PerkinElmer took a second restructuring step by divesting its entire fluid control and containment business group so that it could concentrate on its higher-growth health sciences and optoelectronics businesses; the company's CEO said, "While fluid services is an excellent business, it does not fit with our long-term strategy."[27] Before beginning a restructuring effort in 1995, British-based Hanson PLC owned companies with more than $20 billion in revenues in industries as diverse as beer, exercise equipment, tools, construction cranes, tobacco, cement, chemicals, coal mining, electricity, hot tubs and whirlpools, cookware, rock and gravel, bricks, and asphalt. By early 1997, Hanson had restructured itself into a $3.8 billion enterprise focused more narrowly on gravel, crushed rock, cement, asphalt, bricks, and construction cranes; the remaining businesses were divided into four groups and divested.

During Jack Welch's first four years as CEO of General Electric (GE), the company divested 117 business units, accounting for about 20 percent of GE's assets; these divestitures, coupled with several important acquisitions, provided GE with 14 major business divisions and led to Welch's challenge to the managers of GE's divisions to become number one or number two in their industry. Ten years after Welch became CEO, GE was a different company, having divested operations worth $9 billion, made new acquisitions totaling $24 billion, and cut its workforce by 100,000 people. Then, during the 1990–2001 period, GE continued to reshuffle its business lineup, acquiring over 600 new companies, including 108 in 1998 and 64 during a 90-day period in 1999. Most of the new acquisitions were in Europe, Asia, and Latin America and were aimed at transforming GE into a truly global enterprise. In 2003, GE's new CEO, Jeffrey Immelt, began a further restructuring of GE's business lineup with three initiatives: (1) spending $10 billion to acquire British-based Amersham and extend GE's Medical Systems business into diagnostic pharmaceuticals and biosciences, thereby creating a $15 billion business designated as GE Healthcare; (2) acquiring the entertainment assets of debt-ridden French media conglomerate Vivendi Universal Entertainment (Universal Studios, five Universal theme parks, USA Network, Sci-Fi Channel, the Trio cable channel, and Spanish-language broadcaster Telemundo) and integrate its operations into GE's NBC division (the owner of NBC, 29 television stations, and cable networks CNBC, MSNBC, and Bravo), thereby creating a broad-based $13 billion media business positioned to compete against Walt Disney, Time Warner, Fox, and Viacom; and (3) beginning a withdrawal from the insurance business by divesting several companies in its insurance division and preparing to spin off its remaining life and mortgage insurance businesses through an initial public offering of stock for a new company called Genworth Financial.

In a study of the performance of the 200 largest U.S. corporations from 1990 to 2000, McKinsey & Company found that those companies that actively managed their business portfolios through acquisitions and divestitures created substantially more shareholder value than those that kept a fixed lineup of businesses.[28]

Multinational Diversification Strategies

The distinguishing characteristics of a multinational diversification strategy are a *diversity of businesses* and a *diversity of national markets*.[29] Such diversity makes multinational diversification a particularly challenging and complex strategy to conceive and execute. Managers have to develop business strategies for each industry (with as many multinational variations as conditions in each country market dictate). Then they have to pursue and manage opportunities for cross-business and cross-country collaboration and strategic coordination in ways calculated to result in competitive advantage and enhanced profitability.

Moreover, the geographic operating scope of individual businesses within a diversified multinational corporation (DMNC) can range from one country only to several countries to many countries to global. Thus, each business unit within a DMNC often competes in a somewhat different combination of geographic markets than the other businesses do—adding another element of strategic complexity, and perhaps an element of opportunity.

Illustration Capsule 9.5 shows the scope of four prominent DMNCs.

The Appeal of Multinational Diversification: More Opportunities for Sustained Growth and Maximum Competitive Advantage Potential

Despite their complexity, multinational diversification strategies have great appeal. They contain *two major avenues* for growing revenues and profits: One is to grow by entering additional businesses, and the other is to grow by extending the operations of existing businesses into additional country markets. Moreover, a strategy of multinational diversification also contains six attractive paths to competitive advantage, *all of which can be pursued simultaneously:*

1. *Full capture of economies of scale and experience/learning curve effects.* In some businesses, the volume of sales needed to realize full economies of scale and/or benefit fully from experience/learning curve effects is rather sizable, often exceeding the volume that can be achieved operating within the boundaries of a single country market, especially a small one. *The ability to drive down unit costs by expanding sales to additional country markets is one reason why a diversified multinational may seek to acquire a business and then rapidly expand its operations into more and more foreign markets.*

2. *Opportunities to capitalize on cross-business economies of scope.* Diversifying into related businesses offering economies of scope can drive the development of a low-cost advantage over less diversified rivals. For example, a DMNC that uses mostly the same distributors and retail dealers worldwide can diversify into new businesses using these same worldwide distribution channels at relatively little incremental expense. The cost savings of piggybacking distribution activities can be substantial. Moreover, with more business selling more products in more countries, a DMNC acquires more bargaining leverage in its purchases from suppliers and more bargaining leverage with retailers in securing attractive display space for its products. Consider, for example, the competitive power that Sony derived

Illustration Capsule 9.5

The Global Scope of Four Prominent Diversified Multinational Corporations

Company	Global Scope	Businesses into Which the Company Has Diversified
Sony	Operations in more than 100 countries and sales offices in more than 200 countries	• Televisions, VCRs, DVD players, Walkman MP3 players, radios, digital cameras and video equipment, Vaio PCs, and Trinitron computer monitors; PlayStation game consoles and video game software; Columbia, Epic, and Sony Classical pre-recorded music; Columbia TriStar motion pictures; syndicated television programs; entertainment complexes, and insurance
Nestlé	Operations in 70 countries and sales offices in more than 200 countries	• Beverages (Nescafé and Taster's Choice coffees, Nestea, Perrier, Arrowhead, & Calistoga mineral and bottled waters); milk products (Carnation, Gloria, Neslac, Coffee Mate, Nestlé ice cream and yogurt); pet foods (Friskies, Alpo, Fancy Feast, Mighty Dog); Contadina, Libby's, and Stouffer's food products and prepared dishes; chocolate and confectionery products (Nestlé Crunch, Smarties, Baby Ruth, Butterfinger, KitKat); and pharmaceuticals (Alcon opthalmic products, Galderma dermatological products)
Siemens	Operations in 160 countries and sales offices in more than 190 countries	• Electrical power generation, transmission, and distribution equipment and products; manufacturing automation systems; industrial motors, machinery, and tools; plant construction and maintenance; corporate communication networks; telephones; PCs, mainframes, computer network products, consulting services; mass transit and light rail systems, rail cars, locomotives, lighting products (bulbs, lamps, theater and television lighting systems); semiconductors; home appliances; vacuum cleaners; and financial, procurement, and logistics services
Samsung	Operations in more than 60 countries and sales in more than 200 countries	• Notebook computers, hard disk drives, CD/DVD-ROM drives, monitors, printers, and fax machines; televisions (big-screen TVs, plasma-screen TVs, and LCD-screen TVs); DVD and MP3 players; Cell phones and various other telecommunications products; compressors; home appliances; DRAM chips, flash memory chips, and graphics memory chips; and optical fibers, fiber-optic cables, and fiber-optic connectors

Source: Company annual reports and Web sites.

from these very sorts of economies of scope when it decided to diversify into the video game business with its PlayStation product line. Sony had in place capability to go after video game sales in all country markets where it presently did business in other electronics product categories (TVs, computers, DVD players, VCRs, radios, CD players, and camcorders). And it had the marketing clout and brand-name credibility to persuade retailers to give Sony's PlayStation products prime shelf space and visibility. These strategic-fit benefits helped Sony quickly overtake long-time industry leaders Nintendo and Sega and defend its market leadership against Microsoft's new Xbox.

3. *Opportunities to transfer competitively valuable resources both from one business to another and from one country to another.* A company pursuing related diversification can gain a competitive edge over less diversified rivals by transferring competitively valuable resources from one business to another; a multinational company can gain competitive advantage over rivals with narrower geographic coverage by transferring competitively valuable resources from one country to another. But a strategy of multinational diversification enables simultaneous pursuit of both sources of competitive advantage.

4. *Ability to leverage use of a well-known and competitively powerful brand name.* Diversified multinational companies whose businesses have brand names that are well known and respected across the world possess a valuable strategic asset with competitive advantage potential. For example, Sony's well-established global brand-name recognition gives it an important marketing and advertising advantage over rivals with lesser-known brands. When Sony goes into a new marketplace with the stamp of the Sony brand on its product families, it can command prominent display space with retailers. It can expect to win sales and market share simply on the confidence that buyers place in products carrying the Sony name. While Sony may spend money to make consumers aware of the availability of its new products, it does not have to spend nearly as much on achieving brand recognition and market acceptance as would a lesser-known competitor looking at the marketing and advertising costs of entering the same new product/business/country markets and trying to go head-to-head against Sony. Further, if Sony moves into a new country market for the first time and does well selling Sony PlayStations and video games, it is easier to sell consumers in that country Sony TVs, digital cameras, PCs, MP3 players, and so on—plus, the related advertising costs are likely to be less than they would be without having already established the Sony brand strongly in the minds of buyers.

5. *Ability to capitalize on opportunities for cross-business and cross-country collaboration and strategic coordination.*[30] A multinational diversification strategy allows competitively valuable cross-business and cross-country coordination of certain value chain activities. For instance, by channeling corporate resources directly into a combined R&D/technology effort for all related businesses, as opposed to letting each business unit fund and direct its own R&D effort however it sees fit, a DMNC can merge its expertise and efforts *worldwide* to advance core technologies, expedite cross-business and cross-country product improvements, speed the development of new products that complement existing products, and pursue promising technological avenues to create altogether new businesses—all significant contributors to competitive advantage and better corporate performance.[31] Honda has been very successful in building R&D expertise in gasoline engines and transferring the resulting technological advances to its businesses in automobiles, motorcycles, outboard engines, snow blowers, lawn mowers, garden tillers, and portable power generators. Further, a DMNC can reduce costs through cross-business and cross-country coordination of purchasing and procurement from suppliers, from collaborative introduction and shared use of e-commerce technologies and online sales efforts, and from coordinated product introductions and promotional campaigns. Firms that are less diversified and less global in scope have less such cross-business and cross-country collaborative opportunities.

6. *Opportunities to use cross-business or cross-country subsidization to outcompete rivals.* A financially successful DMNC has potentially valuable organizational resources and multiple profit sanctuaries in both certain country markets and certain businesses that it can draw on to wage a market offensive. In comparison, a one-business domestic company has only one profit sanctuary—its home market. A diversified one-country competitor may have profit sanctuaries in several businesses, but all are in the same country market. A one-business multinational company may have profit sanctuaries in several country markets, but all are in the same business. All three are vulnerable to an offensive in their more limited profit sanctuaries by an aggressive DMNC willing to lowball its prices or spend extravagantly on advertising to win market share at their expense. A DMNC's ability to keep hammering away at competitors with low prices year after year may reflect either a cost advantage growing out of its related diversification strategy or a willingness to accept low profits or even losses in the market being attacked because it has ample earnings from its other profit sanctuaries. For example, Sony's global-scale diversification strategy gives it unique competitive strengths in outcompeting Nintendo and Sega, neither of which are diversified. If need be, Sony can maintain low prices on its PlayStations or fund high-profile promotions for its latest video game products, using earnings from its other business lines to fund its offensive to wrest market share away from Nintendo and Sega in video games. At the same time, Sony can draw on its considerable resources in R&D, its ability to transfer electronics technology from one electronics product family to another, and its expertise in product innovation to introduce better and better video game players, perhaps players that are multifunctional and do more than just play video games. Such competitive actions not only enhance Sony's own brand image but also make it very tough for Nintendo and Sega to match Sony's prices, advertising, and product development efforts and still earn acceptable profits.

The Combined Effects of These Advantages Is Potent A strategy of diversifying into *related* industries and then competing *globally* in each of these industries thus has great potential for being a winner in the marketplace because of the long-term growth opportunities it offers and the multiple corporate-level competitive advantage opportunities it contains. Indeed, *a strategy of multinational diversification contains more competitive advantage potential* (above and beyond what is achievable through a particular business's own competitive strategy) *than any other diversification strategy.*

> **Core Concept**
> A strategy of multinational diversification has more built-in potential for competitive advantage than any other diversification strategy.

The strategic key to maximum competitive advantage is for a DMNC to concentrate its diversification efforts in those industries where there are resource-sharing and resource-transfer opportunities and where there are important economies of scope and brand-name benefits. The more a company's diversification strategy yields these kinds of strategic-fit benefits, the more powerful a competitor it becomes and the better its profit and growth performance is likely to be.

However, it is important to recognize that while, in theory, a DMNC's cross-subsidization capabilities are a potent competitive weapon, cross-subsidization can, in actual practice, be used only sparingly. It is one thing to *occasionally* divert a portion of the profits and cash flows from existing businesses to help fund entry into a new business or country market or wage a competitive offensive against select rivals. It is quite another thing to *regularly* use cross-subsidization tactics and thereby weaken overall company performance. A DMNC is under the same pressures as any other company to demonstrate consistently acceptable profitability across its whole operation.[32] At some juncture, every business and every country market needs to make a profit contribution or become a candidate for abandonment. As a general rule, *cross-subsidization tactics are justified only when there is a good prospect that the short-term impairment to corporate profitability will be offset by stronger competitiveness and better overall profitability over the long term.*

Key Points

The purpose of diversification is to build shareholder value. Diversification builds shareholder value when a diversified group of businesses can perform better under the auspices of a single corporate parent than they would as independent, stand-alone businesses—the goal is not to achieve just a $1 + 1 = 2$ result, but rather to realize important $1 + 1 = 3$ performance benefits. Whether getting into a new business has potential to enhance shareholder value hinges on whether a company's entry into that business can pass the attractiveness test, the cost-of-entry test, and the better-off test.

Entry into new businesses can take any of three forms: acquisition, internal start-up, or joint venture/strategic partnership. Each has its pros and cons, but acquisition is the most frequently used; internal start-up takes the longest to produce home-run results, and joint venture/strategic partnership, though used second most frequently, is the least durable.

There are two fundamental approaches to diversification—into related businesses and into unrelated businesses. The rationale for *related* diversification is *strategic*: Diversify into businesses with strategic fits along their respective value chains, capitalize on strategic-fit relationships to gain competitive advantage, and then use competitive advantage to achieve the desired $1 + 1 = 3$ impact on shareholder value.

The basic premise of unrelated diversification is that any business that has good profit prospects and can be acquired on good financial terms is a good business to diversify into. Unrelated diversification strategies surrender the competitive advantage potential of strategic fit in return for such advantages as (1) spreading business risk over a variety of industries and (2) providing opportunities for financial gain (if candidate acquisitions have undervalued assets, are bargain priced and have good upside potential given the right management, or need the backing of a financially strong parent to capitalize on attractive opportunities). However, the greater the number of businesses a company has diversified into and the more diverse these businesses are, the harder it is for corporate executives to select capable managers to run each business, know when the major strategic proposals of business units are sound, or decide on a wise course of recovery when a business unit stumbles.

Analyzing how good a company's diversification strategy is a six-step process:

1. *Evaluate the long-term attractiveness of the industries into which the firm has diversified.* Industry attractiveness needs to be evaluated from three angles: the attractiveness of each industry on its own, the attractiveness of each industry relative to the others, and the attractiveness of all the industries as a group.

2. *Evaluate the relative competitive strength of each of the company's business units.* Again, quantitative ratings of competitive strength are preferable to subjective

judgments. The purpose of rating the competitive strength of each business is to gain clear understanding of which businesses are strong contenders in their industries, which are weak contenders, and the underlying reasons for their strength or weakness. The conclusions about industry attractiveness can be joined with the conclusions about competitive strength by drawing an industry attractiveness–competitive strength matrix that helps identify the prospects of each business and what priority each business should be given in allocating corporate resources and investment capital.

3. *Check for cross-business strategic fits.* A business is more attractive strategically when it has value chain relationships with sister business units that offer potential to (*a*) realize economies of scope or cost-saving efficiencies; (*b*) transfer technology, skills, know-how, or other resource capabilities from one business to another; (*c*) leverage use of a well-known and trusted brand name; and (*d*) to build new or stronger resource strengths and competitive capabilities via cross-business collaboration. Cross-business strategic fits represent a significant avenue for producing competitive advantage beyond what any one business can achieve on its own.

4. *Check whether the firm's resource strengths fit the resource requirements of its present business lineup.* Resource fit exists when (*a*) businesses add to a company's resource strengths, either financially or strategically; (*b*) a company has the resources to adequately support the resource requirements of its businesses as a group without spreading itself too thin; and (*c*) there are close matches between a company's resources and industry key success factors. One important test of financial resource fit involves determining whether a company has ample cash cows and not too many cash hogs.

5. *Rank the performance prospects of the businesses from best to worst and determine what the corporate parent's priority should be in allocating resources to its various businesses.* The most important considerations in judging business-unit performance are sales growth, profit growth, contribution to company earnings, and the return on capital invested in the business. Sometimes, cash flow generation is a big consideration. Normally, strong business units in attractive industries have significantly better performance prospects than weak businesses or businesses in unattractive industries. Business subsidiaries with the brightest profit and growth prospects and solid strategic and resource fits generally should head the list for corporate resource support.

6. *Crafting new strategic moves to improve overall corporate performance.* This step entails using the results of the preceding analysis as the basis for devising actions to strengthen existing businesses, make new acquisitions, divest weak-performing and unattractive businesses, restructure the company's business lineup, expand the scope of the company's geographic reach multinationally or globally, and otherwise steer corporate resources into the areas of greatest opportunity.

Once a company has diversified, corporate management's task is to manage the collection of businesses for maximum long-term performance. There are four different strategic paths for improving a diversified company's performance: (1) broadening the firm's business base by diversifying into additional businesses, (2) retrenching to a narrower diversification base by divesting some of its present businesses, (3) restructuring the company, and (4) diversifying multinationally.

Exercises

1. Consider the business lineup of General Electric (GE) shown in Illustration Capsule 9.2. What problems do you think the top executives at GE encounter in trying to stay on top of all the businesses the company is in? How might they decide the merits of adding new businesses or divesting poorly performing businesses? What types of advice might they be in a position to give to the general managers of each of GE's business units?

2. The Walt Disney Company is in the following businesses:

    *   Theme parks.
    *   Disney Cruise Line.
    *   Resort properties.
    *   Movie, video, and theatrical productions (for both children and adults).
    *   Television broadcasting (ABC, Disney Channel, Toon Disney, Classic Sports Network, ESPN and ESPN2, E!, Lifetime, and A&E networks).
    *   Radio broadcasting (Disney Radio).
    *   Musical recordings and sales of animation art.
    *   Anaheim Mighty Ducks NHL franchise.
    *   Anaheim Angels major league baseball franchise (25 percent ownership).
    *   Books and magazine publishing.
    *   Interactive software and Internet sites.
    *   The Disney Store retail shops.

    Given the above listing, would you say that Walt Disney's business lineup reflects a strategy of related or unrelated diversification? Explain your answer in terms of the extent to which the value chains of Disney's different businesses seem to have competitively valuable cross-business relationships.

3. Newell Rubbermaid is in the following businesses:

    *   Cleaning and organizations businesses: Rubbermaid storage, organization, and cleaning products; Blue Ice ice substitute; Roughneck storage itemmms; Stain Shield and TakeAlongs food storage containers; and Brute commercial-grade storage and cleaning products (25 percent of annual revenues).
    *   Home and family businesses: Calphalon cookware and bakeware, Cookware Europe, Graco strollers, Little Tikes children's toys and furniture, and Goody hair accessories (20 percent of annual sales).
    *   Home fashions: Levolor and Kirsch window blinds, shades, and hardware in the United States; Swish, Gardinia and Harrison Drape home furnishings in Europe (15 percent of annual revenues).
    *   Office products businesses: Sharpie markers, Sanford highlighters, Eberhard Faber and Berol ballpoint pens, Paper Mate pens and pencils, Waterman and Parker fine writing instruments, and Liquid Paper (25 percent of annual revenues).

    Would you say that Newell Rubbermaid's strategy is one of related diversification, unrelated diversification or a mixture of both? Explain.

4.   Explore the Web sites of the following companies and determine whether the company is pursuing a strategy of related diversification, unrelated diversification, or a mixture of both:

- Berkshire Hathaway
- News Corporation
- Dow Jones & Company
- Kimberly Clark

chapter ten

Strategy, Ethics, and Social Responsibility

When morality comes up against profit, it is seldom profit that loses.

—Shirley Chisholm
Former Congresswoman

But I'd shut my eyes in the sentry box so I didn't see nothing wrong.

—Rudyard Kipling
Author

Values can't just be words on a page. To be effective, they must shape action.

—Jeffrey R. Immelt
CEO, General Electric

Leaders must be more than individuals of high character. They must "lead" others to behave ethically.

—Linda K. Treviño and Michael E. Brown
Professors

Integrity violations are no-brainers. In such cases, you don't need to hesitate for a moment before firing someone or fret about it either. Just do it, and make sure the organization knows why, so that the consequences of breaking the rules are not lost on anyone.

—Jack Welch
Former CEO, General Electric

There is one and only one social responsibility of business—to use its resources and engage in activities designed to increase its profits so long as it stays within the rules of the game, which is to say engages in free and open competition, without deception or fraud.

—Milton Friedman
Nobel Prize–winning economist

Corporations are economic entities, to be sure, but they are also social institutions that must justify their existence by their overall contribution to society.

—Henry Mintzberg, Robert Simons, and Kunal Basu
Professors

C learly, a company has a responsibility to make a profit and grow the business—in capitalistic, or market, economies, management's fiduciary duty to create value for shareholders is not a matter for serious debate. Just as clearly, a company and its personnel also have a duty to obey the law and play by the rules of fair competition. But does a company have a duty to operate according to the ethical norms of the societies in which it operates—should it be held to some standard of ethical conduct? And does it have a duty or obligation to contribute to the betterment of society independent of the needs and preferences of the customers it serves? Should a company display a social conscience and devote a portion of its resources to bettering society?

The focus of this chapter is to examine what link, if any, there should be between a company's efforts to craft and execute a winning strategy and its duties to (1) conduct its activities ethically and (2) demonstrate socially responsible behavior by being a committed corporate citizen and directing corporate resources to the betterment of employees, the communities in which it operates, and society as a whole.

WHAT DO WE MEAN BY *BUSINESS ETHICS?*

Business ethics is the application of ethical principles and standards to business behavior.[1] Business ethics does not really involve a special set of ethical standards applicable only to business situations. Ethical principles in business are not materially different from ethical principles in general. Why? Because business actions have to be judged in the context of society's standards of right and wrong, not by a special set of rules that businesspeople decide to apply to their own conduct. If dishonesty is considered to be unethical and immoral, then dishonest behavior in business—whether it relates to customers, suppliers, employees or shareholders—qualifies as equally unethical and immoral. If being ethical entails not deliberately harming others, then recalling a defective or unsafe product is ethically necessary and failing to undertake such a recall or correct the problem in future shipments of the product is likewise unethical. If society deems bribery to be unethical, then it is unethical for company personnel to make payoffs to government officials to facilitate business transactions or bestow gifts and other favors on prospective customers to win or retain their business.

Core Concept
Business ethics concerns the application of general ethical principles and standards to the actions and decisions of companies and the conduct of company personnel.

WHERE DO ETHICAL STANDARDS COME FROM—ARE THEY UNIVERSAL OR DEPENDENT ON LOCAL NORMS AND SITUATIONAL CIRCUMSTANCES?

Notions of right and wrong, fair and unfair, moral and immoral, ethical and unethical are present in all societies, organizations, and individuals. But there are three schools of thought about the extent to which the ethical standards travel across cultures and whether multinational companies can apply the same set of ethical standards in any and all of the locations where they operate.

The School of Ethical Universalism

According to the school of **ethical universalism,** some concepts of what is right and what is wrong are *universal*; that is, they transcend all cultures, societies, and religions.[2] For instance, being truthful (or not lying, or not being deliberately deceitful) is considered right by the peoples of all nations. Likewise, demonstrating integrity of character, not cheating, and treating people with dignity and respect are concepts that resonate with people of most cultures and religions. In most societies, people believe that companies should not pillage or degrade the environment in the course of conducting their operations. In most societies, people would concur that it is unethical to knowingly expose workers to toxic chemicals and hazardous materials or to sell products known to be unsafe or harmful to the users. *To the extent that there is common moral agreement about right and wrong actions and behaviors across multiple cultures and countries, there exists a set of universal ethical standards to which all societies, all companies, and all individuals can be held accountable.* These universal ethical principles or norms put limits on what actions and behaviors fall inside the boundaries of what is right and which ones fall outside. They set forth the traits and behaviors that are considered virtuous and that a good person is supposed to believe in and to display.

Core Concept
According to the school of *ethical universalism,* the same standards of what's ethical and what's unethical resonate with peoples of most societies regardless of local traditions and cultural norms; hence, common ethical standards can be used to judge the conduct of personnel at companies operating in a variety of country markets and cultural circumstances.

Many ethicists believe that the most important moral standards travel well across countries and cultures and thus are *universal*—universal norms include honesty or trustworthiness, respecting the rights of others, practicing the Golden Rule, avoiding unnecessary harm to workers or to the users of the company's product or service, and respect for the environment.[3] In all such instances where there is cross-cultural agreement as to what actions and behaviors are inside and outside ethical and moral boundaries, adherents of the school of ethical universalism maintain that the conduct of personnel at companies operating in a variety of country markets and cultural circumstances can be judged against the resulting set of common ethical standards.

The strength of ethical universalism is that it draws on the collective views of multiple societies and cultures to put some clear boundaries on what constitutes ethical business behavior and what constitutes unethical business behavior no matter what country market or culture a company or its personnel are operating in. This means that whenever basic moral standards really do not vary significantly according to local cultural beliefs, traditions, religious convictions, or time and circumstance, a multinational company can apply a code of ethics more or less evenly across its worldwide operations.[4] It can avoid the slippery slope that comes from having different ethical standards for different company personnel depending on where in the world they are working.

The School of Ethical Relativism

Apart from select universal basics—honesty, trustworthiness, fairness, a regard for worker safety, and respect for the environment—there are meaningful variations in what societies generally agree to be right and wrong in the conduct of business activities. Divergent religious beliefs, historic traditions, social customs, and prevailing political and economic doctrines (whether a country leans more toward a capitalistic market economy or one heavily dominated by socialistic or communistic principles) frequently produce ethical norms that vary from one country to another. The school of **ethical relativism** holds that when there are cross-country or cross-cultural differences in what is deemed fair or unfair, what constitutes proper regard for human rights, and what is considered ethical or unethical in business situations, it is appropriate for local moral standards to take precedence over what the ethical standards may be elsewhere—for instance, in a company's home market. The thesis is that whatever a culture thinks is right or wrong really is right or wrong for that culture.[5] Hence, the school of ethical relativism contends that there are important occasions when cultural norms and the circumstances of the situation determine whether certain actions or behaviors are right or wrong. Consider the following examples.

> **Core Concept**
>
> According to the school of **ethical relativism** different societal cultures and customs have divergent values and standards of right and wrong—thus what is ethical or unethical must be judged in the light of local customs and social mores and can vary from culture or nation to another.

The Use of Underage Labor In industrialized nations, the use of underage workers is considered taboo; social activists are adamant that child labor is unethical and that companies should neither employ children under the age of 18 as full-time employees nor source any products from foreign suppliers that employ underage workers. Many countries have passed legislation forbidding the use of underage labor or, at a minimum, regulating the employment of people under the age of 18. However, in India, Bangladesh, Botswana, Sri Lanka, Ghana, Somalia, Turkey, and 100-plus other countries, it is customary to view children as potential, even necessary, workers.[6] Many poverty-stricken families cannot subsist without the income earned by young family members, and sending their children to school instead of having them participate in the workforce is not a realistic option. In 2000, the International Labor Organization estimated that 211 million children ages 5 to 14 were working around the world.[7] If such children are not permitted to work—due to pressures imposed by activist groups in industrialized nations—they may be forced to seek work in lower-wage jobs in "hidden" parts of the economy of their countries, beg on the street, or even traffic in drugs or engage in prostitution.[8] So if all businesses succumb to the protests of activist groups and government organizations that, based on their values and beliefs, loudly proclaim that underage labor is unethical, then have either businesses or the protesting groups really done something good on behalf of society in general?

The Payment of Bribes and Kickbacks A particularly thorny area facing multinational companies is the degree of cross-country variability in paying bribes.[9] In many countries in Eastern Europe, Africa, Latin America, and Asia, it is customary to pay bribes to government officials in order to win a government contract, obtain a license or permit, or facilitate an administrative ruling.[10] Senior managers in China often use their power to obtain kickbacks and offer bribes when they purchase materials or other products for their companies.[11] In some developing nations, it is difficult for any company, foreign or domestic, to move goods through customs without paying off low-level officials.[12] Likewise, in many countries it is normal to make payments to prospective customers in order to win or retain their business. A *Wall Street Journal* article reported that 30 to 60 percent of all business transactions in Eastern Europe involved paying bribes, and the costs of bribe payments averaged 2 to 8 percent of revenues.[13] Three recent annual issues of the *Global Corruption Report*, sponsored by Berlin-based Transparency International, provide credible evidence that corruption among public officials and in business transactions is widespread across the world.[14] Some people stretch to justify the payment of bribes and kickbacks on grounds that bribing government officials to get goods through customs or giving kickbacks to customers to retail their business or win an order is simply a payment for services rendered, in the same way that people tip for service at restaurants.[15] But this argument rests on moral quicksand, even though it is a clever and pragmatic way to rationalize why such facilitating payments should be viewed as a normal and maybe unavoidable cost of doing business in some countries.

Companies that forbid the payment of bribes and kickbacks in their codes of ethical conduct and that are serious about enforcing this prohibition face a particularly vexing problem in those countries where bribery and kickback payments have been entrenched as a local custom for decades and are not considered unethical by the local population.[16] Refusing to pay bribes or kickbacks (so as to comply with the company's code of ethical conduct) is very often tantamount to losing business. Frequently, the sales and profits are lost to more unscrupulous companies, with the result that both ethical companies and ethical individuals are penalized. However, winking at the code of ethical conduct and going along with the payment of bribes or kickbacks not only undercuts enforcement of and adherence to the company's code of ethics but can also risk breaking the law. U.S. companies are prohibited by the Foreign Corrupt Practices Act (FCPA) from paying bribes to government officials, political parties, political candidates, or others in all countries where they do business; the FCPA requires U.S. companies with foreign operations to adopt accounting practices that ensure full disclosure of a company's transactions so that illegal payments can be detected. The 35 member countries of the Organization for Economic Cooperation and Development (OECD) in 1997 adopted a convention to combat bribery in international business transactions; the Anti-Bribery Convention obligated the countries to criminalize the bribery of foreign public officials, including payments made to political parties and party officials. So far, however, there has been only token enforcement of the OECD convention and the payment of bribes in global business transactions remains a common practice in many countries.

Ethical Relativism Equates to Multiple Sets of Ethical Standards   The existence of varying ethical norms such as those cited above explains why the adherents of ethical relativism maintain that there are few absolutes when it comes to business ethics and thus few ethical absolutes for consistently judging a company's conduct in various countries and markets. Indeed, the thesis of ethical relativists is that while there are sometimes general moral prescriptions that apply in most every society and business circumstance there are plenty of situations where ethical norms must be contoured to fit the local customs, traditions, and the notions of fairness shared by the parties involved. They argue that a one-size-fits-all template for judging the ethical appropriateness of business actions and the behaviors of company personnel simply does not exist—in other words, ethical problems in business cannot be fully resolved without appealing to the shared convictions of the parties in question.[17] European and American managers may want to impose standards of business conduct that give heavy weight to such core human rights as personal freedom, individual security, political participation, the ownership of property, and the right to subsistence as well as the obligation to respect the dignity of each human person, adequate health and safety standards for all employees, and respect for the environment; managers in China have a much weaker commitment to these kinds of human rights. Japanese managers may prefer ethical standards that show respect for the collective good of society. Muslim managers may wish to apply ethical standards compatible with the teachings of Mohammed. Individual companies may want to give explicit recognition to the importance of company personnel living up to the company's own espoused values and business principles. Clearly, there is merit in the school of ethical relativism's view that what is deemed right or wrong, fair or unfair, moral or immoral, ethical or unethical in business situations depends partly on the context of each country's local customs, religious traditions, and societal norms. Hence, there is a kernel of truth in the argument that businesses need some room to tailor their ethical standards to fit local situations. A company has to be very cautious about exporting its home-country values and ethics to foreign countries where it operates—"photocopying" ethics is disrespectful of other cultures and neglects the important role of moral free space.

> Under ethical relativism, there can be no one-size-fits-all set of authentic ethical norms against which to gauge the conduct of company personnel.

Pushed to Extreme, Ethical Relativism Breaks Down   While the relativistic rule of "When in Rome, do as the Romans do" appears reasonable, it nonetheless presents a big problem—when the envelope starts to be pushed, as will inevitably be the case, *it is tantamount to rudderless ethical standards.* Consider, for instance, the following example: In 1992, the owners of the SS *United States,* an aging luxury ocean liner constructed with asbestos in the 1940s, had the liner towed to Turkey, where a contractor had agreed to remove the asbestos for $2 million (versus a far higher cost in the United States, where asbestos removal safety standards were much more stringent).[18] When Turkish officials blocked the asbestos removal because of the dangers to workers of contracting cancer, the owners had the liner towed to the Black Sea port of Sevastopol, in the Crimean Republic, where the asbestos removal standards were quite lax and where a contractor had agreed to remove more than 500,000 square feet of carcinogenic asbestos for less than $2 million. There are no moral grounds for arguing that exposing workers to carcinogenic asbestos is ethically correct, irrespective of what a country's law allows or the value the country places on worker safety.

A company that adopts the principle of ethical relativism and holds company personnel to local ethical standards necessarily assumes that what prevails as local morality is an adequate guide to ethical behavior. This can be ethically dangerous—it leads to the conclusion that if a country's culture is accepting of bribery or environmental degradation or exposing workers to dangerous conditions (toxic chemicals or bodily harm), then so much the worse for honest people and protection of the environment and safe working conditions. Such a position is morally unacceptable. Even though bribery of government officials in China is a common practice, when Lucent Technologies found that managers in its Chinese operations had bribed government officials, it fired the entire senior management team.[19]

> Managers in multinational enterprises have to figure out how to navigate the gray zone that arises when operating in two cultures with two sets of ethics.

Moreover, from a global markets perspective, ethical relativism results in a maze of conflicting ethical standards for multinational companies wanting to address the very real issue of what ethical standards to enforce companywide. On the one hand, multinational companies need to educate and motivate their employees worldwide to respect the customs and traditions of other nations, and, on the other hand, they must enforce compliance with the company's own particular code of ethical behavior. It is a slippery slope indeed to resolve such ethical diversity without any kind of higher-order moral compass. Imagine, for example, that a multinational company in the name of ethical relativism takes the position that it is okay for company personnel to pay bribes and kickbacks in countries where such payments are customary but forbids company personnel from making such payments in those countries where bribes and kickbacks are considered unethical or illegal. Or that the company says it is ethically fine to use underage labor in its plants in those countries where underage labor is acceptable and ethically inappropriate to employ underage labor at the remainder of its plants. Having thus adopted conflicting ethical standards for operating in different countries, company managers have little moral basis for enforcing ethical standards companywide—rather, the clear message to employees would be that the company has no ethical standards or principles of its own, preferring to let its practices be governed by the countries in which it operates. This is scarcely strong moral ground to stand on.

Ethics and Integrative Social Contracts Theory

Core Concept
According to *integrated social contracts theory,* universal ethical principles or norms based on the collective views of multiple cultures and societies combine to form a "social contract" that all individuals in all situations have a duty to observe. Within the boundaries of this social contract, local cultures or groups can specify other impermissible actions; however, universal ethical norms always take precedence over local ethical norms.

Social contract theory provides a middle position between the opposing views of universalism (that the same set of ethical standards should apply everywhere) and relativism (that ethical standards vary according to local custom).[20] According to **integrative social contracts theory,** the ethical standards a company should try to uphold are governed both by (1) a limited number of universal ethical principles that are widely recognized as putting legitimate ethical boundaries on actions and behavior in *all* situations and (2) the circumstances of local cultures, traditions, and shared values that further prescribe what constitutes ethically permissible behavior and what does not. However, *universal ethical norms take precedence over local ethical norms.* In other words, universal ethical principles apply in those situations where most all societies—endowed with rationality and moral knowledge—have common moral agreement on what is wrong and thereby put limits on what actions and behaviors fall inside the boundaries of what is right and which ones fall outside. *These mostly uniform agreements about what is morally right and wrong form a "social contract" or contract with society that is binding on all individuals, groups, organizations, and businesses in terms of establishing right and wrong and in drawing the line between ethical and unethical behaviors.* But these universal ethical principles or norms nonetheless still leave some moral free space for the people in a particular country (or local culture or even a company) to make specific interpretations of what other actions may or may not be permissible within the bounds defined by universal ethical principles. Hence, while firms, industries, professional associations, and other business-relevant groups are contractually obligated to society to observe universal ethical norms, they have the discretion to go beyond these universal norms and specify other behaviors that are out of bounds and place further limitations on what is considered ethical. Both the legal and medical professions have standards regarding what kinds of advertising are ethically permissible and what kinds are not. Food products companies are beginning to establish ethical guidelines for judging what is and is not appropriate advertising for food products that are inherently unhealthy and may cause dietary or obesity problems for people who eat them regularly or consume them in large quantities.

The strength of integrated social contracts theory is that it accommodates the best parts of ethical universalism and ethical relativism. It is indisputable that cultural differences impact how business is conducted in various parts of the world and that these cultural differences sometimes give rise to different ethical norms. But it is just as indisputable that some ethical norms are more authentic or universally applicable than others, meaning that, in many instances of cross-country differences, one side may be more "ethically correct" or "more right" than another. In such instances, resolving cross-cultural differences entails applying universal, or first-order, ethical norms and overriding the local, or second-order, ethical norms. A good example is the payment of bribes and kickbacks. Yes, bribes and kickbacks seem to be common in some countries, but does this justify paying them? Just because bribery flourishes in a country does not mean that it is an authentic or legitimate ethical norm. Virtually all of the world's major religions (Buddhism, Christianity, Confucianism, Hinduism, Islam, Judaism, Sikhism, and Taoism) and all moral schools of thought condemn bribery and corruption.[21] Bribery is commonplace in India but interviews with Indian CEOs whose companies constantly engaged in payoffs indicated disgust for the practice and they expressed no illusions about its impropriety.[22] Therefore, a multinational company might reasonably conclude that the right ethical standard is one of refusing to condone bribery and kickbacks on the part of company personnel no matter what the local custom is and no matter what the sales consequences are.

Granting an automatic preference to local country ethical norms presents vexing problems to multinational company managers when the ethical standards followed in a foreign country are lower than those in its home country or are in conflict with the company's code of ethics. Sometimes there can be no compromise on what is ethically permissible and what is not. *This is precisely what integrated social contracts theory maintains—universal or first-order ethical norms should always take precedence over local or second-order norms.* Integrated social contracts theory offers managers in multinational companies clear guidance in resolving cross-country ethical differences: Those parts of the company's code of ethics that involve universal ethical norms must be enforced worldwide, but within these boundaries there is room for ethical diversity and opportunity for host country cultures to exert *some* influence in setting their own moral and ethical standards. Such an approach detours the somewhat scary case of a self-righteous multinational company trying to operate as the standard-bearer of moral truth and imposing its interpretation of its code of ethics worldwide no matter what. And it avoids the equally scary case for a company's ethical conduct to be no higher than local ethical norms in situations where local ethical norms permit practices that are generally considered immoral or when local norms clearly conflict with a company's code of ethical conduct. But even with the guidance provided by integrated social contracts theory, there are many instances where cross-country differences in ethical norms create gray areas in which it is tough to draw a line in the sand between right and wrong decisions, actions, and business practices.

THE THREE CATEGORIES OF MANAGEMENT MORALITY

Three categories of managers stand out with regard to ethical and moral principles in business affairs:[23]

- *The moral manager*—Moral managers are dedicated to high standards of ethical behavior, both in their own actions and in their expectations of how the company's business is to be conducted. They see themselves as stewards of ethical behavior and believe it is important to exercise ethical leadership. Moral managers may well be ambitious and have a powerful urge to succeed, but they pursue success in business within the confines of both the letter and the spirit of what is ethical and legal—they typically regard the law as an ethical minimum and have a habit of operating well above what the law requires.

- *The immoral manager*—Immoral managers have no regard for so-called ethical standards in business and pay no attention to ethical principles in making decisions and conducting the company's business. Their philosophy is that good businesspeople cannot spend time watching out for the interests of others and agonizing over "the right thing to do." In the minds of immoral managers, nice guys come in second and the competitive nature of business requires that you either trample on others or get trampled yourself. They believe what really matters is single-minded pursuit of their own best interests—they are living examples of capitalistic greed, caring only about their own or their organization's gains and successes. Immoral managers may even be willing to short-circuit legal and regulatory requirements if they think they can escape detection. And they are always on the lookout for legal loopholes and creative ways to get around rules and regulations that block or constrain actions they deem in their own or their company's self-interest. Immoral managers are thus the bad guys—they have few scruples, little or no integrity, and are willing to do most anything they believe they can get away with. It doesn't bother them much to be seen by others as wearing the black hats.

- *The amoral manager*—Amoral managers appear in two forms: the intentionally amoral manager and the unintentionally amoral manager. Intentionally amoral managers are of the strong opinion that business and ethics are not to be mixed. They are not troubled by failing to factor ethical considerations into their decisions and actions because it is perfectly legitimate for businesses to do anything they wish so long as they stay within legal and regulatory bounds—in other words, if particular actions and behaviors are legal and comply with existing regulations, then they qualify as permissible and should not be seen as unethical. Intentionally amoral managers view the observance of high ethical standards (doing more than what is required by law) as too Sunday-schoolish for the tough competitive world of business, even though observing some higher ethical considerations may be appropriate in life outside of business. Their concept of right and wrong tends to be lawyer-driven—how much can we get by with and can we go ahead even if it is borderline? Thus intentionally amoral managers hold firmly to the view that anything goes, so long as actions and behaviors are not clearly ruled out by prevailing legal and regulatory requirements.

> **Core Concept**
> Amoral managers believe that businesses ought to be able to do whatever current laws and regulations allow them to do without being shackled by ethical considerations—they think that what is permissible and what is not is governed entirely by prevailing laws and regulations, not by societal concepts of right and wrong.

Unintentionally amoral managers do not pay much attention to the concept of business ethics either, but for different reasons. They are simply casual about, careless about, or inattentive to the fact that certain kinds of business decisions or company activities are unsavory or may have deleterious effects on others— in short, they go about their jobs as best they can without giving serious thought to the ethical dimension of decisions and business actions. They are ethically unconscious when it comes to business matters, partly or mainly because they have just never stopped to consider whether and to what extent business decisions or company actions sometimes spill over to create adverse impacts on others. Unintentionally amoral managers may even see themselves as people of integrity and as personally ethical. But, like intentionally amoral managers, they are of the firm view that businesses ought to be able to do whatever the current legal and regulatory framework allows them to do without being shackled by ethical considerations.

By some accounts, the population of managers is said to be distributed among all three types in a bell-shaped curve, with immoral managers and moral managers occupying the two tails of the curve, and the amoral managers (especially the intentionally amoral managers) occupying the broad middle ground.[24] Furthermore, within the population of managers, there is experiential evidence to support that while the average manager may be amoral most of the time, he or she may slip into a moral or immoral mode on occasion, based on a variety of impinging factors and circumstances.

Evidence of Managerial Immorality in the Global Business Community

There is considerable evidence that a sizable majority of managers are either amoral or immoral. The *2005 Global Corruption Report,* sponsored by Transparency International, found that corruption among public officials and in business transactions is widespread across the world. Table 10.1 shows some of the countries where corruption is believed to be lowest and highest—even in the countries where business practices are deemed to be least corrupt, there is considerable room for improvement in the extent to which managers observe ethical business practices. Table 10.2 presents data showing the perceived likelihood that companies in the 21 largest exporting countries are paying bribes to win business in the markets of 15 emerging-country markets—Argentina, Brazil, Colombia, Hungary, India, Indonesia, Mexico, Morocco, Nigeria, the Philippines, Poland, Russia, South Africa, South Korea, and Thailand.

Table 10.1   **Corruption Perceptions Index, Selected Countries, 2004**

Country	2004 CPI Score*	High–Low Range	Number of Surveys Used	Country	2004 CPI Score*	High–Low Range	Number of Surveys Used
Finland	9.7	9.2–10.0	9	Taiwan	5.6	4.7–6.0	15
New Zealand	9.6	9.2–9.7	9	Italy	4.8	3.4–5.6	10
Denmark	9.5	8.7–9.8	10	South Africa	4.6	3.4–5.8	11
Sweden	9.2	8.7–9.5	11	South Korea	4.5	2.2–5.8	14
Switzerland	9.1	8.6–9.4	10	Brazil	3.9	3.5–4.8	11
Norway	8.9	8.0–9.5	9	Mexico	3.6	2.6–4.5	11
Australia	8.8	6.7–9.5	15	Thailand	3.6	2.5–4.5	14
Netherlands	8.7	8.3–9.4	10	China	3.4	2.1–5.6	16
United Kingdom	8.6	7.8–9.2	12	Saudi Arabia	3.4	2.0–4.5	5
Canada	8.5	6.5–9.4	12	Turkey	3.2	1.9–5.4	13
Germany	8.2	7.5–9.2	11	India	2.8	2.2–3.7	15
Hong Kong	8.0	3.5–9.4	13	Russia	2.8	2.0–5.0	15
United States	7.5	5.0–8.7	14	Philippines	2.6	1.4–3.7	14
Chile	7.4	6.3–8.7	11	Vietnam	2.6	1.6–3.7	11
France	7.1	5.0–9.0	12	Argentina	2.5	1.7–3.7	11
Spain	7.1	5.6–8.0	11	Venezuela	2.3	2.0–3.0	11
Japan	6.9	3.5–9.0	15	Pakistan	2.1	1.2–3.3	7
Israel	6.4	3.5–8.1	10	Nigeria	1.6	0.9–2.1	9
Uruguay	6.2	5.6–7.3	6	Bangladesh	1.5	0.3–2.4	5

* The CPI scores range between 10 (highly clean) and 0 (highly corrupt); the data were collected between 2002 and 2004 and reflects a composite of 18 data sources from 12 institutions, as indicated in the number of surveys used. The CPI score represents the perceptions of the degree of corruption as seen by businesspeople, academics, and risk analysts. CPI scores were reported for 146 countries.

Source: Transparency International, *2005 Global Corruption Report,* www.globalcorruptionreport.org (accessed October 31, 2005), pp. 235–38.

Table 10.2   **The Degree to Which Companies in Major Exporting Countries Are Perceived to Be Paying Bribes in Doing Business Abroad**

Rank/Country	Bribe-Payer Index (10 = Low; 0 = High)	Rank/Country	Bribe-Payer Index (10 = Low; 0 = High)
1. Australia	8.5	12. France	5.5
2. Sweden	8.4	13. United States	5.3
3. Switzerland	8.4	14. Japan	5.3
4. Austria	8.2	15. Malaysia	4.3
5. Canada	8.1	16. Hong Kong	4.3
6. Netherlands	7.8	17. Italy	4.1
7. Belgium	7.8	18. South Korea	3.9
8. Britain	6.9	19. Taiwan	3.8
9. Singapore	6.3	20. China (excluding Hong Kong)	3.5
10. Germany	6.3	21. Russia	3.2
11. Spain	5.8		

Note: The bribe-payer index is based on a questionnaire developed by Transparency International and a survey of some 835 private-sector leaders in 15 emerging countries accounting for 60 percent of all imports into non-Organization for Economic Cooperation and Development countries—actual polling was conducted by Gallup International.

Source: Transparency International, *2003 Global Corruption Report*, www.globalcorruptionreport.org (accessed November 1, 2005), p. 267.

The *2003 Global Corruption Report* cited data indicating that bribery occurred most often in (1) public works contracts and construction, (2) the arms and defense industry, and (3) the oil and gas industry. On a scale of 1 to 10, where 10 indicates negligible bribery, even the "cleanest" industry sectors—agriculture, light manufacturing, and fisheries—only had "passable" scores of 5.9, indicating that bribes are quite likely a common occurrence in these sectors as well (see Table 10.3).

The corruption, of course, extends beyond just bribes and kickbacks. For example, in 2005, four global chip makers (Samsung and Hynix Semiconductor in South Korea, Infineon Technologies in Germany, and Micron Technology in the United States) pleaded guilty to conspiring to fix the prices of dynamic random access memory (DRAM) chips sold to such companies as Dell, Apple Computer, and Hewlett-Packard—DRAM chips generate annual worldwide sales of around $26 billion and are used in computers, electronics products, and motor vehicles.[25] So far, the probe has resulted in fines of $730 million, jail terms for nine executives, and pending criminal charges for three more employees for their role in the global cartel; the guilty companies face hundreds of millions of dollars more in damage claims from customers and from consumer class-action lawsuits.

A global business community that is apparently so populated with unethical business practices and managerial immorality does not bode well for concluding that many companies ground their strategies on exemplary ethical principles or for the vigor with which company managers try to ingrain ethical behavior into company personnel. And, as many business school professors have noted, there are considerable numbers of amoral business students in our classrooms. So efforts to root out shady and corrupt business practices and implant high ethical principles into the managerial process of crafting and executing strategy is unlikely to produce an ethically strong global business climate anytime in the near future, barring major effort to address and correct the ethical laxness of company managers.

Table 10.3   **Bribery in Different Industries**

Business Sector	Bribery Score (10 = Low; 0 = High)
Agriculture	5.9
Light manufacturing	5.9
Fisheries	5.9
Information technology	5.1
Forestry	5.1
Civilian aerospace	4.9
Banking and finance	4.7
Heavy manufacturing	4.5
Pharmaceuticals/medical care	4.3
Transportation/storage	4.3
Mining	4.0
Power generation/transmission	3.7
Telecommunications	3.7
Real estate/property	3.5
Oil and gas	2.7
Arms and defense	1.9
Public works/construction	1.3

Note: The bribery scores for each industry are based on a questionnaire developed by Transparency International and a survey of some 835 private sector leaders in 15 emerging countries accounting for 60 percent of all imports into non-Organization for Economic Cooperation and Development countries—actual polling was conducted by Gallup International.

Source: Transparency International, *2003 Global Corruption Report,* www.globalcorruption report.org (accessed November 1, 2005), p. 268.

DO COMPANY STRATEGIES NEED TO BE ETHICAL?

Company managers may formulate strategies that are ethical in all respects, or they may decide to employ strategies that, for one reason or another, have unethical or at least gray-area components. While most company managers are usually careful to ensure that a company's strategy is within the bounds of what is legal, the available evidence indicates they are not always so careful to ensure that all elements of their strategies are within the bounds of what is generally deemed ethical. Senior executives with strong ethical convictions are normally proactive in insisting that all aspects of company strategy fall within ethical boundaries. In contrast, senior executives who are either immoral or amoral may use shady strategies and unethical or borderline business practices, especially if they are clever at devising schemes to keep ethically questionable actions hidden from view.

During the past five years, there has been an ongoing series of revelations about managers who have ignored ethical standards, deliberately stepped out of bounds, and been called to account by the media, regulators, and the legal system. Ethical misconduct has occurred at Enron, Tyco International, HealthSouth, Rite Aid, Citicorp, Bristol-Myers, Squibb, Adelphia, Royal Dutch/Shell, Parmalat (an Italy-based food products company), Mexican oil giant Pemex, Marsh & McLennan and other insurance brokers, several leading brokerage houses and investment banking firms, and a host of mutual fund companies. The consequences of crafting strategies that cannot pass the test of moral scrutiny are manifested in the sharp drops in the stock prices of the guilty companies that have cost shareholders billions of dollars; the frequently devastating public relations hits that the accused companies have taken, the sizes of the fines that have been levied (often amounting to several hundred million dollars); the growing legion of criminal indictments and convictions of company executives; and the numbers of executives who have either been dismissed from their jobs, shoved into early retirement, and/or suffered immense public embarrassment. The fallout from all these scandals has resulted in heightened management attention to legal and ethical considerations in crafting strategy. Illustration Capsule 10.1 details the ethically flawed strategy at the world's leading insurance broker, and the consequences to those concerned.

What Are the Drivers of Unethical Strategies and Business Behavior?

The apparent pervasiveness of immoral and amoral businesspeople is one obvious reason why ethical principles are an ineffective moral compass in business dealings and why companies may resort to unethical strategic behavior. But apart from thinking that maintains "The business of business is business, not ethics," three other main drivers of unethical business behavior also stand out:[26]

- Faulty oversight such that overzealous or obsessive pursuit of personal gain, wealth, and other selfish interests is overlooked by or escapes the attention of higher-ups (most usually the board of directors).
- Heavy pressures on company managers to meet or beat performance targets.
- A company culture that puts the profitability and good business performance ahead of ethical behavior.

Overzealous Pursuit of Personal Gain, Wealth, and Selfish Interests

People who are obsessed with wealth accumulation, greed, power, status, and other selfish interests often push ethical principles aside in their quest for self-gain. Driven by their ambitions, they exhibit few qualms in skirting the rules or doing whatever is necessary to achieve their goals. The first and only priority of such corporate bad apples is to look out for their own best interests and if climbing the ladder of success means having few scruples and ignoring the welfare of others, so be it. A general disregard for business ethics can prompt all kinds of unethical strategic maneuvers and behaviors at companies. Top executives, directors, and majority shareholders at cable-TV company Adelphia Communications ripped off the company for amounts totaling well over $1 billion, diverting hundreds of millions of dollars to fund their Buffalo Sabres hockey team, build a private golf course, and buy timber rights—among other things—and driving the company into bankruptcy. Their actions, which represent one of the biggest instances of corporate looting and self-dealing in American business, took place despite the company's public pontifications about the principles it would observe in trying to care for customers, employees, stockholders, and the local communities where it operated. Andrew Fastow, Enron's chief financial officer (CFO), set himself up as the manager of one of Enron's off-the-books partnerships and as the part-owner of another, allegedly earning extra compensation of $30 million for his owner-manager roles in the two partnerships; Enron's board of directors agreed to suspend the company's conflict-of-interest rules designed to protect the company from this very kind of executive self-dealing (but directors and perhaps Fastow's superiors were kept in the dark about how much Fastow was earning on the side).

Marsh & McLennan's Ethically Flawed Strategy

In October 2004, *Wall Street Journal* headlines trumpeted that a cartel among insurance brokers had been busted. Among the ringleaders was worldwide industry leader Marsh & McLennan Companies Inc., with 2003 revenues of $11.5 billion and a U.S. market share of close to 20 percent. The gist of the brokers' plan was to cheat corporate clients by rigging the bids brokers solicited for insurance policies and thereby collecting big fees (called contingent commissions) from major insurance companies for steering business their way. Two family members of Marsh & McLennan CEO Jeffery Greenberg were CEOs of major insurance companies to which Marsh sometimes steered business. Greenberg's father was CEO of insurance giant AIG (which had total revenues of $81 billion and insurance premium revenues of $28 billion in 2003), and Greenberg's younger brother was CEO of ACE Ltd., the 24th biggest property-casualty insurer in the United States, with 2003 revenues of $10.7 billion and insurance premium revenues of more than $5 billion worldwide. Prior to joining ACE, Greenberg's younger brother had been president and chief operating officer of AIG, headed by his father.

Several months prior to the cartel bust, a Marsh subsidiary, Putnam Investments, had paid a $110 million fine for securities fraud and another Marsh subsidiary, Mercer Consulting, was placed under Securities and Exchange Commission (SEC) investigation for engaging in pay-to-play practices that forced investment managers to pay fees in order to secure Mercer's endorsement of their services when making recommendations to Mercer's pension fund clients.

The cartel scheme arose from the practice of large corporations to hire the services of such brokers as Marsh & McLennan, Aon Corporation, A. J. Gallaher & Company, Wells Fargo, or BB&T Insurance Services to manage their risks and take out appropriate property and casualty insurance on their behalf. The broker's job was to solicit bids from several insurers and obtain the best policies at the lowest prices for the client.

Marsh's insurance brokerage strategy was to solicit artificially high bids from some insurance companies so that it could guarantee that the bid of a preferred insurer on a given deal would win the bid. Marsh brokers called underwriters at various insurers, often including AIG and ACE, and asked for "B" quotes—bids that were deliberately high. Insurers asked for B quotes knew that Marsh wanted another insurer to win the business, but they were willing to participate because on other policy solicitations Marsh could end up steering the business to them via Marsh's same strategy. Sometimes Marsh even asked underwriters that were providing B quotes to attend a meeting with Marsh's client and make a presentation regarding their policy to help bolster the credibility of their inflated bid.

Since it was widespread practice among insurers to pay brokers contingent commissions based on the volume or profitability of the business the broker directed to them, Marsh's B-quote solicitation strategy allowed it to steer business to those insurers paying the largest contingent commissions—these contingent commissions were in addition to the fees the broker earned from the corporate client for services rendered in conducting the bidding process for the client. A substantial fraction of the policies that Marsh unlawfully steered were to two Bermuda-based insurance companies that it helped start up and in which it also had ownership interests (some Marsh executives also indirectly owned shares of stock in one of the companies); indeed, these two insurance companies received 30–40 percent of their total business from policies steered to them by Marsh.

At Marsh, steering business to insurers paying the highest contingent commission was a key component of the company's overall strategy. Marsh's contingent commissions generated revenues of close to $1.5 billion over the 2001–2003 period, including $845 million in 2003. Without these commission revenues, Marsh's $1.5 billion in net profits would have been close to 40 percent lower in 2003.

Within days of headlines about the cartel bust, Marsh's stock price had fallen by 48 percent (costing shareholders about $11.5 billion in market value) and the company was looking down the barrel of a criminal indictment. To stave off the criminal indictment (something no insurance company had ever survived), board members forced Jeffrey Greenberg to resign as CEO. Another top executive was suspended. Criminal charges against several Marsh executives for their roles in the bid-rigging scheme were filed several weeks thereafter.

In an attempt to lead industry reform, Greenberg's successor quickly announced a new business model for Marsh that included not accepting any contingent commissions from insurers. Marsh's new strategy and business model involved charging fees only to its corporate clients for soliciting bids, placing their insurance, and otherwise managing clients' risks and crises. This eliminated Marsh's conflict of interest in earning fees from both sides of the transactions it made on behalf of its corporate clients. Marsh also committed to provide up-front disclosure to clients of the fees it would earn on their business (in the past such fees had been murky and incomplete). Even so, there were indications that close to 10 lawsuits, some involving class action, would soon be filed against the company.

Meanwhile, all major commercial property-casualty insurers were scrambling to determine whether their payment of contingent commissions was ethical, since such arrangements clearly gave insurance brokers a financial incentive to place insurance with companies paying the biggest contingent commissions, not those with the best prices or terms. Prosecutors of the cartel had referred to the contingent commissions as kickbacks.

Sources: Monica Langley and Theo Francis, "Insurers Reel from Bust of a 'Cartel,'" *The Wall Street Journal,* October 18, 2004, pp. A1, A14; Monica Langley and Ian McDonald, "Marsh Averts Criminal Case with New CEO," *The Wall Street Journal,* October 26, 2004, pp. A1, A10; Christopher Oster and Theo Francis, "Marsh and Aon Have Holdings in Two Insurers," *The Wall Street Journal,* November 1, 2004, p. C1; and Marcia Vickers, "The Secret World of Marsh Mac," *BusinessWeek,* November 1, 2004, pp. 78–89.

According to a civil complaint filed by the Securities and Exchange Commission, the CEO of Tyco International, a well-known $35.6 billion manufacturing and services company, conspired with the company's CFO to steal more than $170 million, including a company-paid $2 million birthday party for the CEO's wife held on Sardinia, an island off the coast of Italy; a $7 million Park Avenue apartment for his wife; and secret low-interest and interest-free loans to fund private businesses and investments and purchase lavish artwork, yachts, estate jewelry, and vacation homes in New Hampshire, Connecticut, Massachusetts, and Utah. The CEO allegedly lived rent-free in a $31 million Fifth Avenue apartment that Tyco purchased in his name, directed millions of dollars of charitable contributions in his own name using Tyco funds, diverted company funds to finance his personal businesses and investments, and sold millions of dollars of Tyco stock back to Tyco itself through Tyco subsidiaries located in offshore bank-secrecy jurisdictions. Tyco's CEO and CFO were further charged with conspiring to reap more than $430 million from sales of stock, using questionable accounting to hide their actions, and engaging in deceptive accounting practices to distort the company's financial condition from 1995 to 2002. At the trial on the charges filed by the SEC, the prosecutor told the jury in his opening statement, "This case is about lying, cheating and stealing. These people didn't win the jackpot—they stole it." Defense lawyers countered that "every single transaction . . . was set down in detail in Tyco's books and records" and that the authorized and disclosed multimillion-dollar compensation packages were merited by the company's financial performance and stock price gains. The two Tyco executives were convicted and sentenced to jail.

Prudential Securities paid a total of about $2 billion in the 1990s to settle misconduct charges relating to practices that misled investors on the risks and rewards of limited-partnership investments. Providian Financial Corporation, despite an otherwise glowing record of social responsibility and corporate citizenship, paid $150 million in 2001 to settle claims that its strategy included systematic attempts to cheat credit card holders. Ten prominent Wall Street securities firms in 2003 paid $1.4 billion to settle charges that they knowingly issued misleading stock research to investors in an effort to prop up the stock prices of client corporations. A host of mutual-fund firms made under-the-table arrangements to regularly buy and sell stock for their accounts at special after-hours trading prices that disadvantaged long-term investors and had to pay nearly $2.0 billion in fines and restitution when their unethical practices were discovered by authorities during 2002–2003. Salomon Smith Barney, Goldman Sachs, Credit Suisse First Boston, and several other financial firms were assessed close to $2 billion in fines and restitution for the unethical manner in which they contributed to the scandals at Enron and WorldCom and for the shady practice of allocating shares of hot initial public offering stocks to a select list of corporate executives who either steered or were in a position to steer investment banking business their way.

Heavy Pressures on Company Managers to Meet or Beat Earnings Targets   When companies find themselves scrambling to achieve ambitious earnings growth and meet the quarterly and annual performance expectations of Wall Street analysts and investors, managers often feel enormous pressure to do whatever it takes to sustain the company's reputation for delivering good financial performance. Executives at high-performing companies know that investors will see the slightest sign of a slowdown in earnings growth as a red flag and drive down the company's stock price. The company's credit rating could be downgraded if it has used lots of debt to finance its growth. The pressure to watch the scoreboard and never miss a quarter—so as not to upset the expectations of Wall Street analysts and fickle stock market investors—prompts managers to cut costs wherever savings show up immediately, squeeze extra sales out of early deliveries, and engage in other short-term maneuvers to make the numbers. As the pressure builds to keep performance numbers looking good, company personnel start stretching the rules further and further, until the limits of ethical conduct are overlooked.[27] Once ethical boundaries are crossed in efforts to "meet or beat the numbers," the threshold for making more extreme ethical compromises becomes lower.

Several top executives at WorldCom (the remains of which is now part of Verizon Communications), a company built with scores of acquisitions in exchange for WorldCom stock, allegedly concocted a fraudulent $11 billion accounting scheme to hide costs and inflate revenues and profit over several years; the scheme was said to have helped the company keep its stock price propped up high enough to make additional acquisitions, support its nearly $30 billion debt load, and allow executives to cash in on their lucrative stock options. At Qwest Communications, a company created by the merger of a go-go telecom start-up and U.S. West (one of the regional Bell companies), management was charged with scheming to improperly book $2.4 billion in revenues from a variety of sources and deals, thereby inflating the company's profits and making it appear that the company's strategy to create a telecommunications company of the future was on track when, in fact, it was faltering badly behind the scenes. Top-level Qwest executives were dismissed, and in 2004 new management agreed to $250 million in fines for all the misdeeds.

At Bristol-Myers Squibb, the world's fifth-largest drug maker, management apparently engaged in a series of numbers-game maneuvers to meet earnings targets, including such actions as:

- Offering special end-of-quarter discounts to induce distributors and local pharmacies to stock up on certain prescription drugs—a practice known as channel stuffing.

- Issuing last-minute price increase alerts to spur purchases and beef up operating profits.

- Setting up excessive reserves for restructuring charges and then reversing some of the charges as needed to bolster operating profits.

- Making repeated asset sales small enough that the gains could be reported as additions to operating profit rather than being flagged as one-time gains. (Some accountants have long used a rule of thumb that says a transaction that alters quarterly profits by less than 5 percent is "immaterial" and need not be disclosed in the company's financial reports.)

Such numbers games were said to be a common "earnings management" practice at Bristol-Myers and, according to one former executive, "sent a huge message across the organization that you make your numbers at all costs."[28]

Company executives often feel pressured to hit financial performance targets because their compensation depends heavily on the company's performance. During the late 1990s, it became fashionable for boards of directors to grant lavish bonuses, stock option awards, and other compensation benefits to executives for meeting specified performance targets. So outlandishly large were these rewards that executives had strong personal incentives to bend the rules and engage in behaviors the allowed the targets to be met. Much of the accounting hocus-pocus at the root of recent corporate scandals has entailed situations in which executives benefited enormously from misleading accounting or other shady activities that allowed them to hit the numbers and receive incentive awards ranging from $10 million to $100 million. At Bristol-Myers Squibb, for example, the pay-for-performance link spawned strong rules-bending incentives. About 94 percent of one top executive's $18.5 million in total compensation in 2001 came from stock-option grants, a bonus, and long-term incentive payments linked to corporate performance; about 92 percent of a second executive's $12.9 million of compensation was incentive-based.[29]

The fundamental problem with a "make the numbers and move on" syndrome is that a company doesn't really serve its customers or its shareholders by going overboard in pursuing bottom-line profitability. In the final analysis, shareholder interests are best served by doing a really good job of serving customers (observing the rule that customers are king) and by improving the company's competitiveness in the marketplace—these outcomes are the most reliable drivers of higher profits and added shareholder value. Cutting ethical corners or stooping to downright illegal actions in the name of profits first carries exceptionally high risk for shareholders—the steep stock-price decline and tarnished brand image that accompany the discovery of scurrilous behavior leaves shareholders with a company worth much less than before—and the rebuilding task can be arduous, taking both considerable time and resources.

Company Cultures That Put the Bottom Line Ahead of Ethical Behavior

When a company's culture spawns an ethically corrupt or amoral work climate, people have a company-approved license to ignore what's right and engage in most any behavior or employ most any strategy they think they can get away with. Such cultural norms as "No one expects strict adherence to ethical standards," "Everyone else does it," and "It is politic to bend the rules to get the job done" permeate the work environment.[30] At such companies, ethically immoral or amoral people play down observance of ethical strategic actions and business conduct. Moreover, the pressures to conform to cultural norms can prompt otherwise honorable people to make ethical mistakes and succumb to the many opportunities around them to engage in unethical practices.

A perfect example of a company culture gone awry on ethics is Enron.[31] Enron's leaders encouraged company personnel to focus on the current bottom line and to be innovative and aggressive in figuring out what could be done to grow current revenues and earnings. Employees were expected to pursue opportunities to the utmost. Enron executives viewed the company as a laboratory for innovation; the company hired the best and brightest people and pushed them to be creative, look at problems and opportunities in new ways, and exhibit a sense of urgency in making things happen. Employees were encouraged to make a difference and do their part in creating an entrepreneurial environment in which creativity flourished, people could achieve their full potential, and everyone had a stake in the outcome. Enron employees got the message—pushing the limits and meeting one's numbers were viewed as survival skills. Enron's annual "rank and yank" formal evaluation process, in which the 15 to 20 percent lowest-ranking employees were let go or encouraged to seek other employment, made it abundantly clear that hitting earnings targets and being *the* mover and shaker -in the marketplace were what counted. The name of the game at Enron became devising clever ways to boost revenues and earnings, even if it sometimes meant operating outside established policies and without the knowledge of superiors. In fact, outside-the-lines behavior was celebrated if it generated profitable new business. Enron's energy contracts and its trading and hedging activities grew increasingly more complex and diverse as employees pursued first this avenue and then another to help keep Enron's financial performance looking good.

As a consequence of Enron's well-publicized successes in creating new products and businesses and leveraging the company's trading and hedging expertise into new market arenas, Enron came to be regarded as exceptionally innovative. It was ranked by its corporate peers as the most innovative U.S. company for three consecutive years in *Fortune* magazine's annual surveys of the most-admired companies. A high-performance/high-rewards climate came to pervade the Enron culture, as the best workers (determined by who produced the best bottom-line results) received impressively large incentives and bonuses (amounting to as much as $1 million for traders and even more for senior executives). On Car Day at Enron, an array of luxury sports cars arrived for presentation to the most successful employees. Understandably, employees wanted to be seen as part of Enron's star team and partake in the benefits that being one of Enron's best and smartest employees entailed. The high monetary rewards, the ambitious and hard-driving people that the company hired and promoted, and the competitive, results-oriented culture combined to give Enron a reputation not only for trampling competitors at every opportunity but also for practicing internal ruthlessness. The company's super-aggressiveness and win-at-all-costs mind-set nurtured a culture that gradually and then more rapidly fostered the erosion of ethical standards, eventually making a mockery of the company's stated values of integrity and respect. When it became evident in the fall of 2001 that Enron was a house of cards propped up by deceitful accounting and a myriad of unsavory practices, the company imploded in a matter of weeks—the biggest bankruptcy of all time cost investors $64 billion in losses (between August 2000, when the stock price was at its five-year high, and November 2001), and Enron employees lost their retirement assets, which were almost totally invested in Enron stock.

More recently, a team investigating an ethical scandal at oil giant Royal Dutch/ Shell Group that resulted in the payment of $150 million in fines found that an ethically flawed culture was a major contributor to why managers made rosy forecasts that they couldn't meet and why top executives engaged in maneuvers to mislead investors by overstating Shell's oil and gas reserves by 25 percent (equal to 4.5 billion barrels of oil). The investigation revealed that top Shell executives knew that a variety of internal practices, together with unrealistic and unsupportable estimates submitted by overzealous, bonus-conscious managers in Shell's exploration and production group, were being used to overstate reserves. An e-mail written by Shell's top executive for exploration and production (who was caught up in the ethical misdeeds and later forced to resign) said, "I am becoming sick and tired about lying about the extent of our reserves issues and the downward revisions that need to be done because of our far too aggressive/optimistic bookings."[32]

Illustration Capsule 10.2 describes Philip Morris USA's new strategy for growing the sales of its leading Marlboro cigarette brand—judge for yourself whether the strategy is ethical or shady in light of the undisputed medical links between smoking and lung cancer.

Approaches to Managing a Company's Ethical Conduct

The stance a company takes in dealing with or managing ethical conduct at any given point can take any of four basic forms:[33]

- The unconcerned, or nonissue, approach.
- The damage control approach.
- The compliance approach.
- The ethical culture approach.

The differences in these four approaches are discussed briefly below and summarized in Table 10.4 on page 335.

Illustration Capsule 10.2
Philip Morris USA's Strategy for Marlboro Cigarettes: Ethical or Unethical?

In late 2005, Philip Morris USA and its corporate parent, Altria Group Inc., wrapped up a year of promotions and parties to celebrate the 50th year of selling Marlboro cigarettes. Marlboro commanded a 40 percent share of the U.S. market for cigarettes and was also one of the world's top cigarette brands. Despite sharp advertising restrictions agreed to by cigarette marketers in 1998 and a big jump in state excise taxes on cigarettes since 2002, Marlboro's sales and market share were climbing, thanks to a new trailblazing marketing strategy.

Marlboro had become a major brand in the 1960s and 1970s via a classic mass-marketing strategy anchored by annual ad budgets in the millions of dollars. The company's TV, magazine, and billboard ads for Marlboros always featured a rugged cowboy wearing a Stetson, riding a horse in a mountainous area, and smoking a Marlboro—closely connecting the brand with the American West gave Marlboro a distinctive and instantly recognized brand image. The Marlboro ad campaign was a gigantic success, making Marlboro one of the world's best-known and valuable brands.

But following the ad restrictions in 1998, Philip Morris had to shift to a different marketing strategy to grow Marlboro's sales. It opted for an approach aimed at generating all kinds of marketing buzz for the Marlboro brand and creating a larger cadre of loyal Marlboro smokers (who often felt persecuted by social pressures and antismoking ordinances). Philip Morris directed company field reps to set up promotions at local bars where smokers could sign up for promotional offers like price discounts on Marlboro purchases, a Marlboro Miles program that awarded points for each pack purchased, and sweepstakes prizes that included cash, trips, and Marlboro apparel; some prizes could be purchased with Marlboro Miles points. It also began to sponsor live concerts and other events to generate additional sign-ups among attendees. A Web site was created to spur Internet chatter among the Marlboro faithful and to encourage still more sign-ups

for special deals and contests (some with prizes up to a $1 million)—an online community quickly sprang up around the brand. Via all the sign-ups and calls to an 800 number, Philip Morris created a database of Marlboro smokers that by 2005 had grown to 26 million names. Using direct mail and e-mail, the company sent the members of its database a steady stream of messages and offers, ranging from birthday coupons for free breakfasts to price discounts to chances to attend local concerts, enjoy a day at nearby horse tracks, or win a trip to the company's ranch in Montana (where winners got gifts, five-course meals, massages, and free drinks and could go snowmobiling, fly fishing, or horseback riding).

Meanwhile, Philip Morris also became considerably more aggressive in retail stores, launching an offensive initiative to give discounts and incentives to retailers who utilized special aisle displays and signage for its cigarette brands. One 22-store retail chain reported that, by agreeing to a deal to give Philip Morris brands about 66 percent of its cigarette shelf space, it ended up paying about $5.50 per carton less for its Marlboro purchases than it paid for cartons of Camels supplied by rival R. J. Reynolds. Some Wal-Mart stores were said to have awarded Philip Morris as much as 80 percent of its cigarette shelf space.

Thus, despite being besieged by the costs of defending lawsuits and paying out billions to governments as compensation for the increased health care costs associated with smoking, Philip Morris and other cigarette makers were making very healthy profits: operating margins of nearly 28 percent in 2005 (up from 26 percent in 2004) and net income of about $11.4 billion on sales of $66.3 billion in the United States and abroad.

However, health care officials were highly critical of Philip Morris's marketing tactics for Marlboro, and the U.S. Department of Justice had filed a lawsuit claiming, among other things, that the company knowingly marketed Marlboros to underage people in its database, a charge denied by the company.

Source: Based largely on information in Nanette Byrnes, "Leader of the Packs," *BusinessWeek,* October 31, 2005, pp. 56, 58.

The Unconcerned, or Nonissue, Approach   The unconcerned approach is prevalent at companies whose executives are immoral and unintentionally amoral. Senior executives at companies using this approach ascribe to the view that notions of right and wrong in matters of business are defined entirely by government via the prevailing laws and regulations. They maintain that trying to enforce ethical standards above and beyond what is legally required is a nonissue because businesses are entitled to conduct their affairs in whatever

Table 10.4   **Four Approaches to Managing Business Ethics**

	Unconcerned, or Nonissue Approach	Damage Control Approach	Compliance Approach	Ethical Culture Approach
Underlying beliefs	• The business of business is business, not ethics. • All that matters is whether an action is legal. • Ethics has no place in the conduct of business. • Companies should not be morally accountable for their actions.	• The company needs to make a token gesture in the direction of ethical standards (a code of ethics).	• The company must be committed to ethical standards and monitoring ethics performance. • Unethical behavior must be prevented and punished if discovered. • It is important to have a reputation for high ethical standards.	• Ethics is basic to the culture. • Behaving ethically must be a deeply held corporate value and become a way of life. • Everyone is expected to walk the talk.
Ethics management approaches	• There's no need to make decisions concerning business ethics—if its legal, it is okay. • No intervention regarding the ethical component of decisions is needed.	• The company must act to protect against the dangers of unethical strategies and behavior. • Ignore unethical behavior or allow it to go unpunished unless the situation is extreme and requires action.	• The company must establish a clear, comprehensive code of ethics. • The company must provide ethics training for all personnel. • Have formal ethics compliance procedures, an ethics compliance office, and a chief ethics officer.	• Ethical behavior is ingrained and reinforced as part of the culture. • Much reliance on co-worker peer pressure—"That's not how we do things here." • Everyone is an ethics watchdog—whistle-blowing is required. • Ethics heroes are celebrated; ethics stories are told.
Challenges	• Financial consequences can become unaffordable. • Some stakeholders are alienated.	• Credibility problems with stakeholders can arise. • The company is susceptible to ethical scandal. • The company has a subpar ethical reputation—executives and company personnel don't walk the talk.	• Organizational members come to rely on the existing rules for moral guidance—fosters a mentality of what is not forbidden is allowed. • Rules and guidelines proliferate. • The locus of moral control resides in the code and in the ethics compliance system rather than in an individual's own moral responsibility for ethical behavior.	• New employees must go through strong ethics induction program. • Formal ethics management systems can be underutilized. • Relying on peer pressures and cultural norms to enforce ethical standards can result in eliminating some or many of the compliance trappings and, over time, induce moral laxness.

Source: Adapted from Gedeon J. Rossouw and Leon J. van Vuuren, "Modes of Managing Morality: A Descriptive Model of Strategies for Managing Ethics," *Journal of Business Ethics* 46, no. 4 (September 2003), pp. 392–93.

manner they wish so long as they comply with the letter of what is legally required. Hence, there is no need to spend valuable management time trying to prescribe and enforce standards of conduct that go above and beyond legal and regulatory requirements. In companies where senior managers are immoral, the prevailing view may well be that under-the-table dealing can be good business if it can be kept hidden or if it can be justified on grounds that others are doing it too. Companies in this mode usually engage in most any business practices they believe they can get away with, and the strategies they employ may well embrace elements that are either borderline from a legal perspective or ethically shady and unsavory.

The Damage Control Approach   Damage control is favored at companies whose managers are intentionally amoral but who are wary of scandal and adverse

> The main objective of the damage control approach is to protect against adverse publicity and any damaging consequences brought on by headlines in the media, outside investigation, threats of litigation, punitive government action, or angry or vocal stakeholders.

public relations fallout that could cost them their jobs of tarnish their careers. Companies using this approach, not wanting to risk tarnishing the reputations of key personnel or the company, usually make some concession to window-dressing ethics, going so far as to adopt a code of ethics—so that their executives can point to it as evidence of good-faith efforts to prevent unethical strategy making or unethical conduct on the part of company personnel. But the code of ethics exists mainly as nice words on paper, and company personnel do not operate within a strong ethical context—there's a notable gap between talking ethics and walking ethics. Employees quickly get the message that rule bending is tolerated and may even be rewarded if the company benefits from their actions.

Company executives that practice the damage control approach are prone to look the other way when shady or borderline behavior occurs—adopting a kind of "See no evil, hear no evil, speak no evil" stance (except when exposure of the company's actions put executives under great pressure to redress any wrongs that have been done). They may even condone questionable actions that help the company reach earnings targets or bolster its market standing—such as pressuring customers to stock up on the company's product (channel stuffing), making under-the-table payments to win new business, stonewalling the recall of products claimed to be unsafe, badmouthing the products of rivals, or trying to keep prices low by sourcing goods from disreputable suppliers in low-wage countries that run sweatshop operations or use child labor. But they are usually careful to do such things in a manner that lessens the risks of exposure or damaging consequences. This generally includes making token gestures to police compliance with codes of ethics and relying heavily on spin to help extricate the company or themselves from claims that the company's strategy has unethical components or that company personnel have engaged in unethical practices.

The Compliance Approach   Anywhere from light to forceful compliance is favored at companies whose managers (1) lean toward being somewhat amoral but are highly concerned about having ethically upstanding reputations or (2) are moral and see strong compliance methods as the best way to impose and enforce ethical rules and high ethical standards. Companies that adopt a compliance mode usually do some or all of the following to display their commitment to ethical conduct: make the code of ethics a visible and regular part of communications with employees, implement ethics training programs, appoint a chief ethics officer or ethics ombudsperson, have ethics committees to give guidance on ethics matters, institute formal procedures for investigating alleged ethics violations, conduct ethics audits to measure and document compliance, give ethics awards to employees for outstanding efforts to create an ethical climate and improve ethical performance, and/or try to deter violations by setting up ethics hotlines for anonymous callers to use in reporting possible violations.

Emphasis here is usually on securing broad compliance and measuring the degree to which ethical standards are upheld and observed. However, violators are disciplined and sometimes subjected to public reprimand and punishment (including dismissal), thereby sending a clear signal to company personnel that complying with ethical standards needs to be taken seriously. The driving force behind the company's commitment to eradicate unethical behavior normally stems from a desire to avoid the cost and damage associated with unethical conduct or else a quest to gain favor from stakeholders (especially ethically conscious customers, employees, and investors) for having a highly regarded reputation for ethical behavior. One of the weaknesses of the compliance approach is that moral control resides in the company's code of ethics and in the ethics compliance system rather than in (1) the strong peer pressures for ethical behavior that come from ingraining a highly ethical corporate culture and (2) an individual's own moral responsibility for ethical behavior.[34]

The Ethical Culture Approach   At some companies, top executives believe that high ethical principles must be deeply ingrained in the corporate culture and function as guides for "how we do things around here." A company using the ethical culture approach seeks to gain employee buy-in to the company's ethical standards, business principles, and corporate values. The ethical principles embraced in the company's code of ethics and/or in its statement of corporate values are seen as integral to the company's identity and ways of operating—they are at the core of the company's soul and are promoted as part of business as usual. The integrity of the ethical culture approach depends heavily on the ethical integrity of the executives who create and nurture the culture—it is incumbent on them to determine how high the bar is to be set and to exemplify ethical standards in their own decisions and behavior. Further, it is essential that the strategy be ethical in all respects and that ethical behavior be ingrained in the means that company personnel employ to execute the strategy. Such insistence on observing ethical standards is what creates an ethical work climate and a workplace where displaying integrity is the norm.

Many of the trappings used in the compliance approach are also manifest in the ethical culture mode, but one other is added—strong peer pressure from coworkers to observe ethical norms. Thus, responsibility for ethics compliance is widely dispersed throughout all levels of management and the rank-and-file. Stories of former and current moral heroes are kept in circulation, and the deeds of company personnel who display ethical values and are dedicated to walking the talk are celebrated at internal company events. The message that ethics matters—and matters a lot—resounds loudly and clearly throughout the organization and in its strategy and decisions. However, one of the challenges to overcome in the ethical culture approach is relying too heavily on peer pressures and cultural norms to enforce ethics compliance rather than on an individual's own moral responsibility for ethical behavior—absent unrelenting peer pressure or strong internal compliance systems, there is a danger that over time company personnel may become lax about its ethical standards. Compliance procedures need to be an integral part of the ethical culture approach to help send the message that management takes the observance of ethical norms seriously and that behavior that falls outside ethical boundaries will have negative consequences.

Why a Company Can Change Its Ethics Management Approach

Regardless of the approach they have used to managing ethical conduct, a company's executives may sense that they have exhausted a particular mode's potential for managing ethics and that they need to become more forceful in their approach to ethics management. Such changes typically occur when the company's ethical failures have made the headlines and created an embarrassing situation for company officials or when the business climate changes. For example, the recent raft of corporate scandals, coupled with aggressive enforcement of anticorruption legislation such as the Sarbanes-Oxley Act of 2002 (which addresses corporate governance and accounting practices), has prompted numerous executives and boards of directors to clean up their acts in accounting and financial reporting, review their ethical standards, and tighten up ethics compliance procedures. Intentionally amoral managers using the unconcerned approach to ethics management may see less risk in shifting to the damage control approach (or, for appearance's sake, maybe a "light" compliance mode). Senior managers who have employed the damage control mode may be motivated by bad experiences to mend their ways and shift to a compliance mode. In the wake of so many corporate scandals, companies in the compliance mode may move closer to the ethical culture approach.

WHY SHOULD COMPANY STRATEGIES BE ETHICAL?

There are two reasons why a company's strategy should be ethical: (1) because a strategy that is unethical in whole or in part is morally wrong and reflects badly on the character of the company personnel involved and (2) because an ethical strategy is good business and in the self-interest of shareholders.

The Moral Case for an Ethical Strategy

Managers do not dispassionately assess what strategic course to steer. Ethical strategy making generally begins with managers who themselves have strong character (i.e., who are honest, have integrity, are ethical, and truly care about how they conduct the company's business). Managers with high ethical principles and standards are usually advocates of a corporate code of ethics and strong ethics compliance, and they are typically genuinely committed to certain corporate values and business principles. They walk the talk in displaying the company's stated values and living up to its business principles and ethical standards. They understand that there is a big difference between adopting values statements and codes of ethics that serve merely as window dressing and those that truly paint the white lines for a company's actual strategy and business conduct. As a consequence, ethically strong managers consciously opt for strategic actions that can pass moral scrutiny—they display no tolerance for strategies with ethically controversial components.

The Business Case for an Ethical Strategy

There are solid business reasons to adopt ethical strategies even if most company managers are not of strong moral character and personally committed to high ethical standards. Pursuing unethical strategies not only damages a company's reputation but can also have costly, wide-ranging consequences. Some of the costs are readily visible; others are hidden and difficult to track down—as shown in Figure 10.1. The costs of

Figure 10.1 **The Business Costs of Ethical Failures**

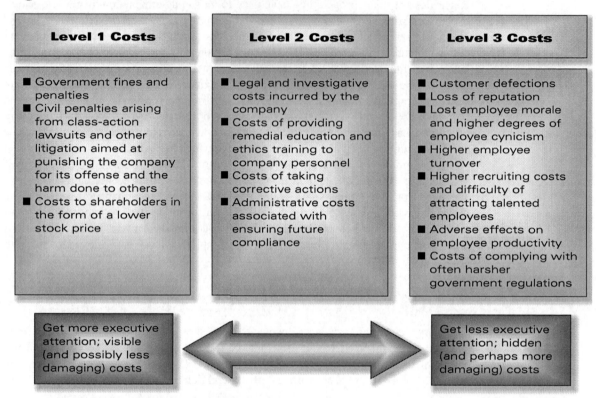

Source: Adapted from Terry Thomas, John R. Schermerhorn, and John W. Dienhart, "Strategic Leadership of Ethical Behavior," *Academy of Management Executive* 18, no. 2 (May 2004), p. 58.

fines and penalties and any declines in the stock price are easy enough to calculate. The administrative cleanup (or Level 2) costs are usually buried in the general costs of doing business and can be difficult to ascribe to any one ethical misdeed. Level 3 costs can be quite difficult to quantify but can sometimes be the most devastating—the aftermath of the Enron debacle left Arthur Andersen's reputation in shreds and led to the once-revered accounting firm's almost immediate demise, and it remains to be seen whether Marsh & McLennan can overcome the problems described in Illustration Capsule 10.1. Merck, once one of the world's most respected pharmaceutical firms, has been struggling against the revelation that senior management deliberately concealed that its Vioxx painkiller, which the company pulled off the market in September 2004, was tied to much greater risk of heart attack and strokes—some 20 million people in the United States had taken Vioxx over the years, and Merck executives had reason to suspect as early as 2000 (and perhaps earlier) that Vioxx had dangerous side effects.[35]

Rehabilitating a company's shattered reputation is time-consuming and costly. Customers shun companies known for their shady behavior. Companies with reputations for unethical conduct have considerable difficulty in recruiting and retaining talented employees. Most hardworking, ethically upstanding people are repulsed by a work environment where unethical behavior is condoned; they don't want to get entrapped in a compromising

> Conducting business in an ethical fashion is in a company's enlightened self-interest.

Illustration Capsule 10.3

A Test of Your Business Ethics

As a gauge of your own ethical and moral standards, take the following quiz and see how you stack up against other members of your class. For the test to be valid, you need to answer the questions candidly, not on the basis of what you think the ethically correct answer is.

1. Do you think that it would be unethical for you to give two Super Bowl tickets to an important customer? Would your answer be different if the customer is likely to place a large order that would qualify you for a large year-end sales bonus?

   _____Yes _____No _____Unsure (it depends)

   _____Need more information

2. Would it be wrong to accept a case of fine wine from an important customer? Would your answer be different if you have just convinced your superiors to authorize a special price discount on a big order that the customer has just placed?

   _____Yes _____No _____Unsure (it depends)

   _____Need more information

3. Is it unethical for a high school or college coach to accept a "talent fee" or similar type of payment from a maker of sports apparel or sports equipment when the coach has authority to determine which brand of apparel or equipment to use for his or her team and subsequently chooses the brand of the company making the payment? Is it unethical for the maker of the sports apparel or equipment to make such payments in expectation that the coach will reciprocate by selecting the company's brand? (Would you answer be different if everybody else is doing it?)

   _____Yes _____No _____Unsure (it depends)

   _____Need more information

4. Is it unethical to accept an invitation from a supplier to spend a holiday weekend skiing at the supplier company's resort home in Colorado? (Would your answer be different if you were presently considering a proposal from that supplier to purchase $1 million worth of components?)

   _____Yes _____No _____Unsure (it depends)

   _____Need more information

5. Is it unethical for a food products company to incorporate ingredients that have trans fats in its products, given that trans fats are known to be very unhealthy for consumers and that alternative ingredients (which might be somewhat more expensive) can be used in producing the product?

   _____Yes _____No _____Unsure (it depends)

   _____Need more information

6. Would it be wrong to keep quiet if you, as a junior financial analyst, had just calculated that the projected return on a possible project was 18 percent and your boss (a) informed you that no project could be approved without the prospect of a 25 percent return and (b) told you to go back and redo the numbers and "get them right"?

   _____Yes _____No _____Unsure (it depends)

   _____Need more information

7. Would it be unethical to allow your supervisor to believe that you were chiefly responsible for the success of a new company initiative if it actually resulted from a team effort or major contributions by a co-worker?

   _____Yes _____No _____Unsure (it depends)

   _____Need more information

8. Would it be unethical for you, as the chief company official in India to (a) authorize a $25,000 payment to a local government official to facilitate governmental approval to construct a $200 million petrochemical plant and (b) disguise this payment by instructing accounting personnel to classify the payment as part of the cost of obtaining a building permit? (As you can see from Table 10.1, corruption is the norm in India, and bribes and kickbacks are often a "necessary" cost of doing business there.)

   _____Yes _____No _____Unsure (it depends)

   _____Need more information

9. Is it unethical for a motor vehicle manufacturer to resist recalling some of its vehicles when governmental authorities present it with credible evidence that the vehicles have safety defects?

   _____Yes _____No _____Unsure (it depends)

   _____Need more information

10. Is it unethical for a credit card company to aggressively try to sign up new accounts when, after an introductory period of interest-free or low-interest charges on unpaid monthly balances, the interest rate on unpaid balances jumps to 1.5 percent or more monthly (even though such high rates of 18 percent or more annually are disclosed in fine print)?

    _____Yes _____No _____Unsure (it depends)

    _____Need more information

11. Is it unethical to bolster your résumé with exaggerated claims of your credentials and prior job accomplishments in hopes of improving your chances of gaining employment at another company?

    _____Yes _____No _____Unsure (it depends)

    _____Need more information

12. Is it unethical for a company to spend as little as possible on pollution control when, with some extra effort and expenditures, it could substantially reduce the amount of pollution caused by its operations?

    _____Yes _____No _____Unsure (it depends)

    _____Need more information

Answers: The answers to questions 1, 2, and 4 probably shift from no/unsure to a definite yes when the second part of the circumstance comes into play. We think a strong case can be made that the answers to the remaining 9 questions are yes, although it can be argued that more information about the circumstances might be needed in responding to questions 5, 7, 9, and 12.

situation, nor do they want their personal reputations tarnished by the actions of an unsavory employer. A 1997 survey revealed that 42 percent of the respondents took into account a company's ethics when deciding whether to accept a job.[36] Creditors are usually unnerved by the unethical actions of a borrower because of the potential business fallout and subsequent risk of default on any loans. To some significant degree, therefore, companies recognize that ethical strategies and ethical conduct are good business. Most companies have strategies that pass the test of being ethical, and most companies are aware that both their reputations and their long-term well-being are tied to conducting their business in a manner that wins the approval of suppliers, employees, investors, and society at large.

As a test your own business ethics and where you stand on the importance of companies having an ethical strategy, take the test on page 340.

LINKING A COMPANY'S STRATEGY TO ITS ETHICAL PRINCIPLES AND CORE VALUES

Many companies have officially adopted a code of ethical conduct and a statement of company values—in the United States, the Sarbannes-Oxley Act, passed in 2002, requires that companies whose stock is publicly traded have a code of ethics or else explain in writing to the Securities and Exchange Commission why they do not. But there's a big difference between having a code of ethics and a values statement that serve merely as a public window dressing and having ethical standards and corporate values that truly paint the white lines for a company's actual strategy and business conduct. If ethical standards and statements of core values are to have more than a cosmetic role, boards of directors and top executives must work diligently to see that they are scrupulously observed in crafting the company's strategy and conducting every facet of the company's business. In other words, living up to the ethical principles and displaying the core values in actions and decisions must become a way of life at the company.

Indeed, the litmus test of whether a company's code of ethics and statement of core values are cosmetic is the extent to which they are embraced in crafting strategy and in operating the business day to day. It is up to senior executives to walk the talk and make a point of considering two sets of questions whenever a new strategic initiative is under review:

- Is what we are proposing to do fully compliant with our code of ethical conduct? Is there anything here that could be considered ethically objectionable?
- Is it apparent that this proposed action is in harmony with our core values? Are any conflicts or concerns evident?

Unless questions of this nature are posed—either in open discussion or by force of habit in the minds of strategy makers, then there's room for strategic initiatives to become disconnected from the company's code of ethics and stated core values. If a company's executives are ethically principled and believe strongly in living up to the company's stated core values, there's a good chance they will pose these types of questions and reject strategic initiatives that don't measure up. There's also a good chance that strategic actions will be scrutinized for their compatibility with ethical standards and core values when the latter are so deeply ingrained in a company's culture and in the

Core Concept
More attention is paid to linking strategy with ethical principles and core values in companies headed by moral executives and in companies where ethical principles and core values are a way of life.

everyday conduct of company personnel that they are automatically taken into account in all that the company does. However, in companies with window-dressing ethics and core values or in companies headed by immoral or amoral managers, any strategy-ethics-values link stems mainly from a desire to avoid the risk of embarrassment, scandal, and possible disciplinary action should strategy makers get called on the carpet and held accountable for approving an unethical strategic initiative.

STRATEGY AND SOCIAL RESPONSIBILITY

The idea that businesses have an obligation to foster social betterment, a much-debated topic in the past 40 years, took root in the 19th century when progressive companies in the aftermath of the industrial revolution began to provide workers with housing and other amenities. The notion that corporate executives should balance the interests of all stakeholders—shareholders, employees, customers, suppliers, the communities in which they operated, and society at large—began to blossom in the 1960s. A group of chief executives of America's 200 largest corporations, calling themselves the Business Roundtable, promoted the concept of corporate social responsibility. In 1981, the Roundtable's "Statement on Corporate Responsibility" said:[37]

> Balancing the shareholder's expectations of maximum return against other priorities is one of the fundamental problems confronting corporate management. The shareholder must receive a good return but the legitimate concerns of other constituencies (customers, employees, communities, suppliers and society at large) also must have the appropriate attention . . . [Leading managers] believe that by giving enlightened consideration to balancing the legitimate claims of all its constituents, a corporation will best serve the interest of its shareholders.

Today, corporate social responsibility is a concept that resonates in Western Europe, the United States, Canada, and such developing nations as Brazil and India.

What Do We Mean by Social Responsibility?

Core Concept
The notion of *social responsibility* as it applies to businesses concerns a company's *duty* to operate in an honorable manner, provide good working conditions for employees, be a good steward of the environment, and actively work to better the quality of life in the local communities where it operates and in society at large.

The essence of socially responsible business behavior is that a company should balance strategic actions to benefit shareholders against the *duty* to be a good corporate citizen. The thesis is that company managers are obligated to display a *social conscience* in operating the business and specifically take into account how management decisions and company actions affect the well-being of employees, local communities, the environment, and society at large. Acting in a socially responsible manner thus encompasses more than just participating in community service projects and donating money to charities and other worthy social causes. Demonstrating social responsibility also entails undertaking actions that earn trust and respect from all stakeholders—operating in an honorable and ethical manner, striving to make the company a great place to work, demonstrating genuine respect for the environment, and trying to make a difference in bettering society. As depicted in Figure 10.2, the menu for demonstrating a social conscience and choosing specific ways to exercise social responsibility includes:

- *Efforts to employ an ethical strategy and observe ethical principles in operating the business*—A sincere commitment to observing ethical principles is

Figure 10.2 **Demonstrating a Social Conscience: The Five Components of Socially Responsible Business Behavior**

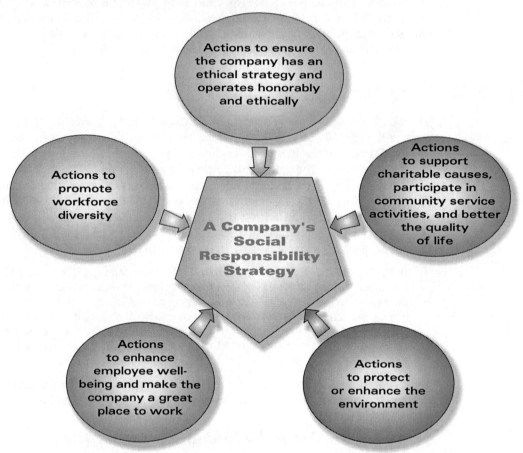

Source: Adapted from material in Ronald Paul Hill, Debra Stephens, and Iain Smith, "Corporate Social Responsibility: An Examination of Individual Firm Behavior," *Business and Society Review* 108, no. 3 (September 2003), p. 348.

necessary here simply because unethical strategies and conduct are incompatible with the concept of good corporate citizenship and socially responsible business behavior.

- *Making charitable contributions, donating money and the time of company personnel to community service endeavors, supporting various worthy organizational causes, and reaching out to make a difference in the lives of the disadvantaged*—Some companies fulfill their corporate citizenship and community outreach obligations by spreading their efforts over a multitude of charitable and community activities; for instance, Microsoft and Johnson & Johnson support a broad variety of community art, social welfare, and environmental programs. Others prefer to focus their energies more narrowly. McDonald's, for example, concentrates on sponsoring the Ronald McDonald House program (which provides a home away from home for the families of seriously ill children receiving treatment at nearby hospitals), preventing child abuse and neglect, and participating in local community service activities; in 2004, there were 240 Ronald McDonald Houses in 25 countries and more than 6,000 bedrooms available nightly. British Telecom gives 1 percent of its profits directly to communities, largely for education—teacher training, in-school workshops, and digital technology. Leading prescription drug maker GlaxoSmithKline and other pharmaceutical companies either donate or heavily discount medicines for distribution in the least-developed nations. Numerous health-related businesses take a leading role in community activities that promote effective health care. Many companies work closely with community officials to minimize the impact of hiring large numbers of new employees (which could put a strain on local schools and utility services) and to provide outplacement services for laid-off workers. Companies frequently reinforce their philanthropic efforts by encouraging employees to support charitable causes and participate in community affairs, often through programs to match employee contributions.

- *Actions to protect or enhance the environment and, in particular, to minimize or eliminate any adverse impact on the environment stemming from the company's own business activities*—Social responsibility as it applies to environmental protection means doing more than what is legally required. From a social responsibility perspective, companies have an obligation to be stewards of the environment. This means using the best available science and technology to achieve higher-than-required environmental standards. Even more ideally, it means putting time and money into improving the environment in ways that extend past a company's own industry boundaries—such as participating in recycling projects, adopting energy conservation practices, and supporting efforts to clean up local water supplies. Retailers such as Home Depot in the United States and B&Q in the United Kingdom have pressured their suppliers to adopt stronger environmental protection practices.[38]

> Business leaders who want their companies to be regarded as exemplary corporate citizens must not only see that their companies operate ethically but they must personally display a social conscience in making decisions that affect employees, the environment, the communities in which they operate, and society at large.

- *Actions to create a work environment that enhances the quality of life for employees and makes the company a great place to work*—Numerous companies go beyond providing the ordinary kinds of compensation and exert extra efforts to enhance the quality of life for their employees, both at work and at home. This can include varied and engaging job assignments, career development programs and mentoring, rapid career advancement, appealing compensation incentives, ongoing training to ensure future employability, added decision-making authority, onsite day care, flexible work schedules for single parents, workplace exercise facilities, special leaves to care for sick family members, work-at-home opportunities, gender pay equity, showcase plants and offices, special safety programs, and the like.

- *Actions to build a workforce that is diverse with respect to gender, race, national origin, and perhaps other aspects that different people bring to the workplace*—Most large companies in the United States have established workforce diversity programs, and some go the extra mile to ensure that their workplaces are attractive to ethnic minorities and inclusive of all groups and perspectives. The pursuit of workforce diversity can be good business—Johnson & Johnson, Pfizer, and Coca-Cola believe that a reputation for workforce diversity makes recruiting employees easier (talented employees from diverse backgrounds often seek out such companies). And at Coca-Cola, where strategic success depends on getting people all over the world to become loyal consumers of the company's beverages, efforts to build a public persona of inclusiveness for people of all races, religions, nationalities, interests, and talents has considerable strategic value. Multinational companies are particularly inclined to make workforce diversity a visible strategic component; they recognize that respecting individual differences and promoting inclusiveness resonate well with people all around the world. At a few companies the diversity initiative extends to suppliers—sourcing items from small businesses owned by women or ethnic minorities.

Crafting a Social Responsibility Strategy: The Starting Point for Demonstrating a Social Conscience

While striving to be socially responsible entails choosing from the menu outlined in the preceding section, there's plenty of room for every company to make its own statement about what charitable contributions to make, what kinds of community service projects to emphasize, what environmental actions to support, how to make the company a good place to work, where and how workforce diversity fits into the picture, and what else it will do to support worthy causes and projects that benefit society. The particular combination of socially responsible endeavors a company elects to pursue defines its **social responsibility strategy.** However, unless a company's social responsibility initiatives become part of the way it operates its business every day, the initiatives are unlikely to catch fire and be fully effective. As an executive at Royal Dutch/Shell put it, corporate social responsibility "is not a cosmetic; it must be rooted in our values. It must make a difference to the way we do business."[39] Thus some companies are integrating social responsibility objectives into their missions and overall performance targets—they see social performance and environmental metrics as an essential component of judging the company's overall future performance. Some 2,500 companies around the world are not only articulating their social responsibility strategies and commitments but they are also issuing annual social responsibility reports (much like an annual report) that set forth their commitments and the progress they are making for all the world to see and evaluate.[40]

> **Core Concept**
> A company's *social responsibility strategy* is defined by the specific combination of socially beneficial activities it opts to support with its contributions of time, money, and other resources.

At Starbucks, the commitment to social responsibility is linked to the company's strategy and operating practices via the tag line "Giving back to our communities is the way we do business"; top management makes the theme come alive via the company's extensive community-building activities, efforts to protect the welfare of coffee growers and their families (in particular, making sure they receive a fair price), a variety of recycling and environmental conservation practices, and the financial support it provides to charities and the disadvantaged through the Starbucks Foundation. At Green Mountain Coffee Roasters, social responsibility includes fair dealing with suppliers and trying to do something about the poverty of small coffee growers; in its dealings with suppliers at small farmer cooperatives in Peru, Mexico, and Sumatra, Green Mountain pays "fair trade" prices for coffee beans (in 2002, the fair trade prices were a minimum of $1.26 per pound for conventional coffee and $1.41 for organically grown versus market prices of 24 to 50 cents per pound). Green Mountain also purchases about 25 percent of its coffee direct from farmers so as to cut out intermediaries and see that farmers realize a higher price for their efforts—coffee is the world's second most heavily traded commodity after oil, requiring the labor of some 20 million people, most of whom live at the poverty level.[41] At Whole Foods Market, a $5 billion supermarket chain specializing in organic and natural foods, the social responsibility emphasis is on supporting organic farming and

> Many companies tailor their strategic efforts to operate in a socially responsible manner to fit their core values and business mission, thereby making their own statement about "how we do business and how we intend to fulfill our duties to all stakeholders and society at large."

sustainable agriculture, recycling, sustainable seafood practices, giving employees paid time off to participate in worthy community service endeavors, and donating 5 percent of after-tax profits in cash or products to charitable causes. At General Mills the social responsibility focus is on service to the community and bettering the employment opportunities for minorities and women. Stonyfield Farm, a producer of yogurt and ice cream products, employs a social responsibility strategy focused on wellness, good nutrition, and earth-friendly actions (10 percent of profits are donated to help protect and restore the earth, and yogurt lids are used as miniature billboards to help educate people about environmental issues); in addition, it is stressing the development of an environmentally friendly supply chain, sourcing from farmers that grow organic products and refrain from using artificial hormones in milk production. Chick-Fil-A, an Atlanta-based fast-food chain with over 1,200 outlets in 38 states, has a charitable foundation; supports 14 foster homes and a summer camp (for some 1,600 campers from 22 states and several foreign countries); funds two scholarship programs (including one for employees that has awarded more than $20 million in scholarships); and maintains a closed-on-Sunday policy to ensure that every Chick-Fil-A employee and restaurant operator has an opportunity to worship, spend time with family and friends, or just plain rest from the workweek.[42] Toys "R" Us supports initiatives addressing the issues of child labor and fair labor practices around the world. Community Pride Food Stores is assisting in revitalizing the inner city of Richmond, Virginia, where the company is based.

It is common for companies engaged in natural resource extraction, electric power production, forestry and paper products, motor vehicles, and chemicals production to place more emphasis on addressing environmental concerns than, say, software and electronics firms or apparel manufacturers. Companies whose business success is heavily dependent on high employee morale or attracting and retaining the best and brightest employees are somewhat more prone to stress the well-being of their employees and foster a positive, high-energy workplace environment that elicits the dedication and enthusiastic commitment of employees, thus putting real meaning behind the claim "Our people are our greatest asset." Ernst & Young, one of the four largest global accounting firms, stresses its "People First" workforce diversity strategy, which focuses on respecting differences, fostering individuality, and promoting inclusiveness so that its 105,000 employees in 140 countries can feel valued, engaged, and empowered in developing creative ways to serve the firm's clients.

Thus, while the strategies and actions of all socially responsible companies have a sameness in the sense of drawing on the five categories of socially responsible behavior shown in Figure 10.2, each company's version of being socially responsible is unique.

The Moral Case for Corporate Social Responsibility

Every action a company takes can be interpreted as a statement of what it stands for.

The moral case for why businesses should actively promote the betterment of society and act in a manner that benefits all of the company's stakeholders—not just the interests of shareholders—boils down to the fact that it's the right thing to do. Ordinary decency, civic-mindedness, and contributing to the well-being of society should be expected of any business. In today's social and political climate, most business leaders can be expected to acknowledge that socially responsible actions are important and that businesses have a duty to be good corporate citizens. But there is a complementary school of thought that business operates on the basis of an implied social contract with the members of society. According to this contract, society grants a business the right to conduct its business affairs and agrees not to unreasonably restrain its pursuit of a fair profit for the goods or services it sells; in return for this "license to operate," a business is obligated to act as a responsible citizen and do its fair share to promote the general welfare. Such a view clearly puts a moral burden on a company to take corporate citizenship into consideration and to do what's best for shareholders within the confines of discharging its duties to operate honorably, provide good working conditions to employees, be a good environmental steward, and display good corporate citizenship.

The Business Case for Socially Responsible Behavior

Whatever the merits of the moral case for socially responsible business behavior, it has long been recognized that it is in the enlightened self-interest of companies to be good citizens and devote some of their energies and resources to the betterment of employees, the communities in which they operate, and society in general. In short, there are several reasons why the exercise of social responsibility is good business:

- *It generates internal benefits (particularly as concerns employee recruiting, workforce retention, and training costs)*—Companies with deservedly good reputations for contributing time and money to the betterment of society are better able to attract and retain employees compared to companies with tarnished reputations. Some employees just feel better about working for a company committed to improving society.[43] This can contribute to lower turnover and better worker productivity. Other direct and indirect economic benefits include lower costs for staff recruitment and training. For example, Starbucks is said to enjoy much lower rates of employee turnover because of its full benefits package for both full-time and part-time employees, management efforts to make Starbucks a great place to work, and the company's socially responsible practices. When a U.S. manufacturer of recycled paper, taking eco-efficiency to heart, discovered how to increase its fiber recovery rate, it saved the equivalent of 20,000 tons of waste paper—a factor that helped the company become the industry's lowest-cost producer.[44] Various benchmarking and measurement mechanisms have shown that workforce diversity initiatives promote the success of companies that stay behind them. Making a company a great place to work pays dividends in recruiting talented workers, more creativity and energy on the part of workers, higher worker productivity, and greater employee commitment to the company's business mission/vision and success in the marketplace.

- *It reduces the risk of reputation-damaging incidents and can lead to increased buyer patronage*—Firms may well be penalized by employees, consumers, and shareholders for actions that are not considered socially responsible. When a major oil company suffered damage to its reputation on environmental and social grounds, the CEO repeatedly said that the most negative impact the company suffered—and the one that made him fear for the future of the company—was that bright young graduates were no longer attracted to work for the company.[45] Consumer, environmental, and human rights activist groups are quick to criticize businesses whose behavior they consider to be out of line, and they are adept at getting their message into the media and onto the Internet. Pressure groups can generate widespread adverse publicity, promote boycotts, and influence like-minded or sympathetic buyers to avoid an offender's products.

> The higher the public profile of a company or brand, the greater the scrutiny of its activities and the higher the potential for it to become a target for pressure-group action.

Research has shown that product boycott announcements are associated with a decline in a company's stock price.[46] Outspoken criticism of Royal Dutch/Shell by environmental and human rights groups and associated boycotts were said to be major factors in the company's decision to tune in to its social responsibilities. For many years, Nike received stinging criticism for not policing sweatshop conditions in the Asian factories of its contractors, causing Nike CEO Phil Knight to observe that "Nike has become synonymous with slave wages, forced overtime, and arbitrary abuse."[47] In 1997, Nike began an extensive effort to monitor conditions in the 800 overseas factories from which it outsourced its shoes; Knight said, "Good shoes come from good factories, and good factories have good labor relations." Nonetheless, Nike has continually been plagued by complaints from human rights activists that its monitoring procedures are flawed and that it is not doing enough to correct the plight of factory workers. In contrast, to the extent that a company's socially responsible behavior wins applause from consumers and fortifies its reputation, the company may win additional patronage; Ben & Jerry's, Whole Foods Market, Stonyfield Farm, and the Body Shop have definitely expanded their customer bases because of their visible and well-publicized activities as socially conscious companies. More and more companies are recognizing the strategic value of social responsibility strategies that reach out to people of all cultures and demographics—in the United States, women are said to having buying power of $3.7 trillion, retired and disabled people close to $4.1 trillion, Hispanics nearly $600 billion, African Americans some $500 billion, and Asian Americans about $255 billion.[48] So reaching out in ways that appeal to such groups can pay off at the cash register. Some observers and executives are convinced that a strong, visible social responsibility strategy gives a company an edge in differentiating itself from rivals and in appealing to those consumers who prefer to do business with companies that are solid corporate citizens. Yet there is only limited evidence that consumers go out of their way to patronize socially responsible companies if it means paying a higher price or purchasing an inferior product.[49]

- *It is in the best interest of shareholders*—Well-conceived social responsibility strategies work to the advantage of shareholders in several ways. Socially responsible business behavior helps avoid or preempt legal and regulatory actions that could prove costly and otherwise burdensome. Increasing numbers of mutual funds and pension benefit managers are restricting their stock purchases to companies that meet social responsibility criteria. According to one survey, one out of every eight dollars under professional management in the United States

> There's little hard evidence indicating shareholders are disadvantaged in any meaningful way by a company's actions to be socially responsible.

involved socially responsible investing.[50] Moreover, the growth in socially responsible investing and identifying socially responsible companies has led to a substantial increase in the number of companies that publish formal reports on their social and environmental activities.[51] The stock prices of companies that rate high on social and environmental performance criteria have been found to perform 35 to 45 percent better than the average of the 2,500 companies comprising the Dow Jones Global Index.[52] A two-year study of leading companies found that improving environmental compliance and developing environmentally friendly products can enhance earnings per share, profitability, and the likelihood of winning contracts.[53] Nearly 100 studies have examined the relationship between corporate citizenship and corporate financial performance over the past 30 years; the majority point to a positive relationship. Of the 80 studies that examined whether a company's social performance is a good predictor of its financial performance, 42 concluded yes, 4 concluded no, and the remainder reported mixed or inconclusive findings.[54] To the extent that socially responsible behavior is good business, then, a social responsibility strategy that packs some punch and is more than rhetorical flourish turns out to be in the best interest of shareholders.

In sum, companies that take social responsibility seriously can improve their business reputations and operational efficiency while also reducing their risk exposure and encouraging loyalty and innovation. Overall, companies that take special pains to protect the environment (beyond what is required by law), are active in community affairs, and are generous supporters of charitable causes and projects that benefit society are more likely to be seen as good investments and as good companies to work for or do business with. Shareholders are likely to view the business case for social responsibility as a strong one, even though they certainly have a right to be concerned whether the time and money their company spends to carry out its social responsibility strategy outweighs the benefits and reduces the bottom line by an unjustified amount.

Companies are, of course, sometimes rewarded for bad behavior—a company that is able to shift environmental and other social costs associated with its activities onto society as a whole can reap large short-term profits. The major cigarette producers for many years were able to earn greatly inflated profits by shifting the health-related costs of smoking onto others and escaping any responsibility for the harm their products caused to consumers and the general public. Most companies will, of course, try to evade paying for the social harms of their operations for as long as they can. Calling a halt to such actions usually hinges upon (1) the effectiveness of activist social groups in publicizing the adverse consequences of a company's social irresponsibility and marshaling public opinion for something to be done, (2) the enactment of legislation or regulations to correct the inequity, and (3) widespread actions on the part of socially conscious buyers to take their business elsewhere.

The Well-Intentioned Efforts of Do-Good Executives Can Be Controversial

While there is substantial agreement that businesses have obligations to non-owner stakeholders and to society at large, and that these must be factored into a company's overall strategy and into the conduct of its business operations, there is much less agreement about the extent to which "do-good" executives should pursue their personal vision of a better world using company funds. One view holds that any money executives authorize for so-called social responsibility initiatives is effectively theft from a company's shareholders who can, after all, decide for themselves what and how much to give to charity and other causes they deem worthy. A related school of thought says that companies should be wary of taking on an assortment of societal obligations because doing so diverts valuable resources and weakens a company's competitiveness. Many academics and businesspeople believe that businesses best satisfy their social responsibilities through conventional business activities, primarily producing needed goods and services at prices that people can afford. They further argue that spending shareholders' or customers' money for social causes not only muddies decision making by diluting the focus on the company's business mission but also thrusts business executives into the role of social engineers—a role more appropriately performed by charitable and nonprofit organizations and duly elected government officials. Do we really want corporate executives deciding how to best balance the different interests of stakeholders and functioning as social engineers? Are they competent to make such judgments?

Take the case of Coca-Cola and Pepsi bottlers. Local bottlers of both brands have signed contracts with public school districts that provide millions of dollars of support for local schools in exchange for vending-machine distribution rights in the schools.[55] While such contracts would seem to be a win–win proposition, protests from parents concerned about children's sugar-laden diets and commercialism in the schools make such contracts questionable. Opponents of these contracts claim that it is the role of government to provide adequate school funding and that the learning environment in local schools should be free of commercialism and the self-serving efforts of businesses to hide behind providing support for education.

In September 1997, the Business Roundtable changed its stance from one of support for social responsibility and balanced consideration of stakeholder interests to one of skepticism with regard to such actions:

> The notion that the board must somehow balance the interests of stockholders against the interests of other stakeholders fundamentally misconstrues the role of directors. It is, moreover, an unworkable notion because it would leave the board with no criteria for resolving conflicts between the interest of stockholders and of other stakeholders or among different groups of stakeholders.[56]

The new Business Roundtable view implied that the paramount duty of management and of boards of directors is to the corporation's stockholders. Customers may be "king," and employees may be the corporation's "greatest asset" (at least in the rhetoric), but the interests of shareholders rule.[57]

However, there are real problems with disconnecting business behavior from the well-being of non-owner stakeholders and the well-being of society at large.[58] Isolating business from the rest of society when the two are inextricably intertwined is unrealistic. Many business decisions spill over to impact non-owner stakeholders and society. Furthermore, the notion that businesses must be managed solely to serve the interests of shareholders is something of a stretch. Clearly, a business's first priority must be to deliver value to customers. Unless a company does a creditable job of satisfying buyer needs and expectations of reliable and attractively priced goods and services, it cannot survive. While shareholders provide capital and are certainly entitled to a return on their investment, fewer and fewer shareholders are truly committed to the companies whose stock they own. Shareholders can dispose of their holdings in a moment's whim or at the first sign of a downturn in the stock price. Mutual funds buy and sell shares daily, adding and dropping companies whenever they see fit. Day traders buy and sell within hours. Such buying and selling of shares is nothing more than a financial transaction and results in no capital being provided to the company to fund operations except when it entails the purchase of newly issued shares of stock. So why should shareholders—a group distant from the company's operations and adding little to its operations except when new shares of stock are purchased—lay such a large claim on how a company should be managed? Are most shareholders really interested in or knowledgeable about the companies they own? Or do they just own a stock for whatever financial returns it is expected to provide?

While there is legitimate concern about the use of company resources for do-good purposes and the motives and competencies of business executives in functioning as social engineers, it is tough to argue that businesses have no obligations to nonowner stakeholders or to society at large. If one looks at the category of activities that fall under the umbrella of socially responsible behavior (Figure 10.2), there's really very little for shareholders or others concerned about the do-good attempts of executives to object to in principle. Certainly, it is legitimate for companies to minimize or eliminate any adverse impacts of their operations on the environment. It is hard to argue against efforts to make the company a great place to work or to promote workforce diversity. And with regard to charitable contributions, community service projects, and the like, it would be hard to find a company where spending on such activities is so out of control that shareholders might rightfully complain or that the company's competitiveness is being eroded. What is likely to prove most objectionable in the social responsibility arena are the specific activities a company elects to engage in and/or the manner in which a company carries out its attempts to behave in a socially responsible manner.

How Much Attention to Social Responsibility Is Enough?

What is an appropriate balance between the imperative to create value for shareholders and the obligation to proactively contribute to the larger social good? What fraction of a company's resources ought to be aimed at addressing social concerns and bettering the well-being of society and the environment? A few companies have a policy of setting aside a specified percentage of their profits (typically 5 percent or maybe 10 percent) to fund their social responsibility strategy; they view such percentages as a fair amount to return to the community as a kind of thank-you or a tithe to the betterment of society. Other companies shy away from a specified percentage of profits or revenues because it entails upping the commitment in good times and cutting back on social responsibility initiatives in hard times (even cutting out social responsibility initiatives entirely if profits temporarily turn into losses). If social responsibility is an ongoing commitment rooted in the corporate culture and enlists broad participation on the part of company personnel, then a sizable portion of the funding for the company's social responsibility strategy has to be viewed as simply a regular and ongoing cost of doing business.

But judging how far a particular company should go in pursuing particular social causes is a tough issue. Consider, for example, Nike's commitment to monitoring the workplace conditions of its contract suppliers.[59] The scale of this monitoring task is significant: in 2005, Nike had over 800 contract suppliers employing over 600,000 people in 50 countries. How frequently should sites be monitored? How should it respond to the use of underage labor? If only children above a set age are to be employed by suppliers, should suppliers still be required to provide schooling opportunities? At last count, Nike had some 80 people engaged in site monitoring. Should Nike's monitoring budget be $2 million, $5 million, $10 million, or whatever it takes?

Consider another example: If pharmaceutical manufacturers donate or discount their drugs for distribution to low-income people in less-developed nations, what safeguards should they put in place to see that the drugs reach the intended recipients and are not diverted by corrupt local officials for reexport to markets in other countries? Should drug manufacturers also assist in drug distribution and administration in these less-developed countries? How much should a drug company invest in R&D to develop medicines for tropical diseases commonly occurring in less-developed countries when it is unlikely to recover its costs in the foreseeable future?

And how much should a company allocate to charitable contributions? Is it falling short of its responsibilities if its donations are less than 1 percent of profits? Is a company going too far if it allocates 5 percent or even 10 percent of its profits to worthy causes of one kind or another? The point here is that there is no simple or widely accepted standard for judging when a company has or has not gone far enough in fulfilling its citizenship responsibilities.

Linking Social Performance Targets to Executive Compensation

Perhaps the most surefire way to enlist a genuine commitment to corporate social responsibility initiatives is to link the achievement of social performance targets to executive compensation. If a company's board of directors is serious about corporate citizenship, then it will incorporate measures of the company's social and environmental performance into its evaluation of top executives, especially the CEO. And if the CEO uses compensation incentives to further enlist the support of down-the-line company personnel in effectively crafting and executing a social responsibility strategy, the company will over time build a culture rooted in social responsible and ethical behavior. According to one survey, 80 percent of surveyed CEOs believe that environmental and social performance metrics are a valid part of measuring a company's overall performance. At Verizon Communications, 10 percent of the annual bonus of the company's top 2,500 managers is tied directly to the achievement of social responsibility targets; for the rest of the staff, there are corporate recognition awards in the form of cash for employees who have made big contributions towards social causes. The corporate social responsibility reports being issued annually by 2,500 companies across the world that detail social responsibility initiatives and the results achieved are a good basis for compensating executives and judging the effectiveness of their commitment to social responsibility.

Key Points

Ethics involves concepts of right and wrong, fair and unfair, moral and immoral. Beliefs about what is ethical serve as a moral compass in guiding the actions and behaviors of individuals and organizations. Ethical principles in business are not materially different from ethical principles in general.

There are three schools of thought about ethical standards:

1. According to the *school of ethical universalism*, the same standards of what's ethical and what's unethical resonate with peoples of most societies regardless of local traditions and cultural norms; hence, common ethical standards can be used to judge the conduct of personnel at companies operating in a variety of country markets and cultural circumstances.

2. According to the *school of ethical relativism* different societal cultures and customs have divergent values and standards of right and wrong—thus, what is ethical or unethical must be judged in the light of local customs and social mores and can vary from culture or nation to another.

3. According to *integrated social contracts theory*, universal ethical principles or norms based on the collective views of multiple cultures and societies combine to form a "social contract" that all individuals in all situations have a duty to observe. Within the boundaries of this social contract, local cultures can specify other impermissible actions; however, universal ethical norms always take precedence over local ethical norms.

Three categories of managers stand out as concerns their prevailing beliefs in and commitments to ethical and moral principles in business affairs: the moral manager; the immoral manager, and the amoral manager. By some accounts, the population of managers is said to be distributed among all three types in a bell-shaped curve, with immoral managers and moral managers occupying the two tails of the curve, and the amoral managers, especially the intentionally amoral managers, occupying the broad middle ground.

The apparently large numbers of immoral and amoral businesspeople are one obvious reason why some companies resort to unethical strategic behavior. Three other main drivers of unethical business behavior also stand out:

1. Overzealous or obsessive pursuit of personal gain, wealth, and other selfish interests.
2. Heavy pressures on company managers to meet or beat earnings targets.
3. A company culture that puts the profitability and good business performance ahead of ethical behavior.

The stance a company takes in dealing with or managing ethical conduct at any given time can take any of four basic forms:

1. The unconcerned, or nonissue, approach.
2. The damage control approach.
3. The compliance approach.
4. The ethical culture approach.

There are two reasons why a company's strategy should be ethical: (1) because a strategy that is unethical in whole or in part is morally wrong and reflects badly on the character of the company personnel involved, and (2) because an ethical strategy is good business and in the self-interest of shareholders.

The term *corporate social responsibility* concerns a company's *duty* to operate in an honorable manner, provide good working conditions for employees, be a good steward of the environment, and actively work to better the quality of life in the local communities where it operates and in society at large. The menu of actions and behavior for demonstrating social responsibility includes:

1. Employing an ethical strategy and observing ethical principles in operating the business.
2. Making charitable contributions, donating money and the time of company personnel to community service endeavors, supporting various worthy organizational causes, and making a difference in the lives of the disadvantaged. Corporate commitments are further reinforced by encouraging employees to support charitable and community activities.
3. Protecting or enhancing the environment and, in particular, striving to minimize or eliminate any adverse impact on the environment stemming from the company's own business activities.
4. Creating a work environment that makes the company a great place to work.
5. Employing a workforce that is diverse with respect to gender, race, national origin, and perhaps other aspects that different people bring to the workplace.

There is ample room for every company to tailor its social responsibility strategy to fit its core values and business mission, thereby making their own statement about "how we do business and how we intend to fulfill our duties to all stakeholders and society at large."

The moral case for social responsibility boils down to a simple concept: It's the right thing to do. The business case for social responsibility holds that it is in the enlightened self-interest of companies to be good citizens and devote some of their energies and resources to the betterment of such stakeholders as employees, the communities in which it operates, and society in general.

Exercises

1. Given the description of Marsh & McLennan's strategy presented in Illustration Capsule 10.1, would it be fair to characterize the payment of contingent commissions by property-casualty insurers as nothing more than thinly disguised kickbacks? Why or why not? If you were the manager of a company that hired Marsh & McLennan to provide risk management services, would you see that Marsh had a conflict of interest in steering your company's insurance policies to insurers in which it has an ownership interest? Given Marsh's unethical and illegal foray into rigging the bids on insurance policies for its corporate clients, what sort of fines and penalties would you impose on the company for its misdeeds (assuming you were asked to recommend appropriate penalties by the prosecuting authorities). In arriving at a figure, bear in mind that Prudential Securities paid a total of about $2 billion in the 1990s to settle civil regulatory charges and private lawsuits alleging that it misled investors on the risks and rewards of limited-partnership investments. Ten Wall Street securities firms in 2003 paid $1.4 billion to settle civil charges for issuing misleading stock research to investors. Prominent mutual-fund firms were assessed nearly $2 billion in fines and restitution for engaging in after-hours stock trading at prearranged prices that were contrary to the interests of long-term shareholders. And several well-known financial institutions, including Citigroup, Merrill Lynch, Goldmans Sachs, and Credit Suisse First Boston agreed to pay several billion dollars in fines and restitution for their role in scandals at Enron and WorldCom and for improperly allocating initial public offerings of stock. Using Internet research tools, determine what Marsh & McLennan ended up paying in fines and restitution for its unethical and illegal strategic behavior and assess the extent to which the conduct of company personnel damaged shareholders.

2. Consider the following portrayal of strategies employed by major recording studios:[60]

    Some recording artists and the Recording Artists' Coalition claim that the world's five major music recording studios—Universal, Sony, Time Warner, EMI/Virgin, and Bertelsmann—deliberately employ strategies calculated to take advantage of musicians who record for them. One practice to which they strenuously object is that the major-label record companies frequently require artists to sign contracts committing them to do six to eight albums, an obligation that some artists say can entail an indefinite term of indentured servitude. Further, it is claimed that audits routinely detect unpaid royalties to musicians under contract; according to one music industry attorney, record companies misreport and underpay artist royalties by 10 to 40 percent and are "intentionally fraudulent." One music writer was recently quoted as saying the process was "an entrenched system whose prowess and conniving makes Enron look like amateur hour." Royalty calculations are based on complex formulas that are paid only after artists pay for recording costs and other expenses and after any advances are covered by royalty earnings.

    A *Baffler* magazine article outlined a hypothetical but typical record deal in which a promising young band is given a $250,000 royalty advance on a new album. The album subsequently sells 250,000 copies, earning $710,000 for the record company; but the band, after repaying the record company for $264,000 in expenses ranging from recording fees and video budgets to catering, wardrobe, and bus tour costs for promotional events related to the album, ends up $14,000 in the hole, owes the record company money, and is thus paid no royalties on any of the $710,000 in revenues the recording company receives from the sale of the band's music. It is also standard practice in the music industry for recording studios to sidestep payola laws by hiring independent promoters to lobby and compensate radio stations for playing certain records. Record companies are often entitled to damages for undelivered albums if an artist leaves a recording studio for another label after seven years. Record companies also retain the copyrights in perpetuity on all music recorded under contract, a practice that artists claim is unfair. The Dixie Chicks, after a year-long feud with Sony over contract terms, ended up refusing to do another album; Sony sued for breach of contract, prompting a countersuit by the Dixie Chicks charging "systematic thievery" to cheat them out of royalties. The suits were settled out of court. One artist said, "The record companies are like cartels."

Recording studios defend their strategic practices by pointing out that fewer than 5 percent of the signed artists ever deliver a hit and that they lose money on albums that sell poorly. According to one study, only 1 of 244 contracts signed during 1994–1996 was negotiated without the artists being represented by legal counsel, and virtually all contracts renegotiated after a hit album added terms more favorable to the artist.

a.   If you were a recording artist, would you be happy with some of the strategic practices of the recording studios? Would you feel comfortable signing a recording contract with studios engaging in any of the practices?

b.   Which, if any, of the practices of the recording studios do you view as unethical?

3.   Recently, it came to light that three of the world's four biggest public accounting firms may have overbilled clients for travel-related expenses. Pricewaterhouse Coopers, KPMG, and Ernst & Young were sued for systematically charging their clients full price for airline tickets, hotel rooms and car-rental expenses, even though they received volume discounts and rebates of up to 40 percent under their contracts with various travel companies. Large accounting firms, law firms, and medical practices have in recent years used their size and purchasing volumes to negotiate sizable discounts and rebates on up-front travel costs; some of these contracts apparently required that the discounts not be disclosed to other parties, which seemingly included clients.

However, it has long been the custom for accounting and law firms to bill their clients for actual out-of-pocket expenses. The three accounting firms, so the lawsuit alleges, billed clients for the so-called full prices of the airline tickets, hotel rooms, and car-rental expenses rather than for the out-of-pocket discounted amounts. They pocketed the differences to the tune of several million dollars annually in additional profits. Several clients, upon learning of the full-price billing practices, claimed fraud and sued.

Do you consider the accounting firms' billing practice to be unethical? Why or why not?

4.   Suppose you found yourself in the following situation: In preparing a bid for a multimillion-dollar contract in a foreign country, you are introduced to a "consultant" who offers to help you in submitting the bid and negotiating with the customer company. You learn in conversing with the consultant that she is well connected in local government and business circles and knows key personnel in the customer company extremely well. The consultant quotes you a six-figure fee.

Later, your local co-workers tell you that the use of such consultants is normal in this country—and that a large fraction of the fee will go directly to people working for the customer company. They further inform you that bidders who reject the help of such consultants have lost contracts to competitors who employed them. What would you do, assuming your company's code of ethics expressly forbids the payments of bribes or kickbacks in any form?

5. Assume that you are the sales manager at a European company that makes sleepwear products for children. Company personnel discover that the chemicals used to flameproof the company's line of children's pajamas might cause cancer if absorbed through the skin. Following this discovery, the pajamas are then banned from sale in the European Union and the United States, but senior executives of your company learn that the children's pajamas in inventory and the remaining flameproof material can be sold to sleepwear distributors in certain East European countries where there are no restrictions against the material's use. Your superiors instruct you to make the necessary arrangements to sell the inventories of banned pajamas and flameproof materials to East European distributors. Would you comply if you felt that your job would be in jeopardy if you didn't?

6. At Salomon Smith Barney (a subsidiary of Citigroup), Credit Suisse First Boston (CSFB), and Goldman Sachs (three of the world's most prominent investment banking companies), part of the strategy for securing the investment banking business of large corporate clients (to handle the sale of new stock issues or new bond issues or advise on mergers and acquisitions) involved (a) hyping the stocks of companies that were actual or prospective customers of their investment banking services, and (b) allocating hard-to-get shares of hot new initial public offerings (IPOs) to select executives and directors of existing and potential client companies, who then made millions of dollars in profits when the stocks went up once public trading began.[61] Former WorldCom CEO Bernard Ebbers reportedly made more than $11 million in trading profits over a four-year period on shares of IPOs received from Salomon Smith Barney; Salomon served as WorldCom's investment banker on a variety of deals during this period. Jack Grubman, Salomon's top-paid research analyst at the time, enthusiastically touted WorldCom stock and was regarded as the company's biggest cheerleader on Wall Street.

To help draw in business from new or existing corporate clients, CSFB established brokerage accounts for corporate executives who steered their company's investment banking business to CSFB. Apparently, CSFB's strategy for acquiring more business involved promising the CEO and/or CFO of companies about to go public for the first time or needing to issue new long-term bonds that if CSFB was chosen to handle their company's IPO of common stock or a new bond issue, then CSFB would ensure they would be allocated shares at the initial offering price of all subsequent IPOs in which CSFB was a participant. During 1999–2000, it was common for the stock of a hot new IPO to rise 100 to 500 percent above the initial offering price in the first few days or weeks of public trading; the shares allocated to these executives were then sold for a tidy profit over the initial offering price. According to investigative sources, CSFB increased the number of companies whose executives were allowed to participate in its IPO offerings from 26 companies in January 1999 to 160 companies in early 2000; executives received anywhere from 200 to 1,000 shares each of every IPO in which CSFB was a participant in 2000. CSFB's accounts for these executives reportedly generated profits of about $80 million for the participants. Apparently, it was CSFB's practice to curtail access to IPOs for some executives if their companies didn't come through with additional securities business for CSFB or if CSFB concluded that other securities offerings by these companies would be unlikely.

Goldman Sachs also used an IPO-allocation scheme to attract investment banking business, giving shares to executives at 21 companies—among the participants were the CEOs of eBay, Yahoo, and Ford Motor Company. eBay's CEO was a participant in over 100 IPOs managed by Goldman during the 1996–2000 period and was on Goldman's board of directors part of this time; eBay paid Goldman Sachs $8 million in fees for services during the 1996–2001 period.

a. If you were a top executive at Salomon Smith Barney, CSFB, or Goldman Sachs, would you be proud to defend your company's actions?

b. Would you want to step forward and take credit for having been a part of the group who designed or approved of the strategy for gaining new business at any of these three firms?

c. Is it accurate to characterize the allocations of IPO shares to "favored" corporate executives as bribes or kickbacks?

CASES

A Guide to Case Analysis

I keep six honest serving men
(They taught me all I knew);
Their names are What and Why and When;
And How and Where and Who.
— *Rudyard Kipling*

In most courses in strategic management, students use cases about actual companies to practice strategic analysis and to gain some experience in the tasks of crafting and implementing strategy. A case sets forth, in a factual manner, the events and organizational circumstances surrounding a particular managerial situation. It puts readers at the scene of the action and familiarizes them with all the relevant circumstances. A case on strategic management can concern a whole industry, a single organization, or some part of an organization; the organization involved can be either profit seeking or not-for-profit. The essence of the student's role in case analysis is to *diagnose* and *size up* the situation described in the case and then to *recommend* appropriate action steps.

Why Use Cases to Practice Strategic Management?

> *A student of business with tact*
> *Absorbed many answers he lacked.*
> *But acquiring a job,*
> *He said with a sob,*
> *"How does one fit answer to fact?"*

The foregoing limerick was used some years ago by Professor Charles Gragg to characterize the plight of business students who had no exposure to cases.[1] The facts are that the mere act of listening to lectures and sound advice about managing does little for anyone's management skills and that the accumulated managerial wisdom cannot effectively be passed on by lectures and assigned readings alone. If anything had been learned about the practice of management, it is that a storehouse of ready-made textbook answers does not exist. Each managerial situation has unique aspects, requiring its own diagnosis, judgment, and tailor-made actions. Cases provide would-be managers with a valuable way to practice wrestling with the actual problems of actual managers in actual companies.

The case approach to strategic analysis is, first and foremost, an exercise in learning by doing. Because cases provide you with detailed information about conditions and problems of different industries and companies, your task of analyzing company after company and situation after situation has the twin benefit of boosting your analytical skills and exposing you to the ways companies and managers actually do things. Most college students have limited managerial backgrounds and only fragmented knowledge about companies and real-life strategic situations. Cases help substitute for on-the-job experience by (1) giving you broader exposure to a variety of industries, organizations, and strategic problems; (2) forcing you to assume a managerial role (as opposed to that of just an onlooker); (3) providing a test of how to apply the tools and techniques of strategic management; and (4) asking you to come up with pragmatic managerial action plans to deal with the issues at hand.

Objectives of Case Analysis

Using cases to learn about the practice of strategic management is a powerful way for you to accomplish five things:[2]

1. *Increase your understanding of what managers should and should not do in guiding a business to success.*

2. *Build your skills in sizing up company resource strengths and weaknesses and in conducting strategic analysis in a variety of industries and competitive situations.*

3. Get valuable practice in identifying strategic issues that need to be addressed, evaluating strategic alternatives, and formulating workable plans of action.

4. Enhance your sense of business judgment, as opposed to uncritically accepting the authoritative crutch of the professor or "back-of-the-book" answers.

5. Gaining in-depth exposure to different industries and companies, thereby acquiring something close to actual business experience.

If you understand that these are the objectives of case analysis, you are less likely to be consumed with curiosity about "the answer to the case." Students who have grown comfortable with and accustomed to textbook statements of fact and definitive lecture notes are often frustrated when discussions about a case do not produce concrete answers. Usually, case discussions produce good arguments for more than one course of action. Differences of opinion nearly always exist. Thus, should a class discussion conclude without a strong, unambiguous consensus on what do to, don't grumble too much when you are *not* told what the answer is or what the company actually did. Just remember that in the business world answers don't come in conclusive black-and-white terms. There are nearly always several feasible courses of action and approaches, each of which may work out satisfactorily. Moreover, in the business world, when one elects a particular course of action, there is no peeking at the back of a book to see if you have chosen the best thing to do and no one to turn to for a provably correct answer. The best test of whether management action is "right" or "wrong" is *results*. If the results of an action turn out to be "good," the decision to take it may be presumed "right." If not, then the action chosen was "wrong" in the sense that it didn't work out.

Hence, the important thing for you to understand about analyzing cases is that the managerial exercise of identifying, diagnosing, and recommending is aimed at building your skills of business judgment. Discovering what the company actually did is no more than frosting on the cake—the actions that company managers actually took may or may not be "right" or best (unless there is accompanying evidence that the results of their actions were highly positive.

The point is this: *The purpose of giving you a case assignment is not to cause you to run to the library or surf the Internet to discover what the company actually did but, rather, to enhance your skills in sizing up situations and developing your managerial judgment about what needs to be done and how to do it.* The aim of case analysis is for *you* to become actively engaged in diagnosing the business issues and managerial problems posed in the case, to propose workable solutions, and to explain and defend your assessments— this is how cases provide you with meaningful practice at being a manager.

Preparing a Case for Class Discussion

If this is your first experience with the case method, you may have to reorient your study habits. Unlike lecture courses where you can get by without preparing intensively for each class and where you have latitude to work assigned readings and reviews of lecture notes into your schedule, a case assignment requires conscientious preparation before class. You will not get much out of hearing the class discuss a case you haven't read, and you certainly won't be able to contribute anything yourself to the discussion. What you have got to do to get ready for class discussion of a case is to study the case, reflect carefully on the situation presented, and develop some reasoned thoughts. Your goal in preparing the case should be to end up with what you think is a sound, well-supported analysis of the situation and a sound, defensible set of recommendations about which managerial actions need to be taken. The Case-TUTOR software downloads that accompany the text and that are available on this same Web site will assist you in preparing the cases— the Case-TUTOR files contain a set of study questions for each case and step-by-step tutorials to walk you through the process of analyzing and developing reasonable recommendations.

To prepare a case for class discussion, we suggest the following approach:

1. ***Skim the case rather quickly to get an overview of the situation it presents.*** This quick overview should give you the general flavor of the situation and indicate the kinds of issues and problems that you will need to wrestle with. If your instructor has provided you with study questions for the case, now is the time to read them carefully.

2. ***Read the case thoroughly to digest the facts and circumstances.*** On this reading, try to gain full command of the situation presented in the case. Begin to develop some tentative answers to the study questions your instructor has provided or that are provided in the Case-TUTOR software package which you can download at the Web site for the text. If your instructor has elected not to give you assignment questions or has elected not to use Case-TUTOR, then start forming your own picture of the overall situation being described.

3. ***Carefully review all the information presented in the exhibits.*** Often, there is an important story in the numbers contained in the exhibits. Expect the information in the case exhibits to be crucial enough to materially affect your diagnosis of the situation.

4. ***Decide what the strategic issues are.*** Until you have identified the strategic issues and problems in the case, you don't know what to analyze, which tools and analytical techniques are called for, or otherwise how to proceed. At times the strategic issues are clear—either being stated in the case or else obvious from reading the case. At other times you will have to dig them out from all the information given; if so, the study questions and the case preparation exercises provided in the Case-TUTOR software will guide you.

5. ***Start your analysis of the issues with some number crunching.*** A big majority of strategy cases call for some kind of number crunching—calculating assorted financial ratios to check out the company's financial condition and recent performance, calculating growth rates of sales or profits or unit volume, checking out profit margins and the makeup of the cost structure, and understanding whatever revenue-cost-profit relationships are present. See Table 1 for a summary of key financial ratios, how they are calculated, and what they show.

6. ***Apply the concepts and techniques of strategic analysis you have been studying.*** Strategic analysis is not just a collection of opinions; rather, it entails applying the concepts and analytical tools described in Chapters 1 through 13 to cut beneath the surface and produce sharp insight and understanding. Every case assigned is strategy related and presents you with an opportunity to usefully apply what you have learned. Your instructor is looking for you to demonstrate that you know *how* and *when* to use the material presented in the text chapters. The case preparation guides on Case-TUTOR will point you toward the proper analytical tools needed to analyze the case situation.

7. ***Check out conflicting opinions and make some judgments about the validity of all the data and information provided.*** Many times cases report views and contradictory opinions (after all, people don't always agree on things, and different people see the same things in different ways). Forcing you to evaluate the data and information presented in the case helps you develop your powers of inference and judgment. Asking you to resolve conflicting information "comes with the territory" because a great many managerial situations entail opposing points of view, conflicting trends, and sketchy information.

8. ***Support your diagnosis and opinions with reasons and evidence.*** The most important things to prepare for are your answers to the question "Why?" For instance, if after studying the case you are of the opinion that the company's managers are doing a poor job, then it is your answer to "Why?" that establishes just how good your analysis of the situation is. If your instructor has provided you with specific study questions for the case or if you are attempting to complete any one of the case preparation exercises on Case-TUTOR, by all means prepare answers that include all the reasons and number-crunching evidence you can muster

to support your diagnosis. Work through the case preparation exercises on Case-TUTOR *conscientiously* or, if you are using study questions provided by the instructor, *generate at least two pages of notes!*

9. ***Develop an appropriate action plan and set of recommendations.*** Diagnosis divorced from corrective action is sterile. The test of a manager is always to convert sound analysis into sound actions—actions that will produce the desired results. Hence, the final and most telling step in preparing a case is to develop an action agenda for management that lays out a set of specific recommendations on what to do. Bear in mind that proposing realistic, workable solutions is far preferable to casually tossing out off-the-top-of-your-head suggestions. Be prepared to argue why your recommendations are more attractive than other courses of action that are open. You'll find the case preparation exercises on Case-TUTOR helpful in performing this step, too.

Table 1

Key Financial Ratios: How to Calculate Them and What They Mean

Ratio	How Calculated	What It Shows
Profitability ratios		
1. Gross profit margin	$\dfrac{\text{Sales} - \text{Cost of goods sold}}{\text{Sales}}$	Shows the percentage of revenues available to cover operating expenses and yield a profit. Higher is better and the trend should be upward.
2. Operating profit margin (or return on sales)	$\dfrac{\text{Sales} - \text{Operating expenses}}{\text{Sales}}$ or $\dfrac{\text{Operating income}}{\text{Sales}}$	Shows the profitability of current operations without regard to interest charges and income taxes. Higher is better and the trend should be upward.
3. Net profit margin (or net return on sales)	$\dfrac{\text{Profits after taxes}}{\text{Sales}}$	Shows after tax profits per dollar of sales. Higher is better and the trend should be upward.
4. Return on total assets	$\dfrac{\text{Profits after taxes} + \text{interest}}{\text{Total assets}}$	A measure of the return on total investment in the enterprise. Interest is added to after tax profits to form the numerator since total assets are financed by creditors as well as by stockholders. Higher is better and the trend should be upward.
5. Return on stockholders' equity	$\dfrac{\text{Profits after taxes}}{\text{Total stockholders' equity}}$	Shows the return stockholders are earning on their investment in the enterprise. A return in the 12-15% range is "average", and the trend should be upward.
6. Earnings per share	$\dfrac{\text{Profits after taxes}}{\text{Number of shares of common stock outstanding}}$	Shows the earnings for each share of common stock outstanding. The trend should be upward, and the bigger the annual percentage gains, the better.
Liquidity Ratios		
1. Current ratio	$\dfrac{\text{Current assets}}{\text{Current liabilities}}$	Shows a firm's ability to pay current liabilities using assets that can be converted to cash in the near term. Ratio should definitely be higher than 1.0; ratios of 2 or higher are better still.
2. Quick ratio (or acid-test ratio)	$\dfrac{\text{Current assets} - \text{Inventory}}{\text{Current liabilities}}$	Shows a firm's ability to pay current liabilities without relying on the sale of its inventories.

Table 1 *continued*

3.	Working capital	Current assets − current liabilities	Bigger amounts are better because the company has more internal funds available to (1) pay its current liabilities on a timely basis and (2) finance inventory expansion, additional accounts receivable, and a larger base of operations without resorting to borrowing or raising more equity capital.

Leverage Ratios

1.	Debt-to-assets ratio	$\dfrac{\text{Total debt}}{\text{Total assets}}$	Measures the extent to which borrowed funds have been used to finance the firm's operations. Low fractions or ratios are better—high fractions indicate overuse of debt and greater risk of bankruptcy.
2.	Debt-to-equity ratio	$\dfrac{\text{Total debt}}{\text{Total stockholders' equity}}$	Should usually be less than 1.0. High ratios (especially above 1.0) signal excessive debt, lower creditworthiness, and weaker balance sheet strength.
3.	Long-term debt-to-equity ratio	$\dfrac{\text{Long-term debt}}{\text{Total stockholders' equity}}$	Shows the balance between debt and equity in the firm's *long-term* capital structure. Low ratios indicate greater capacity to borrow additional funds if needed.
4.	Times-interest-earned (or coverage) ratio	$\dfrac{\text{Operating income}}{\text{Interest expenses}}$	Measures the ability to pay annual interest charges. Lenders usually insist on a minimum ratio of 2.0, but ratios above 3.0 signal better creditworthiness.

Activity Ratios

1.	Days of inventory	$\dfrac{\text{Sales} \div 365}{\text{Inventory}}$	Measures inventory management efficiency. Fewer days of inventory are usually better.
2.	Inventory turnover	$\dfrac{\text{Sales}}{\text{Inventory}}$	Measures the number of inventory turns per year. Higher is better.
3.	Average collection period	$\dfrac{\text{Accounts receivable}}{\text{Total sales} \div 365}$ or $\dfrac{\text{Accounts receivable}}{\text{Average daily sales}}$	Indicates the average length of time the firm must wait after making a sale to receive cash payment. A shorter collection time is better.

Other Important Measures of Financial Performance

1.	Dividend yield on common stock	$\dfrac{\text{Annual dividends per share}}{\text{Current market price per share}}$	A measure of the return that shareholders receive in the form of dividends. A "typical" dividend yield is 2-3%. The dividend yield for fast-growth companies is often below 1% (maybe even 0); the dividend yield for slow-growth companies can run 4-5%.
2.	Price-earnings ratio	$\dfrac{\text{Current market price per share}}{\text{Earnings per share}}$	P-e ratios above 20 indicate strong investor confidence in a firm's outlook and earnings growth; firms whose future earnings are at risk or likely to grow slowly typically have ratios below 12.
3.	Dividend payout ratio	$\dfrac{\text{Annual dividends per share}}{\text{Earnings per share}}$	Indicates the percentage of after-tax profits paid out as dividends.
4.	Internal cash flow	After tax profits + Depreciation	A quick and rough estimate of the cash a company's business is generating after payment of operating expenses, interest, and taxes. Such amounts can be used for dividend payments or funding capital expenditures.

As long as you are conscientious in preparing your analysis and recommendations, and have ample reasons, evidence, and arguments to support your views, you shouldn't fret unduly about whether what you've prepared is "the right answer" to the case. In case analysis there is rarely just one right approach or set of recommendations. Managing companies and crafting and executing strategies are not such exact sciences that there exists a single provably correct analysis and action plan for each strategic situation. Of course, some analyses and action plans are better than others; but, in truth, there's nearly always more than one good way to analyze a situation and more than one good plan of action. So, if you have carefully prepared the case by either completing one of the Case-TUTOR case preparation exercises or developing your own answers to the assignment questions for the case, don't lose confidence in the correctness of your work and judgment.

Participating in Class Discussion of a Case

Classroom discussions of cases are sharply different from attending a lecture class. In a case class students do most of the talking. The instructor's role is to solicit student participation, keep the discussion on track, ask "Why?" often, offer alternative views, play the devil's advocate (if no students jump in to offer opposing views), and otherwise lead the discussion. The students in the class carry the burden for analyzing the situation and for being prepared to present and defend their diagnoses and recommendations. Expect a classroom environment, therefore, that calls for *your* size-up of the situation, *your* analysis, what actions *you* would take, and why *you* would take them. Do not be dismayed if, as the class discussion unfolds, some insightful things are said by your fellow classmates that you did not think of. It is normal for views and analyses to differ and for the comments of others in the class to expand your own thinking about the case. As the old adage goes, "Two heads are better than one." So it is to be expected that the class as a whole will do a more penetrating and searching job of case analysis than will any one person working alone. This is the power of group effort, and its virtues are that it will help you see more analytical applications, let you test your analyses and judgments against those of your peers, and force you to wrestle with differences of opinion and approaches.

To orient you to the classroom environment on the days a case discussion is scheduled, we compiled the following list of things to expect:

1. *Expect the instructor to assume the role of extensive questioner and listener.*

2. *Expect students to do most of the talking. The case method enlists a maximum of individual participation in class discussion. It is not enough to be present as a silent observer; if every student took this approach, there would be no discussion. (Thus, expect a portion of your grade to be based on your participation in case discussions.)*

3. *Be prepared for the instructor to probe for reasons and supporting analysis.*

4. *Expect and tolerate challenges to the views expressed. All students have to be willing to submit their conclusions for scrutiny and rebuttal. Each student needs to learn to state his or her views without fear of disapproval and to overcome the hesitation of speaking out. Learning respect for the views and approaches of others is an integral part of case analysis exercises. But there are times when it is OK to swim against the tide of majority opinion. In the practice of management, there is always room for originality and unorthodox approaches. So while discussion of a case is a group process, there is no compulsion for you or anyone else to cave in and conform to group opinions and group consensus.*

5. *Don't be surprised if you change your mind about some things as the discussion unfolds. Be alert to how these changes affect your analysis and recommendations (in the event you get called on).*

6. *Expect to learn a lot in class as the discussion of a case progresses; furthermore, you will find that the cases build on one another—what you learn in one case helps prepare you for the next case discussion.*

There are several things you can do on your own to be good and look good as a participant in class discussions:

Although you should do your own independent work and independent thinking, don't hesitate before (and after) class to discuss the case with other students. In real life, managers often discuss the company's problems and situation with other people to refine their own thinking.

- *In participating in the discussion, make a conscious effort to contribute, rather than just talk. There is a big difference between saying something that builds the discussion and offering a long-winded, off-the-cuff remark that leaves the class wondering what the point was.*

- *Avoid the use of "I think," "I believe," and "I feel"; instead, say, "My analysis shows —" and "The company should do _____.because _____." Always give supporting reasons and evidence for your views; then your instructor won't have to ask you "Why?" every time you make a comment.*

- *In making your points, assume that everyone has read the case and knows what it says; avoid reciting and rehashing information in the case—instead, use the data and information to explain your assessment of the situation and to support your position.*

  - Bring the printouts of the work you've done on Case-Tutor or the notes you've prepared (usually two or three pages' worth) to class and rely on them extensively when you speak. There's no way you can remember everything off the top of your head—especially the results of your number crunching. To reel off the numbers or to present all five reasons why, instead of one, you will need good notes. When you have prepared thoughtful answers to the study questions and use them as the basis for your comments, *everybody* in the room will know you are well prepared, and your contribution to the case discussion will stand out.

Preparing a Written Case Analysis

Preparing a written case analysis is much like preparing a case for class discussion, except that your analysis must be more complete and put in report form. Unfortunately, though, there is no ironclad procedure for doing a written case analysis. All we can offer are some general guidelines and words of wisdom—this is because company situations and management problems are so diverse that no one mechanical way to approach a written case assignment always works.

Your instructor may assign you a specific topic around which to prepare your written report. Or, alternatively, you may be asked to do a comprehensive written case analysis, where the expectation is that you will (1) *identify* all the pertinent issues that management needs to address, (2) perform whatever *analysis* and *evaluation* is appropriate, and (3) propose an *action plan* and *set of recommendations* addressing the issues you have identified. In going through the exercise of identify, evaluate, and recommend, keep the following pointers in mind.[3]

Identification   It is essential early on in your paper that you provide a sharply focused diagnosis of strategic issues and key problems and that you demonstrate a good grasp of the company's present situation. Make sure you can identify the firm's strategy (use the concepts and tools in Chapters 1–8 as diagnostic aids) and that you can pinpoint whatever strategy implementation issues may exist (again, consult the material in Chapters 9–11 for diagnostic help). Consult the key points we have provided at the end of each chapter for further diagnostic suggestions. Review the study questions for the case on Case-Tutor. Consider beginning your paper with an overview of the company's situation, its strategy, and the significant problems and issues that confront management. State problems/issues as clearly and precisely as you can. Unless it is necessary to do so for emphasis, avoid recounting facts and history about the company (assume your professor has read the case and is familiar with the organization).

Analysis and Evaluation This is usually the hardest part of the report. Analysis is hard work! Check out the firm's financial ratios, its profit margins and rates of return, and its capital structure, and decide how strong the firm is financially. Table 1 contains a summary of various financial ratios and how they are calculated. Use it to assist in your financial diagnosis. Similarly, look at marketing, production, managerial competence, and other factors underlying the organization's strategic successes and failures. Decide whether the firm has valuable resource strengths and competencies and, if so, whether it is capitalizing on them.

Check to see if the firm's strategy is producing satisfactory results and determine the reasons why or why not. Probe the nature and strength of the competitive forces confronting the company. Decide whether and why the firm's competitive position is getting stronger or weaker. Use the tools and concepts you have learned about to perform whatever analysis and evaluation is appropriate. Work through the case preparation exercise on Case-Tutor if one is available for the case you've been assigned.

In writing your analysis and evaluation, bear in mind four things:

1. *You are obliged to offer analysis and evidence to back up your conclusions. Do not rely on unsupported opinions, over-generalizations, and platitudes as a substitute for tight, logical argument backed up with facts and figures.*

2. *If your analysis involves some important quantitative calculations, use tables and charts to present the calculations clearly and efficiently. Don't just tack the exhibits on at the end of your report and let the reader figure out what they mean and why they were included. Instead, in the body of your report cite some of the key numbers, highlight the conclusions to be drawn from the exhibits, and refer the reader to your charts and exhibits for more details.*

3. *Demonstrate that you have command of the strategic concepts and analytical tools to which you have been exposed. Use them in your report.*

4. *Your interpretation of the evidence should be reasonable and objective. Be wary of preparing a one-sided argument that omits all aspects not favorable to your conclusions. Likewise, try not to exaggerate or overdramatize. Endeavor to inject balance into your analysis and to avoid emotional rhetoric. Strike phrases such as "I think," "I feel," and "I believe" when you edit your first draft and write in "My analysis shows," instead.*

Recommendations The final section of the written case analysis should consist of a set of definite recommendations and a plan of action. Your set of recommendations should address all of the problems/ issues you identified and analyzed. If the recommendations come as a surprise or do not follow logically from the analysis, the effect is to weaken greatly your suggestions of what to do. Obviously, your recommendations for actions should offer a reasonable prospect of success. High-risk, bet-the-company recommendations should be made with caution. State how your recommendations will solve the problems you identified. Be sure the company is financially able to carry out what you recommend; also check to see if your recommendations are workable in terms of acceptance by the persons involved, the organization's competence to implement them, and prevailing market and environmental constraints. Try not to hedge or weasel on the actions you believe should be taken.

By all means state your recommendations in sufficient detail to be meaningful—get down to some definite nitty-gritty specifics. Avoid such unhelpful statements as "the organization should do more planning" or "the company should be more aggressive in marketing its product." For instance, if you determine that "the firm should improve its market position," then you need to set forth exactly how you think this should be done. Offer a definite agenda for action, stipulating a timetable and sequence for initiating actions, indicating priorities, and suggesting who should be responsible for doing what.

In proposing an action plan, remember there is a great deal of difference between, on the one hand, being responsible for a decision that may be costly if it proves in error and, on the other hand, casually suggesting courses of action that might be taken when you do not have to bear the responsibility for any of the consequences. A good rule to follow in making your recommendations is: *Avoid recommending anything you would not yourself be willing to do if you were in management's shoes.* The importance of learning to develop good managerial judgment is indicated by the fact that, even though the same information and operating data may be available to every manager or executive in an organization, the quality of the judgments about what the information means and which actions need to be taken does vary from person to person.[4]

It goes without saying that your report should be well organized and well written. Great ideas amount to little unless others can be convinced of their merit—this takes tight logic, the presentation of convincing evidence, and persuasively written arguments.

Preparing an Oral Presentation

During the course of your business career it is very likely that you will be called upon to prepare and give a number of oral presentations. For this reason, it is common in courses of this nature to assign cases for oral presentation to the whole class. Such assignments give you an opportunity to hone your presentation skills.

The preparation of an oral presentation has much in common with that of a written case analysis. Both require identification of the strategic issues and problems confronting the company, analysis of industry conditions and the company's situation, and the development of a thorough, well-thought out action plan. The substance of your analysis and quality of your recommendations in an oral presentation should be no different than in a written report. As with a written assignment, you'll need to demonstrate command of the relevant strategic concepts and tools of analysis and your recommendations should contain sufficient detail to provide clear direction for management. The main difference between an oral presentation and a written case is in the delivery format. Oral presentations rely principally on verbalizing your diagnosis, analysis, and recommendations and visually enhancing and supporting your oral discussion with colorful, snappy slides (usually created on Microsoft's PowerPoint software).

Typically, oral presentations involve group assignments. Your instructor will provide the details of the assignment—how work should be delegated among the group members and how the presentation should be conducted. Some instructors prefer that presentations begin with issue identification, followed by analysis of the industry and company situation analysis, and conclude with a recommended action plan to improve company performance. Other instructors prefer that the presenters assume that the class has a good understanding of the external industry environment and the company's competitive position and expect the presentation to be strongly focused on the group's recommended action plan and supporting analysis and arguments. The latter approach requires cutting straight to the heart of the case and supporting each recommendation with detailed analysis and persuasive reasoning. Still other instructors may give you the latitude to structure your presentation however you and your group members see fit.

Regardless of the style preferred by your instructor, you should take great care in preparing for the presentation. A good set of slides with good content and good visual appeal is essential to a first-rate presentation. Take some care to choose a nice slide design, font size and style, and color scheme. We suggest including slides covering each of the following areas:

- An opening slide covering the "title" of the presentation and names of the presenters.
- A slide showing an outline of the presentation (perhaps with presenters' names by each topic).
- One or more slides showing the key problems and strategic issues that management needs to address.
- A series of slides covering your analysis of the company's situation.
- A series of slides containing your recommendations and the supporting arguments and reasoning for each recommendation—one slide for each recommendation and the associated reasoning has a lot of merit.

You and your team members should carefully plan and rehearse your slide show to maximize impact and minimize distractions. The slide show should include all of the pizzazz necessary to garner the attention of the audience, but not so much that it distracts from the content of what group members are saying to the class. You should remember that the role of slides is to help you communicate your points to the audience. Too many graphics, images, colors, and transitions may divert the audience's attention from what is being said or disrupt the flow of the presentation. Keep in mind that visually dazzling slides rarely hide a shallow or superficial or otherwise flawed case analysis from a perceptive audience. Most instructors will tell you that first-rate slides will definitely enhance a well-delivered presentation but that impressive visual aids, if accompanied by weak analysis and poor oral delivery, still adds up to a substandard presentation.

Researching Companies and Industries via the Internet and Online Data Services

Very likely, there will be occasions when you need to get additional information about some of the assigned cases, perhaps because your instructor has asked you to do further research on the industry or company or because you are simply curious about what has happened to the company since the case was written. These days it is relatively easy to run down recent industry developments and to find out whether a company's strategic and financial situation has improved, deteriorated, or changed little since the conclusion of the case. The amount of information about companies and industries available on the Internet and through online data services is formidable and expanding rapidly.

It is a fairly simple matter to go to company Web sites, click on the investor information offerings and press release files, and get quickly to useful information. Most company Web sites allow you to view or print the company's quarterly and annual reports, its 10K and 10Q filings with the Securities and Exchange Commission, and various company press releases of interest. Frequently, a company's Web site will also provide information about its mission and vision statements, values statements, codes of ethics, and strategy information, as well as charts of the company's stock price. The company's recent press releases typically contain reliable information about what of interest has been going on—new product introductions, recent alliances and partnership agreements, recent acquisitions, summaries of the latest financial results, tidbits about the company's strategy, guidance about future revenues and earnings, and other late-breaking company developments. Some company Web pages also include links to the home pages of industry trade associations where you can find information about industry size, growth, recent industry news, statistical trends, and future outlook. Thus, an early step in researching a company on the Internet is always to go to its Web site and see what's available.

Online Data Services

Lexis-Nexis, Bloomberg Financial News Services, and other on-line subscription services available in many university libraries provide access to a wide array of business reference material. For example, the web-based Lexis-Nexis Academic Universe contains business news articles from general news sources, business publications, and industry trade publications. Broadcast transcripts from financial news programs are also available through Lexis-Nexis, as are full-text 10-Ks, 10-Qs, annual reports, and company profiles for more than 11,000 U.S. and international companies. Your business librarian should be able to direct you to the resources available through your library that will aid you in your research.

Public and Subscription Websites with Good Information

Plainly, you can use a search engine such as Google or Yahoo! or MSN to find the latest news on a company or articles written by reporters that have appeared in the business media. These can be very valuable in running down information about recent company developments. However, keep in mind that the information retrieved by a search engine is "unfiltered" and may include sources that are not reliable or that contain inaccurate or misleading information. Be wary of information provided by authors who are unaffiliated with reputable organizations or publications and articles that were published in off-beat sources or on Web sites with an agenda. Be especially careful in relying on the accuracy of information you find posted on various bulletin boards. Articles covering a company or issue should be copyrighted or published by a reputable source. If you are turning in a paper containing information gathered from the Internet, you should cite your sources (providing the Internet address and date visited); it is also wise to print Web pages for your research file (some Web pages are updated frequently).

The Wall Street Journal, Business Week, Forbes, Barron's, and *Fortune* are all good sources of articles on companies. *The Wall Street Journal Interactive Edition* contains the same information that is available daily in its print version of the paper, but also maintains a searchable database of all *Wall Street Journal* articles published during the past few years. *Fortune* and *Business Week* also make the content of the most current issue available online to subscribers as well as provide archives sections that allow you to search for articles related to a particular keyword that were published during the past few years.

The following Websites are particularly good locations for company and industry information:

Securities and Exchange Commission EDGAR database (contains company 10-Ks, 10-Qs, etc.)	http://www.sec.gov/cgi-bin/srch-edgar
CNN Money	http://money.cnn.com
Hoover's Online	http://hoovers.com
The Wall Street Journal Interactive Edition	http://www.wsj.com
Business Week	http://www.businessweek.com
Fortune	http://www.fortune.com
MSN Money Central	http://moneycentral.msn.com
Yahoo! Finance	http://finance.yahoo.com/

Some of these Internet sources require subscriptions in order to access their entire databases.

Learning Comes Quickly With a modest investment of time, you will learn how to use Internet sources and search engines to run down information on companies and industries quickly and efficiently. And it is a skill that will serve you well into the future. Once you become familiar with the data available at the different Web sites mentioned above and with using a search engine, you will know where to go to look for the particular information that you want. Search engines nearly always turn up too many information sources that match your request rather than two few; the trick is to learn to zero in on those most relevant to what you are looking for. Like most things, once you get a little experience under your belt on how to do company and industry research on the Internet, you will find that you can readily find the information you need.

The Ten Commandments of Case Analysis

As a way of summarizing our suggestions about how to approach the task of case analysis, we have compiled what we like to call "The Ten Commandments of Case Analysis." They are shown in Table 2. If you observe all or even most of these commandments faithfully as you prepare a case either for class discussion or for a written report, your chances of doing a good job on the assigned cases will be much improved. Hang in there, give it your best shot, and have some fun exploring what the real world of strategic management is all about.

Table 2

The Ten Commandments of Case Analysis

To be observed in written reports and oral presentations, and while participating in class discussions.

1. Go through the case twice, once for a quick overview and once to gain full command of the facts; then take care to explore the information in every one of the case exhibits.

2. Make a complete list of the problems and issues that the company's management needs to address.

3. Be thorough in your analysis of the company's situation (either work through the case preparation exercises on Case-TUTOR or make a minimum of 1 to 2 pages of notes detailing your diagnosis).

4. Look for opportunities to apply the concepts and analytical tools in the text chapters—all of the cases in the book have very definite ties to the material in one or more of the text chapters!!!!

5. Do enough number crunching to discover the story told by the data presented in the case. (To help you comply with this commandment, consult Table 1 in this section to guide your probing of a company's financial condition and financial performance.)

6. Support any and all off-the-cuff opinions with well-reasoned arguments and numerical evidence; don't stop until you can purge "I think" and "I feel" from your assessment and, instead, are able to rely completely on "My analysis shows."

7. Prioritize your recommendations and make sure they can be carried out in an acceptable time frame with the available resources.

8. Support each recommendation with persuasive argument and reasons as to why it makes sense and should result in improved company performance.

9. Review your recommended action plan to see if it addresses all of the problems and issues you identified—any set of recommendations that does not address all of the issues and problems you identified is incomplete and insufficient.

10. Avoid recommending any course of action that could have disastrous consequences if it doesn't work out as planned; therefore, be as alert to the downside risks of your recommendations as you are to their upside potential and appeal.

Endnotes

[1] Charles I. Gragg, "Because Wisdom Can't Be Told," in *The Case Method at the Harvard Business School*, ed. M. P. McNair (New York: McGraw-Hill, 1954), p. 11.

[2] Ibid., pp. 12–14; and D. R. Schoen and Philip A. Sprague, "What Is the Case Method?" in *The Case Method at the Harvard Business School*, ed. M. P. McNair, pp. 78–79.

[3] For some additional ideas and viewpoints, you may wish to consult Thomas J. Raymond, "Written Analysis of Cases," in *The Case Method at the Harvard Business School*, ed. M. P. McNair, pp. 139–63. Raymond's article includes an actual case, a sample analysis of the case, and a sample of a student's written report on the case.

[4] Gragg, "Because Wisdom Can't Be Told," p. 10.

Whole Foods Market in 2006: Mission, Core Values, and Strategy

Arthur A. Thompson
The University of Alabama

Founded in 1980 as a local supermarket for natural and health foods in Austin, Texas, Whole Foods Market had by 2006 evolved into the world's largest retail chain of natural and organic foods supermarkets. The company had 180 stores in the United States, Canada, and Great Britain and 2005 sales of $4.7 billion; revenues had grown at a compound annual rate of 20 percent since 1998. John Mackey, the company's cofounder and CEO, believed that Whole Foods' rapid growth and market success had much to do with having "remained a uniquely mission-driven company—highly selective about what we sell, dedicated to our core values and stringent quality standards and committed to sustainable agriculture." The company's stated mission was to promote vitality and well-being for all individuals by offering the highest quality, least processed, most flavorful natural and naturally preserved foods available. But as the company's motto—"Whole Foods, Whole People, Whole Planet"—implied, its core mission extended well beyond food retailing (see Exhibit 1).

John Mackey's vision was for Whole Foods to become a national brand synonymous not just with natural and organic foods but also with being the best food retailer in every community it served. In pursuit of this vision, the company's strategic plan aimed at expanding its retail operations to offer the highest quality and most nutritious foods to more and more customers and promoting organically grown foods, food safety concern, and sustainability of the entire

ecosystem. During its 25-year history, Whole Foods Market had been a leader in the natural and organic foods movement across the United States, helping the industry gain acceptance among growing numbers of consumers. The company's long-term objectives were to have 400 stores and sales of $12 billion by 2010.

THE NATURAL AND ORGANIC FOODS INDUSTRY

The combined sales of natural and organic foods—about $43 billion in 2003—represented 5.5 percent of the roughly $775 billion in total U.S. grocery store sales. *Natural foods* are defined as foods that are minimally processed; largely or completely free of artificial ingredients, preservatives, and other non–naturally occurring chemicals; and as near to their whole, natural state as possible. The U.S. Department of Agriculture's Food and Safety Inspection Service defines *natural food* as "a product containing no artificial ingredient or added color and that is minimally processed." While sales of natural foods products had increased at double-digit rates in the 1990s, growth had slowed to the 7–9 percent range in 2001–2005.

Organic foods were a special subset of the natural foods category and had to be grown and processed without the use of pesticides, antibiotics, hormones,

Exhibit 1 Whole Foods Market's Motto: Whole Foods, Whole People, Whole Planet

Whole Foods

We obtain our products locally and from all over the world, often from small, uniquely dedicated food artisans. We strive to offer the highest quality, least processed, most flavorful and naturally preserved foods. Why? Because food in its purest state—unadulterated by artificial additives, sweeteners, colorings and preservatives—is the best tasting and most nutritious food available.

Whole People

We recruit the best people we can to become part of our team. We empower them to make their own decisions, creating a respectful workplace where people are treated fairly and are highly motivated to succeed. We look for people who are passionate about food. Our team members are also well-rounded human beings. They play a critical role in helping build the store into a profitable and beneficial part of its community.

Whole Planet

We believe companies, like individuals, must assume their share of responsibility as tenants of Planet Earth. On a global basis we actively support organic farming—the best method for promoting sustainable agriculture and protecting the environment and the farm workers. On a local basis, we are actively involved in our communities by supporting food banks, sponsoring neighborhood events, compensating our team members for community service work, and contributing at least five percent of total net profits to not-for-profit organizations.

Source: Information posted at www.wholefoodsmarket.com (accessed November 28, 2005).

synthetic chemicals, artificial fertilizers, preservatives, dyes or additives, or genetic engineering. Organic foods included fresh fruits and vegetables, meats, and processed foods that had been produced using:

1. Agricultural management practices that promoted a healthy and renewable ecosystem that used no genetically engineered seeds or crops, sewage sludge, long-lasting pesticides, herbicides, or fungicides.

2. Livestock management practices that involved organically grown feed, fresh air and outdoor access for the animals, and no use of antibiotics or growth hormones.

3. Food processing practices that protected the integrity of the organic product and did not involve the use of radiation, genetically modified organisms, or synthetic preservatives.

In 1990, passage of the Organic Food Production Act started the process of establishing national standards for organically grown products in the United States, a movement that included farmers, food activists, conventional food producers, and consumer groups. In October 2002, the U.S. Department of Agriculture (USDA) officially established labeling standards for organic products, overriding both the patchwork of inconsistent state regulations for what could be labeled as organic and the different rules of some

43 agencies for certifying organic products. The new USDA regulations established four categories of food with organic ingredients and varying levels of organic purity:

1. *100 percent organic products:* Such products were usually whole foods, such as fresh fruits and vegetables, grown by organic methods—which meant that the product had been grown without the use of synthetic pesticides or sewage-based fertilizers, had not been subjected to irradiation, and had not been genetically modified or injected with bioengineered organisms, growth hormones, or antibiotics. Products that were 100 percent organic could carry the green USDA organic certification seal, provided the merchant could document that the food product had been organically grown (usually by a certified organic producer).

2. *Organic products:* Such products, often processed, had to have at least 95 percent organically certified ingredients. These could also carry the green USDA organic certification seal.

3. *Made with organic ingredients:* Such products had to have at least 70 percent organic ingredients; they could be labeled "made with organic ingredients" but could not display the USDA seal.

4. *All other products with organic ingredients:* Products with less than 70 percent organic ingredients could not use the word *organic* on the front of a package, but organic ingredients could be listed among other ingredients in a less prominent part of the package.

An official with the National Organic Program, commenting on the appropriateness and need for the new USDA regulations, said, "For the first time, when consumers see the word *organic* on a package, it will have consistent meaning."[1] The new labeling program was not intended as a health or safety program (organic products have not been shown to be more nutritious than conventionally grown products, according to the American Dietetic Association), but rather as a marketing solution. An organic label has long been a selling point for shoppers wanting to avoid pesticides or to support environmentally friendly agricultural practices. However, the new regulations required additional documentation on the part of growers, processors, exporters, importers, shippers, and merchants to verify that they were certified to grow, process, or handle organic products carrying the USDA's organic seal. In 2003, Whole Foods was designated as the first national "Certified Organic" grocer by Quality Assurance International, a federally recognized independent third-party certification organization. In 2005, major food processors were lobbying to make the definition of organic foods less restrictive and permit the use of synthetics in so-called 100 percent organic products.

Organic farmland in the United States was estimated at close to 3 million acres, with an estimated 14,000 mostly small-scale farmers growing organic products in 2004. The amount of certified organic cropland had doubled between 1997 and 2001, and livestock pastures increased at an even faster rate. However, less than 1 percent of U.S. farmland was certified organic in 2004. The Rodale Institute, a Pennsylvania-based advocate of organic farming, had set a goal of 100,000 certified organic U.S. farmers by 2013, a number equal to 5 percent of the 2 million U.S. farmers.[2]

A 2004 survey conducted by the Organic Trade Association found that U.S. manufacturers' sales of organic food products hit $10.4 billion in 2003, up from $1 billion in 1990; sales were expected to reach $30 billion in 2007.[3] In 2005, organic products were sold in about 14,500 natural foods stores in the United States and over 75 percent of the nation's conventional grocery stores and supermarkets. Organic foods and beverages were available in nearly every food category in 2005.

RETAILING OF NATURAL AND ORGANIC FOODS

According to the USDA, 2000 was the first year in which more organic food was sold in conventional U.S. supermarkets than in the nation's 14,500 natural foods stores. Since 2002, most mainstream supermarkets had been expanding their selections of natural and organic products, which ranged from potato chips to fresh produce to wines, cereals, pastas, cheeses, yogurt, vinegars, beef, chicken, and canned and frozen fruits and vegetables. Fresh produce was the most popular organic product— lettuce, broccoli, cauliflower, celery, carrots, and apples were the biggest sellers. Meat, dairy, bread, and snack foods were among the fastest-growing organic product categories. Most supermarket chains stocked a selection of natural and organic food items, and the number and variety of items they carried was growing. Leading supermarket chains like Wal-Mart, Kroger, Publix, Safeway, Albertson's, and Supervalu/Save-a-Lot had created special organic and health food sections for nonperishable foods in most of their stores. Kroger, Publix, and several other chains also had special sections for fresh organic fruits and vegetables in their produce cases in many of their stores in 2005. Kroger had reopened several of its supermarkets as Fresh Fare stores, offering shoppers items such as sushi, gourmet takeout food, organic produce, and an extensive selection of fine wines and cheeses; in 2004–2005, there were 20 Fresh Fare stores in California operating under the Ralph's Fresh Fare name and the Fresh Fare concept was being tested in five Michigan locations. A Kroger official indicated that Fresh Fare was not aimed at the customer who shopped exclusively at upscale, natural foods chains like Whole Foods, but rather at the customer who already shopped Kroger but might travel to Whole Foods for things like vegetables, meats, and prepared foods. Two chains— upscale Harris Teeter in the southeastern United States and Whole Foods Market—had launched their own private-label brands of organics. Exhibit 2 shows 2004–2005 data for the leading supermarket retailers in North America.

Exhibit 2   **Leading North American Supermarket Chains, 2004–2005 (ranked by sales revenues)**

Rank/Company	Number of Stores	2004–2005 Sales Revenues (in billions)	Share of Total U.S. Grocery Sales ($775 billion)
1. Wal-Mart Supercenters	1,713	$70.8	9.1%
2. Kroger	2,530	56.2	7.3
3. Albertson's	1,810	39.7	5.1
4. Safeway	1,817	35.8	4.6
5. Costco	434	29.3	3.8
6. Ahold USA*	1,489	27.4	3.5
7. Sam's Clubs	551	22.3	2.9
8. Loblaw	1,050	21.7	n.a.‡
9. Supervalu/Save-a-Lot	1,544	19.5	2.5
10. Publix Super Markets	847	18.6	2.4
11. Delhaize†	1,494	15.8	2.0
27. Whole Foods Market	171	4.7	0.6

Note: Sales revenue numbers represent estimated sales of supermarket items only in the case of Wal-Mart, Sam's Club, and Costco. Sales data for Kroger's (whose supermarket brands also include City Market, King Sooper, Ralph's, and 11 smaller chains) and Albertson's include revenues from company-owned retail outlets (fuel centers, drugstores, apparel, and jewelry) that are not supermarket related.

*Ahold USA , the U.S. division of Netherlands-based Ahold, includes 339 Stop & Shops, 197 Giant Foods (Landover, Maryland), 180 Bruno's units, 292 Bi-Los, 116 Giant Foods (Carlisle, Pennsylvania), and 365 Tops Friendly Markets.

†Delhaize includes 1,214 Food Lion stores, 123 Hannaford Bros. stores, 103 Kash 'n Karry stores, and 54 Harvey's stores.

‡**n.a.** = Not applicable. Loblaw is a Canadian chain, and market shares are based on U.S. supermarket sales.

Sources: Top 75, www.supermarketnews.com (accessed November 28, 2005); www.walmartstores.com (accessed November 28, 2005); and Whole Foods Market press release, November 9, 2005.

Most industry observers expected that conventional supermarkets would continue to expand their offerings and selection as demand for natural and organic foods expanded. Supermarkets were attracted to merchandising natural and organic foods for two reasons: Consumer demand for natural and organic foods was growing at 7–9 percent annually and was expected to accelerate; meanwhile, retail sales of general food products were growing slowly because of intense price pressures and because more and more consumers were eating out rather than cooking at home.

Leading food processors were showing greater interest in organics as well. Heinz had introduced an organic ketchup and owned a 19 percent stake in Hain Celestial Group, one of the largest organic and natural foods producers. Campbell Soup had introduced organic tomato juice. Starbucks, Green Mountain Coffee, and several other premium coffee marketers were marketing organically grown coffees; Coca-Cola's Odwalla juices were organic; and Tyson Foods and several other chicken producers had introduced organic chicken products. Producers of organically grown beef were selling all they could produce, and sales were expected to grow 30 percent annually through 2008. Safeway, Publix, and Kroger were stocking organic beef and chicken in a number of their stores. Whole Foods was struggling to find organic beef and chicken suppliers big enough to supply all its stores. Lite House organic salad dressings had recently been added to the shelves of several mainstream supermarkets. Major food-processing companies like Kraft, General Mills, Groupe Danone (the parent of Dannon Yogurt), Dean Foods, and Kellogg had all purchased organic food producers in an effort to capitalize on sales-growth opportunities for healthy foods that taste good. In the fall of 2005, McDonald's began marketing organic coffee in

650 units in New England. Most observers saw the trend toward organics as in its infancy, believing that organic products had staying power in the marketplace and were not a fad marching by in the night.

Several factors had combined to transform natural and organic foods retailing, once a niche market, into the fastest-growing segment of U.S. food sales:

- Healthier eating patterns on the part of a populace that was becoming better educated about foods, nutrition, and good eating habits. Among those most interested in organic products were aging affluent people concerned about health and better-for-you foods.

- Increasing consumer concerns over the purity and safety of food due to the presence of pesticide residues, growth hormones, artificial ingredients and other chemicals, and genetically engineered ingredients.

- Environmental concerns due to the degradation of water and soil quality.

- A wellness, or health-consciousness, trend among people of many ages and ethnic groups.

An August 2004 report by Mintel indicated that 10 percent of consumers purchased organic products frequently enough to be "organically obsessed" and another 34 percent purchased them "at least occasionally." All age groups were at least as likely to buy organics in 2004 as they were in 2002, but the largest increases were among young adults, ages 18 to 24 (49 percent versus 34 percent in 2002), and 55- to 64-year-olds (45 percent, up from 25 percent in 2002).[4]

A 2005 survey commissioned by Whole Foods found that 65 percent of U.S. consumers had tried organic foods and beverages, up from 54 percent in both 2003 and 2004; 27 percent of respondents indicated they consumed more organic foods and beverages than they did one year ago.[5] Ten percent consumed organic foods several times per week, up from just 7 percent in 2004. The top three reasons why consumers were buying organic foods and beverages were avoidance of pesticides (70.3 percent), freshness (68.3 percent), and health and nutrition (67.1 percent); 55 percent reported buying organic to avoid genetically modified foods. Also, many respondents agreed that organic foods and beverages were "better for my health" (52.8 percent) and better for the environment (52.4 percent). The

categories of organic foods and beverages that were purchased most frequently by those participating in the Whole Foods survey were fresh fruits and vegetables (73 percent), nondairy beverages (32 percent), bread or baked goods (32 percent), dairy items (24.6 percent), packaged goods such as soup or pasta (22.2 percent), meat (22.2 percent), snack foods (22.1 percent), frozen foods (16.6 percent), prepared and ready-to-eat meals (12.2 percent), and baby food (3.2 percent).

The higher prices of organic products were the primary barrier for most consumers in trying or using organic products—75 percent of those participating in the 2005 Whole Foods survey believed organics were too expensive. Other reasons for not consuming more organics were availability (46.1 percent) and loyalty to non-organic brands (36.7 percent).

WHOLE FOODS MARKET

Whole Foods Market was founded in Austin, Texas, when John Mackey, the current CEO, and two other local natural foods grocers in Austin decided the natural foods industry was ready for a supermarket format. The original Whole Foods Market opened in 1980 with a staff of only 19. It was an immediate success. At the time, there were less than half a dozen natural foods supermarkets in the United States. By 1991, the company had 10 stores, revenues of $92.5 million, and net income of $1.6 million. Whole Foods became a public company in 1992, with its stock trading on the Nasdaq; Whole Foods stock was added to the Standard & Poor's (S&P) Mid-Cap 400 Index in May 2002 and to the Nasdaq-100 Index in December 2002. The company had 32,000 employees in 2005 and expected sales of around $5.6 billion in 2006; Mackey believed the company's cash flow from operations in upcoming years would prove more than sufficient to cover the capital costs of the company's aggressive store expansion plan. In November 2005, the company announced a 20 percent increase in its quarterly dividend to $0.30, a special dividend of $4.00 per share, a 2-for-1 stock split, and a $200 million four-year stock buyback program.

Core Values

In 1997, when Whole Foods developed the "Whole Foods, Whole People, Whole Planet" slogan, John

Mackey, known as a go-getter with a "cowboy way of doing things," said:

> This slogan taps into perhaps the deepest purpose of Whole Foods Market. It's a purpose we seldom talk about because it seems pretentious, but a purpose nevertheless felt by many of our Team Members and by many of our customers (and hopefully many of our shareholders too). Our deepest purpose as an organization is helping support the health, well-being, and healing of both people (customers and Team Members) and of the planet (sustainable agriculture, organic production and environmental sensitivity). When I peel away the onion of my personal consciousness down to its core in trying to understand what has driven me to create and grow this company, I come to my desire to promote the general well-being of everyone on earth as well as the earth itself. This is my personal greater purpose with the company and the slogan perfectly reflects it.

Complementing the slogan were five core values shared by both top management and company personnel (see Exhibit 3 on page C-8). In the company's 2003 annual report, John Mackey said:

> Our core values reflect the sense of collective fate among our stakeholders and are the soul of our company. Our Team Members, shareholders, vendors, community and environment must flourish together through their affiliation with us or we are not succeeding as a business. It is leadership's role to balance the needs and desires of all our stakeholders and increase the productivity of Whole Foods Market. By growing the collective pie, we create larger slices for all of our shareholders.

Growth Strategy

Prior to 2002, Whole Foods' growth strategy had been to expand via a combination of opening its own new stores and acquiring small, owner-managed chains. About 35 percent of the company's store base had come from acquisitions; since 1991, the company had acquired 14 chains with 67 stores (see Exhibit 4 on page C-9). Since the natural foods industry was highly fragmented, consisting of close to 20,000 mostly one-store operations and small and regional chains, Whole Foods' management had continued to explore acquisitions that provided access to desirable locations and markets and that had capable personnel that would fit in with Whole Foods. However, since 2002 the company's growth strategy had shifted markedly to opening its own large stores

(50,000 square feet and larger) rather than be acquiring small chains having stores in the range of 5,000 to 20,000 square feet—very few natural foods competitors had stores bigger than 20,000 square feet.

Store Sizes and Locations

Whole Foods' 180 stores (as of January 2006) had an open format and generated average annual sales of about $26 million. Stores opened in fiscal 2004–2005 were averaging sales of over $30 million annually. Stores more than eight years old averaged about 30,000 square feet, stores less than eight years old averaged about 36,000 square feet, and the company's newest stores ranged between 25,000 and 80,000 square feet. The three Harry's Farmers Market stores in Atlanta that Whole Foods acquired in 2001 each measured 75,000–80,000 square feet. Whole Foods' newly opened 58,000-square-foot store on Columbus Circle in New York City was the largest grocery in Manhattan and the company's biggest revenue producer in 2005; Whole Foods opened a three-story 48,500-square-foot store in the Union Square area of Manhattan in March 2005. Whole Foods had a new 74,500-square-foot store in Columbus, Ohio; a flagship 78,000-square-foot store in Austin, Texas; a 62,500-square-foot store in Princeton, New Jersey; a 62,200-square-foot store in Plano, Texas; a 61,000-square-foot store in Omaha, Nebraska; a 56,000-square-foot store in Bellevue, Washington; and a 53,000-square-foot store in Torrance, California. The company was on the verge of opening a 75,000-square-foot store in London, England; a 60,000-square-foot store in Chandler (outside Phoenix); and a 65,000-square-foot store in Plymouth Meeting (a suburb of Philadelphia). In early 2006, 113 of the company's 180 stores were 30,000 square feet or larger. It was the company's practice each year to relocate some of its smaller stores to larger sites with improved visibility and parking. Exhibit 5 on page C-10 provides store-related statistics.

Whole Foods sought to locate its new stores in the upscale areas of urban metropolitan centers—86 percent of the U.S. stores were in the top 50 statistical metropolitan areas. In 2005, Whole Foods had stores in 31 states and 38 of the top 50 U.S. metropolitan areas. In 2002, the company entered Toronto, Canada, and expanded into London and Bristol, England, in 2004. In November 2005, the company had 64 stores averaging 55,000 square feet

Exhibit 3   **Whole Foods Market's Core Values**

Our Core Values

The following list of core values reflects what is truly important to us as an organization. These are not values that change from time to time, situation to situation or person to person, but rather they are the underpinning of our company culture. Many people feel Whole Foods is an exciting company of which to be a part and a very special place to work. These core values are the primary reasons for this feeling, and they transcend our size and our growth rate. By maintaining these core values, regardless of how large a company Whole Foods becomes, we can preserve what has always been special about our company. These core values are the soul of our company.

Selling the Highest Quality Natural and Organic Products Available

- **Passion for Food**—We appreciate and celebrate the difference natural and organic products can make in the quality of one's life.
- **Quality Standards**—We have high standards and our goal is to sell the highest quality products we possibly can. We define quality by evaluating the ingredients, freshness, safety, taste, nutritive value and appearance of all of the products we carry. We are buying agents for our customers and not the selling agents for the manufacturers.

Satisfying and Delighting Our Customers

- **Our Customers**—They are our most important stakeholders in our business and the lifeblood of our business. Only by satisfying our customers first do we have the opportunity to satisfy the needs of our other stakeholders.
- **Extraordinary Customer Service**—We go to extraordinary lengths to satisfy and delight our customers. We want to meet or exceed their expectations on every shopping trip. We know that by doing so we turn customers into advocates for our business. Advocates do more than shop with us, they talk about Whole Foods to their friends and others. We want to serve our customers competently, efficiently, knowledgeably and with flair.
- **Education**—We can generate greater appreciation and loyalty from all of our stakeholders by educating them about natural and organic foods, health, nutrition and the environment.
- **Meaningful Value**—We offer value to our customers by providing them with high quality products, extraordinary service and a competitive price. We are constantly challenged to improve the value proposition to our customers.
- **Retail Innovation**—We value retail experiments. Friendly competition within the company helps us to continually improve our stores. We constantly innovate and raise our retail standards and are not afraid to try new ideas and concepts.
- **Inviting Store Environments**—We create store environments that are inviting and fun, and reflect the communities they serve. We want our stores to become community meeting places where our customers meet their friends and make new ones.

Team Member Happiness and Excellence

- **Empowering Work Environments**—Our success is dependent upon the collective energy and intelligence of all of our Team Members. We strive to create a work environment where motivated Team Members can flourish and succeed to their highest potential. We appreciate effort and reward results.
- **Self-Responsibility**—We take responsibility for our own success and failures. We celebrate success and see failures as opportunities for growth. We recognize that we are responsible for our own happiness and success.
- **Self-Directed Teams**—The fundamental work unit of the company is the self-directed Team. Teams meet regularly to discuss issues, solve problems and appreciate each others' contributions. Every Team Member belongs to a Team.
- **Open & Timely Information**—We believe knowledge is power and we support our Team Members' right to access information that impacts their jobs. Our books are open to our Team Members, including our annual individual compensation report. We also recognize everyone's right to be listened to and heard regardless of their point of view.
- **Incremental Progress**—Our company continually improves through unleashing the collective creativity and intelligence of all of our Team Members. We recognize that everyone has a contribution to make. We keep getting better at what we do.
- **Shared Fate**—We recognize there is a community of interest among all of our stakeholders. There are no entitlements; we share together in our collective fate. To that end we have a salary cap that limits the compensation (wages plus profit incentive bonuses) of any Team Member to fourteen times the average total compensation of all full-time Team Members in the company.

(Continued)

Exhibit 3   **Continued**

Creating Wealth Through Profits & Growth

- **Stewardship**—We are stewards of our shareholders' investments and we take that responsibility very seriously. We are committed to increasing long term shareholder value.
- **Profits**—We earn our profits everyday through voluntary exchange with our customers. We recognize that profits are essential to creating capital for growth, prosperity, opportunity, job satisfaction and job security.

Caring About Our Communities & Our Environment

- **Sustainable Agriculture**—We support organic farmers, growers and the environment through our commitment to sustainable agriculture and by expanding the market for organic products.
- **Wise Environmental Practices**—We respect our environment and recycle, reuse, and reduce our waste wherever and whenever we can.
- **Community Citizenship**—We recognize our responsibility to be active participants in our local communities. We give a minimum of 5% of our profits every year to a wide variety of community and non-profit organizations. In addition, we pay our Team Members to give of their time to community and service organizations.
- **Integrity in All Business Dealings**—Our trade partners are our allies in serving our stakeholders. We treat them with respect, fairness and integrity at all times and expect the same in return.

Source: Information posted at www.wholefoodsmarket.com (accessed November 29, 2005).

in varying stages of development (the new stores of supermarket chains like Safeway and Kroger averaged around 55,000 square feet).

Most stores were in high-traffic shopping locations, some were freestanding, and some were in strip centers. Whole Foods had its own internally developed model to analyze potential markets according to education levels, population density, and income. After picking a target metropolitan area, the company's site consultant did a comprehensive site study and developed sales projections; potential sites had to pass certain financial hurdles. New stores opened 12 to 24 months after a lease was signed.

The cash investment needed to ready a new Whole Foods Market for opening varied with the metropolitan area, site characteristics, store size, and amount of work performed by the landlord; totals ranged from as little as $2 million to as much as $16 million—the average for the past five years was $8.6 million. In addition to the cost of readying a

Exhibit 4   **Major Acquisitions by Whole Foods Market**

Year	Company Acquired	Location	Number of Stores	Acquisition Costs
1992	Bread & Circus	Northeast United States	6	$20 million plus $6.2 million in common stock
1993	Mrs. Gooch's	Southern California	7	2,970,596 shares of common stock
1996	Fresh Fields Markets	East Coast and Chicago area	22	4.8 million shares of stock plus options for 549,000 additional shares
1997	Merchant of Vino	Detroit area	6	Approximately 1 million shares of common stock
1997	Bread of Life	South Florida	2	200,000 shares of common stock
1999	Nature's Heartland	Boston area	4	$24.5 million in cash
2000	Food 4 Thought (Natural Abilities Inc.)	Sonoma County, California	3	$25.7 million in cash, plus assumption of certain liabilities
2001	Harry's Farmer's Market	Atlanta	3	Approximately $35 million in cash
2004	Fresh & Wild	Great Britain	7	$20 million in cash plus 239,000 shares of common stock

Source: Investor relations section of www.wholefoodsmarket.com (accessed November 18, 2004).

Exhibit 5   **Number of Stores in the Whole Foods Markets Chain, 1991–2005, and Selected Store Operating Statistics, 2000–2005**

Year	Number of Stores at End of Fiscal Year
1991	10
1992	25
1993	42
1994	49
1995	61
1996	68
1997	75
1998	87
1999	100
2000	117
2001	126
2002	135
2003	145
2004	163
2005	178

Store Counts	1998	1999	2000	2001	2002	2003	2004	2005
Beginning of fiscal year	75	87	100	117	126	135	145	163
New stores opened	9	9	17	12	11	12	12	15
Stores acquired	6	5	3	0	3	0	7	0
Relocations and closures	(2)	(3)	(1)	(3)	(3)	(5)	(2)	(1)
End of fiscal year	87	100	117	126	135	145	163	178

	Fiscal Year					
	2000	2001	2002	2003	2004	2005
Store sales (000s)	$1,838,630	$2,272,231	$2,690,475	$3,148,593	$3,864,950	$4,701,289
Average weekly sales	$324,710	$353,024	$392,837	$424,095	$482,061	$536,986
Comparable store sales growth	8.6%	9.2%	10.0%	8.6%	14.9%	12.8%
Total square footage of all stores, end of year	3,180,207	3,598,469	4,098,492	4,545,433	5,145,261	5,819,843
Average store size, end of year, in square feet	27,181	28,559	30,359	31,348	31,566	33,200
Gross margin, all-store average	34.5%	34.7%	34.6%	34.2%	34.2%	35.1%
Store contribution, all-store average*	9.4%	9.5%	9.6%	9.2%	9.3%	9.6%

*Defined as gross profit minus direct store expenses, where gross profit equals store revenues less cost of goods sold.

Source: Information posted at www.wholefoodsmarket.com (accessed November 18, 2004, and November 29, 2005).

store for operation, it took approximately $750,000 to stock the store with inventory, a portion of which was financed by vendors. Preopening expenses had averaged approximately $600,000 per store over the past five years.

Product Line

While product and brand selections varied from store to store (because of differing store sizes and clientele), Whole Foods' product line included some 30,000 natural, organic, and gourmet food and non-food items:

- Fresh produce—fruits and vegetables; displays of fresh-cut fruits; and a selection of seasonal, exotic, and specialty products like cactus pears and cippolini onions.

- Meat and poultry—natural and organic meats, house-made sausages, and poultry products from animals raised on wholesome grains, pastureland, and well water (and not grown with the use of by-products, hormones, or steroids).

- Fresh seafood—a selection of fresh fish; shrimp; oysters; clams; mussels; homemade marinades; and exotic items like octopus, sushi, and black-tip shark. A portion of the fresh fish selections at the seafood station came from the company's Pigeon Cove and Select Fish seafood processing subsidiaries. Seafood items coming from distant supply sources were flown in to stores to ensure maximum freshness.

- A selection of daily baked goods—breads, cakes, pies, cookies, bagels, muffins, and scones.

- Prepared foods—soups, canned and packaged goods, oven-ready meals, rotisserie meats, hearth-fired pizza, pastas, patés, salad bars, a sandwich station, and a selection of entrées and side foods prepared daily.

- Fine-quality cheeses, olives (up to 40 varieties in some stores), and chocolates and confections.

- Frozen foods, juices, yogurt and dairy products, smoothies, and bottled waters.

- A wide selection of bulk items in bins.

- Beer and wines—the selection of domestic and imported wines varied from store to store; organic wines were among those available.

- A body care and nutrition department containing a wide selection of natural and organic body care and cosmetics products, along with assorted vitamin supplements, homeopathic remedies, yoga supplies, and aromatherapy products. All items entailed the use of non-animal testing methods and contained no artificial ingredients.

- Natural and organic pet foods (including the company's own private-label line), treats, toys, and pest control remedies.

- Grocery and household products—canned and packaged goods, pastas, soaps, cleaning products, and other conventional household items. Whole Foods' larger stores stocked conventional household products in order to make Whole Foods a one-stop grocery-shopping destination.

- A floral department with sophisticated flower bouquets.

- A 365 Every Day Value line of private-label products that included over 440 items at very competitive price points, a 365 Organic line consisting of 200 items, a 29-item Whole X line of best-of-class premium and superpremium organic products, and a 50-item organic food product line developed for children under the Whole Kids label. Most recently, the company had begun using four other private brands—Whole Catch (for frozen seafood selections), Whole Ranch (for frozen meats), Whole Treats (for candies, cookies, and frozen desserts), and Whole Kitchen (a wide selection of frozen entrées and appetizers).

- Educational products (information on alternative health care) and books relating to healing, cookery, diet, and lifestyle. In some stores, there were cooking classes and nutrition sessions.

Whole Foods was the world's biggest seller of organic produce. Perishables accounted for about 65 percent of Whole Foods' sales, considerably higher than the 40–50 percent that perishables represented at conventional supermarkets. The acquisition of the three 75,000-plus-square-foot Harry's Market superstores in Atlanta, where 75 percent of sales were perishables, had provided the company with personnel having valuable intellectual capital in creatively merchandising all major perishables categories. Management believed that the company's emphasis on fresh fruits and vegetables, bakery goods, meats, seafood, and other perishables differentiated Whole Foods stores from other supermarkets and attracted a broader customer base. According to John Mackey:

First-time visitors to Whole Foods Market are often awed by our perishables. We devote more space to fresh fruits and vegetables, including an extensive selection of organics, than most of our competitors. Our meat and poultry products are natural—no artificial ingredients, minimal processing, and raised without the use of artificial growth hormones, antibiotics or animal by-products in their feed. Our seafood is either wild-caught or sourced from aquaculture farms where environmental concerns are a priority. Also, our seafood is never treated with chlorine or other chemicals, as is common practice in the food retailing industry. With each new store or renovation, we challenge ourselves to create more entertaining, theatrical, and scintillatingly appetizing prepared foods areas. We bake daily, using whole grains and unbleached, unbromated flour and feature European-style loaves, pastries, cookies and cakes as well as gluten-free baked goods for those allergic to wheat. We also offer many vegetarian and vegan products for our customers seeking to avoid all animal products. Our cheeses are free of artificial flavors, colors, and synthetic preservatives, and we offer an outstanding variety of both organic cheeses and cheeses made using traditional methods.[6]

Whole Foods' three-story showcase Union Square store in Manhattan carried locally made New York offerings, seasonal items from the nearby Greenmarket farmers' market, and numerous exotic and gourmet items. A 28-foot international section featured such items as Lebanese fig jam, preserved lemons from Morocco, Indian curries, Thai rice, stuffed grape leaves from Greece, and goulash from Hungary. The prepared foods section had a Grilling Station where shoppers could get grilled-to-order dishes such as swordfish in red pepper Romesco sauce and steak with a mushroom demi-glace.

One of Whole Foods Market's foremost commitments to its customers was to sell foods that met strict standards and that were of high quality in terms of nutrition, freshness, appearance, and taste. (Exhibit 6 shows the company's quality standards.) Whole Foods guaranteed 100 percent satisfaction on all items purchased and went to great lengths to live up to its core value of satisfying and delighting customers. Buyers personally visited the facilities of many of the company's suppliers and were very picky about the items they chose and the ingredients they contained. For the benefit of prospective food suppliers, the company maintained a list of ingredients it considered unacceptable in food products (see Exhibit 6).

Pricing

Because the costs of growing and marketing organic foods ran 25 to 75 percent more than those of conventionally grown items, prices at Whole Foods were higher than at conventional supermarkets. For the most part, Whole Foods sold premium products at premium prices. Because the prices for price-sensitive consumers and some media critics had dubbed Whole Foods as "Whole Paycheck," chiefly because some of its exotic items had eye-popping price tags—for example, Graffitti eggplants grown in Holland were $4 per pound, lobster mushrooms from Oregon were $25 per pound, and a three-ounce can of organic pearl jasmine tea was $14.[7] Its earth-friendly detergents, toilet papers, and other household items frequently were priced higher than the name brands of comparable products found in traditional supermarkets. However, as one analyst noted, "If people believe that the food is healthier and they are doing something good for themselves, they are willing to invest a bit more, particularly as they get older. It's not a fad."[8] Another grocery industry analyst noted that while Whole Foods served a growing niche, it had managed to attract a new kind of customer, one who was willing to pay a premium to dabble in health food without being totally committed to vegetarianism or an organic lifestyle.[9]

Store Description and Merchandising

Whole Foods Market did not have a standard store design. Instead, each store's layout was customized to fit the particular site and building configuration and to best show off the particular product mix for the store's target clientele. For instance, the new 78,000-square-foot Austin store opened in March 2005 was already a top Central Texas tourist destination and downtown Austin landmark; it had an intimate village-style layout; six mini-restaurants within the store; a raw food and juice bar; more than 600 varieties of cheese and 40 varieties of olives; a selection of 1,800 wines; a Candy Island with handmade lollipops and popcorn balls; a hot nut bar with an in-house nut roaster; a World Foods section; a walk-in beer cooler with 800 selections; 14 pastry chefs making a variety of items; a Natural Home

313

Exhibit 6   **Whole Foods Market's Product Quality Standards and Customer Commitments**

Our business is to sell the highest quality foods we can find at the most competitive prices possible. We evaluate quality in terms of nutrition, freshness, appearance, and taste. Our search for quality is a never-ending process involving the careful judgment of buyers throughout the company.

- We carefully evaluate each and every product we sell.
- We feature foods that are free from artificial preservatives, colors, flavors and sweeteners.
- We are passionate about great tasting food and the pleasure of sharing it with each other.
- We are committed to foods that are fresh, wholesome and safe to eat.
- We seek out and promote organically grown foods.
- We provide food and nutritional products that support health and well-being.

Whole Foods Market's Quality Standards team maintains an extensive list of unacceptable ingredients (see below). However, creating a product with no unacceptable ingredients does not guarantee that Whole Foods Market will sell it. Our buyers are passionate about seeking out the freshest, most healthful, minimally processed products available.

As of December 2005, the following 83 chemicals were on Whole Foods' list of unacceptable ingredients:

- acesulfame-K (acesulfame potassium)
- acetylated esters of mono- and diglycerides
- ammonium chloride
- artificial colors
- artificial flavors
- aspartame
- azodicarbonamide
- benzoates in food
- benzoyl peroxide
- BHA (butylated hydroxyanisole)
- BHT (butylated hydroxytoluene)
- bleached flour
- bromated flour
- brominated vegetable oil (BVO)
- calcium bromate
- calcium disodium EDTA
- calcium peroxide
- calcium propionate
- calcium saccharin
- calcium sorbate
- calcium stearoyl-2-lactylate
- caprocaprylobehenin
- carmine (see cochineal)
- certified colors
- cochineal (carmine)
- cyclamates
- cysteine (l-cysteine), as an additive for bread products
- DATEM (diacetyl tartaric and fatty acid esters of mono and diglycerides)
- dimethylpolysiloxane

- dioctyl sodium sulfosuccinate (DSS)
- disodium calcium EDTA
- disodium dihydrogen EDTA
- disodium guanylate
- disodium inosinate
- EDTA
- ethyl vanillin
- ethylene oxide
- ethyoxyquin
- FD & C colors
- fois gras
- GMP (disodium guanylate)
- hexa-, hepta- and octa-esters of sucrose
- hydrogenated oil
- IMP (disodium inosinate)
- irradiated foods
- lactylated esters of mono- and diglycerides
- lead soldered cans
- methyl silicon
- methylparaben
- microparticularized whey protein derived fat substitute
- monosodium glutamate (MSG)
- natamyacin
- nitrates/nitrites
- partially hydrogenated oil
- polydextrose
- potassium benzoate

- potassium bisulfite
- potassium bromate
- potassium metabisulfite
- potassium sorbate
- propionates
- propyl gallate
- propylparaben
- saccharin
- sodium aluminum phosphate
- sodium aluminum sulfate
- sodium benzoate
- sodium bisulfite
- sodium diacetate
- sodium glutamate
- sodium metabisulfite
- sodium nitrate/nitrite
- sodium propionate
- sodium stearoyl-2-lactylate
- sodium sulfite
- solvent extracted oils, as standalone single-ingredient oils (except grapeseed oil)
- sorbic acid
- sucralose
- sucroglycerides
- sucrose polyester
- sulfites (sulfur dioxide)
- TBHQ (tertiary butylhydroquinone)
- tetrasodium EDTA
- vanillin

Whole Foods reserved the right to alter its list of unacceptable ingredients at any time.

Source: Information posted at www.wholefoodsmarket.com (accessed November 29, 2005).

section with organic cotton apparel and household linens; an extensive meat department with an in-house smoker and 50 oven-ready items prepared by in-house chefs; and a theater-like seafood department with more than 150 fresh seafood items and on-the-spot shucking, cooking, smoking, slicing, and frying to order. The Columbus Circle store in Manhattan had a 248-seat café where shoppers could enjoy restaurant-quality prepared foods while relaxing in a comfortable community setting; a Jamba Juice smoothie station that served freshly blended-to-order fruit smoothies and juices; a full-service sushi bar by Genji Express where customers sat on bar stools wrapped in nori enjoying fresh-cut sushi wrapped in organic seaweed; a walk-in greenhouse showcasing fresh-cut and exotic flowers; a wine shop with more than 700 varieties of wine from both large and small vineyards and family estates; and a chocolate enrobing station in the bakery where customers could request just about anything covered in chocolate.

The driving concept of Whole Foods' merchandising strategy was to create an inviting and interactive store atmosphere that turned shopping for food into a fun, pleasurable experience. Management at Whole Foods wanted customers to view company stores as a "third place" (besides home and office) where people could gather, learn, and interact while at the same time enjoying an intriguing food-shopping and eating experience. Stores had a colorful decor, and products were attractively merchandised (see Exhibit 7). According to one industry analyst, Whole Foods had "put together the ideal model for the foodie who's a premium gourmet and the natural foods buyer. When you walk into a Whole Foods store, you're overwhelmed by a desire to look at everything you see."[10]

Most stores featured hand-stacked produce, in-store chefs and open kitchens, scratch bakeries, prepared foods stations, European-style charcuterie departments, Whole Body departments with a wide selection of natural cosmetics (as well as a makeup station) and personal care items, salad bars, sit-down dining areas, gourmet food sections with items from around the world, and ever-changing selections and merchandise displays. Many stores had recipe cards at the end of key aisles. A few stores offered valet parking, home delivery, and massages. Management believed that the extensive and attractive displays of fresh produce, seafood, meats and house-made sausages (up to 40 varieties), baked goods, and prepared

foods in its larger stores appealed to a broader customer base and were responsible for the stores bigger than 30,000 square feet showing higher performance than the smaller stores.

Whole Foods got very high marks from merchandising experts and customers for its presentation—from the bright colors of the produce displays, to the quality of the foods and customer service, to the wide aisles and cleanliness. Management was continually experimenting with new merchandising concepts to keep stores fresh and exciting for customers. According to a Whole Foods regional manager, "We take the best ideas from each of our stores and try to incorporate them in all our other stores. We're constantly making our stores better."[11] Whole Foods' merchandising skills were said to be a prime factor in its success in luring shoppers back time and again—Whole Foods stores had annual sales averaging more than $800 per square foot of space about double the sales per square foot of Kroger and Safeway.

To further a sense of community and interaction with customers, stores typically included customer comment boards and Take Action centers for customers who wanted information on such topics as sustainable agriculture, organics, the sustainability of seafood supplies and overfishing problems, and the environment in general. The Toronto store had biographies of farmers suspended from the ceiling on placards and a board calling attention to Whole Foods' Sustainable Seafood Policy hung above the seafood station.

Marketing and Customer Service

Whole Foods spent about 0.5 percent of its revenues on advertising, a much smaller percentage than conventional supermarkets spent, preferring instead to rely primarily on word-of-mouth recommendations from customers. The corporate marketing budget was allocated to regionwide programs, marketing efforts for individual stores, a national brand awareness initiative, and consumer research. Stores spent most of their marketing budgets on in-store signage and store events such as taste fairs, classes, and product samplings. Store personnel were encouraged to extend company efforts to encourage the adoption of a natural and organic lifestyle by going out into the community and conducting a proactive public relations campaign. Each store also had a separate

Exhibit 7   **Scenes from Whole Foods Stores**

budget for making contributions to philanthropic activities and community outreach programs.

Since one of its core values was to satisfy and delight customers (see Exhibit 3), Whole Foods Market strove to meet or exceed customer expectations on every shopping trip. Competent, knowledgeable, and friendly service was a hallmark of shopping at a Whole Foods Market. The aim was to turn highly satisfied customers into advocates for Whole Foods who talked to close friends and acquaintances about their positive experiences with the company. Store personnel were personable and chatty with shoppers. Customers could get personal attention in every department of the store. When customers asked where an item was located, team members often took them to the spot, making conversation along the way and offering to answer any questions. Team members were quite knowledgeable and enthusiastic about the products in their particular department and tried to take advantage of opportunities to inform and educate customers about natural foods, organics, healthy eating, and food-related environmental issues. They took pride in helping customers navigate the extensive variety to make the best choices. Meat department personnel provided customers with custom cuts, cooking instructions, and personal recommendations.

Store Operations

Depending on store size and traffic volume, Whole Foods stores employed between 80 and 500 team members, who were organized into up to 11 teams, each led by a team leader. Each team within a store was responsible for a different product category or aspect of store operations such as customer service and customer check-out stations. Team leaders screened candidates for job openings on their team, but a two-thirds majority of the team had to approve a new hire—approval came only after a 30-day trial for the candidate.

Whole Foods practiced a decentralized team approach to store operations, with many personnel, merchandising, and operating decisions made by teams at the individual store level. Management believed that the decentralized structure made it critical to have an effective store team leader. The store team leader worked with one or more associate store team leaders, as well as with all the department team leaders, to operate the store as efficiently and profitably as possible. Store team leaders were paid a salary plus a bonus based on the store's economic value added

(EVA) contribution; they were also eligible to receive stock options.[12] Store team leaders reported directly to one of the 10 regional presidents.

Management believed its team members were inspired by the company's mission because it complemented their own views about the benefits of a natural and organic foods diet. In management's view, many Whole Foods team members felt good about their jobs because they saw themselves as contributing to the welfare of society and to the company's customers by selling clean and nutritious foods, by helping advance the cause of long-term sustainable agriculture methods, and by promoting a healthy, pesticide-free environment.

In December 2005, the company had some 32,000 team members, of which approximately 86 percent were full-time. None were represented by unions, although there had been a couple of unionization attempts. John Mackey was viewed as fiercely anti-union and had once said: "The union is like having herpes. It doesn't kill you, but it's unpleasant and inconvenient and it stops a lot of people from becoming your lover."[13] Union leaders were critical of the company's anti-union stance and a Web site (www.wholeworkersunite.org) was devoted to criticizing Mackey, explaining why unionization was good for Whole Foods employees, and compiling instances of the company's anti-union actions. A second Web site (www.michaelbluejay.com) touted so-called scandals at Whole Foods; the material consisted of two articles from publications that criticized Whole Foods' wage rates and Mackey's anti-union stance.

Whole Foods had been ranked by *Fortune* magazine for eight consecutive years (1998–2006) as one of the top 100 companies to work for in America—Whole Foods was one of only 22 companies to make the list every year since its inception. Whole Foods was the only national supermarket chain to ever make the list, although the regional supermarket chain Wegman's was the top-ranked company on the 2005 list. (In scoring companies, *Fortune* places a two-thirds weight on responses to a random survey of employees and a one-third weight on its evaluation of a company's benefits and practices.) A team member at Whole Foods' store in Austin, Texas, said, "I really feel like we're a part of making the world a better place. When I joined the company 17 years ago, we only had four stores. I have always loved—as a customer and now as a Team Member—the camaraderie, support for others, and progressive atmosphere at Whole Foods Market."[14] According to the company's vice president of human resources, "Team members who love to take initiative, while enjoying working as part of a team and being rewarded through shared fate, thrive here."

During 2002, team members across the company actively contributed ideas about the benefits they would like the company to offer; the suggestions were compiled and, through three subsequent votes, put into package form. The benefits plan that was adopted for three years was approved by 83 percent of the 79 percent of the team members participating in the benefits vote. Under the adopted plan, each team member could select his or her own benefits package. The resulting health insurance plan that the company put in place in January 2003 involved the company paying 100 percent of the premium for full-time employees and the establishment of company-funded "personal wellness accounts" that team members could use to pay the higher deductibles; any unused balances in a team member's account could roll over and accumulate for future expenses. Whole Foods expected to repeat its benefits vote every three years.

Every year, management gave team members an opportunity to complete a morale survey covering job satisfaction, opportunity and empowerment, pay, training, and benefits. In 2004, the overall participation rate was 63 percent (versus 71 percent in 2003). Of the team members responding in 2004, 86 percent said they almost always or frequently enjoyed their job (the same percentage as in 2003), and 82 percent said they almost always or frequently felt empowered to do their best work at Whole Foods Market (up slightly from 81 percent in 2003). In response to the question "What is the best thing about working at Whole Foods Market?" common responses included coworkers, customers, flexibility, work environment, growth and learning opportunities, the products Whole Foods sold, benefits, the team concept, and the culture of empowerment.

Compensation and Incentives

Whole Foods' management strove to create a "shared-fate consciousness" on the part of team members by uniting the self-interests of team members with those of shareholders. One way management reinforced this concept was through a gain-sharing program that rewarded a store's team members according to their store's contribution to operating profit (store sales less

cost of goods sold less store operating expenses)—gain-sharing distributions added 5–7 percent to team member wages. The company also encouraged stock ownership on the part of team members through three other programs:

1. *A team member stock option plan*—Team members were eligible for stock options based on seniority, promotion, or the discretion of regional or national executives. Roughly 85 percent of the company's stock options in 2004 were held by non-executives.

2. *A team member stock purchase plan*—Team members could purchase a restricted number of shares at a discount from the market price through payroll deductions.

3. *A team member 401(k) plan*—Whole Foods Market stock was one of the investment options in the 401(k) plan.

All the teams at each store were continuously evaluated on measures relating to sales, operations, and morale; the results were made available to team members and to headquarters personnel.[15] Teams competed not only against the goals they had set for themselves but also against other teams at their stores or in their region—competition among teams was encouraged. In addition, stores went through two review processes—a store tour and a "customer snapshot." Each store was toured periodically and subjected to a rigorous evaluation by a group of 40 personnel from another region; the group included region heads, store team leaders, associate team leaders, and leaders from two operating teams. Customer snapshots involved a surprise inspection by a headquarters official or regional president who rated the store on 300 items; each store had 10 surprise inspections annually, with the results distributed to every store and included in the reward system. Rewards were team-based and tied to performance metrics—all compensation was publicly disclosed.

Whole Foods had a salary cap that limited the compensation (wages plus profit incentive bonuses) of any team member to 14 times the average total compensation of all full-time team members in the company—a policy mandated in the company's core values (see Exhibit 3). The salary cap was raised from 10 to 14 times the average total compensation in 2005—it had been 8 times in 2003; the increases stemmed from the need to attract and retain key executives. For example, if the average total compensation was $50,000, then a cap of

10 times the average meant that an executive could not be paid more than $500,000. Such an amount was below top-level salaries at companies of comparable size and growing as rapidly as Whole Foods. In 2005, the average annual compensation was $73,061 for salaried workers and $25,451 for hourly workers. Any employee could look up anyone else's pay.

Promotions were primarily from within, with people often moving up to assume positions at stores soon to be opened or at stores in other regions.

The Use of Economic Value Added In 1999, Whole Foods adopted an economic value added (EVA) management and incentive system. EVA is defined as net operating profits after taxes minus a charge for the cost of capital necessary to generate that profit. EVA at the store level was based on store contribution (store revenues minus cost of goods sold minus store operating expenses) relative to store investment over and above the cost of capital—see Exhibit 5 for average store contribution percentages. Senior executives managed the company with the goal of *improving* EVA at the store level and companywide; they believed that an EVA-based bonus system was the best financial framework for team members to use in helping make decisions that created sustainable shareholder value. The teams in all stores were challenged to find ways to boost store contribution and EVA—the team member bonuses paid on EVA improvement averaged 6 percent in 2003.

In 2005, over 500 senior executives, regional managers, and the store leaders were on EVA-based incentive compensation plans. The primary measure for payout was EVA improvement. In fiscal year 2001, the company's overall EVA was a negative $30.4 million, but companywide EVA was $2.6 million in fiscal 2003, $15.6 million in fiscal 2004, and a record $25.8 million in 2005.

In addition, management used EVA calculations to determine whether the sales and profit projections for new stores would yield a positive and large enough EVA to justify the investment; EVA was also used to guide decisions on store closings and to evaluate new acquisitions.

Purchasing and Distribution

Whole Foods' buyers purchased most of the items retailed in the company's stores from local, regional, and national wholesale suppliers and vendors. In recent years, the company had shifted much of the buying responsibility from the store level to the regional and national levels in order to put the company in a better position to negotiate volume discounts with major vendors and distributors. Whole Foods Market was the largest account for many suppliers of natural and organic foods. United Natural Foods was the company's biggest supplier, accounting for about 20 percent of Whole Foods' purchases.

Whole Foods owned two produce procurement centers and procured and distributed the majority of its produce itself. However, where feasible, local store personnel sourced produce items from local organic farmers as part of the company's commitment to promote and support organic farming methods. Two subsidiaries, the Pigeon Cove seafood processing facility in Massachusetts and Select Fish, a West Coast seafood processing facility, supplied a portion of the company's seafood requirements. A regional seafood distribution facility had recently been established in Atlanta.

The company operated eight regional distribution centers to supply its stores. The largest distribution center in Austin supplied a full range of natural products to the company's stores in Texas, Louisiana, Colorado, Kansas, and New Mexico; the other seven regional centers distributed mainly produce and private-label goods to area stores. Twelve regional bake houses and five regional commissary kitchens supplied area stores with various prepared foods. A central coffee-roasting operation supplied stores with the company's Allegro brand of coffees.

Community Citizenship and Social Activism

Whole Foods demonstrated its social conscience and community citizenship in two ways: (1) by donating at least 5 percent of its after-tax profits in cash or products to nonprofit or educational organizations and (2) by giving each team member 20 hours of paid community service hours to use for volunteer work for every 2,000 hours worked. Team members at every store were heavily involved in such community citizenship activities as sponsoring blood donation drives, preparing meals for seniors and the homeless, holding fund-raisers to help the disadvantaged, growing vegetables for a domestic violence shelter, participating in housing renovation projects, and working as deliverypeople for Meals on Wheels.

Further, John Mackey indicated the company was sincere in living up to its core values as they related to healthy eating habits and protection of environmental ecosystems. In an effort to "walk the talk," Mackey had initiated the gathering of information about key issues that could affect people's health and well-being—the genetic engineering of food supplies, food irradiation practices, and the organic standards process; Whole Foods disseminated this information via in-store brochures, presentations to groups, and postings on its Web site. Mackey had also charged company personnel with developing position statements on sustainable seafood practices (see Exhibit 8), the merits of organic farming, and wise environmental practices. Whole Foods regularly publicized its position statements in its stores and on its Web site, along with the company's commitment to selling only those meats that had been raised without the use of growth hormones, antibiotics, and animal by-products. Company personnel were conscientious in identifying and implementing "green" actions on Whole Foods' part that enhanced the health of the planet's ecosystems. The company's Web site had a legislative action center that alerted people to pending legislation on these types of issues and made it easy for them to send their comments and opinions to legislators and government officials.

In 2004, *Business Ethics* named Whole Foods Market to its list "100 Best Corporate Citizens."

Whole Foods Market's Financial Performance

From 1991 to 2005, Whole Foods Market's net income rose at a compound average rate of 37.4 percent. The company had been profitable every year except one since 1991, when it became a public company. The one money-losing year in 2000, which involved a net loss of $8.5 million, stemmed from a decision to divest a nutritional supplement business and losses in two affiliated dot-com enterprises (Gaiam.com and WholePeople.com) in which Whole Foods owned a minority interest. The company's stock price had jumped from $30 in December 2000 to $152.50 as of December 1, 2005, and was set for a 2-for-1 stock split in January 2006.

Whole Foods paid its first quarterly dividend of $0.15 per share in January 2004; the quarterly dividend was increased to $0.19 per share in January 2005, to $0.25 per share in April 2005, and to $0.30 per share starting in January 2006 (before the scheduled stock split). The company's business was generating strong, positive cash flows. In fiscal 2004, for instance, cash flow from operations was $330 million, allowing Whole Foods to self-fund $265 million in capital expenditures (of which $155 million was for new stores) and cover cash outlays of $28 million for dividends. In fiscal 2005, Whole Foods realized $411 million in cash flow from operations, which more than covered $324 million

Exhibit 8   Whole Foods' Position on Seafood Sustainability

The simple fact is our oceans are soon to be in trouble. Our world's fish stocks are disappearing from our seas because they have been overfished or harvested using damaging fishing practices. To keep our favorite seafood plentiful for us to enjoy and to keep it around for future generations, we must act now.

As a shopper, you have the power to turn the tide. When you purchase seafood from fisheries using ocean-friendly methods, you reward their actions and encourage other fisheries to operate responsibly.

At Whole Foods Market, we demonstrate our long-term commitment to seafood preservation by:

- Supporting fishing practices that ensure the ecological health of the ocean and the abundance of marine life.
- Partnering with groups who encourage responsible practices and provide the public with accurate information about the issue.
- Operating our own well-managed seafood facility and processing plant, Pigeon Cove Seafood, located in Gloucester, Massachusetts.
- Helping educate our customers on the importance of practices that can make a difference now and well into the future.
- Promoting and selling the products of well-managed fisheries.

Source: Information posted at www.wholefoodsmarket.com (accessed November 26, 2004).

Exhibit 9   **Whole Foods Market, Statement of Operations, Fiscal Years 2002–2005 (in thousands)**

	Fiscal Year 2005	Fiscal Year 2004	Fiscal Year 2003	Fiscal Year 2002
Sales	$4,701,289	$3,864,950	$3,148,593	$2,690,475
Cost of goods sold and occupancy costs	3,048,870	2,523,816	2,070,334	1,758,281
Gross profit	1,652,419	1,341,134	1,078,259	932,194
Direct store expenses	1,199,870	986,040	794,422	677,704
Store contribution	452,549	355,094	283,837	254,490
General and administrative expenses	149,364	119,800	100,693	95,871
Share-based compensation*	19,896			
Pre-opening and relocation costs	37,035	18,648	15,765	17,934
Natural disaster costs[†]	16,521	—	—	—
Operating income	229,733	216,646	167,379	140,985
Interest expense, net	2,223	7,249	8,114	10,384
Investment and other income (loss)	9,623	6,456	5,593	2,056
Income before income taxes	237,133	215,853	164,858	132,657
Provision for income taxes	100,782	86,341	65,943	53,063
Net income	$ 136,351	$ 129,512	$ 98,915	$ 79,594
Basic earnings per share	$2.10	$2.11	$1.68	$1.41
Weighted average shares outstanding	65,045	61,324	59,035	56,385
Diluted earnings per share	$1.98	$1.98	$1.58	$1.32
Weighted average shares outstanding, diluted basis	69,975	67,727	65,330	63,340

*The company began expensing the costs of stock option compensation in 2005.

[†]Costs associated with damage to two stores in New Orleans resulting from Hurricane Katrina.

Sources: Company press release, November 9, 2005, and 2004 10K/A report.

in capital expenditures (of which $208 million was related to opening new stores) and dividend payments of $55 million. During fiscal 2005, Whole Foods also reduced its long-term debt from $164.7 million to $12.9 million. Exhibits 9 and 10 present the company's recent statements of operations and consolidated balance sheets.

COMPETITORS

The food retailing business was intensely competitive. The degree of competition Whole Foods faced varied from locality to locality, and to some extent from store location to store location within a given locale. Competitors included local, regional, and national supermarkets, along with specialty grocery stores and health and natural foods stores. Most supermarkets had offered at least a limited selection of natural and organic foods and some had chosen to expand their offerings aggressively. Whole Foods' executives had said it was to the company's benefit for conventional supermarkets to offer natural and organic foods for two reasons: First, it helped fulfill the company's mission of improving the health and well-being of people and the planet, and, second, it helped create new customers for Whole Foods by providing a gateway experience. They contended that as more

Exhibit 10   **Whole Foods Market, Consolidated Balance Sheet, Fiscal Years 2004–2005 (in thousands)**

	September 25, 2005	September 26, 2004
Assets		
Current assets:		
Cash and cash equivalents	$ 308,524	$ 194,747
Restricted cash	36,922	26,790
Trade accounts receivable	66,682	64,972
Merchandise inventories	174,848	152,912
Deferred income taxes	39,588	29,974
Prepaid expenses and other current assets	45,965	16,702
Total current assets	$ 672,529	$ 486,097
Property and equipment, net of accumulated depreciation and amortization	1,054,605	873,397
Goodwill	112,476	112,186
Intangible assets, net of accumulated amortization	21,990	24,831
Deferred income taxes	22,452	4,193
Other assets	5,244	20,302
Total assets	$1,889,296	$1,521,006
Liabilities and shareholders' equity		
Current liabilities:		
Current installments of long-term debt and capital lease obligations	$ 5,932	$ 5,973
Trade accounts payable	103,348	90,751
Accrued payroll, bonus and other benefits due team members	126,981	100,536
Dividends payable	17,208	9,361
Other current liabilities	164,914	128,329
Total current liabilities	$ 418,383	$ 334,950
Long-term debt and capital lease obligations, less current installments	12,932	164,770
Deferred rent liability	91,775	70,067
Other long-term liabilities	530	1,581
Total liabilities	$ 523,620	$ 571,368
Shareholders' equity:		
Common stock, no par value, 300,000 and 150,000 shares authorized; 68,009 and 62,771 shares issued; 67,954 and 62,407 shares outstanding in 2005 and 2004, respectively	874,972	535,107
Accumulated other comprehensive income	4,405	2,053
Retained earnings	486,299	412,478
Total shareholders' equity	$1,365,676	$ 949,638
Commitments and contingencies		
Total liabilities and shareholders' equity	$1,889,296	$1,521,006

Source: Company press release, November 9, 2005.

people were exposed to natural and organic products, they were more likely to become a Whole Foods customer because Whole Foods was the category leader for natural and organic products, offered the largest selection at competitive prices, and provided the most well-informed customer service.

Whole Foods Market's two biggest competitors in the natural foods and organics segment of the food retailing industry were Wild Oats Markets and Fresh Market. Another competitor with some overlap in products and shopping ambience was Trader Joe's. Supervalu/Save-a-Lot, the ninth largest supermarket chain in North America (see Exhibit 2), had begun an initiative to launch a chain of small natural and organic foods stores called Sunflower Markets.

Wild Oats Markets

Wild Oats Markets—a 113-store natural foods chain based in Boulder, Colorado—ranked second behind Whole Foods in the natural foods and organics segment. The company's stores were in 24 states and British Columbia, Canada; stores were operated under four names: Wild Oats Natural Marketplace, Henry's Marketplace, Sun Harvest, and Capers Community Markets. Founded in 1987, Wild Oats had sales of $1.05 billion in 2004, up from $969 million in 2003. In 1993 and 1994, Wild Oats was named one of the "500 Fastest-Growing Private Companies in America" by *Inc.* magazine. Interest quickly spread to Wall Street, and in 1996 Wild Oats became a public company traded on the Nasdaq under the symbol OATS. Grocery analysts believed that Wild Oats had close to a 3 percent market share of the natural and organic foods market in 2000, compared to about 14 percent for Whole Foods.

Wild Oats' CEO, Perry Odak, formerly the CEO of Ben & Jerry's Homemade until it was acquired by Unilever in 2000, joined the company in 2001 and had launched a turnaround strategy, which was still in progress in 2005. The company's prior CEO and founder, Mike Gilliland, had gone on an aggressive acquisition streak during the late 1990s to expand Wild Oats' geographic coverage; store growth peaked in 1999 with the acquisition of 47 stores. But Gilliland's acquisition binge piled up extensive debt and dropped the company into a money-losing position with too many stores, a dozen different store names, and a dozen different ways of operating. Product selection and customer service were inconsistent from one location to another.

When Odak arrived in March 2001, he streamlined operations, closed 28 unprofitable stores, cut prices, trimmed store staffing by 100 employees, and launched a new, smaller prototype store with a heavier emphasis on fresh food. Merchandising and marketing were revamped. The strategy was to draw in more "crossover" shoppers with lower-priced produce, meat, and seafood, along with a Fresh Look program stressing freshness and affordability to increase store traffic and raise the average purchase above the current $19 level. While the lower prices cut into the company's gross profit margin, management had tried to restore margins by concentrating purchases with fewer vendors and getting better discounts. An agreement was reached in September 2002 for Wild Oats to obtain a substantial part of its store inventories from Tree of Life, one of the leading natural foods distributors. Another of Odak's strategic thrusts was to drive a customer service mindset throughout the organization via training programs and enhanced employee communication. Odak wanted to position Wild Oats as a resource for value-added services and education about health and well-being. In 2002 Wild Oats sold close to 4.45 million shares at $11.50 to raise capital for opening 58 stores in the next three years (13 in 2003, 20 in 2004, and 25 in 2005) and remodeling a number of existing stores. While both Whole Foods and Wild Oats had stores in some of the same urban areas and were targeting some of the same areas for expansion, Wild Oats was targeting city and metropolitan neighborhoods for its new stores where there were no Whole Foods stores.

Wild Oats' new prototype stores were 22,000 to 24,000 square feet and featured a grocery-store layout where produce, dairy, meat, seafood, and baked goods were around the perimeters of the store), an expanded produce section at the front of the store, a deli, a sushi bar, a juice and java bar, a reduced selection of canned and packaged items, and store-within-a-store sections for supplements and specialty personal care products. Wild Oats had completed the remodeling of six stores (as part of its overall store remodeling initiative begun in 2003); it opened 12 new stores in 2004 and closed, sold, or relocated 7 others; it was planning to open 12 stores and remodel 10 others in 2005—both new store numbers were below the original target set when new shareholder capital had been raised in 2002. Wild Oats ended 2004 with 2.45 million square feet of floor space in its 113 stores (versus 5.8 million for Whole Foods); its expansion plans called for a total of 2.6 million square feet of floor space by year-end 2006. Also, in 2004, Wild Oats (1) completed a transition to using United Natural Foods as its primary distributor; (2) consolidated its smaller produce warehouse facilities into a single, 240,000-square-foot, state-of-the-art perishables distribution center in Riverside, California; and (3) completed the centralization and reorganization of its operations to improve efficiency. Like Whole Foods, Wild Oats was expanding its private-label offerings—400 Wild Oats and Henry's products were scheduled for introduction in 2005.

As was the case at Whole Foods, Perry Odak believed that while conventional supermarkets would continue to expand their offerings of natural and organic products, the competitive threat posed by conventional supermarkets was only moderate because their selection was more limited than what Wild Oats stores offered and because they lacked the knowledge and high level of service provided by a natural foods supermarket. In his view, "They are introducing conventional shoppers to natural brands, which will benefit us in the long run."

Wild Oats' sales in 2004 were adversely affected by conventional grocers' overly aggressive promotional activity in Southern California and by intense competition in Texas. This competition resulted in negative comparable store sales throughout the third quarter in approximately one-third of the company's store base. As a result, comparable store customer traffic in the third quarter of 2004 was a negative 4.1 percent. Wild Oats management took "aggressive action" in the form of lower prices and additional promotions to rebuild its customer traffic and sales in regions affected by intense competitive activity. But despite all of the moves that had been made under Perry Odak's leadership, the company was still struggling. After reporting losses of $15.0 million in 2000 before Odak became CEO, Wild Oats recorded losses of $43.9 million in 2001, net income of $5.1 million in 2002, net income of $1.6 million in 2003, and a loss of $40.0 million in 2004. It was expecting a small profit for 2005—through the first nine months of fiscal 2005, Wild Oats reported a small net loss of $148,000 on sales of $841.2 million

(compared to sales of $766.2 million in the first nine months of 2004). Gross margins (sales minus cost of goods sold) at Wild Oats averaged about 28.5 percent in 2002–2005, compared to 34.5 percent at Whole Foods (see Exhibit 5). Wild Oats stores averaged sales per square foot of about $440 annually versus just over $800 for Whole Foods.

Odak's latest initiatives to improve Wild Oats Markets' performance were to offer Wild Oats branded products in other retail environments. The company had reached agreement to test two alternative retail concepts. The first—a test in the Chicago market with Peapod, the country's leading Internet grocer—began in October 2004 and involved offering more than 200 private-label products on the Peapod site to consumers in the greater Chicago metropolitan area. The second, which began in June 2005, was a three-to-five store test of a Wild Oats branded store-within-a-store concept with Stop & Shop, the largest food retailer in the northeastern United States.

In a June 2004 financial move, Wild Oats sold $100 million in 3.25 percent convertible debentures to private investors; the debentures were convertible into Wild Oats common stock, at the option of the holders, at an initial price of $17.70 per share and could be redeemed starting in May 2011. Management intended to use proceeds of the offering to accelerate its growth plans, fund the repurchase of $25 million in common stock, and finance other "general corporate purposes." Wild Oats stock had traded in the $6–$16 range since 2002 and in December 2005 was trading in the $11–$13 range.

Fresh Market

Fresh Market, headquartered in Greensboro, North Carolina, was a 50-store chain operating in 12 southeastern and midwestern states (Alabama, Florida, Georgia, North Carolina, South Carolina, Tennessee, Virginia, Louisiana, Indiana, Illinois, Ohio, and Kentucky).[16] The company was founded by Ray Berry, a former vice president with Southland Corporation who had responsibility over some 3,600 7-Eleven stores. The first Fresh Market store opened in 1982 in Greensboro. Berry borrowed ideas from stores he had seen all over the United States and, as the chain expanded, used his convenience-store experience to replicate the store format and shape the product lines. During the 1982–2000 period, Fresh Market's sales revenues grew at a 25.2 percent compound rate, reaching $193 million in 2000; revenues were an estimated $280 million in 2004. Fresh Market's goal was to be the food destination store for people who enjoy cooking and good eating. The company was founded on the premise of getting customers to return again and again by offering quality products at reasonable prices and providing top-notch customer service.

Fresh Market's product line included meats, seafood, fresh produce, fresh-baked goods, prepared foods, 40 varieties of coffees, a selection of grocery and dairy items, bulk products, cheeses and deli meats, wine and beer, and floral and gift items. Fresh Market stores averaged 18,000 square feet and were located in neighborhoods near educated, high-income residents. Fresh Market differentiated itself with "upscale grocery boutique" items such as free-range chicken; pick-and-pack spices; gourmet coffees; chocolates; hard-to-get H&H bagels from New York City; Ferrara's New York cheesecake; fresh Orsini parmesan cheese; Acqua della Madonna bottled water; and an extended selection of olive oils, mustards, bulk products (granolas, nuts, beans, dried fruits, spices, and snack mixes), wine, and beer. Stores also stocked a small assortment of floral items and gifts (cookbooks, gift cards, cutting boards, and gift baskets) and a bare lineup of general grocery products. None of the meats and seafood and few of the deli products were prepackaged, and each department had at least one employee in the area constantly to help shoppers—the idea was to force interaction between store employees and shoppers. Fresh Market's warm lights, classical background music and terra-cotta-colored tiles made it a cozier place to shop than a typical grocery store. From time to time, stores had cooking classes, wine tastings, and food-sampling events. Fresh Market sponsored an annual fund-raiser for the Juvenile Diabetes Research Foundation called the Root Beer Float. The average store had 75 employees, resulting in labor costs about double those of typical supermarkets.

Merchandisers at Fresh Market's headquarters selected the stores' products, but store managers placed orders directly from third-party distributors. According to Berry, Fresh Market didn't have the concentration of stores that would make running its own warehouses profitable; Berry believed some grocers' distribution operations had grown so big that they drove the retail business, rather than the other way around.

Since 2000, the company had opened 3 to 5 new stores each year, but going forward the company planned to open 8 to 10 new stores annually. Expansion was funded by internal cash flows and bank debt. Financial data was not available because the company was privately owned, but Fresh Market's profitability was believed to be above the industry average. Several public companies had shown interest in buying the chain. In 2001 Ray Berry, then age 60, had said, "If I can get what I think the company's worth three years from now, I'll sell it. But I won't sell it for what it's worth today because I'm having too much fun."

Trader Joe's

Based in Pasadena, California, Trader Joe's was a specialty supermarket chain with over 200 stores in Arizona, California, Connecticut, Delaware, Illinois, Indiana, Maryland, Massachusetts, Michigan, Missouri, Nevada, New Jersey, New Mexico, New York, Ohio, Oregon, Pennsylvania, Virginia, and Washington. Management described the company's mission and business as follows:

> At Trader Joe's, our mission is to bring our customers the best food and beverage values and the information to make informed buying decisions. There are more than 2000 unique grocery items in our label, all at honest everyday low prices. We work hard at buying things right: Our buyers travel the world searching for new items and we work with a variety of suppliers who make interesting products for us, many of them exclusive to Trader Joe's. All our private label products have their own "angle," i.e., vegetarian, Kosher, organic or just plain decadent, and all have minimally processed ingredients.
>
> Customers tell us, "I never knew food shopping could be so much fun!" Some even call us "The home of cheap thrills!" We like to be part of our neighborhoods and get to know our customers. And where else do you shop that even the CEO, Dan Bane, wears a loud Hawaiian shirt.
>
> Our tasting panel tastes every product before we buy it. If we don't like it, we don't buy it. If customers don't like it, they can bring it back for a no-hassle refund.
>
> We stick to the business we know: good food at the best prices! Whenever possible we buy direct from our suppliers, in large volume. We bargain hard and manage our costs carefully. We pay in cash, and on time, so our suppliers like to do business with us.
>
> Trader Joe's Crew Members are friendly, knowledgeable and happy to see their customers. They

325

taste our items too, so they can discuss them with their customers. All our stores regularly cook up new and interesting products for our customers to sample.[17]

Plans called for ongoing development and introduction of new, one-of-a-kind food items at value prices, and continued expansion of store locations across the country.

Prices and product offerings varied somewhat by region and state. Customers could choose from a variety of baked goods, organic foods, fresh fruits and vegetables, imported and domestic cheeses, gourmet chocolates and candies, coffees, fresh salads, meatless entrées and other vegan products, low-fat and low-carbohydrate foods, frozen fish and seafood, heat-and-serve entrées, packaged meats, juices, wine and beer, snack foods, energy bars, vitamins, nuts and trail mixes, and whatever other exotic items the company's buyers had come upon. About 10–15 new, seasonal, or one-time-buy items were introduced each week. Products that weren't selling well were dropped. Trader Joe's had recently worked with its vendors to remove genetically modified ingredients from all of its private-label products. It had also discontinued sale of duck meat because of the cruel conditions under which ducks were grown.

Stores were open, with wide aisles, appealing displays, cedar plank walls, a nautical decor, and crew members wearing colorful Hawaiian shirts. Because of its combination of low prices, emporium-like atmosphere, intriguing selections, and friendly service, customers viewed shopping at Trader Joe's as an enjoyable experience. The company was able to keep the prices of its unique products attractively low (relative to those at Whole Foods, Fresh Market, and Wild Oats) partly because its buyers were always on the lookout for exotic items they could buy at a discount (all products had to pass a taste test and a cost test) and partly because most items were sold under the Trader Joe's label.

Sunflower Markets

Sunflower Markets, out to establish a discount niche in organic and natural foods, entered the market in 2003 with four stores—two in Phoenix, one in Albuquerque, and one in Denver.[18] As of November 2004 the company had opened three additional stores in Arizona and one in Colorado. Based in Longmont, Colorado, Sunflower's strategy borrowed from concepts employed by Trader Joe's and

small farmers' market–type stores. The company's mission statement described its four-pronged strategic approach:

- We Will Always Offer the Best Quality Food at the Lowest Prices in Town. "Better-than-supermarket quality at better-than-supermarket prices" is our motto.

- We Keep Our Overhead Low. No fancy fixtures or high rent. No corporate headquarters . . . just regular people, like you, looking for the best deals we can find.

- We Buy Big. We source directly, we pay our vendors quickly and we buy almost everything by the pallet or truckload. That buying power means big savings for you!

- We Keep It Simple. We don't charge our vendors "slotting allowances" or shelf space fees. Just honest-to-goodness negotiating for the lowest possible price and we pass the savings on to you.

The company's tag line was "Serious Food . . . Silly Prices." According to founding partner Mark Gilliland, "The last thing we want to be is another wanna-be Whole Foods." Gilliland was formerly the founder and president of Wild Oats but was forced out when his aggressive expansion strategy put Wild Oats in a financial bind.

Each Sunflower Market was about 40,000 square feet and had a warehouse-like atmosphere, with no customer service except for check-out personnel. Stores featured many one-of-a-kind items purchased in large lots from brokers. Pallets of goods were placed wherever floor space was available.

In late 2005, Sunflower had begun downsizing some of its stores to the 30,000-square-foot range and reducing the number of sections within each category—for instance, it was decreasing its selections of capers from 19 to 2 varieties.

Supervalu/Save-a-Lot

In early 2006, Minneapolis-based Supervalu, a Fortune 500 company with 2005 sales of $19.5 billion that operated 649 corporate stores (under eight brands) and 841 licensed Save-A-Lot stores in 40 states, was on the front end of launching a new 12,000- to 15,000-square-foot grocery format called Sunflower Market. The first Sunflower Market opened in January 2006 in Indianapolis as a value-priced organic and natural food store. The stores were modeled after Supervalu's Save-A-Lot small-box, limited-assortment format but had a focus on natural and organic products. Sunflower's offerings consisted of 8,000 to 12,000 stock-keeping units (SKUs) of grocery, frozen and dairy items, produce, deli and cheese, bakery, café, hormone- and antibiotic-free meat and seafood, beer and wine, and wellness products. All Sunflower Market stores were to be operated by Supervalu. Supervalu's venture had no connection to Mike Gilliland's Sunflower Market chain; Supervalu had trademarked the Sunflower name some years earlier and had licensed it to Gilliland for use in the Southwest. It was expected that the first wave of Supervalu's Sunflower Market stores would be opened in the Midwest, where Wild Oats and Whole Foods had comparatively few stores.

Jeff Noddle, Supervalu's chairman and CEO, said, "Across the nation, we are seeing a growing demand for affordable organic foods with exceptional taste and nutritional quality. Sunflower Market draws on our expertise in small-box formats, and leverages our supply chain expertise, which enables us to deliver outstanding natural and organic products at a price point consistent with consumer expectations."[19] Supervalu decided to enter the natural and organics market because the 17 to 21 percent annual growth in sales of natural and organic products was eight times higher than the growth of the conventional food market and because of the success of Whole Foods and Wild Oats. Supervalu's research indicated that 96 percent of consumers purchased organic products occasionally and 27 percent of grocery shoppers bought organics weekly. Another Supervalu executive noted, "Organics is not a fad. It is fast becoming a constant in consumers' lives. By offering these items in a convenient neighborhood market at a value price point, we create a compelling proposition for the middle-market consumer." Supervalu management believed that the company's ownership of specialty produce company W. Newell & Co. would enable Sunflower's prices to run 10 to 15 percent below that of conventional and natural food stores. Supervalu was also launching a new 100-plus-item line of private-label organic and natural products under the Nature's Best brand at Sunflower Market and planned to also make the brand available to Supervalu's 2,200 distribution customers.

Independent Natural and Health Food Grocers

In 2005 there were approximately 14,000 small, independent retailers of natural and organic foods, vitamins/supplements, and beauty and personal care products. Most were single-store, owner-managed enterprises. Combined sales of the 14,000 independents were in the $15 billion range in 2004. Two other vitamin/supplement chains, General Nutrition and Vitamin World, dominated the vitamin/supplement segment with about 7,500 store locations. Most of the independent stores had less than 2,500 square feet of retail sales space and generated revenues of less than $1 million annually, but there were roughly 850 natural foods and organic retailers with store sizes exceeding 6,000 square feet and sales of between $1 million and $5 million annually.

Product lines and range of selection at the stores of independent natural and health foods retailers varied from narrow to moderately broad, depending on a store's market focus and the shopper traffic it was able to generate. Inventories at stores under 1,000 square feet could run as little as $10,000, while those at stores of 6,000 square feet or more often ranged from $400,000 to $1.2 million. Many of the independents had some sort of deli or beverage bar, and some even had a small dine-in area with a limited health food menu. Revenues and customer traffic at most independent stores were trending upward, reflecting growing buyer interest in natural and organic products. Most independent retailers had average annual sales per square foot of store space of $200 (for stores under 2,000 square feet) to as much as $470 (for stores greater than 6,000 square feet)—Whole Foods' average was over $800 per square foot in 2005.[20]

Endnotes

[1]As quoted in Elizabeth Lee, "National Standards Now Define Organic Food," *Atlanta Journal and Constitution,* October 21, 2002.

[2]Press release, May 22, 2003, www.newfarm.org (accessed November 24, 2004).

[3]Organic Trade Association, "2004 Manufacturer Survey," www.ota.com (accessed November 28, 2005).

[4]Cited in the Trendspotting section of *Natural Foods Buyer,* Fall 2004, www.newhope.com (accessed November 26, 2004).

[5]Company press release, November 18, 2005.

[6]Letter to shareholders, 2003 annual report.

[7]Prices cited in "Eating Too Fast at Whole Foods," *BusinessWeek,* October 24, 2005, p. 84.

[8]Hollie Shaw, "Retail-Savvy Whole Foods Opens in Canada," *National Post,* May 1, 2002, p. FP9.

[9]See Karin Schill Rives, "Texas-Based Whole Foods Market Makes Changes to Cary, N.C., Grocery Store," *News and Observer,* March 7, 2002.

[10]As quoted in Marilyn Much, "Whole Foods Markets: Austin, Texas Green Grocer Relishes Atypical Sales," *Investors Business Daily,* September 10, 2002.

[11]As quoted in "Whole Foods Market to Open in Albuquerque, N.M.," *Santa Fe New Mexican,* September 10, 2002.

[12]EVA at the store level was based on store contribution (store revenues minus cost of goods sold minus store operating expenses) relative to store investment over and above the cost of capital.

[13]As quoted in John K. Wilson, "Going Whole Hog with Whole Foods," Bankrate.com, December 23, 1999. Mackey made the statement in 1991 when efforts were being made to unionize the company's store in Berkeley, California.

[14]Company press release, January 21, 2003.

[15]Information contained in John R. Wells and Travis Haglock, "Whole Foods Market, Inc." Harvard Business School case study 9-705-476.

[16]Much of the information in this section is based on M. E. Lloyd, "Specialty-Grocer Fresh Market Cultivates Upscale Consumers, Reaps Big Returns," *The Wall Street Journal,* February 20, 2001, p. B11, and information posted at www.freshmarket.com (accessed December 1, 2005).

[17]Information posted at www.traderjoes.com (accessed December 1, 2005).

[18]This section is based on information posted at www.sunflowermarkets.com and in Joe Lewandowski, "Naturals Stores Freshen Their Strategies," *Natural Foods Merchandiser,* January 1, 2004 (accessed November 19, 2004, at www.naturalfoodsmerchandiser.com).

[19] Company press release, October 19, 2005.

[20]*Natural Foods Merchandiser,* June 2004, p. 27.

Case 4

Competition in the Golf Equipment Industry in 2005

John E. Gamble
University of South Alabama

It is not known with certainty when the game of golf originated, but historians believe it evolved from ball-and-stick games played throughout Europe in the Middle Ages. The first known reference to golf in historical documents was a 1452 decree by King James II of Scotland banning the game. The ban was instituted because King James believed his archers were spending too much time playing golf and not enough time practicing archery. King James III and King James IV reaffirmed the ban in 1471 and 1491, respectively, but King James IV ultimately repealed the ban in 1502 after he himself became hooked on the game. The game became very popular with royalty and commoners alike, with the Archbishop of Saint Andrews decreeing in 1553 that the local citizenry had the right to play on the links of Saint Andrews and King James VI declaring in 1603 that his subjects had the right to play golf on Sundays.

The first known international golf tournament was played in Leith, Scotland, in 1682 when Scotsmen George Patterson and James VII prevailed over two Englishmen. By the 1700s golf had become an established sport in the British Isles, complete with golfing societies, published official rules, regularly held tournaments, full-time equipment manufacturers, and equipment exports from Scotland to the American colonies. The course at Saint Andrews became a private golf society in 1754 and was bestowed the title of Royal & Ancient Golf Club of Saint Andrews by King William IV in 1834. The first golf society in the United States was founded in Charleston, South Carolina, in 1786.

By 2000, the U.S. golf economy accounted for approximately $62 billion worth of goods and

services. The golf economy involved core industries such as golf equipment manufacturers, course designers, turf maintenance services, and club management services. The golf economy also included such enabled industries as residential golf communities and hospitality and tourism. In 2000, the size of golf-enabled industries was estimated at approximately $23 billion. The overall size of core golf industries was estimated at nearly $39 billion, with retail sales of golfing supplies totaling nearly $6 billion. The largest segment of the golfing supply industry was golf equipment, at approximately $4 billion in retail sales, followed by golf apparel, at $989 million; golf magazines, at $737 million; and golf books, at $160 million in retail sales.

Even though golf had grown to have a greater total effect on the U.S. economy than, for example, the motion picture industry or the mining industry, at $57.8 billion and $51.6 billion, respectively, the golf equipment industry was faced with serious troubles in 2005. The retail value of the golf equipment industry had declined from approximately $4 billion in 2000 to $3.2 billion projected for 2005. In addition, the number of golfers in the United States playing eight or more times per year had declined by 3 percent between 2000 and 2004. Industry sales were keyed to the number of core golfers playing eight or more times per year since these frequent golfers accounted for the majority of equipment sales. In addition, equipment manufacturers were finding it more difficult to develop technological innovations that would encourage occasional and core golfers to purchase new equipment. Golf's governing body in North America, the United States Golf Association (USGA), had ruled in 1998 that some clubs planned for introduction at that time were too technologically advanced and posed a threat to the game. The primary concern of the USGA was that technologically advanced driving clubs might produce a spring-like effect to help launch the ball as it was struck by a golfer. As a result of its concern, the USGA established a coefficient of restitution (COR) club face performance limitation that created a technology ceiling; all major manufacturers had reached this ceiling by 2005. Once the USGA felt comfortable that it was able to hold golf club innovation in check, it turned its attention to golf balls. In June 2005, the USGA asked all golf ball manufacturers to develop prototypes of golf balls that would fly 25 yards shorter than current models. USGA officials asked that these prototypes be submitted for evaluation by golf's governing body.

The combined effect of technological limitations imposed by the USGA, slowing growth in the number of new golfers, a decline in the number of core golfers, and blurred differentiation between golf equipment brands had set off some notable price competition in the industry and had led to significant declines in industry profitability and market value. Industry leader Callaway Golf Company, which had earned a record $132 million when it enjoyed a large technology-based competitive advantage over rivals in 1997, experienced a $10.1 million loss in 2004. The company's share price declined from a peak of $35 in 1997 to approximately $15 in late 2005. The company's shares had traded as low as $10 before the company was rumored to be an acquisition target during mid-2005. TaylorMade Golf, which was an adidas-Salomon business unit and another technological leader in the industry, suffered a 1 percent decline in sales and an 11 percent decline in operating profits between 2003 and 2004. Industry rivals with less-developed technological capabilities had actually benefited from the USGA COR limitation, since it provided those companies with an opportunity to catch up to TaylorMade and Callaway Golf from a technology standpoint. Revenues for Adams Golf, which had been a niche seller with limited technological capabilities, increased from $41.7 million in 2000 to $56.8 million in 2004 after its products eventually matched the COR of those offered by such industry leaders as Callaway Golf and TaylorMade. The sizable increase in revenues allowed Adams Golf to swing from a $37 million loss in 2000 to a $3.1 million profit in 2004.

Even though the equalization of technological capabilities and market shares had resulted in increased profits for some golf equipment manufacturers, the overall slim operating profit margins in the industry and emergence of price competition were troubling signs for investors seeking growth and preservation of principal. Golf equipment retail sales, units sold, and average selling price by product category for 1997–2004 are presented in Exhibit 1.

INDUSTRY CONDITIONS IN 2005

In 2005, approximately 27.5 million Americans played golf at least once per year. About one-third of golfers were considered core golfers—those playing at least eight times per year and averaging 37 rounds per year. In 2004, there were 10.2 million adult male core golfers and 2.5 million adult female core golfers in the United States. One million of the 2.9 million junior golfers in the United States played eight or more rounds per year. Minority participation was relatively low in the United States, with only 1.3 million African American golfers, 1.1 million Asian American golfers, and 1.0 million Hispanic American golfers participating in 2003. Ninety-one percent of rounds played per year were accounted for by core golfers. Core golfers also accounted for 87 percent of the industry equipment sales, membership fees, and greens fees.

A large percentage of the sales of gloves, shoes, and bags were replacement purchases by existing golfers since those products tended to wear out over time. Similarly, golf balls needed to be replaced regularly because they were frequently lost. However, the sales of new golf clubs were usually dependent on whether existing golfers believed new clubs would improve their games. Many golfers new to the game tended either to purchase used clubs or to borrow a set, but it was not uncommon for core golfers to spend considerable amounts of money on new equipment in anticipation of lower scores. Even though core golfers might play once a week or more, only a small fraction of golfers might be confused for Professional Golfers' Association (PGA) touring professionals while on the course. The average score for adult male golfers on an 18-hole course was 95, with only 8 percent of adult male golfers regularly

(*Continued on page C-72*)

Exhibit 1 Retail Value, Units Sold, and Average Selling Price of Golf Equipment in the United States, 1997–2004 (dollar amounts and units in millions)

Drivers and Woods

Year	Retail Value	Drivers/Woods Sold	Average Selling Price
1997	$676.8	2.93 million	$231
1998	601.1	2.81	214
1999	583.8	2.91	201
2000	599.1	2.94	204
2001	626.6	2.99	210
2002	608.7	3.09	197
2003	660.4	3.28	201
2004	654.1	3.56	184
2004 vs. 2003	−1.0%	8.5%	−8.7%

Irons

Year	Retail Value	Irons Sold	Average Selling Price
1997	$533.4	7.12 million	$74.90
1998	485.4	6.87	70.71
1999	447.9	6.97	64.28
2000	475.3	7.14	66.57
2001	459.3	7.17	64.06
2002	456.4	7.42	61.50
2003	461.4	7.66	60.23
2004	482.6	8.06	59.88
2004 vs. 2003	4.6%	4.6%	−0.6%

Putters

Year	Retail Value	Putters Sold	Average Selling Price
1997	$142.1	1.70 million	$83.49
1998	150.3	1.68	89.20
1999	160.1	1.68	95.13
2000	161.5	1.67	96.52
2001	167.2	1.65	101.44
2002	184.3	1.65	111.38
2003	195.2	1.60	121.92
2004	188.6	1.58	119.67
2004 vs. 2003	−3.4%	−1.6%	−1.8%

Wedges

Year	Retail Value	Wedges Sold	Average Selling Price
1997	$67.6	0.78 million	$86.17
1998	64.3	0.79	81.79
1999	65.0	0.81	80.45
2000	68.3	0.82	82.88
2001	69.4	0.82	84.78
2002	71.2	0.83	85.24
2003	77.0	0.88	86.99
2004	79.3	0.93	85.58
2004 vs. 2003	3.1%	4.8%	−1.6%

(Continued)

Exhibit 1 **Continued**

Golf Balls

Year	Retail Value	Golf Balls Sold	Average Selling Price per Dozen
1997	$458.7	19.97 million	$22.97
1998	487.4	20.06	24.30
1999	518.1	20.46	25.32
2000	530.8	20.80	25.52
2001	555.6	21.32	26.06
2002	529.9	20.81	25.46
2003	496.4	19.85	25.01
2004	506.3	19.98	25.34
2004 vs. 2003	2.0%	0.7%	1.3%

Footwear

Year	Retail Value	Pairs Sold	Average Selling Price
1997	$214.3	2.48 million	$86.49
1998	204.3	2.43	84.13
1999	206.9	2.47	83.77
2000	220.8	2.52	87.68
2001	217.8	2.57	84.62
2002	211.7	2.68	78.95
2003	217.1	2.82	76.97
2004	234.4	3.00	78.22
2004 vs. 2003	8.0%	6.2%	1.6%

Gloves

Year	Retail Value	Gloves Sold	Average Selling Price
1997	$156.7	12.81 million	$12.23
1998	160.6	12.79	12.56
1999	161.6	12.98	12.46
2000	165.4	13.20	12.53
2001	169.2	13.42	12.61
2002	163.7	13.36	12.26
2003	157.1	12.92	12.16
2004	159.3	13.15	12.11
2004 vs. 2003	1.4%	1.8%	−0.4%

Golf Bags

Year	Retail Value	Golf Bags Sold	Average Selling Price
1997	$171.8	1.37 million	$125.82
1998	165.6	1.32	125.13
1999	165.4	1.32	125.22
2000	165.1	1.31	125.56
2001	163.2	1.32	124.02
2002	153.4	1.32	116.27
2003	145.5	1.32	110.58
2004	146.8	1.34	109.55
2004 vs. 2003	0.9%	1.8%	−0.9%

Source: Golf Datatech

breaking a score of 80. The average score for adult female golfers was 106. Throughout the 1990s, it was very common for core golfers to purchase a new driver at $400–$500 at least every other year as clubs with new technological advances were introduced. Most core golfers seemed to believe it was worth the cost of new drivers, putters, and irons if technology could help offset their modest skill levels.

Key Competitive Capabilities in the Golf Equipment Industry

Competitive rivalry in the industry centered on technological innovation in clubhead and shaft design, product performance, company image, and tour exposure. The pace of technological innovation had increased rapidly during the late 1990s as industry leaders Callaway Golf, Ping Golf, TaylorMade Golf, and Titleist each attempted to beat the other to market with clubs touting unique performance characteristics. The breakneck pace of technological change caused product life cycles to decline from about three to four years during the early 1990s to about 12–18 months by 2000. Similarly, the manufacturers of golf balls introduced new products at intervals of 12–18 months to keep the interest of golfers who were looking for products that included innovations and improved performance.

The innovations in clubhead design focused on the use of lightweight metal or carbon composite materials to increase clubhead size without adding weight, to improve weight distribution within the clubhead, and to create a larger club face. After Callaway Golf Company's 1991 launch of the oversized Big Bertha driver, golf equipment manufacturers began to search for materials that would allow the clubhead to increase further in size and have a thinner face. The larger clubhead size and thinness of the club face created a larger "sweet spot," which reduced the negative effects of mis-hit shots. Beginning in the early 2000s, clubhead designers began to reposition weight in the clubhead to produce higher launch angles and to create a draw bias. Higher launch angles tended to help golfers achieve greater distance, while a draw bias helped many golfers hit straighter shots.

A golf club manufacturer's image was based in large part on its reputation for innovation and on endorsements from touring professionals. Most recreational golfers who watched televised golf tournaments or read golf magazines were very aware of what brands of clubs and golf balls their favorite touring professionals used. Also, it was not unusual for recreational golfers to base purchase decisions on the equipment choices of successful golfers on the PGA Tour. All leading golf equipment companies had long-term endorsement agreements with well-known touring professionals and also went to great lengths to make sure their products were used by lesser-known golfers as well.

The Darrell Survey counted and recorded the brand and model of each club in every golfer's bag during every professional tournament. Many golf equipment companies would pay tournament entrants a "tee-up fee" of $1,000 to $2,000 to put a club in their bag during the day of the Darrell Survey count. The tee-up fees allowed some golf club manufacturers to make factual, although misleading, claims in upcoming ads in golf magazines that their products were "number one on the PGA Tour." Endorsements paid to professional golfers totaled nearly $255 million in 2000. The best players in the game commanded multimillion-dollar contracts. Ernie Els's contract with Titleist was worth $3 million per year, while Callaway Golf paid Phil Mickelson a reported $8 million per year to use its clubs in PGA tournaments. Tiger Woods's $125 million five-year contract inked with Nike in 2003 far exceeded that provided to any other PGA touring professional in 2005. Woods's total endorsements were estimated to be worth more than $50 million per year.

Golf equipment companies also relied on personalized service in addition to lucrative endorsement fees to retain endorsements from key touring professionals. All golf equipment companies supported their touring staff members with equipment trailers during tournaments that could make adjustments to clubs prior to and during a tournament or make club substitutions at the pro's request. Some professionals' requests during the tournament might be as simple as asking the manufacturer's support staff to substitute a long iron for an additional fairway wood, while others, who might have struggled during the day, might ask that the shafts be replaced in all of their clubs before the next day's round. Touring staff members also frequented the manufacturer's headquarters to give designers feedback during the development process and to have their equipment customized to their preference. For example, when Tiger Woods became a Nike Golf staff player in 1999, his Nike irons were so highly customized they did not even resemble Nike irons offered to consumers.

Suppliers to the Industry

Most club makers' manufacturing activities were restricted to club assembly since clubhead production was contracted out to investment casting houses located in Asia and shafts and grips were usually purchased from third-party suppliers. Casting houses, such as Advanced International Multitech Company in Taiwan, produced clubheads to manufacturers' specifications and shipped the clubheads to the United States for assembly. Manufacturers were quite selective in establishing contracts with offshore casting houses since the quality of clubhead greatly affected consumers' perception of overall golf club quality and performance. Poor casting could result in clubheads that could easily break or fail to perform to the developers' expectations. Ping Golf was the only golf club producer vertically integrated into clubhead casting.

Differentiation based on shaft performance became more important to golf club manufacturers as technological differences between brands of golf clubs decreased after the USGA enacted its limitation on clubhead size and performance. Most golf club manufacturers developed modestly sized lines of proprietary shafts, which were also produced by outside suppliers. The relatively narrow line of shafts bearing the club manufacturer's name was supplemented with branded shafts produced and marketed by companies such as UST, Fujikura, or Graffaloy. Even though third-party branded shafts were equally available to all manufacturers, they were important in attracting sales to highly discriminating consumers, since these golfers might have as strong a preference for a particular shaft as for a clubhead design. For example, the purchase decision made by a low-handicap golfer considering two drivers might come down to which club could be ordered with a specific shaft.

The USGA limitation on clubhead size and club face performance had helped shaft manufacturers record higher revenues and profits. Like many shaft manufacturers, Aldila had struggled during years when consumers' greatest interest was on clubhead innovations, but a shifting consumer focus on shafts had allowed the company to swing from a $1.7 million loss in 2003 to a $9.3 million profit in 2004. At the end of the company's second quarter 2005, its net profit margins had soared to nearly 19 percent, its current ratio was nearly 4.0, and its stock price had improved to $25 per share from $1 per share in late

2002. Grips had yet to prove to be a point of differentiation, and few golfers showed a strong preference for one brand of grip over another.

Golf Equipment Retailers and the Distribution and Sale of Golf Equipment

Leading golf equipment manufacturers distributed their products through on-course pro shops, off-course pro shops such as Edwin Watts and Nevada Bob's, and online golf retailers such as Golfsmith.com and TGW.com. Most on-course pro shops sold only to members and carried few clubs since their members purchased golf clubs infrequently. Off-course pro shops accounted for the largest portion of retail golf club sales because they carried a wider variety of brands and marketed more aggressively than on-course shops. Off-course pro shops held an advantage over online retailers as well, since golf equipment consumers could inspect clubs and try out demo models before committing to a purchase. Also, both on-course and off-course pro shops were able to offer consumers custom fitting and advice from a PGA member or other individual with the training necessary to properly match equipment to the customer. Most consumers making online purchases had already decided on a brand and model, choosing to buy online to get a lower price or to avoid sales taxes. However, most of the top brands required online retailers to sell their equipment at the same prices as those offered by traditional retailers.

Custom fitting was offered by most manufacturers and large off-course pro shops with the use of specialized computer equipment. Common swing variables recorded and evaluated in determining the proper clubs for golfers included clubhead speed and path, club face angle at impact, ball position, the golfer's weight distribution, ball flight pattern, and ball flight distance. Custom fitting had become very important as golf equipment companies expanded shaft flex options during the early 2000s. In 2005, most iron sets could be equipped with shafts in senior, regular, stiff, or extra-stiff flex. Manufacturers offered drivers with dozens of different shaft configurations. For example, the Callaway Golf Big Bertha Fusion FT-3 Driver could be ordered with Aldila, Fujikura, Graffaloy, UST, or Graphite Design shafts. There were 20 different Aldila shafts available for the Fusion FT-3, each with a unique flex, weight, torque, and kick point. A wide variety of shafts from UST, Graphite Design, Fujikura, and Graffaloy were also available on the Fusion FT-3 driver.

Pro shops generally chose to stock only equipment produced by leading manufacturers and did not carry less expensive, less technologically advanced equipment. Low-end manufacturers sold their products mainly through discounters, mass merchandisers, and large sporting goods stores. These retailers had no custom fitting capabilities and rarely had sales personnel knowledgeable about the performance features of the different brands and models of golf equipment carried in the store. Such retail outlets offered the appeal of low price; they mainly attracted beginning golfers and occasional golfers who were unwilling to invest in more expensive equipment.

RECENT TRENDS IN THE GOLF EQUIPMENT INDUSTRY

Limited Opportunities for Innovation in Clubface Design

Not long after Callaway Golf Company's introduction of the Great Big Bertha titanium driver in 1995, the United States Golf Association (USGA) began to show concern that technologically advanced golf equipment might change the game of golf. The driving distance of John Daly, Tiger Woods, and other PGA members had overwhelmed some golf courses designed in the age of persimmon woods, and it was not unusual for the average driving distance of professional tournament golfers to exceed 300 yards. Many golfers playing on the Champions Tour claimed that new, technologically advanced drivers had helped them hit the longest drives of their careers even though they might be age 60 or over. The USGA believed that the added distance was a product of ultra-thin driver clubfaces that produced a springlike or trampoline effect that could help propel the ball forward.

Beginning in 1998, the USGA limited the coefficient of restitution (COR) for drivers to 0.83 to prevent manufacturers from developing clubs with a so-called springlike effect. The COR—the ratio of incoming to outgoing velocity—was calculated by firing a golf ball at a driver out of a cannonlike

machine at 109 miles per hour. The speed that the ball returned to the cannon could not exceed 83 percent of its initial speed (90.47 miles per hour). Drivers that did not conform to the USGA 0.83 COR threshold were barred from use by recreational or professional golfers in the United States, Canada, and Mexico who intended to play by the USGA's Rules of Golf. The USGA refused to calculate handicaps for golfers who had used nonconforming equipment, but it did not attempt to restrict the club's usage among players who did not choose to establish or maintain handicaps.

A discrepancy existed between the USGA's limitation on driver performance and the Rules of Golf as published by the Royal and Ancient (R&A) Golf Club of Saint Andrews, Scotland, which governed play in most countries outside of North America. The R&A did not measure the COR for driving clubs at the time of the USGA's ruling and did not have a COR limitation for clubhead performance. The two organizations agreed to develop a common worldwide standard for clubhead performance in May 2002, but the USGA unexpectedly withdrew its support from the compromise standard in August 2002. In December 2003, the R&A announced its policy regarding driver performance that would become effective in January 2004. The R&A developed a less complex test for a springlike or trampoline effect that used a pendulum to drop a weight onto the clubface of the driver. The R&A pendulum test required that the clubface and the weight remain in contact for 239 microseconds, with a tolerance of 18 microseconds. The pendulum test was applied only to drivers used in elite professional tournaments. The R&A ruled that recreational golfers and those competing in lesser tournaments were not subject to its Driving Club Condition of Competition. The USGA developed a similar pendulum test to replace its test for COR after the R&A made its December 2003 announcement. However, the USGA's use of a pendulum test did not change its specifications for drivers or make nonconforming drivers available to recreational golfers wishing to maintain a handicap.

Golf club manufacturers disagreed that a springlike effect could be produced by a metal golf club and believed that the USGA's ruling, which affected recreational as well as professional tournament golfers, would discourage new golfers from taking up the game. During the 2000 Masters Tournament in Augusta, Georgia, Callaway Golf's chief engineer, Richard Helmstetter, challenged the suggestion that clubs with a high COR could produce a springlike effect:

> We do a great deal of research at Callaway Golf and I think we are the most technologically advanced golf company in the world. We have been unable to find any evidence at all that a club face, no matter how thin, plays a role like a trampoline in striking the ball. We do think that certain kinds of construction and materials will reduce the loss of energy in the golf ball at impact and give the golfer longer drives, but this is quite different from a trampoline. The club face vibrates during impact at a speed so high that it cannot be timed, we believe, to the compression and release of a golf ball. Consequently, we think that trampoline effect is a misnomer, if not a myth entirely.[1]

Callaway Golf challenged the USGA's COR limitation in 2000 when it introduced for sale in the United States the ERC II driver with a COR of 0.86. The company's management believed that the 6–10 additional yards of carry achieved by recreational golfers using the ERC II posed no threat to the game of golf. Callaway Golf executives did concede that equipment limitations might be set for professional golfers, but saw no need to limit the performance of equipment used by recreational golfers who might gain more pleasure from hitting longer drives. Callaway Golf founder Ely Callaway suggested there were "two games of golf—tournament golf and recreational golf, and the two games differ in many respects . . . We believe that recreational golfers should not be denied the benefits of modern technology that can bring them added enjoyment that comes from occasionally hitting the ball a little bit further."[2]

Upon the announcement that Callaway Golf would make the club available to golfers in the United States, Arnold Palmer supported the company's decision by saying, "I think what Callaway is doing is just right. I have given a lot of thought to conforming and nonconforming clubs. If my daughter, who is a 100s shooter can shoot 90 with a nonconforming driver, I can't imagine that there would be anything wrong with that."[3]

The ERC II was a failure in the United States since the USGA did not agree with Callaway Golf's arguments and recreational golfers were hesitant to purchase a nonconforming club. The club did sell in large numbers in markets where the R&A Rules of Golf governed play. In 2005, all major golf club producers produced two versions of their drivers—high-COR drivers for markets outside North America and a version with a COR of 0.83 for the United States, Mexico, and Canada.

Slowing Growth in the Number of New Golfers and Rounds Played

Golf was the 12th most popular form of recreation in the United States, with approximately 27.5 million participants. In 2003, there were approximately 6.3 million golfers in Europe and 16.7 million golfers in Asia. The industry had seemingly reached maturity as a sport, with the number of new participants each year barely exceeding the number who were giving up the sport. Asia's 2–3 percent annual growth in the number of new golfers made it the only geographic region to experience growth between 1999 and 2003. Poor economic conditions in the United States during 2000 caused many frequent golfers to scale back their participation levels that year, but the number of core and avid core golfers rebounded in 2001 through 2004. However, the overall number of rounds played by golfers declined until 2004, when the number of rounds played increased by nearly 7 percent. Exhibits 2 and 3 present trends in frequency of play and rounds played for the U.S. golf market for various years between 1991 and 2004.

A survey of golfers conducted in June 2003 by the National Golf Foundation found that golfers of all types were finding it more difficult to play golf often. Golfers who were married with children were most likely to comment that job responsibilities, lack of free time, and family responsibilities prohibited them from playing golf on a more regular basis. Job responsibilities and lack of free time were also barriers to playing golf more frequently for married or single golfers who had no children. Older golfers who were either retired or who were working less than 40 hours per week had fewer job and family responsibilities and had ample free time, but were frequently troubled with heath concerns or injuries. About 30 percent of golfers said that high golf fees prevented them from playing golf more often. In fact, a different study on golf participation conducted by the National Golf Foundation in 2003 found that income was the primary predictor of golf participation.

The 2003 National Golf Foundation study on minority golf participation in the United States found there were differences in participation rates

Exhibit 2   **Number of U.S. Golfers by Frequency of Play, 1991, 1994, 1997, 2000–2003 (in thousands)**

Year	Occasional Golfers (1–7 rounds/year)	Core Golfers (8–24 rounds/year)	Avid Core Golfers (25+ rounds per year)	Total Golfers
1991	11,480	6,133	5,348	22,961
1994	11,463	6,058	5,113	22,634
1997	10,619	7,897	5,602	24,118
2000	10,961	7,399	6,276	24,636
2001	14,190	5,676	5,934	25,800
2002	13,624	6,812	5,764	26,200
2003	14,184	7,083	6,133	27,400

Source: National Golf Foundation

among races, but income tended to reduce those differences. For golfers with household incomes lower than $100,000, white non-Hispanics and Asians were nearly twice as likely to play golf as African Americans or Hispanic Americans. Nearly 15 percent of white non-Hispanic Americans and 12.4 percent of Asian Americans with household incomes of less than $100,000 per year played golf, whereas only 8.4 percent of African Americans and 8.0 percent of Hispanic Americans with incomes under $100,000 played golf. However, the percentage of individuals with household incomes less than $100,000 interested in playing golf did not vary to a great degree among U.S. citizens of different races. White non-Hispanic Americans were most interested in golf (29.6 percent), but 23.8 percent of African Americans, 24.2 percent of Asian Americans, and 20.2 percent of Hispanic Americans were also interested in playing golf. About 28 percent of adults with household incomes exceeding $100,000 played golf, regardless of race. At household incomes exceeding $150,000, the National Golf Foundation

study found that Hispanic Americans had the highest golf participation rate, at 32 percent.

Foretelling the findings of the National Golf Foundation's studies on golf participation, former Callaway Golf CEO Ron Drapeau said in a 2002 interview with *Smart Money*, "The cost of golf is a concern: We need to see more affordable municipal-type golf courses, including alternative facilities; 9-hole courses, pitch-and-putt, and par 3 courses. The time it takes to play is also an issue."[4]

The Rise of Counterfeiting in the Golf Equipment Industry

Knockoffs of branded golf equipment had been produced by Chinese manufacturers and sold in the United States since the early 1990s, but they weren't a serious threat to the industry because knockoffs only appeared similar to legitimate products. For example, knockoffs like the Canterbury Big Bursar looked similar to the Callaway Big Bertha driver but

Exhibit 3   **Total Rounds of Golf Played in the United States, 2001–2004 (in millions)**

Year	Rounds Played (in millions)	Percent Change
2001	518.1	—
2002	502.4	−3.0%
2003	494.9	−1.5
2004	528.6	6.8

Source: National Golf Foundation

would never pass for a Big Bertha upon close inspection. Beginning golfers were most likely to purchase knockoffs since they looked similar to brand-name clubs but sold for as much as 75 percent less than clubs made by Callaway Golf, Cobra, TaylorMade, Ping, or Titleist. Serious golfers tended not to purchase knockoff clubs since they were made from poor-quality alloy metals, did not perform as well as branded clubs, and were prone to breaking.

Counterfeit clubs were a much greater threat to the industry since good counterfeits were nearly exact copies of legitimate products and could only be identified as counterfeits by very knowledgeable golfers, trained personnel of golf equipment retailers, or golf equipment producers. Like knockoffs, counterfeits were made from inferior materials, were not produced to the standards of legitimate equipment manufacturers, and were not very durable. However, the extraordinarily low prices that counterfeit clubs were offered at were too great a temptation for many bargain-hunter golfers. In 2005, it was not unusual to see complete sets of new Callaway Golf, TaylorMade, Ping, Titleist, Nike, or Cobra clubs that would retail for more than $2,000 sell on eBay or similar auction Web sites for $150 to $400. Sellers who dealt in counterfeit merchandise could purchase counterfeit sets complete with eight irons, a driver, two or three fairway woods, a putter, a golf bag, and a travel bag for as little as $100 in China. Callaway Golf Company alerted visitors to its Web site to counterfeit clubs sold on eBay or other Internet sites with the following warning: "A full set of authentic Callaway Golf clubs, depending on the models, will retail for $2,500–$3,000 or more. If the deal looks too good to be true, it probably is."[5]

The rise in counterfeiting was attributable to the improved manufacturing capabilities of companies in China and the decision by golf equipment companies to source components from Chinese manufacturers. In 2005, about 60 percent of all golf equipment was produced in China and more than 90 percent of counterfeits came from China. Counterfeiters were able to make very accurate copies of branded golf clubs through reverse engineering or by enticing employees of contract manufacturers to steal clubhead molds that could be used to produce counterfeit clubheads. Similarly, counterfeit shafts and grips could be fabricated to produce complete sets of counterfeit golf clubs. Counterfeiters even copied the details of the packaging golf clubs were shipped in to better disguise the fakes. It was

estimated that counterfeiters in China could produce golf clubs for less than $3 per club.

The golf equipment industry's six leading manufacturers created an alliance in December 2003 to identify and pursue counterfeiters and sellers of counterfeit clubs. TaylorMade Golf, Fortune Brands (parent of Titleist and Cobra Golf), Callaway Golf, Ping Golf, Cleveland Golf, and Nike Golf had successfully shut down many Internet auction sellers in the United States and Canada that listed counterfeit clubs and had gained cooperation from the Chinese government to confiscate counterfeit goods produced in that country. The Chinese government conducted two raids in 2004 that netted approximately $3 million worth of counterfeit golf equipment and the Chinese seized more than $1 million worth of counterfeit clubs in 2005. However, the efforts to shut down Internet sellers of counterfeits and manufacturers of counterfeits had achieved limited success. A Nike executive explained, "Often these aren't legitimate businesses, so you can't take the case to a court of law, you have to hunt them down. Many times it isn't even worth the effort. They simply create a new company and move. It's really frustrating."[6]

PROFILES OF THE LEADING MANUFACTURERS AND MARKETERS OF GOLF EQUIPMENT

Callaway Golf Company

Callaway Golf Company began to take form in 1983 when Ely Reeves Callaway Jr. purchased a 50 percent interest in a Temecula, California, manufacturer and marketer of hickory-shafted wedges and putters for $400,000. Upon acquiring an interest in Hickory Stick USA, Callaway became the company's president and CEO and soon began to transform the little-known maker of reproductions of antique clubs into the world's largest producer of golf clubs. Callaway knew from the outset that the company's prospects for outstanding profits were limited as long as its product line was restricted to hickory-shafted clubs. Callaway noticed that most golf equipment had changed very little since the 1920s and believed that, due to the difficulty of the game of golf (there was so much room for variation in *each* swing of the club and for off-center contact with the ball), recreational golfers would be willing to invest in high-tech, premium-priced equipment if such clubs could improve their game by being more forgiving of a less-than-optimum swing. Ely Callaway's vision was at odds with that of the company's founders and eventually resulted in Callaway's outright purchase of the company. In 1985 Ely Callaway hired Richard C. Helmstetter as the company's chief club designer, who was aided by a team of five aerospace and metallurgical engineers, to develop what Callaway termed a "demonstrably superior and pleasingly different" line of clubs that was set apart from competing brands by its technological innovation. Helmstetter and his team introduced the company's S2H2 (short, straight, hollow hosel) line of irons in 1988 and an S2H2 line of metal woods in 1989. The 1988 S2H2 launch was accompanied by a name change from Callaway Hickory Stick USA to Callaway Golf Company. The S2H2 line of clubs was well received by professional and recreational golfers alike and became the number one driver on the Senior PGA Tour by year-end 1989.

The company's engineers followed up the successful S2H2 line with the Big Bertha—named by Callaway after the World War I German long-distance cannon—which was launched in 1991. The Big Bertha was revolutionary in that it was much larger than conventional woods and lacked a hosel so that the weight could be better distributed throughout the clubhead. This innovative design gave the clubhead a larger sweet spot, which allowed a player to mis-hit or strike the golf ball off-center and not suffer much loss of distance or accuracy. By 1992 Big Bertha drivers were number one on the Senior PGA, LPGA, and Hogan Tours. Callaway Golf Company became a public company on February 28, 1992. By year-end 1992 its annual revenues had doubled to $132 million, and by 1996 Callaway Golf had become the world's largest manufacturer and marketer of golf clubs, with annual sales of more than $683 million.

The company's technological leadership and financial performance eroded during a brief retirement by Ely Callaway between 1996 and 1998, but rebounded soon after Ely Callaway returned as CEO in October 1998. The founder's first efforts upon his return to active management at Callaway Golf were to "direct [the company's] resources—talent,

energy, and money—in an ever-increasing degree toward the creation, design, production, sale and service of new and better products."[7] As part of his turnaround strategy Ely Callaway also initiated a $54.2 million restructuring program that involved a number of cost-reduction actions and operational improvements. Ely's strategies allowed the company to regain its technological leadership with the introduction of Callaway Golf Company's low center-of-gravity Steelhead line of metal woods in 1998, the ERC Forged Titanium Driver in 1999, and variable face thickness X-14 irons and the ERC II Forged Titanium Driver in 2000. Also, the company acquired Odyssey, a leading brand of putters, in 1996 and began manufacturing and marketing golf balls in 2000. Ely Callaway believed that golf balls were a natural product-line extension for the company, pointing out, "We have 7 million people out there playing our products, and 80% of them think they're the best clubs in the world—we have almost a guaranteed 'try' on our new products."[8]

In February 2000 a survey of golf equipment company executives voted Callaway's Big Bertha driver the best golf product of the century by a 2-to-1 margin. The same group of executives called Ely Callaway the most influential golf trade person of the 1990s. Ely Callaway stepped down as president and CEO of the company on May 15, 2001, after being diagnosed with pancreatic cancer. He was replaced by the company's senior executive vice president of manufacturing, Ron Drapeau, and passed away at his home in Rancho Santa Fe, California, on July 5, 2001. Drapeau began his employment with Callaway Golf in late 1996 and had headed the company's Odyssey Golf unit for 18 months before becoming responsible for all of the company's manufacturing operations as vice president of manufacturing in February 1999.

As it had during Ely Callaway's 1996 retirement, the company's performance declined soon after his death in 2001. Callaway's share of drivers began to decline after the USGA instituted its 0.83 COR limitation in 1998, but the company's share of the driver market fell at a faster rate under Drapeau. The 0.83 limitation left Callaway with fewer innovation options since the company had already met the 0.83 threshold at the time the rule went into effect. The key innovation of Callaway's highly successful Great Big Bertha driver launched in 1995 was its titanium construction. Titanium was a much lighter metal than stainless steel, which allowed Callaway

Golf's engineers to create a larger clubhead featuring an expanded sweet spot. After competitors had matched Callaway Golf Company's titanium construction, the company's research and development efforts steered toward identifying materials lighter than titanium. In 2002, Callaway Golf introduced the C4 driver—a 360-cubic-centimeter (cc) driver made from a carbon composite material. The carbon composite material performed exceptionally well and was 75 percent lighter than titanium, which allowed golfers to generate more clubhead speed than with heavier titanium clubs.

Even though the C4 performed up to the R&D staff's expectations, the driver was a failure in the marketplace. The driver met the 0.83 COR limit, as did competing drivers, but golfers were much more impressed with the drivers offered by Titleist, Ping, Cobra, and TaylorMade. The C4 had two shortcomings in the minds of many golfers. First, most of Callaway's rivals chose to push the size of their drivers toward the USGA size limit of 460 cc rather than experiment with lighter materials. The larger clubhead tended to give some golfers more confidence at the tee and produced a higher launch angle, which equated to greater distance. Also, golfers were dissatisfied with the sound of the carbon composite driver, which was rather muffled when it struck a ball. The extra-large, hollow titanium drivers produced by Callaway Golf's rivals tended to produce an exceptionally loud noise when they made contact with the ball. Golf retailers found that many customers that tried C4 and competing demo drivers returned the C4 to their stores stating that "even though they hit the club very well, it didn't sound like they hit it well."

The company also misjudged the importance of a new type of club introduced by rivals that was a substitute for low-lofted, long irons. Hybrid clubs had a clubhead smaller than, but similar to, a fairway wood with a shaft the length of that used in a midlength iron. Golfers of all abilities (even touring professionals) found the hybrid clubs much easier to hit than long irons. TaylorMade's Rescue was the first hybrid to gain a widespread appeal, but almost all manufacturers raced to quickly get hybrid clubs to the market. Callaway Golf's inability to get its hybrid club to market before 2005 caused it to lose significant sales as many golfers purchased TaylorMade, Nike Golf, Adams Golf, and Cobra hybrid clubs to replace 2-, 3-, and 4-irons from their bags. Some golfers replaced fairway woods with hybrids as well.

As Callaway Golf struggled with its golf club business, its golf ball operations also failed to perform to management's expectations. When Ely Callaway announced that the company would enter the golf ball business, the company expected to gain a 10 percent market share within two years and eventually become one of the two top brands of golf balls. The company missed its projections, with its sales growing to just $66 million and its share reaching only 5.7 percent in 2002. In addition, Callaway Golf's golf ball business had lost $90 million between 2000 and 2002 and showed little hope of providing a return on its $170 million investment in golf ball development and plant and equipment. In 2003, the company acquired Top-Flite Golf for $125 million to give it the volume necessary to achieve economies of scale in golf ball production. At the time of its acquisition by Callaway Golf, the maker of Top-Flite golf balls, Strata golf balls, and Ben Hogan golf clubs had sales of $250 million and was in bankruptcy. About $175 million of the company's 2002 revenues were generated from the sale of golf balls.

Even though the Top-Flite acquisition made Callaway Golf the number two golf ball producer behind Titleist, the acquisition led to further financial problems for the company. Integrating Top-Flite's operations into Callaway's golf ball business was more troublesome than expected. Callaway Golf's golf balls were the most technologically advanced in the industry in 2003 and were produced at its state-of-the-art production facility in Carlsbad, California. Top-Flite primarily produced lower-end golf balls for mass merchandisers using an older golf ball production facility with few technological capabilities. Callaway was unable to use Top-Flite's production facility to produce Callaway Golf golf balls until 2005 because Callaway's high-tech golf balls were too complex to be produced in the older Top-Flite plant. In addition, the integration of Top-Flite and Callaway personnel was a challenge because the two companies had dramatically different cultures. Ely Callaway had developed a professional, technology-based culture that encouraged employees to exhibit the highest levels of gentlemanly behavior, while some retailers had likened Top-Flite's freewheeling sales force to carnival barkers.

With Callaway's growing problems in its golf club operations and golf ball business, pressure began to mount on Ron Drapeau to produce results acceptable to investors. Under Drapeau, the company did introduce the highly successful Odyssey 2-Ball putter, which allowed the company to increase its share of the putter market from 30.7 percent in 1999 to 40.2 percent in 2002. In fact, the sales of 2-Ball putters alone were greater than the total revenues for any golf company except Titleist/Cobra, TaylorMade, and Ping in 2003. Callaway Golf had also achieved acceptable results in the irons category of the golf equipment industry, where its share grew from 14.4 percent in 1999 to 16.1 percent in 2002, but its inventory of fairway woods and drivers grew to unacceptable levels as its share of those products declined from 30.9 percent in 1999 to 21.6 percent in 2002. In 2003 and 2004, Drapeau dropped retail prices on its drivers by as much as $100 and even gave some products away to retailers. The price cut on current models was a first in the company's history. Typically, the company did not discount products until a new generation was launched and available in retail stores.

Ron Drapeau stepped down as Callaway Golf CEO in August 2004 to be replaced on an interim basis by longtime board member 71-year-old William Baker. The company did not name a permanent replacement until August 2005, when it hired former Revlon CEO George Fellows to lead the company. While at Revlon as CEO between 1997 and 1999, Fellows had been credited for producing a turnaround year in 1997 after years of losses. However, the company returned to a loss in 1998 and recorded its worst-ever loss in 1999. Some analysts suggested that Fellows did "not [have] a strong résumé" for the job, and others claimed that while Fellows was at Revlon, he "was handed a deck that didn't have 52 cards."[9]

During William Baker's tenure as interim CEO, Callaway Golf continued to struggle with excessive inventory and integration of Top-Flite and Ben Hogan Golf operations. However, the company was able to develop some of its most innovative products prior to George Fellows's arrival. The company's titanium-faced Big Bertha Fusion irons were unlike any made by other golf equipment manufacturers at the time and were said by some retailers to be the best product Callaway Golf had ever developed. The company had also launched new X-18 and X-Tour irons, which contributed to a 28 percent increase in the sales of its irons between the second quarter of 2004 and the second quarter of 2005. The two-piece X-Tour iron was Callaway Golf's first forged iron, which was the preference of touring professionals and some low-handicap golfers. The company also

developed new versions of its 2-Ball putter that produced a 16 percent increase in putter sales between the second quarter of 2004 and the second quarter of 2005 and had created a 460-cc replacement to its ERC Fusion driver. The Fusion FT-3, like the original Big Bertha Fusion featured a titanium clubface and carbon composite shell, but also featured prepositioned weights to produce a draw, fade, or neutral ball path. The success of the FT-3 in the marketplace was critical to Callaway's turnaround since its Big Bertha 454 had met with limited success—leading to a 32 percent decline in net sales of woods for the six months ending June 30, 2005, when compared to the months ending June 30, 2004.

Callaway Golf also added the state-of-the-art HX Tour 56 golf ball to its lineup of Top-Flite and Callaway golf balls in June 2005. The HX Tour 56 was Callaway Golf's most technologically advanced golf ball and accounted for nine victories across all six professional tours since it was released to touring professionals in early 2005. The Tour 56 also was used in three of Phil Mickelson's lowest career 18-hole scores. In addition to the HX Tour 56's nine pro tour wins in 2005, the company's HX Tour golf ball had accounted for 46 global tour wins between 2003 and 2005. Callaway Golf expected the HX Tour 56 to help the golf ball division reverse an 11 percent decline in sales during the first six months of 2005. However, in mid-2005 the company was unable to get large quantities of its HX Tour 56 golf ball to retailers because of production problems in its Top-Flite plant. The company was also unable to ship sufficient quantities of its Fusion FT-3 drivers to retailers due to production problems at supplier foundries. As of late 2005, it was unknown how successful the FT-3 would be in allowing Callaway to recapture lost market share in the driver segment of the golf equipment industry since Callaway had not made the driver available to many retailers.

Even though Callaway Golf had significant hurdles to clear to return to its late-1990s glory, the company's stock price rose by nearly 50 percent in mid-2005 amid talks of a possible takeover. At least two separate groups of investors were pursuing the company with offers as high as $1.2 billion, or $16.25 per share. Prior to the hiring of George Fellows as Callaway Golf's CEO, its board had hired an investment bank to evaluate strategic alternatives for the company. However, upon his acceptance of the job, Fellows commented that the company was worth substantially more than the amounts of the two buyout bids and that he had been hired to turn around the company, not to prepare it for sale. At the end of the company's third quarter in 2005, Fellows announced a broad restructuring plan that would reduce expenses by $70 million by year-end 2006 by consolidating all golf ball operations; integrating sales functions of Callaway, Odyssey, Top-Flite, and Ben Hogan brands; and eliminating an unspecified number of jobs. The restructuring program would result in charges against 2005 and 2006 earnings of $12 million. A financial summary for Callaway Golf Company is presented in Exhibit 4. Exhibit 5 provides the company's revenues by product group for the period 1999 to 2004.

TaylorMade-adidas Golf

TaylorMade was founded in 1979 when Gary Adams mortgaged his home and began production of his "metalwoods" in an abandoned car dealership building in McHenry, Illinois. Both touring pros and golf retailers alike were skeptical of the new club design until they found that the metal woods actually hit the ball higher and farther than persimmon woods. By 1984, TaylorMade metalwoods were the number one wood on the PGA Tour and the company had grown to be the third-largest golf equipment company in the United States. The company was acquired by France-based Salomon SA in 1984, which provided the capital necessary for the company to continue to develop innovative new lines of metal woods. The company also produced irons and putters, but most of TaylorMade's sales were derived from high-margin drivers and fairway woods.

TaylorMade's metalwood drivers were the most technologically advanced in the industry until Callaway Golf's 1991 introduction of the oversized Big Bertha metalwood. During the entire decade of the 1990s, TaylorMade was unable to leapfrog Callaway Golf's innovations and remained a runner-up in the driver segment. Even though TaylorMade was unable to beat Callaway to the market with latest technology, the company was always able to launch drivers nearing the performance of Callaway products within months of a Callaway product introduction. Taylor-Made and its parent were acquired by athletic footwear and apparel company adidas in 1997.

TaylorMade's introduction of a 400-cc driver in 2003 gave it the innovation it had long sought to become the largest seller of drivers and fairway woods. The company's R580 driver was 40 cc larger than

Callaway's competing Great Big Bertha II driver and matched consumers' preference for the largest possible driver. TaylorMade expanded its lead over Callaway Golf in drivers with its 2004 introduction of its r5 series and r7 Quad drivers. The r5 was a 450 cc driver that came in three varieties and used prepositioned weights to produce a draw, slight fade, or straight shots. The r5 was one of the best-selling drivers in the marketplace but was less technologically advanced (and lower-priced) than TaylorMade's r7 Quad driver. The r7's movable weight technology allowed users to use a special tool move four tungsten weights with a total weight of 48 grams to ports in various positions in the clubhead to produce whatever bias the golfer found necessary on a given day. For example, a golfer who was struggling with a low fade could move the heaviest of the four weights to the toe of the clubhead favor a high draw. The golfer could later move the weights to a different position if he or she experienced a different ball flight on a different day. The movable weight system allowed golfers to have a single driver that could produce six ball flight paths.

TaylorMade was also the leading seller of hybrid clubs. TaylorMade introduced its Rescue line of hybrid clubs in 1999, but the clubs did not become a huge success in the marketplace until 2002. In 2005, TaylorMade extended its Rescue line by adding models that featured its movable weight technology. Retailers were uncertain that movable weights would be a strong selling point in hybrids, since hybrids were already marketed as clubs that were easier to hit with than woods or long irons.

TaylorMade had traded positions with Titleist and Ping as the second-largest brand of irons, but it had never challenged Callaway Golf for market share leadership in the category. In late 2005, the company introduced its r7 irons in hopes of repeating the success of the r7 driver. The r7 irons were designed much like Callaway Golf's Fusion irons, with a titanium face mounted to a stainless-steel perimeter-weighted frame. The r7 irons also featured prepositioned tungsten cartridges imbedded into the stainless-steel clubhead to improve launch angles.

TaylorMade was a relatively weak competitor in the putter segment. Its Maxfli golf ball business produced successful models such as the Noodle—which sold more than 2 million dozen per year—but the division had yet to post a profit since its acquisition by adidas-Salomon in 2002. In 2005, the Maxfli brand accounted for less than 5 percent golf ball sales worldwide.

Exhibit 4 **Callaway Golf Company, Financial Summary, 1992–2004 (in thousands, except per share amounts)**

	2004	2003	2002	2001	2000	1999	1998	1997	1996	1995	1994	1993	1992
Net sales	$934,564	$514,032	$792,064	$816,163	$837,627	$719,038	$703,060	$848,941	$683,536	$557,048	$451,779	$256,376	$132,956
Pretax income	(23,713)	67,883	111,671	98,192	128,365	85,497	(38,899)	213,765	195,595	158,401	129,405	69,600	33,175
Pretax income as a percent of sales	–3%	13%	14%	12%	15%	12%	–6%	25%	29%	29%	29%	27%	25%
Net income	$ 10,103	$ 45,523	$ 69,446	$ 58,375	$ 80,999	$ 55,322	($25,564)	$13 2,704	$122,337	$ 97,736	$ 78,022	$ 42,862	$ 19,280
Net income as a percent of sales	1%	9%	9%	7%	10%	8%	–4%	16%	18%	18%	17%	17%*	15%
Fully diluted earnings per share	($0.15)	$0.68	$1.03	$0.82	$1.13	$0.78	($0.38)	$1.85	$1.73	$1.40	$1.07	$0.62	$0.32
Shareholders' equity	$586,317	$589,383	$543,387	$514,349	$511,744	$499,934	$453,096	$481,425	$362,267	$224,934	$186,414	$116,577	$ 49,750

Source: Callaway Golf Company annual reports.

Exhibit 5   **Callaway Golf Company's Net Sales by Product Group, 1999–2004 (in thousands)**

Product Group	2004	2003	2002	2001	2000	1999
Woods	$238.6	$252.4	$310.00	$392.90	$403.00	$429.00
Irons	259.1	280.7	243.5	248.9	299.9	221.3
Balls	231.3	78.4	66.0	54.9	34.0	—
Putters, accessories and other	205.6	202.5	172.6	119.5	100.8	68.7
Net sales	$934.6	$814.0	$792.10	$816.20	$837.60	$719.00

Source: Callaway Golf Company annual reports.

TaylorMade's net sales on a currency-neutral basis grew by 5 percent between 2003 and 2004, but declined by 1 percent after the effects of exchange rates were taken into account. The company's growth in sales was attributable to the popularity of its r7 Quad driver, which recorded wins in the U.S. Open and the PGA Championship. Growth in adidas golf footwear and apparel also contributed to the 5 percent revenue increase. In 2004, the company's Asian sourcing allowed its gross margins to improve to 47.0 percent, from 45.5 percent in 2003, but its operating margins declined from 10.5 percent in 2003 to 9.5 percent in 2004 because of increased marketing expenses. Exhibit 6 presents net sales and operating profit between 2001 and 2004 for TaylorMade-adidas Golf. The table also presents the adidas-Salomon golf division's sales by product category in 2004. Market shares for the leading sellers of drivers and fairway woods, irons, and golf shoes between January 2002 and July 2004 are presented in Exhibit 7.

Titleist/Cobra

The Acushnet Company was a rubber deresinating company founded in 1910 in Acushnet, Massachusetts. The company opened a golf ball division in 1932 when founder Phil Young believed that a bad putt during a round of golf he was playing was a result of a faulty ball rather than his poor putting. Young took the ball to a dentist's office to have it X-rayed and found that the core of the ball was indeed off-center. Believing that Acushnet could develop and manufacture high-quality golf balls, Young teamed with a fellow Massachusetts Institute of Technology graduate, Fred Bommer, to create the Titleist line of balls. Young and Bommer introduced their first Titleist golf ball in 1935, and by 1949 Titleist had become the most played ball on the PGA Tour.

Acushnet's acquisition of John Reuter Jr. Inc. in 1958 and Golfcraft Inc. in 1969 put Titleist into the golf club business. Titleist's Reuter Bulls Eye

Exhibit 6   **Selected Data for Taylor Made-adidas Golf**

	2004	2003	2002	2001
Net sales (in millions)	€633	€637	€707	€545
Operating profit (in millions)	60	67	74	63
Sales by Product				
Metalwoods	48%			
Irons	19			
Apparel	11			
Footwear	7			
Golf balls	6			
Accessories	6			
Putters	3			

Source: adidas-Salomon annual reports.

Exhibit 7   **Market Shares of Leading Sellers of Golf Equipment for Drivers and Fairway Woods, Irons, and Footwear, January 2002–July 2004**

Drivers and fairway woods

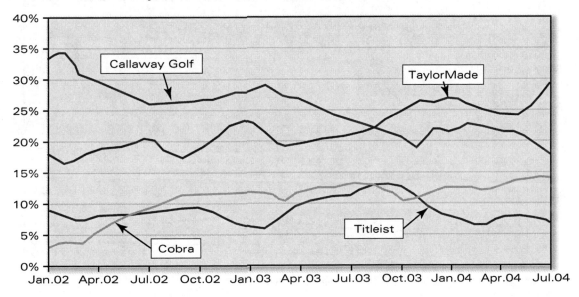

Irons

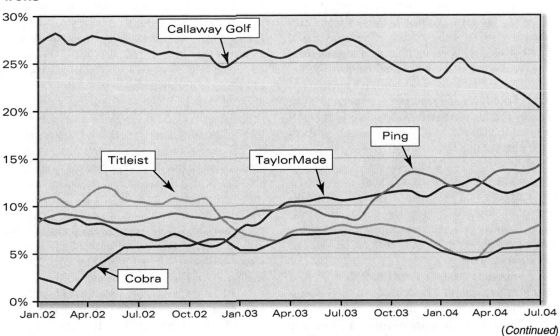

(*Continued*)

Exhibit 7   **Continued**

Footwear

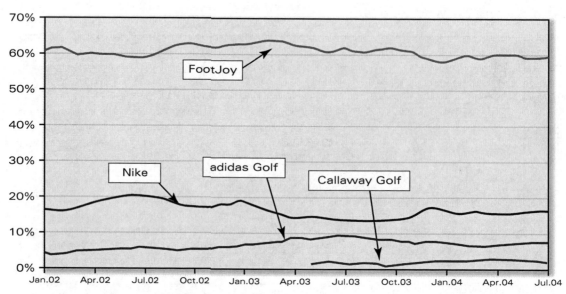

Source: Adidas-Salomon AG Investor Day 2004 Presentation, October 5, 2004.

putter became a favorite on the PGA Tour during the 1960s, and its AC-108 heel-toe weighted irons were among the most popular brands of irons during the early 1970s. The company's Pinnacle line of golf balls was developed in 1980 as a lower-priced alternative to Titleist-branded golf balls. In 1996, The Acushnet Company was acquired by tobacco and spirits producer and marketer American Brands. American Brands increased its presence in the golf equipment industry in 1985 when it acquired Foot-Joy, the number one seller of golf gloves and shoes. In 1996 American Brands acquired Cobra Golf for $715 million. The company changed its name to Fortune Brands in 1997 when it completed the divestiture of tobacco businesses begun in 1994. Fortune Brands' golf and leisure products division had an operating profit of $154 million on sales of $1.2 billion in 2004.

At year-end 2004, Titleist and Cobra were ranked third and fourth, respectively, in total equipment sales, with the sales of each brand totaling nearly $200 million. The sales of Titlist and Pinnacle golf balls amounted to approximately $485 million and accounted for more than 70 percent of industry sales. In addition, FootJoy led the industry in the sale of golf shoes, golf gloves, and golf outerwear, with revenues of $363 million.

Most golfers considered Titleist golf balls to be technologically superior to other brands, although industry analysts and golf retailers considered Callaway Golf's HX technology equally impressive. Titleist's Pro V1 golf ball was the company's most advanced and expensive golf ball and was able to offer maximum distance along with spin rates that allowed low-handicap golfers to stop approach shots near the pin. Lower-grade golf balls were able to offer golfers distance off the tee but were likely to roll across the green on approach shots to the hole. Titleist's line of golf clubs was targeted toward low-handicap golfers. Titleist produced only forged irons, which were difficult for all but the best recreational golfers to hit with since they had a small sweet spot and were very unforgiving of mis-hits. Titleist offered one driver model—the 905, which was a 400-cc driver and a popular choice with professionals and better recreational golfers.

Titleist offered only one hybrid club, which was more ironlike in its design than hybrids offered by Callaway or TaylorMade. Titleist's Vokey forged wedges were frequently used on the PGA Tour and were favorites of many low-handicap golfers. The Titleist Scotty Cameron putter line sold at the highest price points in the industry. Scotty Cameron putter models sold between $270 and $300 and were status symbols at country clubs and golf resorts throughout North America and Asia.

Fortune Brands' Cobra line of golf clubs was targeted to golfers of an average skill level. The brand's drivers pushed the regulatory limits in terms of clubhead size. In 2005, Cobra offered a 460-cc driver with the largest clubface among all major brands, a 454-cc driver, and 414-cc driver. All of the company's King Cobra drivers featured carbon composite top plates and milled titanium clubfaces. Cobra emphasized distance and forgiveness in its advertisements and fielded a long-drive team, which competed in various long-drive competitions held throughout the United States. King Cobra irons sold at slight lower price points than competing brands and were mostly perimeter-weighted models. The Cobra Baffler hybrid club was similar in design to the TaylorMade Rescue and Callaway Golf Heavenwood and sold at a slightly lower price point than models offered by key rivals. The company's wedges and putters were not widely used on the PGA Tour or among recreational golfers.

Titleist management's biggest concern in late 2005 centered on the USGA's interest in lesser-performing golf balls. In a special equipment issue of *Inside the USGA* published in October 2005, the editors worried openly that technology might endanger some of golf's most historic courses. The editors recalled how the wound, rubber-cored Haskell ball developed in 1898 and popularized during the early 1900s eventually "removed for consideration the Myopia Hunt Club, which hosted four U.S. Opens between 1898 and 1908."[10] The USGA editorial staff continued to speculate that the "confluence of golf science and commercial investment . . . accelerated by the injection of large amounts of capital" might possibly have the same effect on such championship courses as Merion or Oakland Hills.[11] The USGA believed it had a responsibility to the protect the game of golf and pointed out in its special issue that the average driving distance of touring professionals had increased by 26 yards between 1990 and 2005. In addition, the USGA commented that improvements in golf clubs and golf balls had contributed to a 1.5 stroke improvement in average handicaps between 1994 and 2005. Titleist management responded to such concerns by pointing out that the average score per round during PGA tournaments had improved by only one stroke between 1980 and 1997. In addition, Titleist management also disagreed with the

contention that historic courses were likely to become obsolete because of technology. Titleist noted on its Web site that the average score during the 2005 PGA Championship at Baltusrol—the site of three U.S Opens dating back to 1967—was .345 higher than the average score posted during when the Springfield, New Jersey, course hosted the 1993 U.S. Open.

Titleist's CEO, Wally Uihlein, attributed the overall scoring improvement among recreational and tournament golfers to "six contributing factors: 1) the introduction of low-spinning high performance golf balls, 2) the introduction of oversize, thin-faced drivers, 3) improved golf course conditioning and agronomy; 4) player physiology—they're bigger and stronger; 5) improved techniques and instruction; and 6) launch monitors and the customization of equipment."[12] In a tit-for-tat reply, the USGA quoted famous golf course designer Pete Dye, who commented, "It's not the strength of the players. My good friend John Daly hits the ball 30 yards farther in 2005 than he did in 1991. Now John will be the first one to tell you he hasn't done too many push-ups in the last 15 years."[13]

Ping Golf

Perimeter weighting came about due to the poor putting of Karsten Solheim, a General Electric mechanical engineer, who took up golf at the age of 47 in 1954. Solheim designed a putter for himself that he found provided more "feel" when he struck the ball. Solheim moved much of the clubhead weight to the heel and toe, leaving a cavity at the rear and center of the club. Perimeter-weighted, or cavity-back, clubs had a larger sweet spot because of a higher moment of inertia or resistance to twisting. The resistance to twisting reduced the gear effect of the clubhead and resulted in straighter, longer shots with irons. In addition to perimeter weighting, Solheim also developed the investment-casting manufacturing process. This process allowed clubheads to be formed from molds rather than forged from steel—the traditional manufacturing process.

Solheim made his putters by hand from 1959 until 1967, when he left GE and founded Karsten Manufacturing. By the 1970s, Karsten manufactured a full line of perimeter-weighted putters and irons that carried the Ping brand. Solheim named the brand Ping because of the sound the perimeter-weighted clubhead made when it struck the ball. Karsten Manufacturing's Ping putters and irons were thought to be among the most technologically advanced throughout the 1980s and reigned as the market leaders. Karsten Manufacturing was renamed Ping Inc. in 1999.

Karsten Solheim was also the pioneer of custom fitting, with his fitting activities predating the official founding of the company. During the 1960s, touring professionals would meet with Solheim to have him custom-fit putters to their body measurements, and by the 1970s Solheim had developed a fitting system for irons. His system used the golfer's physical measurements, stance and swing, and ball flight to select irons with the optimal lie. The company's irons were sold in 10 color-coded lie configurations to best match recreational golfers' unique fit conditions. In a 2005 golf consumer survey, Ping was rated as the industry leader in custom fitting by a 3-to-1 margin. In addition to producing 10 configurations of iron models, Ping invited retailers to three-day training programs in its plant in Phoenix to become better skilled at custom fitting. By 2005, Ping had trained thousands of retailers.

Ping remained an industry leader in the iron segment in 2005, with a number two position in irons behind Callaway Golf. The company offered three lines of irons—the traditional blade S59 irons, which featured minimal perimeter weighting; the i5 line, with a medium degree of perimeter weighting; and the G5 line, which had expanded perimeter weighting. The S59 line was suitable for professionals and low-handicap recreational golfers, while the i5 was designed for average players looking for a lower ball flight. The G5 produced a higher ball flight than other models and was intended for average golfers who were able to produce only modest amounts of clubhead speed. The company produced a broad line of putters and regularly traded positions with Odyssey as the number one brand of putters.

Even though Ping had been known at one time for only its irons and putters, in late 2005 the privately owned company had become the maker of the most sought-after driver in the industry. The company's 460-cc G5 titanium driver had become the best-selling driver in late 2005 as golfers began to question the merit of the r7's movable weight system and found it difficult to locate Callaway Golf's FT-3 Fusion on retailer shelves. The company had failed to develop a hybrid until late 2005, but retailers expected Ping's G5 hybrid to become one of the best-selling hybrid clubs during equipment upgrades in the spring of 2006. The company's wedges were not big sellers in the market.

Nike Golf

Nike management believed that Tiger Woods could not only generate interest in golf but also help generate substantial revenues for a golf equipment company. Nike seized on the instant popularity of Tiger Woods in 1996 by signing the young star to a five-year, $40 million contract to endorse Nike shoes and apparel. In 1999 Woods extended the contract for an additional five years for $90 million to endorse Nike's new golf ball and forthcoming golf clubs. As with its athletic and apparel and footwear, Nike outsourced the production of its golf balls (in this instance to Bridgestone), while it hired a custom-club designer to design and lead its new golf club business. Nike's new driver, irons, and wedges were introduced during the 2002 PGA Merchandise Show. The company's 2002 line of golf clubs achieved only modest success and an improved line, including a 400-cc forged titanium driver, was introduced during the 2003 PGA Merchandise Show. Tiger Woods began endorsing the company's golf ball in 2000 and began using its driver and irons in 2002. Woods again extended his contract to endorse Nike's golf equipment, golf balls, apparel, and footwear in 2003 for $25 million per year for five years.

Nike management's 1996 assessment of Tiger Woods's enduring worldwide popularity was on the mark with PGA tournament viewership doubling when Woods was in contention for a Sunday win. However, Woods's appeal with television viewers did not translate into equipment sales. Nike's entry into the golf equipment industry had proved successful in terms of apparel and footwear sales, where it was the second leading seller of golf shoes behind FootJoy, but Nike Golf held only a 2.6 percent share of the golf club market in 2004. Nike Golf had achieved nearly a 10 percent market share in golf balls in 2004 and might likely benefit from Tiger Woods's miracle chip shot on the 16th hole of the 2005 Masters that put him in a playoff with Chris DiMarco and led to an eventual win. While an estimated television audience of 15 million watched, Woods's Nike Platinum One golf ball slowly rolled across the 16th green, where it clung to the edge of the hole for what seemed like eternity. As the ball perched at the edge of the cup, the Nike logo could not have been aligned with the camera more perfectly if it had been placed there by the company's advertising agency. After being tracked by CBS's cameras for 17 seconds, the ball fell into the cup.

Nike also boasted after the 2005 Masters Tournament that its brand of irons was the most widely used during the tournament. However, with the exception of those used by Woods, all Nike irons were used by former champions who were not expected to be in contention for a win at the Masters, including Billy Casper, who withdrew from the tournament after shooting a first-round score of 106. Casper's withdrawal from the tournament prevented his score from being recorded as an official statistic. It was reported that Nike paid $20,000 tee-up fees during the Masters practice rounds to those willing to use the company's irons during the day. As of late 2005, Nike's 460-cc SasQuatch and Ignite drivers; Slingshot, NDS, Forged, and Combo irons; and CPR hybrids remained poor sellers. Demand for the company's putters and wedges was also low. Nike had more recently signed 13 additional professional golfers to endorsement contracts, including 15-year-old Michelle Wie. Nike's October 2005 agreement with Wie would pay the teenager, who had yet to win a tournament competing against professionals in her 30 attempts, $20 million over four years. Nike did not disclose in its financial statements what percentage of its 2004 revenues of $12.3 billion was made up of golf equipment and apparel sales.

End notes

[1] As quoted in *The Callaway Connection*, Spring 2000, p. 7.
[2] As quoted in "Callaway Golf Introduced ERC II Forged Titanium Driver—Its Hottest and Most Forgiving Driver Ever," *PR Newswire*, October 24, 2000.
[3] Ibid.
[4] As quoted in *Smart Money*, August 2002, p. 34.
[5] Posted at www.callawaygolf.com/EN/customerservice.aspx?pid=9ways.
[6] As quoted in "Teed Off: Counterfeiters Are Cashing In on Big-Name Clubs by Hawking Bogus Merchandise on the Internet," *St. Louis Post-Dispatch*, May 18, 2005, p. C1.
[7] Callaway Golf Company 1998 annual report.
[8] "Callaway Enters the Ball Game," *Show News*, February 5, 2000.
[9] As quoted in "Looking for the Sweet Spot: Prospects Are Rosier for Carlsbad's Callaway Golf, but Some Wonder If New CEO Can Complete the Turnaround," *San Diego Union-Tribune*, August 28, 2005, p. H-1.
[10] As quoted in "Keeping Our Eye on the Ball," *Inside the USGA, Special Issue: Equipment*, October 2005, p. 1.
[11] Ibid, p. 9.
[12] As quoted in a reprint of "Mr. Titleist Talks," *Travel & Leisure Golf*, posted at www.titleist.com, 2005.
[13] As quoted in "Keeping Our Eye on the Ball," p. 16.

DAVID B. YOFFIE

MICHAEL SLIND

Apple Computer, 2006

Early in 2006, following a surge in the stock price for Apple Computer, CEO Steve Jobs savored a moment of triumph over one of his chief rivals in the personal computer (PC) industry. In an e-mail to his employees, he quipped that "Michael Dell wasn't perfect at predicting the future. Based on today's stock market close, Apple is worth more than Dell [Inc., Dell's namesake company]. Stocks go up and down, and things may be different tomorrow, but I thought it was worth a moment of reflection today."[1] Back in 1997, not long before Jobs returned to the company that he had founded, Dell had recommended that Apple throw in the proverbial towel: "I'd shut it down and give the money back to the shareholders."[2] Dell's remark was not without warrant. Apple had just gone through five years of turmoil. But not quite a decade later, Apple was riding high. In the fiscal year 2005, it posted $1.3 billion in net income on $13.9 billion in sales, and recorded an operating margin of 11.8%. Since 2001, its sales had grown at a compound annual rate of 27%. Early in 2006, its stock was trading at an all-time high of $86 a share—up from its 1997 low of $7.[3]

Jobs had made several dramatic moves since returning to Apple. He had pushed the company to turn out innovative products, such as the iMac and the OS X operating system. He had launched the Apple retail chain and had accelerated the outsourcing of key manufacturing tasks. In 2005, he announced an especially striking shift: Apple would source chips from Intel, a company that (along with Microsoft) had formed the basis of its main platform competitor.[4] Through all of these changes, Apple retained a core of fervent customers, although its PC market share remained low.

Meanwhile, with its profit-fueling iPod product line, Apple had ventured aggressively into areas that seemed distant from its traditional focus on designing and selling Macintosh computers. Jobs faced a new variation on an old question: Was Apple's recent success merely another blip in the company's up and down history, or had Jobs finally found a sustainable strategy?

Apple's History

Steve Jobs and Steve Wozniak, a pair of 20-something college dropouts, founded Apple Computer on April Fool's Day, 1976.[5] Working out of the Jobs family's garage in Los Altos, California, they built a computer circuit board that they named the Apple I. Within several months, they had made 200 sales and taken on a new partner—A.C. "Mike" Markkula, Jr., a freshly minted millionaire who had retired from Intel at the age of 33. Markkula, who was instrumental in attracting venture capital, was

Professor David B. Yoffie and Research Associate Michael Slind prepared this case from published sources. This case derives from earlier cases, including "Apple Computer 2002," HBS No. 702-469, by Professor David B. Yoffie and Research Associate Yusi Wang, and "Apple Computer, 2005," HBS No. 705-469, by Professor David B. Yoffie. HBS cases are developed solely as the basis for class discussion. Cases are not intended to serve as endorsements, sources of primary data, or illustrations of effective or ineffective management.

the experienced businessman on the team; Wozniak was the technical genius; and Jobs was the visionary who sought "to change the world through technology."

Jobs made it Apple's mission to bring an easy-to-use computer to every man, woman, and child. In April 1978, the company launched the Apple II, a relatively simple machine that people could use straight out of the box. The Apple II set in motion a computing revolution that drove the PC industry to $1 billion in annual sales in less than three years.[6] (See **Exhibit 1a**—Apple Computer: Selected Financial Information, as well as **1b** and **1c**.) Apple quickly became the industry leader, selling more than 100,000 Apple IIs by the end of 1980. (See **Exhibit 2**—Apple Computer: Worldwide PC Share.) In December 1980, Apple launched a successful IPO. (See **Exhibit 3**—Apple Computer: Daily Closing Share Price.)

Apple's competitive position changed fundamentally in 1981, when IBM entered the PC market. The IBM PC, which used Microsoft's DOS operating system and a microprocessor (also called a CPU) from Intel, seemed bland and gray in comparison with the graphics- and sound-enhanced Apple II. But the IBM PC was a relatively "open" system that other producers could clone. By contrast, Apple relied on proprietary designs that only Apple could produce. As IBM-compatibles proliferated, Apple's revenue continued to grow, but its market share dropped sharply, falling to 6.2% in 1982.[7]

In 1984, Apple introduced the Macintosh, marking a breakthrough in ease of use, industrial design, and technical elegance. Yet the Mac's slow performance and a lack of compatible software limited its sales. Between 1983 and 1984, Apple's net income fell 17%, leaving the company in crisis. In April 1985, Apple's board removed Jobs from an operational role. Several months later, Jobs left Apple to found a new company named NeXT. Those moves left John Sculley, the CEO whom Apple had recruited from Pepsi-Cola in 1983, alone at the helm. Sculley, armed with a Wharton MBA, had led Pepsi's successful charge against Coca-Cola. Now he hoped to use his marketing savvy and operational expertise to help Apple compete against dominant players in its industry.

The Sculley Years, 1985–1993

Sculley sought to exploit Apple's capabilities in graphics and design to make the company a leader in desktop publishing as well as education. He also moved aggressively to bring Apple into the corporate world. Apple's combination of superior software, such as Aldus (later Adobe) PageMaker and Microsoft Excel, and peripherals, such as laser printers, gave the Macintosh unmatched capabilities in desktop publishing. Sales exploded, turning Apple into a global brand. By 1990, sales reached $5.6 billion, while Apple's worldwide market share stabilized at about 8%. In the education market, which contributed roughly half of Apple's U.S. sales, the company held a share of more than 50%. Apple had $1 billion in cash and was the most profitable PC company in the world.

By 1990, Apple controlled the only significant alternative, both in hardware and in software, to the IBM-compatible standard. The company practiced horizontal and vertical integration to a greater extent than any other PC company, with the exception of IBM. Apple typically designed its products from scratch, using unique chips, disk drives, and monitors, as well as unusual shapes for its computers' chassis. While it never backward-integrated into microprocessors—which were supplied exclusively by Motorola—the company manufactured and assembled most of its own products in state-of-the-art factories in California. Apple also developed its own proprietary operating system (OS), which it bundled with the Mac; its own application software (made by Claris, an Apple subsidiary); and many peripherals, including printers.

Analysts generally considered Apple's products to be more versatile than comparable IBM-compatible machines. IBM-compatibles narrowed the gap in ease of use in 1990, when Microsoft released Windows 3.0. But in many core software technologies, such as multimedia, Apple retained a big lead. In addition, since Apple controlled all aspects of its computer, it could offer customers a complete desktop solution, including hardware, software, and peripherals that allowed customers to "plug and play." By contrast, users often struggled to add hardware or software to IBM-compatible PCs. As a result, one analyst noted, "The majority of IBM and compatible users 'put up' with their machines, but Apple's customers 'love' their Macs."[8]

This love affair with the Mac allowed Apple to sell its products at a premium price. Top-of-the-line Macs went for as much as $10,000, and gross profit hovered around an enviable 50%. However, senior executives at Apple realized that trouble was brewing. As IBM-compatible prices dropped, Macs appeared overpriced by comparison. As John Sculley explained, "We were increasingly viewed as the 'BMW' of the computer industry. Our portfolio of Macintoshes were almost exclusively high-end, premium-priced computers. . . . Without lower prices, we would be stuck selling to our installed base." Moreover, Apple's cost structure was high: Apple devoted 9% of sales to research and development (R&D), compared with 5% at Compaq, and only 1% at many other IBM-clone manufacturers. These concerns led Dan Eilers, then vice president of strategic planning at Apple, to conclude: "The company was on a glide path to history."[9] Sculley, for his part, believed that "drastic action" was necessary to get Apple back on track. In his words, there would be no "sacred cows."[10]

Beginning in 1990, Sculley aimed to move Apple into the mainstream by offering "products and prices designed to regain market share."[11] That meant becoming a low-cost producer of computers with mass-market appeal. He also sought to maintain Apple's technological lead by bringing out "hit products" every 6 to 12 months. In October 1990, Apple shipped the Mac Classic, a $999 computer that was designed to compete head-to-head with low-priced IBM clones. One year later, the company launched the PowerBook notebook computer to rave reviews.

Despite these signs of strength, Sculley made a bold move to forge an alliance with its foremost rival, IBM, in 1991. Apple and IBM formed a joint venture, named Taligent, with the goal of creating a revolutionary new operating system. At the time, it cost around $500 million to develop a next-generation OS; subsequent marginal costs were close to zero. The two companies also formed a joint venture, named Kaleida, to create multimedia applications In addition, Apple committed to switching from Motorola's microprocessor line to IBM's new PowerPC chip, while IBM agreed to license its technology to Motorola in order to guarantee Apple a second source. Sculley believed that the PowerPC could help Apple to leapfrog the Intel-based platform.

Meanwhile, Apple undertook another cooperative project, this one involving Novell and Intel. Codenamed Star Trek, it was a highly secretive effort to rework the Mac OS to run on Intel chips. Sculley authorized the project in early 1992, and a working prototype was available by November.

Although Sculley was a marketer by training, he took on the post of chief technology officer (CTO) in March 1990. He believed strongly that Apple had to change the rules of its industry if it was to thrive in the coming decade. In his new role, Sculley championed the Newton, the first product in a category that he called "personal digital assistants" (PDAs). He believed that Apple's expertise in user-friendly software would give it an edge as PCs converged with consumer electronics.

Sculley argued that it was essential for Apple to drive down costs in order to remain competitive. In 1991, as pricing pressure hit Apple, the company moved to reduce its headcount by 10%. Apple also sought to move much of its manufacturing to subcontractors and adopted a tougher line toward distribution and development partners. However, these actions were not enough to sustain Apple's profitability. Its gross margin by this point was heading toward 34%—14 points below the company's 10-year average. When Sculley decided to commute from Connecticut to the West Coast, the board "promoted" him to chairman in June 1993 and appointed Michael Spindler, the company president, as the new CEO. Five months later, Sculley left Apple for good.

The Spindler Years, 1993–1995

Mike Spindler was a German-born engineer who, as head of Apple Europe, had tripled his division's revenue between 1988 and 1990.[12] As head of Apple, Spindler tried to reinvigorate its core markets: education (K-12) and desktop publishing, in which the company held 60% and 80% shares, respectively.[13] Meanwhile, to increase market share overall, Spindler killed the plan to put the Mac OS on Intel-based PCs and announced instead that Apple would license a handful of companies to make Mac clones. Those companies would pay roughly $50 per copy for a Mac OS license.

Yet despite Spindler's efforts, Apple was losing momentum: A 1995 *Computerworld* survey of 140 corporate computer system managers found that none of the Windows users would consider buying a Mac, while more than half the Apple users expected to buy an Intel-based PC.[14] (See **Exhibit 4**— Shipments and Installed Base of PC Microprocessors.) Like Sculley, moreover, Spindler had hoped that a revolutionary new operating system would turn the company around, but prospects for a breakthrough were fading fast. At the end of 1995, Apple and IBM parted ways on Taligent and Kaleida. After spending more than $500 million, neither side wanted to switch to a new technology.[15]

Under Spindler, international growth became a key objective for Apple. In 1992, 45% of its sales came from outside the United States. Spindler targeted China in particular, setting the goal of achieving a 15% or 16% market share in that country by 2000.[16] Apple had just a 2% share China in 1992, but the growth potential of that market was immense. Spindler also moved to slash costs, cutting 16% of Apple's workforce and reducing R&D spending to 6% of sales. But serious problems remained. In its first fiscal quarter of 1996, Apple reported a $69 million loss and announced further layoffs.[17] Two weeks later, Gilbert Amelio, an Apple director, replaced Spindler as CEO.

The Amelio Years, 1996–1997

Amelio, like Spindler, came from an engineering background; he had worked previously in Rockwell International's semiconductor business and at National Semiconductor. Right away, Amelio set out to improve Apple's operations by streamlining its product line, slashing its payroll, and rebuilding cash reserves. He also planned to push Apple into higher-margin segments such as servers, Internet access devices, and PDAs. Four months after Amelio arrived, he proclaimed that Apple would return to its premium-price differentiation strategy. He declared that just as MagLite could sell its flashlights at a huge premium over ordinary flashlights, Apple should be able to sell Macintoshes at a huge premium over Intel-based PCs.[18] He, too, hoped that a new OS would restore the Mac platform to its position as a technological leader. But these efforts were in disarray. Amelio decided to cut Apple's losses by canceling the repeatedly delayed next-generation Mac OS, which had cost more than $500 million in R&D. Instead, in December 1996, he announced that Apple would acquire NeXT Software—and that NeXT's founder, Steve Jobs, would return to Apple as a part-time adviser. NeXT's operating system, NeXTStep, had a lead over Microsoft in a few technical areas, but its market share was tiny and it could not run Mac software.

Amelio led the company through three reorganizations and several deep payroll cuts.[19] Yet, despite these austerity moves, Apple lost $1.6 billion on Amelio's watch. In addition, its share price sank to a 12-year low, and its worldwide market share dropped from 6% to 3%.[20] The Apple board forced Amelio out, and in September 1997 Steve Jobs became the company's interim CEO.

Steve Jobs and the "Apple Turnaround"

After returning as Apple's leader, Steve Jobs moved quickly to shake things up. On August 6, 1997, he announced that Microsoft had agreed to invest $150 million in Apple and had also reaffirmed its commitment to develop core products, such as Microsoft Office, for the Mac through August 2002. While the Apple faithful booed and hissed, the news sent Apple's stock to a 52-week high, and Apple's board soon signaled its faith in Jobs by deferring its search for a permanent CEO.

Jobs abruptly brought the Macintosh licensing program to an end. Since the announcement of the first licensing agreement, clones had reached 20% of Macintosh unit sales, while the value of the Mac market had fallen 11%.[21] Convinced that clones were cannibalizing Apple's sales, Jobs refused to license the latest Mac OS. In addition, Apple spent $110 million to acquire the assets of the leading clone maker, Power Computing, including its Mac OS license.[22] Jobs also consolidated Apple's product range, reducing the number of its lines from 15 to 3.

Jobs's first real coup was the launch of the iMac—"the Internet-age computer for the rest of us"—in August 1998. Priced at $1,299, the iMac lacked a floppy-disk drive but incorporated a low-end CPU, a CD-ROM drive, and a modem, all housed in a distinctive translucent case that came in multiple colors. It also supported "plug-and-play" peripherals, such as printers, that were designed for Windows-based machines. (Previous-generation machines required peripherals that were built for the Apple platform.) Roughly three years after its launch, the iMac had sold about 6 million units, compared with sales of 300 million PCs during the same time frame.

In February 1998, Jobs shut down two divisions: one that produced the Newton and one that was developing a portable PC for education. Apple had spent roughly $500 million to develop those products over six years.[23] In addition, Jobs slashed new project plans by 70%.[24] Under Jobs, Apple continued its restructuring efforts by reducing headcount, closing facilities, and outsourcing manufacturing tasks. For example, the company outsourced the manufacturing of iMacs to Foxconn Electronics, a Taiwan-based assembler. Jobs also revamped Apple's distribution system, eliminating relationships with thousands of smaller outlets and expanding Apple's presence in national chains. In November 1997, Apple launched a website to sell its products directly to consumers for the first time. In announcing that move, Jobs showed a picture of Michael Dell with a bull's-eye plastered on it, and declared, "We're coming after you, buddy."[25] By 2001, Apple's online store—by selling either directly to users or through dealers—accounted for 40% of the company's overall sales.[26] Internally, meanwhile, Jobs worked to streamline operations and reinvigorate innovation. By 2000, Apple pared its inventory down to less than two days' worth of sales. And at a time when other PC companies were cutting research expenditures, Apple in 2003 increased its R&D to nearly 8% of net sales, up from about 5%. (See **Exhibit 5**—PC Manufacturers: Key Operating Measures.)

A chief priority for Jobs was to reenergize Apple's image. Soon after taking the helm, he rehired TBWA Chiat/Day, the agency that had designed ads for the original Mac. Starting with the "Think Different" campaign, which featured iconic figures such as Albert Einstein and John Lennon, Apple began promoting itself as a hip alternative to other computer brands. For Jobs, Apple was not just a technology company; it was a cultural force. Not coincidentally, perhaps, during this period Jobs retained his position as CEO of Pixar, an animation studio that he had cofounded in 1986. In collaboration with Disney, Pixar produced such major films as *Toy Story* and *Monsters, Inc.*[27] (In 2006, Disney bought Pixar, and Jobs assumed a seat on the Disney board.[28])

The Macintosh Business in the 21st Century

Midway through the first decade of the new century, the buzz around Apple focused on a product that was not a personal computer. Surging sales of the iPod drove much of the company's growth and captured the greater part of public attention. Yet Mac sales in 2005 still accounted for 45% of Apple's revenue, and Steve Jobs continued to treat the Macintosh as central to his plans.[29]

As the (second) Jobs era progressed, Apple put an ever-higher premium on creating machines that offered cutting-edge, tightly integrated design—both in their hardware chassis and in the user experience that they delivered. And it charged premium prices as well.[30] The Power Mac G5, introduced in 2003, cost between $1,999 and $3,299. While it had a sleek metal case and featured high-end graphics capability, it did not come with a monitor, even at those prices. For $799 to $2,499, users could buy an Apple Cinema Display, with an anodized aluminum stand and state-of-the-art clarity and brightness. These products appealed to Apple's core customers in creative fields such as graphic design, publishing, and film and music production.

Other Mac models included the iMac G5, a 2-inch-thick device with an integrated monitor (priced at $1,299 to $1,699), and two lines of notebook computers. The most innovative Macintosh offering, as of its introduction in January 2005, was perhaps the Mac Mini, a computer that measured 2 inches high by 6.5 inches square, with prices ranging from $499 to $699. The twist, as Jobs explained, was that the Mini arrived in BYODKM condition: "Bring your own display, keyboard, and mouse."[31] The Mini was Apple's first bid in almost a decade to target price-sensitive customers. All of these products featured distinctive Apple styling, and were designed to offer better, more seamless ways for people to use Macs. "What Apple is great at is figuring out how to invent cool technology [and] making it wonderfully easy to use," Jobs said in 2004.[32] That approach entailed strict, vertical control of hardware, on the one hand, and of operating systems and software, on the other.

On the operating system front, Apple launched OS X in 2001 and issued new versions on a roughly annual basis.[33] Jobs, speaking in 2005, called the move to OS X the second "major transition" in the Mac's history (the first being the shift to PowerPC chips).[34] Based on UNIX, the new operating system offered a more stable environment than previous Mac platforms.[35] With each version of OS X, Apple aimed to generate not only extra revenue, but also new interest in the Mac and greater loyalty to the platform among existing users. A version named Tiger, released in 2005, included improved interoperability with Windows and an advanced search function called Spotlight. In addition, OS X had fewer reported security hazards, giving it another advantage over Windows.[36]

Proprietary, Apple-developed applications made up a growing segment of the company's Mac-based efforts. Many of these applications served creative or entertainment purposes, thereby furthering Jobs's goal to make the Mac central to an emerging digital lifestyle. As Jobs said, "Software is the user experience."[37] Instead of relying on independent software vendors (ISVs) to design that experience, Apple built programs such as those in the iLife suite (iPhoto, iTunes, and so on). In 1998, for example, when Adobe Systems rejected Jobs's request to create a video-editing program for the Mac, Apple launched an internal project to create Final Cut Pro.[38]

Moving in that direction carried certain risks. While Jobs might wish to "control the core technology"[39] in Macs and other Apple devices, his company also depended on cooperation by key ISVs (independent software vendors). In 2003, after Apple developed the Web browser Safari, Microsoft announced that it would no longer develop Internet Explorer for the Mac. Similarly, Adobe announced the same year that it would not create a new Mac version of its flagship Premiere software.[40] Apple did receive assurances in 2005 that Microsoft would develop its Office suite for Mac for another five years, and that Adobe would continue to issue Mac versions of Photoshop and other key programs.[41] But Jobs saw fit to hedge his bets by developing other applications, such as iWork productivity software. All of these decisions, of course, required Apple to assume additional development costs.[42]

While Jobs insisted on maintaining control in many areas, he relinquished control in others. Over the years, Apple had migrated toward standard interfaces (such as the USB port), making the Mac a less closed system. Thus, users of a Mac Mini could use a non-Mac keyboard. Conversely, the owner of a non-Mac PC could attach it to an Apple display.[43]

Adventures in Retail

On May 19, 2001, Apple opened its first retail store in McLean, Virginia.[44] By the end of 2005, it had opened 135 stores, and in 2006 it planned to open about 40 additional retail outlets.[45] Although most of the stores were in the United States, the chain also included stores in Canada, Japan, and the United Kingdom. The move into retail operations was a major departure for Apple. Early on, skeptics likened this retail foray to the Gateway Country chain, which suffered steep losses and finally shut down in 2004.[46] But by the 2005 fiscal year, Apple's retail division accounted for 17% of its revenues.[47] In the first quarter of the following year, which covered the 2005 holiday shopping season, retail sales topped $1 billion—marking a year-over-year increase of 78%.[48]

Through its stores in malls and other shopping districts, Apple reached large numbers of consumers who otherwise had undergone little exposure to the Mac. The company estimated that in the 2005 fiscal year, foot traffic in its stories totaled 50 million. It also estimated that of retail customers who bought a Mac, 50% had switched from using a Windows machine.[49] A key factor in bringing people into the stores, most analysts believed, was the popularity of the iPod. Having entered a store to buy one of Apple's trendy portable music players, consumers could admire the attractive "form factor" of Macintosh products, test-drive the user-friendly OS X, and give salespeople a chance to cross-sell them a computer to go with their iPod. More generally, some observers speculated that an iPod "halo effect" might benefit Apple's core PC business.[50]

Macintosh sales were indeed robust at mid-decade. In the fiscal year 2005, Mac revenues came to $6.275 billion, for a year-over-year increase of 27%.[51] For the calendar year 2005, unit sales totaled 4.7 million, up from 3.5 million in the previous year.[52] Mac sales outpaced the PC market overall, which grew about 16%.[53] (See **Exhibit 6**—Apple Computer: Unit Sales by Product Category.) Yet Apple's share of the worldwide PC market edged up only slightly, and remained in the 2% to 3% range, where it had been for half a decade.[54] To achieve share growth, the company needed to expand its reach within its core markets: small and medium-sized business (accounting for 42% of Mac sales), consumer (25%), and education (33%).[55]

Apple's share of the business market was just 1%, and its premium pricing (together with high switching costs for Windows-based business users) made growth in that sector difficult.[56] The company's strength lay in the consumer market; by one estimate, its share of that segment rose to 5.5% in mid-2005, after a period of hovering around 3%.[57] Equally critical to the company was the education market, in which its share was 10% worldwide and 17% in the United States. Although Apple had seen a surge in education sales in recent years, its share of that market was down sharply from a decade earlier.[58] (See **Exhibit 7**—PC Manufacturers: Share of the U.S. Education Market.)

Putting Intel Inside the Mac

When Jobs contended that the launch of OS X was the second "major transition" in Apple history, he did so in the context of announcing a third crucial shift: Apple, he said in June 2005, would abandon its longstanding use of PowerPC chips in favor of microprocessors made by Intel Corp.[59] In January 2006—half a year ahead of its originally announced schedule—Apple began shipping two products built with Intel Core Duo chips. These "Intel Mac" machines, an updated iMac and a replacement of the PowerBook called the MacBook Pro, represented a startling move for a company that had long positioned itself against the "Wintel" (Windows plus Intel) colossus. By the end of 2006, Jobs said, the entire Macintosh line would be running on Intel chips.[60]

Driving the leap to Intel was Jobs's frustration with the PowerPC chip line. The makers of that line, IBM and Freescale Semiconductor (a spin-off from Motorola), had failed to match Intel's performance, especially in low-power applications. High energy use by PowerPC chips drained batteries, created excess heat, and blocked advances in laptop performance. The latter point was crucial. Portable machines made up 43% of Apple's PC revenue, compared with the industry average of 29%.[61] Intel's dual-core technology (which in effect allowed two chips to occupy one piece of silicon) enabled Apple to build a MacBook Pro that was potentially five times as fast as the PowerBook G4, even as it used 20% less power.[62] And it did so at a cost that allowed the new iMac ($1,299 and up) and the MacBook Pro ($1,999 and up) to match their predecessors in pricing.[63]

The shift to Intel chips also presented a large software transition challenge: ISVs would need to rewrite all of their applications to run efficiently on the new machines. Apple produced an Intel-compatible version of OS X, along with compatible versions of each of its proprietary software titles. But to enable users to run key applications such as Excel and Photoshop, Apple relied on a translation program called Rosetta.[64] Early reviews indicated that Rosetta supported the smooth operation of those programs, albeit at a pace that canceled out the speed gains of the Intel processor.[65]

With "Intel inside," some analysts speculated, Apple might be able to double its PC share to 6%.[66] Reinforcing that possibility was Apple's move in April 2006 to enable users to run Windows on Intel-based Macs. That move, involving a free application called Boot Camp, provided a "safety net" to would-be Windows switchers.[67] Nonetheless, even as Apple moved closer to the Wintel mainstream, it remained an outlier. With its proprietary OS and its relatively tight control of the Mac "ecosystem," Apple continued to ply its own course. But for how long would that strategy remain viable, particularly at a time when the PC industry continued to evolve rapidly?

The Evolving Personal Computer Industry

In 2005, the personal computer industry logged more than $200 billion in sales.[68] Worldwide PC shipments totaled 208 million units, marking a 16% increase over the previous year.[69] From its earliest days in the mid-1970s, the industry had experienced explosive growth, dramatically altering the landscape of competition. Although Apple pioneered the first usable "personal" computing devices, IBM was the company that brought PCs into the mainstream. IBM's brand name and product quality helped it to capture the lion's share of the market in the early 1980s, when its customers included almost 70% of the Fortune 1000. At the time, many PC buyers shunned IBM-compatible clones because of fears about quality, compatibility, reliability, and service.[70]

IBM's dominance of the PC industry started to erode in the late 1980s, as buyers increasingly viewed PCs as commodities. IBM tried to boost its margins by building a more proprietary PC, but instead, it lost more than half of its market share, as well as its claim to being the standard bearer for the industry. By the early 1990s, "Wintel" had replaced "IBM-compatible" as the dominant standard. Throughout the 1990s, thousands of manufacturers, ranging from Compaq and Dell to no-name clone makers, built PCs around standard building blocks from Microsoft and Intel.

By 2005, there were nearly 900 million PCs in use around the world.[71] The United States accounted for about 30% of total shipments, Asia/Pacific (excluding Japan) for about 20%, and Latin America and Japan each for nearly 7%. The largest regional market, which analysts called EMEA (Europe, Middle East, and Africa), absorbed 33% of worldwide PC shipments in 2005.[72] Annual PC unit growth had averaged roughly 15% from the mid-1980s through 2000. In 2001, unit sales actually fell by about 4%, making it the worst year in history for the industry. But strong growth resumed in 2003. Much of that growth occurred in non-U.S. markets and especially in emerging Asian markets.[73] Revenue growth, however, did not keep pace with volume growth. In more mature markets such as the United States, where 60% of households owned PCs, slowing growth was intensifying competition on price.[74] By one estimate, the average selling price for a PC system had declined from $1,699 in 1999 to $1,034 in 2005—that is, by 8% per year (compound annual rate).[75]

PC Manufacturing

The PC was a relatively simple device. Using a screwdriver, a person with relatively little technological sophistication could assemble a PC from four widely available types of components: a microprocessor (the brains of the PC), a motherboard (the main circuit board), memory storage, and peripherals (the monitor, keyboard, mouse, and so on). Most manufacturers also bundled their PCs with an operating system. While the first PC was a desktop machine, by 2006 there was a wide range of forms, including laptops, notebooks, sub-notebooks, workstations (more powerful desktops), and servers (computers that acted as the backbone for PC networks).

In 2006, using off-the-shelf components, it cost roughly $400 to produce a mass-market desktop computer that would retail for $500. The largest cost element was the microprocessor, which ranged in price from $50 to more than $500 for the latest CPU. The other main components of a basic machine—motherboard, hard drive, memory, chassis, power, and packaging—cost between $120 and $250. A keyboard, mouse, modem, CD-ROM and floppy drives, and speakers totaled $50 to $140; a basic monitor cost about $75; and Windows XP and labor added $45 to $60 and $30, respectively. A PC maker could push its retail price down to $300 by using a less powerful CPU, cutting back on hard drive capacity and memory, and offering lower-quality peripherals. Or, by tailoring a machine for computer gaming enthusiasts, a manufacturer could build a PC whose sale price topped $3,000.[76]

As components became increasingly standardized, PC makers cut R&D spending. In the early 1980s, the leading manufacturers spent an average of 5% of sales on R&D. By 2005, not only did the industry leader—Dell Computer—devote less than 1% of sales to R&D, but its executives chided competitors that emphasized product innovation.[77] Of companies that tried to win through R&D, Michael Dell said, "That paradigm belongs in the Smithsonian with the dinosaurs."[78] Rather than invest heavily in R&D, companies such as Dell looked to innovations in manufacturing, distribution, and marketing to give them a competitive edge. Many firms, for example, turned to contract manufacturers to produce both components and entire PCs. Contractors initially shaved costs by handling simple manufacturing operations at flexible, high-volume plants in low-cost locations. Over time, these contractors moved into more complex areas, such as design, prototyping, and testing.

By the early 21st century, a new breed of large contract manufacturers of vertically integrated systems began to build everything for the brand-name companies. These firms were based mainly in China and Taiwan where labor rates were between 3% and 30% of U.S. rates.[79] Companies such as Asus, Compal, FIC, Foxconn, Mitec, and Quanta designed and assembled basic computers in Asia, and then finished production in geographic hubs, such as Mexico or southern California to serve the Americas. CPUs were installed close to the market and immediately before shipment to ensure the lowest possible price. In addition, many PC manufacturers sought to streamline their operations by moving from a build-to-stock model to a build-to-order (or configure-to-order) approach. By moving from a build-to-stock to build-to-order model, a company could dramatically reduce costs.[80] Much of the savings came from cuts in product returns and in factory inventory costs. (An industry rule of thumb was that each extra week of inventory reduced a PC maker's gross margin by one percentage point.[81]) The remaining savings stemmed from a decline in price protection costs, which manufacturers incurred by insuring distributors against revenue losses that would otherwise result from future price cuts. As of 2006, by one estimate, those costs added 3% to the cost structure of a PC, since the prices of key components (CPUs, memory, and hard disk drives) dropped by an average annual rate of 30%.[82]

Buyers and Distribution

PC buyers fell into four broad categories: business, home, government, and education. In 2005, businesses, large and small, consumed roughly 46% of the world's computers; home buyers accounted for 38%; and government and education each constituted about 8%.[83] The major criteria guiding PC purchases varied by market segment. While price was critical to all segments, home users were generally the most sensitive to cost, while business customers—especially small-office/home-office (SOHO) users—made decisions according to combination of service and price. Education buyers focused on a combination of price and software availability.

In the 1980s, most PC buyers were business managers who were relatively unsophisticated first-time customers. Since most IT organizations wanted to avoid buying PCs, managers in corporate departments generally made their own decisions. Yet many were intimidated by the technology and placed great emphasis on service, support, and compatibility in their buying decisions. In general, they bought no more than a few PCs at a time and preferred to buy established brands through full-service dealers. In the early 1990s, however, as customers became more knowledgeable about PCs, a variety of alternative channels emerged. Corporate information technology managers and purchasing departments, often operating under tight budgets, began to buy large numbers of PCs directly from vendors or their distributors. Superstores, such as Wal-Mart and Costco, catered to the consumer and SOHO markets. Web-based retailers, which offered computers and peripherals at steep discounts, also saw a sharp increase in demand. Yet the largest distribution channel was the so-called "white box" channel, which offered generic PCs that were assembled by local entrepreneurs. Roughly one-third of all PCs were white boxes, and in countries such as China that figure was even higher.[84]

PC Manufacturers

In 2006, the three top PC vendors—Dell, Hewlett-Packard, and Lenovo—accounted for more than 40% of all PC shipments. (See **Exhibit 8**—Apple Competitors: Selected Financial Information.) Below this top tier were a number of well-known brands, including Acer, Fujitsu, and Toshiba, but none of these firms had more than a 5% share. (See **Exhibit 9**—PC Manufacturers: Worldwide Market Shares.)

Dell   Michael Dell started selling computers out of his dorm room at the University of Texas-Austin in 1984. Dell Computer's first product was an IBM PC clone, which sold through computer magazines for up to 50% off IBM's price.[85] By 2006, Dell offered a full line of desktops, notebooks, workstations, and servers, in addition to software, service, support, and a growing number of accessories and consumer electronics. The company had almost $56 billion in revenue, of which about two-thirds came from PC sales.[86] Dell executives attributed their success to the company's distinctive business model, which centered on direct sales and build-to-order manufacturing. Dell needed as little as two days after taking an order to ship a computer out the door.[87] Consequently, as of 2005, Dell maintained only about 4 days of inventory, compared with nearly 40 days for Hewlett-Packard.[88] The resulting cost savings allowed Dell to maintain high margins while undercutting rivals' prices considerably. The Dell model also made it possible to offer products that precisely matched customer needs. Using Dell's website, customers could specify the exact configuration of their desired PC and find out immediately how much it would cost. Competitors tried to emulate the direct-sales approach, but none had fully succeeded. Some observers believed that Dell accounted for more than 100% of total PC industry profits.[89] Despite Dell's obvious success, annual revenue growth had slowed dramatically, from 40%–60% during the 1990s to about 15% by 2005.[90] As growth dropped, the company looked both to new product lines (including servers, printers, storage, and flat-panel TVs) and to overseas markets, where its PC share was only 7.8%.[91]

Hewlett-Packard (HP)   Hewlett-Packard, founded in 1939 by former Stanford classmates Bill Hewlett and Dave Packard, focused for many years on making electronic instruments and medical equipment. In the 1980s, the firm added computers and printers to its portfolio. Through products such as its LaserJet printers, it became a leader in the imaging and printing field.[92] Its purchase in 2002 of Compaq, for an estimated $19 billion, vaulted the company to the front ranks of PC makers.[93] Compaq, a pioneer in the IBM PC clone business, had been the leading worldwide PC vendor from 1994 to 2000.[94] Hewlett-Packard, after acquiring that company, marketed PCs under both its own brand and the Compaq brand. In 2005, HP was an $86.7 billion company, with 30% of its revenue coming from the division responsible for PC sales.[95] Its printer unit, meanwhile, was roughly the same size but accounted for 85% of the company's profits.[96] The company's sprawling operations also covered data storage, IT services, and other areas. In March 2005, Mark Hurd (former CEO of PC maker NEC) became the company's chief executive. His predecessor, Carly Fiorina, left after a six-year tenure marked by controversy over the Compaq purchase, among other issues.[97] One of Hurd's first major actions was to reverse Fiorina's decision to combine HP's personal systems (PC) group with its printer unit. Fiorina had also pushed HP aggressively toward a Dell-like direct-sales model. Hurd, by contrast, sought to cut costs across the board and to improve relations with retailers and other resellers, which handled sales of about 60% of HP products.[98]

Lenovo   When it acquired IBM's PC business for $1.75 billion in May 2005, Lenovo was the leading PC vendor in the fast-growing Chinese market, where it had a 26% share in 2004.[99] Legend Group Holdings, which was under the control of the Chinese government, owned a majority stake in the company, and the deal with IBM gave that company a 13% stake as well.[100] The IBM deal resulted in a company with a U.S. headquarters, yet with an eye on creating a global PC business. IBM pledged to sell Lenovo PCs through its worldwide sales force. The $13 billion company sought to combine the very different strengths of Lenovo, a low-end consumer-oriented operation with labor costs of merely $3 per desktop, and IBM, which had excelled in higher-end business sales.[101] The acquisition allowed Lenovo to market computers under IBM's famed ThinkPad and ThinkCentre brands for a five-year period. Back in the mid-1980s, IBM had earned 25% to 30% of the revenues generated by the PC business worldwide.[102] But despite its early lead in the industry, IBM had failed to secure ownership of the PC platform, yielding control of critical components to Microsoft (the OS) and Intel (the microprocessor). Later, IBM failed to keep pace with changes in the structure and economics of the industry, and by 2004 its market share had dwindled to less than 6%. Before its purchase by Lenovo, IBM's PC division had lost money for several years in a row.[103] Lenovo, for its part, made a 5% profit in the 2005 fiscal year.[104] In December 2005, the company chose a new CEO, William Amelio—former head of Dell's Asian operation, and a supply-chain expert—to complete the IBM integration.[105]

Suppliers, Complements, and Substitutes

There were two categories of suppliers to the PC industry: those supplying products (such as memory chips, disk drives, and keyboards) that had many sources; and those supplying products—notably microprocessors and operating systems—that came from just a few sources. Products in the first category were widely available at highly competitive prices. Products in the second category were supplied chiefly by two firms: Intel and Microsoft.

Microprocessors (CPUs) CPUs were the hardware "brains" of a PC. In 2005, the market for Intel-compatible chips was worth $32 billion.[106] While Intel was the sole producer of the 80386 market from 1986 through 1991, the market became more competitive in the 1990s. AMD (Advanced Micro Devices), Transmeta, and Taiwan's Via all challenged Intel with directly competitive products. Still, Intel remained the market leader by virtue of its powerful brand and its large manufacturing scale. Intel usually cut CPU prices by 30% to 60% per year.[107] By 2005, AMD had made significant inroads into Intel's market share, but Intel continued to supply roughly 80% of all PC CPUs.[108]

Operating systems Operating systems were large pieces of software that managed a PC's resources and supported its applications. Following the launch of the IBM PC, Microsoft dominated the PC operating system market. In the 1980s, Microsoft sold MS-DOS, a relatively crude OS, to hardware manufacturers for $15 per PC. In 1990, Microsoft started to challenge Apple's technical supremacy by introducing Windows 3.0. Though widely adopted by users, Windows remained markedly inferior to the Mac OS, at least until the release in 1995 of Windows 95. An instant success, Windows 95 sold roughly 50 million copies in its first year, with Microsoft receiving an average of $40 for every copy sold. Windows XP, released in October 2001, sold 17 million copies in its first eight weeks on the market. Developed at a cost of $1 billion, XP initially garnered Microsoft between $45 and $60 in revenue per copy, according to analysts' estimates.[109] In 2005, more than 90% of all PCs in the world ran on Windows.[110]

Application software The value of an operating system corresponded directly to the quantity and quality of application software that was available on that platform. The Apple II, for example, was a hit among business users because it supported VisiCalc, the first electronic spreadsheet. Other important PC application segments included word processing, presentation graphics, database software, desktop publishing, personal finance, education, entertainment, and the Internet. Throughout the 1990s and into the next decade, the number of applications available on PCs exploded while average selling prices for PC software collapsed. Microsoft was the largest vendor of software for Wintel PCs and, aside from Apple itself, for Macs.[111] However, tens of thousands of ISVs wrote the majority of PC applications.

Alternative technologies By 2006, personal computers were far easier to use than they had been two decades earlier, largely thanks to Apple-driven innovation. They were also entering the price range of consumer electronics for the first time. Nonetheless, a number of analysts believed that PCs had reached the end of the line. Lou Gerstner, then chairman and CEO of IBM, made the point most dramatically in that company's 1998 annual report. In a letter to shareholders, Gerstner wrote, "The PC era is over." Others, such as Microsoft senior executive Craig Mundie, took a more moderate line: "This isn't the post-PC era; it's the PC-plus era."[112] While few observers predicted that personal computers would disappear, many expected that simpler computing devices would supplement and, in some cases, replace PCs. These alternative devices ranged from handheld PDAs to smart phones, TV set-top boxes, and game machines. In 2006, advanced game devices (such as Microsoft Xbox 360 and Sony PlayStation2) allowed consumers not only to run traditional video games, but also to play DVDs and CDs, surf the Web, and play games directly online.

Playing Apple's Tune

In 2006, Apple's fate hinged on two large bets. One bet was the conversion of its Macs to Intel chips. The second bet was the launch of the iPod and an aggressive push into digital music. The iPod, clearly, was a home run. In the quarter ending December 31, 2005, the company reported the largest earnings and revenue totals in its history. Driving that result was the sale of more than 14 million iPods—which marked a 207% increase from a year earlier.[113] Along with the iTunes Music Store, the iPod pointed the way toward a future for Apple that might transcend its heritage as a PC company.

The iPod Phenomenon

Apple launched the iPod, a portable digital music player based on the MP3 compression standard, in November 2001.[114] Five years later, it offered a full line of MP3 players—from the iPod Shuffle (starting $69), which randomly played up to 240 songs; to the iPod Nano (starting at $149), which stored up to 1,000 songs; to the video iPod, whose 60-gigabyte version ($399) could hold 15,000 songs, 25,000 photos, or 150 hours of video.[115] The iPod had many things going for it: high storage capacity (supported by sophisticated engineering that placed a hard drive in its standard versions), sleek design (exemplified by its trademark white earphones), and appealing functionality (embodied in its "click wheel" control).[116] As a result, it became "an icon of the Digital Age," one journalist wrote.[117] It also commanded a premium of up to $50 over other MP3 players.[118]

The economics of the iPod were stellar by consumer electronics standards, with gross margins that ranged from 20% to 30%.[119] In 2005, analysts estimated that Apple paid a bill of materials (BOM) of $143.50 for a video iPod, which retailed for $299. Apple received about $270 of that amount, after the retailers' discount of 10%. The largest expense in the BOM was for the hard drive, which cost $65.[120] In the case of the iPod Nano, which used flash memory instead of a hard drive, margins were higher: According to one analyst, a 2GB Nano (which retailed for $199) had a BOM of $90.[121] Meanwhile, Apple also sought to extract additional value from the exploding iPod accessory market. In the spring of 2006, the company floated the idea of charging 10% of the wholesale price of any accessory that carried its "Made for iPod" logo.[122]

By the end of 2005, Apple had sold 42 million iPods, and the device claimed a 75% share of the U.S. market for portable music players.[123] For Steve Jobs, the success of the iPod had profound significance for Apple: "We're getting a chance to see what Apple engineering and Apple design can really do once we get out from underneath the 5 percent Macintosh operating system share," he said in 2004.[124] Although analysts predicted that the iPod's market share would dip as competition intensified, they also projected a steep rise in the size of the market. By one estimate, the worldwide market for MP3 players would total 100 million units by 2010, and the iPod would likely penetrate 70% of that market.[125] In 2006, major rivals in this market were few and growing fewer. They included Creative Technologies, iRiver, Samsung, and Sony. Late in 2004, Creative announced its goal of claiming 40% of the market with its new product line. But as iRiver CEO Jonathan Sasse admitted in early 2006, "None of us has more than a couple percent market share."[126] During the previous year, both Dell and Rio (which originated the category) had left the market.[127] Meanwhile, other companies, such as Amazon and Microsoft, signaled their intentions to enter the field.[128] Most iPod competitors had converged on the use of Microsoft's WMA standard; in 2005, more than 70 portable music players supported that format.[129] (See **Exhibit 10**—iPod Competitors: Comparison of Models and Prices for MP3 Players.)

Initially, the iPod could "sync" only with Macs. But in August 2002, despite reported reluctance on Jobs's part, Apple introduced an iPod for Windows.[130] In other ways, too, the company's approach to developing and marketing the iPod was less closed than the Macintosh. To make the iPod, Apple depended on a company called PortalPlayer, which manufactured the device's core chip, and on companies such as Hitachi, which supplied hard disk drives. As iPod architecture shifted from hard disk to NAND flash memory, Apple forged arrangements with flash manufacturers. In November 2005, the company agreed to pay $500 million up-front to Intel and Micron to secure "a substantial portion" of the output from their new flash-memory joint venture. It made similar arrangements with Hynix and Samsung. Apple, in fact, reportedly "tied up" 40% of Samsung's NAND output and commanded a 40% discount from the manufacturer.[131] Late in 2005, regulators in South Korea began investigating whether the two companies were conducting an unfair trade practice.[132] Most important, the iPod spawned as many as 1,000 accessories. An iPod leather case, for example, strengthened the iPod "ecosystem," even if Apple made no money from it. Apple reported nearly $900 million in sales of iPod-related services and accessories in 2005. It also announced that 30% of all new U.S. cars would come with iPod-compatible audio systems.

The iTunes System

One key element of the iPod system was the iTunes Music Store, an online service that Apple launched in April 2003. For 99 cents per song, visitors could download music offered by all five major record labels and by thousands of independent music labels. Users could play a downloaded song on their computer, burn it onto their own CD, or transfer it to an iPod. Initially available only to Mac users, the iTunes store became Windows-compatible in October 2003. Within three days of the launch of that service, PC owners had downloaded 1 million copies of free iTunes software and had paid for 1 million songs.[133] The first legal site that allowed music downloads on a pay-per-song basis, iTunes became the dominant online store of its kind. Early in 2006, it held an 83% share of that market, and as of February of that year, it had sold more than 1 billion songs.[134] According to one estimate, iPod owners downloaded an average of 26 iTunes songs per device per year.[135]

The introduction of iTunes had a galvanic impact on iPod sales. Before the advent of iTunes, Apple sold an average of 113,000 iPods per quarter; by the quarter that ended December 2003, iPod sales had shot up to 733,000 units—and then continued to rise.[136] (See **Exhibit 11**—iPod + iTunes: Quarterly Sales.) The direct impact of iTunes on Apple's profitability was far less impressive. "The dirty little secret of all this is there's no way to make money on these stores," Jobs said.[137] Of the 99 cents that Apple collected per song, 65 cents went to the music label that owned it, and 22 cents went toward the cost of credit card processing. That left Apple with only about a dime of revenue per track, from which Apple had to pay for its website, along with other direct and indirect costs.[138] In essence, Jobs had created a razor-and-blade business, only in reverse: Here, the variable element served as a loss leader for a profit-driving durable good.[139]

Central to the iTunes model was a set of standards that guarded both the music labels' intellectual property and the proprietary technology inside the iPod. An Apple-exclusive "digital rights management" (DRM) system called FairPlay protected iTunes songs against piracy by limiting to five the number of computers that could play a downloaded song. FairPlay DRM enabled Jobs to bring music executives onboard the iTunes venture. It also fueled iPod sales, since no competing MP3 player could play FairPlay-protected songs.[140] Observers called iTunes a "Trojan horse" that allowed iPod-specific standards to invade users' music collections and, in effect, to lock out would-be "iPod killers."[141] The iPod, meanwhile, could play content-standard MP3, AAC, and WAV formats. While competitors to iTunes were numerous, most of them used Microsoft's WMA audio format as well as Microsoft's Janus DRM system. AOL, Napster, Rhapsody (from RealNetworks), Sony, Virgin, Wal-Mart, and Yahoo all had deals with major labels that enabled them to offer a large music catalog, and several of them offered both per-song sales (at 99 cent or less per track) and subscription packages that allowed unlimited listening for, say, $9.99 per month. Yet by one estimate, these and other services accounted for just 16% of the online music market.[142]

In 2005, combined iPod and iTunes sales accounted for 39% of total Apple revenue.[143] But several challenges confronted the iPod-iTunes ecosystem. Music companies grew impatient with Apple's non-variable pricing structure and began pursuing other outlets for selling their content. Still, as the largest legal purveyor of online music, Apple was able to ensure continuation of its flat 99-cent song price when it renewed contracts with four of the top music labels in May 2006.[144] Government watchdogs showed signs of impatience with Apple as well. In March 2006, the French National Assembly passed a measure that (if also passed by the French Senate) would require Apple to open up its FairPlay system to users and rivals. While the law would cover all DRM systems, its impact on Apple would be especially onerous; an Apple spokeswoman called it "state-sponsored piracy."[145] Another, perhaps more serious threat came from mobile phone companies. Building on a base of 190 million U.S. cell phones, improved 3G (third-generation) cellular technology, and an ability to bill customers without going through credit card issuers, these companies aimed to usurp the entire MP3 player market by delivering music directly to wireless devices.[146]

In response to such challenges, Apple kept up a steady stream of new offerings. In September 2005, it entered a partnership with Motorola and Cingular Wireless to market an iTunes-supported mobile phone called the ROKR.[147] Although that device was a critical and commercial flop, Motorola came out in January 2006 with another iTunes phone, the SLVR.[148] Meanwhile, signs emerged that Apple might bring out its own iPod phone, perhaps under the trademark "iPhone" or "Mobile Me."[149] In October 2005, Apple introduced a video-enabled iPod and simultaneously began selling for the first time downloadable TV shows, such as "Desperate Housewives" and "Lost," at the iTunes site.[150] Within just three months, the site had sold more than 8 million videos.[151] A deal to be an exclusive distributor of Harry Potter audiobooks reinforced a sense that Apple sought to push its iPod-iTunes model in a new, more expansive direction.[152]

Apple Turns 30

In early 2006, Apple Computer prepared to celebrate its 30th anniversary. As that milestone approached, the company's place within the PC industry arguably appeared harder to define than ever before. One commentator wrote:

> Stop and look at Apple for a second, since it's an odd company. . . . Apple makes its own hardware (iBooks and iMacs), it makes the operating system that runs on that hardware (Mac OS X), and it makes programs that run on that operating system. . . . It also makes the consumer-electronics devices that connect to all those things (the rapidly multiplying iPod family), and it runs the online service that furnishes content to those devices (the iTunes Music Store). If you smooshed together Microsoft, Dell and Sony into one company, you would have something like the diversity of the Apple technological biosphere. . . . Apple is essentially operating its own closed miniature techno-economy.[153]

"Mr. Jobs," another writer noted, "has created a fusion of fashion, brand, industrial design and computing. . . . [I]f he is to successfully revamp Apple, [Jobs] will ultimately win not by taking on PC rivals directly, but by changing the rules of the game."[154] Should Apple remain ensconced within its "closed miniature" world? Or would that course ruin its chance to become an information technology powerhouse? Could the company truly "change the rules" of the game in computing and in next-generation devices? As Apple entered its fourth decade, those questions preoccupied Steve Jobs, who had spent his career doing the unexpected.

Exhibit 1a Apple Computer: Selected Financial Information, 1981–2005 (in millions of dollars, except for employee and stock-related data)

	1981	1986	1991	1996	1998	2000	2002	2003	2004	2005
Net sales	334	1,902	6,309	9,833	5,941	7,983	5,742	6,207	8,279	13,931
Cost of sales	170	891	3,314	8,865	4,462	5,733	4,021	4,387	5,871	9,738
Research and development	21	128	583	604	310	380	447	471	489	534
Selling, general, and administrative	77	610	1,740	1,568	908	1,546	1,557	1,683	1,910	2,393
Operating income (loss)	66	274	447	(1,383)	261	620	46	25	349	1,650
Net income (loss)	39	154	310	(816)	309	786	65	69	276	1,335
Cash, cash equivalents, and short-term investments	73	576	893	1,745	2,300	4,027	4,337	4,566	5,464	8,261
Accounts receivable, net	42	263	907	1,496	955	953	565	950	1,050	1,312
Inventories	104	109	672	662	78	33	45	56	101	165
Net property, plant, and equipment	31	222	448	598	348	313	621	669	707	817
Total assets	255	1,160	3,494	5,364	4,289	6,803	6,298	6,815	8,050	11,551
Total current liabilities	70	138	1,217	2,003	1,520	1,933	1,658	2,357	2,680	3,484
Total shareholders' equity	177	694	1,767	2,058	1,642	4,107	4,095	4,223	5,076	7,466
Cash dividends paid	—	—	57	14	—	—	—	—	—	—
Employees	2,456	5,600	14,432	13,398	9,663	11,728	12,241	13,566	13,426	16,820
International sales/sales	27%	26%	45%	52%	45%	46%	43%	42%	41%	41%
Gross margin	49%	53%	47%	10%	25%	28%	30%	29%	29%	30%
R&D/sales	6%	7%	9%	6%	5%	5%	8%	8%	6%	4%
SG&A/sales	23%	32%	28%	16%	15%	19%	27%	27%	23%	17%
Return on sales	12%	8%	5%	NM	5%	10%	1%	1%	3%	10%
Return on assets	24%	15%	10%	NM	7%	12%	1%	1%	3%	12%
Return on equity	38%	25%	19%	NM	22%	19%	2%	2%	5%	18%
Stock price low	$1.78	$2.75	$10.28	$4.22	$3.28	$7.00	$6.80	$6.56	$10.64	$31.65
Stock price high	$4.31	$5.47	$18.19	$8.75	$10.75	$36.05	$13.06	$12.41	$34.22	$74.98
P/E ratio at year-end	27.7	16.8	21.9	NM	17.5	6.1	79.6	112.5	90.7	46.1
Market value at year-end	1,223.7	2,578.3	6,649.9	2,598.5	5,539.7	4,996.2	5,146.4	7,858.5	25,892.5	60,586.6

Source: Standard & Poor's Compustat® data.

Notes: All information is on a fiscal-year basis, except for share price data, which are on a calendar-year basis.
Apple's fiscal year ends in September.
NM = Not Meaningful.

Exhibit 1b   Apple Computer: Net Sales Data by Product Category (in millions of dollars)

	2002	2003	2004	2005
Power Macintosh[a]	$1,380	$1,237	$1,419	NM
iMac[b]	$1,448	$1,238	$954	NM
Desktops[c]	NM	NM	NM	$3,436
PowerBook	$831	$1,299	$1,589	NM
iBook	$875	$717	$961	NM
Portables[d]	NM	NM	NM	$2,839
Total Macintosh Net Sales	$4,534	$4,491	$4,923	$6,275
iPod	$143	$345	$1,306	$4,540
Other music products[e]	$4	$36	$278	$899
Peripherals and other hardware[f]	$527	$691	$951	$1,126
Software[g]	$307	$362	$502	NM
Service and other net sales	$227	$282	$319	NM
Software, service, and other net sales[h]	NM	NM	NM	$1,091
Total Net Sales	$5,742	$6,207	$8,279	$13,931

Source: Apple financial statements. Apple's fiscal year ends in September.

NM = Not Meaningful.

[a]Includes Xserve product line.

[b]Includes eMac product line.

[c]Includes iMac, eMac, Mac Mini, Power Mac, and Xserve product lines.

[d]Includes iBook and PowerBook product lines.

[e]Includes sales from iTunes Music Store, iPod-related services, and iPod-related accessories.

[f]Includes sales of Apple-branded and third-party displays, wireless connectivity and networking solutions, and other hardware accessories.

[g]Includes sales of Apple-branded operating system and application software and sales of third-party software.

[h]Includes combined sales of software, services, and other net sales.

Exhibit 1c Apple Computer: Operational Data by Segment (in millions of dollars)

	2002	2003	2004	2005
Americas				
Net sales	$3,131	$3,181	$4,019	$6,590
Operating income	278	323	465	798
Depreciation, amortization, and accretion	4	5	6	6
Segment assets	395	494	563	705
Europe				
Net sales	$1,251	$1,309	$1,799	$3,073
Operating income	122	130	280	454
Depreciation, amortization, and accretion	4	4	4	4
Segment assets	165	252	259	289
Japan				
Net sales	$710	$698	$677	$920
Operating income	140	121	115	140
Depreciation, amortization, and accretion	2	3	2	3
Segment assets	50	130	114	199
Retail				
Net sales	$283	$621	$1,185	$2,350
Operating income (loss)	(22)	(5)	39	151
Depreciation, amortization, and accretion	16	25	35	43
Segment assets	141	243	351	555
Other[a]				
Net sales	$367	$398	$599	$998
Operating income	44	51	90	118
Depreciation, amortization, and accretion	2	2	2	2
Segment assets	67	78	124	133

Source: Apple financial statements. Apple's fiscal year ends in September.

[a]"Other" segments include the Asia-Pacific region and Apple's FileMaker business.

Exhibit 2   Apple Computer: Worldwide PC Share, 1980–2005

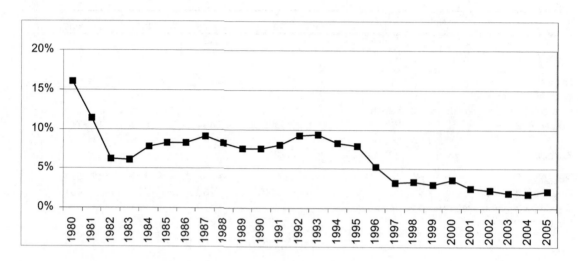

Source: Adapted from InfoCorp., International Data Corp., Dataquest, and Merrill Lynch data.

Exhibit 3   Apple Computer: Daily Closing Share Price, 1980–2006

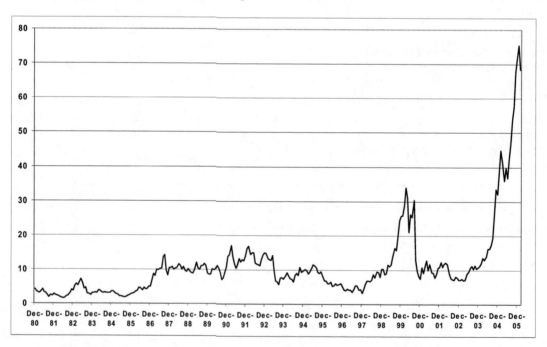

Source: Thomson Datastream.

Exhibit 4   Shipments and Installed Base of PC Microprocessors, 1992–2005 (in millions of units)

Total Shipments	1992	1994	1996	1998	1999	2000	2001	2002	2003	2004	2005
Intel Technologies											
Units shipped	30.6	47.8	76.0	105.0	140	156	146	126	152[a]	170[a]	200[a]
Installed base	122.2	211.4	347.5	542.5	683	839	985	1,111	1,263[a]	1,433[a]	1,633[a]
Motorola (680X0)											
Units shipped	3.9	3.9	0.8	0.2	NM	NM	NM	NM	NM	NM	NM
Installed base	16.5	24.9	26.8	27.5	NM	NM	NM	NM	NM	NM	NM
PowerPC											
Units shipped	0	0.8	4.0	3.5	3.4	4.7	4.1	3.1	3.3[a]	3.5[a]	4.7[a]
Installed base	0	0.8	7.8	14.1	17.5	22.2	26.3	29.4	32.9[a]	36.2[a]	40.9[a]

Source: Adapted from Dataquest, InfoCorp., International Data Corp., Merrill Lynch, and Credit Suisse data, and casewriter estimates.

NM = Not Meaningful.

[a]Between 5% and 10% of total microprocessor shipments go into non-PC end products. In any given year, roughly 30% to 45% of microprocessors in the total installed base involve older technologies that are probably no longer in use. The figures for PowerPC shipments exclude microprocessors destined for Sony PlayStation and Xbox 360 machines.

Exhibit 5   PC Manufacturers: Key Operating Measures, 1997–2005

	1997	2000	2003	2004	2005
Gross Margin (%)					
Apple	21%	28%	29%	29%	30%
Dell	23%	21%	19%	19%	18%
Hewlett-Packard	38%	31%	29%	27%	25%
Inventory Days					
Apple	35.4	1.7	4.1	4.8	4.9
Dell	9.1	5.6	7.7	5.3	4.0
Hewlett-Packard	88.5	56.4	41.2	40.4	38.8
R&D/Sales					
Apple	12.1%	4.8%	7.6%	5.9%	3.8%
Dell	1.2%	1.5%	0.8%	0.9%	0.8%
Hewlett-Packard	7.2%	5.4%	5.0%	4.4%	4.0%

Source: Compiled from company financial reports, Hoover's, Inc., www.hoovers.com.

Note: All information is on a fiscal-year basis. The fiscal year ends in September for Apple, in January for Dell, and in October for Hewlett-Packard.

369

Exhibit 6   Apple Computer: Unit Sales by Product Category, 2003–2005 (in thousands of units)

	2003	Y/Y change	2004	Y/Y change	2005
Desktops[a]	1,761	(8%)	1,625	55%	2,520
Portables[b]	1,251	33%	1,665	21%	2,014
Total Macintosh Unit Sales	3,012	9%	3,290	38%	4,534
Net Sales per Macintosh Unit Sold	$1,491	0%	$1,496	(7%)	$1,384
iPods	939	370%	4,416	409%	22,497
Net Sales per iPod Unit Sold	$367	(19%)	$296	(32%)	$202

Source: Apple financial statements.

[a]Includes iMac, eMac, Mac Mini, Power Mac, and Xserve product lines.

[b]Includes iBook and PowerBook product lines.

Exhibit 7   PC Manufacturers: Share of the U.S. Education Market, 1996–2004

	1996	1998	2000	2002	2003	2004
Dell	4%	11%	26%	35%	42%	44%
Apple	27%	22%	19%	14%	14%	14%
Hewlett-Packard	6%	13%	13%	13%	14%	14%
Gateway	4%	10%	10%	7%	7%	7%
IBM/Lenovo	4%	4%	5%	6%	4%	3%
Total shipments	1.8 million	2.6 million	4.3 million	5.5 million	5.1 million	5.5 million

Source: Adapted from data provided in Chris Whitmore, Sherri Scribner, and Joakim Mahlberg, "Beyond iPod" (analysts' report), Deutsche Bank, September 21, 2005, p. 29.

Exhibit 8 Apple Competitors: Selected Financial Information, 2000–2005 (in millions of dollars)

	2000	2001	2002	2003	2004	2005
Dell						
Total revenues	31,888	31,168	35,404	41,444	49,205	55,908
Cost of sales	25,205	25,422	28,844	33,629	39,856	45,620
R&D	482	321	319	330	463	463
SG&A	3,675	3,236	3,505	4,008	4,761	5,140
Net income	2,177	1,246	2,122	2,645	3,043	3,572
Total assets	13,435	13,535	15,470	19,311	23,215	23,09
Total current liabilities	6,543	7,519	8,933	10,896	14,136	15,927
Total stockholders' equity	5,622	4,694	4,873	6,280	6,485	4,129
Gross margin	21%	18%	19%	19%	19%	18%
R&D/sales	2%	1%	1%	1%	1%	1%
SG&A/sales	12%	10%	10%	10%	10%	9%
Return on sales	7%	4%	6%	6%	6%	6%
Market value at year-end	45,630	70,858	68,968	87,003	104,689	70,488
Hewlett-Packard						
Total revenues	48,782	45,226	56,588	73,061	79,905	86,696
Cost of sales	33,709	32,279	40,134	51,857	58,540	64,718
R&D	2,646	2,670	4,105	3,653	3,543	3,492
SG&A	10,029	9,722	12,345	14,664	14,530	14,674
Net income	3,697	408	(903)	2,539	3,497	2,398
Total assets	34,009	32,584	70,710	74,708	76,138	77,317
Total current liabilities	15,197	13,964	24,310	26,630	28,588	31,460
Total stockholders' equity	14,209	13,953	36,262	37,746	37,564	37,176
Gross margin	31%	29%	29%	29%	27%	25%
R&D/sales	5%	6%	7%	5%	4%	4%
SG&A/sales	21%	21%	22%	20%	18%	17%
Return on sales	8%	1%	-2%	3%	4%	3%
Market value at year-end	62,431	39,848	52,973	70,039	63,327	81,242
Lenovo						
Total revenues	234.1	200.4	208.6	191.7	164.7	2,891.5
Cost of sales	104.4	84.0	85.4	83.7	74.3	2,741.1
R&D	NA	NA	NA	NA	NA	NA
SG&A	74.2	68.6	76.8	66.6	53.9	37.7
Net income	20.8	16.0	(61.8)	16.4	23.8	143.6
Total assets	277.8	279.8	181.3	142.3	167.4	1,157.9
Total current liabilities	24.5	31.3	27.0	20.2	15.3	445.2
Total stockholders' equity	140.6	156.7	96.7	114.3	143.8	667.2
Gross margin	55.4%	58.1%	59.1%	56.3%	54.9%	5.2%
R&D/sales	NA	NA	NA	NA	NA	NA
SG&A/sales	31.7%	34.2%	36.8%	34.8%	32.7%	1.3%
Return on sales	8.9%	8.0%	-29.6%	8.6%	14.4%	5.0%
Market value at year-end	4,696	3,833	2,501	3,200	2,236	3,923

Exhibit 8 (continued)

	2000	2001	2002	2003	2004	2005
Intel						
Total revenues	33,726	26,539	26,764	30,141	34,209	38,826
Cost of sales	9,429	9,649	8,389	8,253	9,591	15,777
R&D	4,006	3,994	4,054	4,365	4,778	5,145
SG&A	8,986	8,260	8,543	8,736	9,466	5,688
Net income	10,535	1,291	3,117	5,641	7,516	8,664
Total assets	47,945	44,395	44,224	47,143	48,143	48,314
Total current liabilities	8,650	6,570	6,595	6,879	8,006	9,234
Total stockholders' equity	37,322	35,830	35,468	37,846	38,579	36,182
Gross margin	72%	64%	69%	73%	72%	59%
R&D/sales	12%	15%	15%	14%	14%	13%
SG&A/sales	27%	31%	32%	29%	28%	15%
Return on sales	31%	5%	12%	19%	22%	22%
Market value at year-end	202,321	211,092	103,836	209,351	147,895	150,484
Microsoft						
Total revenues	22,956	25,296	28,365	32,187	36,835	39,788
Cost of sales	2,334	1,919	4,177	4,596	5,899	5,316
R&D	3,775	4,379	4,307	4,659	7,779	6,184
SG&A	8,925	10,121	10,604	12,278	18,560	16,946
Net income	9,421	7,346	7,829	9,993	8,168	12,254
Total assets	52,150	59,257	67,646	79,571	92,389	70,815
Total current liabilities	9,755	11,132	12,744	13,974	14,969	16,877
Total stockholders' equity	41,368	47,289	52,180	61,020	74,825	48,115
Gross margin	90%	92%	85%	86%	84%	87%
R&D/sales	16%	17%	15%	14%	21%	16%
SG&A/sales	39%	40%	37%	38%	50%	43%
Return on sales	41%	29%	28%	31%	22%	31%
Market value at year-end	231,290	356,806	276,412	296,073	290,720	278,358

Sources: Standard & Poor's Compustat® data and company financial reports. (In the case of Dell, Intel, and Lenovo, 2005 data comes from company financial reports. All other data comes from Compustat. Variations may result from differences in how Compustat and some companies tabulate reported data.)

Notes: All information is on a fiscal-year basis, except for "market value at year-end," which is on a calendar-year basis. The fiscal year ends in January for Dell, in October for Hewlett-Packard, in March for Lenovo, in December for Intel, and in June for Microsoft.

NM = Not Meaningful.

Exhibit 9 PC Manufacturers: Worldwide Market Shares, 2000–2005

	2000	2001	2002	2003	2004	2005
Dell	11.4%	12.9%	15.1%	16.7%	17.9%	18.1%
Hewlett-Packard[a]	7.8%	6.9%	16.0%	16.2%	15.8%	15.6%
Lenovo[b]	—	—	—	—	2.3%	6.2%
Acer	—	—	—	3.1%	3.6%	4.7%
Fujitsu Siemens	5.1%	4.5%	4.2%	4.1%	4.0%	4.1%
IBM[b]	7.1%	6.2%	5.9%	5.8%	5.9%	—
Toshiba	3.0%	2.8%	3.2%	3.1%	3.6%	—
Compaq[a]	13.0%	11.2%	—	—	—	—
Packard Bell NEC	4.5%	3.5%	3.3%	—	—	—
Apple	3.5%	2.5%	2.3%	1.9%	1.9%	2.2%
Total shipments	128.5 million	121.8 million	136.9 million	154.7 million	177.5 million	208.6 million

Source: "PC Market Continues Rapid Growth in Fourth Quarter of 2005 as Annual Shipments Reach New Highs, According to IDC" (press release), International Data Corp., January 18, 2006; IDC data, as cited in Megan Graham-Hackett, "Computers: Hardware" (industry survey), Standard & Poor's, December 8, 2005, p. 2, and in previous editions of that survey; Apple Computer annual financial reports; and casewriter estimates.

Note: Market share data for Apple is derived from Macintosh unit sales, as reported in the company's annual reports. The sampling of market shares for other companies comes mainly from annual listings of the top five PC makers, as measured by IDC. Absence of a figure indicates that a company placed below the top five in a given year.

[a]Hewlett-Packard acquired Compaq in mid-2002. The 2002 market share figure for HP incorporates Compaq sales for the first part of that year.

[b]Lenovo acquired IBM's PC business in mid-2005. The 2005 market share figure for Lenovo incorporates IBM sales for first part of that year.

Exhibit 10 iPod Competitors: Comparison of Models and Prices for MP3 Players (April 2006)

	1 GB (flash drive)	2 GB – 6 GB (hard disk & flash)	20 GB – 60 GB (hard disk drive)
Apple	iPod Shuffle (1 GB) $99 iPod nano (1 GB) $149	iPod nano (2 GB) $199 iPod nano (4 GB) $249	iPod (30 GB) $299 iPod (60 GB) $399
Creative	MuVo TX FM (1 GB) $110 Zen Nano (1 GB) $100	Zen Micro (4 GB) $180 Zen Micro (6 GB) $230	Zen Sleek (20 GB) $230 Zen Vision (30 GB) $300
iRiver	T30 (1 GB) $150 T10 (1 GB) $200	H10 Series (5 GB) $230 H10 Series (6 GB) $280	H10 Series (20 GB) $300
Philips	PSA242 (1 GB) $160	HDD082 (2 GB) $130 HDD1630 (6 GB) $200	HDD6330 (30 GB) $280
Samsung	YP-T7JZ (1 GB) $180 YP-T8Z (1 GB) $200	YP-Z5QS (2 GB) $200 YP-Z5AS (4 GB) $250	YH-J70SB (20 GB) $350
Sony	Walkman Bean (1 GB) $120 Walkman Core (1 GB) $130	—	Network Walkman (20 GB) $350

Source: Company websites, accessed March and April 2006.

Note: Pricing information reflects retail prices as listed on each company's website or, in a few cases, on Amazon.com.

Exhibit 11   iPod + iTunes: Quarterly Sales (of iPod Units and iTunes songs), 2001–2005

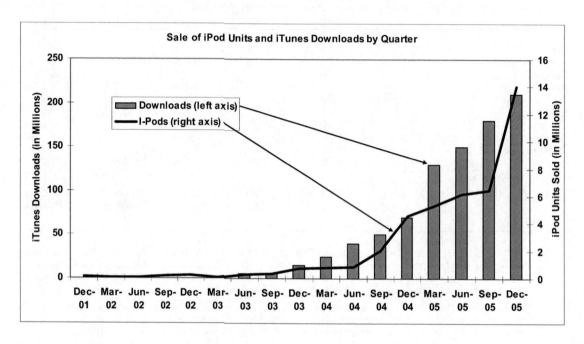

Source: Compiled from Apple financial reports, Apple press releases, and casewriter estimates.

Endnotes

[1] John Markoff, "Michael Dell Should Eat His Words, Apple Chief Suggests," *The New York Times*, January 16, 2006, p. C1.

[2] Jai Singh, "Dell: Apple Should Close Shop," CNET News.com, October 6, 1997.

[3] "Apple Computer: Annual Financials," Hoover's Online, http://premium.hoovers.com/subscribe/ co/fin/annual.xhtml?ID=12644, accessed January 2006; "Apple Computer: Historical Financials," Hoover's, Inc., www.hoovers.com, accessed January 2006

[4] John Markoff and Steve Lohr, "Apple Plans to Switch from I.B.M. to Intel for Chips," *The New York Times*, June 6, 2005, p. C1.

[5] This discussion of Apple's history is based largely on Jim Carlton, *Apple: The Inside Story of Intrigue, Egomania, and Business Blunders* (New York: Times Business/Random House, 1997); David B. Yoffie, "Apple Computer 1992," HBS No. 792-081 (Boston: Harvard Business School Publishing, 1992); and David B. Yoffie and Yusi Wang, "Apple Computer 2002," HBS No. 702-469 (Boston: Harvard Business School Publishing, 2002). Unless otherwise attributed, all quotations and all data cited in this section are drawn from those two cases.

[6] Carlton, *Apple*, p. 10.

[7] Data from Dataquest, cited in Carlton, *Apple*, p. 11.

[8] Yoffie, "Apple Computer 1992."

[9] Yoffie, "Apple Computer 1992."

[10] Ibid.

[11] Ibid.

[12] Carlton, *Apple*, p. 123.

[13] Ibid, p. 273.

[14] David B. Yoffie, "Apple Computer 1996," HBS No. 796-126 (Boston: Harvard Business School Publishing, 1996).

[15] Charles McCoy, "Apple, IBM Kill Kaleida Labs Venture," *The Wall Street Journal*, November 20, 1995.

[16] David B. Yoffie, "Apple Computer in China—1993," HBS Case No. 794-100 (Boston: Harvard Business School Publishing, 1993).

[17] Louise Kehoe, "Apple Shares Drop Sharply," *The Financial Times*, January 19, 1996.

[18] John Simons, "A Bushel of Hope for Apple," *U.S. News & World Report*, July 29, 1996.

[19] Dawn Kawamoto and Anthony Lazarus, "Apple Lays Off Thousands," CNET News.com, March 14, 1997.

[20] Jim Carlton and Lee Gomes, "Apple Computer Chief Amelio Is Ousted," *The Wall Street Journal*, July 10, 1997.

[21] Laurie J. Flynn, "Apple Sending Clone Makers Mixed Signals," *The New York Times*, August 11, 1997.

[22] Dawn Kawamoto, "Apple Paid More Than Planned for Power," CNET News.com, May 11, 1998.

[23] Carlton, *Apple*, pp. 238, 235.

[24] Pete Burrows, "A Peek at Steve Jobs' Plan," *BusinessWeek*, November 17, 1997.

[25] Jim Davis, "Power Macs, Sales Plan Unveiled," *CNET News.com*, November 10, 1997, http://news.com. com/2100-1001-205179.html, accessed March 2006.

[26] Dennis Sellers, "Notes from Apple's Earning[s] Conference Call," Macworld.com, July 17, 2001, http://www.macworld.com/news/2001/07/17/apple/index.php, accessed April 2006.

[27] "Steve Jobs" (executive profile), Apple Computer website, http://www.apple.com/pr/bios/jobs.html, accessed April 2006.

[28] "$7.4 Billion Seals Disney-Pixar Deal," *Hollywood Reporter*, January 31, 2006, accessed via Factiva.

[29] "Apple Computer: Annual Financials," Hoover's Online.

[30] All product and price information for Macintosh computers is drawn from the Apple Computer website, http://www.apple.com/hardware, accessed February 2006.

[31] David Pogue, "Price Tags Get Smaller at Apple," *The New York Times*, January 12, 2005, p. G1.

[32] Walter S. Mossberg, "Boss Talk: The Music Man; Apple CEO Steve Jobs Talks About the Success of iTunes, Mac's Future, Movie Piracy," *The Wall Street Journal*, June 14, 2004, p. B1.

[33] Brent Schlender, "How Big Can Apple Get?" *Fortune*, February 21, 2005, p. 66.

[34] "Apple's Intel Switch: Jobs' Keynote Transcript," CNET News.com, June 15, 2005, accessed via Factiva.

[35] "A Talk with Apple's Mr. Marketer," BusinessWeek Online, January 22, 2002, accessed via Factiva.

[36] Brent Schlender, "How Big Can Apple Get?" *Fortune*, February 21, 2005, p. 66.

[37] Ibid.

[38] Ibid.

[39] Mossberg, "Boss Talk."

[40] "Microsoft Will No Longer Make Mac Web Browser," Reuters News, June 16, 2003, accessed via Factiva; Matthew Yi, "Beyond iPod, Apple Grows Healthy Software Business," *The San Francisco Chronicle*, January 31, 2005, p. E1.

[41] Thomas Claburn and Darrell Dunn, "Apple Bets Its Chips," *InformationWeek*, January 15, 2006, p. 26; Nick Wingfield and Don Clark, "With Intel Inside, Macs May Be Faster, Smaller," *The Wall Street Journal*, June 7, 2005, p. B1.

[42] Schlender, "How Big Can Apple Get?"

[43] On interoperability of Mac and non-Mac devices, see pages on the Apple website devoted to the Mac Mini (http://www.apple.com/macmini/accessories.html) and to Apple displays (http://www.apple.com/displays), both accessed April 2006.

[44] "Apple to Open 25 Stores in 2001" (press release), Apple Computer, May 15, 2001, http://www.apple.com/pr/library/2001/may/15retail.html, accessed February 2005.

[45] John Dvorak, "Tech View: The Real Apple Success Story," Dow Jones News Service, January 11, 2006, accessed via Factiva; Jenn Abelson and Chris Reidy, "Apple Plans Flagship Store in Back Bay," *The Boston Globe*, February 10, 2006, p. C1.

[46] Alex Salkever, "What Apple Stores Aren't Doing," BusinessWeek Online, April 7, 2004, accessed via Factiva; John Markoff, "Oh, Yeah, He Also Sells Computers," *The New York Times*, April, 25, 2004, p. 3-1

[47] "Apple Computer: Annual Financials," Hoover's Online.

[48] Nick Turner and Patrick Seitz, "Apple's Intel Machines Ahead of Schedule," *Investor's Business Daily*, January 11, 2006, p. A4.

[49] Arik Hesseldahl, "Apple's Growing Army of Converts," BusinessWeek Online, November 10, 2005, accessed via Factiva; Salkever, "What Apple Stores Aren't Doing."

[50] Chris Whitmore, Sherri Scribner, and Joakim Mahlberg, "Beyond iPod" (analyst' report), Deutsche Bank, September 21, 2005, p. 31; Megan Graham-Hackett, "Computers: Hardware" (industry survey), Standard & Poor's, December 8, 2005, p. 8; Hesseldahl, "Apple's Growing Army of Converts."

[51] Apple Computer, Form 10-K for the fiscal year ending September 24, 2005, November 29, 2005, p. 31.

[52] Michael K. Ozanian, "This Apple Is Too Shiny," Forbes, January 30, 2006, p. 43.

[53] Patrick Seitz, "A Reversal of Fortune in PCs," Investor's Business Daily, October 21, 2005, p. A13; Chris Whitmore et al., "Beyond iPod," p. 25.

[54] Bill Shope and Elizabeth Borbolla, "IT Hardware: Top Issues for 2006 and Industry Primer" (analysts' report), JP Morgan, January 30, 2006, p. 27; Graham-Hackett, "Computers: Hardware," pp. 6-8.

[55] Whitmore et al., "Beyond iPod," p. 24.

[56] Ibid, pp. 30–31.

[57] Ibid, p. 27.

[58] Ibid, pp. 28–29.

[59] "Apple's Intel Switch: Jobs' Keynote Transcript."

[60] Nick Turner and Patrick Seitz, "Apple's Intel Machines Ahead of Schedule," Investor's Business Daily, January 11, 2006, p. A4; Thomas Clayburn and Darrell Dunn, "Apple Bets Its Chips," InformationWeek, "January 16, 2006, p. 26; Daniel Drew Turner, "Apple Shows New Intel Notebooks, Software," eWeek, January 10, 2006.

[61] Peter Burrows, "Tougher Days, Bolder Apple," BusinessWeek, June 20, 2005, p. 38.

[62] Stephen Fenech, "Apple's New Core: New Macs with Intel Dual Processors Revealed," Daily Telegraph (London), January 18, 2006, p. 11.

[63] Pricing information is drawn from the Apple website, http://www.apple.com/hardware, accessed February 2006.

[64] John Markoff and Laurie J. Flynn, "Apple's Next Test: Get Developers to Write Programs for Intel Chips," The New York Times, June 7, 2005, p. C1.

[65] Walter S. Mossberg and Katherine Boehret, "The Mossberg Solution: The iMac Gets a Brain Transplant," The Wall Street Journal, January 18, 2006, p. D1.

[66] McGrath, "Apple Banks on iPod to Open Doors for Intel-Powered Mac." (The analyst cited is Tim Bajarin, president of Creative Strategies of Campbell, California.)

[67] Nick Wingfield, "Apple Releases Software to Run Windows on Macs," Dow Jones News Wire, April 5, 2006, accessed via Factiva.

[68] Mahon and Gerhardy, "Q4 2005 Global Technology Data Book," p. 15.

[69] "PC Market Continues Rapid Growth in Fourth Quarter of 2005 as Annual Shipments Reach New Highs, According to IDC" (press release), International Data Corp., January 18, 2006, http://www.idc.com/getdoc.jsp?containerId=prUS20051406, accessed March 2006.

[70] Unless otherwise attributed, historical information in this section on the personal computer industry derives from David B. Yoffie and Yusi Wang, "Apple Computer 2002," HBS No. 702-469 (Boston: Harvard Business School Publishing, 2002) and other earlier cases written by David B. Yoffie.

[71] "Mobile PCs in Use Surpass 200M" (press release), Computer Industry Almanac, Inc., June 20, 2005, http://www.c-i-a.com/pr0605.htm, accessed March 2006.

[72] "Gartner Says EMEA Region Became Largest PC Market in the World Based on Unit Shipments in 2005" (press release), Gartner, Inc., January 18, 2006.

[73] Graham-Hackett, "Computers: Hardware," pp. 1–2, 6–7.

[74] Ibid, p. 14.

[75] IDC (International Data Corp.) data, as cited in Graham-Hackett, "Computers: Hardware," p. 7.

[76] Component costs and wholesale prices are based on casewriter communications with a computer industry insider. Retail pricing is based on survey of online PC vendors.

[77] See **Exhibit 5**—"PC Manufacturers: Key Operating Measures," in this case."

[78] Michael Dell quoted in Thomas A. Stewart and Louise O'Brien, "Execution Without Excuses: The HBR Interview" (interview of Michael Dell and Kevin Rollins), *Harvard Business Review*, March 2005, p. 104.

[79] Judith Banister, "Manufacturing Employment and Compensation in China," U.S. Bureau of Labor Statistics, November 2005, http://www.bls.gov/fls/chinareport.pdf, accessed March 2006; "Hourly Compensation Costs for Production Workers in Manufacturing, 32 Countries or Areas, 22 Manufacturing Industries, 1992–2004," U.S. Bureau of Labor Statistics, February 2006, http://www.bls.gov/fls/flshcindnaics.htm, accessed March 2006.

[80] Robert P. Anastasi et al., "The Computer Sales Channel," The Robinson-Humphrey Co., Inc., August 25, 1997, p. 11.

[81] Shope and Borbolla, "IT Hardware," pp. 28–29.

[82] Ibid

[83] Casewriter communications with computer industry insider.

[84] Ibid.

[85] "Dell Inc.," Hoover's Online, accessed March 2006; Andy Serwer, "Dell's Midlife Crisis: The Powerhouse PC Maker has Hit a Sudden Speed Bump," *Fortune*, November 28, 2005, p. 147.

[86] "Dell Inc.," Hoover's Online, accessed March 2006; Jay Palmer, "Rebooting Dell," *Barron's*, September 12, 2005, p. 21

[87] The two-day figure is derived from an attempted consumer transaction at the Dell website, www.dell.com, March 2006.

[88] Dell and Hewlett-Packard 2005 financial reports; Hoover's Online. See also Exhibit 5—"PC Manufacturers: Key Operating Measures," in this case.

[89] Palmer, "Rebooting Dell."

[90] Ibid

[91] Serwer, "Dell's Midlife Crisis."

[92] "Hewlett-Packard Company," Hoover's Online; "History and Facts," Hewlett-Packard website, http://www.hp.com/hpinfo/abouthp/histnfacts, accessed March 2006.

[93] Graham-Hackett, "Computers: Hardware," p. 8; Ben Elgin, "Can Anyone Save HP?" *BusinessWeek*, February 21, 2005, p. 28.

[94] Graham-Hackett, "Computers: Hardware," p. 8.

[95] Hewlett-Packard Form 10-K, filed December 15, 2005 (for the year ending October 31, 2005, p. 34.

[96] Peter Burrows, "HP Says Goodbye to Drama," *BusinessWeek*, September 12, 2005, p. 83.

[97] "Hewlett-Packard Company," Hoover's Online; Bill Saporito and Chris Taylor, "Why Carly's Out," *Time*, February 21, 2005, p. 34.

[98] Burrows, "HP Says Goodbye to Drama"; Elgin, "Can Anyone Save HP?"

[99] "Lenovo Group Limited," Hoover's Online; Steve Hamm, with Dexter Roberts and Louise Lee, "East Meets West, Big-Time: Lenovo's Deal for IBM's PC Unit Led to a Merger of Talent—and a Threat to Dell," *BusinessWeek*, May 9, 2005, p. 74.

[100] Michelle Kessler, "Lenovo Chief Says It's Still the Same IBM ThinkPad," *USA Today*, July 25 , 2005, p. B1; "Lenovo Group Limited," Hoover's Online.

[101] Hamm, "East Meets West"; Charles Forelle, "Remote Control: How IBM's Ward Will Lead China's Largest PC Company from Other Side of the Globe," *The Wall Street Journal*, April 21, 2005, p. B1.

[102] Data from InfoCorp, cited in Yoffie, "Apple Computer 1992," p. 17.

[103] Forelle, "Remote Control"; Kessler, "Lenovo Chief Says It's Still the Same IBM ThinkPad."

[104] Kessler, "Lenovo Chief Says It's Still the Same IBM ThinkPad."

[105] John G. Spooner, "Lenovo Gains CEO, Operations Expert," eWeek.com, December 21, 2005, http://www.eweek.com/article2/0,1895,1904307,00.asp, accessed March 2005.

[106] Intel Corporation, Form 10-K, filed February 27, 2006 (for the year ending December 31, 2005); Advanced Micro Devices, Inc., Form 10-K, filed February 24, 2006 (for the year ending December 25, 2005).

[107] Graham-Hackett, "Computers: Hardware," p. 14; Amrit Tewary and Elayne Sheridan, "Semiconductors" (industry survey), Standard & Poor's, September 1, 2005, p. 17.

[108] Graham-Hackett, "Computers: Hardware," p. 13.

[109] David B. Yoffie, Dharmesh M. Mehta, and Rudina I. Suseri, "Microsoft in 2005," HBS Case No. 705-505, (Boston: Harvard Business School Publishing, 2006).

[110] Graham-Hackett, "Computers: Hardware," p. 13.

[111] On Microsoft as a maker of Macintosh software, see Microsoft's Mactopia website, http://www.microsoft.com/mac/macbu.

[112] John Markoff, "Fight of the (Next) Century: Converging Technologies Put Sony and Microsoft on a Collision Course," *The New York Times*, March 7, 1999.

[113] "Apple Reports First Quarter Results" (press release), Apple Computer, January 18, 2006, http://www.apple.com/pr/library/2006/jan/18results.html, accessed January 2006.

[114] For a general overview of the origin and impact of the iPod, see Rob Walker, "The Guts of the New Machine," *The New York Times Magazine*, November 30, 2003, p. 78.

[115] All product and price information for the current line of iPod devices is drawn from the Apple Computer website, http://www.apple.com/ipod/ipod.html, accessed February 2006.

[116] Walker, "The Guts of the New Machine."

[117] Peter Burrows and Ronald Glover, with Heather Green, "Steve Jobs' Magic Kingdom," *BusinessWeek*, February 6, 2006, p. 62.

[118] Peter Burrows, "Beating the iPod Crunch," BusinessWeek Online, November 22, 2005, accessed via Factiva.

[119] Whitmore et al., "Beyond iPod," pp. 18-19; Bill Shope, Elizabeth Borbolla, and Mark Moskowitz, "Apple Computer: iPod Economics II" (analysts' report), JP Morgan, May 26, 2005, p. 46; Ozanian, "This Apple Is Too Shiny."

[120] Adam Benjamin and Blayne Curtis, "Video iPod Teardown: Who's In and Who's Not" (analysts' report), Jeffreys & Company, Inc., October 19, 2005, p. 2, https://jefferies.bluematrix.com/docs/pdf/31086.pdf, accessed March 2005.

[121] Chris Crotty, "iSuppli Teardown Reveals Apple's Surprising Choices for iPod nano" (press release), iSuppli Corp., September 26, 2005, http://www.isuppli.com/marketwatch/default.asp?id=316, accessed March 2006.

[122] Ina Fried, "Apple Seeks 'Tax' on iPod Accessories," CNET News.com, March 16, 2006, http://news.com.com/Apple+seeks+tax+on+iPod+accessories/2100-1041_3-5620959.html, accessed March 2006.

[123] Fenech, "Apple's New Core"; Ozanian, "This Apple Is Too Shiny."

[124] Markoff, "Oh, Yeah, He Also Sells Computers."

[125] Whitmore et al., "Beyond iPod," pp. 13-15.

[126] Paul Taylor, "The iPod's Rivals Seek to Take a Bite Out of Apple," *Financial Times*, January 13, 2006.

[127] Tom Sanders, "Dell Dumps Hard-Drive MP3 Players," VNUNet United Kingdom, February 7, 2006, accessed via Factiva; John Borland, "The Day Rio's Music Died," CNET News.com, August 26, 2006, accessed via Factiva.

[128] Brian Garrity, "Apple on Top, but Under Fire," *Billboard*, March 11, 2006; "Rivals Eye Big Bit of iPod Sales," *Irish Independent*, February 2, 2006.

[129] Saul Hansell, "Gates vs. Jobs: The Rematch," *The New York Times*, November 14, 2004, p. 3-1; Shope et al., "iPod Economics II," p. 20.

[130] "Apple Unveils New iPods" (press release), Apple Compute, July 18, 2002, accessed via Factiva; Markoff, "Oh, Yeah, He Also Sells Computers."

[131] Arik Hesseldahl, "Unpeeling Apple's Nano," BusinessWeek Online, September 22, 2005, accessed via Factiva.

[132] Jung-A Song, "Watchdog Scrutinizes Samsung Chips Deal," *Financial Times*, November 24, 2005, p. 31.

[133] Chris Taylor, "The 99¢ Solution," *Time*, November 17, 2003, p. 66.

[134] Laurie J. Flynn, "Profit Rises at Apple, but Shares Tumble," *The New York Times*, January 19, 2006, p. C1; "Apple Music Store Downloads Top One Billion Songs" (press release), Apple Computer, http://www.apple.com/pr/library/2006/feb/23itms.html, accessed February 2006.

[135] Shope et al., "iPod Economics II," p. 47.

[136] Ibid, p. 7.

[137] Taylor, "The 99¢ Solution."

[138] Shope et al., "iPod Economics II," p. 26.

[139] Ibid, pp. 8–10.

[140] Ibid, pp. 10–13.

[141] Taylor, "The 99¢ Solution"; Walker, "The Guts of the New Machine."

[142] Shope et al., "iPod Economics II," pp. 18-24; Devin Leonard, "The Player: Rivals Won't Find It Easy Competing with the iPod's Closed System," *Fortune*, March 26, 2006, p. 54.

[143] "Apple Computer: Annual Financials," Hoover's Online.

[144] Kevin Allison and Joshua Chaffin, "Apple Sets Tune for Pricing of Song Downloads," *Financial Times*, May 2, 206, p. 15.

[145] Rob Pegararo, "France Takes a Shot at iTunes," *The Washington Post*, March 26, 2006, p. F6; Shiraz Sidhva, "French Bill Aims for DRM Sharing," Hollywood Reporter Online, March 22, 2006, accessed via Factiva.

[146] Bill Albert, "Bites Off the Apple," *Barron's*, June 27, 2005, p. B19; Roger O. Crockett, with Heather Green, Tom Lowry, Moon Ihlwan, and Andy Rein, "iPod Killers? New Rivals Take Aim at the Champ," *BusinessWeek*, April 27, 2005, p. 58.

[147] "Apple, Morotola & Cingular Launch World's First Mobile Phone with iTunes" (press release), Apple Computer, September 7, 2006, http://www.apple.com/pr/library/2005/sep/07rokr.html, accessed April 2006.

[148] Mike Angell, "Motorola Rokr Phone Not Basking in iPod's Glow," *Investor's Business Daily*, October 25, 2005, p. A4; Peter Lewis, "Moto's ROKR Is a STINKR," *Fortune*, October 3, 2005, p. 170.

[149] Burrows, "More Apple Miracles in 2006?"; Ryan Kim, "Apple May Link Cell Phone, iPod," *The San Francisco Chronicle*, January 17, 2006, p. C3.

[150] "Apple Unveils the New iPod" (press release), Apple Computer, October 12, 2006, http://www.apple.com/pr/library/2005/oct/12ipodr.html, accessed April 2006.

[151] Stephen Fenech, "Apple's New Core," *The Daily Telegraph* (London), January 18, 2006, p. 11.

[152] "Harry Potter Digital Audiobooks Debut Exclusively on iTunes Music Store" (press release), Apple Computer, September 7, 2005, http://www.apple.com/pr/library/2005/sep/07potter.html, accessed April 2006.

[153] Lev Grossman, "How Apple Does It," *Time*, October 24, 2005, p. 66.

[154] Markoff, "Oh, Yeah, He Also Sells Computers."

Harley-Davidson in 2004

John E. Gamble
University of South Alabama

Roger Schäfer
University of South Alabama

Harley-Davidson's management had much to be proud of as the company wrapped up its Open Road Tour centennial celebration, which began in July 2002 in Atlanta, Georgia, and ended on the 2003 Memorial Day Weekend in Harley's hometown of Milwaukee, Wisconsin. The 14-month Open Road Tour was a tremendous success, drawing large crowds of Harley owners in each of its five stops in North America and additional stops in Australia, Japan, Spain, and Germany. Each stop along the tour included exhibits of historic motorcycles, performances by dozens of bands as diverse as Lynyrd Skynyrd, Earl Scruggs, and Nickelback, and brought hundreds of thousands of Harley enthusiasts together to celebrate the company's products. The Ride Home finale brought 700,000 biker-guests from four points in the United States to Milwaukee for a four-day party that included concerts, factory tours, and a parade of 10,000 motorcycles through downtown Milwaukee. The company also used the Open Road Tour as a platform for its support of the Muscular Dystrophy Association (MDA), raising $7 million for the MDA during the 14-month tour. Photos from the Open Road Tour and Harley's new V-Rod model are presented in Exhibit 1.

Harley-Davidson's centennial year was also a year to remember for the company's being named to *Fortune*'s annual list "The 100 Best Companies to Work For" and judged third in automotive quality behind Rolls-Royce and Mercedes-Benz by Harris Interactive, a worldwide market research and consulting firm best known for the Harris Poll. Consumer loyalty to Harley-Davidson motorcycles was unmatched by almost any other company. As

a Canadian Harley dealer explained, "You know you've got strong brand loyalty when your customers tattoo your logo on their arm."[1] The company's revenues had grown at a compound annual rate of 16.6 percent since 1994 to reach $4.6 billion in 2003—marking its 18th consecutive year of record revenues and earnings. In 2003, the company sold more than 290,000 motorcycles, giving it a commanding share of the market for motorcycles in the 651+ cubic centimeters (cc) category in the United States and the leading share of the market in the Asia/Pacific region. The consistent growth had allowed Harley-Davidson's share price to appreciate by more than 15,000 percent since the company's initial public offering in 1986. In January 2004, the company's CEO, Jeffrey Bleustein, commented on the centennial year and the company's prospects for growth as it entered its second century:

> We had a phenomenal year full of memorable once-in-a-lifetime experiences surrounding our 100th Anniversary. As we begin our 101st year, we expect to grow the business further with our proven ability to deliver a continuous stream of exciting new motorcycles, related products, and services. We have set a new goal for the company to be able to satisfy a yearly demand of 400,000 Harley-Davidson motorcycles in 2007. By offering innovative products and services, and by driving productivity gains in all facets of our business, we are confident that we can deliver an earnings growth rate in the mid-teens for the foreseeable future.[2]

However, not everyone was as bullish on Harley-Davidson's future, with analysts pointing out that the company's plans for growth were too dependent on aging baby boomers. The company had achieved its record growth during the 1990s and

Exhibit 1   **Photos from Harley-Davidson's Open Road Tour and Its VRSC V-Rod**

Source: Harley-Davidson Web site.

early 2000s primarily through the appeal its image held for baby boomers in the United States. Some observers wondered how much longer boomers would choose to spend recreational time touring the country by motorcycle and attending motorcycle rallies. The company had yet to develop a motorcycle that appealed in large numbers to motorcycle riders in their 20s or cyclists in Europe, both of whom preferred performance-oriented bikes over cruisers or touring motorcycles. Another concern of analysts watching the company was Harley-Davidson's short-term oversupply of certain models

Exhibit 2   **Summary of Harley-Davidson's Financial Performance, 1994–2003 (in thousands, except per share amounts)**

	2003	2002	2001
Income statement data			
Net sales	$4,624,274	$4,090,970	$3,406,786
Cost of goods sold	2,958,708	2,673,129	2,253,815
Gross profit	1,665,566	1,417,841	1,152,971
Operating income from financial services	167,873	104,227	61,273
Selling, administrative and engineering	(684,175)	(639,366)	(551,743)
Income from operations	1,149,264	882,702	662,501
Gain on sale of credit card business	—	—	—
Interest income, net	23,088	16,541	17,478
Other income (expense), net	(6,317)	(13,416)	(6,524)
Income from continuing operations before provision for income taxes and accounting changes	1,166,035	885,827	673,445
Provision for income taxes	405,107	305,610	235,709
Income from continuing operations before accounting changes	760,928	580,217	437,746
Income (loss) from discontinued operations, net of tax	—	—	—
Income before accounting changes	760,928	580,217	437,746
Cumulative effect of accounting changes, net of tax	—	—	—
Net income (loss)	$ 760,928	$ 580,217	$ 437,746
Weighted average common shares:			
Basic	302,271	302,297	302,506
Diluted	304,470	305,158	306,248
Earnings per common share from continuing operations:			
Basic	$ 2.52	$ 1.92	$ 1.45
Diluted	2.50	1.90	1.43
Dividends paid	0.195	0.135	0.115
Balance sheet data			
Working capital	$1,773,354	$1,076,534	$ 949,154
Current finance receivables, net	1,001,990	855,771	656,421
Long-term finance receivables, net	735,859	589,809	379,335
Total assets	4,923,088	3,861,217	3,118,495
Short-term finance debt	324,305	382,579	217,051
Long-term finance debt	670,000	380,000	380,000
Total debt	$ 994,305	$ 762,579	$ 597,051
Shareholders' equity	$2,957,692	$2,232,915	$1,756,283

Source: Harley-Davidson Inc. 2003, 2002, and 1998 10-K reports.

brought about by the 14-month production run for its 100th anniversary models. The effect of the extended production period shortened the waiting list for most models from over a year to a few months and left some models on showroom floors for immediate purchase. The combined effects of a market focus on a narrow demographic group, the difficulty experienced in gaining market share in Europe, and short-term forecasting problems led to a sell-off of Harley-Davidson shares going into 2004. Exhibit 2 presents a summary of Harley-Davidson's financial and operating performance for 1994–2003. Its market performance for 1994 through January 2004 is presented in Exhibit 3.

	2000	1999	1998	1997	1996	1995	1994
	$2,943,346	$2,482,738	$2,087,670	$1,762,569	$1,531,227	$1,350,466	$1,158,887
	1,979,572	1,666,863	1,414,034	1,176,352	1,041,133	939,067	800,548
	963,774	815,875	673,636	586,217	490,094	411,399	358,339
	37,178	27,685	20,211	12,355	7,801	3,620	—
	(485,980)	(427,701)	(360,231)	(328,569)	(269,449)	(234,223)	(204,777)
	514,972	415,859	333,616	270,003	228,446	180,796	153,562
	18,915	—	—	—	—	—	—
	17,583	8,014	3,828	7,871	3,309	96	1,682
	(2,914)	(3,080)	(1,215)	(1,572)	(4,133)	(4,903)	1,196
	548,556	420,793	336,229	276,302	227,622	175,989	156,440
	200,843	153,592	122,729	102,232	84,213	64,939	60,219
	347,713	267,201	213,500	174,070	143,409	111,050	96,221
	—	—	—	—	22,619	1,430	8,051
	347,713	267,201	213,500	174,070	166,028	112,480	104,272
	—	—	—	—	—	—	—
	$ 347,713	$ 267,201	$ 213,500	$ 174,070	$ 166,028	$ 112,480	$ 104,272
	302,691	304,748	304,454	151,650	150,683	149,972	150,440
	307,470	309,714	309,406	153,948	152,925	151,900	153,365
	$ 1.15	$ 0.88	$ 0.70	$ 1.15	$ 0.95	$ 0.74	$ 0.64
	1.13	0.86	0.69	1.13	0.94	0.73	0.63
	0.098	0.088	0.078	0.135	0.110	0.090	0.070
	$ 799,521	$ 430,840	$ 376,448	$ 342,333	$ 362,031	$288,783	$189,358
	530,859	440,951	360,341	293,329	183,808	169,615	—
	234,091	354,888	319,427	249,346	154,264	43,829	—
	2,436,404	2,112,077	1,920,209	1,598,901	1,299,985	980,670	676,663
	89,509	181,163	146,742	90,638	8,065	—	—
	355,000	280,000	280,000	280,000	250,000	164,330	—
	$ 444,509	$ 461,163	$ 426,742	$ 391,572	$ 285,767	$185,228	$ 10,452
	$1,405,655	$1,161,080	$1,029,911	$ 826,668	$ 662,720	$494,569	$433,232

COMPANY HISTORY

Harley-Davidson's history began in Milwaukee, Wisconsin, in 1903 when 20-year-old Arthur Davidson convinced his father to build a small shed in their backyard where Arthur and 21-year-old William Harley could try their hand at building a motorcycle. Various types of motorized bicycles had been built since 1885, but the 1901 development of a motorcycle with an integrated engine by a French company inspired Davidson and Harley to develop their own motorcycle. The two next-door neighbors built a two-horsepower engine that they fit onto a

Exhibit 3   **Yearly Performance of Harley-Davidson Inc.'s Stock Price, 1994 to January 2004**

(a) Trend in Harley-Davidson Inc.'s Common Stock Price

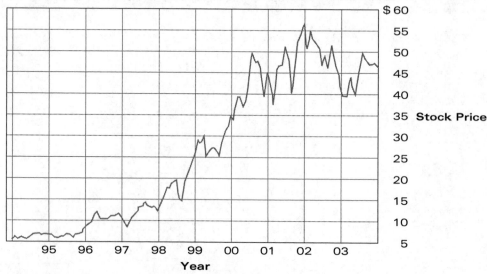

(b) Performance of Harley-Davidson Inc.'s Stock Price versus the S&P 500 Index

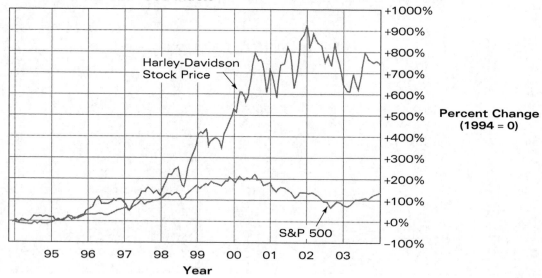

modified bicycle frame. At first the motorcycle could not pull itself and a rider up a steep hill, but after some additional tinkering, the first Harley-Davidson motorcycle could run as fast as 25 miles per hour. Milwaukee residents were amazed as Harley and Davidson rode the motorcycle down local streets, and by the end of the year the partners were able to produce and sell three of their motorcycles. Walter Davidson joined his brother and William Harley during the year to help assemble and race the company's motorcycles. In 1905, a Harley-Davidson motorcycle won a 15-mile race in Chicago with a time of 19:02, and by 1907 the company had developed quite a reputation in motorcycle racing with numerous wins in Milwaukee-area races. In 1907, another Davidson brother, William, joined the company and the company began

386

adding dealers. Harley-Davidson's dealers helped the company sell 150 motorcycles in 1907.

In 1909, Harley-Davidson developed a more powerful seven-horsepower motorcycle engine to keep its edge in racing, an innovation that turned out to define the look of the company's motorcycles for the next century. Twin cylinders joined at a 45-degree angle became a trademark Harley-Davidson engine design characteristic and created a distinctive "potato-potato-potato" sound. Harley designed his V-twin engine with two pistons connected to a single crankpin, whereas later designs used crankpins for each piston. The single-crankpin design had been called an inferior design because it caused the pistons to come into firing positions at uneven intervals, which produced an uneven cadence in sound and excessive vibrations. Nevertheless, the vibrations and distinctive rumble of a Harley engine were accepted by the market in the early 1900s and continued to appeal to motorcyclists in the early 2000s.

The stronger engine allowed the company to produce 17,000 motorcycles for the U.S. military during World War I and become the largest motorcycle producer in the world in 1920, with 2,000 dealers in 67 countries. A number of features that make up Harley-Davidson's image originated during the 1920s, including the teardrop gas tank, the "Hog" nickname, and the "Flathead" engine design. Harley-Davidson was one of two U.S. motorcycle companies to survive the Great Depression—the other being Indian—by relying on exports and sales to police departments and the U.S. military. The 1930s saw Harley-Davidson win more races and develop additional elements of its differentiated image, including the art deco eagle design painted on its gas tanks, three-tone paint, and the "Knucklehead" engine rocker boxes. Harley-Davidson's 1936 EL model, or "Knucklehead," became its first highly styled motorcycle and formed the foundation of style elements that remained present in the highly demanded 2004 Softail Fat Boy. The company suspended production of civilian motorcycles in 1941 to produce almost 90,000 motorcycles for the U.S. military during World War II.

The recreational motorcycle market grew dramatically after World War II, as ex-GIs purchased motorcycles and led enthusiasm for riding. Harley-Davidson introduced new models for enthusiasts, including the Hydra-Glide in 1949, the K-model in 1952, the Sportster in 1957, and the Duo-Glide in 1958. The combination of racing success

(Harley-Davidson riders won 18 of 24 races and set six new racing records in 1950 alone) and innovative new Harley-Davidson models led to rival company Indian's demise in 1953. Harley-Davidson would remain the sole U.S. manufacturer of motorcycles until 1998, when the Indian brand was revived.

Harley-Davidson continued to win races throughout the 1960s, but its reputation began to erode soon after its acquisition by American Machine and Foundry Company (AMF) in 1969. Harley-Davidson under AMF was known for its leaking engines, unreliable performance, and poor customer service. At one point during AMF's ownership of the company, more than one-half of its bikes had to be repaired before leaving the factory. The company attempted to offset its declining sales of road bikes with the introduction of dirt bikes and snowmobiles in the early 1970s, but by the late 1970s AMF lost faith in the acquisition and slated it for divestiture. When no buyers for the company emerged, 13 executives engineered a leveraged buyout of Harley-Davidson in 1981. Harley-Davidson struggled under the heavy debt load and came within four hours of bankruptcy in 1985, before then-CEO Richard Teerlink was able to convince new creditors to step in and restructure Harley with less costly financing terms. Teerlink also launched a restructuring program that updated manufacturing methods, improved quality, and expanded the model line.

U.S. tariffs imposed on 651+cc Japanese motorcycles also aided Harley-Davidson in gaining financial strength and competitiveness in the heavyweight segment of the U.S. motorcycle industry. Harley-Davidson completed an initial public offering in 1985 and petitioned the International Trade Commission to terminate tariffs on Japanese heavyweight motorcycles in 1987 when its market share in the U.S. heavyweight category had improved to 25 percent from 16 percent in 1985. In 1998, the company purchased Wisconsin-based Buell Motorcycle, a performance brand using Harley-Davidson engines that began as a venture between Erik Buell and Harley-Davidson in 1992. Harley-Davidson opened its 358,000-square-foot Kansas City, Missouri, plant in 1998 to produce Sportster, Dyna Glide, and V-Rod models and built an assembly plant in Brazil in 1999 to aid in its Latin American expansion. The new capacity allowed Harley-Davidson to set production records each year during the early 2000s to reach 290,000 units by year-end 2003.

OVERVIEW OF THE MOTORCYCLE INDUSTRY

Demand for motorcycles in developed countries such as the United States, Germany, France, Spain, and Great Britain, grew dramatically at the end of World War II as veterans who enjoyed riding motorcycles during the war purchased their own bikes upon return to civilian life. Groups of enthusiasts began to form motorcycle clubs that allowed them to socialize and participate in rallies and races. Two of the earliest motorcycle rallies in the United States were the Daytona Bike Week and the Sturgis Rally. The first Daytona 200, which occurs during Bike Week, was run in 1937 on a 3.2-mile beach and road course. The first Sturgis, South Dakota, race took place in 1938 when nine participants raced a half-mile track and performed such stunts as jumping ramps and crashing through plywood walls. These and other such events grew dramatically in popularity beginning in the 1970s, with both Daytona Bike Week and the Sturgis Rally each drawing over 200,000 bikers in 2003. The Sturgis Rally was said to be among the most raucous motorcycle rallies in the United States, with plenty of public drunkenness and lewd behavior accompanying the seven days of races. Such behavior was common enough that the Rally Web site (www. sturgis.com) provided the fines and bonds associated with such offenses as indecent exposure, disorderly conduct, open container in public, and possession of controlled substances.

The rowdy and rebellious image of bikers is traced to some of the motorcycle clubs that began after World War II. The outlaw image of cyclists first developed in 1947 when *Life* magazine photographers captured images of an impromptu rally at Hollister, California, by a motorcycle group calling themselves the Boozefighters. The group became quite rowdy during their motorcycling exhibition, but *Life* reporters embellished the story significantly, claiming the Boozefighters descended on the town and proceeded to terrorize its residents by drag-racing down the main street, tossing beer bottles, and riding motorcycles through the front doors of the town's saloon. The imagery of the drunken Fourth of July attack on the town became etched deeper into the minds of the world when the story became the subject of *The Wild One,* a 1954 movie starring Marlon Brando. When asked by a local resident what he was rebelling against, Brando's character, Johnny, replied, "Whaddya got?"[3] The general public came to dislike bikers because of incidents like the one in Hollister and because of the Hollywood treatment of the event, but the Hells Angels made many people fearful of bikers and put motorcycle gangs under the close scrutiny of law enforcement at local, state, and federal levels.

The Hells Angels were established in 1948 in Fontana, California, by a group of young cyclists who had read of the Hollister rampage and wished to start their own outlaw biker group. The Hells Angels, who took their name and symbols from various World War II flying units, became notorious during the 1960s when they became linked to drug trafficking and other organized crime activities. Sonny Barger, a founder of the Oakland, California, chapter in the late 1950s, became the United States' most infamous biker after organizing a disastrous security effort for the 1969 Rolling Stones concert in Altamont at which one concertgoer was stabbed and killed by Hells Angels members. Barger, who had been convicted of attempted murder, possession of narcotics with intent to sell, and assault with a deadly weapon, commented in an interview with the British Broadcasting Corporation (BBC) that he pressed a pistol into Keith Richards' ribs and ordered him to continue to play after the Rolling Stones' guitarist threatened to end the show because of Hells Angels' rough tactics with fans.[4]

The Hells Angels and rival motorcycle clubs like the Pagans, the Banditos, and the Outlaws, rode only Harleys, which hurt Harley-Davidson's image with the public in the 1960s. Honda successfully exploited Harley's outlaw image with the slogan "You meet the nicest people on a Honda" to become the largest seller of motorcycles in the United States during the late 1960s and early 1970s.[5] The image of the Hells Angels had spilled over to the entire industry and contributed to declines in motorcycle demand in the United States and Europe during the 1960s before a new Hollywood film resurrected interest in motorcycles. *Easy Rider* (1969) portrayed bikers as less villainous rebels and appealed greatly to young people in the United States and Europe. The movie eventually gained cult status and helped charge a demand for motorcycles that began in the 1970s and continued through 2003. The red-white-and-blue 1951 Harley "Captain America" chopper ridden by Peter Fonda's Wyatt character helped

Harley-Davidson break the outlaw image and come to represent less malevolent rebellion.

Industry Conditions in 2003

In 2003, more than 950,000 motorcycles were sold in the United States and 28 million motorcycles were in operation worldwide. The industry was expected to grow by approximately 5 percent annually through 2007 with light motorcycles, Mopeds, and scooters accounting for most of the expected growth. A general increase in incomes in such emerging markets as China, India, and Southeast Asia was the primary force expected to drive industry growth. Demand growth for the heavyweight motorcycle category had outpaced smaller motorcycles in the United States during the 1990s and into 2003, but analysts projected that demand for larger motorcycles would decline as the population aged and became less able to travel on two-wheelers. In 2002, demand for heavyweight motorcycles in the United States grew by 17 percent compared to an industrywide growth rate of 10 percent.

The industry was segmented into various groups on the basis of engine size and vehicle style. Mopeds, scooters, and some small motorcycles were equipped with engines having displacements of 50 cubic centimeters (cc) or less. These motorbikes were best suited for urban areas where streets were narrow and parking was limited or for developing countries where personal incomes were limited and consumers could make only small investments in transportation. Motorcycles used for basic transportation or for motocross events were typically equipped with engines ranging from 125cc to 650cc. Larger street bikes required more power and usually had engines over 650cc. Large motorcycles with engine displacements greater than 651cc accounted for the largest portion of demand in North America and Europe as riders increasingly chose motorcycles with more horsepower and better performance. Exhibit 4 presents registrations of 651+cc motorcycles in the United States, Europe, and Asia-Pacific for 1998–2003. Even though Europe had fewer registrations of 651+cc motorcycles than the United States, it was the world's largest market for motorcycles, with 1.1 million registrations of 125+cc motorcycles in 2002. Registrations of motorcycles with engine displacements greater than 125cc in the largest European markets are presented in Exhibit 5.

Segmentation within the 651+cc Category

Motorcycles in the 651+cc segment were referred to as heavyweights and were grouped into four categories. Standard heavyweight motorcycles were designed for low-cost transportation and lacked many of the features and accessories of more expensive classes of heavyweights. Performance bikes had streamlined styling, low-profile fairings, and seat and handlebar configurations that required the rider to lean forward; they were characterized by responsive handling, rapid acceleration, and high top-end speeds. Custom motorcycles ranged from motorcycles with a custom paint scheme to highly personalized bikes painted with murals or other designs, chromed frames and other components, and accessories not found on stock motorcycles. The chopper, among the more unusual custom styles, was limited only by designers' imaginations but typically had extended forks, high handlebars, a narrow front tire, and a rigid "hardtail" frame design that lacked rear shocks and was stretched longer than normal motorcycles. Another notable feature of custom choppers was that they were almost always built from stock Harley-Davidson motorcycles, sometimes retaining only the engine.

Custom bikes were the largest segment of the U.S. heavyweight market for motorcycles and had become a curiosity for noncyclists. The Discovery Channel regularly aired two programs dedicated to the topic of choppers and other custom vehicles. The names of two custom motorcycle shops, West Coast Choppers (WCC) and Orange County Choppers, frequently made the Internet search engine Lycos's list of 50 most-searched terms. Jesse James, a descendent of the famous American Old West outlaw and owner of West Coast Choppers, also made Lycos's list of most-searched terms. WCC charged between $60,000 and $150,000 for its custom motorcycles, which were usually sold to celebrities such as movie stars, professional athletes, and rock musicians.

Touring bikes were set apart from other categories by creature comforts and accessories that included large fairings, storage compartments, CD players, cruise control, and other features typically found on cars rather than on motorcycles. Touring bikes were popular in the United States since many baby boomers wished to enjoy biking, but with some

Exhibit 4   **Market Shares of the Leading Producers of Motorcycles by Geographic Region for the Heavyweight Segment, 1998–2003 (engine displacement of 651+cc)**

	2003	2002	2001	2000	1999	1998
New U.S. registrations (thousands of units)						
Total market new registrations	461.2	442.3	394.3	340	275.6	227.1
Harley-Davidson new registrations	228.4	209.3	177.4	155.1	134.5	109.1
Buell new registrations	3.5	2.9	2.6	4.2	3.9	3.2
Total company new registrations	231.9	212.2	180.0	159.3	138.4	112.3
Percentage market share						
Harley-Davidson motorcycles	49.5%	47.5%	45.0%	45.6%	48.8%	48.1%
Buell motorcycles	0.8	0.7	0.7	1.2	1.4	1.4
Total Harley-Davidson	50.3%	48.2%	45.7%	46.8%	50.2%	49.5%
Honda	18.4%	19.8%	20.5%	18.5%	16.4%	20.3%
Suzuki	9.8	9.6	10.8	9.3	9.4	10.0
Kawasaki	6.7	6.9	8.0	9.0	10.3	10.1
Yamaha	8.5	8.9	7.9	8.4	7.0	4.2
Other	6.3	6.6	7.1	8.0	6.7	5.9
Total	100.0%	100.0%	100.0%	100.0%	100.0%	100.0%
New European registrations (thousands of units)						
Total market new registrations	323.1	303.5	292.1	293.4	306.7	270.2
Total Harley-Davidson new registrations	26.3	20.1	19.6	19.9	17.8	15.7
Percentage market share						
Total Harley-Davidson	8.1%	6.6%	6.7%	6.8%	5.8%	5.8%
Honda	16.7	21.0	17.4	21.8	22.2	24.1
Yamaha	16.0	17.7	16.4	17.3	18.0	16.3
BMW	15.3	15.1	15.1	13.0	13.0	13.4
Suzuki	15.5	14.8	16.5	14.3	15.4	17.2
Other	28.4	24.8	27.9	26.8	25.6	23.2
Total	100.0%	100.0%	100.0%	100.0%	100.0%	100.0%
New Asia-Pacific registrations (thousands of units)						
Total market new registrations	58.9	63.9	62.1	62.7	63.1	69.2
Total Harley-Davidson new registrations	15.2	13.0	12.7	12.2	11.6	10.3
Percentage market share						
Total Harley-Davidson	25.8%	21.3%	20.4%	19.5%	18.5%	14.8%
Honda	17.8	19.1	17.3	20.4	22.4	28.0
Kawasaki	13.8	15.8	15.6	18.9	19.0	22.1
Yamaha	11.4	13.6	15.8	17.0	19.0	16.0
Suzuki	10.7	10.1	12.8	10.4	9.3	7.9
Other	20.5	20.1	18.1	13.8	11.8	11.2
Total	100.0%	100.0%	100.0%	100.0%	100.0%	100.0%

Source: Harley-Davidson Inc. 10-K reports and annual reports.

Exhibit 5   **Registrations of New Motorcycles in Major European Markets, 1998–2003 (engine displacement of 125+cc)**

Country	1998	1999	2000	2001	2002	2003
Germany	175,937	187,192	170,636	158,270	145,369	138,712
Italy	79,400	103,800	122,085	126,400	129,261	130,224
France	88,500	109,105	103,900	106,802	113,852	N/A
Great Britain	84,500	98,186	93,634	91,543	93,557	N/A
Spain	35,600	39,200	38,052	31,829	35,252	N/A

N/A = Not available.

Sources: Association des Constructeurs Europeens de Motocycles, Brussels; Industrieverband Motorrad Deutschland e.V.

comfort. Comfortable saddles, upright riding positions, and other features found on touring bikes were especially welcomed by those who took cross-country or other long-distance journeys on their motorcycles. Custom and touring motorcycles were less popular outside of the United States since cyclists in other countries were more likely to travel only short distances and did not necessarily identify with the individualist or outlaw image associated with heavyweights in the United States. The largest segment of the heavyweight motorcycle category outside the United States was the performance bike category since most riders in other countries preferred sleek styling and were more interested in speed and handling rather than in comfort and tradition. In addition, motorcyclists in Europe and Asia tended to choose performance bikes over motorcycles in the custom and touring categories because of the high relative prices of such motorcycles. Exhibit 6 presents a regional comparison of motorcycle registrations by heavyweight category for 1998 through 2002.

Competition in the Global Motorcycle Industry

Rivalry in the motorcycle industry centered on performance, styling, breadth of product line, image and reputation, quality of after-the-sale service, and price. Most motorcycle manufacturers had good reputations for performance and styling with the greatest variance between brands occurring in pricing, variety of models, and quality of dealer service. Most cyclists preferred not to purchase specific brands, even if they were attracted to specific models, if the company's dealers did not have trained mechanics or had a reputation for shoddy workmanship or poor parts availability. There was also a great degree of price variability in the industry with comparable models of Japanese motorcycles typically carrying retail prices far below that of U.S.- or European-made motorcycles.

Exhibits 7 and 8 illustrate the difficulty U.S. and European manufacturers had experienced in attracting price-sensitive buyers in Europe. The Japanese producers were able to offer high-performance motorcycles at prices below those of Harley-Davidson, Ducati, Triumph, or Moto Guzzi. BMW had achieved considerable success in Europe, especially in Germany, because of exceptional performance and reputation, a strong dealer network, and regional loyalty to the brand.

Motorcycle manufacturers, like automobile manufacturers, maintained relationships with suppliers to produce or assemble components such as upholstery, tires, engine parts, brake parts, wiring harnesses, shocks, and rims. Almost without exception, the manufacturer designed and manufactured its engines and frames. Design and assembly of motorcycles took place in the manufacturers' home country, and completed motorcycles were exported to country markets where dealer networks had been established.

Consumers typically evaluated brands by talking to other cyclists, reading product reviews, perusing company Web sites, noting ads in print and other media, and noting a manufacturer's performance in competitive events. Typically, consumers had some

Exhibit 6 **Regional Comparison of the 651+cc Motorcycle Market by Segment,* 1998–2002 (percent of units registered)**

	1998	1999	2000	2001	2002
United States					
Custom	58.4%	57.7%	56.6%	58.9%	60.3%
Touring	20.4	21.7	21.1	20.3	20.2
Performance	19.4	18.9	20.4	19.1	17.3
Standard	1.8	1.8	2.0	1.7	2.2
	100.0%	100.0%	100.0%	100.0%	100.0%
Europe					
Custom	22.8%	20.2%	17.6%	17.8%	13.8%
Touring	5.3	5.5	5.2	5.2	4.8
Performance	59.8	58	61.7	59.8	61.2
Standard	12.1	16.3	15.5	17.2	20.2
	100.0%	100.0%	100.0%	100.0%	100.0%
Asia-Pacific					
Custom	18.3%	28.6%	26.7%	23.9%	n/a
Touring	3.9	4.7	3.7	7.2	n/a
Performance	76.1	64.5	66.2	65.5	n/a
Standard	1.7	2.2	3.5	3.4	n/a
	100.0%	100.0%	100.0%	100.0%	n/a

*Category definitions:

Custom: Characterized by "American styling." Often personalized by accessorizing.

Touring: Designed primarily for long trips, with an emphasis on comfort, cargo capacity, and reliability. Often have features such as two-way radios (for communication with passenger), stereo, and cruise control.

Performance: Characterized by quick acceleration, top speed, and handling. Commonly referred to as "sport bikes."

Standard: A basic, no-frills motorcycle with an emphasis on low price.

Source: Harley-Davidson Inc. 2003 and 2002 10-K reports.

ability to negotiate prices with dealers, but most preferred to buy from dealers with good service departments, large parts inventories, and attractive financing programs. Similarly, strong motorcycle dealers preferred to represent manufacturers with good reputations and strong consumer demand, responsive customer service and parts delivery, formal training programs for service technicians, and financing divisions that offered competitive rates and programs.

Consumers purchased motorcycles for various reasons. Some individuals, especially in developing countries, were looking for low-cost transportation. Lightweight motorcycles, mopeds, and scooters were priced inexpensively compared to cars and used far less gasoline. However, motorcycles provided no protection from the elements and were used only for fair-weather transportation by most riders who also owned a car. In the United States and Europe, most consumers who purchased a motorcycle also owned a car and preferred to travel by motorcycle on weekends or other times they were not working. Some in Europe did choose to commute to and from work on motorcycles when weather permitted because of limited parking available in large European cities and the high cost of fuel. Many motorcycle owners, particularly so in the United States, looked at riding as a form of recreation and had given up other sports or hobbies to spend time touring on motorcycles. Many middle-aged bikers in the United States had

Exhibit 7   **Market Shares of the Leading Sellers of Motorcycles in Germany, 2001–2003 (engine displacement of 125+cc)**

Brand	2001 Market Share	2002 Market Share	2003 Market Share
BMW	16.0%	18.1%	19.5%
Suzuki	21.7	20.3	19.2
Yamaha	16.3	16.0	15.9
Honda	16.8	17.3	15.5
Kawasaki	11.1	10.7	10.6
KTM	3.1	3.8	4.4
Harley-Davidson	3.6	3.7	4.2
Ducati	2.8	2.8	2.9
Triumph	2.5	1.8	2.0
Aprilia	1.7	1.5	1.4
Moto Guzzi	0.6	0.7	0.9
Buell	0.4	0.3	0.6
MV/Cagiva	1.2	0.8	0.6
MZ	0.5	0.4	0.3
Sachs	0.3	0.2	0.2
Other	1.4	1.6	1.9
Total	100.0%	100.0%	100.0%

Sources: Kraftfahrtbundesamt; Industrieverband Motorrad Deutschland e.V.

Exhibit 8   **Best-Selling Motorcycle Models in Germany, November 2003**

Rank	Brand	Model	Manufacturers' Recommended Price ($ US)	Year-to-Date 2003 Registrations	Heavyweight Classification
1	BMW	R 1150 GS	$14,500	6,242	Enduro/Touring
2	Suzuki	GSF 1200 (KL)	7,399	4,023	Performance
3	BMW	F 650 GS	8,190	3,524	Enduro/Touring
4	Suzuki	SV 650	6,299	3,444	Standard
5	Yamaha	FZS 600	6,499	3,294	Standard
6	Suzuki	GSF 600	6,299	3,182	Standard
7	Suzuki	GSX-R 1000	10,599	2,836	Performance
8	Kawasaki	Z1000	8,499	2,825	Performance
9	BMW	R 1150 RT	16,290	2,607	Touring
10	BMW	R 1150 R	9,990	2,539	Performance

Sources: Kraftfahrtbundesamt; Industrieverband Motorrad Deutschland e.V.

purchased motorcycles after giving up sports and activities requiring more athleticism or endurance.

REGULATION AND LEGAL CHALLENGES

The motorcycle industry was subject to laws and regulations in all countries where motorcycles were operated. The European Parliament and the European Council included motorcycles in their agreement to reduce exhaust gas values during their March 2002 meeting. The agreement required producers of motorcycles and scooters to reduce pollutants by 60 percent for all new cycles produced after April 2003. A further 60 percent reduction would be required for motorcycles produced after January 2006. Demand for motorcycles in Europe was impacted to a great degree by the implementation of the euro in 2002; prices of motorcycles increased substantially in some countries when the currency exchange took effect. For instance, because Germany's currency was much stronger than that of many other European Union countries, prices of most products and services increased in Germany after the change to the euro since the euro attempted to equalize the differences between currencies. The difficulty in obtaining a driver's license for motorcycles in some European countries also affected demand for motorcycles. German laws required separate automobile and motorcycle licenses for riders of motorcycles larger than 125cc, and France required those applying for motorcycle licenses to have first held an automobile license for two years. Austria's licensing laws were the most restrictive, requiring applicants to first hold an automobile license for five years and to complete six training sessions prior to obtaining a motorcycle license. Motorcycles that produced excessive noise were also under attack in most European countries.

In the United States, motorcycle producers were subject to certification by the Environmental Protection Agency (EPA) for compliance with emission and noise standards, as well as agencies in some states imposing more stringent noise and emission standards. The California Air Resources Board (CARB) had outlined new tailpipe emission standards that would go into effect in 2004 and 2008. The EPA developed new emission standards that would go into effect in 2006 and 2010 to match national standards with those in California. Motorcycle producers in the United States were also required to meet the product safety standards imposed by the National Highway Traffic Safety Administration (NHTSA).

Also in the United States, many motorcyclists found that their health insurance providers excluded coverage for any injuries sustained while on a motorcycle. The American Motorcyclists Association (AMA) had successfully petitioned the U.S. Senate to pass a bill in October 2003 that would prohibit insurance companies from denying coverage to someone hurt while riding a motorcycle, a snowmobile, or an all-terrain vehicle. Insurance companies had based their policies on NHTSA statistics that found motorcycling to be much more dangerous than traveling by car. While traffic fatalities per 100 million vehicle miles traveled hit a historic low in 2002, motorcycle fatalities had increased for a fifth consecutive year, to reach 3,244 deaths. There were 42,815 traffic fatalities in 2002 involving occupants of automobiles. Fatalities involving motorcyclists ages 50 and older increased by 26 percent during 2002—a higher rate of increase than any other age demographic. State legislatures in some states where helmets were optional had attempted to force motorcyclists who chose not to wear helmets to become mandatory organ donors. However, the AMA and its membership had successfully stopped all such attempts to pass mandatory organ donor laws.

HARLEY-DAVIDSON'S STRATEGY FOR COMPETING IN THE MOTORCYCLE INDUSTRY

Harley-Davidson was reincorporated in 1981 after it was purchased from AMF by 13 of its managers through a leveraged buyout (LBO). The management team's main focus at the time was to preserve jobs, but its members soon realized the company would need to be rebuilt from the ground up to survive. The company's market share in the United States had fallen to 3 percent, primarily because its products were unreliable and had poorer performance relative to less-expensive Japanese motorcycles. In addition, its network of dealers ran greasy, run-down shops that many people didn't feel comfortable visiting. Upon assessing the company's situation, the management team concluded that a strong allegiance to the Harley brand by many bikers was the company's only resource strength. However, when managers began to meet with customers, they found that long-time Harley riders felt cheated by the company and were angry about the lack of attention to product quality and customer service under AMF ownership. Some of the most loyal Harley riders refused to call models produced in the 1970s Harleys, preferring to label them as AMFs. After the LBO, Harley management tried to win over previous customers by attending any function at which motorcyclists congregated. The company's director of communications at the time commented in a 2003 interview with a trade publication, "At first we found that our customers didn't like us, and they didn't trust us."[6] However, the distrust subsided when Harley owners saw their suggestions being implemented by the company.

Harley-Davidson's turnaround strategy including improving product quality by adopting Japanese management practices, abandoning a reliance on advertising in favor of promotions at motorcycle rallies, and improving its dealer network to broaden its appeal to new customers. After hearing complaints about dealers from Harley riders at rallies and other bike events, Harley-Davidson conducted a pilot program with two dealers in Milwaukee that called for the dealers to build clean, attractive stores to showcase the company's improved motorcycles and display apparel and other merchandise that cyclists might wish to purchase. The two dealerships recaptured their investments within 18 months, while other dealers struggled. The pilot program led to new or remodeled dealerships across the Harley-Davidson network and helped the company enter into a new product category. Harley showrooms offered a large assortment of clothing items and accessories—for example, leather jackets, T-shirts, helmets, and boots—in addition to new motorcycles. In 2003 Harley-Davidson introduced 1,200 new clothing items and licensed its name to more than 100 manufacturers making everything from Harley-Davidson Edition Ford F-150 pickups to Harley Barbie dolls. Apparel and accessories were so important

to the company and its dealers that in 2003 every dealer had a fitting room.

Cultivating Loyalty Through HOG Membership

After Harley-Davidson's product quality issues had been resolved, the company focused on cultivating the mystique of Harley ownership. The company formed Harley Owners Groups (HOGs) in 1983 to provide Harley owners with local chapters through which they could socialize and ride with other owners. Harley-Davidson established HOGs in cities where dealers were located, but did not interfere with HOG operations or try to use the organization in a self-serving way. The company's primary interest in setting up the chapters was to give motorcycle buyers a sense of community. Management understood that once new owners came to feel they belonged to the Harley community, they would bring new buyers to the company without any encouragement from Harley-Davidson.

The company provided each new Harley buyer with a free membership to a HOG where they could not only meet other area bikers but also learn the ins and outs of the biker world. HOGs also organized rides, raised money for charities, and participated in nationwide HOG events. Owners were required to renew their free memberships each year to ensure that only active participants would be on chapter roles. The HOG organization started with 33,000 members in 1983 and had grown to 793,000 members in 1,200 chapters in 2003. The company sponsored about 100 HOG rallies in 2003, with thousands of additional events organized by local chapters.

Harley's Image and Appeal with Baby Boomers

Even though Harley sold many motorcycles to construction workers, mechanics, and other blue-collar workers, Harley riders included a great many accountants, lawyers, bankers, and corporate executives. In 2003, Harley-Davidson's typical customer was a 46-year-old male earning $78,000 per year. The company had successfully added upscale consumers to its list of customers without alienating traditional bikers. Some of the more traditional bikers did complain about the new breed of "bean counter Harley owners," sometimes calling them "rubbers"—rich urban bikers. Such concern had been calmed to some degree by William G. Davidson's continuing involvement with the company. "Willie G." was the grandson of the company's cofounder and, as chief designer, had designed every motorcycle for the company since the 1960s. Willie G. was an "old-school" biker himself and rationalized the company's alliance with upscale baby boomers with comments such as "There's a lot of beaners, but they're out on the motorcycles, which is a beautiful thing."[7]

Part of the appeal of HOG membership was that new motorcyclists could experience freedom of the open road, much like a Hells Angel might, if only during occasional weekends when the weather was nice. Some middle-aged professionals purchased Harleys because riding was an opportunity to recreate and relax without being reminded of their daily responsibilities. Belonging to a HOG or other riding group was different from joining a country club or other club dominated by upper-income families; as the CEO of a Fortune 500 company explained, "Nobody cares what anybody else does. We share a common bond of freedom on a bike." This same Harley owner claimed that after a few hours of riding, he forgets he's a CEO.[8] Another affluent Harley owner suggested that Harley owners from all walks of life shared the brotherhood of the open road: "It doesn't matter if you make $10,000 a year or $300,000."[9] Others suggested that Harley ownership gave you an identity and provided you with a close group of friends in an increasingly anonymous culture.

However, other Harley owners were lured by the appeal of Harley-Davidson's outlaw image. The editor of *AARP Magazine* believed that baby boomers purchased Harleys because of a desire to feel "forever young."[10] The *AARP Magazine* editor said that riding a Harley helped take boomers back to a time when they had less responsibility. "You saw 'Easy Rider.' As a kid, you had a bit of a wild period in the '70s and you associate the motorcycle with that. But you got married. You had kids and a career. Now you can afford this. It's a safe way to live out a midlife crisis. It's a lot safer than running off with a stewardess."[11] In fact, many of Harley-Davidson's competitors have claimed that Harley sells lifestyles, not motorcycles. Harley-Davidson CEO Jeffrey Bleustein commented on the appeal of the company's motorcycles by stating, "Harley-Davidson stands for freedom, adventure, individual expression and being a little on the edge, a little bit naughty. People are drawn to the brand for those reasons."[12]

The desire to pose as a Hells Angel, Peter Fonda's Wyatt character, or Brando's Johnny helped Harley-Davidson sell more than 290,000 motorcycles and over $200 million in general merchandise in 2003. Many of Harley-Davidson's 1,400 dealers dedicated as much as 75 percent of their floor space to apparel and accessories, with most suggesting that between 25 and 40 percent of their annual earnings came from the sale of leather jackets, chaps, boots, caps, helmets, and other accessories. One dealer offered her opinion of what drove merchandise sales by commenting, "Today's consumer tends to be a little more affluent, and they want the total look."[13] The dealer also said that approximately 5 percent of the dealership's apparel sales were to non–bike owners who wanted the biker image. Even though some high-income baby boomers wanted to be mistaken from a distance for Hells Angels' "1 percenters"—the most rebellious 1 percent of the population—for most it was all show. When looking out at the thousands of leather-clad bikers attending Harley-Davidson's 2003 Memorial Day centennial celebration in Milwaukee, a Harley owner said, "The truth is, this is mostly professional people . . . People want to create an image. Everybody has an alter side, an alter ego. And this is a chance to have that."[14]

Another Harley owner who had ridden his Heritage Softail from his home in Sioux Falls, South Dakota, to attend the centennial event commented on his expectations for revelry during the four-day celebration by pointing out, "Bikers like to party pretty big. It's still a long way to go before you forget the image of the Hells Angels."[15] However, weekend bikers were quite different from the image they emulated. The Hells Angels continued to be linked to organized crime into 2003, with nine Hells Angels members being convicted in September 2003 of drug trafficking and murdering at least 160 people, most of whom were from rival gangs.[16] Similarly, Hells Angels organizations in Europe had been linked to drug trafficking and dozens of murders.[17] Fifty-seven Angels in the United States were arrested in December 2003 for crimes such as theft of motorcycles, narcotics trafficking, and firearms and explosives trafficking following a two-year investigation of the motorcycle club by the Bureau of Alcohol, Tobacco, Firearms and Explosives.[18]

Harley-Davidson balanced its need to promote freedom and rebellion against its need to distance the company from criminal behavior. Its Web site pointed out that "the vast majority of riders throughout the history of Harley-Davidson were law-abiding citizens," and the company archivist proposed, "Even those who felt a certain alienation from society were not lawless anarchists, but people who saw the motorcycle as a way to express both their freedom and their identity."[19] When looking at the rows of Harleys glistening in the sun in front of his Southern California roadside café, the longtime proprietor of one of the biggest biker shrines in the United States commented, "There used to be some mean bastards on those bikes. I guess the world has changed."[20] A Harley-Davidson dealer commented that dealers considered hardcore bikers "1 percenters" because they made up less than 1 percent of a dealer's annual sales. The dealer found that very affluent buyers made up about 10 percent of sales, with the remainder of customers making between $40,000 and $100,000 per year.[21]

Harley-Davidson's Product Line

Unlike Honda and Yamaha, Harley-Davidson did not produce scooters and mopeds, nor did it manufacture motorcycles with engine displacements less than 651cc. In addition, Harley-Davidson did not produce dirt bikes or performance bikes like those offered by Kawasaki and Suzuki. Of the world's major motorcycle producers, BMW produced bikes that most closely resembled Harley-Davidson's traditional line, although BMW also offered a large number of performance bikes. In 2004, Harley-Davidson's touring and custom motorcycles were grouped into five families: Sportster, Dyna Glide, Softail, Touring, and the VRSC V-Rod. The Sportster, Dyna Glide, and VRSC models were manufactured in the company's Kansas City, Missouri, plant, while Softail and Touring models were manufactured in York, Pennsylvania. Harley-Davidson considered the Sportster, Dyna Glide, and VRSC models custom bikes, while Softails and Touring models fell into the Touring industry classification. Sportsters and Dyna Glides each came in four model variations, while Softails came in six variations and Touring bikes came in seven basic configurations. The VRSC V-Rod came in two basic styles. Harley-Davidson produced three models of its Buell performance bikes in its East Troy, Wisconsin, plant. In 2004, Harley Sportsters carried retail prices ranging from $6,495 to $8,675; Dyna Glide models sold at price points between $11,995 and $16,580; VRSC V-Rods

sold between $16,895 and $17,995; Softails were offered between $13,675 and $17,580; and the Road King and Electra Glide touring models sold at prices between $16,995 and $20,405. Consumers could also order custom Harleys through the company's Custom Vehicle Operations (CVO) unit, started in 1999. Customization and accessories on CVO models could add as much as $10,000 to the retail price of Harley-Davidson motorcycles. Images of Harley-Davidson's five product families and CVO models can be viewed at www.harley-davidson.com.

Honda, Kawasaki, Suzuki, and Yamaha had all introduced touring models that were very close replicas of Harley Sportsters, Dyna Glides, Road Kings, and Electra Glides. The Japanese producers had even copied Harley's signature V-twin engine and had tuned their dual-crankpin designs in an attempt to copy the distinctive sound of a Harley-Davidson engine. However, even with prices up to 50 percent less on comparable models, none of the Japanese producers had been able to capture substantial market share from Harley-Davidson in the United States or in their home markets. (Refer back to Exhibit 4 for a breakdown of market shares in the heavyweight segment in the U.S., European, and Asia-Pacific regions.) Indian Motorcycle Corporation had experienced similar difficulties gaining adequate market share in the U.S. heavyweight segment and ceased its operations for a second time in September 2003.

Harley-Davidson's difficulties in luring buyers in the performance segment of the industry were similar to challenges that Japanese motorcycle producers had encountered in their attempts to gain market share in the custom and touring categories of the U.S. heavyweight motorcycle segment. Harley-Davidson had co-developed and later purchased Buell to have a product that might appeal to motorcyclists in the United States who were in their 20s and did not identify with the *Easy Rider* or Hells Angels images or who did not find Harley-Davidson's traditional styling appealing. Harley management also believed that Buell's performance street-racer-style bikes could help it gain market share in Europe, where performance bikes were highly popular. The Buell brand competed exclusively in the performance category against models offered by Honda, Yamaha, Kawasaki, Suzuki, and lesser-known European brands such as Moto Guzzi, Ducati, and Triumph. Buell prices began at $4,595 for its Blast model to better compete with Japanese motorcycles on price as well as on performance and styling. Buell's Lighting and Firebolt models were larger, faster motorcycles and retailed for between $9,000 and $11,000. The VSRC V-Rod, with its liquid-cooled, Porsche-designed engine, was also designed to appeal to buyers in the performance segment of the industry, both in the United States and Europe.

As of 2004, Harley-Davidson had not gained a significant share of the performance motorcycle segment in the United States or Europe. Some industry analysts criticized Harley-Davidson's dealers for the lackluster sales of V-Rod and Buell models since most dealers did little to develop employees' sales techniques. Demand for Harleys had exceeded supply since the early 1990s, and most dealers' sales activities were limited to taking orders and maintaining a waiting list. In addition, most Harley-Davidson dealers had been able to charge $2,000 to $4,000 over the suggested retail price for new Harley-Davidson motorcycles, although most dealers had begun to sell Harleys at sticker price in 2003. Harley-Davidson's revenues by product group are shown below:

Harley-Davidson Revenues by Product Group (in millions)

	2003	2002	2001
Harley-Davidson motorcycles	$3,621.5	$3,161.0	$2,671.3
Buell motorcycles	76.1	66.9	61.7
Total motorcycles	$3,697.6	$3,227.9	$2,733.0
Motorcycle Parts and Accessories	712.8	629.2	509.6
General Merchandise	211.4	231.5	163.9
Other	2.5	2.4	0.3
Net revenue	$4,624.3	$4,091.0	$3,406.8

Source: Harley-Davidson Inc. 2002 and 2003 annual reports.

The number of Harley-Davidson and Buell motorcycles shipped annually between 1998 and 2003 is presented in Exhibit 9.

Distribution and Sales in North America, Europe, and Asia-Pacific

Harley-Davidson's dealers were responsible for operating showrooms where motorcycles could be examined and test-ridden, stocking parts and accessories that existing owners might need, operating service departments, and selling biking merchandise such as apparel, boots, helmets, and various Harley-Davidson-branded gift items. Some Harley owners felt such strong connections to the brand that they either gave or asked for Harley gifts for birthdays, weddings, and anniversaries. Some Harley owners had even been married at Harley-Davidson dealerships or at HOG rallies. Harley-Davidson dealers were also responsible for distributing newsletters and promoting rallies for local HOG chapters. The

10,000-member Buell Riders Adventure Group (BRAG) was also supported by Harley-Davidson dealers.

Harley mechanics and other dealership personnel were trained at the Harley-Davidson University (HDU) in Milwaukee, where they took courses in such subjects as retail management, inventory control, merchandising, customer service, diagnostics, maintenance, and engine service techniques. More than 17,000 dealership employees took courses at the company's university in 2002. Harley-Davidson also provided in-dealership courses through its Web-based distance learning program. In 2002, HDU held 665 instructor-led classes, 115 online classes, and had participation in their courses by 96 percent of the company's dealers.

The company also held demo rides in various locations throughout the United States, and many Harley dealers offered daily rentals designed to help novices decide whether they really wanted a motorcycle. Some dealers also rented motorcycles for longer periods to individuals who wished to take long-distance trips. Harley-Davidson motorcycles could

Exhibit 9   **Annual Shipments of Harley-Davidson and Buell Motorcycles, 1998–2003**

	2003	2002	2001	2000	1999	1998
Harley-Davidson						
Sportster	57,165	51,171	50,814	46,213	41,870	33,892
Custom*	151,405	141,769	118,303	100,875	87,806	77,434
Touring	82,577	70,713	65,344	57,504	47,511	39,492
	291,147	263,653	234,461	204,592	177,187	150,818
Domestic	237,656	212,833	186,915	158,817	135,614	110,902
International	53,491	50,820	47,546	45,775	41,573	39,916
	291,147	263,653	234,461	204,592	177,187	150,818
Buell						
Buell (exc. Blast)	8,784	6,887	6,436	5,043	7,767	6,334
Buell Blast	1,190	4,056	3,489	5,416	—	—
	9,974	10,943	9,925	10,189	7,767	6,334

*Custom includes Softail, Dyna Glide, and VRSC.

Source: Harley-Davidson Inc. 2002 and 2003 annual reports.

also be rented from third parties like EagleRider—the world's largest renter of Harleys, with 29 locations in the United States and Europe. Harley-Davidson's Riders Edge motorcycle training courses were also offered by quite a few dealers in North America, Europe, and Asia-Pacific. The company had found that inexperienced riders and women were much more likely to purchase motorcycles after taking a training course. Harley-Davidson management believed the 25-hour Riders Edge program had contributed to the company's increased sales to women, which had increased from 2 percent of total sales prior to the adoption of the program to 9 percent in 2003.

In 2003, Harley-Davidson motorcycles were sold by 644 independently owned and operated dealerships across the United States. Buell motorcycles were also sold by 436 of these dealers. There were no Buell-only dealerships, and 81 percent of Harley dealers in the United States sold Harley-Davidson motorcycles exclusively. The company also sold apparel and merchandise in about 50 nontraditional retail locations such as malls, airports, and tourist locations. The company's apparel was also available seasonally in about 20 temporary locations in the United States where there was significant tourist traffic. The company also had three nontraditional merchandise outlets in Canada, where it had 76 independent dealers and one Buell

dealership. Thirty-two of its Canadian Harley dealers also sold Buell motorcycles.

Harley-Davidson had 161 independent dealers in Japan, 50 dealers and three distributors in the Australia/New Zealand market and seven other dealers scattered in smaller East and Southeast Asian markets. Only 73 of Harley-Davidson's Asia-Pacific also sold Buell motorcycles. The company also had two dealers that sold Buell but not Harley-Davidson motorcycles. Harley-Davidson motorcycles were sold in 17 Latin American countries by 32 dealerships. The company did not have a dealer for its Buell motorcycles in Latin America, but had 13 retail stores carrying only apparel and merchandise in the region.

The company's European distribution division based in the United Kingdom served 32 countries in Europe, the Middle East, and Africa. The European region had 436 independent dealers, with 313 choosing to also carry Buell motorcycles. Buell motorcycles were also sold in Europe by 10 dealers that were not Harley dealers. Harley-Davidson also had 26 nontraditional merchandise retail locations in Europe.

Exhibit 10 presents the company's revenues by geographic region, along with the division of assets in the United States and abroad and a breakdown of financial services revenues by region. The company's financial services unit provided retail financing

Exhibit 10   **Harley-Davidson's Net Revenues and Long-Lived Assets by Business Group and Geographic Region, 2000–2003**

	2003	2002	2001	2000
Motorcycles net revenue				
United States	$3,807,707	$3,416,432	$2,809,763	$2,357,972
Europe	419,052	337,463	301,729	285,372
Japan	173,547	143,298	141,181	148,684
Canada	134,319	121,257	96,928	93,352
Other foreign countries	89,649	72,520	57,185	57,966
	$4,624,274	$4,090,970	$3,406,786	$2,943,346
Financial services income				
United States	$ 260,551	$ 199,380	$ 172,593	$ 132,684
Europe	8,834	4,524	1,214	655
Canada	10,074	7,596	7,738	6,796
	$ 279,459	$ 211,500	$ 181,545	$ 140,135
Long-lived assets				
United States	$1,400,772	$1,151,702	$1,021,946	$ 856,746
Other foreign countries	41,804	36,138	33,234	27,844
	$1,442,576	$1,187,840	$1,055,180	$ 884,590

Source: Harley-Davidson Inc. 2002 and 2003 10-K reports.

to consumers and wholesale financial services to dealers, including inventory floor plans, real estate loans, computer loans, and showroom remodeling loans.

CHALLENGES CONFRONTING HARLEY-DAVIDSON AS IT ENTERED ITS SECOND CENTURY

As Harley-Davidson entered its second century in 2004, the company not only celebrated a successful centennial celebration that brought more than 700,000 of Harley's most loyal customers to Milwaukee but also a successful year with record shipments, revenues, and earnings. New capacity had allowed the company's shipments to increase to more than 290,000 units, which drove annual revenues to $4.6 billion and net earnings to nearly $761 million. The company's planned 350,000-square-foot expansion of its York, Pennsylvania, plant would allow the

company to increase production to 400,000 units by 2007. However, there was some concern that the company might not need the additional capacity.

Some market analysts had begun to believe Harley-Davidson's stock was approaching its apex because of the aging of its primary baby boomer customer group. Between 1993 and 2003, the average age of the company's customers had increased from 38 to 46. The average age of purchasers of other brands of motorcycles in 2003 was 38. Some analysts suspected, that within the next 5 to 10 years, fewer baby boomers would be interested in riding motorcycles and Harley's sales might begin to decline. Generation X buyers were not a large enough group to keep Harley's sales at the 2003 level, which would cause the company to rely on Generation Y (or echo boomer) consumers. However, most Generation Y motorcyclists had little interest in the company's motorcycles and did not identify with the *Easy Rider* or outlaw biker images that were said to appeal to baby boomers. The company's V-Rod motorcycle had won numerous awards for its styling and performance, but its $17,000-plus price tag kept most 20-year-olds away from Harley showrooms. Similarly, Buell motorcycles were critically acclaimed in terms of performance and styling but had been unable to draw performance-minded consumers in the United States or Europe away from Japanese street-racing-style bikes to any significant degree.

Europe was the largest market for motorcycles overall, and the second largest market for heavyweight motorcycles, but Harley-Davidson had struggled in building share in the region. In some ways the company's 6+ percent market share in Europe was impressive since only 4.8 percent of motorcycles purchased in 2002 were touring cycles and custom cycles accounted for only 13.8 percent of motorcycles sold in Europe during 2002. The V-Rod's greatest success was in Europe, but neither the V-Rod nor any other HD model had become one of the top-10 best-selling models in any major European market.

There was also some concern that Harley-Davidson's 14-month production run had caused an unfavorable short-term production problem since the company's waiting list, which required a two-year wait in the late 1990s, had fallen to about 90 days beginning in mid-2003. The overavailability of 2003 models had caused Harley-Davidson's management to adopt a 0 percent down payment financing program that began at midyear 2003 and would run through February 2004. When asked about the program during a television interview, Harley-Davidson CEO Jeffery Bleustein justified it by noting, "It's not zero percent financing, as many people understood it to be, its zero dollars down, and normal financing. The idea there was to get the attention of some of the people who aren't riding Harleys and are used to a world of other motorcycles where there's always a financing program of some sort going on. We just wanted to get their attention."[22] By year-end 2003, dealer inventories had declined to about 2,000 units and many dealers again began charging premiums over list price, but not the $2,000–$4,000 premiums charged in prior years.

Endnotes

[1]As quoted in "Analyst Says Harley's Success Had Been to Drive into Buyers' Hearts," *Canadian Press Newswire,* July 14, 2003.
[2]As quoted in January 21, 2004, press release.
[3]As quoted in "Wings of Desire," *The Independent,* August 27, 2003.
[4]As quoted in "Born to Raise Hell," *BBC News Online,* August 14, 2000.
[5]"Wheel Life Experiences," *Whole Pop Magazine Online.*
[6]As quoted in "Will Your Customers Tattoo Your Logo?" *Trailer/Body Builders,* March 1, 2003, p. 5.
[7]As quoted in "Will Harley-Davidson Hit the Wall?" *Fortune,* July 22, 2002.
[8]As quoted in "Even Corporate CEOs Buy Into the Harley-Davidson Mystique, *Milwaukee Journal-Sentinel,* August 24, 2003.
[9]As quoted in "Harley-Davidson Goes Highbrow at Annual Columbia, S.C., H.O.G. Rally," *The State,* September 26, 2003.
[10]As quoted in "Even Corporate CEOs."
[11]Ibid.
[12]As quoted in "Milwaukee-Based Harley-Davidson Rides into Future with Baby Boomers Aboard," *The News-Sentinel,* August 5, 2003.
[13]As quoted in "Harley-Davidson Fans Sport Motorcycle Style," *Detroit Free Press,* August 28, 2003.
[14]As quoted in "Bikers Go Mainstream 100 Years On," *Global News Wire,* September 11, 2003.
[15]Ibid.
[16]"Nine Montreal Hells Angels Sentenced to 10 to 15 Years in Prison," *CNEWS,* September 23, 2003.
[17]"Hells Angels: Easy Riders or Criminal Gang?," *BBC News,* January 2, 2004.
[18]"Feds Raid Hells Angels' Clubhouses," *CBSNews.com,* December 4, 2003.
[19]As quoted in "Wings of Desire," *Global News Wire,* August 27, 2003.
[20]Ibid.
[21]Interview with Mobile, Alabama, Harley-Davidson dealership personnel.
[22]As quoted in a CNNfn interview conducted on *The Money Gang,* June 11, 2003.

H A R V A R D | **B U S I N E S S** | **S C H O O L**

9-803-133
REV: MARCH 11, 2003

JAMES L. HESKETT

Southwest Airlines 2002: An Industry Under Siege

Amid Crippled Rivals, Southwest Again Tries To Spread Its Wings; Low-Fare Airline Maintains Service, Mulls Expansion In Risky Bid for Traffic

> —Front Page Headline, *The Wall Street Journal*, October 11, 2001

The Age of "Wal-Mart" Airlines Crunches the Biggest Carriers; Low-Cost Rivals Win Converts As Business Travelers Seek Alternatives to Lofty Fares

> —Front Page Headline, *The Wall Street Journal*, June 18, 2002

Vaunted Southwest Slips In On-Time Performance; Airline Famous for Reliability Now Ranks Next-to-Last

> —Page D1 Headline, *The Wall Street Journal*, September 25, 2002

Having weathered an unimaginable series of events during the past 15 months, the top management team at Southwest Airlines engaged in a series of discussions late in 2002 intended to insure sound strategic decisions in the face of industry setbacks, volatile responses on the part of competitors, the preservation of a culture formed around a charismatic founder/leader who had turned over the CEO's job to a successor, and a series of government directives that made it increasingly difficult for Southwest to implement an operating strategy that had differentiated it from its competition. As Colleen Barrett, president and chief operating officer, put it at one gathering of the top management team, "Recent events have made it increasingly difficult to live up to the promise to customers in our ads that 'You are now free to move about the country.'"

Changes in the airline operating environment after the terrorist attacks of September 11, 2001 were thought by some on Southwest's management team to make it more difficult for the airline to maintain its distinctive competitive position. For example, industry bailout efforts by Congress were intended to help Southwest's competitors that were in the worst financial condition. The need to respond to constantly changing security directives made it harder for employees to create and convey the Southwest SPIRIT. More recently, Southwest's organization had increased efforts to maintain its relatively high on-time arrival performance levels while its competitors' levels had risen. Southwest's managers attributed this largely to the addition of time to competitors' flight schedules, but it was creating the perception that Southwest's service levels were declining in relation to those of its competitors.

A series of important management decisions had positioned Southwest to resume its pre-9/11 growth. Just what form that growth might take was subject to discussion.

The Southwest Story

Southwest Airlines was founded in 1967 by Rollin King and Herb Kelleher in response to a need for increased capacity on major travel routes between major Texas cities. Although the routes were served by large "through" carriers such as American Airlines and Braniff International, often there were insufficient seats on flights making intermediate stops in Texas while arriving from cities outside Texas or departing for destinations outside the state. Because of the demand for seats on the intrastate legs of those flights, fares were high.

The Founding Strategy

Because federal regulation of the airline industry made it difficult to start an airline providing interstate service, Southwest's founders decided to create an intrastate carrier connecting Dallas, Houston, and San Antonio, Texas, roughly an hour's flying time apart from one another. Their strategy was centered around costs low enough to enable Southwest to establish fares below the cost of driving a vehicle over the same route. With three new Boeing 737s bought at favorable prices because of overproduction, Southwest finally flew its first flights on June 18, 1971 on two legs of what would become a triangular route connecting the three metro areas. Based at Love Field in Dallas and with a need to get attention, the airline's new president, Lamar Muse, adopted the "love" theme in executing its strategy. As a result, drinks served on board were called "love potions," ticket machines were called "love machines," and cabin "hostesses" (there were no males at that time) were selected for their striking appearance and dressed in suits with "hot pants" and boots (the fashion rage at the time). The hostesses were featured in what today would be called highly sexist ads extolling the distinctive features of the airline, such as stewardesses with seductive voices intoning "what you get at Southwest is me."

Southwest's point-to-point service enabled it to achieve high levels of on-time service. Its frequent departures enabled passengers to catch a later flight if they happened to miss one, a feature valued by frequent business fliers to whom Southwest hoped to cater. And its selection of older, less congested airports located more conveniently for business travelers allowed Southwest to achieve faster turnaround times at lower costs.

To achieve frequent departures with just four planes and three cities, turnaround times had to be minimized. This required that employees be given the latitude to do whatever might be necessary to get a plane turned around in the targeted time of 15 minutes; thus, early union contract job descriptions were negotiated with the open-ended clause "and whatever else might be needed to perform the service," a practice that remained in succeeding years.

All of this was done with an emphasis on fun for employees and travelers. Ground and in-flight personnel were encouraged to be creative in the way they delivered required announcements to passengers. Some sang the messages; others delivered them in dialect (such as an Arnold Schwarzenegger-like "You vill sit back. You vill relax. You vill enjoy this flight. Hasta la vista, baby") or in Donald Duck-speak. On early flights, passengers who could produce the largest holes in their socks were recognized and rewarded. In-flight contests were conducted to see how many passengers could be fitted into the bathroom at one time. And holidays were celebrated with costumes and giveaways. This emphasized the selection of employees who could be empathetic and bring pleasing personalities to the job.

Competitive Response

Southwest's principal competitors, Braniff International Airways and Trans Texas Airways (later Texas International Airlines), responded immediately. They first asked the Texas courts to enjoin issuance of Southwest's intrastate operating certificate. Then they lobbied and litigated to get the local and federal government (and courts) to force Southwest to abandon Love Field near downtown Dallas and move with other airlines to the newly opened Dallas-Fort Worth International Airport much farther from downtown Dallas. On yet another front, they initiated low-price fare "sales" intended to make it difficult for Southwest to get a foothold in the market. They failed on all three initiatives.

In one pivotal incident, on February 1, 1973, before Southwest had achieved profitability, Braniff International initiated a 60-day "half-price sale" of tickets between Dallas and Houston, offering tickets at $13 (substantially below the full cost of the service) as opposed to Southwest's $26 fare. With little knowledge of whether the sale would be extended until Southwest might be forced to discontinue service, Southwest's management countered with an ad proclaiming that "nobody's going to shoot Southwest out of the sky for a lousy $13" and offering customers an unusual alternative. They could ask to pay either $26 or $13 for exactly the same seats on Southwest flights. Those requesting $26 tickets were rewarded with gifts such as ice buckets or fifths of whiskey. The ploy worked. Fully 80% of customers requested $26 tickets. The first day of the offer generated the most traffic on Southwest up to that point. Barrett remarked, "At least for one month, we became Chivas Regal's biggest distributor." Within days, Braniff announced the discontinuance of its sale. Yet another of the legends for which the company would become known was forged.

Southwest's Takeoff

When Congress passed the Airline Deregulation Act in 1978, making it possible for airlines to begin flying new interstate routes without regulatory permission, Southwest was ready to extend its route network. Its only constraint would prove to be the so-called Wright Amendment, attached to the International Air Transportation Competition Act of 1979. It restricted interstate flights out of Love Field to the four states contiguous to Texas and was supported by those who had sought unsuccessfully to force Southwest earlier to move its operations to Dallas-Fort Worth International Airport. When Southwest did initiate service to noncontiguous states in 1982, it was from its Texas stations other than Love Field, a practice that it continued to follow subsequently.

Shortly after deregulation, however, a policy was adopted that, in spite of expansion opportunities, an effort would be made to manage the annual growth rate in aircraft capacity to about 10% to 15%. This was done to insure that the organization could maintain a strong balance sheet and, as senior managers often said, "manage in good times in order to survive in bad times."

In its only significant departure from its growth policy, in 1993 Southwest acquired Morris Air, a regional carrier based in Salt Lake City established on the Southwest model, and retained seven of Morris's operating stations, all new to the Southwest network. The routes of the two airlines were complementary and enabled Southwest to extend its service for the first time into the Northwest. The acquisition did, however, require the consolidation of two organizations with somewhat different management philosophies. For example, Morris Air's leadership had been successful in its efforts to avoid unionization while Southwest, embracing the idea of partnering with unions, had become the most heavily unionized airline in the industry and the most strike free.[1] Morris Air was only the

---

[1] Few of Morris's senior management people remained with Southwest. June Morris joined Southwest's board of directors. The only other Morris senior officer who joined Southwest was David Neeleman. He remained only a few months. After

second acquisition Southwest had made at that time, the other having been the acquisition of Muse Air in 1985, which was operated for a short time as a separate and independent company.

Southwest's growth was steady in the face of increasing requests from cities hoping to experience what had become known in government circles as "the Southwest effect." This effect inevitably resulted from Southwest's policy of pricing its service to compete with auto travel. It required that a fare structure be established that was often 70% below that being offered by other airlines at the time of Southwest's entry into a market. The result was often a 1,000% increase in traffic on the newly served city-pair markets in one year or less. Even at a time when the list of cities requesting the airline's service had grown to more than 50, Southwest chose to enter only two or three new cities each year in addition to filling out its existing network of point-to-point flights. (**Exhibit 1** contains a 2002 route map along with information about markets served by the airline.)

Southwest's strategy created a winning model for profits as well. After breaking even less than two years after its founding in 1971, the airline had enjoyed 30 consecutive years of profit beginning in 1973, a record unmatched by any airline in the world. (Financial and related information can be found in **Exhibits 2** and **3**.) Its stock, floated in an initial over-the-counter offering in 1971 and later on the American and New York Stock Exchanges with the trading symbol LUV, turned in, according to *Money* Magazine, the best performance of any stock in the Standard & Poor's 500 during that time.

This performance was bound to attract other airlines founded on some of the same beliefs. One such airline was People Express, based in Newark, New Jersey and established in 1980 with a lean organization including almost no staff. It was designed to provide a low-fare, bare-bones service aimed at college students and other pleasure travelers who were willing to pay for all amenities such as checked baggage and on-board refreshments in return for the lowest fares in markets served by the airline. The company grew rapidly both through internal growth and the acquisition of other struggling airlines. However, its failure to meet profit goals led to an unsuccessful effort to reposition the airline for business travelers at about the same time that full-fare competitors began to use their sophisticated reservation and yield-management systems to price services more competitively. While People's leadership blamed larger competitors for its subsequent demise, others felt that management had sown the seeds of its own destruction through simultaneous efforts to grow through acquisition, revamp its information systems, and reposition itself in the marketplace.

Although Southwest had been dismissed as a niche player and was able to "fly under the radar" for a number of years, by the mid-1990s major airlines were responding with the equivalent of lower-fare "fighting brands" such as Continental Lite in the southeast United States, the United Shuttle on the West Coast, and Delta Express and US Airways MetroJet on the East Coast. As they spread their routes, competition from these airlines temporarily depressed Southwest's profitability in 1995. However, it was thought that because they were spawned by full-service airlines with attendant problems of inherited management beliefs, cultures, and labor policies or route structures designed in part to connect through parents' hubs, lower-fare rivals created by the largest airlines were unable to achieve acceptable levels of profit. Southwest's management was so proud of its employees' culture that it periodically hosted "best practice" teams from all industries that wanted to discuss hiring,

---

serving out his five-year noncompete with the merged airlines, he formed JetBlue Airline in 1999. The best-financed start-up in airline history, JetBlue became profitable just six months after it began operations and was thought by some to be a potential future Southwest competitor. JetBlue, a nonunion organization operating substantially longer flights than Southwest, sought to differentiate customer service and high aircraft and labor productivity through extensive use of technology. For example, everything from passenger ticketing and check-in to in-flight entertainment was based on technological solutions. Similarly, information technology was used extensively as a substitute for front-line coordination of the efforts of ground crews to achieve "the perfect 30-minute turnaround" (later abandoned in favor of 35 to 55 minutes, depending on the nature of the flight). Some jobs, such as those of flight attendant, were designed to be short term in nature. For a comparison of Southwest and JetBlue, see Jody Hoffer Gittell, *The Southwest Airlines Way* (New York: McGraw-Hill, 2003).

training, and employee-relations practices. More recently, Barrett had discontinued the practice because, in her words, "I felt that we were devoting too much time, energy, attention, and resources educating the outside world about our culture—as opposed to devoting that time, energy, attention, and resources internally on enhancing and enriching our own culture."

In the 1990s other airlines around the world began to model their strategies around Southwest's, often after a visit by their managements to Dallas. The most successful of these included RyanAir, Easy Jet, and GO in Europe as well as Air Asia in the Far East.

Strategy

Important elements of the Southwest strategy, some of which were a reflection of the constraints the company faced early in its existence, included a number of things that Southwest did not do. For example, it did not employ the hub-and-spoke route system adopted by many other airlines. Hub-and-spoke systems were designed to feed large volumes of passengers into hubs where they could be redistributed to connecting flights, all of which was intended to increase average load factors (available seats utilized) and revenues per available seat mile flown. However, they were considered less convenient for passengers who preferred point-to-point flying. And they exacerbated the "domino effect" that one late flight could have on several others. Just as important, they were more costly to staff because of the extreme peaks and valleys in the traffic through each hub at "connect" times, an effect that also increased crowding and confusion for connecting passengers.

A point-to-point route system also enabled Southwest to speed the turnaround of its aircraft not required to wait for connecting flights and thereby gain greater utilization from a fleet containing only Boeing 737s. The newest of these were purchased for something less than the list price of $41 million under a contract with Boeing signed in June 2000 for as many as 436 Boeing 737s to be delivered through 2012 (on the schedule shown in **Exhibit 4**).

By mid-2001, Southwest's turnaround time had grown to an average of 24 minutes, a figure that was thought to be at least 30 minutes faster than the average for the industry as a whole. Contributing to Southwest's performance on turnaround time, in addition to its route system, were (1) an absence of meals on all Southwest flights, (2) a limited amount of checked luggage on Southwest's typically 60- to 90-minute flights, (3) a near-uniform configuration for all of its 737 aircraft, (4) a team-oriented approach to ground services with team measures for turning around planes and employees willing to do whatever necessary to get a plane pushed off on time, (5) a high-speed boarding process (described below), (6) a "handoff" of flights from one ground crew to another involving detailed information about numbers of passengers and bags as well as special passenger needs so that the receiving ground crew could make preparations in advance of a flight's arrival, and (7) the utilization of agents with the latitude to bring a wide variety of resources to bear on the flight-servicing process.

Southwest neither connected with other airlines nor sold "interline" tickets. Because it targeted business and pleasure fliers with relatively simple itineraries and short trips, these features were not thought necessary. Further, it did not assign seats. Instead, passengers were issued colorful reusable plastic boarding passes numbered so that 30 passengers could be boarded at a time in the sequence of their numbers. Once on board, passengers took any available seat, thus providing an incentive for an early arrival at the gate. This routine eliminated the time-consuming reconciliation of the double assignment of seats on full flights. And it allowed Southwest agents to keep the plane doors open for last-minute arrivals at the gate. But it led to what Barrett described as "the number one complaint about Southwest's service, particularly among the uninitiated," the absence of assigned seats.

Rather than spread its flights thinly over an extensive system, Southwest's strategy for opening markets was to limit markets served and provide high-frequency departures each day to a given destination. The intensity of this schedule reduced the consequences of a missed flight and enabled Southwest to retain tardy passengers.

Southwest was a maverick in its ticketing processes. Although its flight information was displayed in four computer reservation and ticketing systems operated by other airlines in the early 1990s, it paid $1 per booking only to the SABRE system, the only one with sufficient clout to demand payment. This allowed travel agents using SABRE to print tickets, even though a booking still necessitated a telephone call by an agent booking the ticket. Travel agents hated it because of the extra work for less commission on a lower-priced ticket. But the policy was thought to save the airline in excess of $30 million per year in computer reservation booking fees paid to airline ticketing systems and increased direct business resulting from travel agents advising customers to book Southwest flights themselves. In 1994, Southwest was ejected from all systems except SABRE. In response, the company's management was compelled to innovate new means of protecting its own ticket-distribution system over the following eight years. For example, it implemented a highly successful "ticketless" (paperless) travel program and later the development of Southwest.com as a means of using the Internet to sell travel directly to customers. These innovations had the combined effect of increasing sales and further lowering overall distribution costs.

Southwest's frequent-flier program was the simplest in the industry—fly eight flights, get one free. It had been preceded by a discount ticket program in the early 1970s in which purchasers of 10 flights received a booklet with 11 tickets, often cited by Kelleher as "the world's first frequent-flier program."

By mid-2001, Southwest's operations had grown to encompass 32,500 employees (more than 1,000 married to one another), operating a total of 360 Boeing 737 aircraft (with an average daily utilization of nearly 12 hours per aircraft) connecting 58 airports with 2,650 flights per day. It realized 7.5% of revenue passenger miles flown by the eight largest U.S. airlines and supplied an estimated 90% of all available seat miles in the "low-fare" segment of the market. It was the only airline to have been first in on-time performance, lowest in lost baggage, and highest in customer satisfaction for the same year, according to statistics maintained by the U.S. Department of Transportation, having achieved the feat five years in a row. And it had achieved an enviable financial performance. Chairman Kelleher commented: "Most people think of us as this flamboyant airline, but we're really very conservative from the fiscal standpoint. We have the best balance sheet in the industry. We've always made sure that we never overreached ourselves. We never got dangerously in debt, and never let costs get out of hand. And that gave us a real edge."[2]

Leadership, Values, and Culture

A visit to Southwest Airlines' headquarters at Love Field yielded vivid impressions of the company's leadership, values, and culture. The walls of the three-story building (with a five-story addition) were covered with literally thousands of framed photos and awards, many of them showing Southwest employees in their party cloths ranging from black tie and formals to jeans. Many others portrayed employees engaged in community activities together in their free time, often at Ronald McDonald houses for children across the country.

---

[2] Katrina Booker, "The Chairman of the Board Looks Back," *Fortune*, May 28, 2001.

In the hallways, jeans, Texas greetings, and hugs were the order of the day. As one of his colleagues put it, "Jim [executive vice president of operations] Wimberly's idea of dressing up is to wear socks." In response to the question, "What's the most enjoyable thing about your job?" posed by the casewriter, one staffer replied after a moment's thought, "I guess just coming to work every day." The response reflected the fact that Southwest Airlines had placed in the top five employers in *Fortune* Magazine's "100 Best Places to Work in the U.S." every year it had competed for the award.

Leadership

Many of the framed photos at headquarters included Kelleher, one of the founders, who had gained fame for his unorthodox but effective style of leadership at Southwest over the years. He could be seen on a customized Harley-Davidson presented to him by his pilot group, at an arm wrestling contest with the executive of another company in order to settle litigation over the use of an advertising slogan, or at the maintenance hangar (by his account, at 2 a.m.) dressed in a long dress with a purple boa and large purple hat to settle a performance challenge made to the maintenance crew. Kelleher's style of leadership was so charismatic and infectious that many claimed his retirement would present a serious challenge to his successors and to Southwest's culture.

By June 2001, Kelleher had turned the day-to-day operating responsibilities over to Jim Parker, former vice president–general counsel and now CEO; Barrett, his long-time associate, former executive vice president–customers, and now president and chief operating officer; and a team of other senior executives, most with long service with the airline. (**Exhibit 5** contains an organization chart as of late 2002.) Less visible to the general public, Kelleher nevertheless retained the position of chairman, with oversight responsibilities for growth strategies and government and airline industry relations. In the transition, responsibility for Southwest's unique culture remained with Barrett.

Parker had been persuaded by Kelleher to join his law firm and later (in 1986) to come to work at Southwest. He was described by one account as "modest and easygoing. Workplace colleagues say he brews the office coffee in the morning, makes his own photocopies, wears khakis and golf shirts to work."[3] In addition to devoting his time to strategic issues, he assumed personal responsibility for the negotiation of numerous labor contracts.

Barrett, who had joined Southwest with Kelleher, had begun her career as Kelleher's secretary, gradually taking on responsibility for "customers" (passengers and marketing as well as employees) and, in a way, anchoring the leadership team behind the scenes while Kelleher performed a much more public role. Shy and unassuming, Barrett spent most of her waking moments engaged in Southwest business. Little was done on the internal or external customer service front without her tacit approval.

Values and Culture

For years, Southwest had been operated on "The Basic Principles" of (1) focus on the situation, issue, or behavior, not on the person; (2) maintain the self-confidence and self-esteem of others; (3) maintain constructive relationships with your employees, peers, and managers; (4) take initiative to make things better; and (5) lead by example. Its core values were profitability, low cost, family, fun, love, hard work, individuality, ownership, legendary service, egalitarianism, common sense/good judgment, simplicity, and altruism.

---

[3] Micheline Maynard, "Southwest, Without the Stunts," *The New York Times*, July 7, 2002, Section 3, p. 2.

In 1990, an informal group organized years before by Barrett became the core of a committee formed to plan the airline's 20th anniversary celebration. It rapidly evolved into what became known as the Culture Committee. Before, according to Donna Conover, who was named executive vice president–customer service as part of the June 2001 transition plan, "Colleen [Barrett] was the Culture Committee." Championed by Barrett and headed by a member of her staff, Susan (Sunny) Stone in 2002, the committee's goal was to "help create the Southwest Spirit and Culture where needed; to enrich it and make it better where it already exists; and to liven it up in places where it might be 'floundering.' In short, this group's goal is to do WHATEVER IT TAKES to create, enhance, and enrich the special Southwest Sprit and Culture that has made this such a wonderful Company/Family."

The committee comprised 96 employees nominated by their peers from all levels and locations in the Southwest organization, each with responsibility for attending three meetings annually to plan various events as well as for actively participating in three of the events. These ranged from employee appreciation events throughout the system to flight/operations "midnight madness" parties and breakfasts to a Christmas SPIRIT packing exercise in which goody packages were prepared for employees who had to work on Christmas. After several years, members graduated to "alumni" status and retained responsibility for attending two events each year. By 2002, there were more than 250 Culture Committee alumni. The biggest problem apparently was in finding members willing to transition to alumni status.

The biggest companywide event of the year was the annual awards banquet, for which employees from all over the system were brought to Dallas and honored for their length of service. As Conover put it, "People sort of need to come home once in awhile." In addition, the Culture Committee sponsored a Heroes of the Heart celebration at headquarters on February 14 each year. Awards were made to groups nominated by others in the organization that had gone "above and beyond" to deliver Southwest service.

The company's values and culture infused everything that it did. For example, Southwest had become well known for its efforts in partnering with unions (essentially invited into Southwest by its management), airports, and suppliers. Negotiations with unions, including the Teamsters and other national organizations, were entered with the idea of providing the best possible pay and benefits in return for flexible work rules. Efforts were made to maintain good working relations at airports from the top management to the staff in the control towers, where Southwest managers regularly appeared with donuts and coffee. Joint problem solving had become more important as problems with airport security had grown. And Southwest engaged in joint problem-solving exercises with those supplying everything from fuel to the peanuts served on planes.

The work of the Culture Committee increased in importance with the growth of the airline. For example, in contrast to the extensive preparations for Halloween at headquarters (described below), the casewriter observed few decorations on the same day at Southwest's Baltimore gates but more as he approached Dallas through Houston.

Organization

A small management team headed up Southwest's organization (as shown in **Exhibit 5**). At the very top, the team consisted of Kelleher, Parker, and Barrett, plus three executive vice presidents responsible for operations (Wimberly), customer service (Conover), and corporate staff services (Gary Kelly). Reporting to this team of six were those managing such functions as marketing, government relations, human resources (called People Department), schedule planning, legal, and others. Top managers spent an unusual amount of time with one another, making decisions on a cross-functional basis. This philosophy pervaded the organization.

In contrast to competitors, the organization was staffed more heavily with managers responsible for coordinating all functions at the front-line operating level. All personnel involved in turning a plane around could be asked by them to help out wherever needed. Failure to do so according to schedule resulted in a "team late." Rather than assess individual responsibility, teams were then tasked to figure out how to avoid the problem in the future. As a result, pilots sometimes handled baggage or helped cabin attendants in picking up the cabin while gate attendants might be seen putting provisions on board for the departing flight. The theme driving this effort, according to Conover, was "doing whatever it takes" instead of "it's not my job." As she put it, "You can talk later about who should have done what."

The idea of dedicating an operations agent to each flight was somewhat unusual in the industry; other airlines regarded it as an extra expense, even though Southwest's gate crews, even including the operations agents, were among the most productive in the industry (as suggested by data in **Exhibit 6**). Employees typically became operations agents after serving in customer service or ramp positions. They could then become prime candidates for other front-line management jobs.

Throughout the organization, stress was placed on the value of "family" in the organization. This led to unusual practices in hiring new recruits, a process that Kelleher once described as "a near-religious experience." Southwest was well known, for example, for its group interviews, involving groups of 30 or more candidates for entry-level positions. Candidates were often asked to stand and describe such things as their most embarrassing moment. The interview team then watched both the presenter and those in the audience for signs of interest, concern, and empathy for the presenter. The interview team often included frequent-flier customers as well, particularly when customer-contact people were being selected. As one such customer put it when asked why he would take off time from his company to spend a day hiring Southwest employees, "I thought I might learn something and have a little fun doing it. And besides, it's my airline."

All of this was part of a process "to hire for attitude," in Conover's words. When asked if this policy extended to pilots, she replied, "Oh, my gosh, yes. That is such a close-knit group, but we're going to have people [other than the internal recruiter and chief pilot] look at them too. They have to have the right attitude."

All ground operations (station) employees experienced one to two weeks of technical orientation at individual stations before going to class in Dallas for a week to study everything from the use of company systems to the organization's values.

Southwest's employees received total compensation roughly equivalent to that of their counterparts in other airlines, but they typically worked more productively for it. This resulted in costs for Southwest that were substantially lower than those of other major airlines (as shown in **Exhibit 7**). In addition, all employees became members of Southwest's profit-sharing plan after the end of their six-month probation period, during which it was determined whether they represented a good fit with their peers. Contributions on their behalf began vesting after 12 months, although benefits began accruing from day one of their employment. No contribution to the plan was required of employees. Company contributions, depending on profits, ranged up to 14.7% of salary in 2000. By late 2002, the profit-sharing plan owned about 10% of Southwest's 763 million outstanding shares. Conover commented, "We don't get enough credit for the plan among our employees. After about five years, you begin to realize how important it is." Nevertheless, the turnover at all levels of the Southwest organization was significantly less than in other airlines. Other than for entry-level positions, the company hired from the outside talent pool only for specialized jobs, such as in information technology.

The Impact of the Events of 9/11

On the morning of September 11, 2001, as reports of plane crashes came in to Southwest's headquarters, senior executives assembled in the "control center," which was actually the board-room. Everyone waited as Southwest's planes one by one reached the ground safely across the United States. When Greg Wells, director of dispatch, reported that the last Southwest plane had landed safely, there was a huge sense of relief. At that moment, Kelleher commented, "We'll never be exactly the same industry again." Little did anyone know how true that would be.

Conover described the thought sequence following Kelleher's announcement:

First you realize that we've got them on the ground. Then you ask, "Will we ever get them back in the air again?" Then the attitude quickly changed to "We've got to get back to work." There was never any talk about laying employees off. This attitude is so inbred in us that we didn't even think "it's going to be tough."

The most important decision we made in the hours following the attacks was not to fly before Friday [three days after the tragedy]. The government was urging airlines to fly as soon as Thursday to demonstrate our resilience, and our competitors were preparing to do so. But we decided that after all that had happened, we couldn't put our employees through a ramp-up that we might have to postpone.

Immediate Responses

Perhaps the most remarkable response to 9/11 at Southwest was one that did not occur. No member of management could recall a conversation about a possible layoff of employees or a cutback in flights. This was not a trivial matter. As CFO Kelly pointed out, "Even though we had roughly a billion dollars 'in the bank,' it was in commercial paper; we couldn't get at it because the markets were closed for several trading days, and we didn't know what it would be worth when the markets reopened."

Overnight, security issues made the handling of passengers, baggage, and other matters more complicated and time consuming. In a way, the challenge was proportional to the number of passengers boarded, and by September 11 Southwest was boarding more passengers than any U.S. airline except Delta. One response was to add more customer service agents to the boarding process for each flight, increasing the average of employees to staff a departure from 3.5 to 5.5. As Conover put it, "We knew we had to do it to get over the hump. For the first four or five months, when things were not pretty, customers could at least find a human being. Then we let attitude take over. As we learned how to handle the problem, employees began saying 'We've got too many people here.' At that point we let attrition get us back to our former staffing levels."

Less than 48 hours after the attacks, Joyce Rogge, Southwest's senior vice president–marketing, stressed the need to get a message in the form of a public service announcement to the general public, one that would appeal to American patriotism and resiliency while recognizing the bravery of people who had suffered through the 9/11 attacks. Late on the Sunday afternoon after the attacks, she recorded Barrett's voice on an inexpensive dictaphone machine with a message that was used as a voice-over for a hastily produced television ad showing Barrett's name and title on a typed title card in front of an American flag. It was devoid of the usual Southwest humor. Subsequent television and radio ads profiled Southwest employees, assuring the public that when they were ready to fly, Southwest would be there and ready to fly them.

Heightened Security and Regulation

An even greater challenge was faced by Southwest's governmental affairs office, led by Ron Ricks, who had logged 16 years in his position after serving at the same law firm where Kelleher, Parker, and Barrett had been employed before coming to Southwest.

In the 60 days following 9/11, Southwest received roughly 200 directives from the Federal Aviation Agency (FAA), the FBI, and the CIA. Many of these would later be consolidated under the Transportation Security Administration (TSA) created by Congress later in the year, but it did not exist during this period. As Ricks put it, "It wasn't just the sheer volume of directives. A typical directive required that we implement a new security procedure overnight. The directive would contain complex 'terms of art,' hard for a 22-year-old customer service agent to understand and act on. The alternatives were 'Do it or don't operate.'" Many directives were rescinded by later directives, some no more than 24 hours after the order they rescinded. As Wimberly put it, "Overnight, we became a branch of government."

Once the TSA was created by Congress, it was staffed with people drawn from the Secret Service, FBI, CIA, and Tobacco and Firearms agencies. This contributed to continuing confusion about directives issued by the TSA. Ricks commented, "Their perceived mandate was that they were fighting a war on terrorism. We were in a mind-set of being in a war too. And we didn't know anything about that kind of war. We just concluded that we couldn't substitute our judgment for theirs."

Dave Ridley, vice president of ground operations, held a daily call with all 59 Southwest stations. He would go over "today's directive" and how Southwest would deal with it. For example, one directive required that in the absence of baggage screening, all bags were to be opened at the counter by Southwest employees, apparently with little thought about questions of logistics, employee safety, and what to do if (nonthreatening) illegal contraband were found in the bags.

Southwest's passengers typically had less accompanying baggage than those on other major airlines. However, they carried a relatively high percentage on board. When the FAA limited carry-on luggage to one bag and a personal item, the number of bags checked per passenger began rising. This added work for Southwest's baggage handling crews and in some cases necessitated enlarging crews to meet plane turnaround schedules.

Certain security directives placed Southwest at a competitive disadvantage. For example, many of Southwest's best customers, because of the "last-second" manner of their travel, fit the profile of those most likely to be thoroughly searched. Barrett estimated that as many as 15% of Southwest's passengers were being flagged for screening, a figure much higher than for other airlines.

Several of the directives dealt with the tracking of passengers and their baggage from curb to seat. But because it had never had assigned seats, Southwest's relatively simple systems were not designed to provide more detailed information and had to be reprogrammed.

The need to identify passengers requiring detailed screening forced Southwest to abandon its distinctive, colorful, reusable plastic boarding passes in favor of paper passes on which information targeting selected passengers could be printed.

Industry Bailout and Taxation

A rapidly conceived bailout for an industry in financial as well as physical peril occupied a great deal of Kelleher's and Ricks's time as well. In the immediate wake of 9/11, Southwest's competitors, many of which had little in the way of a financial cushion, began announcing cutbacks in both service and employment. In total, roughly 20% of all flights flown by seven of the eight other largest carriers were discontinued, and more than 15% of those employed by seven of the eight other largest carriers (at least 100,000) were laid off.[4]

In response to immediate airline needs, an effort was made in the U.S. House of Representatives to pass by voice vote a hastily prepared Air Transportation Safety and Systems Stabilization Act. Southwest executives learned of it the next day. Largely based on "need" (thereby freezing Southwest out of the benefit), the bill did not pass. Ricks commented, "Southwest did not advocate a bailout but did take the position that if the government decided as a matter of public policy that economic reimbursement for our losses was a good thing, then the program should be implemented in a nondiscriminatory way." Ultimately, a bill was passed that provided for up to $10 billion in loan guarantees to airlines seeking financing assistance. In addition, it provided for $5 billion to be distributed among all aviation providers based on seat miles (one seat flown one mile) available on September 10, 2001. Out of the latter pool, Southwest received $278 million.

On another front, discussions were under way concerning various methods of taxing airlines to help defray added costs to the government for airline security, especially following the assumption of airport security staffing by the federal government in November 2001. On this front, two taxes were ultimately established. The first, a tax of $2.50 on each segment flown by a passenger, hit the lowest-fare airlines the hardest. However, as Ricks commented, "After 9/11, everyone became a low-fare carrier. Therefore, the potential for a penalty to Southwest was somewhat mitigated on this score. We think the size of the tax is a reason why traffic is slow to return to the airlines. But Congress realized that it couldn't pay for obligations it had assumed without it." (Monthly traffic trends for major U.S. airlines are shown in **Exhibit 8**.)

A second tax was assessed each airline to help pay for increased costs to the government for security. Whatever each airline was paying for security prior to the takeover was to be turned over to the government.

New Competitive Position

In spite of new challenges and taxes, the decision by Southwest's management to maintain and ultimately to increase schedules and employment after 9/11 had a profound effect on its competitive position in the industry. Market share rose immediately (as shown in **Exhibit 8**). Given the immediate plunge in the value of competitors' stock from 11% to 74%, Southwest's market value quickly became greater than that for all of the other eight largest airlines combined and maintained that position for months, in spite of the fact that its earnings had suffered substantial declines as a result of lower ticket prices, higher costs, and new taxes.

Labor Relations

Several labor contract negotiations coincided with Southwest's apparently successful emergence from the 9/11 crisis. Claims of lower wages than those paid by other airlines in the face of profitable

---

[4] Among the other eight largest U.S. airlines, only Alaska Airlines did not furlough employees following September 11, 2001.

company performance emboldened several unions to seek more favorable contracts. Stating that "There's really nothing more important that we do than have a relationship with our employees," Parker continued his personal responsibility for negotiations.[5]

In spite of the fact that unions took a tougher stance than in the past, an acceptable two-year extension of the pilots' 10-year agreement (to 2006) was achieved. The mechanics, after rejecting Southwest's first offer (in a somewhat unusual move), agreed to a second offer. Similar contracts were expected to be signed with other unions. Nevertheless, it raised a question about the degree to which growth had challenged Southwest's policy of relating closely to its employees. Observers continued to conclude that the company's labor relations were still far superior to those of its competitors. As Jonathan Weaks, president of the Southwest Airlines Pilots Association (the pilots' union), put it, "We don't want to be just another airline."[6]

Short-Term Challenges: Operating Procedures

In response to the 9/11 crisis, other airlines had increased estimated-schedule flight times to reflect increased passenger- and baggage-processing times. With disappointing load factors, many flights as a result regularly arrived 20 minutes or more before their scheduled times. Southwest's management, on the other hand, had not changed its schedules in the hope that this would continue to benefit aircraft utilization. In spite of this, average turnaround times in recent months had risen from 24 to 27 minutes, a matter of real concern to management, and Southwest's reported on-time performance had slipped below that of its rivals (as shown in **Exhibit 9**).

Southwest's management had discussed several possible responses at various meetings in late October 2002. Among these, one possibility was that of just sitting tight, essentially concentrating on doing the best possible job with the resources at hand in a price-competitive environment and despite sluggish demand for the service. The price of this alternative would be depressed profits and possibly declining morale.

A second response would be simply to reschedule the airline, building more liberal flight and turnaround times into the schedule. However, too often schedules became self-fulfilling prophecies. If this proved to be true, results could be quite costly with serious profit implications.

Third, efforts could be made to redesign passenger- and baggage-handling processes once again. Southwest's practice of boarding passengers in groups just minutes before flight time, then holding the door of the aircraft open for late arrivals, was somewhat at odds with the government directive to single out passengers for a thorough search of luggage at the gate. Southwest gate agents were instructed to encourage passengers so identified to assemble at the gate for searching as early as possible in the relatively rapid boarding process. Even so, passengers were often still being searched after everyone else had boarded. Those singled out often ended up getting inferior seats even if they arrived at the gate early in order to get a good choice. One solution to this problem, that of adding extra government security guards at Southwest's gates (probably at the airline's expense), would substantially increase boarding costs.

Fourth, passenger boarding policies could be altered. Other airlines were requiring passengers to be on hand at the gate with greater lead times before boarding in order to accommodate new security procedures. This would further restrict Southwest's passengers, a direct contradiction of its past policies and its advertising strategy of freedom "to move about the country."

---

[5] Maynard, p. 2.

[6] Ibid.

Finally, open seating could be abandoned, insuring that passengers would get a seat they had chosen when they booked the seat. This would require "retraining" regular passengers, some of whom actually preferred open seating. Further, it would likely add delays, especially to full flights on which the probability of assigning the same seat to two people would be greater.

Whatever was done would have to be implemented with customers', employees', and the government's needs in mind. Conover, in charge of customers (both travelers and employees), commented on the success of Southwest's responses to changing requirements to date: "Now, both government and our employees think we're invincible. That's great, but it's almost a disservice. It has been tough trying to maintain customer service levels and relationships in a whole new environment. We sometimes wonder if we're in control of our destiny any longer."

Long-Term Challenges: Growth Strategies

Immediately after 9/11, Southwest deferred 19 aircraft deliveries, borrowed a billion dollars, and developed a contingency operating schedule. Initially, little thought was given to strategic growth plans. The primary focus, instead, was on stabilizing operations, even though decisions were made to go ahead immediately with a previously planned opening of the Norfolk station and begin accepting in early 2002 deliveries of new aircraft. But by late 2002 questions regarding appropriate long-term growth strategies began to surface once again.

Over the years, the average flight length at Southwest had gradually increased from an average of 228 miles in the first year of operations, 1971, to about 450 miles in 1998. On Thanksgiving Day, 1998, Southwest experimented with its first nonstop transcontinental flight, between Baltimore and Oakland, necessitating a flight time of about five hours. The plane was filled with passengers who had paid $99 for the flight; almost half of the passengers had never flown Southwest before. The only problem experienced by the crew was the lack of space to store the trash that accumulated during the flight. Many observers, who attributed much of Southwest's success to the focus of its operating strategy up to that time, feared that the test might mark the first crack in the strategy.

Passenger reactions to the flight were positive. Those who typically flew multiple segments to get to a distant destination were enthusiastic about getting there two hours sooner. They provided "permission" to the airline's management to introduce other long-haul flights. By late 2002, Southwest was operating 213 flights per day over 1,200 miles in length. (**Exhibit 10** contains information about Southwest's network and flights.) Some crew members preferred to work longer flights, enough to be able to staff new flights; others, according to Pete McGlade, vice president–schedule planning, "signed on with Southwest because they like more landings and takeoffs per day of work."

Because longer flights experienced high-load factors, utilized the existing infrastructure, and did not require additional catering or on-board staffing (with only snack service, the usual three cabin attendants could serve a full planeload of 137 passengers), they generated healthy profits per passenger and operating economics at least comparable to those of shorter flights. This comparison held true only if long-haul flights were operated from cities served by a substantial number of other Southwest flights.

By mid-2002, the average aircraft stage (flight) length had grown to 550 miles. Southwest's experience with longer flights raised the question of the degree to which the airline should rely on them in its future growth plans. There were a number of opportunities to connect existing stations three or more flying hours apart on the Southwest system. The alternative would be to continue to add new cities to the airline's 59-station network from among more than 100 cities that were requesting Southwest service.

Questions were raised from time to time about limits to Southwest's growth and, when growth was resumed, whether the airline could resume its 14% growth per year between 1980 and 2000. However, one Wall Street analyst, examining Southwest's route structure and the density of existing service, concluded that it could double its size without opening one new station.

A Late October Visit to Southwest Airlines Headquarters

On October 30, 2002, two appropriately contrasting events took place simultaneously during the casewriter's visit to Southwest's Love Field headquarters in Dallas. The first, a three-hour emergency exercise, was called unexpectedly by Wimberly at 8 a.m. It involved a simulated report of the crash of a Southwest flight from Houston short of the runway in New Orleans just 30 minutes earlier. The hypothetical drill specified that there were survivors and that they were being evacuated to local hospitals. (Southwest in its entire history had never experienced a fatal accident.) The resulting exercise involved hundreds of people mobilized in the form of teams responsible for care (family assistance), employee assistance, business continuation, dispatch, corporate communications, an executive office taskforce (which assembled in the board room under Wimberly's direction), family notification, manifest, medical services, mortuary assistance, purchasing, reservations, security, technical support, and building services. Many were assembled in a Go Team that boarded a plane pulled up behind corporate headquarters for a simulated flight to New Orleans, during which they were briefed once again concerning their duties upon arrival. They then departed the plane and walked through the processes and decisions for which they would be responsible in the event of a real emergency. It was one of a series of emergency exercises planned for the coming months.

At the same time, many other employees continued their preparations for the annual Halloween celebration, which had been cancelled in 2001 in deference to 9/11. Each department was busy preparing its own decorations and a skit reflecting a particular theme. The legal department was building a biker's bar from which to present its show. In the executive office, employees were rehearsing for the Rocky Horror Airport Experience presented by Transylvania Scareways. And the maintenance hangar was draped with a large sign proclaiming the name of the show to be presented there, "Hogs and Kisses," featuring the department's Harley moto-ballet team. Little work appeared to be getting done anywhere in the building. The following day employees would take hundreds of their children out of school so they could attend a full schedule of skits with their parents.

Exhibit 1   Southwest Airlines Routes and Market Data, November 2002

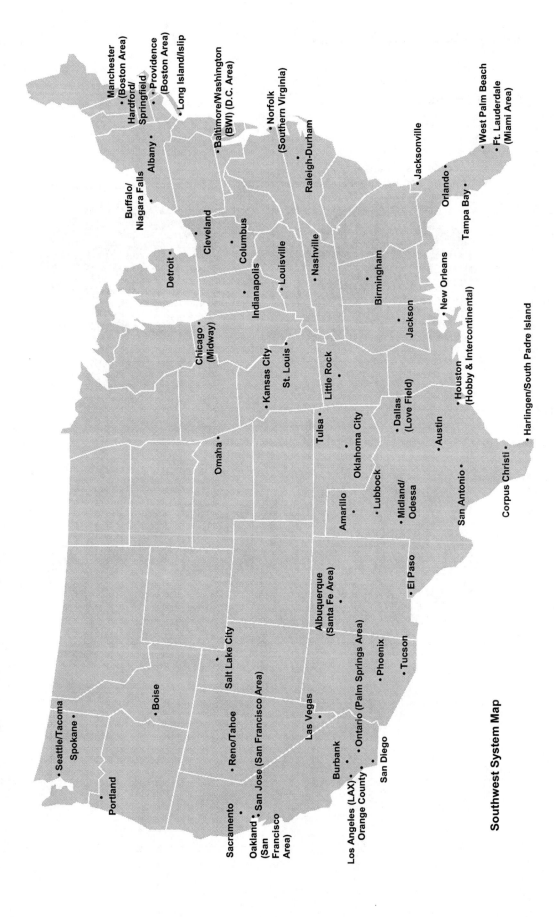

Southwest System Map

Exhibit 1 (continued)

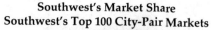

Southwest's Market Share
Southwest's Top 100 City-Pair Markets

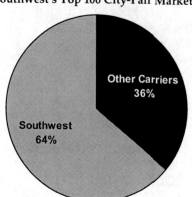

Southwest's Capacity by Region

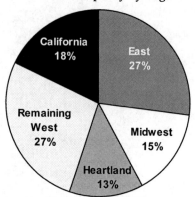

Southwest's Top 10 Airports
Daily Departures

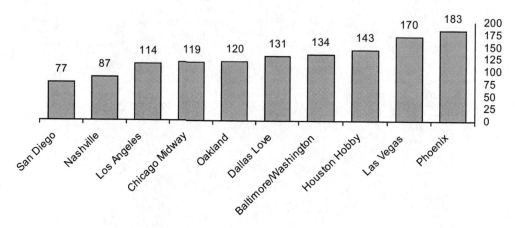

Source: Southwest Airlines Co. 2001 Annual Report.

418

Exhibit 2   Selected Financial and Other Information, Southwest Airlines, 1998–2001 (in thousands, except per share amounts)

	2001	2000	1999	1998
Operating revenues:				
Passenger[a]	$ 5,378,702	$ 5,467,965	$ 4,562,616	$ 4,010,029
Freight	91,270	110,742	102,990	98,500
Other[a]	85,202	70,853	69,981	55,451
Total operating revenues	5,555,174	5,649,560	4,735,587	4,163,980
Operating expenses	4,924,052	4,628,415	3,954,011	3,480,369
Operating income	631,122	1,021,145	781,576	683,611
Other expenses (income), net	(196,537)	3,781	7,965	(21,501)
Income before income taxes	827,659	1,017,364	773,611	705,112
Provision for income taxes[b]	316,512	392,140	299,233	271,681
Net income[b]	$ 511,147	$ 625,224[c]	$ 474,378	$ 433,431
Net income per share, basic[b]	$.67	$.84[c]	$.63	$.58
Net income per share, diluted[b]	$.63	$.79[c]	$.59	$.55
Cash dividends per common share	$.0180	$.0147	$.0143	$.0126
Total assets	$ 8,997,141	$ 6,669,572	$ 5,563,703	$ 4,715,996
Long-term debt	$ 1,327,158	$ 760,992	$ 871,717	$ 623,309
Stockholders' equity	$ 4,014,053	$ 3,451,320	$ 2,835,788	$ 2,397,918
Consolidated Financial Ratios[d]				
Return on average total assets	6.5%	10.1%[c]	9.2%	9.7%
Return on average stockholders' equity	13.7%	19.9%[c]	18.1%	19.7%
Consolidated Operating Statistics[e]				
Revenue passengers carried	64,446,773	63,678,261	57,500,213	52,586,400
Revenue passenger miles (RPMs, 000s)	44,493,916	42,215,162	36,479,322	31,419,110
Available seat miles (ASMs, 000s)	65,295,290	59,909,965	52,855,467	47,543,515
Passenger load factor	68.1%	70.5%	69.0%	66.1%
Average length of passenger haul	690	663	634	597
Trips flown	940,426	903,754	846,823	806,822
Average passenger fare[a]	$83.46	$85.87	$79.35	$76.26
Passenger revenue yield per RPM[a]	12.09¢	12.95¢	12.51¢	12.76¢
Operating revenue yield per ASM	8.51¢	9.43¢	8.96¢	8.76¢
Operating expenses per ASM	7.54¢	7.73¢	7.48¢	7.32¢
Fuel cost per gallon (average)	70.86¢	78.69¢	52.71¢	45.67¢
Number of employees at year end	31,580	29,274	27,653	25,844
Size of fleet at year end[f]	355	344	312	280
Common stock price range	$23.32-$11.25	$23.33-$10.00	$15.72-$9.58	$10.56-$6.81
Common stock price close[g]	$18.48	$22.35	$10.75	$10.08

Source: Southwest Airlines Co. 2001 Annual Report.

[a]Includes effect of reclassification of revenue reported in 1999 through 1995 related to the sale of flight segment credits from Other to Passenger due to the accounting change implementation in 2000.

[b]Pro forma for 1992 assuming Morris, an S-Corporation prior to 1993, was taxed at statutory rates.

[c]Excludes cumulative effect of accounting change of $22.1 million ($.03 per share).

[d]The selected consolidated financial data and consolidated financial ratios for 1992 have been restated to include the financial results of Morris Air Corporation (Morris).

[e]Prior to 1993, Morris operated as a charter carrier; therefore, no Morris statistics are included for 1992.

[f]Includes leased aircraft.

[g]The closing price on December 6, 2002 was $16.27.

Exhibit 3 Southwest Airlines, Consolidated Balance Sheets, December 31, 2000 and 2001 (in thousands, except per share amounts)

	December 31,	
	2001	2000
ASSETS		
Current assets:		
Cash and cash equivalents	$2,279,861	$ 522,995
Accounts and other receivables	71,283	138,070
Inventories of parts and supplies, at cost	70,561	80,564
Deferred income taxes	46,400	28,005
Prepaid expenses and other current assets	52,114	61,902
Total current assets	$2,520,219	$ 831,536
Property and equipment, at cost:		
Flight equipment	7,534,119	6,831,913
Ground property and equipment	899,421	800,718
Deposits on flight equipment purchase contracts	468,154	335,164
	8,901,694	7,967,795
Less allowance for depreciation	2,456,207	2,148,070
	6,445,487	5,819,725
Other assets	31,435	18,311
	$8,997,141	$6,669,572
LIABILITIES AND STOCKHOLDERS' EQUITY		
Current liabilities:		
Accounts payable	$ 504,831	$ 312,716
Accrued liabilities	547,540	499,874
Air traffic liability	450,407	377,061
Aircraft purchase obligations	221,840	–
Short-term borrowings	475,000	–
Current maturities of long-term debt	39,567	108,752
Total current liabilities	$2,239,185	$1,298,403
Long-term debt less current maturities	1,327,158	760,992
Deferred income taxes	1,058,143	852,865
Deferred gains from sale and leaseback of aircraft	192,342	207,522
Other deferred liabilities	166,260	98,470
Commitments and contingencies		
Stockholders' equity		
Common stock, $1.00 par value: 2,000,000 shares authorized; 766,774 and 507,897 shares issued in 2001 and 2000, respectively	766,774	507,897
Capital in excess of par value	50,409	103,780
Retained earnings	3,228,408	2,902,007
Accumulated other comprehensive income (loss)	(31,538)	–
Treasury stock, at cost: 3,735 shares in 2000	–	(62,364)
Total stockholders' equity	4,014,053	3,451,320
	$8,997,141	$6,669,572

Source: Southwest Airlines Co. 2001 Annual Report.

Exhibit 4   Aircraft Utilization and Fleet Size, 1997–2001, and Firm Aircraft Orders and Options as of December 31, 2001

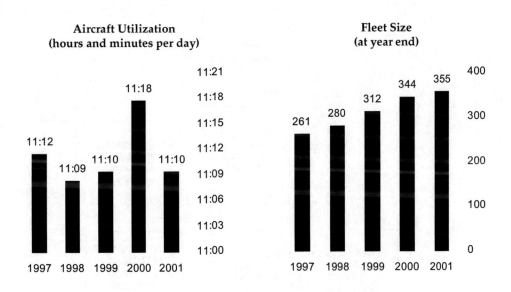

Boeing 737-700 Firm Orders and Options

Type	2002	2003	2004	2005	2006	2007	2008	2009-2012	Total
Firm orders	11	21	23	24	22	25	6	–	132
Options	–	–	13	20	20	9	25	–	87
Purchase rights	=	=	=	=	=	20	20	177	217
Total	11	21	36	44	42	54	51	177	436

Source: Southwest Airlines Co. 2001 Annual Report.

Exhibit 5   Southwest Airlines' Organization, November 2002

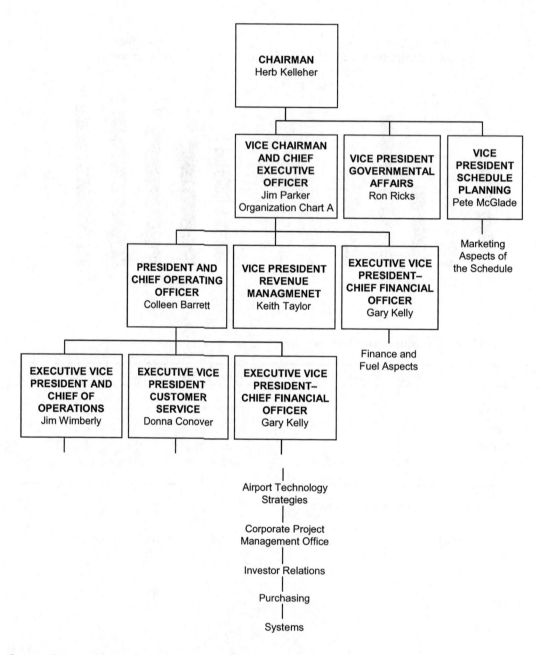

Source: Company documents.

Exhibit 6 Passengers Boarded per Employee, Major U.S. Airlines, First Quarter 2001 and 2002

Airline	First Quarter, 2001	First Quarter, 2002
Southwest	604.6	509.8
JetBlue	542.3	495.6
America West	369.8	353.2
US Air	309.9	318.8
Alaska Air	309.4	303.8
Delta	295.1	287.3
Northwest	240.6	251.2
Continental	235.1	247.4
American	194.9	241.8
United	184.6	182.2

Source: U.S. Department of Transportation.

Exhibit 7 Revenue and Cost per Passenger Seat Mile, Major U.S. Airlines, First Quarter 2001 and 2002 (in cents per mile)

Airline	First Quarter 2001			First Quarter 2002		
	Revenue/ Seat Mile[a]	Cost/Seat Mile[b]	Revenue-Cost (in cents/mile)	Revenue/ Seat Mile	Cost/Seat Mile	Revenue-Cost (in cents/mile)
Alaska Air	9.50	10.22	−.72	9.23	10.17	−.94
American	10.62	11.22	−.60	9.08	11.33	−2.25
America West	8.00	8.59	−.59	7.25	9.51	−2.26
Continental	10.04	10.39	−.35	9.12	10.73	−1.61
Delta	9.64	10.34	−.70	8.70	10.54	−1.84
JetBlue	8.54	7.41	1.13	8.22	6.82	1.40
Northwest	10.04	10.96	−.92	9.47	10.35	−.88
Southwest	8.95	7.65	1.30	7.57	7.29	.28
United	9.51	11.51	−2.00	8.48	11.41	−2.93
US Air	11.02	14.08	−3.06	9.88	14.77	−4.89

Source: U.S. Department of Transportation. The first quarter typically is the least profitable for most U.S. airlines.

[a]Revenue per seat mile is total revenue per available seat mile, occupied or not, in cents. As a result, it is a measure of both prices and capacity utilization.

[b]Cost per seat mile is total operating expenses divided by available seat miles, occupied or not, in cents.

Exhibit 8   Passenger Miles Flown, Major U.S. Airlines, First Quarter 2001 and 2002 (in billions)

Airline	First Quarter, 2001	First Quarter, 2002
American	68.6	72.1
United	74.6	64.1
Delta	62.4	56.8
Northwest	47.4	43.0
Continental	37.7	34.9
Southwest	27.8	27.0
US Air	29.6	24.8
America West	12.7	11.1
Alaska Air	7.5	7.7
JetBlue	1.6	3.4
Totals	369.9	344.9

Source: U.S. Department of Transportation.

Exhibit 9   Trends in Reported Percentage of On-Time Arrivals, Major U.S. Airlines, June 2001–July 2002

Airline	June 2001	June 2002	July 2002
Alaska Air	71.7%	77.1%	79.3%
American	78.9	81.6	81.6
America West	77.1	82.2	80.4
Continental	79.4	82.3	83.9
Delta	75.7	79.2	79.8
JetBlue	N.A.[a]	N.A.	N.A.
Northwest	81.0	80.0	80.1
Southwest	83.0	79.8	79.4
United	77.8	80.4	84.3
US Air	77.8	82.9	84.6

Source: U.S. Department of Transportation.

[a]Not available.

Exhibit 10   Southwest Airlines' Route and Flight Information, November 2002

PROFILE OF A HYPOTHETICAL NETWORK CONNECTING ALL CITIES
ON THE SOUTHWEST ROUTE SYSTEM, NOVEMBER 2002

Distance	Number of Possible Route Segments[a] (city pairs)
100–400 miles	186
400–800 miles	366
800–1,200 miles	350
More than 1,200 miles	753
Total	1,655

PROFILE OF ACTUAL ROUTES SERVED BY SOUTHWEST FLIGHTS, NOVEMBER 2002

Distance	Route Segments (city pairs)	Flights
100–400 miles[b]	103	1,503
400–800 miles[c]	100	770
800–1,200 miles[d]	70	298
More than 1,200 miles[e]	65	221
Total	338	2,792

Source: Company documents.

[a]The total possible number excludes all routes under 100 miles (reflecting the shortest route actually flown between Islip, Long Island and Providence of 108 miles) and routes from Dallas Love Field, which Southwest was prohibited from flying by law (the Wright Amendment).

[b]Numbers of flights between these city pairs ranged from two per day between Austin and Harlingen, Texas (as well as many other city pairs) to 61 per day between Dallas Love Field and Houston Hobby Airport.

[c]Numbers of flights between these city pairs ranged from two per day between Albuquerque, New Mexico and Salt Lake City (as well as many other city pairs) to 32 per day between Kansas City and Chicago.

[d]Numbers of flights between these city pairs ranged from two per day between Hartford, Connecticut and Tampa, Florida (as well as many other city pairs) to 12 per day between Las Vegas and Kansas City.

[e]Numbers of flights between these city pairs ranged from two per day between Albany, New York and Las Vegas (as well as many other city pairs) to 11 per day between Phoenix and St. Louis.

Starbucks' Global Quest in 2006: Is the Best Yet to Come?

Amit J. Shah
Frostburg State University

Arthur A. Thompson
The University of Alabama

Thomas F. Hawk
Frostburg State University

In early 2006, Howard Schultz, Starbucks' founder, chairman of the board, and global strategist, could look with satisfaction on the company's phenomenal growth and market success. Since 1987, Starbucks had transformed itself from a modest nine-store operation in the Pacific Northwest into a powerhouse multinational enterprise with 10,241 store locations, including some 2,900 stores in 30 foreign countries (see Exhibit 1). During Starbucks' early years when coffee was a 50-cent morning habit at local diners and fast-food establishments, skeptics had ridiculed the notion of $3 coffee as a yuppie fad. But the popularity of Starbucks' Italian-style coffees, espresso beverages, teas, pastries, and confections had made Starbucks one of the great retailing stories of recent history and the world's biggest specialty coffee chain. In 2003, Starbucks made the Fortune 500, prompting Schultz to remark, "It would be arrogant to sit here and say that 10 years ago we thought we would be on the Fortune 500. But we dreamed from day one and we dreamed big."[1]

Having positioned Starbucks as the dominant retailer, roaster, and brand of specialty coffees and coffee drinks in North America and spawned the creation of the specialty coffee industry, management's long-term objective was now to establish Starbucks as the most recognized and respected brand in the world. New stores were being opened at the rate of roughly 32 per week in 2005, and management

expected to have 15,000 Starbucks stores open worldwide going into 2006. Believing that the scope of Starbucks' long-term opportunity had been underestimated, Schultz had recently increased the targeted number of stores from 25,000 to 30,000 worldwide by 2013, at least half of which were to be outside the United States.[2] He noted that Starbucks had only an overall 7 percent share of the coffee-drinking market in the United States and perhaps a 1 percent share internationally. According to Schultz, "That still leaves lots of room for growth. Internationally, we are still in our infancy."[3] Although coffee consumption worldwide was stagnant, coffee was still the second-most-consumed beverage in the world, trailing only water.[4]

Starbucks reported revenues in fiscal 2005 of $6.4 billion, up 205 percent from $2.1 billion in fiscal 2000; after-tax profits in 2005 were $494.5 million, an increase of 423 percent from the company's fiscal 2000 net earnings of $94.6 million.

COMPANY BACKGROUND

Starbucks got its start in 1971 when three academics, English teacher Jerry Baldwin, history teacher Zev Siegel, and writer Gordon Bowker—all coffee aficionados—opened Starbucks Coffee, Tea, and Spice in touristy Pikes Place Market in Seattle. The three partners shared a love for fine coffees and exotic teas and believed they could build a clientele in Seattle that would appreciate the best coffees and

Exhibit 1   **Number of Starbucks Store Locations Worldwide, 1987–2005**

Fiscal Year	Number of Store Locations at End of Fiscal Year	Fiscal Year	Number of Store Locations at End of Fiscal Year
1987	17	1997	1,412
1988	33	1998	1,886
1989	55	1999	2,135
1990	84	2000	3,501
1991	116	2001	4,709
1992	165	2002	5,886
1993	272	2003	7,225
1994	425	2004	8,569
1995	676	2005	10,241
1996	1,015		

Licensed Locations of Starbucks Stores, 2005

Asia-Pacific		Europe–Middle East–Africa		Americas	
Japan	572	Spain	39	United States	2,435
China	185	Saudi Arabia	38	Canada	118
Taiwan	153	Greece	38	Mexico	60
South Korea	133	United Arab Emirates	37	Hawaii	51
Philippines	83	Kuwait	32	Puerto Rico	11
Malaysia	62	Turkey	24	Peru	6
New Zealand	41	Switzerland	21	The Bahamas	2
Indonesia	32	France	16		2,683
	1,261	Lebanon	10		
		Austria	9		
		Qatar	8		
		Bahrain	8		
		Cyprus	7		
		Oman	4		
		Jordan	4		
		United Kingdom	2		
			297		

Source: 2005 10-K report.

teas, much like what had already emerged in the San Francisco Bay area. They each invested $1,350 and borrowed another $5,000 from a bank to open the Pikes Place store. The inspiration and mentor for the Starbucks venture in Seattle was a Dutch immigrant named Alfred Peet, who had opened Peet's Coffee and Tea, in Berkeley, California, in 1966. Peet's store specialized in importing fine coffees and teas and dark-roasting its own beans the European way to bring out the full flavors. Customers were encouraged to learn how to grind the beans and make their own freshly brewed coffee at home. Baldwin, Siegel, and Bowker were well acquainted with Peet's expertise, having visited his store on numerous occasions and listened to him expound on quality coffees and the importance of proper bean-roasting techniques.

The Pikes Place store featured modest, hand-built, classic nautical fixtures. One wall was devoted to whole-bean coffees, while another had shelves of coffee products. The store did not offer fresh-brewed coffee by the cup, but tasting samples were sometimes available. Initially, Siegel was the only paid employee. He wore a grocer's apron, scooped out beans for customers, extolled the virtues of fine, dark-roasted coffees, and functioned as the partnership's retail expert. The other two partners kept their day jobs but came by at lunch or after work to help out. During the start-up period, Baldwin kept the books and developed a growing knowledge of coffee; Bowker served as the "magic, mystery, and romance man."[5] The store was an immediate success, with sales exceeding expectations, partly because of interest stirred by a favorable article in the *Seattle Times*. For most of the first year, Starbucks ordered its coffee-bean supplies from Peet's, but then the partners purchased a used roaster from Holland, set up roasting operations in a nearby ramshackle building, and developed their own blends and flavors.

By the early 1980s, the company had four Starbucks stores in the Seattle area and had been profitable every year since opening its doors. But then Zev Siegel experienced burnout and left the company to pursue other interests. Jerry Baldwin took over day-to-day management of the company and functioned as chief executive officer; Gordon Bowker remained involved as an owner but devoted most of his time to his advertising and design firm, a weekly newspaper he had founded, and a microbrewery that he was launching known as the Redhook Ale Brewery.

Howard Schultz Enters the Picture

In 1981, Howard Schultz, vice president and general manager of U.S. operations for a Swedish maker of stylish kitchen equipment and coffeemakers, decided to pay Starbucks a visit—he was curious about why Starbucks was selling so many of his company's products. The morning after his arrival in Seattle, he was escorted to the Pikes Place store by Linda Grossman, the retail merchandising manager for Starbucks. A solo violinist was playing Mozart at the door (his violin case open for donations). Schultz was immediately taken by the powerful and pleasing aroma of the coffees, the wall displaying coffee beans, and the rows of coffeemakers on the shelves. As he talked with the clerk behind the counter, the clerk scooped out some Sumatran coffee beans, ground them, put the grounds in a cone filter, poured hot water over the cone, and shortly handed Schultz a porcelain mug filled with freshly brewed coffee. After only taking three sips of the brew, Schultz was hooked. He began asking the clerk and Grossman questions about the company, about coffees from different parts of the world, and about the different ways of roasting coffee.

A bit later, he was introduced to Jerry Baldwin and Gordon Bowker, whose offices overlooked the company's coffee-roasting operation. Schultz was struck by their knowledge about coffee, their commitment to providing customers with quality coffees, and their passion for educating customers about the merits of dark-roasted coffees. Baldwin told Schultz, "We don't manage the business to maximize anything other than the quality of the coffee."[6] The company purchased only the finest arabica coffees and put them through a meticulous dark-roasting process to bring out their full flavors. Baldwin explained that the cheap robusta coffees used in supermarket blends burned when subjected to dark roasting. He also noted that the makers of supermarket blends preferred lighter roasts, which allowed higher yields (the longer a coffee was roasted, the more weight it lost).

Schultz was also struck by the business philosophy of the two partners. It was clear that Starbucks stood not just for good coffee but also for the dark-roasted flavor profiles that the founders were passionate about. Top-quality, fresh-roasted, whole-bean coffee was the company's differentiating feature and a bedrock value. It was also clear to Schultz that Starbucks was strongly committed to educating its customers to appreciate the qualities of fine coffees. The company depended mainly on word of mouth to get more people into its stores, then built customer loyalty cup by cup as buyers gained a sense of discovery and excitement about the taste of fine coffee.

On his trip back to New York the next day, Howard Schultz could not stop thinking about Starbucks and what it would be like to be a part of the Starbucks enterprise. Schultz recalled, "There was something magic about it, a passion and authenticity I had never experienced in business."[7] The appeal of living in the Seattle area was another strong plus. By the time he landed at Kennedy Airport, he knew in his heart he wanted to go to work for Starbucks. At the first opportunity, Schultz asked Baldwin whether there was any way he could fit into Starbucks. While Schultz and Baldwin had established an easy, comfortable personal rapport, it still took a year, numerous meetings at which Schultz presented his ideas, and a lot of convincing to get Baldwin, Bowker, and their silent partner from San Francisco to agree to hire him. Schultz pursued a job at Starbucks far more vigorously than Starbucks pursued hiring Schultz. There was some nervousness about bringing in an outsider, especially a high-powered New Yorker who had not grown up with the values of the company. Nonetheless, Schultz continued to press his ideas about the tremendous potential of expanding the Starbucks enterprise outside Seattle and exposing people all over America to Starbucks coffee. He argued that there had to be more than just the few thousand coffee lovers in Seattle who would enjoy the company's products.

At a meeting with the three owners in San Francisco in the spring of 1982, Schultz once again presented his ideas and vision for opening Starbucks stores across the United States and Canada. He thought the meeting went well and flew back to New York, believing a job offer was in the bag. However, the next day Jerry Baldwin called Schultz and indicated that the owners had decided against hiring him because geographic expansion was too risky and they did not share Schultz's vision for Starbucks. Schultz was despondent, seeing his dreams of being a part of Starbucks' future go up in smoke. Still, he believed so deeply in Starbucks' potential that he decided to make a last-ditch appeal; he called Baldwin back the next day and made an impassioned, reasoned case for why the decision was a mistake. Baldwin agreed to reconsider. The next morning Baldwin called Schultz and told him the job of heading marketing and overseeing the retail stores was his. In September 1982, Howard Schultz took over his new responsibilities at Starbucks.

Starbucks and Howard Schultz: The 1982–1985 Period

In his first few months at Starbucks, Howard Schultz spent most of his waking hours in the four Seattle stores—working behind the counters, tasting different kinds of coffee, talking with customers, getting to know store personnel, and learning the retail aspects of the coffee business. By December, Jerry Baldwin concluded that Schultz was ready for the final part of his training, that of actually roasting the coffee. Schultz spent a week getting an education about the colors of different coffee beans, listening for the telltale second pop of the beans during the roasting process, learning to taste the subtle differences among Baldwin and Bowker's various roasts, and familiarizing himself with the roasting techniques for different beans.

Schultz made a point of acclimating himself to the informal dress code at Starbucks, gaining credibility and building trust with colleagues, and making the transition from the high-energy, coat-and-tie style of New York to the more casual, low-key ambience of the Pacific Northwest (see Exhibit 2 for a rundown on Howard Schultz's background). Schultz made real headway in gaining the acceptance and respect of company personnel while working at the Pikes Place store one day during the busy Christmas season that first year. The store was packed and Schultz was behind the counter ringing up sales of coffee when someone shouted that a shopper had just headed out the door with some stuff—two expensive coffeemakers it turned out, one in each hand. Without thinking, Schultz leaped over the counter and chased the thief up the cobblestone street outside the store, yelling, "Drop that stuff! Drop it!" The thief was startled enough to drop both pieces and run away. Howard picked up the merchandise and returned to the store, holding the coffeemakers up like trophies. Everyone applauded. When Schultz returned to his office later that afternoon, his staff had strung up a banner that read: "Make my day."[8]

Schultz was overflowing with ideas for the company. Early on, he noticed that first-time customers sometimes felt uneasy in the stores because of their lack of knowledge about fine coffees and because store employees sometimes came across as a little arrogant or superior to coffee novices. Schultz worked with store employees on customer-friendly sales skills and developed brochures that made it easy for customers to learn about fine coffees. However, Schultz's biggest inspiration and vision for Starbucks' future came during the spring of 1983 when the company sent him to Milan, Italy, to attend an international housewares show. While walking from his hotel to the convention center, he spotted an espresso bar and went inside to look around. The cashier beside the door nodded and smiled. The

Exhibit 2 **Biographical Sketch of Howard Schultz**

- His parents both came from working-class families residing in Brooklyn, New York, for two generations. Neither completed high school.
- He grew up in a government-subsidized housing project in Brooklyn, was the oldest of three children, played sports with the neighborhood kids and developed a passion for baseball, and became a die-hard Yankees fan.
- His father was a blue-collar factory worker and taxicab driver who held many low-wage, no-benefits jobs; his mother remained home to take care of the children during their preschool years, then worked as an office receptionist. The family was hard pressed to make ends meet.
- He had a number of jobs as a teenager—paper route, counter job at luncheonette, an after-school job in the garment district in Manhattan, a summer job steaming yarn at a knit factory. He always gave part of his earnings to his mother to help with family expenses.
- He saw success in sports as his way to escape life in the projects; he played quarterback on the high school football team.
- He was offered a scholarship to play football at Northern Michigan University (the only offer he got) and he took it. When his parents drove him to the campus to begin the fall term, it was his first trip outside New York. It turned out that he didn't have enough talent to play football, but he got loans and worked at several jobs to keep himself in school. He majored in communications, took a few business courses on the side, and graduated in 1975 with a B average—the first person in his family to graduate from college.
- He went to work for a ski lodge in Michigan after graduation, then left to go back to New York, landing a sales job at Xerox Corporation. He left Xerox to work for Swedish coffee-equipment maker Hammarplast, U.S.A., becoming vice president and general manager in charge of U.S. operations and managing 20 independent sales representatives.
- He married Sheri Kersch in July 1982 and later became the father of two children.
- His father contracted lung cancer in 1982 at age 60 and died in 1988, leaving his mother with no pension, no life insurance, and no savings.
- He became a principal owner of Seattle SuperSonics NBA team in 2001 and also a principal owner of Seattle Storm of WNBA.
- He owned about 32 million shares of Starbucks worth about $950 million in December 2005.

Source: Howard Schultz and Dori Jones Yang, *Pour Your Heart Into It* (New York: Hyperion, 1997).

barista behind the counter greeted Howard cheerfully and moved gracefully to pull a shot of espresso for one customer and handcraft a foamy cappuccino for another, all the while conversing merrily with those standing at the counter. Schultz thought the barista's performance was "great theater." Just down the way on a side street, he entered in an even more crowded espresso bar where the barista, whom he surmised to be the owner, was greeting customers by name; people were laughing and talking in an atmosphere that plainly was comfortable and familiar. In the next few blocks, he saw two more espresso bars. That afternoon, when the trade show concluded for the day, Schultz walked the streets of Milan to explore more espresso bars. Some were stylish and upscale; others attracted a blue-collar clientele. Most had few chairs, and it was common for Italian opera to be playing in the background. What struck Schultz was how popular and vibrant the Italian coffee bars were.

Energy levels were typically high, and they seemed to function as an integral community gathering place. Each one had its own unique character, but they all had a barista who performed with flair and maintained a camaraderie with the customers.

Schultz remained in Milan for a week, exploring coffee bars and learning as much as he could about the Italian passion for coffee drinks. Schultz was particularly struck by the fact that there were 1,500 coffee bars in Milan, a city about the size of Philadelphia, and a total of 200,000 in all of Italy. In one bar, he heard a customer order a caffe latte and decided to try one himself—the barista made a shot of espresso, steamed a frothy pitcher of milk, poured the two together in a cup, and put a dollop of foam on the top. Schultz liked it immediately, concluding that lattes should be a feature item on any coffee bar menu even though none of the coffee experts he had talked to had ever mentioned them.

Schultz's 1983 trip to Milan produced a revelation: The Starbucks stores in Seattle completely missed the point. There was much more to the coffee business than just selling beans and getting people to appreciate grinding their own beans and brewing fine coffee in their homes. What Starbucks needed to do was serve fresh-brewed coffee, espressos, and cappuccinos in its stores (in addition to beans and coffee equipment) and try to create an American version of the Italian coffee bar culture. Going to Starbucks should be an experience, a special treat, a place to meet friends and visit. Re-creating the authentic Italian coffee bar culture in the United States could be Starbucks' differentiating factor.

Schultz Becomes Frustrated

On Howard Schultz's return from Italy, he shared his revelation and ideas for modifying the format of Starbucks' stores with Jerry Baldwin and Gordon Bowker. But instead of winning their approval for trying out some of his ideas, Schultz encountered strong resistance. They argued that Starbucks was a retailer, not a restaurant or coffee bar. They feared that serving drinks would put them in the beverage business and diminish the integrity of Starbucks' mission as a purveyor of fine coffees. They pointed out that Starbucks had been profitable every year and there was no reason to rock the boat in a small, private company like Starbucks. But a more pressing reason not to pursue Schultz's coffee bar concept emerged shortly—Baldwin and Bowker were excited by an opportunity to purchase Peet's Coffee and Tea. The acquisition was finalized in early 1984, and to fund it Starbucks had to take on considerable debt, leaving little in the way of financial flexibility to support Schultz's ideas for entering the beverage part of the coffee business or expanding the number of Starbucks stores. For most of 1984, Starbucks managers were dividing their time between operations in Seattle and the Peet's enterprise in San Francisco. Schultz found himself in San Francisco every other week supervising the marketing and operations of the five Peet stores. Starbucks employees began to feel neglected and, in one quarter, did not receive their usual bonus due to tight financial conditions. Employee discontent escalated to the point where a union election was called. The union won by three votes. Baldwin was

shocked at the results, concluding that employees no longer trusted him. In the months that followed, he began to spend more of his energy on Peet's operation in San Francisco.

It took Howard Schultz nearly a year to convince Jerry Baldwin to let him test an espresso bar. Baldwin relented when Starbucks opened its sixth store in April 1984. It was the first store designed to sell beverages, and it was the first store located in downtown Seattle. Schultz asked for a 1,500-square-foot space to set up a full-scale Italian-style espresso bar, but Jerry agreed to allocating only 300 square feet in a corner of the new store. As a deliberate experiment to see what would happen, the store opened with no fanfare. By closing time on the first day, some 400 customers had been served, well above the 250-customer average of Starbucks' best-performing stores. Within two months the store was serving 800 customers per day. The two baristas could not keep up with orders during the early-morning hours, resulting in lines outside the door onto the sidewalk. Most of the business was at the espresso counter, while sales at the regular retail counter were only adequate.

Schultz was elated at the test results, expecting that Jerry's doubts about entering the beverage side of the business would be dispelled and that he would gain approval to pursue the opportunity to take Starbucks to a new level. Every day he went into Baldwin's office to show him the sales figures and customer counts at the new downtown store. But Baldwin was not comfortable with the success of the new store, believing that it felt wrong and that espresso drinks were a distraction from the core business of marketing fine arabica coffees at retail. Baldwin rebelled at the thought that people would see Starbucks as a place to get a quick cup of coffee to go. He adamantly told Schultz, "We're coffee roasters. I don't want to be in the restaurant business . . . Besides, we're too deeply in debt to consider pursuing this idea."[9] While he didn't deny that the experiment was succeeding, he didn't want to go forward with introducing beverages in other Starbucks stores. Schultz's efforts to persuade Baldwin to change his mind continued to meet strong resistance, although to avoid a total impasse Baldwin finally did agree to let Schultz put espresso machines in the back of possibly one or two other Starbucks stores.

Over the next several months, Schultz made up his mind to leave Starbucks and start his own company. His plan was to open espresso bars in high-traffic downtown locations, serve espresso drinks and coffee by the cup, and try to emulate the friendly, energetic atmosphere he had encountered in Italian espresso bars. Baldwin and Bowker, knowing how frustrated Schultz had become, supported his efforts to go out on his own and agreed to let him stay in his current job and office until definitive plans were in place. Schultz left Starbucks in late 1985.

Schultz's Il Giornale Venture

With the aid of a lawyer friend who helped companies raise venture capital and go public, Howard Schultz began seeking out investors for the kind of company he had in mind. Ironically, Jerry Baldwin committed to investing $150,000 of Starbucks' money in Schultz's coffee bar enterprise, thus becoming Schultz's first investor. Baldwin accepted Schultz's invitation to be a director of the new company, and Gordon Bowker agreed to be a part-time consultant for six months. Bowker, pumped up about the new venture, urged Schultz to take pains to make sure that everything about the new stores—the name, the presentation, the care taken in preparing the coffee—be calculated to elevate customer expectations and lead them to expect something better than competitors offered. Bowker proposed that the new company be named Il Giornale Coffee Company (pronounced *il jor NAHL ee*), a suggestion that Schultz accepted. In December 1985, Bowker and Schultz made a trip to Italy, where they visited some 500 espresso bars in Milan and Verona, observing local habits, taking notes about decor and menus, snapping photographs, and videotaping baristas in action.

About $400,000 in seed capital was raised by the end of January 1986, enough to rent an office, hire a couple of key employees, develop a store design, and open the first store. But it took until the end of 1986 to raise the remaining $1.25 million needed to launch at least eight espresso bars and prove that Schultz's strategy and business model were viable. Schultz made presentations to 242 potential investors, 217 of whom said no. Many who heard Schultz's hour-long presentation saw coffee as a commodity business and thought that Schultz's espresso bar concept lacked any basis for sustainable competitive advantage (no patent on dark roast, no

advantage in purchasing coffee beans, no ways to bar the entry of imitative competitors). Some noted that coffee couldn't be turned into a growth business—consumption of coffee had been declining since the mid-1960s. Others were skeptical that people would pay $1.50 or more for a cup of coffee, and the company's unpronounceable name turned some off. Being rejected by so many of the potential investors he approached was disheartening (some who listened to Schultz's presentation didn't even bother to call him back; others refused to take his calls). Nonetheless, Schultz maintained an upbeat attitude and displayed passion and enthusiasm in making his pitch. He ended up raising $1.65 million from about 30 investors; most of the money came from nine people, five of whom became directors.

The first Il Giornale store opened in April 1986. It had 700 square feet and was located near the entrance of Seattle's tallest building. The decor was Italian, and there were Italian words on the menu. Italian opera music played in the background. The baristas wore white shirts and bow ties. All service was stand-up—there were no chairs. National and international papers were hung on rods on the wall. By closing time on the first day, 300 customers had been served—mostly in the morning hours. But while the core idea worked well, it soon became apparent that several aspects of the format were not appropriate for Seattle. Some customers objected to the incessant opera music, others wanted a place to sit down, and many did not understand the Italian words on the menu. These "mistakes" were quickly fixed, but an effort was made not to compromise the style and elegance of the store. Within six months, the store was serving more than 1,000 customers a day. Regular customers had learned how to pronounce the company's name. Because most customers were in a hurry, it became apparent that speedy service was essential.

Six months after opening the first store, Schultz opened a second store in another downtown building. A third store was opened in Vancouver, British Columbia, in April 1987. Vancouver was chosen to test the transferability of the company's business concept outside Seattle. Schultz's goal was to open 50 stores in five years, and he needed to dispel his investors' doubts about geographic expansion early on to achieve his growth objective. By mid-1987, sales at the three stores were running at a rate equal to $1.5 million annually.

Il Giornale Acquires Starbucks

In March 1987 Jerry Baldwin and Gordon Bowker decided to sell the whole Starbucks operation in Seattle—the stores, the roasting plant, and the Starbucks name. Bowker wanted to cash out his coffee business investment to concentrate on his other enterprises; Baldwin, who was tired of commuting between Seattle and San Francisco and wrestling with the troubles created by the two parts of the company, elected to concentrate on the Peet's operation. As he recalls, "My wife and I had a 30-second conversation and decided to keep Peet's. It was the original and it was better."[10]

Schultz knew immediately that he had to buy Starbucks; his board of directors agreed. Schultz and his newly hired finance and accounting manager drew up a set of financial projections for the combined operations and a financing package that included a stock offering to Il Giornale's original investors and a line of credit with local banks. While a rival plan to acquire Starbucks was put together by another Il Giornale investor, Schultz's proposal prevailed—and within weeks Schultz had raised the $3.8 million needed to buy Starbucks. The acquisition was completed in August 1987. The new name of the combined companies was Starbucks Corporation. Howard Schultz, at the age of 34, became Starbucks' president and CEO.

STARBUCKS AS A PRIVATE COMPANY: 1987–1992

The following Monday morning, Howard Schultz returned to the Starbucks offices at the roasting plant, greeted all the familiar faces, and accepted their congratulations. Then he called the staff together for a meeting on the roasting plant floor:

> All my life I have wanted to be part of a company and a group of people who share a common vision . . . I'm here today because I love this company. I love what it represents . . . I know you're concerned . . . I promise you I will not let you down. I promise you I will not leave anyone behind . . . In five years, I want you to look back at this day and say "I was there when it started. I helped build this company into something great."[11]

Schultz told the group that his vision was for Starbucks to become a national company with values and guiding principles that employees could be proud of. He indicated that he wanted to include people in the decision-making process and that he would be open and honest with them.

Schultz believed that building a company that valued and respected its people, inspired them, and shared the fruits of success with those who contributed to the company's long-term value was essential, not just an intriguing option. His aspiration was for Starbucks to become the world's most respected brand name in coffee and for the company to be admired for its corporate responsibility. In the next few days and weeks, Schultz came to see that the unity and morale at Starbucks had deteriorated badly in the 20 months he had been at Il Giornale. Some employees were cynical and felt unappreciated. There was a feeling that prior management had abandoned them and a wariness about what the new regime would bring. Schultz decided to make building a new relationship of mutual respect between employees and management a priority.

The new Starbucks had a total of nine stores. The business plan Schultz had presented investors called for the new company to open 125 stores in the next five years—15 the first year, 20 the second, 25 the third, 30 the fourth, and 35 the fifth. Revenues were projected to reach $60 million in 1992. But the company lacked experienced management. Schultz had never led a growth effort of such magnitude and was just learning what the job of CEO was all about, having been the president of a small company for barely two years. Dave Olsen, a Seattle coffee bar owner Schultz had recruited to direct store operations at Il Giornale, was still learning the ropes in managing a multistore operation. Ron Lawrence, the company's controller, had worked as a controller for several organizations. Other Starbucks employees had only the experience of managing or being a part of a six-store organization. When Starbucks' key roaster and coffee buyer resigned, Schultz put Dave Olsen in charge of buying and roasting coffee. Lawrence Maltz, who had 20 years' experience in business and eight years' experience as president of a profitable public beverage company, was hired as executive vice president and charged with heading operations, finance, and human resources.

In the next several months, a number of changes were instituted. To symbolize the merging of the two companies and the two cultures, a new logo was created that melded the designs of the Starbucks logo and the Il Giornale logo. The Starbucks stores were equipped with espresso machines and remodeled to look more Italian than Old World nautical. Il Giornale green replaced the traditional Starbucks brown. The result was a new type of store—a cross between a retail coffee-bean store and an espresso bar/café that has now become Starbucks' signature.

By December 1987, the mood of the employees at Starbucks had turned upbeat. They were buying into the changes that Schultz was making and began to trust management. New stores were on the verge of opening in Vancouver and Chicago. One Starbucks store employee, Daryl Moore, who had started working at Starbucks in 1981 and who had voted against unionization in 1985, began to question the need for a union with his fellow employees. Over the next few weeks, Moore began a move to decertify the union. He carried a decertification letter around to Starbucks' stores securing the signatures of employees who no longer wished to be represented by the union. He got a majority of store employees to sign the letter and presented it to the National Labor Relations Board, which then decertified the union representing store employees. Later, in 1992, the union representing Starbucks' roasting plant and warehouse employees was also decertified.

Market Expansion Outside the Pacific Northwest

Starbucks' entry into Chicago proved far more troublesome than management anticipated. The first Chicago store opened in October 1987 and three more stores were opened over the next six months. Customer counts at the stores were substantially below expectations. Chicagoans did not take to dark-roasted coffee as fast as Schultz had anticipated. The first downtown store opened onto the street rather than into the lobby of the building where it was located; in the winter months, customers were hesitant to go out in the wind and cold to acquire a cup of coffee. It was more expensive to supply fresh coffee to the Chicago stores out of the Seattle warehouse (the company solved the problem of freshness and quality assurance by putting freshly roasted beans in special FlavorLock bags that used vacuum packaging techniques with a one-way valve to allow carbon dioxide to escape without allowing air and moisture in). Rents were higher in Chicago than in Seattle,

and so were wage rates. The result was a squeeze on store profit margins. Gradually, customer counts improved, but Starbucks lost money on its Chicago stores until, in 1990, prices were raised to reflect higher rents and labor costs, more experienced store managers were hired, and a critical mass of customers caught on to the taste of Starbucks products.

Portland, Oregon, was the next market Starbucks entered, and Portland coffee drinkers took to its products quickly. By 1991, the Chicago stores had become profitable and the company was ready for its next big market entry. Management decided on California because of its host of neighborhood centers and the receptiveness of Californians to high-quality, innovative food. Los Angeles was chosen as the first California market to enter. L.A. was selected principally because of its status as a trendsetter and its cultural ties to the rest of the country. L.A. consumers embraced Starbucks quickly, and the *Los Angeles Times* named Starbucks as the best coffee in America even before the first area store opened. The entry into San Francisco proved more troublesome because San Francisco had an ordinance against converting stores to restaurant-related uses in certain prime urban neighborhoods; Starbucks could sell beverages and pastries to customers at stand-up counters but could not offer seating in stores that had formerly been used for general retailing. However, the city council was soon convinced by café owners and real estate brokers to change the code. Still, Starbucks faced strong competition from Peet's and local espresso bars in the San Francisco market.

Starbucks' store expansion targets proved easier to meet than Schultz had originally anticipated, and he upped the numbers to keep challenging the organization. Starbucks opened 15 new stores in fiscal 1988, 20 in 1989, 30 in 1990, 32 in 1991, and 53 in 1992—producing a total of 161 stores, significantly above the 1987 objective of 125 stores.

From the outset, the strategy was to open only company-owned stores; franchising was avoided so as to keep the company in full control of the quality of its products and the character and location of its stores. But company ownership of all stores required Starbucks to raise new venture capital to cover the cost of new store expansion. In 1988, the company raised $3.9 million; in 1990, venture capitalists provided an additional $13.5 million; and in 1991, another round of venture capital financing generated $15 million. Starbucks was able to raise the needed funds despite posting losses of $330,000 in 1987,

$764,000 in 1988, and $1.2 million in 1989. While the losses were troubling to Starbucks' board of directors and investors, Schultz's business plan had forecast losses during the early years of expansion. At a particularly tense board meeting where directors sharply questioned Schultz about the lack of profitability, Schultz said:

> Look, we're going to keep losing money until we can do three things. We have to attract a management team well beyond our expansion needs. We have to build a world-class roasting facility. And we need a computer information system sophisticated enough to keep track of sales in hundreds and hundreds of stores.[12]

Schultz argued for patience as the company invested in the infrastructure to support continued growth well into the 1990s. He contended that hiring experienced executives ahead of the growth curve, building facilities far beyond current needs, and installing support systems laid a strong foundation for rapid, profitable growth on down the road. His arguments carried the day with the board and with investors, especially since revenues were growing by approximately 80 percent annually and customer traffic at the stores was meeting or exceeding expectations.

Starbucks became profitable in 1990; profits had increased every year since 1990 except for fiscal year 2000 (because of $58.8 million in investment write-offs in four dot-com enterprises). Exhibit 3 provides a financial and operating summary for 2000–2005. Exhibit 4 shows the performance of the company's stock price. The stock had split 2-for-1 five times. In September 2005, Starbucks' board of directors approved the repurchase of up to 5 million shares of common stock; a total of 35.7 million shares had been repurchased since the company went public.

HOWARD SCHULTZ'S STRATEGY TO MAKE STARBUCKS A GREAT PLACE TO WORK

Howard Schultz deeply believed that Starbucks' success was heavily dependent on customers having a very positive experience in its stores. This meant having store employees who were knowledgeable about the company's products, who paid attention to detail in preparing the company's espresso drinks, who eagerly communicated the company's passion for coffee, and who possessed the skills and personality to deliver consistent, pleasing customer service. Many of the baristas were in their 20s and worked part-time, going to college on the side or pursuing other career activities. The challenge to Starbucks, in Schultz's view, was how to attract, motivate, and reward store employees in a manner that would make Starbucks a company that people would want to work for and that would generate enthusiastic commitment and higher levels of customer service. Moreover, Schultz wanted to send all Starbucks employees a message that would cement the trust that had been building between management and the company's workforce.

One of the requests that employees had made to the prior owners of Starbucks was to extend health care benefits to part-time workers. Their request had been turned down, but Schultz believed that expanding health care coverage to include part-timers was the right thing to do. His father had recently passed away with cancer and he knew from his own experience of having grown up in a family that struggled to make ends meet how difficult it was to cope with rising medical costs. In 1988, Schultz went to the board of directors with his plan to expand the company's health care coverage to include part-timers who worked at least 20 hours per week. He saw the proposal not as a generous gesture but as a core strategy to win employee loyalty and commitment to the company's mission. Board members resisted because the company was unprofitable and the added costs of the extended coverage would only worsen the company's bottom line. But Schultz argued passionately that it was the right thing to do and wouldn't be as expensive as it seemed. He observed that if the new benefit reduced turnover, which he believed was likely, then it would reduce the costs of hiring and training—which equaled about $3,000 per new hire; he further pointed out that it cost $1,500 a year to provide an employee with full benefits. Part-timers, he argued, were vital to Starbucks, constituting two-thirds of the company's workforce. Many were baristas who knew the favorite drinks of regular customers; if the barista left, that connection with the customer was broken. Moreover, many part-time employees were called upon to open the stores early, sometimes at 5:30 or 6:00 a.m.; others had to work until closing, usually 9:00 p.m. or later. Providing these employees with health care benefits, he argued, would signal that the company honored their value and contribution.

The board approved Schultz's plan, and part-timers working 20 or more hours were offered the same health coverage as full-time employees starting in late 1988. Starbucks paid 75 percent of an employee's health care premium; the employee paid 25 percent. Over the years, Starbucks extended its health coverage to include preventive care, crisis counseling, dental care, eye care, mental health, and chemical dependency. Coverage was also offered for unmarried partners in a committed relationship. Since most Starbucks' employees were young and comparatively healthy, the company had been able to provide broader coverage while keeping monthly payments relatively low. The value of Starbucks' health care program struck home when one of the company's store managers and a former barista walked into Schultz's office and told him he had AIDS:

> I had known he was gay but had no idea he was sick. His disease had entered a new phase, he explained, and he wouldn't be able to work any longer. We sat

Exhibit 3   Financial and Operating Summary for Starbucks Corporation, Fiscal Years 2000–2005 (dollars in 000s)

	Fiscal Years Ending[1]					
	October 2, 2005	October 3, 2004	September 30, 2003	September 29, 2002	September 30, 2001	October 1, 2000
Results of operations data						
Net revenues:						
Retail	$5,391,927	$4,457,378	$3,449,624	$2,792,904	$2,229,594	$1,823,607
Specialty	977,373	836,869	625,898	496,004	419,386	354,007
Total net revenues	$6,369,300	$5,294,247	$4,075,522	$3,288,908	$2,648,980	$2,177,614
Cost of sales and related company costs	2,605,212	2,191,440	1,681,434	1,350,011	1,112,785	961,885
Store operating expenses	2,165,911	1,790,168	1,379,574	1,109,782	867,957	704,898
Other operating expenses	197,024	171,648	141,346	106,084	72,406	78,445
Depreciation and amortization expenses	340,169	289,182	244,671	205,557	163,501	130,232
General and administrative expenses	357,114	304,293	244,550	234,581	179,852	110,202
Income from equity ventures	76,745	59,071	36,903	33,445	27,740	20,300
Operating income	$ 780,615	$ 606,587	$ 420,850	$ 316,338	$ 280,219	$ 212,252
Internet-related investment losses[2]					2,940	58,792
Gain on sale of investment[3]				13,361		
Net earnings	$ 494,467	$ 388,973	$ 265,355	$ 210,463	$ 178,794	$ 94,564
Net earnings per common share—diluted[4]	$0.61	$0.49	$0.34	$0.54	$0.46	$0.24
Cash dividends per share	0	0	0	0	0	0
Balance sheet data						
Current assets	$1,209,334	$1,350,895	$ 924,029	$ 772,643	$ 593,925	$ 459,819
Current liabilities	1,226,996	746,259	608,703	462,595	445,264	313,251
Working capital[5]	(17,662)	604,636	335,767	328,777	165,045	146,568
Total assets	3,514,065	3,386,541	2,776,112	2,249,435	1,807,574	1,491,546
Long-term debt (including current portion)	3,618	4,353	5,076	5,786	6,483	7,168
Shareholders' equity	$2,090,634	$2,470,211	$2,068,689	$1,712,456	$1,366,355	$1,148,399

(Continued)

Exhibit 3 **Continued**

	Fiscal Years Ending[1]					
	October 2, 2005	October 3, 2004	September 30, 2003	September 29, 2002	September 30, 2001	October 1, 2000
Store operations data						
Percentage change in comparable store sales[6]						
United States	9%	11%	9%	7%	5%	9%
International	6	6	7	1	3	12
Consolidated	8	10	8	6	5	9
Systemwide stores opened during the year[7,8]						
United States						
Company-operated stores	574	514	506	503	498	388
Licensed stores	596	417	315	264	268	342
International						
Company-operated stores	161	141	124	117	151	96
Licensed stores	341	272	256	293	291	177
Total	1,672	1,344	1,201	1,177	1,208	1,003
Systemwide stores open at year-end[8]						
United States[9]						
Company-operated stores	4,867	293	3,779	3,209	2,706	2,208
Licensed stores	2,435	1,839	1,422	1,033	769	501
International						
Company-operated stores	1,133	972	831	707	590	411
Licensed stores	1,806	1,465	1,193	937	644	381
Total	10,241	8,569	7,225	5,886	4,709	3,501

[1]The company's fiscal year ends on the Sunday closest to September 30. All fiscal years presented include 52 weeks, except fiscal 2004, which includes 53 weeks.

[2]In fiscal 2000, the company wrote off most of its investment in four ill-fated dot-com businesses. In fiscal 2001, the company wrote off an additional $2.9 million in Internet-related investments.

[3]On October 10, 2001, the company sold 30,000 of its shares of Starbucks Coffee Japan Ltd. at approximately $495 per share, net of related costs, which resulted in a gain of $13.4 million.

[4]Earnings per share data for fiscal years presented above have been restated to reflect the 2-for-1 stock splits in fiscal 2006 and 2001.

[5]Working capital deficit as of October 2, 2005, was primarily due to lower investments from the sale of securities to fund common stock repurchases and increased current liabilities from short-term borrowings under the revolving credit facility.

[6]Includes only Starbucks company-operated retail stores open 13 months or longer. Comparable store sales percentage for fiscal 2004 excludes the extra sales week.

[7]Store openings are reported net of closures.

[8]International store information has been adjusted for the fiscal 2005 acquisitions of licensed operations in Germany, southern China, and Chile by reclassifying historical information from licensed store to company-operated stores.

[9]United States stores open at fiscal 2003 year end included 43 SBC and 21 Torrefazione Italia Company–operated stores and 74 SBC franchised stores.

Source: 10-K reports for 2005, 2004, 2003, 2002, and 2000. Notes reflect 2005 10-K report.

together and cried, for I could not find meaningful words to console him. I couldn't compose myself. I hugged him.

At that point, Starbucks had no provision for employees with AIDS. We had a policy decision.

Because of Jim, we decided to offer health-care coverage to all employees who have terminal illnesses, paying medical costs in full from the time they are not able to work until they are covered by government programs, usually twenty-nine months.

Exhibit 4   **The Performance of Starbucks' Stock, 1992–2005**

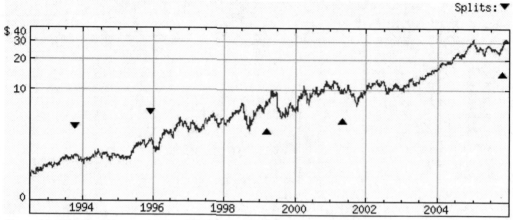

Source: http://finance.yahoo.com (accessed December 28, 2005).

After his visit to me, I spoke with Jim often and visited him at the hospice. Within a year he was gone. I received a letter from his family afterward, telling me how much they appreciated our benefit plan.[13]

In 1994 Howard Schultz was invited to the White House. He met one-on-one with President Bill Clinton to brief him on the Starbucks' health care program.

The Creation of an Employee Stock Option Plan

By 1991 the company's profitability had improved to the point where Schultz could pursue a stock option plan for all employees, a program he believed would have a positive, long-term effect on the success of Starbucks.[14] Schultz wanted to turn all Starbucks employees into partners, give them a chance to share in the success of the company, and make clear the connection between their contributions and the company's market value. Even though Starbucks was still a private company, the plan that emerged called for granting stock options to all full-time and part-time employees in proportion to their base pay. The plan, dubbed Bean Stock, was presented to the board in May 1991. Though board members were concerned that increasing the number of shares might unduly dilute the value of the shares of investors who had put up hard cash, the plan received unanimous approval. The first grant was

made in October 1991, just after the end of the company's fiscal year in September; each partner was granted stock options worth 12 percent of base pay. Each October since then, Starbucks has granted employees options equal to 14 percent of base pay, awarded at the stock price at the start of the fiscal year (October 1). When the Bean Stock program was presented to employees, Starbucks dropped the term *employee* and began referring to all of its people as *partners* because everyone, including part-timers working at least 20 hours per week, was eligible for stock options after six months. At the end of fiscal year 2004, Starbucks' employee stock option plan included 38.4 million shares in outstanding options; new options for about 9 million shares were being granted annually.[15]

Starbucks Stock Purchase Plan for Employees

In 1995, Starbucks implemented an employee stock purchase plan. Eligible employees could contribute up to 10 percent of their base earnings to quar-terly purchases of the company's common stock at 85 percent of the going stock price. As of fiscal 2005, about 14.8 million shares had been issued since inception of the plan, and new shares were being purchased at a rate close to 1 million shares annually by some 18,800 active employee participants (out of almost 55,100 employees who were eligible to participate).[16] During fiscal 2004, the U.K. Share Incentive Plan, a new employee stock purchase plan was introduced, discontinuing the original plan established in 2002. As of fiscal 2005, 10,732 shares had been issued.[17]

The Workplace Environment

Starbucks' management believed the company's pay scales (around $9–$12 per hour) and fringe benefit package allowed it to attract motivated people with above-average skills and good work habits. Store employees were paid several dollars above the hourly minimum wage. Whereas most national retailers and fast-food chains had turnover rates for store employees ranging from 150 to 400 percent a year, the turnover rates for Starbucks baristas ran about 65 percent. Starbucks' turnover for store managers was about 25 percent, compared to about 50 percent for other chain retailers. Starbucks executives believed that efforts to make the company an attractive, caring place to work were responsible for its relatively low turnover rates. One Starbucks store manager commented, "Morale is very high in my store among the staff. I've worked for a lot of companies, but I've never seen this level of respect. It's a company that's very true to its workers, and it shows. Our customers always comment that we're happy and having fun. In fact, a lot of people ask if they can work here."[18]

Starbucks' management used annual "Partner View" surveys to solicit feedback from the company's workforce of over 115,000 people worldwide, learn their concerns, and measure job satisfaction. In the latest sample survey of 1,400 employees, 79 percent rated Starbucks' workplace environment favorably relative to other companies they were familiar with, 72 percent reported being satisfied with their present job, 16 percent were neutral, and 12 percent were dissatisfied. But the 2002 survey revealed that many employees viewed the benefits package as only "average," prompting the company to increase its match of 401(k) contributions for those who had been with the company more than three years and to have these contributions vest immediately.

Exhibit 5 contains a summary of Starbucks' fringe benefit program. Starbucks was named by *Fortune* magazine as one of the "100 Best Companies to Work For" in 1998, 1999, 2000, 2002, 2003, 2004, and 2005. In 2005, Starbucks was ranked 11th, up from 34th in 2004. In October 2005, Starbucks had approximately 115,000 employees worldwide, of which 97,500 were in the United States. It had 91,200 employees in its U.S. company-owned stores. Employees at 10 stores in Canada were represented by a union.

Starbucks' Corporate Values and Business Principles

During the early building years, Howard Schultz and other Starbucks' senior executives worked to instill some key values and guiding principles into

Exhibit 5   Elements of Starbucks' Fringe Benefit Program

• Medical insurance	• Sick time
• Dental and vision care	• Paid vacations (first-year workers got one vacation week and two personal days)
• Mental health and chemical dependency coverage	• 401(k) retirement savings plan—the company matched from 25% to 150%, based on length of service, of each employee's contributions up to the first 4% of compensation.
• Short- and long-term disability	• Stock purchase plan—eligible employees could buy shares at a discounted price through regular payroll deductions
• Life insurance	• Free pound of coffee each week
• Benefits extended to committed domestic partners of Starbucks employees	• 30% product discounts
• Stock option plan (Bean Stock)	• Tuition reimbursement program

Source: Compiled by the case researchers from company documents and other sources.

the Starbucks culture. The cornerstone value in the effort "to build a company with soul" was that the company would never stop pursuing the perfect cup of coffee—it would continue buying the best beans and roasting them to perfection. Schultz remained steadfastly opposed to franchising; he wanted the company to be able to control the quality of its products and build a culture common to all stores. He was adamant about not selling artificially flavored coffee beans: "We will not pollute our high-quality beans with chemicals." If a customer wanted hazelnut-flavored coffee, Starbucks would add hazelnut syrup to the drink, rather than adding hazelnut flavoring to the beans during roasting. Running flavored beans through the grinders would result in chemical residues being left behind to alter the flavor of beans ground afterward; plus, the chemical smell given off by artificially flavored beans was absorbed by other beans in the store. Furthermore, Schultz didn't want the company to pursue supermarket sales because it would mean pouring Starbucks' beans into clear plastic bins where they could get stale, thus compro-mising the company's legacy of fresh, dark-roasted, full-flavored coffee.

Starbucks' management was also emphatic about the importance of employees paying attention to what pleased customers. Employees were trained to go out of their way—even to take heroic measures if necessary—to make sure customers were fully satisfied. The theme was "Just say yes" to customer requests. Further, employees were encouraged to speak their minds without fear of retribution from upper management—senior executives wanted employees to be straight with them, verbalizing what Starbucks was doing right, what it was doing wrong, and what changes were needed. Management wanted employees to be involved in and contribute to the process of making Starbucks a better company.

A values-and-principles crisis arose at Starbucks in 1989 when customers started requesting nonfat (skim) milk in making cappuccinos and lattes. Howard Schultz, who read all customer comments cards, and Dave Olsen, head of coffee quality, conducted taste tests of lattes and cappuccinos made with nonfat milk and concluded they were not as good as those made with whole milk. Howard Behar, recently hired as head of retail store operations, indicated that management's opinions didn't matter; what mattered was giving customers what they wanted.

Schultz said, "We will never offer nonfat milk. It's not who we are." Behar, however, stuck to his guns, maintaining that use of nonfat milk should at least be tested—otherwise, it appeared as if all the statements management had made about the importance of really and truly pleasing customers were a sham. A fierce internal debate ensued. One dogmatic defender of the quality and taste of Starbucks' coffee products buttonholed Behar outside his office and told him that using nonfat milk amounted to "bastardizing" the company's products. Numerous store managers maintained that offering two kinds of milk was operationally impractical. Schultz found himself in a quandary, torn between the company's commitment to quality and its goal of pleasing customers. Then, one day after visiting one of the stores in a residential neighborhood and watching a customer leave to go to a competitor's store because Starbucks did not make lattes with nonfat milk, Schultz authorized Behar to begin testing.[19] Within six months, all 30 stores were offering drinks made with nonfat milk. Currently, about half the lattes and cappuccinos Starbucks sells are made with nonfat milk.

Schultz's approach to offering employees good compensation and a comprehensive benefits package was driven by his belief that sharing the company's success with the people who made it happen helped everyone think and act like an owner, build positive long-term relationships with customers, and do things efficiently. He had vivid recollection of his father's employment experience—bouncing from one low-paying job to another, working for employers who offered few or no benefits and who conducted their business with no respect for the contributions of the workforce—and he had no intention of Starbucks being that type of company. He vowed that he would never let Starbucks employees suffer a similar fate, saying:

> My father worked hard all his life and he had little to show for it. He was a beaten man. This is not the American dream. The worker on our plant floor is contributing great value to the company; if he or she has low self-worth, that will have an effect on the company.[20]

The company's employee benefits program was predicated on the belief that better benefits attract good people and keep them longer. Schultz's rationale, based on his father's experience of going from one low-wage, no-benefits job to another, was that if you treat your employees well, they in turn will treat customers well.

STARBUCKS' MISSION STATEMENT

In early 1990, the senior executive team at Starbucks went to an off-site retreat to debate the company's values and beliefs and draft a mission statement. Schultz wanted the mission statement to convey a strong sense of organizational purpose and to articulate the company's fundamental beliefs and guiding principles. The draft was submitted to all employees for review and several changes were made based on employee comments. The resulting mission statement, which remained unchanged in 2005, is shown in Exhibit 6.

Following adoption of the mission statement, Starbucks' management implemented a "Mission Review" to solicit and gather employee opinions as to whether the company was living up to its stated mission. Employees were urged to report their concerns to the company's Mission Review team if they thought particular management decisions were not supportive of the company's mission statement. Comment cards were given to each newly hired employee and were kept available in common areas with other employee forms. Employees had the option of signing the comment cards or not. Hundreds of cards were submitted to the Mission Review team each year. The company promised that a relevant manager would respond to all signed cards within two weeks. Howard Schultz reviewed all the comments, signed and unsigned.

STARBUCKS' STORE EXPANSION STRATEGY

In 1992 and 1993 Starbucks developed a three-year geographic expansion strategy that targeted areas that not only had favorable demographic profiles but also could be serviced and supported by the company's operations infrastructure. For each targeted region, Starbucks selected a large city to serve as a hub; teams of professionals were located in hub cities to support the goal of opening 20 or more stores in the hub in the first two years. Once stores blanketed the hub, then additional stores were opened in smaller, surrounding spoke areas in the region. To oversee the expansion process, Starbucks created zone vice presidents to direct the development of each region and to implant the Starbucks culture in the newly opened stores. All of the new zone vice presidents Starbucks recruited came with extensive operating and marketing experience in chain store retailing.

Starbucks' strategy in major metropolitan cities was to blanket the area with stores, even if some stores cannibalized another store's business.[21] While a new store might draw 30 percent of the business of an existing store two or so blocks away, management believed its "Starbucks everywhere" approach cut down on delivery and management costs, shortened customer lines at individual stores, and increased foot traffic for all the stores in an area.

In 2002, new stores generated an average of $1.2 million in first-year revenues, compared to $700,000 in 1995 and only $427,000 in 1990. The steady increases in new-store revenues were due partly to growing popularity of premium coffee drinks and

Exhibit 6 **Starbucks' Mission Statement**

Establish Starbucks as the premier purveyor of the finest coffee in the world while maintaining our uncompromising principles while we grow.

The following six guiding principles will help us measure the appropriateness of our decisions:

- Provide a great work environment and treat each other with respect and dignity.
- Embrace diversity as an essential component in the way we do business.
- Apply the highest standards of excellence to the purchasing, roasting, and fresh delivery of our coffee.
- Develop enthusiastically satisfied customers all of the time.
- Contribute positively to our communities and our environment.
- Recognize that profitability is essential to our future success.

partly to Starbucks' growing reputation. In more and more instances, Starbucks' reputation reached new markets even before stores opened. Moreover, existing stores continued to post sales gains in the range of 2–10 percent annually. In 2005, Starbucks posted same-store sales increases averaging 8 percent (refer back to Exhibit 3), the 14th consecutive year the company had achieved sales growth of 5 percent or greater at existing stores. Starbucks' revenues had climbed an average of 20 percent annually since 1992.

One of Starbucks' core competencies was identifying good retailing sites for its new stores. The company was regarded as having the best real estate team in the coffee bar industry and a sophisticated system for identifying not only the most attractive individual city blocks but also the exact store location that was best; it also worked hard at building good relationships with local real estate representatives in areas where it was opening multiple store locations. The company's site location track record was so good that, as of 1997, it had closed only 2 of the 1,500 sites it had opened; its track record in finding successful store locations was still intact as of 2005 (although specific figures were not available).

International Expansion

In markets outside the continental United States (including Hawaii), Starbucks had a two-pronged store expansion plan: Either open company-owned and company-operated stores, or else license a reputable and capable local company with retailing know-how in the target host country to develop and operate new Starbucks stores. In most countries, Starbucks used a local partner/licensee to help it recruit talented individuals, set up supplier relationships, locate suitable store sites, and cater to local market conditions. Starbucks looked for partners/licensees that had strong retail/restaurant experience, had values and a corporate culture compatible with Starbucks', were committed to good customer service, possessed talented management and strong financial resources, and had demonstrated brand-building skills.

Starbucks had created a new subsidiary, Starbucks Coffee International, to orchestrate overseas expansion and begin to build the Starbucks brand name globally via licensees. (Refer back to Exhibit 1 for the number of licensed international stores in

each country.) Starbucks' management expected to have a total of 10,000 stores in 60 countries by the end of 2005. As of August 2005, Starbucks was located in 34 countries, with 1,049 company-operated stores and 1,734 licensed locations outside the United States. The company's first store in France opened in early 2004 in Paris. China was expected to be Starbucks' biggest market outside the United States in the years to come. Thus far, Starbucks' products were proving to be a much bigger hit with consumers in Asia than in Europe. In 2003, the Starbucks Coffee International division was only marginally profitable, with pretax earnings of only $3.8 million on sales of $603 million. However, the profitability picture improved in 2004, with pretax profits rising to $51.7 million on sales of $803 million. And it did even better in fiscal 2005, with pretax earnings of $86.4 million on sales of $1.03 billion.

So far, Starbucks had avoided franchising, preferring licensing because it permitted tighter controls over the operations of licensees. Often, Starbucks opened foreign stores as a minority partner with local companies. In 2005, Starbucks assumed 100 percent equity ownership of previously licensed operations in Germany and Chile (where it had been a 20 percent equity partner), and it boosted its ownership of stores in southern China from 20 percent to 51 percent.

In May 2005, Starbucks announced the first step into expanding its consumer products channel in the South Pacific region by launching the sales of its Frappuccino line in Japan and Taiwan. The combined ready-to-drink markets in these countries represented more than $10 billion in annual sales.[22] Marketing of Frappuccino products also began in South Korea through agreements with leading local distributors; the ready-to-drink coffee segment in South Korea represented $320 million in annual consumer sales.[23]

Employee Training and Recognition

To accommodate its strategy of rapid store expansion, Starbucks put in systems to recruit, hire, and train baristas and store managers. Starbucks' vice president for human resources used some simple guidelines in screening candidates for new positions, "We want passionate people who love coffee . . . We're looking for a diverse workforce, which reflects our community. We want people who enjoy what they're doing and for whom work is an extension of themselves."[24]

Every partner/barista hired for a retail job in a Starbucks store received at least 24 hours training in his or her first two to four weeks. The topics included classes on coffee history, drink preparation, coffee knowledge (four hours), customer service (four hours), and retail skills, plus a four-hour workshop titled "Brewing the Perfect Cup." Baristas spent considerable time learning about beverage preparation—grinding beans, steaming milk, learning to pull perfect (18- to 23-second) shots of espresso, memorizing the recipes of all the different drinks, practicing making the different drinks, and learning how to customize drinks to customer specifications. There were sessions on operating the cash register, cleaning the milk wand on the espresso machine, explaining the Italian drink names to unknowing customers, selling home espresso machines, making eye contact with customers, and taking personal responsibility for the cleanliness of the store. Everyone was drilled in the Star Skills, three guidelines for on-the-job interpersonal relations: (1) maintain and enhance self-esteem, (2) listen and acknowledge, and (3) ask for help. And there were rules to be memorized: Milk must be steamed to at least 150 degrees Fahrenheit but never more than 170 degrees; every espresso shot not pulled within 23 seconds must be tossed; never let coffee sit in the pot more than 20 minutes; always compensate dissatisfied customers with a Starbuck coupon that entitles them to a free drink.

In response to feedback through 2003 Partner View Survey, Starbucks expanded its training and career development offerings by adding the following:[25]

> *Coffee Masters Program:* A set of courses in which partners deepen their coffee knowledge and expertise. More than 7,000 partners have taken advantage of this training either partially or fully.
>
> *Servant Leadership Workshop:* A workshop that emphasizes trust, collaboration, people development, and ethics. Approximately 6,200 partners attended this workshop.
>
> *Career Power and Career Power for Coaches Workshop:* A workshop designed to provide partners and their managers with an opportunity to reflect on their personal values,

career dreams, and development through coaching and feedback. More than 200 partners in Seattle attended the workshop.

Management trainees attended classes for 8 to 12 weeks. Their training covered not only the coffee knowledge and information imparted to baristas but also the details of store operations, practices and procedures as set forth in the company's operating manual, information systems, and the basics of managing people. Starbucks' trainers were all store managers and district managers with on-site experience. Among their major objectives were to ingrain the company's values, principles, and culture and to pass on their knowledge about coffee and their passion about Starbucks.

When Starbucks opened stores in a new market, it launched a major recruiting effort. Eight to 10 weeks before opening a store, the company placed ads to hire baristas and begin their training. It sent a Star team of experienced managers and baristas from existing stores to the area to lead the store-opening effort and to conduct one-on-one training following the company's formal classes and basic orientation sessions at the Starbucks Coffee School in San Francisco.

To recognize the partner contributions, Starbucks had created 19 different awards programs ranging from frequent awards to high-level cash awards. Some of the high-level awards included Manager of the Quarter for store manager leadership, Green Apron Awards for outstanding customer service, and Green Bean Awards for exceptional support for company's environmental mission.

Real Estate, Store Design, Store Planning, and Construction

Starting in 1991, Starbucks created its own in-house team of architects and designers to ensure that each store would convey the right image and character. Stores had to be custom-designed because the company didn't buy real estate and build its own free-standing structures like McDonald's or Wal-Mart; rather, each space was leased in an existing structure, making each store differ in size and shape. Most stores ranged in size from 1,000 to 1,500 square feet and were located in office buildings, downtown and suburban retail centers, airport terminals, university campus areas, and busy neighborhood shopping areas convenient for pedestrian foot traffic and/or drivers. Only a select few were in suburban malls.

Over the years, Starbucks had experimented with a broad range of store formats. Special seating areas were added to help make Starbucks a desirable gathering place where customers could meet and chat or simply enjoy a peaceful interlude in their day. Flagship stores in high-traffic, high-visibility locations had fireplaces, leather chairs, newspapers, couches, and lots of ambience. The company also experimented with drive-through windows in locations where speed and convenience were important to customers and with kiosks in supermarkets, building lobbies, and other public places.

A "stores of the future" project team was formed in 1995 to raise Starbucks' store design to a still higher level and come up with the next generation of Starbucks stores. The vision of what a Starbucks store should be like included such concepts as an authentic coffee experience that conveyed the artistry of espresso making, a place to think and imagine, a spot where people could gather and talk over a great cup of coffee, a comforting refuge that provided a sense of community, a third place for people to congregate beyond work or the home, a place that welcomes people and rewards them for coming, and a layout that could accommodate both fast service and quiet moments. The team researched the art and literature of coffee throughout the ages, studied coffee-growing and coffeemaking techniques, and looked at how Starbucks' stores had already evolved in terms of design, logos, colors, and mood. The team came up with four store designs—one for each of the four stages of coffeemaking: growing, roasting, brewing, and aroma—each with its own color combinations, lighting scheme, and component materials. Within each of the four basic store templates, Starbucks could vary the materials and details to adapt to different store sizes and settings (downtown buildings, college campuses, neighborhood shopping areas). In late 1996, Starbucks began opening new stores based on one of four formats and color schemes. But as the number of stores increased rapidly in 2000–2003, greater store diversity and layout quickly became necessary. Exhibit 7 shows the diverse nature of Starbucks stores.

To better control average store opening costs, the company centralized buying, developed standard contracts and fixed fees for certain items, and consolidated work under those contractors who displayed good cost control practices. The retail operations group outlined exactly the minimum amount of equipment each core store needed so that standard items could be ordered in volume from vendors at 20 to 30 percent discounts, then delivered just-in-time to the store site either from company warehouses or the vendor. Modular designs for display cases were developed. And the whole store layout was developed on a computer, with software that allowed the costs to be estimated as the design evolved. All this cut store opening costs significantly and reduced store development time from 24 to 18 weeks.

In August 2002, Starbucks teamed up with T-Mobile USA, the largest U.S. carrier-owned Wi-Fi service, to experiment with providing Internet access capability and enhanced digital entertainment to patrons at over 1,200 Starbucks locations. The objective was to heighten the "third-place" Starbucks experience, entice customers into perhaps buying a second latte or espresso while they caught up on e-mail, listened to digital music, put the finishing touches on a presentation, or accessed their corporate intranet. Since the August 2002 introduction of Wi-Fi at Starbucks, wireless Internet service had been added at over 1,700 more stores. Internal research showed that the average connection lasted approximately 45 minutes and that more than 90 percent of accesses were during the off-peak store hours.

During the early start-up years, Starbucks avoided debt and financed new stores entirely with equity capital. But as the company's profitability improved and its balance sheet strengthened, Schultz's opposition to debt as a legitimate financing vehicle softened. In 1996 the company completed its second debt offering, netting $161 million from the sale of convertible debentures for use in its capital construction program. This debt was successfully converted into common stock in 1997. Over the next eight years, strong internal cash flows allowed Starbucks to finance virtually all of its store expansion with internal funds; in 2005, the company had less than $3 million in long-term debt on its balance sheet despite having $1.8 billion in net investment in facilities and equipment, but it did have long-term liabilities of $193.6 million associated with lease obligations at its stores.

Store Ambience

Starbucks management viewed each store as a billboard for the company and as a contributor to

Exhibit 7   **Scenes from Starbucks Stores**

building the company's brand and image. Each detail was scrutinized to enhance the mood and ambience of the store, to make sure everything signaled "best-of-class" and reflected the personality of the community and the neighborhood. The thesis was "Everything matters." The company went to great lengths to make sure the store fixtures, the merchandise displays, the colors, the artwork, the banners, the music, and the aromas all blended to create a consistent, inviting, stimulating environment that evoked the romance of coffee, that signaled the company's passion for coffee, and that rewarded customers with ceremony, stories, and surprise. Starbucks was recognized for its sensitivity to neighborhood conservation with the Scenic America's award for excellent design and "sensitive reuse of spaces within cities."

To try to keep the coffee aromas in the stores pure, Starbucks banned smoking and asked employees to refrain from wearing perfumes or colognes. Prepared foods were kept covered so that customers would smell coffee only. Colorful banners and posters in tune with seasons and holidays kept the look of Starbucks stores fresh. Company designers came up with artwork for commuter mugs and T-shirts in different cities that were in keeping with each city's personality (peach-shaped coffee mugs for Atlanta, pictures of Paul Revere for Boston and the Statue of Liberty for New York). To make sure that Starbucks' stores measured up to standards, the company used "mystery shoppers" who posed as customers and rated each location on a number of criteria.

THE PRODUCT LINE AT STARBUCKS

Starbucks stores offered a choice of regular or decaffeinated coffee beverages, a special "coffee of the day," and an assortment of made-to-order Italian-style hot and cold espresso drinks. In addition, customers could choose from a wide selection of fresh-roasted whole-bean coffees (which could be ground or not on the premises for take-home in distinctive packages), fresh pastries, juices, hot and iced teas, coffeemaking equipment, coffee mugs and other accessories, and music CDs. From time to time, stores ran special promotions touting the company's special Christmas Blend coffee, shade-grown coffee from Mexico, organically grown coffees, and various

rare and exotic coffees from across the world. In 2003, Starbucks began offering customers a choice of using its exclusive Silk soymilk specifically designed to accentuate its handcrafted beverages using espresso roast coffee and Tazo chai teas; the organic, kosher soymilk appealed to some customers as a substitute for milk or skim milk in various coffee and tea beverages.

The company's retail sales mix in 2005 was 77 percent beverages, 15 percent food items, 4 percent whole-bean coffees, and 4 percent coffeemaking equipment and accessories.[26] The product mix in each store varied, depending on the size and location of each outlet. Larger stores carried a greater variety of whole coffee beans, gourmet food items, teas, coffee mugs, coffee grinders, coffeemaking equipment, filters, storage containers, and other accessories. Smaller stores and kiosks typically sold a full line of coffee beverages, a limited selection of whole-bean coffees, and a few hardware items.

The idea for selling music CDs (which, in some cases, were special compilations that had been put together for Starbucks to use as store background music) originated with a Starbucks store manager who had worked in the music industry and selected the new "tape of the month" Starbucks played as background in its stores. He had gotten compliments from customers wanting to buy the music they heard and suggested to senior executives that there was a market for the company's music tapes. Research through two years of comment cards turned up hundreds asking Starbucks to sell the music it played in its stores. The Starbucks CDs proved a significant seller and addition to the product line; some of the CDs were specifically collections designed to tie in with new blends of coffee that company was promoting. Starbucks had also co-produced a Ray Charles CD, *Genius Loves Company,* which became a multiplatinum album with significant sales from Starbucks stores.

In 2000, Starbucks acquired Hear Music, a San Francisco–based company, to give it added capability in enhancing its music CD offerings. In 2004, Starbucks introduced Hear Music media bars, a service that offered custom CD burning at select Starbucks stores, and it opened several Starbucks Hear Music Coffeehouses—a first-of-its-kind coffee and music establishment where customers could enjoy a freshly brewed cup of coffee while downloading music from the company's 200,000-plus song library and, if they wished, have the downloaded songs burned onto a CD for purchase.

In 2005, in an average week, an estimated 30 million-plus customers patronized Starbucks, up from about 5 million in 1998. U.S. stores did about half of their business by 11:00 a.m. Loyal customers patronized a Starbucks store 15 to 20 times a month, spending perhaps $50–$75 monthly. Some customers were Starbucks fanatics, coming in daily. Baristas became familiar with regular customers, learning their names and their favorite drinks. Christine Nagy, a field director for Oracle Corporation in Palo Alto, California, told a *Wall Street Journal* reporter, "For me, it's a daily necessity or I start getting withdrawals."[27] Her standard order was a custom drink: a decaf grande nonfat no-whip no-foam extra-cocoa mocha; when the barista saw her come through the door, she told the reporter, "They just say 'We need a Christine here.' " Since the inception of Starbucks Cards in 2001, 52 million Starbucks customers had purchased the reloadable cards that allowed them to pay for their purchases with a quick swipe at the cash register and also to earn and redeem rewards. The use of Starbucks Cards was a growing means of payment in Starbucks stores. In fiscal 2004, the company reached approximately $1 billion in total life-to-date activations and reloads on Starbucks cards. Due to its success in the United States the Starbucks Card was being launched internationally, with the initial rollouts starting in Japan and Greece.

In the fall of 2003, Starbucks, in partnership with Bank One, introduced the Duetto Visa card, which added Visa card functionality to the reloadable Starbucks Cards. By charging purchases to the Visa account of their Duetto card anywhere Visa credit cards were accepted, cardholders earned 1 percent back in Duetto Dollars, automatically loaded on their Starbucks card account after each billing cycle. Duetto Dollars could be used to purchase beverages, food, and store merchandise at any Starbucks location. The Duetto card was an example of the ongoing effort by Starbucks' management to introduce new products and experiences for customers that belonged exclusively to Starbucks; senior executives drummed the importance of always being open to reinventing the Starbucks experience.

So far, Starbucks had spent very little money on advertising, preferring instead to build the brand cup-by-cup with customers via word of mouth and the appeal of its storefronts. The company spent a total of $87.7 million on advertising in fiscal 2005, up from $49.6 million in fiscal 2003.

Joint Ventures and Acquisitions

In 1994, after months of meetings and experimentation, PepsiCo and Starbucks entered into a joint venture to create new coffee-related products for mass distribution through Pepsi channels, including cold coffee drinks in a bottle or can. Howard Schultz saw this as a major paradigm shift with the potential to cause Starbucks' business to evolve in heretofore unimaginable directions; he thought it was time to look for ways to move Starbucks out into more mainstream markets. Cold coffee products had historically met with poor market reception, except in Japan, where there was an $8 billion market for ready-to-drink coffee-based beverages. Nonetheless, Schultz was hoping the partners would hit upon a new product to exploit a good-tasting coffee extract that had been developed by Starbucks' recently appointed director of research and development. The joint venture's first new product, Mazagran, a lightly flavored carbonated coffee drink, was a failure; a market test in southern California showed that some people liked it and some hated it. While people were willing to try it the first time, partly because the Starbucks name was on the label, repeat sales proved disappointing. Despite the clash of cultures and the different motivations of PepsiCo and Starbucks, the partnership held together because of the good working relationship that evolved between Howard Schultz and Pepsi's senior executives. Then Schultz, at a meeting to discuss the future of Mazagran, suggested, "Why not develop a bottled version of Frappuccino?"[28] Starbucks had come up with Frappuccino in the summer of 1995, and the cold coffee drink had proved to be a big hot-weather seller; Pepsi executives were enthusiastic. After months of experimentation, the joint venture product research team came up with a shelf-stable version of Frappaccino that tasted quite good. It was tested in West Coast supermarkets in the summer of 1996; sales ran 10 times projections, with 70 percent being repeat business. Sales of Frappuccino reached $125 million in 1997 and achieved national supermarket penetration of 80 percent. Starbucks' management believed that the market for Frappuccino would ultimately exceed $1 billion.

In October 1995 Starbucks partnered with Dreyer's Grand Ice Cream to supply coffee extract for a new line of coffee ice cream made and distributed by Dreyer's under the Starbucks brand. The new line, featuring such flavors as Dark Roast Expresso Swirl, JavaChip, Vanilla MochaChip, Biscotti Bliss, and Caffe Almond Fudge, hit supermarket shelves in April 1996, and by July 1996 Starbucks' coffee-flavored ice cream was the top-selling superpremium brand in the coffee segment. In 1997, two new low-fat flavors were added to complement the original six flavors, along with two flavors of ice cream bars; all were well received in the marketplace.

The partnerships with Pepsi and Dreyer's produced about $20 million in revenues for Starbucks in fiscal 2005 (equal to about 2 percent of total specialty sales).

In 2004, Starbucks teamed with Jim Beam Brands to invent a Starbucks Coffee Liqueur that would be sold in bars, liquor stores, and restaurants; projections were for systemwide gross sales of over $8 million annually. Launched in February 2005, Starbucks Coffee Liqueur was the top-selling new spirit product through August 2005, according to Nielsen. In October 2005, again collaborating with Jim Beam Brands, Starbucks introduced Starbucks Cream Liqueur, a blend of cream, spirits, and a hint of Starbucks coffee. With 22 million cordial consumers in the U.S. market, the cream liqueur category was nearly three times the size of coffee liqueur category. Both Starbucks Coffee Liqueur and Starbucks Cream Liqueur were packaged in a 750-milliliter bottle priced at $22.99.

In April 2005, Starbucks purchased Ethos Water for $8 million in cash. The acquisition was made to expand the line of beverages in Starbucks' stores in the United States.

Licensed Stores and Specialty Sales

Starbucks had a licensing agreement with Kraft Foods to market and distribute Starbucks whole-bean and ground coffees in grocery and mass-merchandise channels across the United States. Kraft managed all distribution, marketing, advertising, and promotions and paid a royalty to Starbucks based on a percentage of net sales. The coffee that Starbucks sold in supermarkets featured distinctive, elegant packaging, prominent positions in grocery aisles, and the same premium quality as that it sold in its stores. Product freshness was guaranteed by Starbucks' FlavorLock packaging, and the price per pound paralleled the

prices in Starbucks' retail stores. Flavor selections in supermarkets were more limited than those at Starbucks stores. Going into 2006, Starbucks coffees were available in some 31,300 grocery and warehouse clubs (such as Sam's and Costco) with 30,000 in the United States and 1,300 in the international markets. Revenues from this category comprised 24 percent of specialty revenues in fiscal 2005.

Starbucks executives recognized that supermarket distribution entailed several risks, especially in exposing Starbucks to first-time customers. Starbucks had built its reputation around the unique retail experience in its stores where all beverages were properly prepared—it had no control over how customers would perceive Starbucks when they encountered it in grocery aisles. A second risk concerned coffee preparation at home. Rigorous quality control and skilled baristas ensured that store-purchased beverages would measure up, but consumers using poor equipment or inappropriate brewing methods could easily conclude that Starbucks packaged coffees did not live up to their reputation.

Starbucks had also entered into a limited number of licensing agreements for store locations in areas where it did not have ability to locate its own outlets. The company had an agreement with Marriott Host International that allowed Host to operate Starbucks retail stores in airport locations, and it had an agreement with Aramark Food and Services to put Starbucks stores on university campuses and other locations operated by Aramark. Starbucks received a license fee and a royalty on sales at these locations and supplied the coffee for resale in the licensed locations. All licensed stores had to follow Starbucks' detailed operating procedures, and all managers and employees who worked in these stores received the same training given to Starbucks managers and store employees. As of 2005, there were 2,435 licensed or franchised stores in the United States and 1,806 licensed stores in other countries. Licensing revenues increased from $241 million in fiscal 2001 to $673 million in fiscal 2005; domestic stores accounted for $515 million of the revenues from licensing in 2005.

Starbucks had a specialty sales group that provided its coffee products to restaurants, airlines, hotels, universities, hospitals, business offices, country clubs, and select retailers. One of the early users of Starbucks coffee was Horizon Airlines, a regional carrier based in Seattle. In 1995, Starbucks entered into negotiations with United Airlines to serve Starbucks coffee on all United flights. There was much internal debate at Starbucks about whether such a move made sense for Starbucks and the possible damage to the integrity of the Starbucks brand if the quality of the coffee served did not measure up (since there was different coffeemaking equipment on different planes). It took seven months of negotiations for Starbucks and United to arrive at a mutually agreeable way to handle quality control on United's various types of planes.

In recent years, the specialty sales group had won the coffee accounts at Hyatt, Hilton, Sheraton, Radisson, and Westin hotels, resulting in packets of Starbucks coffee being in each room with coffee-making equipment. Starbucks had entered into an agreement with Wells Fargo to provide coffee service at some of the bank's locations in California. A 1997 agreement with U.S. Office Products gave Starbucks an entrée to provide its coffee to workers in 1.5 million business offices. In addition, Starbucks supplied an exclusive coffee blend to Nordstrom's for sale only in Nordstrom stores, operated coffee bars in Barnes & Noble bookstores, and, most recently, had begun coffee bar operations in Chapters bookstores (Chapters was a Toronto book retailer that had sites throughout Canada) and Borders bookstores that had cafés. Starbucks also had an alliance with SYSCO Corporation to service the majority of its food-service and restaurant accounts. In fiscal 2005, Starbucks was supplying its coffees to 15,500 food-service accounts worldwide, producing fiscal 2005 revenues of $304 million, up from $179 million in 2001.

Other Starbucks initiatives included a 24-hour Starbucks Hear Music digital music channel available to all XM satellite radio subscribers and the availability of wireless broadband Internet service in company-owned stores in the United States and Canada. Collectively, these other initiatives accounted for 3 percent of specialty revenue in fiscal 2005.

Starbucks experimented with a mail order catalog and with online sales at its Web site, but it discontinued those operations in 2003 when sales fell off (chiefly because of the growing availability of Starbucks coffees in supermarkets and the company's expanding number of store locations).

STARBUCKS COFFEE PURCHASING STRATEGY

Starbucks personnel traveled regularly to coffee-producing countries—Colombia, Sumatra, Yemen, Antigua, Indonesia, Guatemala, New Guinea, Costa Rica, Sulawesi, Papua, Kenya, Ethiopia, Java, and Mexico—building relationships with growers and exporters, checking on agricultural conditions and crop yields, and searching out varieties and sources that would meet Starbucks' exacting standards of quality and flavor. The coffee-purchasing group, working with personnel in roasting operations, tested new varieties and blends of beans from different sources.

Coffee was grown in 70 tropical countries and was the second-most-traded commodity in the world after petroleum. The global value of the 2000–2001 coffee bean crop was about $5.6 billion. By World Bank estimates, some 25 million small farmers made their living growing coffee. Commodity-grade coffee, which consisted of robusta and commercial quality arabica beans, was traded in a highly competitive market as an undifferentiated product. Coffee prices were subject to considerable volatility due to weather, economic and political conditions in the growing countries, new agreements establishing export quotas, and periodic efforts to bolster prices by restricting coffee supplies. Starbucks used fixed-price purchase commitments to limit its exposure to fluctuating coffee prices in upcoming periods and, on occasion, purchased coffee futures contracts to provide price protection. In years past, there had been times when unexpected jumps in coffee prices had put a squeeze on Starbucks' margins, forcing an increase in the prices of the beverages and beans sold at retail.

Starbucks sourced approximately 50 percent of its beans from Latin America, 35 percent from the Pacific Rim, and 15 percent from East Africa. Sourcing from multiple geographic areas not only allowed Starbucks to offer a greater range of coffee varieties to customers but also spread the company's risks regarding weather, price volatility, and changing economic and political conditions in coffee-growing countries.

During 2002, a global oversupply of more than 2 billion pounds drove the prices of commodity coffees to historic lows of $0.40–$0.50 per pound. The specialty coffee market, which represented about 10 percent of worldwide production, consisted primarily of high-quality arabica beans. Prices for specialty coffees were determined by the quality and flavor of the beans and were almost always higher than prevailing prices for commodity-grade coffee beans. Starbucks purchased only high-quality arabica coffee beans, paying an average of $1.20 per pound in 2004. Its purchases represented about 1 percent of the world's coffee bean crop. The company's green coffee costs reached a historic low in 2002 and had gradually increased since then. Given the price volatility risk, the company entered into fixed-price purchase commitments in order to secure an adequate supply of quality green coffee. As of October 2005, the company had over $375 million in fixed-price purchase commitments, which along with existing inventory was expected to provide an adequate supply of green coffee through fiscal 2006.[29]

Believing that the continued growth and success of its business depended on gaining access to adequate supplies of high-quality coffees year-in and year-out, Starbucks had been a leader in promoting environmental and social stewardship in coffee-origin countries. Starbucks' coffee sourcing strategy was to contribute to the sustainability of coffee growers and help conserve the environment. In sourcing green coffee beans, Starbucks was increasingly dealing directly with farmers and cooperatives, and its policy was to pay prices high enough to ensure that small coffee growers, most of whom lived on the edge of poverty, were able to cover their production costs and provide for their families. About 40 percent of Starbucks purchases were made under three-to five-year contracts, which management believed enabled the company to purchase its future coffee bean requirements at predictable prices over multiple crop years. Coffee purchases negotiated through long-term contracts increased from 3 percent in 2001 to 36 percent in 2002. Farmers who met important quality, environmental, social, and economic criteria, which Starbucks had developed with the support of Conservation International's Center for Environmental Leadership in Business, were rewarded with financial incentives and preferred supplier status. In fiscal 2004, the company opened its Farmer Support Center in Costa Rica to support existing and potential Starbucks coffee suppliers and their communities.

Starbucks had $375 million in fixed-price purchase commitments in October 2005 but was not planning to increase this commitment in the near future due to a significant jump in the prices of green coffee beans (in some cases the going prices for green beans were above the fixed purchase prices). The high commodity prices for coffee beans made farmers less willing to enter into fixed-price arrangements.

Fair Trade Certified Coffee

A growing number of small coffee growers were members of democratically run cooperatives that were registered with the Fair Trade Labeling Organi-

zations International; these growers could sell their beans directly to importers, roasters, and retailers at favorable guaranteed "Fair Trade" prices. The idea behind guaranteed prices for Fair Trade coffees was to boost earnings for small coffee growers enough to allow them to afford basic health care, education, and home improvements. Starbucks marketed Fair Trade Certified coffee at most of its retail stores and through other locations that sold Starbucks coffees. In October 2005, Starbucks introduced Café Estima Blend Fair Trade Certified Coffee as the coffee of the week to support Fair Trade Month 2005. Starbucks expected to purchase 10 million pounds of Fair Trade Certified coffee in 2005, and it planned to purchase 12 million pounds in 2006.

Environmental Best Practices

Since 1998, Starbucks had partnered with Conservation International to promote coffee cultivation methods that protected biodiversity and maintained a healthy environment. A growing percentage of the coffees that Starbucks purchased were grown "organically" without the use of pesticides, herbicides, or chemical fertilizers; organic cultivation methods resulted in clean groundwater and helped protect against degrading of local ecosystems, many of which were fragile or in areas where biodiversity was under severe threat. Another environmental conservation practice involved growing organic coffee under a natural canopy of shade trees interspersed with fruit trees and other crops; this not only allowed farmers to get higher crop yields from small acreages but also helped protect against soil erosion on mountainsides.

COFFEE ROASTING OPERATIONS

Starbucks considered the roasting of its coffee beans to be something of an art form, entailing trial-and-error testing of different combinations of time and temperature to get the most out of each type of bean and blend. Recipes were put together by the coffee department, once all the components had been tested. Computerized roasters guaranteed consistency. Each batch was roasted in a powerful gas oven for 12 to 15 minutes. Highly trained and experienced roasting personnel monitored the process, using both smell and hearing, to help check when the beans were perfectly done—coffee beans make a popping sound when ready. Starbucks' standards were so exacting that roasters tested the color of the beans in a blood-cell analyzer and discarded the entire batch if the reading wasn't on target. After roasting and cooling, the coffee was immediately vacuum-sealed in bags with one-way valves that let out gases naturally produced by fresh-roasted beans without letting oxygen in—one-way valve technology extended the shelf life of packaged Starbucks coffee to 26 weeks. As a matter of policy, however, Starbucks removed coffees on its shelves after three months, and, in the case of coffee used to prepare beverages in stores, the shelf life was limited to seven days after the bag was opened.

At the end of fiscal 2005, Starbucks had roasting plants in Kent, Washington; York, Pennsylvania; Minden, Nevada; and the Netherlands. In addition to roasting capability, the Kent, York, Minden, and Netherlands plants also had additional space for warehousing and shipping coffees. The roasting plants and distribution facilities in Kent supplied stores west of the Mississippi and in the Asia-Pacific region. The newly constructed Minden plant and distribution center was used to supply stores in the Mountain West and Midwest. The roasting and distribution facility in York, which could be expanded to 1 million square feet, supplied stores mainly east of the Mississippi. The 94,000-square-foot facility in the Netherlands supplied stores in Europe and the Middle East.

STARBUCKS' CORPORATE SOCIAL RESPONSIBILITY STRATEGY

Howard Schultz's effort to "build a company with soul" included broad-based initiatives to contribute positively to the communities in which Starbucks had stores and to the environment. The guiding theme of Starbucks' social responsibility strategy was "Giving back to our communities is the way we do business." The Starbucks Foundation was set up in 1997 to orchestrate the company's philanthropic activities. Since 1991 Starbucks had been a major contributor to CARE, a worldwide relief and development organization that sponsored health, education, and humanitarian aid programs in almost all of the third world countries where Starbucks purchased its coffee supplies. Stores featured CARE in promotions and had organized concerts to benefit CARE. A second major philanthropic effort involved providing financial support to community literacy organizations. In 1995 Starbucks began a program to improve the conditions of workers in coffee-growing countries, establishing a code of conduct for its growers and providing financial assistance for agricultural improvement projects. In 1997, Star-bucks formed an alliance with Appropriate Technology International to help poor, small-scale coffee growers in Guatemala increase their income by improving the quality of their crops and their market access; the company's first-year grant of $75,000 went to fund a new processing facility and set up a loan program for a producer cooperative.

Starbucks had an Environmental Committee that looked for ways to reduce, reuse, and recycle waste, as well as contribute to local community environmental efforts. There was also a Green Store Task Force that looked at how Starbucks stores could conserve on water and energy usage and generate less solid waste. Customers who brought their own mugs to stores were given a 10-cent discount of beverage purchases (in 2002, customers used commuter mugs in making purchases about 12.7 million times). Coffee grounds, which were a big portion of the waste stream in stores, were packaged and given to customers, parks, schools and plant nurseries as a soil amendment. Company personnel purchased paper products with high levels of recycled content and unbleached fiber to help Starbucks minimize its environmental footprint. Stores participated in Earth Day activities each year with in-store promotions and volunteer efforts to educate employees and customers about the impacts their actions had on the environment. Suppliers were encouraged to provide the most energy-efficient products within their category and eliminate excessive packaging; Starbucks had recently instituted a Code of Conduct for suppliers of noncoffee products that addressed standards for social responsibility, including labor and human rights. No genetically modified ingredients were used in any food or beverage products that Starbucks served, with the exception of milk. (U.S. labeling requirements do not require milk producers to disclose the use of hormones aimed at increasing the milk production of dairy herds.)

Starbucks stores participated regularly in local charitable projects of one kind or another, donating drinks, books, and proceeds from store-opening benefits. Employees were encouraged to recommend and apply for grants from the Starbucks Foundation to benefit local community literacy organizations.

Exhibit 8   **Starbucks' Environmental Mission Statement**

Starbucks is committed to a role of environmental leadership in all facets of our business.

We fulfill this mission by a commitment to:

- Understanding of environmental issues and sharing information with our partners.
- Developing innovative and flexible solutions to bring about change.
- Striving to buy, sell, and use environmentally friendly products.
- Recognizing that fiscal responsibility is essential to our environmental future.
- Instilling environmental responsibility as a corporate value.
- Measuring and monitoring our progress for each project.

On the Fourth of July weekend in 1997, three Starbucks employees were murdered in the company's store in the Georgetown area of Washington, D.C.; Starbucks offered a $100,000 reward for information leading to the arrest of the murderer(s). The company announced it would reopen the store in early 1998 and donate all future net proceeds of the store to a Starbucks Memorial Fund that would make annual grants to local groups working to reduce violence and aid the victims of violent crimes. In 2005, Starbucks made a $5 million, five-year commitment to long-term relief and recovery efforts for victims of Hurricane Katrina and committed $5 million to support educational programs in China.

Starbucks felt so deeply about its responsibilities that it even developed an environmental mission statement to expand on its corporate mission statement (see Exhibit 8). In 2002, Starbucks also began issuing an annual Corporate Social Responsibility Report (the reports for recent years can be viewed in the Investors section at www.starbucks.com). Going into 2004, Starbucks had received 20 awards from a diverse group of organizations for its philanthropic, community service, and environmental activities.

THE SPECIALTY COFFEE INDUSTRY

While the market for traditional commercial grade coffees had stagnated since the 1970s, the specialty coffee segment had expanded, as interested, educated, upscale consumers became increasingly inclined to upgrade to premium coffees with more robust flavors. Whereas retail sales of specialty coffees amounted to only $45 million in 1969, by 1994 retail sales of specialty coffees had increased to $2 billion, much of which stemmed from sales in coffee bars or the shops of coffee bean retailers (like Peet's). The increase was attributed to wider consumer awareness of and appreciation for fine coffee, the emergence of coffee bars featuring a blossoming number of premium coffee beverages, and the adoption of a healthier lifestyle that prompted some consumers to replace alcohol with coffee. Coffee's image changed from one of just a breakfast or after-dinner beverage to a drink that could be enjoyed at any time in the company of others. Many coffee drinkers took to the idea of coffee bars where they could enjoy a high-caliber coffee beverage and sit back and relax with friends or business associates.

Some industry experts expected the gourmet coffee market in the United States would be saturated by 2005. But the international market was much more wide open as of early 2004. The United States, Germany, and Japan were the three biggest coffee-consuming countries.

COMPETITORS

Starbucks' primary competitors were restaurants, specialty coffee shops, doughnut shops, supermarkets, convenience stores, and others that sold hot coffee and specialty coffee drinks. In 2003, there were an estimated 14,000 specialty coffee outlets in the United States, with some observers predicting there would as many as 18,000 locations selling specialty coffee drinks by 2015.

Starbucks' success was prompting a number of ambitious rivals to scale up their expansion plans. Still, no other specialty coffee rival had as many as 400 stores, but there were at least 20 small local and regional chains that aspired to compete against Starbucks in their local market arenas, most notably Caribou Coffee (337 stores in 14 states and the District of Columbia), Tully's Coffee (98 stores in 4 states), Gloria Jean's (280 mall locations in 35 states and several foreign countries), New World Coffee (30 locations), Brew HaHa (13 locations in Delaware and Pennsylvania), Bad Ass Coffee (about 60 locations in 18 states, Japan, and South Korea),

Second Cup Coffee (the largest chain based in Canada), and Qwiky's (India). Caribou Coffee went public in late 2005, with a stock offering that raised about $68 million. McDonald's had begun opening McCafés. While it had been anticipated in the late 1990s that local and regional chains would merge in efforts to get bigger and better position themselves as an alternative to Starbucks, such consolidation had not occurred as of 2003. But numerous retail entrepreneurs had picked up on the growing popularity of specialty coffees and opened coffee bars in high-pedestrian-traffic locations to serve espresso, cappuccino, latte, and other coffee drinks. Growing numbers of restaurants were upgrading the quality of the coffee they served.

Starbucks also faced competition from nation wide coffee manufacturers—such as Kraft General Foods (the parent of Maxwell House), Procter & Gamble (the marketer of Folger's and Millstone brands), and Nestlé—that distributed their coffees through supermarkets. Both General Foods and Procter & Gamble had introduced premium blends of their Maxwell House and Folgers coffees on supermarket shelves, pricing them several dollars below Starbucks' offerings. But Starbucks' most important competitors in supermarkets were the increasing numbers of rival brands of specialty coffees—Green Mountain, Allegro, Peaberry, Brothers, and dozens of other brands. Because many consumers were accustomed to purchasing their coffee supplies at supermarkets, it was easy for them to choose whatever specialty coffee brand or brands were featured in their local supermarkets over Starbucks.

FUTURE CHALLENGES

In fiscal 2006, Starbucks planned to open 1,800 new stores globally. Top management believed that it could grow revenues by about 20 percent annually and net earnings by 20–25 percent annually for the next three to five years. Howard Schultz and CEO Jim Donald viewed China as a huge market opportunity, along with Brazil, India, and Russia. Howard Schultz believed that, to sustain its growth and make Starbucks one of the world's preeminent global brands, the company had to challenge the status quo, be innovative, take risks, and adapt its vision of who it was, what it did, and where it was headed. If the challenge was met successfully, in all likelihood the company's best years lay on the strategic road ahead.

Endnotes

[1]As quoted in Cora Daniels, "Mr. Coffee," *Fortune,* April 14, 2003, p. 139.
[2]2004 annual report, letter to shareholders.
[3]2002 annual report, letter to shareholders.
[4]Ibid.
[5]Howard Schultz and Dori Jones Yang, *Pour Your Heart Into It* (New York: Hyperion, 1997), p. 33.
[6]Ibid., p. 34.
[7]Ibid., p. 36.
[8]As told in ibid., p. 48.
[9]Ibid., pp. 61–62.
[10]As quoted in Jennifer Reese, "Starbucks: Inside the Coffee Cult," *Fortune,* December 9, 1996, p. 193.
[11]Schultz and Yang, *Pour Your Heart Into It,* pp. 101–2.
[12]Ibid., p. 142.
[13]Ibid., p. 129.
[14]As related in ibid., pp. 131–36.
[15]2004 annual report, p. 36.
[16]Ibid.
[17]2005 Starbucks 10-K report, p. 67.
[18]Ben van Houten, "Employee Perks: Starbucks Coffee's Employee Benefit Plan," *Restaurant Business,* May 15, 1997, p. 85.
[19]As related in Schultz and Yang, *Pour Your Heart Into It,* p. 168.
[20]As quoted in Ingrid Abramovitch, "Miracles of Marketing," *Success* 40, no. 3, p. 26.
[21]Daniels, "Mr. Coffee," p. 140.
[22]Company press releasse, May 31, 2005, and October 25, 2005
[23]Company press release, October 25, 2005.
[24]Kate Rounds, "Starbucks Coffee," *Incentive* 167, no. 7, p. 22.
[25]CSR annual report, Starbucks, fiscal 2004.
[26]Fiscal 2005 annual report, p. 14.
[27]David Bank, "Starbucks Faces Growing Competition: Its Own Stores," *The Wall Street Journal,* January 21, 1997, p. B1.
[28]As related in Schultz and Yang, *Pour Your Heart Into It,* p. 224.
[29]Starbucks 2005 form 10-K report, p. 6.

Case 8

Netflix versus Blockbuster versus Video-on-Demand

Braxton Maddox
The University of Alabama

Arthur A. Thompson
The University of Alabama

Heading into 2006, Netflix had convinced most skeptics that its pioneering business model for renting DVDs online could be profitable. Netflix had attracted some 3.6 million subscribers who paid monthly fees ranging from $9.99 to $47.99; subscribers went to Netflix's Web site, selected one or more movies from its library of 55,000 titles, and received the DVDs by first-class mail within one to three business days. Subscribers could keep a DVD for as long as they wished, with no due dates or late fees, although they were limited to having a certain number of DVDs in their possession at any one time (the number depended on which fee plan they had chosen). A unique aspect of Netflix's business model was that it provided subscribers with all the benefits of a typical movie rental store but without the hassle of having to drive to the store, pick out DVDs, and return the rentals by a specified time.

However, Netflix's rapid growth and profit outlook had a major downside—they had induced movie rental leader Blockbuster to enter the online movie rental segment and try to horn in on the market opportunity that Netflix was exploiting. Amazon.com was also looking at entering the market. Wal-Mart had pursued online movie rentals for a short time, but in May 2005 it decided to enter into an arrangement with Netflix whereby Wal-Mart would refer customers interested in online DVD rentals to Netflix while Netflix would steer customers wanting to purchase a movie DVD to www.walmart.com. Wal-Mart's existing DVD rental customers were offered the option of becoming Netflix subscribers at the current Wal-Mart rate for one year from their sign-up date. Wal-Mart was motivated to team up with Netflix because its own online movie rental business presented an assortment of troublesome operating problems and was unprofitable, and because it saw more opportunity in focusing on the growing numbers of customers who were buying movie DVDs at www.walmart.com. Entry barriers into online DVD rentals were relatively low, but the barriers to profitability were considered rather high because of the need to attract a subscriber base of 2 to 4 million in order to operate at a profit.

Reed Hastings, founder and CEO of Netflix, was concerned about how to outcompete Blockbuster, and he was also concerned about the competitive threat posed by video-on-demand (VOD). Several new competitors were gearing up to offer movies on a pay-per-view basis to Internet customers with high-speed broadband connections. Providing VOD had been technically possible for a number of years, but VOD had not garnered substantial usage because movie studios were leery of the potential for movie pirating and doubtful of whether they could profit from a VOD business model. Nonetheless, the major Hollywood studios had formed a joint venture called MovieLink to offer VOD to the public. And several ambitious start-up companies, like San Francisco–based GreenCine, were offering online movie viewing to consumers who had Microsoft's Windows Media Player installed on their PCs and a broadband Internet connection. Once they downloaded a movie, consumers could play it on their desktop or laptop PCs or connect the PC to a TV.

Hastings's challenge was how to sustain Netflix's growth and put together a strategy that would protect Netflix's industry-leading position against mounting competition. In Hastings's view, "No one is going to out-hare Netflix. Our danger is in a tortoise attack."

COMPANY BACKGROUND AND STRATEGY

After successfully founding his first company, Pure Software, in 1991, Reed Hastings engineered several acquisitions and grew Pure Software into one of the 50 largest software companies in the world—the company's principal product was a debugging tool for engineers. When Pure Software was acquired by Rational Software in 1997 for $750 million, Hastings used the money from selling his shares of Pure Software to help fund his pursuit of another, entirely different business venture. Sensing the opportunity for online movie rentals in a climate where

the popularity of the Interet was mushrooming, he founded Netflix in 1997, launched the online subscription service in 1999, and attracted a subscriber base of over 2 million in just four years (America Online took six years to acquire the same number of subscribers). Exhibit 1 shows trends in Netflix's subscriber growth.

By 2005, in what proved to be a rapidly evolving marketplace, Netflix had made a name for itself. It was the world's largest online DVD movie rental service, with 2005 revenues approaching $700 million and a selection of movie titles that far exceeded those available in local brick-and-mortar movie rental stores. Its strategy and market success were predicated on providing an expansive selection of DVDs, an easy way to choose movies, and fast, free delivery—the goal was to deliver customer value by eliminating the hassle involved in choosing, renting, and returning movies. Netflix's DVD lineup included everything from the latest big Hollywood releases to hard-to-locate documentaries to independent films to TV shows and how-to videos.

Exhibit 1 **Subscriber Data for Netflix, 2000–2005**

	1999	2000	2001	2002	2003	2004	First Nine Months, 2005
Total subscribers at beginning of period	0	107,000	292,000	456,000	857,000	1,487,000	2,610,000
Gross subscriber additions during period	127,000	515,000	566,000	1,140,000	1,571,000	2,716,000	2,573,000
Subscriber cancellations during the period	20,000	330,000	402,000	739,000	941,000	1,593,000	1,591,000
Total subscribers at end of period	107,000	292,000	456,000	857,000	1,487,000	2,610,000	3,592,000
Net subscriber additions during the period	107,000	185,000	164,000	401,000	630,000	1,123,000	982,000
Free trial subscribers*	n.a.	n.a.	56,000	61,000	71,000	124,000	169,000
Subscriber acquisition cost	$110.79	$49.96	$37.16	$31.39	$31.79	$36.09	$36.92

n.a. = Not available.

*First-time subscribers automatically were eligible for a free two-week trial; membership fees began after the two-week trial expired (unless the membership was canceled).

Members had the choice of eight subscription plans:

- $9.99, unlimited DVDs, one title out at a time.
- $11.99, four DVDs a month, two titles out at a time.
- $14.99, unlimited DVDs, two titles out at a time.
- $17.99, unlimited DVDs, three titles out at a time.
- $23.99, unlimited DVDs, four titles out at a time.
- $29.99, unlimited DVDs, five titles out at a time.
- $35.99, unlimited DVDs, six titles out at a time.
- $41.99, unlimited DVDs, seven titles out at a time.
- $47.99, unlimited DVDs, eight titles out at a time.

The most popular plan in 2005 was $17.99 a month. Subscribers could cancel anytime. Subscribers were drawn to Netflix's policies of no late fees and no due dates (which eliminated the hassle of getting DVDs back to local rental stores by the designated due date), and the convenience of being provided a postage-paid return envelope for mailing the DVDs back to Netflix. Netflix provided subscribers extensive information about DVD movies, including critic reviews, member reviews, online trailers, ratings, and personalized movie recommendations. Subscribers could create a "wish list" of all the movies they wanted to see, change the list at any time, and use the list to order their next round of movies.

Netflix's Cinematch Software Technology

Netflix had developed proprietary software technology, called Cinematch, which enabled it to provide subscribers with personalized movie recommendations every time they visited the Netflix Web site. These personalized recommendations were based on a subscriber's individual likes and dislikes (determined by their wish list, rental history, and movie ratings). Cinematch was an Oracle database that organized Netflix's library of movies into clusters of similar movies and analyzed how customers rated them after they rented them. Those customers who rated similar movies in similar clusters were then matched as like-minded viewers. When a customer was online, Cinematch looked at the clusters the subscriber had rented from in the past, determined which movies the customer had yet to rent in that cluster, and recommended only those movies in the cluster that had been highly rated by viewers. The recommendations helped subscribers quickly identify films they might like to rent and allowed Netflix to promote lesser-known, high-quality films to subscribers who otherwise might have missed spotting them in the company's massive 55,000-film library (to which new titles were continuously being added).

In December 2005 Netflix had more than 1 billion movie ratings from customers in its database, and the average subscriber had rated more than 200 movies. On average, more than 85 percent of the movie titles in the Netflix library of offerings were rented each quarter, an indication of the effectiveness of the company's Cinematch software in steering subscribers to movies of interest. Netflix management believed that over 50 percent of its rentals came from the recommendations generated by Cinematch.

Shipping

Netflix had 37 regional shipping centers scattered across the United States, giving it one-business-day delivery capability for 90 percent of its subscribers. Additional shipping centers were on the drawing board.

Netflix had developed sophisticated software to track its inventory and minimize delivery times. Netflix's system allowed the distribution centers to communicate to determine the fastest way of getting DVDs to customers. When a customer placed an order for a specific DVD, the system first looked for that DVD at the shipping center closest to the customer. If that center didn't have the DVD in stock, the system then moved the next closest center and checked there. The search continued until the DVD was found, at which point the shipping center was provided with the information needed to initiate the order fulfillment and shipping process. If the DVD was unavailable anywhere in the system, it was wait-listed. The system then moved to the customer's next choice and the process started all over. And no matter where the DVD was sent from, the system knew to print the return label on the prepaid envelope to send the DVDs to the shipping center closest to the customer to reduce return mail times and permit more efficient use of the company's DVD inventory.

In 2005, Netflix was shipping more than 1 million DVDs a day. It had an inventory of around 20 million DVDs (which was growing as the subscriber base increased). In the first nine months of 2005, Netflix spent $84.2 million on the acquisition of new DVDs; it had an arrangement with movie studios to purchase new-release DVDs for an upfront fee plus a percentage of revenue earned from rentals for a defined period. The company's September 30, 2005, balance sheet indicated that its DVD holdings had a net value of $52.7 million (after depreciation). New-release DVDs were amortized over one year; the useful life of back-library titles (some of which qualified as classics) were amortized over periods of one to three years (since they continued to be rented from time to time because of the Cinematch recommendations). DVDs that the company expected to sell at the end of their useful lives carried a salvage value of $3 per DVD; DVDs that the company did not expect to sell were assigned a salvage value of zero.

Target Customers and Customer Satisfaction

The company's subscriber base consisted of three types of customers: those who liked the convenience of home delivery, bargain hunters who were enthused about being able to watch 10 or more movies a month at an economical price (on the $17.99 plan, 12 movies a month equated to a rental fee of $1.50 per movie), and movie buffs who wanted access to a wide selection of films.

In a survey by Netflix, customers said they rented twice as many movies per month as they did prior to joining Netflix. New Netflix customers also said they were immediately more satisfied with their home-entertainment experience than they were prior to joining Netflix. And 9 out of 10 customers said they were so satisfied with the service that they recommended the service to family and friends. Netflix was the top-rated Web site for customer satisfaction according to a spring 2005 survey by ForeSee Results and FGI Research. In the fall of 2005, *Fast Company* magazine named Netflix the winner of its annual Customers First Award.

Growth Strategy

Netflix's growth strategy had three primary components:

- Continue to innovate and enhance the consumer experience.
- Use Netflix's market-leading position to lead the transition to high-definition DVDs and eventually digital downloading.
- Focus on rapid subscriber growth in order to
  —Maintain market leadership.
  —Realize economies of scale.

Netflix's strategic intent was to be the world's largest and most influential movie supplier.

Netflix's Performance

The company's recent operating statistics and financial statement data are shown in Exhibits 2 and 3. Netflix's decline in profit in 2005 reflected the adverse effects of lower subscription prices that had been instituted in late 2004. Concerned about mounting competitive pressures—particularly from Blockbuster, which announced its entry into the online rental segment in August 2004—Netflix had halted expansion into Britain and Canada and dropped the monthly subscription price on its most popular plan from $21.99 to $17.99 starting November 1, 2004. At the lower $17.99 price, Netflix believed it could continue to grow its subscriber base but would only be able to break even (given the $48 per year revenue loss for many of its subscribers). Blockbuster responded in December 2004 with a price drop from $19.99 to $14.99 per month on its most popular plan, which allowed three DVDs out at a time.

Following Blockbuster's announced entry into online movie rentals and Netflix's November price cut, investors immediately grew nervous about Netflix's profitability and competitive staying power—the company's stock price dropped sharply from around $35 per share in late July 2004 to $10 to $12 per share in the November 2004–February 2005 period. Starting March 2005, the stock began a climb back to the $25 to $30 range, as investors took comfort in Netflix's continued growth in subscribers, the partnership arrangement with Wal-Mart (which had eliminated a prime competitive threat), the company's return to profitability in the second and third quarters of 2005, and upbeat management forecasts for 2006.

Exhibit 2   **Netflix's Statement of Operations, 2000–2005 (in thousands of $, except per share data)**

	Year Ended December 31,					
	2000	2001	2002	2003	2004	First Nine Months, 2005
Statement of Operations Data						
Revenues:						
Subscriptions	$ 35,894	$ 74,255	$150,818	$270,410	$500,611	$489,213
Sales	—	1,657	1,988	1,833	5,617	3,741
Total revenues	35,894	75,912	152,806	272,243	506,228	492,954
Cost of revenues:						
Subscriptions	24,861	49,088	77,044	147,736	273,401	291,821
Sales	—	819	1,092	624	3,057	2,542
Total cost of revenues	24,861	49,907	78,136	148,360	276,458	294,363
Gross profit	11,033	26,005	74,670	123,883	229,770	198,591
Operating expenses:						
Fulfillment	10,247	13,452	19,366	31,274	56,609	51,798
Technology and development	16,823	17,734	14,625	17,884	22,906	22,674
Marketing	25,727	21,031	35,783	49,949	98,027	95,008
General and administrative	6,990	4,658	6,737	9,585	16,287	17,925
Restructuring charges	—	671	—	—	—	—
Stock-based compensation	9,714	6,250	8,832	10,719	16,587	10,995
Total operating expenses	69,501	63,796	85,343	119,411	210,416	198,400
Operating income (loss)	(58,468)	(37,791)	(10,673)	4,472	19,354	191
Other income (expense):						
Interest and other income	1,645	461	1,697	2,457	2,592	3,788
Interest and other expense	(1,451)	(1,852)	(11,972)	(417)	(170)	(54)
Net income before income taxes	(58,274)	(39,182)	(20,948)	6,512	21,776	3,925
Provision for income taxes	—	—	—	—	181	109
Net income (loss)	$(58,274)	$(39,182)	$ (20,948)	$ 6,512	$ 21,595	$ 3,816
Net income (loss) per share:						
Basic	$ (20.61)	$ (10.73)	$ (0.74)	$ 0.14	$ 0.42	$ 0.07
Diluted	(20.61)	(10.73)	(0.74)	0.10	0.33	0.06
Weighted-average shares outstanding:						
Basic	2,828	3,652	28,204	47,786	51,988	53,237
Diluted	2,828	3,652	28,204	62,884	64,713	64,928

Source: Netflix's 2004 10-K Report and company press release, October 19, 2005.

Netflix expected to end 2005 with about 4 million subscribers, revenues of close to $685 million (versus $506 million in 2004), and net income of $5 to $10 million (versus $21.6 million in 2004); the lower profits in 2005 were a direct result of having lowered subscription fees in November 2004.

Netflix reported a loss of $8.8 million in the first quarter of 2005, a profit of $5.7 million in the second quarter, and a profit of $6.9 million in the third quarter. Management's latest forecast for 2006 called for 5.65 million subscribers at year-end, revenues of at least $940 million, and pretax income

Exhibit 3   **Selected Balance Sheet and Cash Flow Data for Netflix, 2000–2005 (in thousands of $)**

	2000	2001	2002	2003	2004	September 30, 2005
Selected Balance Sheet Data						
Cash and cash equivalents	$ 14,895	$ 16,131	$ 59,814	$ 89,894	$174,461	$181,886
Short-term investments	—	—	43,796	45,297	—	—
Current assets	n.a.	19,552	107,075	138,946	187,346	191,198
Net investment in DVD library	n.a.	3,633	9,972	22,238	42,158	52,735
Total assets	52,488	41,630	130,530	176,012	251,793	278,302
Current liabilities	n.a.	26,208	40,426	63,019	94,910	98,755
Working capital*	(1,655)	(6,656)	66,649	75,927	92,436	93,163
Notes payable, less current portion	1,843	—	—	—	—	—
Subordinated notes payable	—	2,799	—	—	—	—
Redeemable convertible preferred stock	101,830	101,830	—	—	—	—
Stockholders' equity	(73,267)	(90,504)	89,356	112,708	156,283	178,672
Cash flow data						
Net cash provided by operating activities	$(22,706)	$ 4,847	$ 40,114	$ 89,792	$147,571	$ 99,245
Net cash used in investing activities	(24,972)	(12,670)	(67,301)	(64,677)	(68,381)	(99,307)
Net cash provided by financing activities	48,375	9,059	70,870	4,965	5,599	7,487

*Defined as current assets minus current liabilities.

Sources: 2002 10-K report, 2004 10-K report, and company press release October 19, 2005.

of $50 to $60 million. One Wall Street analyst had recently forecast that Netflix could have 7 million subscribers by the end of 2007. Adams Media Research and Netflix had projected that there would be more than 20 million online subscribers for DVD movie rentals within the next five to seven years.

MARKET TRENDS IN MOVIE DVDs

The digital video disc (DVD) player was one of the most successful consumer electronic products of all time. As of December 2005, more than 160 million DVD players had been sold since launch and more than 80 million U.S. households had DVD players (many had more than one). DVD playback had

worked its way into a number of electronic devices, and DVD recording was expected to be an essential driver of the DVD market. DVD recorders were forecast to surpass sales of play-only DVD players by 2007, with an expected compound annual growth rate of 126 percent.

Consumers could obtain movie DVDs through a wide variety of channels:

- Retail outlets such as Wal-Mart, Target, Circuit City, Best Buy, Office Depot, and Staples.
- Rental outlets such as Blockbuster and Movie Gallery.
- Web sites of both brick-and-mortar retailers (Wal-Mart) and Internet-only retailers such as Amazon.com.
- Online rental services such as Netflix and GreenCine.

- PC downloads from Web sites such as Movielink or file-sharing programs such as Kazaa.

According to Kagan Research, consumer spending for in-home movie viewing increased from about $22.6 billion in 2003 to about $25.1 billion in 2004 and was projected to increase to about $33.8 billion by 2009.[1] These numbers represented rental fees and household purchases of videocassettes and DVDs. According to Adams Media Research, DVD sales and rentals amounted to a $23.4 billion market in the United States in 2005, up from $22.0 billion in 2004.[2]

But despite growing sales of DVD players, there were some other factors at work in the marketplace:[3]

- Growth in the sales of DVDs was slowing from double-digit growth to forecasts of single-digit growth in 2006. Online rentals of movie DVDs, computer downloads of music and movie files, video-on-demand (VOD) services, and growing popularity of high-definition TV programs were cited as factors.

- The flood of new and old TV shows on DVDs that had recently hit the marketplace had cut into the sales of movie DVDs—the multidisc sets of TVs shows were more expensive than many new releases of movie DVDs.

- A growing number of households were purchasing digital video recorders (DVRs), which made it simple to record a TV program or movie and then replay it at a convenient time. Many DVR owners were highly attracted to recording movies (and other programs) shown in high definition and then watching them at their convenience.

- Cable companies like Comcast were offering VOD options for many of their premium movie channels. The Starz Entertainment Group claimed that its research showed that Comcast customers who were using the Starz on Demand VOD service tended to reduce their purchases and rentals of movie DVDs due to the ease of using the VOD service.

- Cable and satellite TV companies were expected to expand their VOD services over the next several years and make many more movie titles available to their customers.

- Cable customers with DVRs could readily substitute use of VOD movie offerings from their cable TV provider for purchasing or renting movie DVDs.

- Online rentals and VOD services were not only cutting into sales of movie DVDs but also taking business away from video rental stores. Just as Netflix posed a competitive threat to Blockbuster and Movie Gallery in the United States, market research in Great Britain indicated that one out of every five DVDs rented was rented online.

- Hollywood movie producers were hoping that next-generation, high-definition optical-disc-format DVDs would rejuvenate sales of movie DVDs, but it remained to be seen whether such hopes were well founded, given the growing popularity of DVRs, VOD, and online rentals.

Another factor acting to spur watching movies at home was rapidly growing sales of wide-screen TVs with a 16:9 scale as opposed to the old-style 4:3 scale. Most TV manufacturers had introduced a variety of high-tech TV models with screen sizes up to 72 inches. Prices for wide-screen TVs were dropping rapidly, and picture quality was exceptionally good, if not stunning, on increasing numbers of models. Consumers with wide-screen TVs typically found watching movies at home much more appealing, as compared to those having TVs with 27-inch to 36-inch screens.

BLOCKBUSTER INC.

Blockbuster was the world leader in the videocassette, DVD, and video game rental market, with an estimated 40 percent share of the roughly $13 billion rental market. Founded in Dallas, Texas, in 1985, Blockbuster had grown to over 9,000 company-operated and franchised stores worldwide—in 2005, it had 4,660 company-operated stores in the United States, 2,585 company-operated stores outside the United States, and 1,831 franchised stores (400 of which were in the United States). The company's revenues were derived from rentals of videocassettes for VCRs (11.4 percent of 2004 revenues), DVDs (53.5 percent), video games (8.2 percent), and sales of videotapes, DVDs, and video games (25.3 percent). Revenue from rentals and sales of tapes for VCRs was falling sharply, mainly because more and more households were converting from VCRs to DVD players. Blockbuster's rental revenues from tapes for VCRs had fallen from $1.43 billion in 2003 to $692 million in 2004 to just $150 million in the first nine months of 2005. Its DVD rental revenues had risen from $2.6 billion in 2003 to $3.24 billion in 2004 and accounted for 61.8 percent of rental revenues in first nine months of 2005 (up from 54.9 percent for the comparable period in 2004).

Recent Strategic Moves at Blockbuster's Retail Stores

In September 2000, Blockbuster began marketing DIRECTV system equipment in its U.S. stores; in June 2001, the partnership with DIRECTV was extended to marketing a co-branded pay-per-view movie service that made Blockbuster one of the early entrants into the pay-per-view segment of the home entertainment industry.

In 2002, Blockbuster announced a strategic vision of becoming the complete source for movies and games—rental and retail. Already the leader in movie and game rental market, the company set its sights on increasing its share of the growing retail market by launching a variety promotional programs and expanding its in-store selection of movies and gaming equipment, including hardware, software and accessories. In 2003, it began offering an in-store movie rental subscription program, the Blockbuster Freedom Pass, in approximately 25 percent of its stores. For a flat monthly fee, the Freedom Pass allowed members to rent an unlimited supply of movies without due dates or extended viewing fees for as long as they subscribed to the pass. The Freedom Pass program was rolled out to all U.S. company-operated stores in 2004, and the name was changed to Blockbuster Movie Pass. For $24.99 per month, members could take up to two movies out at a time; for $29.99 per month, they could choose the three-movies-at-a-time option. Both plans entitled customers to watch all the movies they wanted, with no specified return dates and no extended viewing fees. Once customers purchased the pass, their credit card or check card was automatically charged the monthly fee; subscriptions could be cancelled at any time.

To expand its presence in the gaming marketplace, in 2002 Blockbuster purchased the U.K.-based video game retailer Gamestation and proceeded to grow the chain from 64 to more than 150 stores. In the United States, the company began offering a Game Freedom Pass rental subscription program in all of its U.S. company-operated stores. Customers could purchase a single-month pass for just $19.99 and get unlimited game rentals for 30 consecutive days with a maximum of one game rented at any given time, and no extended viewing fees during the 30 days; a gamer could keep one game for the entire 30 consecutive days or change out the game daily—or even multiple times a day.

Several other initiatives in video games were launched in 2004–2005. Blockbuster began carrying PlayStation portable handheld games for rent in all stores. And it had boosted its games offering by creating a special "Game Rush" section within certain high-traffic Blockbuster stores where customers could rent, sell, and buy new and used game software and hardware. During peak hours, Game Rush sections were staffed by trained game specialists. Blockbuster believed that about half its U.S. stores were suited to having a Game Rush section.

However, despite all these and other strategic initiatives, Blockbuster was a troubled company in 2005. Sales revenues were stagnant at around $6 billion annually (see Exhibit 4), and the company had lost money in five of the past six years. Blockbuster reported net losses of $1.62 billion in 2002, $979 million in 2003, $1.25 billion in 2004, and $606 million through the first nine months of 2005. It had split off from media conglomerate Viacom in October 2004; part of the split-off arrangement involved paying a special one-time $5 dividend (totaling $905 million) to all shareholders, including Viacom (which owned 81.5 percent of Blockbuster's shares prior to the divestiture deal).

Blockbuster's Online Rental Business

Blockbuster entered the online rental segment in August 2004, offering customers a choice of three monthly plans (all with unlimited rentals and no due dates or late fees): (1) a $19.99 plan with three DVDs out at a time, (2) a $29.99 plan with five DVDs out at a time, and (3) a $39.99 plan with eight DVDs out at a time. Customers could choose from 25,000 titles, ranging from classics to new releases. In addition, subscribers were e-mailed two "e-coupons" each month for two free in-store rentals; all Blockbuster Online members were eligible for exclusive deals and discounts at participating Blockbuster stores.

Exhibit 4 **Selected Financial and Operating Statistics for Blockbuster Inc.,**
2002–2005 ($ in millions, except for per share data)

	First Nine Months, 2005	2004	2003	2002
Selected statement of operations data				
Revenues				
Rentals	$3,165.2	$ 4,428.6	$4,533.5	$4,460.4
Merchandise sales	1,114.0	1,532.6	1,281.6	1,019.7
Other	54.6	92.0	96.6	85.8
Total	4,333.8	6,053.2	5,911.7	5,565.9
Cost of rental revenues	1,046.8	1,250.7	1,362.1	1,513.8
Gross margin on rentals	66.9%	71.8%	70.0%	66.1%
Cost of merchandise sold	861.9	1,190.7	1,027.7	844.9
Gross margin on merchandise sales	22.6%	22.3%	19.8%	17.1%
Gross profit	2,425.1	3,611.8	3,521.9	3,207.2
Gross profit margin	56.0%	59.7%	59.6%	57.6%
Operating expenses				
General and administrative	2,147.4	2,835.2	2,605.9	2,369.5
Share-based compensation	—	18.3		
Advertising	227.1	257.4	179.4	249.2
Depreciation	173.0	247.4	266.0	239.1
Impairment of goodwill and other long-lived assets	356.8	1,504.4	1,304.9	—
Amortization of intangibles	1.8	2.3	2.4	1.7
Total	2,906.1	4,865.0	4,358.6	2,859.5
Operating income	(481.0)	(1,253.2)	(836.7)	347.7
Interest expense	(70.0)	(38.1)	(33.1)	(49.5)
Interest income	2.8	3.6	3.1	4.1
Income (loss) before income taxes	(551.0)	(1,286.1)	(867.1)	305.2
Net profit (loss)	$ (606.1)	$(1,248.8)	$ (978.7)	$ 195.9
Earnings per share (diluted)	$(3.30)	$(6.89)	$(5.41)	$1.08
Dividends per share	$0.04	$5.08	$0.08	$0.08
Selected balance sheet data				
Cash and cash equivalents	$ 190.2	$ 330.3	$ 233.4	$ 152.5
Merchandise inventories	352.2	516.6	415.1	452.1
Current assets	866.5	1,217.7	960.3	958.9
Total assets	3,030.4	3,863.4	4,822.0	6,243.8
Current liabilities	1,989.5	1,449.4	1,323.4	1,477.6
Long-term debt, less current portion	300.0	1,044.9	0.7	328.9
Stockholders' equity	465.9	1,062.9	3,188.4	4,100.9
Selected cash flow data				
Net cash flow provided by operations	$ 492.4	$ 1,215.4	$1,430.3	$ 1,462.3
Net cash flow (used for)/provided by investing activities	(741.2)	(1,112.3)	(1,024.6)	(1,314.6)
Net cash flow (used for)/provided by financing activities	112.8	(18.8)	(335.5)	(199.2)
Worldwide Store Data				
Same-store revenue increase (decrease)	(2.9)%	(3.2)%	(2.2)%	5.1%
Company-owned stores, end-of-year	7,245	7,265	7,105	6,907
Franchised stores, end-of-year	1,831	1,829	1,762	1,638
Total stores, end-of-year	9,076	9,094	8,867	8,545

Source: Blockbuster's 2003 10-K report, 2004 10-K report, and third-quarter 2005 10-Q report.

Rentals were shipped from 11 distribution centers to subscribers via first-class mail and usually arrived in one to three business days. Subscribers were provided with a postage-paid envelope for returning the DVDs. Subscribers could create and maintain a personal queue of movies they wished to rent at Blockbuster's Web site. When Blockbuster received return DVDs from subscribers, it automatically shipped the next available titles in the subscriber's rental queue. Management said the online rental service was the latest in a series of initiatives being implemented by Blockbuster to transform itself from a neighborhood movie rental store into an "anywhere, anytime" entertainment destination that eventually would enable customers to rent, buy, or trade movies and games, new or used, in-store and online. The initial response to Blockbuster Online was promising; John Antonico, Blockbuster's CEO, said, "After six weeks, we had more subscribers than Netflix had in a year and a half of existence."

On December 22, 2004, Blockbuster cut the price on its most popular subscription plan from $19.99 per month to $14.99 and announced it was expanding the copy-depth of new-release movies, boosting the number of titles available for online rental to 30,000, and expanding the selection of TV shows, anime, Hollywood classics, Asian cinema, music performance, documentaries, fitness, and how-to categories among others. It also announced that it was increasing the number of shipping centers to 23 and implementing new technology with the U.S. Postal Service that would shorten delivery times.

Developments at Blockbuster in 2005

In a move to revitalize stagnant store sales (see the worldwide store data section of Exhibit 4) and combat the attractiveness of the no-due-dates/no-late-fees policies of Netflix, Blockbuster in January 2005 discontinued its practice of charging late fees on DVD rental returns at its retail stores. However, it held on to the practice of specified due dates—one week for games and two days or one week for movies. If customers kept the rental beyond the due date, they were automatically granted an extra one-week goodwill period at no additional charge. If a customer chose to keep his or her rental past the end of the seventh day after the due date per the posted rental terms, Blockbuster converted the rental to a sale and charged the customer for the movie or game, minus the original rental fee. If the customer later decided he or she did not want to own the movie or game and returned the product within 30 days, Blockbuster reversed the sale and charged a minimal restocking fee of $1.25 (some franchise stores charged a higher restocking fee).

Blockbuster ran extensive ads in December 2004 and January 2005 touting its new no-late-fee policy. To help compensate for the estimated $250 to $300 million that late fees were expected to contribute to Blockbuster's revenues in 2005, management planned to lower its ongoing marketing, operating, and promotional costs. Nonetheless, John Antioco, CEO of Blockbuster, was under fire from shareholders and some members of the company's board of directors for instituting the no-late-fee policy, given the big revenue erosion impact, Blockbuster's string of huge losses, and the need to increase store inventories of DVDs to compensate for the extra time that customers were keeping the DVDs. Investors and board members were also skeptical about Blockbuster's move in the online rental market segment because of the heavy costs (estimated at $100 to $200 million) and what some considered as dim prospects for profitability. About 160 Blockbuster franchisees decided to discontinue the no-late-fees policy in 2005, even though the program was popular with customers, because of the extra expenses involved in stocking additional copies of popular titles.

In May 2005, disgruntled Blockbuster shareholders ignored management's recommendations and elected an opposing slate of three new directors to the company's board, one of whom was running against CEO John Antioco. When Antioco indicated that he would leave his position as CEO as a consequence of being defeated in his reelection bid, the newly constituted board opted to expand from six to eight members, appointed Antioco to one of the two newly created seats, and made him chairman. It was understood, however, that Antioco would not continue on as CEO past 2005 if the board was not satisfied with the progress being made to restore Blockbuster to profitability.

During his contentious campaign against the opposing slate of directors, Antonico had defended his strategy for Blockbuster:

A key feature of our growth strategy is the recently introduced "End of Late Fees" program, which directly addresses the major problem customers had with their movie rental experience. The program also positions us better to compete with home entertainment options that do not have late fees, including retail DVD, pay-per-view and VOD. To date, the "End of Late Fees" program is producing the desired results. Since the first of January when we introduced the program, we have had positive growth in active membership for the first time in nearly two years.

Another critically important initiative—and the only significant investment we intend to make this year—is our online rental business. Blockbuster is uniquely positioned to compete in this fast growing business. Given the views of leading industry experts that within three years online rental could represent 20% to 30% of movie rental revenues, it is imperative that we pursue this opportunity, which we believe will mean hundreds of millions of dollars in future operating income for our company.

We are prioritizing new initiatives, investing wisely for the future and cutting costs aggressively. We have cut 2005 capital spending by over $100 million from last year and reduced corporate overhead by $70 million on an annualized basis. Additionally, to reduce costs further and better focus our resources, we have put our game initiative, as well as the marketing of our movie trading business, on hold until 2006.

Regarding our dividend policy, during 2004 Blockbuster paid a one-time dividend of $5 per share in addition to its normal quarterly dividends. As a result, our shareholders received a total of $920 million in dividends in 2004. We have consistently said that once we have successfully executed our business initiatives and delivered on our strategic plan, we would consider paying increased quarterly dividends or repurchasing stock.[4]

In characterizing the company's direction, Antonico said, "Our mission right now is to transform Blockbuster from a place you go to rent movies to a place you go to rent or buy movies or games new or used, pay by the day, pay by the month, online or in-store."

In August 2005, Blockbuster Online's pricing was raised. Customers could choose from among three plans:

- $9.99, unlimited DVDs, one title out at a time.
- $14.99, unlimited DVDs, two titles out at a time.
- $17.99, unlimited DVDs, three titles out at a time.

The $17.99 plan was the most popular; all plans included a free two-week trial. The company said it had 1 million online subscribers and during 2005 had added about as many net new subscribers as Netflix. As of mid-2005, online subscribers could choose from over 40,000 titles, with new titles added weekly. Blockbuster had 30 distribution centers, and more than 200 local Blockbuster stores were fulfilling online orders for nearby customers (to help shorten delivery times). More local stores were being added daily to fulfill online orders.

Also in 2005, Blockbuster integrated its in-store and online subscription programs—members paid the same fees and had the same privileges. To conserve cash and bolster Blockbuster's lackluster balance sheet, the company's board of directors elected not to pay the $0.02 per share dividend for the third quarter of 2005. Blockbuster management had plans to reduce costs by over $100 million in 2006 and an additional $50 million in 2007 through a combination of overhead reductions, lower marketing expenditures, and operational savings from divesting a subsidiary that acquired and distributed products for the theatrical, home entertainment, and television markets. Management further planned to cut capital expenditures from $140 million in 2005 to $90 million in 2006, principally because of fewer new store openings.

MOVIE GALLERY INC.

In 2005, Movie Gallery was the second-largest North American home video retailer, with more than 4,700 stores located in all 50 U.S. states, Mexico, and Canada. It specialized in the rental and sale of DVD and VHS movies and video games. Since the company's initial public offering in August 1994, Movie Gallery had grown from 97 stores in 1994 to nearly 2,500 stores at year-end 2004 via new store openings and a series of acquisitions. It had revenues of $791 million in 2004 and earnings of $49.5 million. In April 2005, Movie Gallery beat out Blockbuster in a bidding war to acquire Hollywood Entertainment, which had 2004 revenues of $1.78 billion and operated 2,000 Hollywood Video stores and 700 Game Crazy stores.

The company's stores operating under the Movie Gallery brand primarily targeted small towns and suburban areas. Movie Gallery's scale of operations and resource capabilities enabled it to compete effectively against the independently owned stores and small regional chains in these areas; it was regarded as the industry's lowest-cost operator. The strategy of the Movie Gallery stores was to take advantage of purchasing economics, effective labor strategies, and a strong, proven business model to generate cash flow and continued growth.

The stores operating under the Hollywood Video and Game Crazy brands primarily targeted urban centers and surrounding suburban neighborhoods—much the same places that Blockbuster targeted. The strategy of these stores was predicated on exceptional customer service, innovative marketing and merchandising programs, a strong brand image, and solid in-store execution.

Movie Gallery was formed in 1985 by Joe Malugen and Harrison Parrish in Dothan, Alabama. Through its wholly owned subsidiary M.G.A., the company's founders began operating video specialty stores in southern Alabama and the Florida panhandle, and franchising the Movie Gallery store concept. By June 1987 the company owned five stores and had a franchise operation of 45 stores. In 1988, Movie Gallery began to consolidate the franchisees into company-owned stores; by 1992, it had a total of 37 stores and annual revenues of $6 million.

In August 1994, Movie Gallery completed an initial public offering of its stock and used the proceeds to acquire small video chains, primarily in the Southeast. Additional shares were issued in 1995 to open new stores and continue making acquisitions. By mid-1996 Movie Gallery had made over 100 separate acquisitions and built a chain of over 850 stores. In 1999, Movie Gallery announced plans to build 100 new stores and completed an 88-store acquisition of Blowout Entertainment; it went into 2000 with more than 950 locations in 31 states.

In 2000, Movie Gallery again set its goal at opening 100 new stores and relocating 25. This goal was met and surpassed. In late 2001, Movie Gallery expanded its store base by 30 percent by acquiring Video Update, its largest single-chain acquisition to date. The Video Update acquisition, which included 100 retail locations in Canada, marked Movie Gallery's emergence as a leader in video rentals in North America. Movie Gallery continued to execute an aggressive growth strategy, reaching the 2,000-store mark in 2003.

Following the April 2005 acquisition of Hollywood Entertainment, Movie Gallery strengthened its presence in Western Canada by acquiring the 61-store VHQ Entertainment chain. VHQ also operated VHQ Online (www.VHQonline.ca), a flat-fee, direct-to-home movie delivery service.

Movie Gallery had not launched an online DVD rental service, but its large and diverse geographic spread and its ambitions to be "the dominant entertainment source for video and video game rental and sale in rural and secondary markets in the United States" made it a likely entry candidate.

In the first nine months of 2005, Movie Gallery reported revenues of $1.31 billion and a net loss of $6.3 million. Movie Gallery anticipated fourth-quarter 2005 revenues of $675 to $705 million and same-store revenues in the range of -5 to -9 percent, as compared to the fourth quarter of 2004. In June 2005, management revised the new store development plan for the Movie Gallery and Hollywood Entertainment, cutting the plans for 500 new stores in 2005 to 300 stores; in the fall of 2005 it was on track to meet the target of 300 new store openings. Movie Gallery intended to further reduce its annual capital expenditures for new store development and open approximately 150 new stores in 2006, primarily in rural and secondary markets. It was also exploring various strategic alternatives for its Game Crazy business, including a potential sale, strategic partnership, or joint venture.

VIDEO-ON-DEMAND

Some analysts saw video-on-demand as a huge threat to Netflix because it could kill the market for DVD rentals. Growing numbers of households had high-speed Internet access, thus allowing technologically-savvy consumers to download movies to their PCs and then use the capabilities of Windows Media Center (which was standard on many newly purchased PCs shipped in 2005) to show the downloaded movies on their TVs. Alternatively, they could simply use a credit card to pay a fee to online movie suppliers to watch the movie on their PCs via streaming video.

However, VOD was materializing more slowly than expected because of wrangles with getting movie studios to license more movies for digital downloads—most movie studios feared that any contribution on their part to wider digital downloading of movies would facilitate even greater movie pirating (via file-sharing software) and cause them to lose significant revenues from both declining movie attendance and movie DVD sales. The file-sharing software used to pirate music files over the Internet also allowed people to pirate movies—in 2004, an estimated 400,000 to 600,000 movies were being illegally downloaded each day, costing film companies hundreds of millions in lost sales. More than half of the college-educated adults 35 and under in the United States had broadband connections at home, making it easy to trade copyrighted music and movie files. To try to deter illegal movie downloading, the Motion Picture Association of America in 2004 launched a major ad campaign in daily newspapers and consumer magazines across the country, as well as in more than 100 college newspapers, explaining why movie piracy was illegal, how it impacted jobs and the economy, and what the consequences were for engaging in illegal trafficking. Additionally, antipiracy messages appeared in motion picture theaters across the country.

Movielink's VOD Service

In 2005, Movielink (www.movielink.com), headquartered in Santa Monica, California, was the leading broadband video-on-demand (VOD) service. It offered an extensive selection of new and classic hit movies, foreign films, and other hard-to-find content. The business was a joint venture of Metro-Goldwyn-Mayer Studios, Paramount Pictures, Sony Pictures Entertainment, Universal Studios, and Warner Bros. Studios. Movielink drew its content offerings from the vast libraries of those studios, as well as Walt Disney Pictures, Twentieth Century Fox, Miramax, Artisan, and others on a non-exclusive basis.

After browsing the selection of movies, customers registered and rented movies using a valid credit card. There were no late fees or return times, and Movielink did not require a subscription or membership. Instead, each movie was independently priced by the content provider and charged per rental—fees were as low as $1.99 per movie. "We're excited about the opportunity to work with Movielink and its growing customer base of broadband households," said Peter Levinsohn, Fox's president of worldwide pay television and digital media.

Movielink was available to U.S. Internet users with broadband connections. Consumers could browse Movielink's site and view trailers of available titles without charge. Once customers were ready to rent a title, they registered with Movielink and paid for their rental via credit card. Movielink's Movies in Minutes software let customers either begin watching titles within 2–10 minutes after beginning the download or store them on their hard drives for up to 30 days and experience unlimited viewing for any 24-hour period on a PC, a television connected to the PC, or a laptop computer. Customers could also use Movielink's MultiPlay software feature to re-rent titles for additional 24-hour viewing periods for up to 30 days after the initial rental. Thirty days after the download, movie files were automatically deleted from the customer's hard drive.

Movielink had partnered with Verizon to launch a co-branded movie downloading service for Verizon Online's consumer broadband subscribers. Verizon Online's consumer DSL and FiOS Internet Service customers could purchase and download movies to watch at home or rent movies through Verizon's special agreement with Movielink.

GreenCine's Combination Online Rental-VOD Movie Offering

GreenCine was an online DVD rental company that also offered its subscribers two other options for watching movies—VOD and DivX downloads, both priced at $4.99 per movie and both allowing customers to watch the movie as many times as they wished over a 10-day period (GreenCine's adult movies had a 30-day use period). GreenCine had 10,000 on-demand movie titles that included independent, international, documentary, classic, and adult movies covering 32 genres.

GreenCine's online rental customers could select from a library of 25,000 titles and choose from among seven plans:

- $9.95, unlimited DVDs, 1 title out at a time.
- $14.95, unlimited DVDs, 2 titles out at a time.
- $21.95, unlimited DVDs, 3 titles out at a time.
- $27.95, unlimited DVDs, 4 titles out at a time.
- $33.95, unlimited DVDs, 5 titles out at a time.
- $49.95, unlimited DVDs, 8 titles out at a time.
- $59.95, unlimited DVDs, 10 titles out at a time.

Like Netflix, GreenCine offered a free two-week trial period. It had one distribution center and delivery could run two to three days. GreenCine sent members an e-mail alert when a movie was mailed out and when it received a movie that the member had returned.

Headquartered in the San Francisco Bay area, GreenCine touted itself as a movie source for people who liked the arts and were fond of off-the-wall, offbeat, eclectic, and unusual movies. Its collection featured independent, foreign, anime, and art house movies, as well as HK action and classic titles. The company's Web site said, "If what you like to see is off-center, or dead center, in terms of taste, Green-Cine is for you."

NETFLIX'S OUTLOOK

Reed Hastings believed that Netflix's prospects were exceptionally bright. In a December 2005 interview with *Inc.* magazine, he said:

> Netflix has at least another decade of dominance ahead of it. But movies over the Internet are coming, and at some point it will become big business. We started investing 1% to 2% of revenue every year in downloading, and I think it's tremendously exciting because it will fundamentally lower our mailing costs. We want to be ready when video-on-demand happens. That's why the company is called Netflix, not DVD-by-Mail.[5]

But two new developments cast shadows on this prognosis. In January 2006, *The Wall Street Journal* reported that cable TV companies and major movie studios were considering strategies to release movies through VOD cable services the same day that the DVDs were available in retail stores and rental outlets.[6] The move was precipitated by deals that Walt Disney and NBC Universal had recently made to make television shows available on Apple Computer's video-capable iPod. With movie box-office attendance and revenues lagging, movie studios were anxious to pursue highly lucrative sales of movie DVDs and prevent that revenue stream from eroding. Historically, movie studios had released new movies first to theaters and then several weeks or months later made them available on DVD, cable video-on-demand services, and other platforms (each a few weeks apart)—a strategy that they believed maximized revenue.

Also in January 2006, Google announced that it would begin allowing consumers to buy videos from major content partners through the Google site.[7] Consumers would be able to pay to download and view videos, such as television shows, on their computers from Google content partners that included CBS Corporation, the National Basketball Association, and other partners soon to be named.

Endnotes

[1]As cited in Blockbuster's 2004 10-K report, p. 1.

[2]As cited in Sarah McBride, Peter Grant, and Merissa Marr, "Movies May Hit DVD Cable Simultaneously," *The Wall Street Journal*, January 4, 2006, p. B1.

[3]Based on information in Shane C. Buettner, "DVD Sales Peaking," posted at Ultimate AV, www.guidetohometheater.com (accessed December 29, 2005).

[4]Excerpt from company press release, April 18, 2005.

[5]Interview with *Inc.* magazine's Patrick J. Sauer, posted at www.inc.com (accessed December 29, 2005).

[6]McBride, Grant, and Marr, "Movies May Hit DVD Cable Simultaneously," p. B1.

[7]Kevin J. Delaney and Nick Wingfield, "Google to Offer Video, Software That Rivals Microsoft's," *The Wall Street Journal*, January 5, 2006, p. A9.

Procter & Gamble's Acquisition of Gillette

John E. Gamble

University of South Alabama

Between 2001 and 2005, Procter & Gamble's revenues increased by more than 40 percent to reach $56.7 billion; its profits more than doubled to approach $7.3 billion; and its number of billion-dollar brands such as Crest, Bounty, Charmin, Tide, Ivory, and Folgers increased from 10 to 16. The company's outstanding financial performance during the four-year period generated adequate free cash flows to fund dividend payments of $11 billion and allowed its market capitalization to increase by more than 100 percent. The company also utilized free cash flows to build its lineup of marquee brands through the acquisitions of Clairol in 2001 and Wella hair care products in 2003.

At the close of its fiscal year ending September 30, 2005, Procter & Gamble executed its largest acquisition ever with the $57 billion takeover of the Gillette Company. The acquisition delivered five additional billion-dollar brands to Procter & Gamble's business mix and made it the global leader in the market for razors and blades. In addition, Gillette's Duracell business unit was the world's number-one seller of alkaline batteries to consumers, its Oral B business was the worldwide leader in manual and electric toothbrushes, and the Braun unit produced and marketed the best-selling brand of foil electric shavers for men and the number-one hair epilator for women. The Gillette Company's sales of Gillette, Foamy, Satin Care, Right Guard, Soft & Dri, and Dry Idea also made it a leading producer of personal care products.

The $57 billion acquisition price represented a 20 percent premium over Gillette's market

capitalization one week prior to the January 28, 2005, merger announcement and would allow Gillette shareholders to exchange each Gillette share held for 0.975 shares of Procter & Gamble (P&G) stock. P&G planned to buy back $18 billion to $22 billion of its outstanding common shares within 12 to 18 months of the completion of the October 1, 2005, merger. The share buyback plan would have the effect of financing the acquisition with 60 percent equity and 40 percent debt.

P&G management expected a $1 + 1 = 3$ effect from the merger since the acquisition of Gillette would give P&G a stronger business lineup and brand portfolio and provide significant cost-sharing opportunities between the two companies' businesses. Procter & Gamble's ability to introduce Gillette brands to new country markets served by its distribution system caused management to increase its near-term annual sales growth objective from 4–6 percent to 5–7 percent. In addition, P&G management had identified approximately $1 billion in annual cost savings resulting from value chain synergies between P&G businesses and Gillette business units. The company planned an immediate workforce reduction of 6,000 employees who would no longer be needed because of duplication of responsibilities and activities.

By all appearances, the Gillette acquisition seemed to offer P&G attractive new consumer products segments and ample strategic-fit opportunities that would benefit the overall performance of both business groups, but P&G shareholders had reason to question whether the company's bid for Gillette was too rich. According to an analysis by Goldman Sachs and UBS, the 20 percent purchase-price premium P&G offered to Gillette shareholders was within the range offered in other recent consumer goods mergers, but the acquisition price seemed high when comparing the merger price sales and earnings before interest and taxes (EBIT) multiples to those of other recent mergers. The $57 billion price offered for Gillette was 5.5 times greater than Gillette's most recent sales and 18.8 times greater than its most recent EBIT. The sales multiple for other acquisitions examined by Goldman Sachs/ UBS ranged from 1.1 to 4.1. EBIT multiples for previous consumer goods acquisitions included in the investment firms' analysis ranged from 8.4 to 17.6. Projections that the addition of Gillette's business units to P&G's lineup would dilute P&G's EPS for up to three years was also worrisome to investors who believed the 0.975 exchange ratio was overly generous. However, as Procter & Gamble closed its first quarter as a merged company on December 31, 2005, the company was performing at the high end of analysts' expectations. In addition, the merged company's ample free cash flows had allowed it to acquire four leading detergent brands sold in Southeast Asia from Colgate-Palmolive. The new brands would dramatically improve P&G's market share in its weakest region in Asia.

COMPANY HISTORIES AND OVERVIEW OF THE MERGER

Procter & Gamble

The Procter & Gamble Company (P&G) was begun when immigrants William Procter and James Gamble settled in Cincinnati, Ohio, in 1837 and soon thereafter married sisters. At the urging of their father-in-law, the two men, one a candle maker and other a soap maker, created a partnership to manufacture and market their products in the Cincinnati area. The company's sales reached $1 million in 1859, but the company had yet to produce and market a national brand until 1879, when James Norris Gamble, son of the founder and a trained chemist, developed Ivory soap. Ivory quickly transformed Procter & Gamble into a national consumer products company with 30 brands and production facilities across the United States and Canada by 1890. The company added a food products division in 1911 when it introduced

Crisco and began a chemicals division to formalize research procedures and develop new products in 1917. P&G entered the hair care business in 1934 when it developed the first detergent-based shampoo. The company introduced popular-selling brands like Tide, Crest, Pampers, and Downy throughout the 1940s, 1950s, and 1960s.

The company expanded its presence in the cosmetics, fragrances, and toiletries industry in the 1980s with the acquisitions of Richardson-Vicks and Noxell. Richardson-Vicks was the producer of Oil of Olay and Pantene products, and Noxell manufactured and marketed Cover Girl, Noxema, and Clarion products. The company acquired Old Spice in 1990, Max Factor in 1991, Giorgio Beverly Hills in 1994, and Tambrands in 1997. Acquisitions during the 2000s included Clairol in 2001 and Wella shampoos and hair care products in 2003. In 2005, the company sold more than 300 brands in 160 countries. The company's business lineup included 16 billion-dollar brands, and P&G was the global market share leader in 7 of the 12 product categories in which it competed. Its closest rival was the market share leader in only two global markets.

P&G's businesses were organized into three product-based segments: Household Care; Health, Baby, and Family Care; and Beauty Care. The company's Household Care segment included fabric care, home care, snacks, coffee, and commercial services businesses. The Health, Baby, and Family Care division businesses included oral care, personal health care, pharmaceuticals, and pet health and nutrition. Beauty Care businesses manufactured and marketed retail and professional hair care products, feminine care products, cosmetics, fine fragrances, and personal cleansing products. The company's best-known brands in each of its business units are presented in Exhibit 1.

The Gillette Company

The history of shaving dates back to at least 3000 BC, when the first copper-bladed razors were fashioned. Razors through the 1800s were knifelike in their appearance and were prone to leaving gashes or nicks in the skin. The razor of the 21st century can be traced to the efforts of King C. Gillette and William Nickerson, who collaborated to invent the first razor with a safe, inexpensive, disposable blade. The invention

Exhibit 1   **P&G's Best-Known Brands Prior to Gillette Acquisition**

Household Care		
Brand Name	**Product Categories**	**Markets**
Ariel	Laundry detergent	Latin America, Europe, Middle East, Africa
Bounce	Dryer sheets	North America, Latin America, Asia
Dawn	Dishwashing liquid	North America, Latin America
Downy	Fabric softener	North America, Latin America, Europe, Middle East, Africa
Folgers	Whole bean, ground, and instant coffees	North America, Latin America
Gain	Laundry detergent	North America
Millstone	100% premium arabica bean coffees with over 65 varieties	North America
Mr. Clean	Multipurpose cleaner	North America, Asia
Pringles	Snack foods	North America, Latin America, Europe, Middle East, Africa, Asia
Swiffer	Sweeper system	North America, Latin America, Europe, Middle East, Africa
Tide	Laundry detergent	North America, Latin America, Europe, Middle East, Africa, Asia

Beauty Care		
Brand Name	**Product Categories**	**Markets**
Always	Sanitary pads	North America, Latin America, Europe, Middle East, Africa
Aussie	Shampoo and styling products	North America, Europe, Middle East, Africa
CoverGirl	Full line of beauty products for face, lips, eyes, and nails	North America, Latin America, Europe, Middle East, Africa, Asia
Giorgio	Fragrances	North America, Latin America, Europe, Middle East, Africa, Asia
Head & Shoulders	Shampoo	North America, Latin America, Europe, Middle East, Africa, Asia
Herbal Essences	Line of shampoos, conditioners, styling aids, and body washes	North America, Europe, Middle East, Africa, Latin America, Asia
Hugo Boss	Fragrances	North America, Latin America, Europe, Middle East, Africa, Asia
Infusium	Line of therapeutic, premium hair care products	North America, Latin America
Ivory	Line of detergent, dishwashing liquid, and body soap	North America, Latin America, Europe, Middle East, Africa, Asia
Max Factor	Full line of beauty products for face, lips, eyes, and nails	North America, Latin America, Europe, Middle East, Africa, Asia
Miss Clairol	Permanent hair color	North America, Europe, Middle East, Africa, Latin America, Asia
Nice 'n Easy	Permanent hair color	North America, Europe, Middle East, Africa, Latin America, Asia
Noxzema	Line of skin care products	North America, Latin America, Europe, Middle East, Africa
Olay	Line of skin care and cleansing products	North America, Latin America, Europe, Middle East, Africa, Asia

(Continued)

Exhibit 1   **Continued**

Beauty Care		
Brand Name	**Product Categories**	**Markets**
Old Spice	Line of shaving and fragrance products for men	North America, Latin America, Europe, Middle East, Africa, Asia
Pantene	Shampoos, conditioners, hairsprays, and styling aids	North America, Latin America, Europe, Middle East, Africa, Asia
Pert Plus	2-in-1 shampoo/conditioner, individual shampoos and conditioners	North America, Latin America, Europe, Middle East, Africa, Asia
Scope	Mouthwash	North America, Latin America
Secret	Antiperspirant	North America, Latin America, Europe, Middle East, Africa
Tampax	Tampons	North America, Latin America, Europe, Middle East, Africa, Asia
Vidal Sassoon	Hair washes, therapies, stylers, and specialty products	North America, Latin America, Europe, Middle East, Africa, Asia

Family Care		
Brand Name	**Product Categories**	**Markets**
Bounty	Paper towels	North America, Latin America
Charmin	Bathroom tissue	North America, Latin America, Europe, Middle East, Africa
Iams	Complete line of premium dog and cat foods	North America, Europe, Middle East, Africa, Latin America
Puffs	Facial tissues	North America, Latin America
PUR	Water filtration systems, including pitchers and faucet mounts	North America

Baby Care		
Brand Name	**Product Categories**	**Markets**
Luvs	Disposable diapers and wipes	North America, Latin America
Pampers	Disposable diapers, wet wipes, and bibs	North America, Latin America, Europe, Middle East, Africa, Asia

Health Care		
Brand Name	**Product Categories**	**Markets**
Crest	Toothpastes and toothbrushes	North America, Latin America, Europe, Middle East, Africa, Asia
NyQuil	Nighttime relief for temporary relief of cold/flu symptoms	North America, Latin America, Europe, Middle East, Africa
Pepto-Bismol	Antacidum that relieves most common stomach discomforts	North America, Latin America
Prilosec OTC	Over-the-counter medication used to treat frequent heartburn	North America
Vicks	Line of temporary cold symptom relief products and throat drops	North America, Latin America, Europe, Middle East, Africa, Asia

Source: www.pg.com.

471

led to the founding of the Gillette Company in 1901, which sold its first razors in 1903. The double-edged safety razor proved so popular with men that Gillette began to expand abroad in 1905, with the company opening a European headquarters in London. On the company's 25th anniversary in 1926, King C. Gillette heralded the success of the company's safety razor by stating, "There is no other article for individual use so universally known or widely distributed. In my travels, I have found it in the most northern town in Norway and in the heart of the Sahara Desert."[1]

In 2005, Gillette had expanded into five business segments: Blades and Razors, Duracell, Oral Care, Braun, and Personal Care. The company has maintained manufacturing operations in 14 countries and sold its products in over 200 countries. Five of Gillette's brands each accounted for more than $1 billion in annual sales. In addition to its blades and razors business unit holding the number-one position worldwide, Duracel was the global leader in alkaline battery sales to consumers, Oral B was the worldwide leader in manual and electric toothbrushes, and Braun was the best-selling brand of foil electric shavers for men and the number-one hair epilator for women. The company's Personal Care segment sold shaving creams, skin care products, and antiperspirants under the Gillette, Foamy, Satin Care, Right Guard, Soft & Dri, and Dry Idea brand names.

Rationale for Merger

Both P&G and Gillette management agreed that a merger between the two companies would offer four key benefits: (1) The companies had complementary strengths in product innovation and selling activities, (2) the merger would result in a stronger lineup of brands, (3) a merged company would generate additional opportunities for scale economies, and (4) a stronger lineup of brands would enhance relationships and bargaining power with retail buyers. Immediately upon consummation of the merger, management was to take Gillette products into developing markets such as China that were served by P&G, but not by Gillette. In addition, company managers planned to share R&D costs between P&G and Gillette products and to reduce more than $1 billion in non-value-adding costs in both business groups through synergies in purchasing and asset utilization. The companies' managers also agreed that both companies had similar cultures, visions, and values, which should facilitate their integration.

The acquisition would also better balance P&G's sales between Beauty Care, Health Care, Baby Care, Family Care, and Household Care, with approximately 50 percent of the combined company's revenues originating from the sales of Beauty and Health and 50 percent coming from the sales of Baby, Family, and Household. Also, the acquisition would give P&G 10 billion-dollar brands in Beauty and Health and 12 billion-dollar brands in Baby, Family, and Household. The merged company's nearly $2 billion R&D budget would be more than most of P&G's direct rivals combined, which should allow it to turn some if its 13 $500 million brands into billion-dollar brands. The combination of merger benefits led P&G management to increase its annual sales growth objectives through 2010 from 4–6 percent to 5–7 percent.

COMPETITIVE POSITION AND PERFORMANCE OF P&G AND GILLETTE BUSINESS UNITS

Procter & Gamble

In 2005, P&G's five business units held an average global market share of 30 percent and held 50–60 percent market shares in the Western Europe Baby Care and Feminine Care markets and the North American Fabric Care market. The company's management believed that P&G had a $15 billion opportunity for organic growth in its existing lineup of brands through continued international expansion. In 2005, emerging markets accounted for only 23 percent of P&G's sales, but accounted for 86 percent of the world's population. The combined GDPs of emerging markets represented 25 percent of the global GDP, but were expected to grow to 30 percent of global GDP by 2009.

P&G Beauty Care sales grew by 14 percent based on volume and 12 percent based on revenues in fiscal 2005, with its net earnings increasing by 22 percent for the year. The Beauty Care division held five billion-dollar brands. Pantene was the world's leading hair care brand in 2005, with sales of more than $2 billion and a 10 percent global share of the market. Head & Shoulders was the world's second best-selling brand of shampoo, with just under

10 percent of the market in 2005. P&G's fragrance lines had also experienced notable growth with the sales of Hugo Boss and Lacoste, each growing by more than 1,000 percent since 2001. Overall, the division's net sales had increased from $12.2 billion in fiscal 2003 to $19.5 billion in fiscal 2005, while net earnings for the division grew from $1.9 billion to $2.9 billion during the three-year period.

Net sales grew by 11 percent and net earning grew by 28 percent in fiscal 2005 for P&G's Family Care and Baby Care divisions. The Baby Care division held a 37 percent global market share in the category with products such as its Pampers line of disposable diapers and baby wipes. Billion-dollar brands in the Family Care division included Crest, Bounty, Charmin, and Iams. Health Care sales grew by 11 percent as well during fiscal 2005, but net income for the business segment increased by only 8 percent during the year. The company's best-known pharmaceutical products were Actonel and Prilosec OTC. Prilosec OTC held 35 percent of the U.S. heartburn treatment market, while Actonel had achieved a 33 percent global market share in the osteoporosis prevention market. The combined sales of all Baby, Family, and Health products increased from $15.7 billion in 2003 to $19.7 billion in 2005. Net income attributable to the divisions increased from $1.6 billion in fiscal 2003 to $2.3 billion in fiscal 2005.

The company's Household Care division recorded sales and earnings of $18.4 and $2.5 billion

in fiscal 2005, respectively. The division's sales had grown from $15.2 billion in 2003, while net earnings contribution had increased from $2.3 billion. The company's top 10 household care products in 2005 were Folgers, Tide, Ariel, Downy, Pringles, and Dawn—all bringing in sales of more than $1 billion each. Gain, Ace, Mr. Clean, and Swifter were other best-selling P&G household products brands.

Approximately 52 percent of P&G's fiscal 2005 sales were from outside North America, with 24 percent originating in Western Europe, 5 percent coming from Northeast Asia, and 23 percent originating from developing geographies. The company's gross margins had improved from 49.0 percent in 2003 to 51.0 percent in 2005. Free cash flow and free cash flow productivity (the ratio of free cash flow to net income) had declined slightly between 2004 and 2005. Exhibit 2 presents a financial summary for Procter & Gamble.

The Gillette Company

The strong competitive position of Gillette's business units in their respective consumer segments was among the most enticing attributes of the company as an acquisition target for P&G. Gillette held the number-one position in each of its primary product categories in 2005, including a 70 percent market share in the global razor and razor blade market, a 40 percent global market share in alkaline

Exhibit 2 **Financial Summary for Procter & Gamble, Fiscal 2000–Fiscal 2005 (in millions, except per share amounts)**

	Year Ended June 30					
	2005	2004	2003	2002	2001	2000
Net sales	$56,741	$51,407	$43,377	$40,238	$39,244	$39,951
Operating income	10,927	9,827	7,853	6,678	4,736	5,954
Net earnings	7,257	6,481	5,186	4,352	2,922	3,542
Diluted net earnings per common share	$ 2.66	$ 2.32	$ 1.85	$ 1.54	$ 1.03	$ 1.23
Dividends per common share	1.03	0.93	0.82	0.76	0.70	0.64
Total assets	61,527	57,048	43,706	40,776	34,387	34,366
Long-term debt	12,887	12,554	11,475	11,201	9,792	9,012
Free cash flow*	6,541	7,338	7,218	6,063	3,318	1,657
Free cash flow productivity†	90.1%	113.2%	139.2%	139.3%	113.6%	46.8%

*Free cash flow represents operating cash flow less capital spending.
†Free cash flow productivity is the ratio of free cash flow to net earnings.
Source: Procter & Gamble 2002 and 2005 10-Ks and 2005 S-4.

batteries, a 36 percent market share of the worldwide market for manual and electric toothbrushes. Net sales for the entire company grew by 13 percent to $10.5 billion in 2004, while gross profit increased by 16 percent and net income grew by 22 percent in 2004. In 2004, 37.8 percent of Gillette's sales were in North America, 33.8 percent came from European markets, 11.2 percent originated in Africa and the Middle East, 9.6 percent came from Asia, and 7.4 percent were in Latin America.

The Gillette Company's management believed that its growth and margin opportunities were better than those available to other consumer staple producers because of consumers' preference for branded products. The overall private-label market share for consumer staple items in the United States was 15 percent, according to a 2003 ACNielsen survey. Some categories experienced even greater pricing pressure from private-label brands, with store brands capturing 18 percent of U.S. food and beverage sales in 2003. Sales of private-label razor blades represented only 5.3 percent of the market in 2003, private-label toothbrushes held only a 6.5 percent market share, and private-label alkaline batteries had captured only 12.7 percent of the U.S. market in 2003. P&G was similarly protected from private-label brands in many categories, with private-label antiperspirants accounting for just 0.4 percent of U.S. sales of such products in 2003.

Gillette had also been successful in urging consumers to trade up to higher-price-point personal care items. For example, the company sold low-cost Gillette double-edged blades for safety razors, entry-level shaving systems like the Gillette Sensor 3, and premium shaving systems such as the battery-powered M Power Mach 3. Consumers in developed markets such as the United States were increasingly trading up to higher-priced and higher-margin personal care products. In 2004, 56 percent of the U.S. blade market was held by brands charging more than $1.50 per blade, 37 percent of the market sold at price points between $0.45 and $1.50, and only 7 percent of the market was held by brands selling at less than $0.45 per blade. Gillette saw great opportunity for higher-end shaving systems in emerging markets since such shavers held only 8 percent of sales in regions such as Asia, Latin America, and Africa–Middle East. The company saw similar opportunities in the markets for power toothbrushes, alkaline batteries, and electric shavers. The transition

to higher-priced personal care products was already evident in growing economies such as Russia, where the sales of blades priced over $1.50 grew by 33 percent in 2004 to account for 41 percent of all blade sales. The sales of the lowest-priced blades declined by 19 percent in Russia during 2004.

Buyers of premium personal care products also tended to be highly loyal, with only 23 percent of Mach3 users indicating in a 2003 NCS-USA survey that they would try another brand if Mach3 shavers were out of stock during their trip to the supermarket. Seventy-two percent of men using less expensive disposable shavers indicated that they would purchase whatever brand was available. Women surveyed in the NCS-USA survey were equally loyal to Gillette shavers, with only 22 percent of Venus users suggesting they would purchase a different brand if no Venus blades were in stock.

The company had recorded its second consecutive year of record results in 2004, with its turnaround that began in 2000 fully completed. The company's net sales had grown at a 9 percent compounded annual growth rate between 2001 and 2004, while earnings per share had grown at a 19 percent compounded annual growth rate during the four-year period. The company's gross margins had also improved by 350 basis points between 2001 and 2004, and free cash flow had improved dramatically after the turnaround began in 2000. The company's total free cash flow between 1997 and 2000 was only $1.9 billion, while free cash flow generated between 2001 and 2004 exceeded $7 billion. Exhibit 3 presents a financial summary for the Gillette Company.

P&G'S SHARE PRICE OFFER

Most analysts understood the attractiveness of a Gillette acquisition for P&G. The two companies both enjoyed strong market positions and competed in relatively attractive consumer goods segments. Also, both companies had achieved outstanding recent financial performance—including the generation of free cash flows that would support further growth. In addition, the two companies management teams believed that P&G and Gillette had similar organizational cultures, which should prove to aid in the integration of the two companies and help P&G

Exhibit 3   **Financial Summary for the Gillette Company, 2000–2004 (in millions, except per share amounts)**

	2004	2003	2002	2001	2000
Net sales	$10,477	$ 9,252	$8,453	$8,084	$8,310
Operating income	2,465	2,003	1,809	1,498	1,512
Net earnings	1,691	1,385	1,216	910	392
Diluted net earnings per common share	1.68	1.35	1.15	0.86	0.37
Dividends per common share	0.65	0.65	0.65	0.65	0.65
Total assets	10,731	10,041	9,883	9,961	10,246
Long-term debt	2,142	2,453	2,457	1,654	1,650
Free cash flow*	1,630	2,232	1,672	1,468	811
Free cash flow productivity[†]	96.4%	161.2%	137.5%	161.3%	206.9%

*Free cash flow represents operating cash flow less capital spending.

[†]Free cash flow productivity is the ratio of free cash flow to net earnings.

Source: Gillette 2001 and 2004 10-Ks.

deliver its expected $1 billion–plus cost savings from cross-business strategic fits. There was also reason to believe that the combined company's key product categories would grow at high enough rates to support future increases in shareholder value. Gillette's calculation of compounded annual growth rates for consumer goods categories between 2000 and 2004 is presented in Exhibit 4. Exhibit 5 provides perpetuity growth rates for selected consumer product categories as prepared by Merrill Lynch for P&G shareholders evaluating the merger.

Merrill Lynch analysts expected the integration of the two companies and the elimination of duplicate value chain activities to take as long as three years, which might have a dilution effect on P&G's earnings per share (EPS). Specifically, Merrill Lynch's analysis indicated P&G's EPS might be higher between 2006 and 2008 if it were to continue to operate without the inclusion of Gillette's products. Merrill Lynch also suggested P&G's EPS might show positive effects from the merger if integration went quicker than expected and cost savings from synergies between

Exhibit 4   **Gillette's Compounded Annual Growth Rates for Consumer Products Categories, 2000–2004**

Consumer Product Category	Growth Rate for Global Market (CAGR for 2000–2004)
Blades and razors	8.2%
Oral care—toothbrushes	7.3
Skin care	6.8
Chocolate confectionery	6.5
Pet food/pet cares	6.5
Baked goods	4.9
Hair care	4.4
Alkaline batteries	3.7
Oral care—toothpaste	3.5
Laundry detergent	3.4
Carbonated soft drinks	3.4

Source: Gillette presentation to the CAGNY Conference, February 24, 2005.

Exhibit 5   **Gillette's Perpetuity Growth Rates for Selected Consumer Product Categories**

Consumer Product Category	Perpetuity Growth Rate Range
Blades and razors	2.8%–3.8%
Personal care	1.5%–2.5%
Duracell	(0.1%)–0.9%
Oral care	2.4%–3.4%
Braun	0.5%–1.5%

Source: P&G 2005 S-4.

brands were captured in fewer than three years. The projected impact of the Gillette acquisition on P&G's financial performance as calculated by Merrill Lynch is shown in Exhibit 6.

The $57 billion price P&G's board of directors agreed to pay for Gillette would give Gillette shareholders a 20.1 percent premium over Gillette's trading price one week prior to the January 28, 2005, merger announcement. P&G believed that the 20.1 percent share price premium would provide Gillette's board of directors with an adequate incentive to approve the merger and prevent outsiders from interfering with the outright purchase of the company. The $57 billion deal also represented a 5.5 multiple of Gillette's 2004 net sales and an 18.8 multiple of the company's 2004 earnings before interest, taxes, depreciation, and amortization (EBITDA). A comparison of purchase-price multiples and stock-price premiums for selected consumer goods acquisitions as prepared for Gillette shareholders by Goldman Sachs and UBS is presented in Exhibit 7. While the 20.1 percent per share purchase-price premium is within the range for other acquisitions examined by

Exhibit 6   **Projected Range of Impact on P&G Performance by Gillette Acquisition**

	Fiscal Year Ending June 30		
	2006E	2007E	2008E
Earnings per share	$(0.25)–$(0.30)	$(0.10)–$0.05	$(0.05)–$0.15
Earnings per share excluding one-time charges	$(0.21)–$(0.26)	$(0.09)–$0.06	$(0.05)–$0.15
Earnings per share excluding one-time charges and new amortization	$(0.16)–$(0.21)	$(0.03)–$0.12	$ 0.00–$0.20

Source: P&G 2005 S-4.

Exhibit 7   **Gillette's Purchase-Price Multiples and Stock-Price Premiums for Selected Consumer Goods Acquisitions**

	Purchase-Price Multiples for Selected Consumer Goods Acquisitions		Per Share Purchase-Price Premium based on Stock Price
	Sales	EBITDA	One Week Prior to Announcement
Median	2.2x	13.0x	19.30%
Mean	2.2x	13.2x	29.10%
Range	1.1x–4.1x	8.4x–17.6x	5.3%–92.6%
Gillette at $54.05	5.5x	18.8x	20.1%*

*Relative to closing price on Wednesday, January 19, 2005.
Source: P&G 2005 S-4.

Exhibit 8   **Transaction Value and Per Share Purchase-Price Premiums Paid in Selected Consumer Goods Acquisitions, 1994–2004**

Announcement Date	Acquirer	Target	Transaction Value (in billions)	Premium to Share Price One Week Prior to Announcement
6/2000	Phillip Morris	Nabisco	$19.2	103.2%
8/1994	Johnson & Johnson	Neutrogena	1.0	76.3
11/2004	Constellation Brands	Robert Mondavi	1.4	52.3
3/2003	Procter & Gamble	Wella	7.0	47.3
10/2003	Tchibo	Beiersdorf	13.0	45.7
6/2000	Unilever	Bestfoods	23.7	39.9
12/2000	PepsiCo	Quaker Oats	15.1	24.0
				Average 55.5%

Source: P&G 2005 S-4.

UBS and Goldman Sachs, the purchase-price multiple exceeds that of prior acquisitions.

Merrill Lynch's analysis of the per share purchase-price premiums paid to acquire selected consumer goods between 1994 and 2004 left room for debate as to whether P&G's 20.1 percent offer was fair to Gillette shareholders. Merrill Lynch's purchase-price evaluation based on Gillette's January 26, 2005, closing price indicates the price might be considered low, although calculations based on Gillette's 52-week low and three-year average stock price was near the average paid in other acquisitions (see Exhibits 8 and 9).

Exhibit 9   **Multiples and Premium for P&G's Share Price Offer for Gillette as Calculated by Merrill Lynch**

	Gillette at Offer Price
2004 sales	5.5x
2004 EBITDA	18.8
Premium to:	
1 day (based on Gillette closing price of ($45.00 on 1/26/05)	20.1%
52-week high	18.7%
52-week low	45.9
3-year average	52.4

Source: P&G 2005 S-4.

Since P&G's shares traded for a higher price at the time of the merger than Gillette shares, Gillette shareholders received a fraction of a P&G share in exchange for their Gillette holdings. The relationship between P&G's prevailing stock price and Gillette's price resulted in an exchange ratio of 0.975. For example, a Gillette stockholder owning 1,000 Gillette shares would receive 975 P&G shares upon the completion of the merger. Fractional shares were not awarded, so a Gillette shareholder owning 100 shares would receive only 97 P&G shares.

Merrill Lynch also calculated a range of appropriate exchange ratios based on Gillette's expected contribution to the combined company's net income and the amount of levered free cash flow provided by Gillette brands (see Exhibit 10). Levered free cash flow represents free cash flow less additional debt service taken on as a result of the acquisition of Gillette. Based on the analysts' estimates of net income contributed by Gillette brands, P&G would be required to capture at least two-thirds of the expected synergies between the company's brands to approach the 0.975 exchange ratio offered to Gillette shareholders. Using the estimates based on levered free cash flow, the 0.975 exchange ratio could be justified if at least some expected synergies were achieved.

Exhibit 11 shows the financial projections used in Merrill Lynch's exchange ratio calculations to estimate the importance of Gillette's brands to the combined company's performance through 2008.

Exhibit 10   **Merrill Lynch's Estimation of Appropriate Exchange Ratios**

	Assuming No Expected Synergies Are Achieved	
	Low Estimate	High Estimate
Exchange ratio based on net income contribution for Gillette brands	0.654	0.684
Exchange ratio based on levered free cash flow provided by Gillette brands	0.848	0.875
	Assuming 50% of Expected Synergies Are Achieved	
	Low Estimate	High Estimate
Exchange ratio based on net income contribution for Gillette brands	0.876	0.886
Exchange ratio based on levered free cash flow provided by Gillette brands	1.108	1.152
	Assuming 2/3 of Expected Synergies Are Achieved	
	Low Estimate	High Estimate
Exchange ratio based on net income contribution for Gillette brands	0.941	0.963
Exchange ratio based on levered free cash flow provided by Gillette brands	1.190	1.252

Source: P&G 2005 S-4.

Exhibit 11   **Financial Projections**

	Procter & Gamble's Contribution to Combined Company	Gillette's Contribution to Combined Company
Sales		
CY* 2004E	83.6%	16.4%
CY 2005E	83.8	16.2
EBITDA		
CY 2004E	80.0	20.0
CY 2005E	79.1	20.9
EBIT		
CY 2004E	80.9	19.1
CY 2005E	79.7	20.3
Net Income		
CY 2004E	80.3	19.7
CY 2005E	78.9	21.1
CY 2006E	78.4	21.6
CY 2007	78.3	21.7
CY 2008	78.3	21.7

*Contributions based on calendar year (CY), since P&G's fiscal year ends June 30 and Gillette's fiscal year ends December 31.

Source: P&G 2005 S-4.

P&G'S EARLY POSTMERGER PERFORMANCE

As the 2005 calendar year ended and P&G closed out its first quarter as a merged company, its managers were pleased that the company's performance seemed to be exceeding analysts' predictions. The company anticipated that its audited reports would show sales growth for the quarter ending December 31, 2005, to come in at 25–26 percent. Prior to the consummation of the merger, the company's managers and financial advisers had projected sales growth for the quarter to be in the 23–26 percent range. The company's managers attributed the increase in revenues to 6–7 percent organic sales growth in its Household Care and Beauty Care business units. Much of that increase was attributable to the performance of Gillette's blades and razors, Duracell, and Braun brands, which had grown by an estimated 17 percent during the quarter. Prior to the merger, Gillette's brands had been expected to grow at a low-single-digit rate.

Procter & Gamble managers also expected that final tabulations for the quarter would report a quarterly EPS of $0.68–$0.69, which was at the very top end of the $0.66–$0.69 projected for the quarter. The achievement of best-case quarterly EPS estimate led P&G managers to predict EPS dilution for the 2006 fiscal year to be no more than $0.20 to $0.26 per share. In assessing the impact of the merger on P&G performance for 2006, Merrill Lynch analysts had expected EPS dilution to fall between $0.25 and $0.30 per share.

P&G announced on January 4, 2006, that it would acquire the Fab, Trojan, Dynamo, and Paic laundry detergent brands marketed in Hong Kong, Singapore, Thailand, and Malaysia from Colgate-Palmolive. The new brands would boost P&G's market share in the category from 2.1 percent to 12.9 percent in Singapore, from 0.3 percent to 7.9 percent in Thailand, from 0.3 percent to 12.5 percent in Malaysia, and from 1.2 percent to 12.5 percent in Hong Kong. The company's market performance relative to the S&P 500 from January 1996 to December 2005 is presented in Exhibit 12. The exhibit also provides a comparison of P&G's stock performance relative to the S&P 500 for the January–December 2005 period.

Exhibit 12   **Performance of Procter & Gamble's Stock Price, January 1996–December 2005**

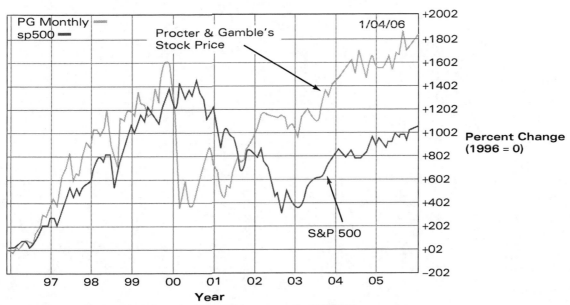

(a) Performance of Procter & Gamble's Stock Price versus the S&P 500.

(Continued)

479

Exhibit 12   **Continued**

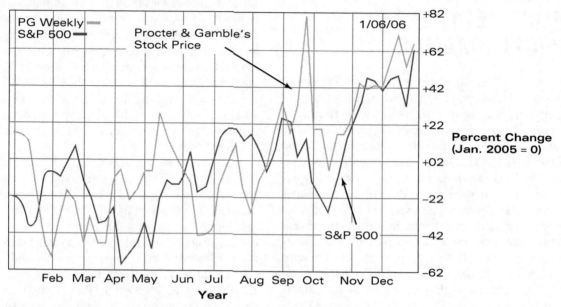

(b) Performance of Procter & Gamble's Stock Price versus the S&P 500 between January 2005 and December 2005.

Endnotes

[1]As quoted in "Gillette at a Glance," http://www.gillette.com/company/
gilletteataglance.asp

Vivendi: Revitalizing a French Conglomerate

After nearly two decades under the leadership of Guy Dejouany, the November 1995 board meeting of Compagnie Générale des Eaux (CGE) marked not only the end of an era, but the transfer of control to a new captain, Jean-Marie Messier. Besides the obvious difference in age between the seventy-six year old Dejouany and the thirty-eight year old Messier, the contrast between the two in terms of leadership style and strategic direction could not have been sharper.

In 1976 when Guy Dejouany took control, CGE was primarily a water utility company with some activities in waste treatment. As the 1980s progressed, reacting to what he saw as "unique opportunities,"[1] Dejouany used the cash flow from the core utility businesses to expand into a wide range of ventures. By November 1995, revenues were eleven times the 1976 levels and the company had diversified into a wide variety of businesses including real estate, healthcare, and telecommunications. CGE was one of the largest French companies; indeed, it was in the top 100 companies in the world. (See **Exhibit 1**.)

By the mid-1990s, however, CGE had serious financial problems. In 1995 the company experienced a net loss of 3.6 billion French francs (Frf). The company's real estate investments had collapsed, and debt levels ballooned. The stagnant share price caused investors to question whether the problems were a blip on the radar or reflected a more fundamental problem in the direction of the company.

After two years as a partner at the investment banking firm Lazard Frères, including five months in New York, Messier understood all too well the demands of the capital markets and the push for "shareholder value." From the beginning it was clear that Dejouany's handpicked dauphin aimed to take the company in a radically new direction.

II. Water Utility Business

The "heart and historical roots of CGE were in the management of the municipal water services in France, not in telecommunications or real estate" explained an executive in CGE's water

---

[1] *Compagnie Générale des Eaux Annual Report 1989*

John M. Turner, MBA '97, with the assistance of Research Associate Elizabeth J. Gordon prepared this case under the supervision of Professor Cynthia A. Montgomery as the basis for class discussion rather than to illustrate either effective or ineffective handling of an administrative situation.

business.[2] As reflected in its name, Compagnie Générale des Eaux, which translates as General Water, CGE built a franchise based on water purification and distribution throughout France.

Historical Roots   From its first contract to supply water to the city of Lyon, awarded by Imperial decree in 1853, CGE expanded rapidly throughout the 19th century into many other local municipalities in France including Nantes (1854), Paris (1860), and Nice (1864). As opposed to other countries where water utilities were strictly controlled by the central government, in France each of the 36,500 communes of the country individually controlled water supply and cost to consumers.[3] Expanding its service offering to local municipalities, CGE first entered wastewater treatment in 1884 with a contract with the French city of Reims. In order to cope with growing populations and aging infrastructure, CGE launched the SADE construction subsidiary in 1918 to construct, install, and rehabilitate water systems of local municipalities. The next acquisition was the piping company Tuyaux Bonna in 1924.

Capitalizing on the large cash flows that these near monopoly businesses generated, the company expanded rapidly in the domestic market. By 1995, 85% of French water distribution was privately controlled, of which 40% was contracted to CGE and 20% to its largest competitor, Lyonnaise des Eaux.[4]

During this same period, CGE began to expand into other municipal services. By 1953, the hundredth anniversary of the firm, the company was engaged in household waste collection. In the 1960s it moved into the management of district heating networks and the operation of waste incineration and composting plants. These businesses continued to expand rapidly during the 1970s. By 1997, waste treatment and energy represented 25% of total revenue. (See **Exhibits 2** and **3**.)

Although international expansion in the water treatment industry was limited until the 1970s, CGE signed its first contract with Venice in 1880. By the 1980s more international water markets began to open up to the firm. As the executive vice president of the water division commented:

> Madame Thatcher and the World Bank were responsible for the explosion of international opportunities in the 1980s. Thatcher believed in privatization. The World Bank came to the realization that it was stupid to invest in infrastructure without investing in efficiency.[5]

By the 1990s CGE was operating in many countries including China, Mexico, Argentina, Thailand, Philippines, and the United Kingdom. By 1997, 23% of water distribution and construction related revenues originated outside France.[6] International push was underway in both waste treatment and energy as well.

Economics of the Business   While CGE pursued a variety of different contractual relationships with local municipalities for water treatment, the vast majority in the domestic market were negotiated using *affermage* agreements.[7] In an *affermage* agreement, the municipality retained ownership of assets and CGE managed and serviced the existing facilities. By contrast, in a *concession* agreement, assets were owned by a private company. Most *affermage* contracts lasted 10 to 15 years,

---

[2] Company interviews, July 1997.

[3] "Profit Stream," *The Economist*, March 29, 1997, p.70.

[4] *SBC Warburg Analyst Report*, May 1996, p. 33.

[5] Company interviews, July 1997

[6] P. Coiffet, *Paribas Analyst Report*, May 1998, p. 65

[7] *Compagnie Générale des Eaux Annual Report 1996*, p. 24.

while *concession* agreements were often negotiated for a 20 to 30 year period. In contrast to domestic contracts, municipalities in the international sphere, especially in developing countries, were increasingly requiring investment in assets by service providers such as CGE.

Historically, relationships with local political leaders were at the heart of the contract negotiation process. Given the enormous stakes involved for long-term outsourcing of an entire population's water needs, securing long-term contracts had an enormous value to companies such as CGE. Local communities historically required a close relationship with the company that secured the contract. To fill this need, CGE's water business was highly decentralized, with 50 subsidiaries in France alone. Often, highly connected individuals such as former political leaders were chosen to run CGE's subsidiaries.

III. Legacy of Guy Dejouany

In 1976 when Guy Dejouany stepped to the helm of CGE, 80% of the company's 15 billion Frf. in revenues were centered in the core businesses of water management, waste treatment and electricity. As the 1980s progressed, Dejouany used the cash flow from the core utility businesses to expand those businesses as well as enter into a wide range of other ventures. Two decades later, after annual sales growth of 26%, the company had reached 166 billion Ffr. in revenue of which only 46% were still composed of these core activities. CGE had diversified into a wide variety of businesses including real estate, transport, healthcare, and telecommunications. Not only had the breadth and size of sales expanded, but also the number of subsidiaries in which these sales were contained had grown exponentially from 280 in 1976 to 2,714 in 1996.

Dejouany Management Style   From the beginning, Guy Dejouany was personally involved in all the company's operations. As CGE grew, so too did the number of individuals reporting to him. By 1995, Dejouany's direct reports had grown from a handful to 70. Meanwhile, corporate staff was kept at a minimum. Henri Proglio, a 25-year veteran of the company, a member of Messier's executive committee and director of the waste and water businesses, described Dejouany's management style:

> Dejouany lived this company! He was a real operational guy that knew everything that occurred in any part of any business. Keen on details, he managed through a very personal style of trust with individual managers. Sure, it was a special sort of governance, but it worked.[8]

For Dejouany, the 1980s were a period of "unprecedented opportunity" in France in which CGE could make the "great leap forward."[9] The French economy as a whole was growing rapidly and the hopes of an expanded market with the European Community were attractive opportunities for the firm. In particular, management believed that the lack of venture capital and the weak capital market in France placed the cash-generating CGE in a unique position to take advantage of the changes. Given the highly decentralized decision-making process at the firm, subsidiary heads and division heads acquired businesses and started businesses on a massive scale.

Some insight into the managers at CGE can be gained through an understanding of their backgrounds. Most, if not all, of the senior managers were educated at one of two schools, Ecole Nationale d'Administration or Polytechnique. Both schools encourage a "Colbertist" management style, founded on a nationalist economic doctrine run by a central power. Jean-Baptiste Colbert, the controller general of finance under King Louis XIV, concentrated his efforts on "reorganizing

---

[8] Interview, July 1997.

[9] "Chairman's Review of Operations," *Compagnie Générale des Eaux Annual Reports, 1989 and 1990.*

industry and commerce in a centralized fashion and busied himself with nearly everything, from matters of finance, production, and trade, to military affairs, arts and education."[10]   Although "Colbertism" has evolved since the sixteenth century, centralization of the economy and state ownership of industry remained the rule in France, thus perpetuating, in the eyes of some, a "ruling class."[11] There was much crossing back and forth between the private and public sectors according to a judge who has written about this issue, with leaders of the main industrial groups having attended the same schools and served in government together.[12]

Reward systems at CGE, as in most of the French economy, were predominately based on salary rather than performance bonuses. Under Dejouany, bonuses for top managers were decided on the basis of his management discretion. Stock options linking company performance to pay were completely absent except for a handful of top managers and directors. During Dejouany's tenure, French management, not only at CGE, rejected linking salary to short-term financial indicators/measures.

Reflecting on the Dejouany's approach to management, Guillaume Hannezo, the CFO of CGE commented:

> Through capturing the entrepreneurial spirit in the company, Dejouany was able to create a tremendous set of diversified companies. But, the process lacked a formal asset allocation system. Growth in the 1980s and early 1990s was spontaneous growth. This has resulted in some very good and some very bad stories for CGE.[13]

Diversification   If Dejouany's vision was the guiding force behind CGE's aggressive campaign of diversification in the 1970s and 1980s, cash flow from the core utilities businesses made the diversification financially feasible.

Many of CGE's decisions to diversify into new businesses were based on Dejouany's personal relationships and experiences. Like many venture capitalists or entrepreneurs, the quality of the people often topped his list of considerations for entering a new business. For example, at the beginning of the 1980s, Dejouany met Christian Pellerin who convinced him of the high profit potential for real estate development, especially in new areas such as La Défense in Paris. Much the same approach was taken with CGE's expansion into telecommunications. In 1984-1985, several highly talented engineers were hired away from France Telecom, the government owned telephone monopoly. Dejouany was immediately impressed by the entrepreneurial spirit of the newly hired engineers and was equally impressed by the potential for new competitors in the deregulated European telecommunications market.   He granted the team a budget to launch a new telecommunications business and soon the division began to grow. Again, central to Dejouany's approach was trust in a group of individuals and their judgment of the market.

Diversification also occurred for other reasons. For example, CGE's construction subsidiary, purchased for the apparent synergy of a similar customer base, was bought as a "poison pill" after St. Gobain, the French glass and materials company, attempted to take over CGE in 1981. Personal experience also played a large role in Dejouany's decisions to enter businesses. As a result of a family member's poor service experience in a French hospital, Dejouany saw the potential for developing a chain of hospitals in France that could deliver a higher level of service. Given that hospitals, as part

---

[10] A.M. Doro, "Les Affaires," *Across the Board*, July/August 1997, p. 44.

[11] *Ibid.*

[12] *Ibid.*

[13] Company interviews, July 1997.

of the state healthcare system in France, were linked to the local municipalities, Dejouany saw a great potential to leverage the company's existing relationships.

Expansion of Cross-Shareholdings   Another source of diversification for CGE came in the mid-80s when the company dramatically increased its portfolio investments or "cross-shareholdings." By the mid-1990s roughly 11 billion Ffr. of CGE's assets were tied up in the shares of other publicly traded French companies such as St. Gobain, Alcatel Alsthom, Accor, Paribas, and Société Générale. On average these assets returned only 3.4% during this period.[14]   At the same time, other large industrial concerns and banks such as AXA, Banque Nationale de Paris and Société Générale became shareholders in CGE. This cross-ownership of shares is known as "noyaux durs" in France.

The origins of these cross-shareholdings can be traced to the period 1986-1988 during a time of "cohabitation" in French government between a socialist president, François Mitterand, and a more conservative Prime Minister, Jacques Chirac. Soon after taking power in 1981, Mitterand nationalized 15 companies. The negative results of these nationalizations and a legislative shift in power to the conservatives forced the reprivatization of the same companies in 1986. Afraid of the inability of the weak French capital markets to absorb the large quantity of newly issued shares domestically and hesitant to open ownership of France's "crown jewels" to foreigners, the French government encouraged large, privately owned firms to soak up the new shares offered during the privatizations. This web of cross-ownership, initially designed as a temporary measure, has evolved into a quasi-permanent structure that continued to exist into the late 1990s.

The cross-shareholding often carried the added punch of enhanced voting rights for participating companies. Thus, while other large French companies held only 18.3% of CGE's stock, they owned 24.3% of the voting rights as late as 1998.[15] Such a large percentage of voting rights in a few hands had a significant impact on control at the board of directors' level. This power was enhanced by the fact that CEOs from cross-shareholding companies often served on each others' boards.

IV. Emerging Problems for CGE in the 1990s

By 1991 cracks were starting to appear in the untarnished picture of CGE's growth. As a result of the large capital expenditures incurred during the diversification of the 1980s, debt levels increased and return on invested capital dropped. The company's cash position worsened. A disintegration of the real estate market in 1991, followed by a scandal in the water business threatened the economic stability of the firm.

Cash Crisis   In the Chairman's Review in the 1992 Annual Report Dejouany first mentioned the difficult real estate market: "The main factors behind the crisis were…high interest rates…and an all-out recession. However, the situation has been made worse…by speculative, anticipatory moves which created excess supply."

Compagnie Immobilière Phenix (Phenix) was the main CGE company involved in real estate, a sector that CGE had seriously entered only in the late 1980s. By the end of 1995, Phenix had cost the company between 50-60 billion Ffr.[16] Consequently, CGE as a whole suffered its first loss ever (see **Exhibits 4-6**). A cash crunch occurred as successful start-up companies, such as Société Francaise du

---

[14] *Cholet-Dupont Analyst Report*, March 1997, p. 10.

[15] The company had an agreement with St. Gobain to unwind their cross-shareholdings by the end of first quarter 1999. This would reduce the stock held by other companies to 10% of the total, representing 15% of the voting rights.

[16] Figure from Stephane Richard, President of CGIS, interview, July 1997.

Radio Telephone (SFR), the telephone venture, required more cash than the water business generated. By 1995 the firm's debt/equity ratio reached 155%, making CGE one of the most highly leveraged companies in France.

Some members of the management team believed that the disaster in real estate was clearly the exception rather than the rule at CGE. As one manager commented:

> Trust was central to Dejouany's management style…He made one big mistake of trusting one man who was the head of real-estate… Without this gambler in real estate, the old personal model of management of Dejouany could have continued…It was a viable model.[17]

Others within CGE believed that the real-estate disaster only signaled a more fundamental set of governance issues within the company.[18]

Shareholders punished CGE shares. From 1991 to 1995, the stock price moved sideways and significantly underperformed the CAC 40, the French equivalent of the Dow Jones Industrial Average.

1995 Corruption Scandal   In the spring of 1995 an alleged bribery scandal involving large payments by CGE to Socialist politicians in the French island territory, La Réunion, splashed onto the front pages of the national newspapers, *Le Monde* and *Le Figaro*. Even the 76 year old CEO Guy Dejouany was placed under criminal investigation, although he was cleared of all charges in July of 1996.[19] While this was a dramatic case, the practice of "political contributions" to local leaders during a negotiation process was not uncommon in the long history of the water business.[20]

In the past, the water contract negotiation process had been only loosely regulated. In the 1990s, significant legislative reforms were made to tighten up the process. In 1993, a new law required water companies and municipalities to provide greater transparency and open bidding in contract negotiation.[21] By 1995, another legislative act, the Barnier Law, eliminated traditional *droits d'entrée* (literally "admissions fees") that were often requested by local municipalities when initially opening water facilities to private management.[22]

After assuming the chairmanship in 1996, Jean-Marie Messier made his position clear about how CGE would conduct business with municipalities. Addressing the scandal in the monthly company newsletter, *Générale Info*: "There can be no hesitation in our choice between losing a contract and agreeing to illegal payments—it is far better to lose the contracts."[23]

Despite the problems, by 1996 the water business generated 41 billion Ffr. in sales, making it one of France's 30 largest firms on a standalone basis. Through its aggressive domestic and international expansion, CGE supplied roughly 65 million people with water and wastewater treatment services. While the water business accounted for roughly one quarter of CGE's sales, its operating income of 3.1 billion Ffr. accounted for nearly 80% of CGE's operating profit due to the company's massive losses in construction/property and the start-up costs in telecommunications.

---

[17] Company interviews, July 1997.

[18] Company interviews, July 1997.

[19] *Reuters European Business Report*, July 23, 1996.

[20] A. Sage, "Bribes Scandal Hits the Bourse ," *The Observer Business Page*, June 19, 1994

[21] *SBC Warburg Analyst Report*, May 1996, p. 34.

[22]*Ibid.*, p. 35.

[23] "Message from Jean-Marie Messier," *Générale Info*, December 20,1996, p. 1.

V. Business Context of France in 1990s

After years of sustained economic growth and optimism surrounding the European Community initiative of 1992, France entered an economic slide that accelerated in the mid-1990s. In 1995, the country's real GDP growth was 2.1%, sinking to 1.5% in 1996. Investment growth was negative and consumer spending weak.[24] By 1997, unemployment in France reached a post-war record of 12.8%. Economic growth had flattened, and economic pessimism permeated both the public and private sectors.

Not only did CGE have to operate in the difficult economic environment, but, as the largest employer in France in 1995 with more than 217,000 employees, the company was under pressure to maintain employment levels. Rigid labor regulations and strong unions made the cost of employing new workers high compared to the more flexible labor markets of foreign competitors. The cost of firing new workers could be even higher. Government attempts in 1995 to liberalize the labor market led to nationwide strikes and economic gridlock.

Capital Markets   A lack of transparency and a weak corporate governance system made investors wary of French equities. The weakness in the French equity markets was compounded by the absence of an established domestic pension system as a source for much needed investment capital. A banker described the results of these conditions: "It was the reign of cross-shareholdings, and of the mutual protection of chief executives."[25]

By 1997, foreign investors' confidence in the opportunities in the French market had grown somewhat, raising the overall level of foreign ownership of the French equity market to 35%.[26] Large institutional investors such as CALPERS and Fidelity had made a substantial portion of new foreign investment. Pressure from such outside institutional investors combined with domestic pressure had initiated a push for corporate governance reform. The most far-reaching reforms, the Vienot Code, were formulated by a group of French CEOs, chaired by the CEO of Société Générale, Marc Vienot. The goal of these reforms has been to increase financial transparency and make French markets more shareholder friendly.

Enormous pressures were being placed on France to "conform" to market capitalism. In the past, as a country, France had placed greater importance on social stability than free market purism. With increased global interdependence and trade liberalization, there was some question as to the sustainability of a separate French approach. The *Economist* highlighted the dilemma:

> How peculiar is France?...can France-alone among nations-run a vigorous economy and at the same time pay for grand national projects, inefficient state industries and a generous welfare state? French voters evidently believe theirs is indeed an exceptional country: last month they put in office a Socialist-Communist government whose leading lights had railed in their campaigns against the 'socially ferocious' Anglo-Saxon capitalism that they see prevailing elsewhere.[27]

As a leading French company, CGE continually faced these conflicting economic tensions.

---

[24] "France: Economic Trends and Outlook" from TradePort Web site funded by U.S. Department of Commerce, *www.tradeport.org/ts/countries/france/trends.shtml*.

[25] A. Jack, *op.cit.*, p. 13.

[26] Martin Laprad, assistant to Marc Vienot, CEO of Société Générale, in an interview on July 8, 1997.

[27] "Vive la différence?" *The Economist*, July 26, 1997, p. 17.

VI. A New CEO: Jean-Marie Messier

In November of 1995, on the personal urging of CEO Guy Dejouany, Jean-Marie Messier was selected as the new chairman and CEO for the company. Although several directors argued that he was too young to run the company,[28] Dejouany pushed the nomination of Messier, a man with limited management experience, who promised to take the company in a different direction. A senior manager who worked with them both described their contrasting styles: "Dejouany adores complexity. Messier, on the other hand, loves to make complex things simple because he's a modern manager who is convinced that that is the best way to make himself understood."[29]

Vision   Central to Messier's new operating principles was that CGE must return to its core activities. He identified these as Utilities (water, waste, energy, and transport), Communications (telecommunications and multimedia), and Construction and Property. Looking forward, his plan was to reduce the importance of Construction and Property while building the role of Communications. Divisional projections for the year 2000 showed almost 50% of the revenue would come from Utilities, 27% from Communications, and 25% from Construction and Property.[30] (See **Exhibits 7-9**.) Complete divestment from real estate had been eliminated as an option in the near-term because Messier believed that the market would not allow a quick liquidation of these assets.

Divestment   With a debt equity ratio of 155% in 1995, CGE needed to reduce its leverage. Guided by his vision of the core businesses, Messier reduced debt by selling assets that he considered peripheral to these central activities. In 1995, 6 billion Ffr. of assets were sold. The pace of divestments rapidly accelerated in 1996 and 1997 with 13.3 billion Ffr. and more than 12 billion Ffr. respectively. While some sales involved real estate disposals to large American "vulture" funds such as the Blackstone Group, significant divestitures were made in other non-core businesses, most notably health care and catering.[31] However, in 1998, CGE's portfolio of assets still contained considerable diversity, including Parc Asterix, a French amusement park, and Sogeparc, a parking garage company.

Shareholdings of other major French companies (see "noyaux durs" above) continued to play a role at CGE. (See **Exhibits 10-11**.) In the first two years under Messier's leadership, the 11.5 billion Ffr. in peripheral assets held in other companies' stock had been reduced.[32] However, CGE's portfolio still included shares in St. Gobain and Alcatel Alsthom, among others. At the same time, CGE's largest competitor, Lyonnaise des Eaux had pledged to dissolve all of its cross-shareholdings by the end of 1997.

Partnerships   Messier created alliances with cash rich partners to supplement CGE's resources in fast growth areas with high capital requirements. For example, large capital investments were required to compete in the market for cellular and fixed line telephony. Messier restructured the telecommunications operations, SFR, to create Cegetel, which, in May 1997, formed an alliance with British Telecom and a German partner, Mannesmann. In the end, CGE kept 44% of the company's capital, with British Telecom receiving a 26% stake for the contribution of 8.85 billion Ffr. The venture received capital from other partners including Southwestern Bell in both mobile and fixed

---

[28] M. Michelson, "Lazard Banker made Crown Prince at Gle. des Eaux," *Reuters European Business Report,* November 23, 1994.

[29] "A hand-picked heir," *Institutional Investor, International Edition,* May 1996, p. 76.

[30] Pierre Coiffet, *Paribas Analyst Report,* May 1998.

[31] Blackstone Real Estate purchased Descartes Towers, a large building in La Défénse. Non real estate disposals included mobile phone, sanitation and pest control, oil and refrigeration businesses in 1996 and linen management, healthcare and cable television businesses in 1997.

[32] The company planned to further reduce these holdings to 3 billion Frf. by the end of the first quarter of 1999.

telephony, and Vodafone, in the mobile telephone market alone. Also in 1997, Messier entered into a partnership with the French railroads, SNCF, to utilize their internal phone systems, "the second largest long distance telecommunications infrastructure in France (after France Telecom)."[33] This deal provided the digital optical fiber network needed to provide broadband services necessary for the corporate market.

Restructuring   Messier began a series of mergers to consolidate many of the 2,714 subsidiaries that composed CGE. Changes occurred first in the loss-making property division. After acquiring the highly successful management team from another real estate group, George V, CGE consolidated all seven of its property subsidiaries under the newly formed company Compagnie Générale de Immobilier (CGIS). Secondly, in 1997 CGE reduced its stake in Société Générale d'Entreprises (SGE), its main construction subsidiary, to 51%, and in Eiffage, another construction subsidiary to 5%. Management philosophy also changed: SGE was no longer to pursue volume, but rather profitability. In addition, the division was rationalized and businesses in industries such as road-building and electrical contracting were reorganized into sectors within SGE. [34]

In the three segments of the utilities business even more dramatic consolidations took place. Originally, multiple subsidiaries were created to get as close as possible to the municipalities that CGE was serving. As reforms in the contract negotiation process took place, and the firm's marketing focus shifted to the end-consumer, management believed that the multiple subsidiary approach had become inefficient. Guillaume Hannezo, the CFO, commented:

> It no longer makes sense to have four or five subsidiaries competing for the same business. For example, in water, there are 32 water subsidiaries operating in France. Each subsidiary provides separate billing, repairs, and administrative staff. We are going to reduce the number to 10 regional branches which will have clearly defined geographic territories. Each regional branch will have roughly two million customers. This will lead to significant savings.[35]

Parallel consolidations were occurring in energy and waste. Already in the energy division, the two main subsidiaries, Compagnie Générale de Chauffe and Esy-Montenay had been merged. Through the elimination of a series of overlapping operations and combined purchasing, the company planned to achieve efficiencies and raise return on investment from 5.5% to 8%. Similar efficiencies were planned for the waste division where the various subsidiaries would be concentrated in eight regional entities controlled by a newly formed subsidiary.

VII. New Structures and Systems

In addition to the financial housecleaning and internal restructuring of CGE, Messier planned other changes. He established a corporate office, developed policies for capital allocation, and addressed the issue of how to improve the management of CGE's human resources. Messier also initiated programs to focus the company on the creation of shareholder value.

Establishing a Corporate Office   First, Messier established a clearer reporting structure in the company. Instead of 70 direct reports, he would have only a dozen. For the first time in nearly a decade, an organizational chart was produced to clearly define the relationships between the remaining subsidiaries. A newly formed Executive Committee, composed of key directors from the main businesses, began meeting as a team on a bi-monthly basis. Each business had its own head,

---

[33] Coiffet, *op. cit.*, p. 127.

[34] *Ibid*, pp. 133-138.

[35] Interview, July 1997.

team, and clearly identified objectives. As Messier described: "This has eliminated internal competition. It has also increased the transparency of performance of each business and placed the emphasis on improving productivity in everyday operations."[36]

Secondly, Messier opened a new headquarters off the Champs Elysees in Paris to house the 215 members of the corporate staff. Those occupying this office included finance, legal, human resources, and investor relations. For the first time, the headquarters of the water division was not combined with corporate headquarters.

Some members of senior management felt that the new headquarters presented a radical change from the status quo. Specifically, the tasks of capital and human resource allocation were changing dramatically. As Hannezo commented:

> In the past, we developed by "capilarité,"[37] rather than through systematic growth. This process was perverse. You end up entering businesses that are only tangentially linked to the core, such as the spider eradication business that I recently discovered that we owned in Australia. The new corporate office will help to discipline our free cash flow.[38]

CGE planned to handle asset allocation at the corporate level. Clear targets would be set by corporate for each division's return on invested capital. Management believed that a restructured reporting organization would help to make these numbers more meaningful. Given the widely varying types of businesses and risks contained in those businesses, clearly defined costs of capital would be assigned to each. For example, the stable water utility business would not be assigned the same target as riskier telecommunications business. Under the new system, the independence of each subsidiary's treasury would also be greatly reduced. All investments greater than 70 million Ffr. would need the approval of corporate headquarters.[39]

Although one of the long-term goals of the new CGE structure was to reduce the cross-subsidization of businesses, in the short term the internal transfer of cash would be needed. Messier and his corporate staff expected that the cash flow from the utilities divisions would be used to support the suffering real estate and property divisions. In response to the question of future cross-subsidization, Guillaume Hannezo replied with a smile: "We [corporate headquarters] need to be loved for ourselves and the discipline that we provide, not for the money that we have!"[40]

Employee Mobility/Firm Culture   Human resource allocation would be another key role of the new headquarters. Under Dejouany, employees of one business had little or no contact with employees from another business. In fact, employees from very distinct businesses such as waste and telecommunications barely considered that they worked for the same company. An extreme example of this was demonstrated during one of Messier's first visits to Asia. According to the director of external relations:

> Last year, our first company-wide meeting in Asia got started one hour late because all of the employees from the various divisions, even their directors, had to

---

[36] Jean-Marie Messier, "Chairman's Message," Speech to Vivendi Shareholders' Meeting, May 15, 1998, from Vivendi Web site, *http://www.vivendi.com/english/fi_et_strat/message.html*.

[37] In French this refers to the formation of the capillaries in the body.

[38] Interview, July 1997

[39] *Ibid.*

[40] *Ibid.*

exchange business cards, because many had never met before. This is despite the fact that many worked in the same cities.[41]

CGE's efforts to increase employee mobility were divided into two separate programs, one for selected managers and one for all employees.

The first policy created mobility for 200 specially selected top managers. Opportunities would be provided for these managers to circulate among the various divisions during the early portions of their careers in order to create a group of better-trained general mangers for CGE. In addition, there was the hope that these managers would establish a new "CGE culture." By June 1997 these managers had been selected and had attended two general meetings. There were 100 moves made as well. A senior human resources manager pointed out that creating mobility for managers at CGE was quite challenging:

> Before, mobility was extremely rare. Mobility is still difficult to arrange for several reasons. First, not only are the businesses of CGE very different, but the 'business culture' from one business to another is strikingly different. In addition, rigid social regulations (retirement/pay) make arranging transfers cumbersome.[42]

Another effort to create mobility was through the "Internal Job Transfer Charter" signed in November 1996. As a result of the extremely high level of unemployment in France in the 1990s, labor unions negotiated preferential treatment for all CGE employees when a job opened in any CGE division. In addition, employees whose jobs were cut due to restructuring were given support in the form of job transfers, or early retirement.

Incentive Systems   Serious discussion of creating a performance-related management incentive system started in the summer of 1997. Once the new, more transparent reporting organization and new financial targets were put into place, management would need an incentive to meet the new goals. Variable financial rewards were almost completely absent under the previous system. Senior management discretion rather than any objective approach determined the incentives. Given the different origins of many of the subsidiaries, no attempt had been made in the past to apply a uniform management performance system.

Under the new remuneration scheme, the pay of the managers of the eight major business units would be linked to their respective return on investment targets. The job of pushing variable pay further down into the various organizational units would be left to the individual business heads. In 1997 the company also introduced a one-time stock option plan for the company's top 25 managers. Further, CGE's ongoing stock option program, which granted options which would vest in five years' time, increased from 200 participants in 1995 to 600 participants by 1998.

Few companies in France have been able to implement variable pay systems similar to those used by their competitors in Britain and the United States. From a social point of view, incentives based on profitability were particularly difficult to institute if cost reductions required layoffs. Gaz de France was one company that had established an innovative incentive system. Its managers accepted a 10% drop in base pay in order to have the opportunity to receive a performance bonus as high as 30%. Some industry observers thought variable compensation plans could meet strong resistance in France, particularly in slow growth or labor intensive companies. Not only would layoffs be expensive and difficult under French law, but also work force reduction could lead to labor unrest.

---

[41] Interview, July 1997.
[42] Company interviews, July 1997.

Creating Shareholder Value   Although Messier had been CEO of the company for only two years by the end of 1997, financial analysts and shareholders had rewarded his performance and, through purchase of the company's shares, expressed confidence in the new directions that CGE had taken. Since January of 1996 when Messier assumed the leadership of the company, the stock had appreciated 71.8%[43]. Over this period, the stock outperformed the main French stock market index, the CAC40 (see **Exhibit 12.**)

Efforts were begun to spread the message of shareholder value to the employees. For example, the concept of shareholder value was explained to the select group of 200 managers, mentioned above, during one of their meetings during 1997. The managers were expected to return to their divisions and hold similar meetings to present the concept to subordinates. Given the long history not only at CGE but also in all of France of balancing the needs of all "stakeholders," especially employees, Messier's message has received varying degrees of understanding and acceptance inside CGE. A senior manager who attended the meeting expressed the following sentiments:

> The idea of shareholder value is quite new…I don't think that it is very well understood, even by the basic people. Last week we had the annual meeting for the top managers…people found the shareholder value concept too complicated…the calculations appeared a bit mysterious.[44]

In 1996 an employee shareholding scheme was introduced. A year later, 21,000 people were participating in the plan. The total amount invested was 528 million Ffr. CGE introduced a number of measures to encourage employees' participation, including additional payments contributed by the company. As of 1998, 2.5% of the company's shares were owned by employees.

Strategic Direction   In his speech to the 1998 annual meeting, Messier elaborated his view of the company's strategic direction. The utilities business, while maintaining its strong domestic position, would be focused on international expansion and the development of multi-service contracts. Construction and property, while not expected to have a decisive financial effect, would once again be focused on becoming attractive to investors. In the communications businesses, Messier would look to build a strong domestic base, becoming a force second only to the national phone company, and a major player internationally as well. In the chairman's message that year Messier said: "Cegetel plus Havas plus our special partnership with Canal Plus—by networking these varied talents [the company] intends to play a major part in the communications industry."[45]

Cegetel, one of the core components of this business, was projected to provide net sales of 20 billion Ffr. in 1998. In early 1998, in partnership with Bertelsmann, the German publisher, Cegetel took a 55% stake in AOL France. In an interview with *CommunicationsWeek International*, Messier commented: "The Internet is at the heart of Cegetel's strategy…it represents a new market where companies like CGE have great opportunities."[46]

Later that year, CGE proposed a merger with Havas, France's largest media group, in which CGE already held a third of the shares. A publisher strong in business and education markets, Havas also increased CGE's interest in Canal+, the largest pay television service in Europe. When the merger was first proposed, a suit was filed by a minority shareholder group contending that shareholders in the target company were not being well treated. The shareholder group lost the court

---

[43] Data from Bloomberg Financial Analysis, December 31, 1995 to December 31, 1997.

[44] Company interviews, July 1997.

[45] Jean-Marie Messier, "Chairman's message," *op.cit.*

[46] K. Cukier, "A break with tradition: The Net's new visionaries rethink the role of the telco," *Communications Week International*, p. 14.

fight, but CGE in time added a cash premium of 8.7 billion Ffr., equal to 107 Ffr. per share, or 14.5 percent of the original offer. [47]

It was expected that the new division of the communications unit would provide proprietary content for the Internet partnership with AOL and Cegetel. In addition, many analysts believed that Messier and Eric Licoys, his former Lazard colleague and the newly appointed head of Havas, could add substantial value to the business through financial and operational restructuring. Additional agreements with Bertelsmann were also expected.

IX. Vivendi

The May 1998 annual shareholders meeting came two and a half years after Jean-Marie Messier assumed the chairmanship of CGE. During the meeting, Messier reviewed his vision for the company, and the reduction of debt and return to profitability that had occurred under his leadership. Looking forward, Messier asked the shareholders to approve CGE's merger with Havas and the renaming of the resulting company as Vivendi. In doing so, he explained that the merger represented the company's commitment to building a stronger presence in communications, expanding beyond the traditional base of water, utilities, and property management. Going forward, the water sector alone would have the exclusive use of the name Générale des Eaux.

In the annual report for 1997, Messier commented on the new name for the enterprise:

> A new name holds a great deal of symbolic force. Vivendi, the name we have chosen, is warm and vivacious. It evokes the characteristics shared by all our businesses—life itself, the quality of life, and movement. Vivendi is easy to pronounce and remember in all languages. It underpins our ambition as an international company and will unite under one banner the individual names of our different businesses worldwide.[48]

The name change was not just cosmetic. In 1997, Messier, with the board's approval, made the first change ever in the firm's articles of incorporation by adding communications as a line of business.

---

[47] J. Tagliabue, "Compliments of U.S. Investors; New Activism Shakes Europe's Markets," *The New York Times*, April 25, 1998 Section D, p. 1.

[48] *Compagnie Générale des Eaux Annual Report 1997*, p. 3.

Exhibit 1 Top 20 Largest French Companies

France Rank	World Rank	Company/ business	Revenue ($ mil)	Net Income ($ mil)	Assets ($ mil)	Market Value ($ mil)	Stock Price ($)	EPS 1997 ($)	EPS 1998E ($)	Yield (%)	Employees (thousands)
1	10	AXA-UAP/insurance	76,869	1,357	403,132	37,727	113.66	4.17	4.54	2.0	80.6
2	28	Elf Aquitaine Group/energy	43,570	960	42,252	38,172	138.70	3.74	5.72	2.7	84.6
3	39	Renault Group/automobiles	35,621	930	38,936	12,527	52.24	3.91	3.61	1.7	141.3
4	44	Total Group/energy	32,738	1,304	25,335	29,904	124.01	5.31	5.20	2.6	54.4
5	45	Suez Lyonnaise Group/service	32,625	688	79,031	31,512	170.41	5.53	6.29	2.2	175.0
6	47	Peugeot Groupe/automobiles	32,002	-474	31,623	9,778	195.11	-9.42	9.30	0.4	140.2
7	48	Alcatel Alsthom/elec. & electron	31,845	799	42,045	34,865	213.64	5.09	7.14	1.3	189.5
8	56	Carrefour Group/retailing	29,001	614	14,518	23,477	610.20	15.96	17.97	1.2	113.3
9	58	GAN-Assur Nationales/insurance	28,935	49	152,281	4,386	29.49	0.33	1.67	0.0	33.6
10	59	Société Générale Group/banking	28,723	1,047	411,055	19,519	197.78	10.86	12.04	2.7	55.5
11	60	Vivendi/services	28,632	924	43,122	27,148	200.62	7.16	7.31	1.9	193.3
12	64	France Telecom/telecomm	26,853	2,546	50,545	55,929	55.93	2.55	2.52	2.9	156.6
13	69	BNP Group/banking	26,118	1,021	339,819	18,188	85.29	4.84	5.19	2.1	52.7
14	89	Crédit Lyonnais Group/banking	22,409	181	250,279	5,120	98.14	3.47	5.97	0.0	50.8
15	109	Promodès Group/retailing	18,960	277	8,355	9,310	486.36	14.49	16.61	0.9	50.8
16	110	Saint-Gobain/bldg. materials	18,346	964	22,668	17,577	196.95	11.13	9.69	2.4	106.8
17	126	Groupe Paribas/banking	16,124	892	245,188	15,725	103.65	10.18	7.29	3.4	20.0
18	134	Bouygues Group/constuction	15,603	129	13,621	4,633	180.59	5.25	3.86	2.4	77.1
19	136	Rhône-Poulenc Group/chemicals	15,412	-855	27,529	20,091	55.41	-2.55	1.88	1.7	68.4
20	138	Pinault-Printemps-Redoute/retailing	15,279	489	11,302	19,305	822.00	21.79	23.59	1.2	59.5

Source: *Forbes*, July 28, 1997, p. 188

Note: All figures except per-share items are in millions of dollars. Revenue, Net Income, and 1997 EPS are converted at an average rate for the fiscal year; assets are converted at fiscal year-end rate. Revenue figures are for groups or consolidated operations and exclude excise taxes and duties. For companies with January, February or March fiscal year-ends, 1997 figures are used unless otherwise noted. Market value is as of May 29, 1998.

Exhibit 2   CGE 1997 Organization Chart

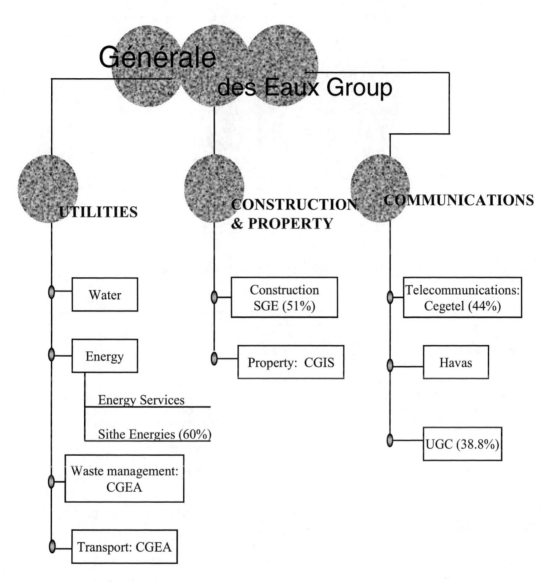

Source: CGE 1997 Annual Report.

Exhibit 3   Breakdown of 1997 Turnover by Division

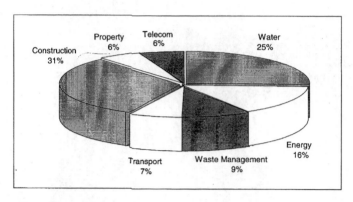

Source: Paribas Analyst's Report, May 1998.

Exhibit 4   Vivendi Consolidated Statement of Income 1995-1997 (in FFm)

	1997	1996	1995
Net sales	167,115.6	165,913.8	162,961.1
Other revenue	6,262.0	5,274.8	4,310.9
Purchases	(97,153.3)	(92,549.0)	(91,713.0)
Wages and social security costs	(44,346.1)	(47,493.9)	(46,491.6)
Taxes other than income taxes	(3,120.4)	(3,261.6)	(3,092.6)
Other operating expenses	(15,967.8)	(16,097.3)	(15,412.4)
Depreciation	(8,619.1)	(7,941.6)	(8,861.9)
Operating income	4,170.9	3,845.2	1,700.5
Financial expense	(1,184.4)	(2,087.2)	(2,724.8)
Financial provisions	(792.3)	(65.9)	(673.7)
Net financial expense	(1,976.7)	(2,153.1)	(3,398.5)
Operating income less net financial expense	2,194.2	1,692.1	(1,698.0)
Exceptional items	11,660.1	2,629.5	843.6
Depreciation	(5,896.5)	(1,712.5)	(2,211.0)
Amortization of goodwill	(2,458.0)	(962.8)	(1,020.8)
Net exceptional expense	3,305.6	(45.8)	(2,388.2)
Employee profit-sharing	(264.5)	(260.8)	(310.9)
Income taxes	(1,277.0)	(1,189.8)	(1,437.8)
Net income/expense) before equity interest and minority interest	3,958.3	195.7	(5,834.9)
Equity in net earnings of affiliated companies	679.3	1,387.2	876.1
Minority interest	754.9	369.8	1,272.5
Net income/(expense)	5,392.5	1,952.7	(3,686.3)

Source: CGE 1997 Annual Report.

Exhibit 5   Vivendi Consolidated Balance Sheet 1995-1997 (in Ffm)

	1997	1996	1995
ASSETS			
Intangible assets other than goodwill	11,334.5	11,771.8	11,039.3
Goodwill	24,726.8	15,648.3	16,946.0
Owned property, plant and equipment	81,597.9	82,791.7	77,590.0
Publicly-owned utility networks financed and			
managed by the group	7,015.7	8,216.1	7,530.0
Accumulated depreciation	(33,588.7)	(33,618.8)	(29,610.9)
Tangible assets	55,024.9	57,389.0	55,509.1
Investments accounted for by the equity method	16,466.6	12,186.6	10,987.0
Unconsolidated investments	5,086.7	3,541.9	3,705.5
Portfolio investments held as fixed assets	8,222.9	9,722.2	10,789.2
Other investments held as fixed assets and other			
financial assets	15,644.6	14,967.9	11,575.0
Financial assets	45,420.8	40,468.6	37,056.7
Total fixed assets	136,507.0	125,277.7	120,551.1
Inventories	27,296.8	25,919.7	26,825.5
Accounts receivable	66,348.5	65,623.4	63,227.4
Short-term financial receivables	10,281.3	10,584.7	9,942.6
Cash and marketable securities	17,785.4	12,838.2	11,265.3
Total current assets	121,712.0	114,966.0	111,260.8
TOTAL ASSETS	258,219.0	240,243.7	231,811.9
SHAREHOLDERS' EQUITY AND LIABILITIES			
Capital stock	13,404.5	12,261.3	11,739.6
Additional paid-in capital	21,235.1	15,469.4	13,517.2
Retained earnings	10,271.7	5,951.2	4,918.8
Shareholders' equity	44,911.3	33,681.9	30,175.6
Minority interest	11,428.9	5,417.7	6,044.8
Grants related to assets and deferred income	3,035.0	2,408.8	1,769.8
Total provisions	35,617.0	28,679.9	28,861.9
Provision for replacement and full warranty and			
amortization of capital employed in publicly-owned			
networks	10,221.8	10,047.8	13,287.8
Provision for liabilities and charges	25,395.2	18,632.1	15,574.1
Subordinated securities	1,216.9	1,252.1	1,298.6
Project financing	5,918.2	5,715.0	6,070.5
Other long-term debt	38,166.7	38,228.0	40,703.4
Total long-term debt	44,084.9	43,943.0	46,773.9
Other long-term liabilities	4,050.2	3,556.5	3,264.2
Total capital employed	144,294.2	118,939.9	118,188.8
Accounts payable	91,651.4	86,733.4	80,190.7
Short-term debt	22,223.4	34,570.4	33,432.4
Total current liabilities	111,874.8	121,303.8	113,623.1
TOTAL SHAREHOLDERS' EQUITY AND LIABILITIES	258,219.0	240,243.7	231,811.9

Source: CGE 1997 Annual Report

Exhibit 6   Vivendi Consolidated Statement of Changes in Financial Position (in millions of French francs)

Uses	1997	1996	1995
Capital expenditure and acquisition of investments	36,484.0	16,246.2	16,662.5
Property assets held as fixed assets	947.2	263.6	3,882.9
Deferred charges	2,778.2	2,050.0	1,472.2
Acquisition of other financial fixed assets	273.8	3,332.9	1,751.1
Repayment of long-term debt	344.8[a]	4,128.0	1,416.6
Dividends paid to parent company shareholders and to the minority interest in consolidated subsidiaries	1,437.8	1,342.6	1,213.8
Total	42,265.8	27,363.3	26,399.1

Sources	1997	1996	1995
Gross cash flow from operations (including net gains from disposal of fixed assets)	9,509.7	7,533.8	4,869.7
Issue of parent company stock	7,118.3	2,473.9	1,670.9
Minority interest in capital increases of subsidiaries	14,883.3	3,848.3	1,568.1
Proceeds from disposal of fixed assets	23,038.0	7,658.5	5,324.1
Increase in other long-term liabilities	1,961.9	835.7	1,160.1
Change in working capital	(14,245.4)	5,013.1	11,806.2
Total	42,265.8	27,363.3	26,399.1

Source: CGE 1997 Annual Report

[a]Including FF67.9m for reimbursement of subordinated securities.

Exhibit 7   Vivendi Revenue, 1994-2000E by Division (FFm)

	1994	1995	1996	1997	1998E	1999E	2000E
Water	37,319	38,877	41,091	42,400	43,500	44,900	46,400
Energy	20,503	24,551	25,852	25,400	30,600	33,600	37,000
Waste management	11,440	12,733	14,599	15,050	17,300	18,576	20,000
Urban transport	3,412	3,595	6,308	11,100	13,532	14,885	16,374
(=) Utilities	**72,674**	**79,756**	**87,849**	**93,950**	**104,932**	**111,961**	**119,774**
Construction	59,292	56,966	54,351	52,500	50,727	50,000	50,000
Property	9,998	8,660	8,222	9,500	10,300	10,900	11,600
Communications (Cegetel)	4,193	4,530	5,929	10,900	13,348	18,194	24,219
Media (Havas)[a]	1,339	1,783	1,451	0	38,290	40,608	43,638
Others + parent company	8,662	11,266	8,112	266	0	0	0
Total	156,158	162,961	165,915	167,116	217,597	231,663	249,231

Source: Analyst's Report, Paribas, May 1998

Exhibit 8   Vivendi Operating Profit, 1994 to 2000E (FFm)

	1994	1995	1996	1997	1998E	1999E	2000E
Water	2,499	2,918	3,064	2,800	2,965	3,300	3,800
Energy	1,755	1,786	2,000	1,800	1,940	2,100	2,320
Waste management	895	871	725	1,100	1,275	1,585	189
Urban transport	193	186	187	292	360	525	705
(=) Utilities	**5,342**	**5,761**	**5,976**	**5,992**	**6,540**	**7,510**	**8,720**
Construction	638	203	-22	282	341	423	525
Property	-1,734	-3,822	-1,352	-582	-530	-150	100
Communications (Cegetel)	-798	-843	-1,098	-1,200	450	2,347	4,264
Media (Havas)[a]	-479	-476	-470	-100	985	1,911	2,481
Others + parent company	708	877	811	-221	-350	0	0
Total	3,677	1,700	3,845	4,171	7,436	12,041	16,090

Source: Analyst's Report, Paribas, May 1998

Exhibit 9   Vivendi Cash Flow, 1994 to 2000E (FFm)

	1994	1995	1996	1997	1998E	1999E	2000E
Water	3,900	3,800	3,900	3,300	3,900	4,420	4,900
Energy	2,300	2,000	2,300	1,800	2,900	3,400	3,700
Waste management	1,250	1,304	1,200	1,600	1,950	2,300	2,550
Urban transport	300	320	325	500	600	800	900
(=) Utilities	**7,750**	**7,424**	**7,725**	**7,200**	**9,350**	**10,920**	**12,050**
Construction	2,100	1,000	500	1,292	1,691	1,771	1,800
Property	-2,100	-4,800	-2,900	-192	300	700	800
Communications (Cegetel)	-205	-112	900	1,600	3,316	4,114	7,064
Media (Havas)[a]	-266	213	-400	0	1,609	2,870	3,135
Others + parent company	1,712	1,145	1,709	-390	713	800	200
Total	8,991	4,870	7,534	9,510	16,979	21,175	25,049

Source: Analyst's Report, Paribas, May 1998

[a]Havas is consolidated over 9 months in 1998 and 12 months in 1999.

Exhibit 10   Cross Ownership—"Noyaux Durs"—1997

Investors	% Owned	% Voting	Company	% Owned	Market Value (Ffrm)
Saint Gobain	7.68	13.70	Saint Gobain	7.83	5,991
UAP-Axa	6.66	4.30	Alcatel Alsthom	1.62	2,011
Alcatel Alsthom	2.05	3.68	UAP-Axa	0.23	321
BNP Group	0.84	1.50	Société Générale	1.27	989
Société Générale	0.92	1.16	Sogeparc	19.90	553
	18.15%	24.34%	Eiffage	18.70	570
			Washington Baltimore through FACIC[a]	10.00	1,214
			Other		816
					12,445

Source: CGE Annual Report 1997

[a]Subsidiary of Southwestern Bell Corporation.

Exhibit 11   Composition of CGE Shareholders—1995 to 1997

	31/08/95	31/08/96	31/01/97	31/12/97
General public (France)	24.64%	24.31%	22.57%	26.85
Industrial and institutional investors (France)	34.86	34.00	32.59	26.38
Foreign investors	36.07	38.17	42.15	43.37
Employees	2.09	2.11	1.87	1.95
Self-controlled	2.34	1.41	0.82	1.45
Total	100%	100%	100%	100%

Source: CGE 1997 Annual Report,

Exhibit 12   Vivendi Versus CAC 40 Index Annual Total Returns to Shareholders: January 1994 to
May 1998

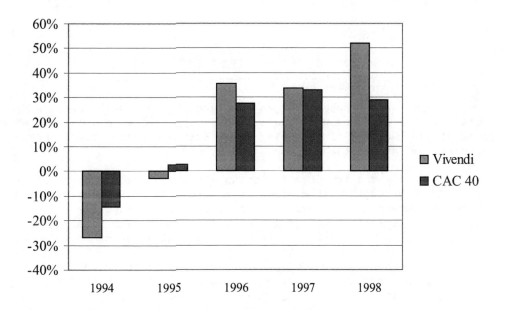

Source: Datastream

JOHNSON & JOHNSON: THE TYLENOL TRAGEDY

In early October 1982, executives at the McNeil Consumer Products division of Johnson & Johnson were confronted with a major problem. Seven people had died after having taken Extra-Strength Tylenol brand capsules that proved to have contained cyanide.

During the few days following the deaths, the company had recalled Extra-Strength Tylenol capsule stocks from retail outlets, and had offered consumers an exchange of bottles of Tylenol capsules for Tylenol tablets (not directly involved in the poisonings). The recalled and exchanged capsules were estimated to have a retail value of some $80 million.

Tylenol was the leading brand of pain reliever in the U.S. marketplace. Tylenol's share of that approximately $1 billion product category was estimated at 37%. Anacin (American Home Products), Bayer (Sterling Drugs), Bufferin (Bristol-Myers), and Excedrin (Bristol-Myers) each was estimated to have a 10%-15% share, with other brands sharing the remaining 15%-20% of the market. The Tylenol line (capsules and tablets, regular and extra-strength) was estimated to account for about $500 million in annual sales, about 8% of J&J sales. Industry experts noted that the brand's share of the company's profits was much greater.

As the first week following the initial death ended, only some short-term effects of the tragedy were known. The longer-term impacts remained a matter of considerable speculation.

The following events had taken place:

o Investigation by law enforcement agencies pointed to the poisoning as the work of outsiders at some point in the distribution process, rather than something that occurred during the internal production process. However, no individual(s) had been apprehended.

o All the cyanide-related deaths had taken place in the Chicago area. A separate strychnine-contamination incident had been reported in California.

This material was prepared from public sources by HBS Professor Stephen A. Greyser. It is not intended to reflect appropriate or inappropriate administrative behavior.

-2-

o   Several local and national governmental units
    had initiated legislation prospectively re-
    quiring tamper-resistant packaging for over-
    the-counter medicines.

o   The Proprietary Association, a group of over-
    the-counter drug companies, met to discuss more
    secure packaging for non-prescription remedies.

o   Some observers -- including the Food and Drug
    Administration Commissioner -- were quoted as
    saying they doubted that packaging could be
    made absolutely tamper-proof.

o   Although retailers removed Tylenol from their
    shelves, some left the space open (rather than
    filling it in with other brands) and some put
    labels over shelves with Tylenol tablets noting
    that tablets were not affected -- indicators of
    the trade's confidence in the brand and the
    company.

o   Early reports of retail sales following the
    tragedy suggested that some consumers were
    avoiding the product category while others
    bought other brands.

o   A $15 million damage suit against Johnson &
    Johnson and the Jewel Food Stores (where the
    affected capsule was purchased) -- the first
    such legal action -- was filed in Chicago by
    a family in which a death occurred.

o   No competitors of Tylenol had overtly undertaken
    changes in their marketing activities.

o   Johnson & Johnson stock had plunged from over 46
    at the time of the announcement of the first death
    to under 39, before rising to 42 5/8 during a
    generally "up" market.

Among the questions being raised about the incident were these:

o What does "responsible corporate behavior" constitute in such a situation?

o Under what conditions, if any, would past Tylenol
   consumers be likely to return to using the brand?

o Would the Tylenol capsule product alone be affected --
   or the brand's tablet product as well?

o Would a much wider group of over-the-counter drug
   products be affected by consumer concern over the
   Tylenol situation?

o What medium-to-longer term actions should McNeil
   Consumer Products Co./Johnson & Johnson be taking
   or considering?

o Is there a role for industry-wide action -- among
   pain-relievers or all OTC products? How, if at all,
   would such action benefit Johnson & Johnson?

o What (further) government actions could be expected?
   Would they help the company?

o What insights for the short-term and long-term futures
   of the Tylenol brand name and Johnson & Johnson could
   be drawn from such past incidents as the cranberry
   cancer scare of 1959, the Rely tampon situation, the
   Bon Vivant botulism deaths, and other product-related
   dangers or deaths?

o Under what conditions would a "return to the marketplace" or a re-launch of Tylenol make sense?

ARTICLES

What is Strategy?

by Michael E. Porter

 Harvard Business Review

Reprint 96608

Harvard Business Review

NOVEMBER-DECEMBER 1996

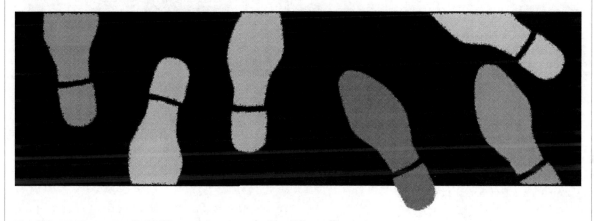

I. Operational Effectiveness Is Not Strategy

For almost two decades, managers have been learning to play by a new set of rules. Companies must be flexible to respond rapidly to competitive and market changes. They must benchmark continuously to achieve best practice. They must outsource aggressively to gain efficiencies. And they must nurture a few core competencies in the race to stay ahead of rivals.

What Is Strategy?

by Michael E. Porter

Positioning – once the heart of strategy – is rejected as too static for today's dynamic markets and changing technologies. According to the new dogma, rivals can quickly copy any market position, and competitive advantage is, at best, temporary.

But those beliefs are dangerous half-truths, and they are leading more and more companies down the path of mutually destructive competition. True, some barriers to competition are falling as regulation eases and markets become global. True, companies have properly invested energy in becoming leaner and more nimble. In many industries, however, what some call *hypercompetition* is a self-inflicted wound, not the inevitable outcome of a changing paradigm of competition.

The root of the problem is the failure to distinguish between operational effectiveness and strategy. The quest for productivity, quality, and speed has spawned a remarkable number of management tools and techniques: total quality management, benchmarking, time-based competition, outsourcing, partnering, reengineering, change management. Although the resulting operational improvements have often been dramatic, many companies have been frustrated by their inability to translate those gains into sustainable profitability. And bit by bit, almost imperceptibly, management tools have taken the place of strategy. As managers push to improve on all fronts, they move farther away from viable competitive positions.

Operational Effectiveness: Necessary but Not Sufficient

Operational effectiveness and strategy are both essential to superior performance, which, after all, is the primary goal of any enterprise. But they work in very different ways.

Michael E. Porter is the C. Roland Christensen Professor of Business Administration at the Harvard Business School in Boston, Massachusetts.

A company can outperform rivals only if it can establish a difference that it can preserve. It must deliver greater value to customers or create comparable value at a lower cost, or do both. The arithmetic of superior profitability then follows: delivering greater value allows a company to charge higher average unit prices; greater efficiency results in lower average unit costs.

Ultimately, all differences between companies in cost or price derive from the hundreds of activities required to create, produce, sell, and deliver their products or services, such as calling on customers, assembling final products, and training employees. Cost is generated by performing activities, and cost advantage arises from performing particular activities more efficiently than competitors. Similarly, differentiation arises from both the choice of activities and how they are performed. Activities, then, are the basic units of competitive advantage. Overall advantage or disadvantage results from all a company's activities, not only a few.[1]

Operational effectiveness (OE) means performing similar activities *better* than rivals perform them. Operational effectiveness includes but is not limited to efficiency. It refers to any number of practices that allow a company to better utilize its inputs by, for example, reducing defects in products or developing better products faster. In contrast, strategic positioning means performing *different* activities from rivals' or performing similar activities in *different ways*.

Differences in operational effectiveness among companies are pervasive. Some companies are able

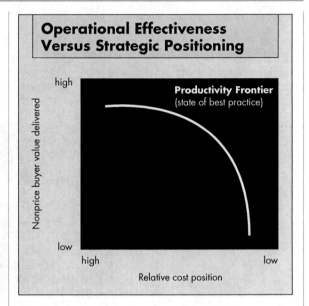

Operational Effectiveness Versus Strategic Positioning

Productivity Frontier (state of best practice)

Nonprice buyer value delivered — high / low

Relative cost position — high / low

tional effectiveness are an important source of differences in profitability among competitors because they directly affect relative cost positions and levels of differentiation.

Differences in operational effectiveness were at the heart of the Japanese challenge to Western companies in the 1980s. The Japanese were so far ahead of rivals in operational effectiveness that they could offer lower cost and superior quality at the same time. It is worth dwelling on this point, because so much recent thinking about competition depends on it. Imagine for a moment a *productivity frontier* that constitutes the sum of all existing best practices at any given time. Think of it as the maximum value that a company delivering a particular product or service can create at a given cost, using the best available technologies, skills, management techniques, and purchased inputs. The productivity frontier can apply to individual activities, to groups of linked activities such as order processing and manufacturing, and to an entire company's activities. When a company improves its operational effectiveness, it moves toward the frontier. Doing so may require capital investment, different personnel, or simply new ways of managing.

The productivity frontier is constantly shifting outward as new technologies and management approaches are developed and as new inputs become available. Laptop computers, mobile communications, the Internet, and software such as Lotus Notes, for example, have redefined the productivity

A company can outperform rivals only if it can establish a difference that it can preserve.

to get more out of their inputs than others because they eliminate wasted effort, employ more advanced technology, motivate employees better, or have greater insight into managing particular activities or sets of activities. Such differences in opera-

This article has benefited greatly from the assistance of many individuals and companies. The author gives special thanks to Jan Rivkin, the coauthor of a related paper. Substantial research contributions have been made by Nicolaj Siggelkow, Dawn Sylvester, and Lucia Marshall. Tarun Khanna, Roger Martin, and Anita McGahan have provided especially extensive comments.

frontier for sales-force operations and created rich possibilities for linking sales with such activities as order processing and after-sales support. Similarly, lean production, which involves a family of activities, has allowed substantial improvements in manufacturing productivity and asset utilization.

For at least the past decade, managers have been preoccupied with improving operational effectiveness. Through programs such as TQM, time-based competition, and benchmarking, they have changed how they perform activities in order to eliminate inefficiencies, improve customer satisfaction, and achieve best practice. Hoping to keep up with shifts in the productivity frontier, managers have embraced continuous improvement, empowerment, change management, and the so-called learning organization. The popularity of outsourcing and the virtual corporation reflect the growing recognition that it is difficult to perform all activities as productively as specialists.

As companies move to the frontier, they can often improve on multiple dimensions of performance at the same time. For example, manufacturers that adopted the Japanese practice of rapid changeovers in the 1980s were able to lower cost and improve differentiation simultaneously. What were once believed to be real trade-offs – between defects and costs, for example – turned out to be illusions created by poor operational effectiveness. Managers have learned to reject such false trade-offs.

Constant improvement in operational effectiveness is necessary to achieve superior profitability. However, it is not usually sufficient. Few companies have competed successfully on the basis of operational effectiveness over an extended period, and staying ahead of rivals gets harder every day. The most obvious reason for that is the rapid diffusion of best practices. Competitors can quickly imitate management techniques, new technologies, input improvements, and superior ways of meeting customers' needs. The most generic solutions – those that can be used in multiple settings – diffuse the fastest. Witness the proliferation of OE techniques accelerated by support from consultants.

OE competition shifts the productivity frontier outward, effectively raising the bar for everyone. But although such competition produces absolute improvement in operational effectiveness, it leads to relative improvement for no one. Consider the $5 billion-plus U.S. commercial-printing industry. The major players – R.R. Donnelley & Sons Company, Quebecor, World Color Press, and Big Flower Press – are competing head to head, serving all types of customers, offering the same array of printing technologies (gravure and web offset), investing heavily in the same new equipment, running their presses faster, and reducing crew sizes. But the resulting major productivity gains are being captured by customers and equipment suppliers, not retained in superior profitability. Even industry-

Japanese Companies Rarely Have Strategies

The Japanese triggered a global revolution in operational effectiveness in the 1970s and 1980s, pioneering practices such as total quality management and continuous improvement. As a result, Japanese manufacturers enjoyed substantial cost and quality advantages for many years.

But Japanese companies rarely developed distinct strategic positions of the kind discussed in this article. Those that did – Sony, Canon, and Sega, for example – were the exception rather than the rule. Most Japanese companies imitate and emulate one another. All rivals offer most if not all product varieties, features, and services; they employ all channels and match one anothers' plant configurations.

The dangers of Japanese-style competition are now becoming easier to recognize. In the 1980s, with rivals operating far from the productivity frontier, it seemed possible to win on both cost and quality indefinitely. Japanese companies were all able to grow in an expanding domestic economy and by penetrating global markets. They appeared unstoppable. But as the gap in operational effectiveness narrows, Japanese companies are increasingly caught in a trap of their own making. If they are to escape the mutually destructive battles now ravaging their performance, Japanese companies will have to learn strategy.

To do so, they may have to overcome strong cultural barriers. Japan is notoriously consensus oriented, and companies have a strong tendency to mediate differences among individuals rather than accentuate them. Strategy, on the other hand, requires hard choices. The Japanese also have a deeply ingrained service tradition that predisposes them to go to great lengths to satisfy any need a customer expresses. Companies that compete in that way end up blurring their distinct positioning, becoming all things to all customers.

This discussion of Japan is drawn from the author's research with Hirotaka Takeuchi, with help from Mariko Sakakibara.

leader Donnelley's profit margin, consistently higher than 7% in the 1980s, fell to less than 4.6% in 1995. This pattern is playing itself out in industry after industry. Even the Japanese, pioneers of the new competition, suffer from persistently low profits. (See the insert "Japanese Companies Rarely Have Strategies.")

The second reason that improved operational effectiveness is insufficient – competitive convergence – is more subtle and insidious. The more benchmarking companies do, the more they look alike. The more that rivals outsource activities to efficient third parties, often the same ones, the more generic those activities become. As rivals imitate one another's improvements in quality, cycle times, or supplier partnerships, strategies converge and competition becomes a series of races down identical paths that no one can win. Competition based on operational effectiveness alone is mutu-

ally destructive, leading to wars of attrition that can be arrested only by limiting competition.

The recent wave of industry consolidation through mergers makes sense in the context of OE competition. Driven by performance pressures but lacking strategic vision, company after company has had no better idea than to buy up its rivals. The competitors left standing are often those that outlasted others, not companies with real advantage.

After a decade of impressive gains in operational effectiveness, many companies are facing diminishing returns. Continuous improvement has been etched on managers' brains. But its tools unwittingly draw companies toward imitation and homogeneity. Gradually, managers have let operational effectiveness supplant strategy. The result is zero-sum competition, static or declining prices, and pressures on costs that compromise companies' ability to invest in the business for the long term.

II. Strategy Rests on Unique Activities

Competitive strategy is about being different. It means deliberately choosing a different set of activities to deliver a unique mix of value.

Southwest Airlines Company, for example, offers short-haul, low-cost, point-to-point service between midsize cities and secondary airports in large cities. Southwest avoids large airports and does not fly great distances. Its customers include business travelers, families, and students. Southwest's frequent departures and low fares attract price-sensitive customers who otherwise would travel by bus or car, and convenience-oriented travelers who would choose a full-service airline on other routes.

Most managers describe strategic positioning in terms of their customers: "Southwest Airlines serves price- and convenience-sensitive travelers,"

The essence of strategy is choosing to perform activities differently than rivals do.

for example. But the essence of strategy is in the activities – choosing to perform activities differently or to perform different activities than rivals. Otherwise, a strategy is nothing more than a marketing slogan that will not withstand competition.

A full-service airline is configured to get passengers from almost any point A to any point B. To reach a large number of destinations and serve passengers with connecting flights, full-service airlines employ a hub-and-spoke system centered on major airports. To attract passengers who desire more comfort, they offer first-class or business-class service. To accommodate passengers who must change planes, they coordinate schedules and check and transfer baggage. Because some passengers will be traveling for many hours, full-service airlines serve meals.

Southwest, in contrast, tailors all its activities to deliver low-cost, convenient service on its particular type of route. Through fast turnarounds at the gate of only 15 minutes, Southwest is able to keep planes flying longer hours than rivals and provide frequent departures with fewer aircraft. Southwest does not offer meals, assigned seats, interline baggage checking, or premium classes of service. Automated ticketing at the gate encourages customers to bypass travel agents, allowing Southwest to avoid their commissions. A standardized fleet of 737 aircraft boosts the efficiency of maintenance.

Southwest has staked out a unique and valuable strategic position based on a tailored set of activities. On the routes served by Southwest, a full-service airline could never be as convenient or as low cost.

Ikea, the global furniture retailer based in Sweden, also has a clear strategic positioning. Ikea targets young furniture buyers who want style at low cost. What turns this marketing concept into a strategic positioning is the tailored set of activities that make it work. Like Southwest, Ikea has chosen to perform activities differently from its rivals.

Consider the typical furniture store. Showrooms display samples of the merchandise. One area might contain 25 sofas; another will display five dining tables. But those items represent only a fraction of the choices available to customers. Dozens of books displaying fabric swatches or wood samples or alternate styles offer customers thousands of product varieties to choose from. Salespeople often escort customers through the store, answering questions and helping them navigate this maze of choices. Once a customer makes a selection, the order is relayed to a third-party manufacturer. With luck, the furniture will be delivered to the customer's home within six to eight weeks. This is a value chain that maximizes customization and service but does so at high cost.

In contrast, Ikea serves customers who are happy to trade off service for cost. Instead of having a sales associate trail customers around the store,

Ikea uses a self-service model based on clear, in-store displays. Rather than rely solely on third-party manufacturers, Ikea designs its own low-cost, modular, ready-to-assemble furniture to fit its positioning. In huge stores, Ikea displays every product it sells in room-like settings, so customers don't need a decorator to help them imagine how to put the pieces together. Adjacent to the furnished showrooms is a warehouse section with the products in boxes on pallets. Customers are expected to do their own pickup and delivery, and Ikea will even sell you a roof rack for your car that you can return for a refund on your next visit.

Although much of its low-cost position comes from having customers "do it themselves," Ikea offers a number of extra services that its competitors do not. In-store child care is one. Extended hours are another. Those services are uniquely aligned with the needs of its customers, who are young, not wealthy, likely to have children (but no nanny), and, because they work for a living, have a need to shop at odd hours.

The Origins of Strategic Positions

Strategic positions emerge from three distinct sources, which are not mutually exclusive and often overlap. First, positioning can be based on

Finding New Positions: The Entrepreneurial Edge

Strategic competition can be thought of as the process of perceiving new positions that woo customers from established positions or draw new customers into the market. For example, superstores offering depth of merchandise in a single product category take market share from broad-line department stores offering a more limited selection in many categories. Mail-order catalogs pick off customers who crave convenience. In principle, incumbents and entrepreneurs face the same challenges in finding new strategic positions. In practice, new entrants often have the edge.

Strategic positionings are often not obvious, and finding them requires creativity and insight. New entrants often discover unique positions that have been available but simply overlooked by established competitors. Ikea, for example, recognized a customer group that had been ignored or served poorly. Circuit City Stores' entry into used cars, CarMax, is based on a new way of performing activities – extensive refurbishing of cars, product guarantees, no-haggle pricing,

sophisticated use of in-house customer financing – that has long been open to incumbents.

New entrants can prosper by occupying a position that a competitor once held but has ceded through years of imitation and straddling. And entrants coming from other industries can create new positions because of distinctive activities drawn from their other businesses. CarMax borrows heavily from Circuit City's expertise in inventory management, credit, and other activities in consumer electronics retailing.

Most commonly, however, new positions open up because of change. New customer groups or purchase occasions arise; new needs emerge as societies evolve; new distribution channels appear; new technologies are developed; new machinery or information systems become available. When such changes happen, new entrants, unencumbered by a long history in the industry, can often more easily perceive the potential for a new way of competing. Unlike incumbents, newcomers can be more flexible because they face no trade-offs with their existing activities.

producing a subset of an industry's products or services. I call this *variety-based positioning* because it is based on the choice of product or service varieties rather than customer segments. Variety-based positioning makes economic sense when a company can best produce particular products or services using distinctive sets of activities.

Jiffy Lube International, for instance, specializes in automotive lubricants and does not offer other

Strategic positions can be based on customers' needs, customers' accessibility, or the variety of a company's products or services.

car repair or maintenance services. Its value chain produces faster service at a lower cost than broader line repair shops, a combination so attractive that many customers subdivide their purchases, buying oil changes from the focused competitor, Jiffy Lube, and going to rivals for other services.

The Vanguard Group, a leader in the mutual fund industry, is another example of variety-based positioning. Vanguard provides an array of common stock, bond, and money market funds that offer predictable performance and rock-bottom expenses. The company's investment approach deliberately sacrifices the possibility of extraordinary performance in any one year for good relative performance in every year. Vanguard is known, for example, for its index funds. It avoids making bets on interest rates and steers clear of narrow stock groups. Fund managers keep trading levels low, which holds expenses down; in addition, the company discourages customers from rapid buying and selling because doing so drives up costs and can force a fund manager to trade in order to deploy new capital and raise cash for redemptions. Vanguard also takes a consistent low-cost approach to managing distribution, customer service, and marketing. Many investors include one or more Vanguard funds in their portfolio, while buying aggressively managed or specialized funds from competitors.

The people who use Vanguard or Jiffy Lube are responding to a superior value chain for a particular type of service. A variety-based positioning can serve a wide array of customers, but for most it will meet only a subset of their needs.

A second basis for positioning is that of serving most or all the needs of a particular group of customers. I call this *needs-based positioning*, which comes closer to traditional thinking about targeting a segment of customers. It arises when there are groups of customers with differing needs, and when a tailored set of activities can serve those needs best. Some groups of customers are more price sensitive than others, demand different product features, and need varying amounts of information, support, and services. Ikea's customers are a good example of such a group. Ikea seeks to meet all the home furnishing needs of its target customers, not just a subset of them.

A variant of needs-based positioning arises when the same customer has different needs on different occasions or for different types of transactions. The same person, for example, may have different needs when traveling on business than when traveling for pleasure with the family. Buyers of cans – beverage companies, for example – will likely have different needs from their primary supplier than from their secondary source.

It is intuitive for most managers to conceive of their business in terms of the customers' needs they are meeting. But a critical element of needs-based positioning is not at all intuitive and is often overlooked. Differences in needs will not translate into meaningful positions unless the best set of activities to satisfy them *also* differs. If that were not the case, every competitor could meet those same needs, and there would be nothing unique or valuable about the positioning.

In private banking, for example, Bessemer Trust Company targets families with a minimum of $5 million in investable assets who want capital preservation combined with wealth accumulation. By assigning one sophisticated account officer for every 14 families, Bessemer has configured its activities for personalized service. Meetings, for example, are more likely to be held at a client's ranch or yacht than in the office. Bessemer offers a wide array of customized services, including investment management and estate administration, oversight of oil and gas investments, and accounting for racehorses and aircraft. Loans, a staple of most private banks, are rarely needed by Bessemer's clients and make up a tiny fraction of its client balances and income. Despite the most generous compensation of account officers and the highest personnel cost as a percentage of operating expenses, Bessemer's differentiation with its target families produces a return on equity estimated to be the highest of any private banking competitor.

Citibank's private bank, on the other hand, serves clients with minimum assets of about $250,000 who, in contrast to Bessemer's clients, want convenient access to loans–from jumbo mortgages to deal financing. Citibank's account managers are primarily lenders. When clients need other services, their account manager refers them to other Citibank specialists, each of whom handles prepackaged products. Citibank's system is less customized than Bessemer's and allows it to have a lower manager-to-client ratio of 1:125. Biannual office meetings are offered only for the largest clients. Both Bessemer and Citibank have tailored their activities to meet the needs of a different group of private banking customers. The same value chain cannot profitably meet the needs of both groups.

The third basis for positioning is that of segmenting customers who are accessible in different ways. Although their needs are similar to those of other customers, the best configuration of activities to reach them is different. I call this *access-based positioning.* Access can be a function of customer geography or customer scale – or of anything that requires a different set of activities to reach customers in the best way.

Segmenting by access is less common and less well understood than the other two bases. Carmike Cinemas, for example, operates movie theaters exclusively in cities and towns with populations under 200,000. How does Carmike make money in markets that are not only small but also won't support big-city ticket prices? It does so through a set of activities that result in a lean cost structure. Carmike's small-town customers can be served through standardized, low-cost theater complexes requiring fewer screens and less sophisticated projection technology than big-city theaters. The company's proprietary information system and management process eliminate the need for local administrative staff beyond a single theater manager. Carmike also reaps advantages from centralized purchasing, lower rent and payroll costs (because of its locations), and rock-bottom corporate overhead of 2% (the industry average is 5%). Operating in small communities also allows Carmike to practice a highly personal form of marketing in which the theater manager knows patrons and promotes attendance through personal contacts. By being the dominant if not the only theater in its markets–the main competition is often the high school football team – Carmike is also able to get its pick of films and negotiate better terms with distributors.

Rural versus urban-based customers are one example of access driving differences in activities. Serving small rather than large customers or densely rather than sparsely situated customers are other examples in which the best way to configure marketing, order processing, logistics, and after-sale service activities to meet the similar needs of distinct groups will often differ.

Positioning is not only about carving out a niche. A position emerging from any of the sources can be broad or narrow. A focused competitor, such as Ikea, targets the special needs of a subset of customers and designs its activities accordingly. Focused competitors thrive on groups of customers who are overserved (and hence overpriced) by more broadly targeted competitors, or underserved (and hence underpriced). A broadly targeted competitor– for example, Vanguard or Delta Air Lines – serves a wide array of customers, performing a set of activities designed to meet their common needs. It

The Connection with Generic Strategies

In *Competitive Strategy* (The Free Press, 1985), I introduced the concept of generic strategies – cost leadership, differentiation, and focus – to represent the alternative strategic positions in an industry. The generic strategies remain useful to characterize strategic positions at the simplest and broadest level. Vanguard, for instance, is an example of a cost leadership strategy, whereas Ikea, with its narrow customer group, is an example of cost-based focus. Neutrogena is a focused differentiator. The bases for positioning – varieties, needs, and access – carry the understanding of those generic strategies to a greater level of specificity. Ikea and Southwest are both cost-based focusers, for example, but Ikea's focus is based on the needs of a customer group, and Southwest's is based on offering a particular service variety.

The generic strategies framework introduced the need to choose in order to avoid becoming caught between what I then described as the inherent contradictions of different strategies. Trade-offs between the activities of incompatible positions explain those contradictions. Witness Continental Lite, which tried and failed to compete in two ways at once.

ignores or meets only partially the more idiosyncratic needs of particular customer groups.

Whatever the basis – variety, needs, access, or some combination of the three – positioning requires a tailored set of activities because it is always a function of differences on the supply side; that is, of differences in activities. However, positioning is not always a function of differences on the demand, or customer, side. Variety and access positionings, in particular, do not rely on *any* customer differences. In practice, however, variety or access differences often accompany needs differences. The tastes – that is, the needs – of Carmike's small-town customers, for instance, run more toward comedies, Westerns, action films, and family entertainment. Carmike does not run any films rated NC-17.

Having defined positioning, we can now begin to answer the question, "What is strategy?" Strategy is the creation of a unique and valuable position, involving a different set of activities. If there were only one ideal position, there would be no need for strategy. Companies would face a simple imperative – win the race to discover and preempt it. The essence of strategic positioning is to choose activities that are different from rivals'. If the same set of activities were best to produce all varieties, meet all needs, and access all customers, companies could easily shift among them and operational effectiveness would determine performance.

III. A Sustainable Strategic Position Requires Trade-offs

Choosing a unique position, however, is not enough to guarantee a sustainable advantage. A valuable position will attract imitation by incumbents, who are likely to copy it in one of two ways.

First, a competitor can reposition itself to match the superior performer. J.C. Penney, for instance, has been repositioning itself from a Sears clone to a more upscale, fashion-oriented, soft-goods retailer. A second and far more common type of imitation is straddling. The straddler seeks to match the benefits of a successful position while maintaining its existing position. It grafts new features, services, or technologies onto the activities it already performs.

For those who argue that competitors can copy any market position, the airline industry is a perfect test case. It would seem that nearly any competitor could imitate any other airline's activities. Any airline can buy the same planes, lease the gates, and match the menus and ticketing and baggage handling services offered by other airlines.

Continental Airlines saw how well Southwest was doing and decided to straddle. While maintaining its position as a full-service airline, Continental also set out to match Southwest on a number of point-to-point routes. The airline dubbed the new service Continental Lite. It eliminated meals and first-class service, increased departure frequency, lowered fares, and shortened turnaround time at the gate. Because Continental remained a full-service airline on other routes, it continued to use travel agents and its mixed fleet of planes and to provide baggage checking and seat assignments.

But a strategic position is not sustainable unless there are trade-offs with other positions. Trade-offs occur when activities are incompatible. Simply put, a trade-off means that more of one thing necessitates less of another. An airline can choose to serve meals – adding cost and slowing turnaround time at the gate – or it can choose not to, but it cannot do both without bearing major inefficiencies.

Trade-offs create the need for choice and protect against repositioners and straddlers. Consider Neutrogena soap. Neutrogena Corporation's variety-based positioning is built on a "kind to the skin," residue-free soap formulated for pH balance. With a large detail force calling on dermatologists, Neutrogena's marketing strategy looks more like a drug company's than a soap maker's. It advertises in medical journals, sends direct mail to doctors, attends medical conferences, and performs research at its own Skincare Institute. To reinforce its positioning, Neutrogena originally focused its distribution on drugstores and avoided price promotions. Neutrogena uses a slow, more expensive manufacturing process to mold its fragile soap.

In choosing this position, Neutrogena said no to the deodorants and skin softeners that many customers desire in their soap. It gave up the large-volume potential of selling through supermarkets and using price promotions. It sacrificed manufacturing efficiencies to achieve the soap's desired attributes. In its original positioning, Neutrogena made a whole raft of trade-offs like those, trade-offs that protected the company from imitators.

Trade-offs arise for three reasons. The first is inconsistencies in image or reputation. A company known for delivering one kind of value may lack credibility and confuse customers – or even undermine its reputation – if it delivers another kind of value or attempts to deliver two inconsistent things at the same time. For example, Ivory soap, with its position as a basic, inexpensive everyday soap would have a hard time reshaping its image to match Neutrogena's premium "medical" reputation. Efforts to create a new image typically cost tens or even hundreds of millions of dollars in a major industry – a powerful barrier to imitation.

Second, and more important, trade-offs arise from activities themselves. Different positions (with their tailored activities) require different product configurations, different equipment, different employee behavior, different skills, and different management systems. Many trade-offs reflect inflexibilities in machinery, people, or systems. The more Ikea has configured its activities to lower costs by having its customers do their own assembly and delivery, the less able it is to satisfy customers who require higher levels of service.

However, trade-offs can be even more basic. In general, value is destroyed if an activity is overdesigned or underdesigned for its use. For example, even if a given salesperson were capable of providing a high level of assistance to one customer and none to another, the salesperson's talent (and some of his or her cost) would be wasted on the second customer. Moreover, productivity can improve when variation of an activity is limited. By providing a high level of assistance all the time, the salesperson and the entire sales activity can often achieve efficiencies of learning and scale.

Finally, trade-offs arise from limits on internal coordination and control. By clearly choosing to compete in one way and not another, senior management makes organizational priorities clear. Companies that try to be all things to all customers, in contrast, risk confusion in the trenches as employees attempt to make day-to-day operating decisions without a clear framework.

Positioning trade-offs are pervasive in competition and essential to strategy. They create the need for choice and purposefully limit what a company offers. They deter straddling or repositioning, because competitors that engage in those approaches undermine their strategies and degrade the value of their existing activities.

Trade-offs ultimately grounded Continental Lite. The airline lost hundreds of millions of dollars, and the CEO lost his job. Its planes were delayed leaving congested hub cities or slowed at the gate by baggage transfers. Late flights and cancellations generated a thousand complaints a day. Continental Lite could not afford to compete on price and still pay standard travel-agent commissions, but neither could it do without agents for its full-service business. The airline compromised by cutting commissions for all Continental flights across the board. Similarly, it could not afford to offer the same frequent-flier benefits to travelers paying the much lower ticket prices for Lite service. It compromised again by lowering the rewards of Continental's entire frequent-flier program. The results: angry travel agents and full-service customers.

Continental tried to compete in two ways at once. In trying to be low cost on some routes and full service on others, Continental paid an enormous straddling penalty. If there were no trade-offs between the two positions, Continental could have succeeded. But the absence of trade-offs is a dangerous half-truth that managers must unlearn. Quality is not always free. Southwest's convenience, one kind of high quality, happens to be consistent with low costs because its frequent departures are facilitated by a number of low-cost practices – fast gate turnarounds and automated ticketing, for example. However, other dimensions of airline quality – an assigned seat, a meal, or baggage transfer – require costs to provide.

In general, false trade-offs between cost and quality occur primarily when there is redundant or wasted effort, poor control or accuracy, or weak coordination. Simultaneous improvement of cost and differentiation is possible only when a company begins far behind the productivity frontier or when the frontier shifts outward. At the frontier, where

Trade-offs are essential to strategy. They create the need for choice and purposefully limit what a company offers.

companies have achieved current best practice, the trade-off between cost and differentiation is very real indeed.

After a decade of enjoying productivity advantages, Honda Motor Company and Toyota Motor Corporation recently bumped up against the frontier. In 1995, faced with increasing customer resistance to higher automobile prices, Honda found that the only way to produce a less-expensive car was to skimp on features. In the United States, it replaced the rear disk brakes on the Civic with lower-cost drum brakes and used cheaper fabric for the back seat, hoping customers would not notice. Toyota tried to sell a version of its best-selling Corolla in Japan with unpainted bumpers and cheaper seats. In Toyota's case, customers rebelled, and the company quickly dropped the new model.

For the past decade, as managers have improved operational effectiveness greatly, they have internalized the idea that eliminating trade-offs is a good thing. But if there are no trade-offs companies will never achieve a sustainable advantage. They will have to run faster and faster just to stay in place.

As we return to the question, What is strategy? we see that trade-offs add a new dimension to the answer. Strategy is making trade-offs in competing. The essence of strategy is choosing what *not* to do. Without trade-offs, there would be no need for choice and thus no need for strategy. Any good idea could and would be quickly imitated. Again, performance would once again depend wholly on operational effectiveness.

IV. Fit Drives Both Competitive Advantage and Sustainability

Positioning choices determine not only which activities a company will perform and how it will configure individual activities but also how activities relate to one another. While operational effectiveness is about achieving excellence in individual activities, or functions, strategy is about *combining* activities.

Southwest's rapid gate turnaround, which allows frequent departures and greater use of aircraft, is essential to its high-convenience, low-cost positioning. But how does Southwest achieve it? Part of the answer lies in the company's well-paid gate and ground crews, whose productivity in turnarounds is enhanced by flexible union rules. But the bigger part of the answer lies in how Southwest performs other activities. With no meals, no seat assignment, and no interline baggage transfers, Southwest avoids having to perform activities that slow down other airlines. It selects airports and routes to avoid congestion that introduces delays. Southwest's strict limits on the type and length of routes make standardized aircraft possible: every aircraft Southwest turns is a Boeing 737.

Fit locks out imitators by creating a chain that is as strong as its strongest link.

What is Southwest's core competence? Its key success factors? The correct answer is that everything matters. Southwest's strategy involves a whole system of activities, not a collection of parts. Its competitive advantage comes from the way its activities fit and reinforce one another.

Fit locks out imitators by creating a chain that is as strong as its *strongest* link. As in most companies with good strategies, Southwest's activities complement one another in ways that create real economic value. One activity's cost, for example, is lowered because of the way other activities are performed. Similarly, one activity's value to customers can be enhanced by a company's other activities. That is the way strategic fit creates competitive advantage and superior profitability.

Types of Fit

The importance of fit among functional policies is one of the oldest ideas in strategy. Gradually, however, it has been supplanted on the management agenda. Rather than seeing the company as a whole, managers have turned to "core" competencies, "critical" resources, and "key" success factors. In fact, fit is a far more central component of competitive advantage than most realize.

Fit is important because discrete activities often affect one another. A sophisticated sales force, for example, confers a greater advantage when the company's product embodies premium technology and its marketing approach emphasizes customer assistance and support. A production line with high levels of model variety is more valuable when combined with an inventory and order processing system that minimizes the need for stocking finished goods, a sales process equipped to explain and encourage customization, and an advertising theme that stresses the benefits of product variations that meet a customer's special needs. Such complementarities are pervasive in strategy. Although some fit among activities is generic and applies to many companies, the most valuable fit is strategy-specific because it enhances a position's uniqueness and amplifies trade-offs.[2]

There are three types of fit, although they are not mutually exclusive. First-order fit is *simple consistency* between each activity (function) and the overall strategy. Vanguard, for example, aligns all activities with its low-cost strategy. It minimizes portfolio turnover and does not need highly compensated money managers. The company distributes its funds directly, avoiding commissions to brokers. It also limits advertising, relying instead on public relations and word-of-mouth recommendations. Vanguard ties its employees' bonuses to cost savings.

Consistency ensures that the competitive advantages of activities cumulate and do not erode or cancel themselves out. It makes the strategy easier to communicate to customers, employees, and shareholders, and improves implementation through single-mindedness in the corporation.

Second-order fit occurs when *activities are reinforcing.* Neutrogena, for example, markets to upscale hotels eager to offer their guests a soap recommended by dermatologists. Hotels grant Neutrogena the privilege of using its customary packaging while requiring other soaps to feature the hotel's name. Once guests have tried Neutrogena in a luxury hotel, they are more likely to purchase it at the drugstore or ask their doctor about it. Thus Neutrogena's medical and hotel marketing activities reinforce one another, lowering total marketing costs.

In another example, Bic Corporation sells a narrow line of standard, low-priced pens to virtually all major customer markets (retail, commercial, promotional, and giveaway) through virtually all available channels. As with any variety-based positioning serving a broad group of customers, Bic emphasizes a common need (low price for an acceptable pen) and uses marketing approaches with a broad reach (a large sales force and heavy television advertising). Bic gains the benefits of consis-

Mapping Activity Systems

Activity-system maps, such as this one for Ikea, show how a company's strategic position is contained in a set of tailored activities designed to deliver it. In companies with a clear strategic position, a number of higher-order strategic themes (in dark purple) can be identified and implemented through clusters of tightly linked activities (in light purple).

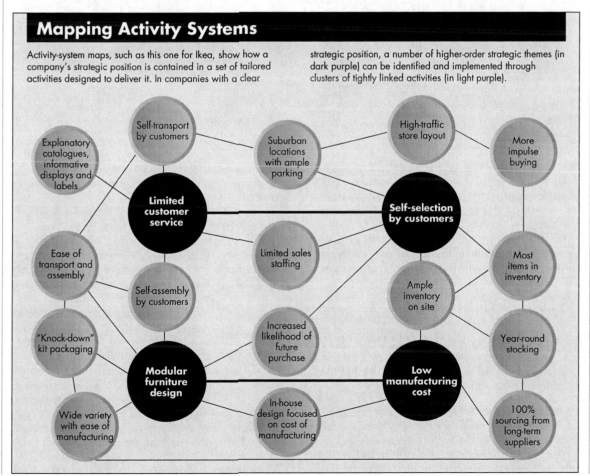

Vanguard's Activity System

Activity-system maps can be useful for examining and strengthening strategic fit. A set of basic questions should guide the process. First, is each activity consistent with the overall positioning – the varieties produced, the needs served, and the type of customers accessed? Ask those responsible for each activity to identify how other activities within the company improve or detract from their performance. Second, are there ways to strengthen how activities and groups of activities reinforce one another? Finally, could changes in one activity eliminate the need to perform others?

Wary of small growth funds

A broad array of mutual funds excluding some fund categories

Limited international funds due to volatility and high costs

Use of redemption fees to discourage trading

Very low expenses passed on to client

Employee bonuses tied to cost savings

No-loads

In-house management for standard funds

Efficient investment management approach offering good, consistent performance

Emphasis on bonds and equity index funds

No broker-dealer relationships

No marketing changes

Strict cost control

Very low rate of trading

Long-term investment encouraged

Shareholder education cautioning about risk

No commissions to brokers or distributors

Direct distribution

No first-class travel for executives

Straightforward client communication and education

On-line information access

Only three retail locations

Limited advertising budget

Reliance on word of mouth

Vanguard actively spreads its philosophy

tency across nearly all activities, including product design that emphasizes ease of manufacturing, plants configured for low cost, aggressive purchasing to minimize material costs, and in-house parts production whenever the economics dictate.

Yet Bic goes beyond simple consistency because its activities are reinforcing. For example, the company uses point-of-sale displays and frequent pack-

The competitive value of individual activities cannot be separated from the whole.

aging changes to stimulate impulse buying. To handle point-of-sale tasks, a company needs a large sales force. Bic's is the largest in its industry, and it handles point-of-sale activities better than its rivals do. Moreover, the combination of point-of-sale

activity, heavy television advertising, and packaging changes yields far more impulse buying than any activity in isolation could.

Third-order fit goes beyond activity reinforcement to what I call *optimization of effort*. The Gap, a retailer of casual clothes, considers product availability in its stores a critical element of its strategy. The Gap could keep products either by holding store inventory or by restocking from warehouses. The Gap has optimized its effort across these activities by restocking its selection of basic clothing almost daily out of three warehouses, thereby minimizing the need to carry large in-store inventories. The emphasis is on restocking because the Gap's merchandising strategy sticks to basic items in relatively few colors. While comparable retailers achieve turns of three to four times per year, the Gap turns its inventory seven and a half times per year. Rapid restocking, moreover, reduces the cost of implementing the Gap's short model cycle, which is six to eight weeks long.[3]

Coordination and information exchange across activities to eliminate redundancy and minimize wasted effort are the most basic types of effort optimization. But there are higher levels as well. Product design choices, for example, can eliminate the need for after-sale service or make it possible for customers to perform service activities themselves. Similarly, coordination with suppliers or distribution channels can eliminate the need for some in-house activities, such as end-user training.

In all three types of fit, the whole matters more than any individual part. Competitive advantage grows out of the *entire system* of activities. The fit among activities substantially reduces cost or increases differentiation. Beyond that, the competitive value of individual activities–or the associated skills, competencies, or resources – cannot be decoupled from the system or the strategy. Thus in competitive companies it can be misleading to explain success by specifying individual strengths, core competencies, or critical resources. The list of strengths cuts across many functions, and one strength blends into others. It is more useful to think in terms of themes that pervade many activities, such as low cost, a particular notion of customer service, or a particular conception of the value delivered. These themes are embodied in nests of tightly linked activities.

Fit and Sustainability

Strategic fit among many activities is fundamental not only to competitive advantage but also to the sustainability of that advantage. It is harder for a rival to match an array of interlocked activities than it is merely to imitate a particular sales-force approach, match a process technology, or replicate a set of product features. Positions built on systems of activities are far more sustainable than those built on individual activities.

Consider this simple exercise. The probability that competitors can match any activity is often

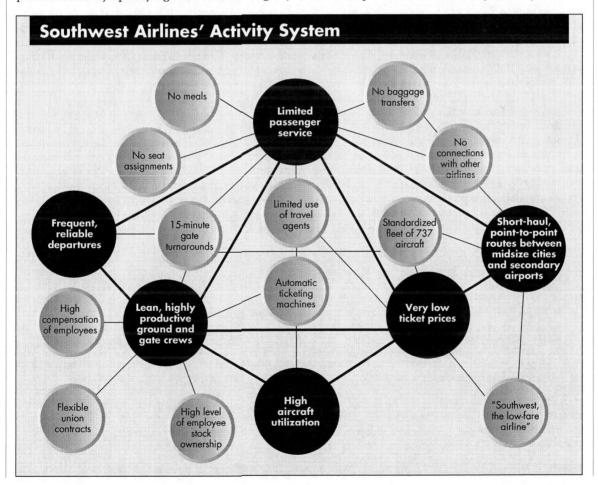

Southwest Airlines' Activity System

No meals

No baggage transfers

Limited passenger service

No seat assignments

No connections with other airlines

Frequent, reliable departures

15-minute gate turnarounds

Limited use of travel agents

Standardized fleet of 737 aircraft

Short-haul, point-to-point routes between midsize cities and secondary airports

High compensation of employees

Lean, highly productive ground and gate crews

Automatic ticketing machines

Very low ticket prices

Flexible union contracts

High level of employee stock ownership

High aircraft utilization

"Southwest, the low-fare airline"

less than one. The probabilities then quickly compound to make matching the entire system highly unlikely (.9×.9= .81; .9×.9×.9×.9= .66, and so on). Existing companies that try to reposition or straddle will be forced to reconfigure many activities.

Strategic positions should have a horizon of a decade or more, not of a single planning cycle.

And even new entrants, though they do not confront the trade-offs facing established rivals, still face formidable barriers to imitation.

The more a company's positioning rests on activity systems with second- and third-order fit, the more sustainable its advantage will be. Such systems, by their very nature, are usually difficult to untangle from outside the company and therefore hard to imitate. And even if rivals can identify the relevant interconnections, they will have difficulty replicating them. Achieving fit is difficult because it requires the integration of decisions and actions across many independent subunits.

A competitor seeking to match an activity system gains little by imitating only some activities and not matching the whole. Performance does not improve; it can decline. Recall Continental Lite's disastrous attempt to imitate Southwest.

Finally, fit among a company's activities creates pressures and incentives to improve operational effectiveness, which makes imitation even harder. Fit means that poor performance in one activity will degrade the performance in others, so that weaknesses are exposed and more prone to get at-

tention. Conversely, improvements in one activity will pay dividends in others. Companies with strong fit among their activities are rarely inviting targets. Their superiority in strategy and in execution only compounds their advantages and raises the hurdle for imitators.

When activities complement one another, rivals will get little benefit from imitation unless they successfully match the whole system. Such situations tend to promote winner-take-all competition. The company that builds the best activity system—Toys R Us, for instance—wins, while rivals with similar strategies—Child World and Lionel Leisure—fall behind. Thus finding a new strategic position is often preferable to being the second or third imitator of an occupied position.

The most viable positions are those whose activity systems are incompatible because of trade-offs. Strategic positioning sets the trade-off rules that define how individual activities will be configured and integrated. Seeing strategy in terms of activity systems only makes it clearer why organizational structure, systems, and processes need to be strategy-specific. Tailoring organization to strategy, in turn, makes complementarities more achievable and contributes to sustainability.

One implication is that strategic positions should have a horizon of a decade or more, not of a single planning cycle. Continuity fosters improvements in individual activities and the fit across activities, allowing an organization to build unique capabilities and skills tailored to its strategy. Continuity also reinforces a company's identity.

Conversely, frequent shifts in positioning are costly. Not only must a company reconfigure individual activities, but it must also realign entire sys-

Alternative Views of Strategy

The Implicit Strategy Model of the Past Decade

☐ One ideal competitive position in the industry
☐ Benchmarking of all activities and achieving best practice
☐ Aggressive outsourcing and partnering to gain efficiencies
☐ Advantages rest on a few key success factors, critical resources, core competencies
☐ Flexibility and rapid responses to all competitive and market changes

Sustainable Competitive Advantage

☐ Unique competitive position for the company
☐ Activities tailored to strategy
☐ Clear trade-offs and choices vis-à-vis competitors
☐ Competitive advantage arises from fit across activities
☐ Sustainability comes from the activity system, not the parts
☐ Operational effectiveness a given

tems. Some activities may never catch up to the vacillating strategy. The inevitable result of frequent shifts in strategy, or of failure to choose a distinct position in the first place, is "me-too" or hedged activity configurations, inconsistencies across functions, and organizational dissonance.

What is strategy? We can now complete the answer to this question. Strategy is creating fit among a company's activities. The success of a strategy depends on doing many things well–not just a few–and integrating among them. If there is no fit among activities, there is no distinctive strategy and little sustainability. Management reverts to the simpler task of overseeing independent functions, and operational effectiveness determines an organization's relative performance.

V. Rediscovering Strategy

The Failure to Choose

Why do so many companies fail to have a strategy? Why do managers avoid making strategic choices? Or, having made them in the past, why do managers so often let strategies decay and blur?

Commonly, the threats to strategy are seen to emanate from outside a company because of changes in technology or the behavior of competitors. Although external changes can be the problem, the greater threat to strategy often comes from within. A sound strategy is undermined by a misguided view of competition, by organizational failures, and, especially, by the desire to grow.

Managers have become confused about the necessity of making choices. When many companies operate far from the productivity frontier, trade-offs appear unnecessary. It can seem that a well-run company should be able to beat its ineffective rivals on all dimensions simultaneously. Taught by popular management thinkers that they do not have to make trade-offs, managers have acquired a macho sense that to do so is a sign of weakness.

Unnerved by forecasts of hypercompetition, managers increase its likelihood by imitating everything about their competitors. Exhorted to think in terms of revolution, managers chase every new technology for its own sake.

The pursuit of operational effectiveness is seductive because it is concrete and actionable. Over the past decade, managers have been under increasing pressure to deliver tangible, measurable performance improvements. Programs in operational effectiveness produce reassuring progress, although superior profitability may remain elusive. Business publications and consultants flood the market with information about what other companies are doing, reinforcing the best-practice mentality. Caught up in the race for operational effectiveness, many managers simply do not understand the need to have a strategy.

Companies avoid or blur strategic choices for other reasons as well. Conventional wisdom within an industry is often strong, homogenizing competition. Some managers mistake "customer focus" to mean they must serve all customer needs or respond to every request from distribution channels. Others cite the desire to preserve flexibility.

Organizational realities also work against strategy. Trade-offs are frightening, and making no choice is sometimes preferred to risking blame for a bad choice. Companies imitate one another in a type of herd behavior, each assuming rivals know something they do not. Newly empowered employees, who are urged to seek every possible source of improvement, often lack a vision of the whole and the perspective to recognize trade-offs. The failure to choose sometimes comes down to the reluctance to disappoint valued managers or employees.

The Growth Trap

Among all other influences, the desire to grow has perhaps the most perverse effect on strategy. Trade-offs and limits appear to constrain growth. Serving one group of customers and excluding others, for instance, places a real or imagined limit on revenue growth. Broadly targeted strategies emphasizing low price result in lost sales with customers sensitive to features or service. Differentiators lose sales to price-sensitive customers.

Managers are constantly tempted to take incremental steps that surpass those limits but blur a company's strategic position. Eventually, pressures to grow or apparent saturation of the target market lead managers to broaden the position by extending product lines, adding new features, imitating competitors' popular services, matching processes, and even making acquisitions. For years, Maytag Corporation's success was based on its focus on reliable, durable washers and dryers, later extended to include dishwashers. However, conventional wis-

Reconnecting with Strategy

Most companies owe their initial success to a unique strategic position involving clear trade-offs. Activities once were aligned with that position. The passage of time and the pressures of growth, however, led to compromises that were, at first, almost imperceptible. Through a succession of incremental changes that each seemed sensible at the time, many established companies have compromised their way to homogeneity with their rivals.

The issue here is not with the companies whose historical position is no longer viable; their challenge is to start over, just as a new entrant would. At issue is a far more common phenomenon: the established company achieving mediocre returns and lacking a clear strategy. Through incremental additions of product varieties, incremental efforts to serve new customer groups, and emulation of rivals' activities, the existing company loses its clear competitive position. Typically, the company has matched many of its competitors' offerings and practices and attempts to sell to most customer groups.

A number of approaches can help a company reconnect with strategy. The first is a careful look at what it already does. Within most well-established companies is a core of uniqueness. It is identified by answering questions such as the following:

☐ Which of our product or service varieties are the most distinctive?

☐ Which of our product or service varieties are the most profitable?
☐ Which of our customers are the most satisfied?
☐ Which customers, channels, or purchase occasions are the most profitable?
☐ Which of the activities in our value chain are the most different and effective?

Around this core of uniqueness are encrustations added incrementally over time. Like barnacles, they must be removed to reveal the underlying strategic positioning. A small percentage of varieties or customers may well account for most of a company's sales and especially its profits. The challenge, then, is to refocus on the unique core and realign the company's activities with it. Customers and product varieties at the periphery can be sold or allowed through inattention or price increases to fade away.

A company's history can also be instructive. What was the vision of the founder? What were the products and customers that made the company? Looking backward, one can reexamine the original strategy to see if it is still valid. Can the historical positioning be implemented in a modern way, one consistent with today's technologies and practices? This sort of thinking may lead to a commitment to renew the strategy and may challenge the organization to recover its distinctiveness. Such a challenge can be galvanizing and can instill the confidence to make the needed trade-offs.

---

dom emerging within the industry supported the notion of selling a full line of products. Concerned with slow industry growth and competition from broad-line appliance makers, Maytag was pressured by dealers and encouraged by customers to extend its line. Maytag expanded into refrigerators and cooking products under the Maytag brand and acquired other brands – Jenn-Air, Hardwick Stove, Hoover, Admiral, and Magic Chef – with disparate positions. Maytag has grown substantially from $684 million in 1985 to a peak of $3.4 billion in 1994, but return on sales has declined from 8% to 12% in the 1970s and 1980s to an average of less than 1% between 1989 and 1995. Cost cutting will improve this performance, but laundry and dishwasher products still anchor Maytag's profitability.

Neutrogena may have fallen into the same trap. In the early 1990s, its U.S. distribution broadened to include mass merchandisers such as Wal-Mart Stores. Under the Neutrogena name, the company expanded into a wide variety of products – eye-

makeup remover and shampoo, for example – in which it was not unique and which diluted its image, and it began turning to price promotions.

Compromises and inconsistencies in the pursuit of growth will erode the competitive advantage a company had with its original varieties or target customers. Attempts to compete in several ways at once create confusion and undermine organizational motivation and focus. Profits fall, but more revenue is seen as the answer. Managers are unable to make choices, so the company embarks on a new round of broadening and compromises. Often, rivals continue to match each other until desperation breaks the cycle, resulting in a merger or downsizing to the original positioning.

Profitable Growth

Many companies, after a decade of restructuring and cost-cutting, are turning their attention to growth. Too often, efforts to grow blur uniqueness, create compromises, reduce fit, and ultimately undermine competitive advantage. In fact, the growth imperative is hazardous to strategy.

What approaches to growth preserve and reinforce strategy? Broadly, the prescription is to concentrate on deepening a strategic position rather than broadening and compromising it. One approach is to look for extensions of the strategy that leverage the existing activity system by offering features or services that rivals would find impossible or costly to match on a stand-alone basis. In other words, managers can ask themselves which activities, features, or forms of competition are feasible or less costly to them because of complementary activities that their company performs.

Deepening a position involves making the company's activities more distinctive, strengthening fit, and communicating the strategy better to those customers who should value it. But many companies succumb to the temptation to chase "easy" growth by adding hot features, products, or services without screening them or adapting them to their strategy. Or they target new customers or markets in which the company has little special to offer. A company can often grow faster – and far more profitably – by better penetrating needs and varieties where it is distinctive than by slugging it out in potentially higher growth arenas in which the company lacks uniqueness. Carmike, now the largest theater chain in the United States, owes its rapid growth to its disciplined concentration on small markets. The company quickly sells any big-city theaters that come to it as part of an acquisition.

Globalization often allows growth that is consistent with strategy, opening up larger markets for a focused strategy. Unlike broadening domestically,

separate units with different strategic positions. On the other, it has created an umbrella appliance company for all its brands to gain critical mass. With shared design, manufacturing, distribution, and customer service, it will be hard to avoid homogenization. If a given business unit attempts to compete with different positions for different products or customers, avoiding compromise is nearly impossible.

The Role of Leadership

The challenge of developing or reestablishing a clear strategy is often primarily an organizational one and depends on leadership. With so many forces at work against making choices and trade-offs in organizations, a clear intellectual framework to guide strategy is a necessary counterweight. Moreover, strong leaders willing to make choices are essential.

In many companies, leadership has degenerated into orchestrating operational improvements and making deals. But the leader's role is broader and far more important. General management is more than the stewardship of individual functions. Its core is strategy: defining and communicating the company's unique position, making trade-offs, and forging fit among activities. The leader must provide the discipline to decide which industry changes and customer needs the company will respond to, while avoiding organizational distractions and maintaining the company's distinctiveness. Managers at lower levels lack the perspective and the confidence to maintain a strategy. There will be constant pressures to compromise, relax trade-offs, and emulate rivals. One of the leader's jobs is to teach others in the organization about strategy – and to say no.

Strategy renders choices about what not to do as important as choices about what to do. Indeed, setting limits is another function of leadership. Deciding which target group of customers, varieties, and needs the company should serve is fundamental to developing a strategy. But so is deciding not to serve other customers or needs and not to offer certain features or services. Thus strategy requires constant discipline and clear communication. Indeed, one of the most important functions of an explicit, communicated strategy is to guide employees in making choices that arise because of trade-offs in their individual activities and in day-to-day decisions.

At general management's core is strategy: defining a company's position, making trade-offs, and forging fit among activities.

expanding globally is likely to leverage and reinforce a company's unique position and identity.

Companies seeking growth through broadening within their industry can best contain the risks to strategy by creating stand-alone units, each with its own brand name and tailored activities. Maytag has clearly struggled with this issue. On the one hand, it has organized its premium and value brands into

Emerging Industries and Technologies

Developing a strategy in a newly emerging industry or in a business undergoing revolutionary technological changes is a daunting proposition. In such cases, managers face a high level of uncertainty about the needs of customers, the products and services that will prove to be the most desired, and the best configuration of activities and technologies to deliver them. Because of all this uncertainty, imitation and hedging are rampant: unable to risk being wrong or left behind, companies match all features, offer all new services, and explore all technologies.

During such periods in an industry's development, its basic productivity frontier is being established or reestablished. Explosive growth can make such times profitable for many companies, but profits will be temporary because imitation and strategic convergence will ultimately destroy industry profitability. The companies that are enduringly successful will be those that begin as early as possible to define and embody in their activities a unique competitive position. A period of imitation may be inevitable in emerging industries, but that period reflects the level of uncertainty rather than a desired state of affairs.

In high-tech industries, this imitation phase often continues much longer than it should. Enraptured by technological change itself, companies pack more features – most of which are never used – into their products while slashing prices across the board. Rarely are trade-offs even considered. The drive for growth to satisfy market pressures leads companies into every product area. Although a few companies with fundamental advantages prosper, the majority are doomed to a rat race no one can win.

Ironically, the popular business press, focused on hot, emerging industries, is prone to presenting these special cases as proof that we have entered a new era of competition in which none of the old rules are valid. In fact, the opposite is true.

Improving operational effectiveness is a necessary part of management, but it is *not* strategy. In confusing the two, managers have unintentionally backed into a way of thinking about competition that is driving many industries toward competitive convergence, which is in no one's best interest and is not inevitable.

Managers must clearly distinguish operational effectiveness from strategy. Both are essential, but the two agendas are different.

The operational agenda involves continual improvement everywhere there are no trade-offs. Failure to do this creates vulnerability even for companies with a good strategy. The operational agenda is the proper place for constant change, flexibility, and relentless efforts to achieve best practice. In contrast, the strategic agenda is the right place for defining a unique position, making clear trade-offs, and tightening fit. It involves the continual search for ways to reinforce and extend the company's position. The strategic agenda demands discipline and continuity; its enemies are distraction and compromise.

Strategic continuity does not imply a static view of competition. A company must continually improve its operational effectiveness and actively try to shift the productivity frontier; at the same time, there needs to be ongoing effort to extend its uniqueness while strengthening the fit among its activities. Strategic continuity, in fact, should make an organization's continual improvement more effective.

A company may have to change its strategy if there are major structural changes in its industry. In fact, new strategic positions often arise because of industry changes, and new entrants unencumbered by history often can exploit them more easily. However, a company's choice of a new position must be driven by the ability to find new trade-offs and leverage a new system of complementary activities into a sustainable advantage.

---

1. I first described the concept of activities and its use in understanding competitive advantage in *Competitive Advantage* (New York: The Free Press, 1985). The ideas in this article build on and extend that thinking.

2. Paul Milgrom and John Roberts have begun to explore the economics of systems of complementary functions, activities, and functions. Their focus is on the emergence of "modern manufacturing" as a new set of complementary activities, on the tendency of companies to react to external changes with coherent bundles of internal responses, and on the need for central coordination – a strategy – to align functional managers. In the latter case, they model what has long been a bedrock principle of strategy. See Paul Milgrom and John Roberts, "The Economics of Modern Manufacturing: Technology, Strategy, and Organization," *American Economic Review* 80 (1990): 511-528; Paul Milgrom, Yingyi Qian, and John Roberts, "Complementarities, Momentum, and Evolution of Modern Manufacturing," *American Economic Review* 81 (1991) 84-88; and Paul Milgrom and John Roberts, "Complementarities and Fit: Strategy, Structure, and Organizational Changes in Manufacturing," *Journal of Accounting and Economics*, vol. 19 (March-May 1995): 179-208.

3. Material on retail strategies is drawn in part from Jan Rivkin, "The Rise of Retail Category Killers," unpublished working paper, January 1995. Nicolaj Siggelkow prepared the case study on the Gap.

Reprint 96608   To place an order, call 1-800-545-7685.

9-707-493
REV: JANUARY 17, 2007

MICHAEL E. PORTER

Understanding Industry Structure

The essence of the job of the strategist is to cope with competition. The arena in which competition takes place is the industry, in which a company and its rivals vie for business. Each industry has a distinctive structure that shapes the nature of competitive interaction that unfolds there. Understanding the underlying structure of a company's industry, now and in the future, is a core discipline in strategy formation.

On the surface, every industry is different. Consider the global automobile industry; the worldwide market for art masterpieces; the booming private equity industry; and the heavily regulated healthcare delivery industry in Europe. At one level, these industries appear to have little in common. Industries also differ in another crucial aspect: they register sharply different levels of average profitability in the long run. For example, **Exhibit 1** shows a histogram of long-run return on invested capital in the United States for more than 400 industries. The most profitable industries generate much higher returns than the least profitable. Equally significant differences arise in other countries, both advanced and emerging.

To understand industry competition and profitability, however, one must look beyond their differences and view industries at a deeper level. In any industry, there are five basic competitive forces—diagrammed in **Figure A**—whose collective strength determines the long-run profit potential

Figure A   Forces that Shape Competition in an Industry

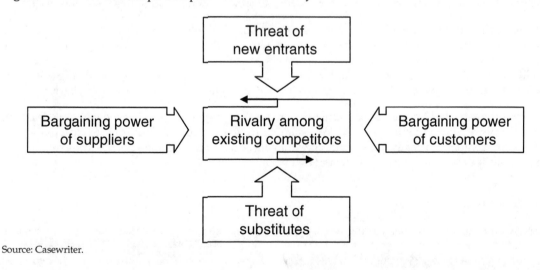

Source: Casewriter.

Professor Michael E. Porter prepared this note based on the classic article "How Competitive Forces Shape Strategy," *Harvard Business Review*, July-August 1979, Product Number 79208. Professor Jan W. Rivkin assisted in the preparation of this note which is an update and extension of the article.

of the industry. The forces range from intense in industries like airlines, textiles, and steel, where almost no company earns attractive returns on investment, to mild in industries like medical supplies, soft drinks, and toiletries, where there is room for quite high returns. Many things can affect industry profitability in the short run—including the weather and the business cycle—but it is industry structure manifested in the competitive forces that sets industry profitability over the long run.

Understanding competitive forces, and their causes, gives a strategist a way to size up any industry, regardless of whether it is a product or a service, emerging or mature, high tech or low tech. An analysis of industry structure reveals the roots of an industry's profitability at any point in time while providing a framework for anticipating and influencing changes in industry competition (and profitability) over time. As we will see, defending against the competitive forces or shaping them in a company's favor becomes an important component of strategy.

Forces that Shape Competition

Managers tend to view competition too narrowly, as manifested only in today's direct competitors. As **Figure A** emphasizes, however, competition goes well beyond the established industry rivals. Customers, suppliers, potential entrants, and substitute products are all competitors in the fight for profits, competitors whose influence may be more or less important depending on the industry. The extended rivalry that results from the interplay of these competitive forces gives rise to industry profitability.

Different forces take on prominence in shaping competition in each industry. In the market for commercial aircraft, the key forces are the fierce rivalry between dominant producers Airbus and Boeing and the bargaining power of the airlines that place huge orders for aircraft. In the movie theater industry, the critical forces are the proliferation of substitute forms of entertainment and the power of the movie producers and distributors who supply the critical input, movies themselves.

The strongest competitive force or forces set the profitability of an industry and become the most important to strategy formulation. For example, even an industry where new entry is not a threat will earn low returns if it faces a superior or lower-cost substitute product—as Kodak and Fuji, the world's leading producers of photographic film, learned with the advent of digital photography. In such a situation, coping with the substitute product becomes the number one strategic priority.

Every industry has an underlying structure, or set of economic and technical characteristics, that gives rise to these competitive forces. We examine industry structure from the perspective of an incumbent company already present in the industry. The analysis can be readily extended to understand the challenges facing a potential entrant.

Threat of Entry

New entrants to an industry bring new capacity and a desire to gain market share. The threat of new entry puts a cap on the profit potential of an industry. When the threat is high, profits cannot rise too high without attracting new competitors. Especially when new entrants are diversifying from other markets, they can leverage existing capabilities to shake up competition, as Microsoft did when it entered the market for Internet browsers.

The threat of entry into an industry depends on the barriers to entry that are present and on the reaction from existing competitors that entrants can expect. If entry barriers are low and newcomers expect little retaliation from the entrenched competitors, the threat of entry is high and industry profitability is moderated.

There are seven major sources of barriers to entry:

1. *Supply-side economies of scale*—These economies arise when firms that produce at larger volumes enjoy lower costs per unit, because they can spread fixed costs over more units, employ more efficient technology, or command better terms from suppliers. Supply-side scale economies deter entry by forcing the aspirant either to come in at a large scale or to accept a cost disadvantage. Scale economies in research, production, consumer marketing, and OEM sales are probably the key barriers to entry in the microprocessor industry, protecting incumbents such as Intel. Economies of scale can also arise in logistics, financing, and information technology infrastructure.

2. *Demand-side benefits of scale*—These benefits, also known as network effects, arise in industries where a buyer's willingness to pay for a company's product increases with the number of other buyers who also patronize the company. Buyers may trust larger companies more for a crucial product; recall the old adage that no one ever got fired for buying from IBM when it was the dominant computer maker. Buyers may also value being in a "network" with a larger set of fellow customers. For instance, each online auction participant is attracted to eBay rather than other auction sites because eBay offers more potential trading partners. Many computer users prefer Microsoft's Windows operating system because other users, with whom they want to be compatible, also opt for Windows. In addition, computer users prefer Windows because its larger base of users has attracted a greater number of independent programmers, who in turn develop more software applications that customers value. Demand-side benefits of scale discourage entry by limiting the willingness of customers to buy from a newcomer and reducing the price the newcomer can command until it builds up a large base of customers.

3. *Customer switching costs*—Switching costs are fixed costs that buyers face when they change suppliers. They may arise because a buyer who switches vendors must alter product specifications, retrain employees to use a new product, or build up new procedures or systems, for example. The larger are switching costs, the harder it will be for an entrant to gain customers.

4. *Capital requirements*—The need to invest large financial resources in order to compete creates a barrier to entry. Capital may be necessary not only for fixed facilities but also for customer credit, inventories, and start-up losses. The barrier is particularly great if the capital is required for unrecoverable expenditures such as up-front advertising or R&D. While major corporations have the financial resources to invade almost any industry, the huge capital requirements in certain fields, such as mineral extraction, limit the pool of likely entrants. In fields such as tax preparation services, in contrast, capital requirements are minimal and potential entrants plentiful.

It is important, however, not to overstate the degree to which capital requirements alone deter entry. If industry returns are attractive and are expected to remain so, and if capital markets are efficient, investors will provide entrants with the funds they need. This is especially true today, when deep pools of private equity stand ready to fund attractive ventures.

5. *Incumbency advantages independent of size*—Incumbent companies may have cost or quality advantages not available to potential rivals, no matter what their size. These advantages can stem from proprietary technology, access to the best raw material sources, government

subsidies, favorable geographic locations, or cumulative experience that has allowed incumbents to learn how to produce efficiently. Sometimes such advantages are legally enforceable, as they are through patents.

6. *Unequal access to distribution channels*—The newcomer on the block must, of course, secure distribution of its product or service. A new food item, for example, must displace others from the supermarket shelf via price breaks, promotions, intense selling efforts, or some other means. The more limited the wholesale or retail channels are and the more that existing competitors have tied them up, the tougher entry into an industry will be. Sometimes access to distribution is so high a barrier that a new entrant must create its own distribution channels. Thus, upstart low-cost airlines in Europe have avoided distribution through travel agents, who tend to favor established higher-fare carriers, and have encouraged passengers to book their own flights via Internet web sites.

7. *Restrictive government policy*—Government can limit or even foreclose entry to industries via controls such as license requirements, patent protection, foreign investment barriers, and limits on access to local raw material sources. Regulated industries like liquor retailing and taxi services are visible examples in most developed countries; more subtle government restrictions operate in fields like health care and coal mining. The government can also heighten entry barriers indirectly through controls such as pollution and safety regulations, which raise the standards newcomers must meet. (Of course, government policies may also make entry easier—for instance, by funding basic research and making it available to all firms, new and old.)

The expectations of potential new entrants about the reaction of existing competitors will also influence their decision to enter or stay out of an industry. Newcomers are likely to have second thoughts about entry if:

- Incumbents have previously responded vigorously against new entrants.

- Incumbents possess substantial resources to fight back, including excess cash and unused borrowing power, available productive capacity, or clout with distribution channels and customers.

- Incumbents seem likely to cut prices because they want to retain market shares or because the industry as a whole has excess capacity.

- Industry growth is slow so that newcomers must gain volume by taking it from incumbents.

Entry barriers should be assessed *relative* to the capabilities of potential entrants, who may be foreign firms or companies in related industries. And, as some of our examples illustrate, the strategist must be mindful of how newcomers might find creative ways to circumvent apparent barriers.

The Power of Suppliers

Suppliers can exert bargaining power by raising prices, shifting costs downstream to industry participants, or limiting the quality of the goods and services they provide. Powerful suppliers can thereby squeeze profitability out of an industry that is unable to pass on cost increases in its own prices. Microsoft, for instance, has contributed to the erosion of profitability among personal computer makers by raising prices on operating systems. The PC makers, competing fiercely for customers who can easily switch among them, have limited freedom to raise *their* prices accordingly.

An industry will depend on multiple groups of suppliers, including suppliers of labor. The power of each important supplier group depends on a number of structural characteristics of the industry. A supplier group is powerful if:

- It is more concentrated than the industry it sells to. Microsoft's near-monopoly in operating systems, coupled with fragmentation among PC-making customers, exemplifies this situation.

- Industry participants face switching costs in changing suppliers. For example, they might have invested heavily in specialized ancillary equipment or in learning how to operate a supplier's equipment (as in Bloomberg terminals used by financial professionals or computer-aided design software packages). Or they may have connected their production lines to supplier's manufacturing facilities (as in some production of beverage containers). When switching costs are high, industry participants find it hard to play suppliers off against one another, and suppliers are then positioned to extract profits from an industry.

- Suppliers offer products that are differentiated. Pharmaceutical makers, each with patented drugs that offer different medical benefits, have more power over hospitals, health maintenance organizations, and other drug buyers, for example, than do suppliers who produce me-too products.

- There are no substitutes to what the supplier group provides. Pilots' unions, for example, exercise considerable supplier power over airlines partly because there are no good alternatives to a well-trained pilot in the cockpit.

- The supplier group can credibly threaten to integrate forward into the industry. Here, if industry participants make too much money relative to suppliers, they will only induce suppliers to enter the market.

- The supplier group does not depend heavily on the industry. Suppliers serving many industries will not hesitate to extract maximum profits from each one. If a particular industry accounts for a large portion of a supplier group's volume or profit, however, suppliers' fortunes will be closely tied to that industry. They will want to protect the industry through reasonable pricing and assistance in activities like R&D and lobbying.

The Power of Customers

Analogous to suppliers, powerful customers can force down prices, demand higher quality or more service (thereby driving up costs), and play competitors off against each other—all at the expense of industry profits. As with suppliers, groups of customers may differ in their bargaining power. Customers are powerful if (1) they have clout relative to industry participants and especially if (2) they emphasize price reductions as the means to exercise their clout.

A customer group has clout if:

- It is concentrated or purchases in volumes that are large relative to the size of a single vendor. Large-volume buyers are particularly powerful if heavy fixed costs characterize an industry—as they do in telecommunications equipment, large-scale software development, and bulk chemicals; this amplifies the need to keep capacity filled.

- The industry's products are standard or undifferentiated. If buyers believe they can always find equivalent suppliers, they tend to play one vendor against another. In overnight delivery, shippers pit UPS, Federal Express, and DHL against each other.

- Buyers face few switching costs in changing vendors.

- Buyers have a credible threat of integrating backward to produce the industry's product themselves if vendors are too profitable. The makers of soft drinks and beer have long controlled the power of can makers by threatening to make, and at times actually making, cans themselves.

A customer group is price-sensitive if:

- The products it purchases from the industry represent a significant fraction of its cost or expenditures. Here buyers are likely to bargain hard for a favorable price, as consumers do for home mortgages. Where the product sold by an industry is a small fraction of buyers' costs or expenditures, buyers are usually much less price sensitive.

- The customer group earns low profits, is strapped for cash, or is otherwise under pressure to trim its purchasing costs. Highly profitable or cash-rich buyers, in contrast, are generally less price sensitive (that is, of course, if the item does not represent a large fraction of their costs). Internet content providers, for instance, became far more selective and powerful buyers of computer equipment after the Internet bubble burst and capital became scarcer.

- The quality of the buyers' products or services is little affected by the industry's product. Where the quality of the buyers' products is very much affected by the industry's product, buyers are generally less price sensitive. When buying or renting production-quality cameras, for instance, makers of major motion pictures opt for equipment made by vendors with strong reputations for quality. They pay limited attention to price.

- The buyer's overall costs are not significantly affected by the industry. Where an industry's product or service can pay for itself many times over, the buyer is usually more interested in quality than in price. This is true in businesses like the logging of oil wells, where an accurate survey can save thousands of dollars in drilling costs, and in services like investment banking and public accounting, where poor performance can be costly and embarrassing.

Most of these sources of buyer power apply to consumers, not just to industrial and commercial buyers. Consumers tend to be more price sensitive if they are purchasing products that are undifferentiated, expensive relative to their incomes, and of a sort where product performance has limited consequences. Channels can also be analyzed the same way, with one important addition. Channels gain significant bargaining power over upstream manufacturers when they influence the purchasing decisions of downstream customers, as they do in consumer electronics and jewelry retailing and in agricultural equipment distribution. Where channels are powerful, exclusive arrangements often arise as producers attempt to mitigate this clout.

The Threat of Substitutes

A substitute performs the same or a similar function as an industry's product but by a different means. Videoconferencing is a substitute for travel, plastic is a substitute for aluminum, and email is a substitute for express mail, for example. Substitutes are easy to overlook because they may look very different from the industry's product: to someone searching for a Father's Day gift, neckties and power tools may be substitutes. Substitutes nearly always exist. Many times, one substitute is to do without a product, and another is for customers to perform a service for themselves.

Substitute products or services limit an industry's profit potential by placing a ceiling on the prices that the companies in an industry can charge. An industry must distance itself from substitutes via performance or marketing or it will suffer in terms of earnings and possibly growth.

The more attractive is the price-performance trade-off offered by substitute products, the tighter is the lid placed on the industry's profit potential. Sugar producers confronted with the large-scale commercialization of high-fructose corn syrup, a sugar substitute, learned this lesson in the 1970s and 1980s. More recently, conventional providers of long-distance telephone service have suffered from the advent of Internet-based phone services such as Skype and Vonage. Similarly, video rental outlets are struggling with the emergence of video-on-demand services offered by cable and satellite television service providers and the rise of Internet video sites such as Google Video and YouTube.

Substitutes not only limit profits in normal times; they also reduce the bonanza an industry can reap in good times while constraining the size of the industry. In emerging economies, for example, the surge in demand for wired telephone lines has been capped as many consumers have opted to make a mobile telephone their first and only phone line.

Substitute products that deserve the most strategic attention are those that (a) are subject to trends improving their price-performance trade-off with the industry's product, or (b) are produced by industries reaping high profits which may erode with competition. Substitutes can rapidly come into play if intensifying competition in their industry causes price reduction or performance improvement. For example, fierce competition among Internet portals in the late 1990s led to quick introduction of free email services by the likes of Yahoo!, Microsoft, and Lycos, affecting substitutes like fax machines and express mail service.

Rivalry among Existing Competitors

Rivalry among existing competitors takes many familiar forms: price discounting, new product introductions, advertising campaigns, service escalation, and so forth. The degree to which rivalry undermines an industry's profit potential depends, first, on the basis on which companies compete and, second, on the intensity with which they compete. Price is typically the most destructive basis of competition for industry profitability. Price reductions transfer profits directly from an industry to its customers, and they are usually easy for competitors to see and match, making successive rounds of retaliatory cuts more likely. Conversely, competition on services or features can allow industry competitors to support good margins.

Industry competition gravitates to price if:

- The product or service lacks differentiation or switching costs. This makes it easy for buyers to shift vendors and encourages competitors to believe that a modest price cut will bring many new customers. Years of airline price wars reflect these circumstances in that industry.

- Fixed costs are high and marginal costs are low. This creates intense pressures for competitors to cut prices below their average costs, even close to their marginal costs, in order to steal incremental customers who will make some contribution to covering fixed costs. Many basic materials businesses, like paper and aluminum, suffer from this problem, especially when demand slackens.

- Capacity must be expanded in large increments. The need for large capacity expansions, as in the chloride and vinyl chloride businesses, disrupts the industry's supply-demand balance and often leads to periods of overcapacity and price cutting.

- The product is perishable. Perishability creates a strong temptation to cut prices and sell a product while it still has value. More products and services are perishable than is commonly thought. Just as tomatoes are perishable because they rot quickly, models of computers are perishable because they quickly becomes obsolete; airline seats are perishable because they are worthless if not sold by flight time; and information may be perishable if it diffuses and thereby loses its value. Indeed, many services are perishable in the sense that unused capacity can never be recovered.

Regardless of whether price is a primary basis of competition, the intensity of competition is greatest if:

- Competitors are numerous or are roughly equal in size and power. In such a situation, rivals find it hard to avoid poaching business. Without an industry leader, practices desirable for the industry go unenforced.

- Industry growth is slow. Slow growth precipitates fights for market share. Slow or negative growth in popular music in the 2000s has intensified rivalry, and pressure on profitability is driving consolidation in the industry.

- Exit barriers are high. Exit barriers, the flip side of entry barriers, arise because of very specialized assets or management's devotion to a particular business. These barriers keep companies competing even though they may be earning low or even negative returns on investment. Excess capacity remains in use, and the profitability of the healthy competitors suffers as the sick ones hang on.

- Rivals are highly committed to the business but have diverse approaches, origins, and "personalities." With different ideas about how to compete, rivals continually run head-on into each other. Clashes of personalities and egos have sometimes exaggerated rivalry in fields such as the media and high technology.

Industry Structure in Context

Industry structure, manifested in the strength of the five competitive forces, determines an industry's long-run profit potential because the forces shape the division of value among industry actors—whether profit is constrained by substitutes or new entrants, bargained away by customers or suppliers, or competed away by rivals. By considering all five forces, a strategist keeps overall structure in mind instead of gravitating to any one element. In addition, attention is paid to long-run industry conditions rather than fleeting factors; industry structure is reflected in profitability over a business cycle, not in a single year.

In assessing industry competition, analysts are often drawn to a number of industry attributes. These attributes can be highly salient, but their significance depends on their effect on the competitive forces. Consider, for instance:

Industry growth rate A common mistake is to assume that fast-growing industries are attractive industries. Growth *does* tend to mute rivalry because an expanding pie offers opportunities for all competitors. The full effect of growth, however, depends on how growth influences overall industry structure. Fast growth can put suppliers in a powerful position, and high growth with low entry barriers will draw in entrants. Even without new entry, a high growth rate certainly does not guarantee profitability if customers are powerful or substitutes are attractive. Indeed, some fast-growth businesses such as the personal computer industry have been among the least profitable industries in recent years.

Government   Government involvement is not inherently good or bad for industry profitability, nor is government best understood as a sixth force. Instead, it is often most fruitful to analyze each specific government policy to see whether it improves or undermines industry structure. Either effect is possible. For instance, patents raise barriers to entry, boosting industry profit potential. Conversely, government policies favoring unions may raise supplier power and diminish profit potential. Bankruptcy rules that allow failing companies to reorganize rather than exit can lead to excess capacity and intense rivalry. The best way to understand the influence of government on competition is to analyze how present government policies affect the competitive forces.

Technology and innovation   Technology or innovations alone are not themselves enough to make an industry structurally attractive (or unattractive). The impact of technology on industry attractiveness depends on how the technology affects the full set of competitive forces. Mundane, low-technology industries are often far more profitable than sexy industries such as software and internet technology that attract competitors.

The role of complementary products and services   Often an industry's product or service is used together with others produced by different industries. Computer hardware and software, for instance, are valuable together and worthless when separated. Personal digital assistants (PDAs) are valuable on their own, but their value is enhanced by thousands of applications that third-party developers have created. When the value of two products together is greater than the sum of each product's value in isolation, we say that the two are complements.

In recent years, strategy researchers have highlighted the role of complements, especially in high-technology industries.[1] By no means, however, do complements appear only in high-tech industries. The value of a car, for example, is greater when the driver also has access to gasoline stations, paved roads, spare parts, auto insurance, a car navigation system, and so forth.

Complements are always important in affecting the overall demand for an industry's product. Especially when demand is small or stagnant, firms should encourage the provision of complements, and sometimes produce complementary products themselves or partner with other firms to do so. Michelin, for example, began publishing its now-famous guidebooks in order to encourage travel by car and boost demand for its tires. More recently, Intel invested in companies that produce equipment for videoconferencing via computers. Intel's leaders realized that such computers would require high-end microprocessors, most likely made by Intel.

While the availability of complements boosts demand, complements have an ambiguous effect on overall industry structure. In computers, for example, operating systems and microprocessors are complements. Each industry would benefit if the other industry were more competitive, with lower prices and less profit. Hence makers of operating systems and microprocessors have incentives to spur on rivalry in each other's industry. Similarly, operating systems are complements to application software. Microsoft eagerly provides tool sets that make it easier to write applications for Windows, which lowers the barriers to entry into the application software industry. As these examples illustrate, complements are neither inherently good or inherently bad for industry profit potential.

---

[1] See especially Adam Brandenburger and Barry Nalebuff, *Co-opetition* (New York: Currency/Doubelday, 1996). For treatments focused on high-tech industries, see Annabel Gawer and Michael Cusumano, *Platform Leadership* (Boston: Harvard Business School Press, 2002); and David S. Evans, Andrei Hagiu, and Richard Schmalensee, *Invisible Engines: How Software Platforms Drive Innovation and Transform Industries* (Cambridge: MIT Press, 2006).

Rather, their effect on industry profitability depends on how they influence the five competitive forces.

Effective strategists look for opportunities to alter conditions in complementary industries in their favor—by boosting demand, improving overall structure, or advancing a firm's relative standing within its industry. In the market for PDAs, for example, Palm beat out other makers largely because it promoted third-party applications and enabled its product to synch with desktop computers— thereby making computers a complement for PDAs rather than a substitute. In the early days of the videocassette recorder, sets of firms led by JVC and Sony battled to determine whose recording standard would be dominant. JVC realized that prerecorded tapes were a key complement to a VCR. The company convinced movie studios to favor its standard when releasing taped films to video stores. This effort to influence a complementary product helped to tip the VCR market toward JVC even though Sony's standard was probably superior from a technical perspective.

Changes in Industry Structure

So far, we have discussed the competitive forces at a single point in time. Industry structure proves to be relatively stable, and industry profitability differences are remarkably persistent in practice. However, industry structure is constantly undergoing modest adjustment and occasionally changes abruptly. Shifts in structure sometimes emanate from outside an industry due to technological, customer, or other developments. In other cases, choices or innovations from within the industry culminate in a new structure. Sometimes industry structural change boosts the profit potential of an industry; sometimes change reduces it. The five competitive forces provide a framework for identifying those industry developments that are most important and for anticipating their impact on industry attractiveness.

Shifting threat of new entry   Changes to any of the seven entry barriers described above can raise or lower the threat of new entry. The expiration of a patent, for instance, may unleash new entrants. On the first day that Merck's patents for the cholesterol reducer Zocor expired, three pharmaceutical makers entered the market for the drug. Conversely, proliferation of products in the ice cream industry has filled up the limited freezer space in grocery stores, making it harder for new ice cream makers to gain access to distribution in North America and Europe.

Strategic decisions of leading competitors often have a major impact on the threat of entry. Starting in the 1970s, for example, retailers such as Wal-Mart, Kmart, and Toys R Us began to adopt new distribution and inventory-control technologies with large fixed costs, including automated distribution centers, bar coding, and point-of-sale terminals. These investments increased the economies of scale in retailing and made it more difficult for small retailers to enter the business (and for existing small players to survive).

Changing supplier and buyer power   As the factors underlying supplier and buyer power change with time, their power rises or declines. In the global appliance industry, for instance, competitors including Electrolux, General Electric, and Whirlpool have been squeezed by the consolidation of retail channels (e.g., the decline of appliance specialty stores and the rise of big-box retailers such as Best Buy and Home Depot in the United States). At the same time, rising global demand for appliance-grade steel, driven by such things as the rapid growth of China, has made suppliers more powerful, at least in the short run.

Shifting substitution threat   The most common reason that substitutes become more or less threatening over time is that advances in technology create new substitutes or shift price-performance comparisons in one direction or another. The earliest microwave ovens, for example, were large and priced above $2,000, making them poor substitutes for conventional ovens. With technological advances, they are now serious substitutes. Flash computer memory has improved enough recently to be a meaningful substitute for low-capacity hard disk drives.

New bases of rivalry Rivalry often intensifies naturally over time. As an industry matures, growth slows. Competitors become more similar as industry conventions emerge, technology diffuses, and consumer tastes converge. Industry profitability falls, and weaker competitors are driven from the business. This story has been played out in industry after industry; televisions, snowmobiles, aerosol packaging, and telecommunications equipment are just a few examples.

It is not inevitable, however, that industries will trend toward more intense rivalry, and especially toward price-based rivalry. The U.S. casino industry has seen enormous competitive activity in recent decades, but most of it has been directed toward new geographic segments and niches (e.g., riverboats, trophy properties, Native American reservations, international expansion, and novel customer groups such as families). Head-to-head rivalry that lowers prices or boosts payouts to customers has been limited.

Mergers and acquisitions can also alter the nature of rivalry in an industry. In the global petroleum industry, for instance, mergers of Exxon and Mobil, British Petroleum and Amoco, Chevron and Texaco, and Conoco and Phillips have raised concerns among consumer advocates and some policymakers about the possibility of muted competition. Technological innovation is another factor in reshaping rivalry. In the retail brokerage industry, the advent of the Internet triggered far more intense competition on commissions and fees than in the past.

Implications for Strategy

Understanding the forces that shape competition in an industry is the starting point for developing strategy. It reveals the most salient aspects of the competitive environment and the crucial constraints to overall profitability. It highlights the industry changes that pose the greatest threats and opportunities.

Industry structure also provides a baseline for sizing up a company's strength and weaknesses: where does the company stand versus buyers, suppliers, entrants, rivals, and substitutes? Most importantly, an understanding of industry structure guides managers toward possibilities for strategic action, including (1) positioning the company vis-à-vis the current competitive forces; (2) anticipating shifts in the forces and exploiting them; and (3) shaping the balance of forces to create a new more favorable structure or one that favors the company.

Positioning the Company

Industry structure reveals insights for positioning. Here, strategy can be viewed as building defenses against the competitive forces or as finding a position in an industry where the forces are weakest.

Consider, for instance, the position of PACCAR in the market for heavy trucks. The heavy truck industry is structurally challenging. Many buyers are large fleets or leasing companies, with a keen interest and the clout to drive down the price for one of their largest purchases. Many trucks are built to regulated standards and offer similar features, so price competition is rampant. Capital intensity causes rivalry among competitors to be fierce, especially during the cyclical downturns in demand.

Unions exercise considerable supplier power. Though there are few direct substitutes for an 18-wheeler, truck buyers face important substitutes for their service, such as cargo delivery by rail.

In this tough setting, PACCAR, a Bellevue, Washington-based company with about 20% of the North American heavy truck market, has chosen to concentrate on owner-operators: drivers who own their own trucks and contract directly with shippers or are subcontractors to larger trucking companies. Such individuals have limited bargaining power, and take great pride in and live for long stretches in their trucks. Owner-operators tend to be willing to pay more for amenities and customization. PACCAR has invested heavily to develop an array of special features: luxurious sleeper cabins, plush leather seats, noise-insulated cabins, sleek exterior styling, and so on. At the company's extensive network of dealers, prospective buyers use software to select among thousands of options. Orders are conveyed to PACCAR's factories, where customized trucks are built to order, not to stock, and delivered in 6 to 8 weeks. Customers pay PACCAR a 10% premium for its trucks, and not only because its Kenworth- and Peterbilt-branded trucks are considered status symbols at truck stops. PACCAR's trucks also have aerodynamic designs that reduce fuel consumption, and they maintain their resale value better than other trucks. PACCAR's roadside assistance program and its IT-supported system for distributing spare parts reduce the time a truck is out of service (a crucial consideration for an owner-operator). PACCAR complements its other activities by helping owner-operators with financing their trucks.

PACCAR illustrates the essence of positioning a company within a given industry structure. PACCAR has found a portion of its industry where competitive forces are weaker—where it can avoid buyer power and price-based rivalry. And it has tailored every single internal function to cope well with the forces in that part of the industry. As a result, PACCAR has been profitable for 68 straight years and has earned a long-run return on equity above 20%.

Exploiting Industry Change

Industry change brings with it the opportunity to spot and claim promising strategic new positions. The rise of Dell's direct distribution model in the personal computer industry, for example, exploited a number of industry trends. An increase in customer knowledge of PCs led more corporate customers to want unique specifications and not require third-party resellers. Increasing reliance on standardized and modular inputs, coupled with declining component prices, opened an opportunity for Dell to build customized computers to order.

To tap the opportunities posed by industry change, a strategist needs a sophisticated understanding of competitive forces and their underpinnings. Consider, for instance, the evolution of the music industry during the past decade. With the advent of the Internet and digital distribution of music, some analysts predicted the birth of thousands of music labels (that is, record companies that develop artists and bring their music to market). This, the analysts argued, would break a pattern that had held since Edison invented the phonograph: between three and six major record companies have always dominated the industry. The Internet would remove distribution of music as a barrier to entry, unleashing a flood of new players.

A careful analysis, however, would have revealed that physical distribution was not the crucial barrier to entry. Rather, entry was barred by other benefits that large music labels enjoyed. Large labels could pool the risks of developing new artists over many bets, cushioning themselves from the impact of inevitable failures. Even more important, they had advantages in breaking through the clutter and getting their new artists heard. To do so, they could promise radio stations and record stores access to well-known artists in exchange for promotion of new artists. New entrants would find this nearly impossible to match. Since digital distribution became a significant issue, new music labels have been rare and the number of major record companies has *declined*—from six in 1997 to four today.

This is not to say that the music industry is structurally unchanged by digital distribution. Piracy and unauthorized downloading created illegal but potent substitutes. The labels tried for years to develop technical platforms for digital distribution themselves, but major companies hesitated to sell their music through a platform owned by a rival. Into this vacuum stepped Apple with its iTunes music store, launched in 2003. iTunes and its recent imitators have become a potentially powerful channel.

When industries are in flux, the framework for analyzing industry structure can not only point a company toward promising positions within its existing industry but can also help the company weigh diversification into other industries. The framework provides a road map for answering the extremely difficult question inherent in diversification decisions: "What is the potential of this business?" Using the framework, creative strategists may be able to spot an industry with a good future before this good future is reflected in the prices of acquisition candidates. Industry structure analysis may also reveal industries that are not necessarily attractive for the average entrant, but where the company itself has reason to believe that it can surmount entry barriers at lower cost than most firms or has a unique ability to cope with the competitive forces there.

Shaping Industry Structure

Exploiting structural change is recognizing, and reacting to, the inevitable. But companies also have the ability to *shape* industry structure. A company can lead its industry toward new ways of competing that alter the five forces for the better. As rivals follow, the entire industry can be transformed. In the process, many industry participants may benefit. Yet the innovator may benefit more by shifting competition in directions where it can excel.

All of the competitive forces are subject to influence. To neutralize supplier power, for example, companies in an industry may establish clear standards for producing inputs, sponsor second-source suppliers, or backward-integrate into production of some inputs. To counter customer power, companies may enhance services that also raise switching costs. Product or service features can be designed that open up more distance from substitutes or establish weapons other than price as the basis for competition. To scare off entrants, incumbents can raise the fixed cost of competing—for instance, by escalating their R&D or marketing expenditures.

As an example of shaping industry structure, consider the long-running efforts of Intel in the market for computer microprocessors. Intel's immediate customers are computer makers like Dell, Hewlett-Packard, and Lenovo. Over the years, however, it has spent billions of dollars on its "Intel Inside" advertising campaign focused on computer users—its customers' customers. This has created brand loyalty to Intel's microprocessors among consumers, and the loyalty makes it harder for PC makers to switch to rival chip producers like AMD. In selling microprocessors, Intel has also maintained what it calls a "level playing field": all PC makers, regardless of size, buy microprocessors from Intel at the same price, with no volume discounts. This makes entry easier for PC makers and controls the growth of customer power. By investing enormous sums in R&D and fabrication plants and by making its own products obsolete quickly, Intel has made entry into microprocessors very costly and has made performance, not just price, an important dimension of rivalry. Performance-based rivalry tends to favor large competitors like Intel, with the greatest ability to invest in performance improvements. Nevertheless, rival AMD has gained ground as Intel's execution has slipped.

Sysco, the leading food service distributor in North America, offers another revealing example. Food service distributors purchase food and related items from food processors and farmers. They then deliver them to restaurants, cafeterias, schools, and other food service institutions. With low barriers to entry, the industry has historically been highly fragmented, with numerous local competitors. Rivals try to cultivate customer relationships, but buyers are price sensitive because food represents a large share of costs. Buyers can also choose the substitute approaches of buying direct or using retail sources. Food suppliers wield bargaining power: they are often large, and they own strong brand names that food preparers and consumers recognize. Average profitability in the industry has been modest.

Sysco recognized that, with its size and national reach, it might change this state of affairs. It led moves to introduce private-label distributor brands, mitigating supplier power. It emphasized value-added services such as credit, menu planning, and inventory management to shift rivalry away from just price. These moves, together with stepped up investments in information technology and regional distribution centers, substantially raised the bar for new entrants, while making the substitutes less attractive. Not surprising, the industry has been consolidating, and industry profitability appears to be rising.

Industry leaders have a special responsibility for improving industry structure. Doing so often requires resources, credibility, and clout that only large players possess. Moreover, an improved industry structure is partly a "public good": it may benefit every firm in the industry, not just the company that initiated the improvement. Often, only a significant firm in an industry has enough motivation to invest for the common good, for leaders are likely to benefit the most from industry improvement. A common error among industry leaders is to focus more on preserving the status quo or improving one's own position than on leading the industry in favorable directions.

There is also a dark side to shaping industry structure that is equally important to understand. Ill-advised changes in practices and ways of competing can undermine industry structure, instead of improving it. Facing pressures to gain market share or enamored with innovation for its own sake, managers can spark new kinds of competition that no incumbent can win. When taking actions to improve their own company's competitive advantage, industry leaders should ask whether they are setting in motion dynamics that will undermine industry structure in the long run. In the early days of the personal computer industry, for instance, IBM tried to make up for its late entry by offering an open architecture that would set industry standards and attract complementary makers of application software and peripherals. In the process, it gave ownership of the critical pieces of the PC—the operating system and the microprocessor—to Microsoft and Intel. By standardizing PCs, it encouraged price-based rivalry. Consequently, IBM became the temporarily dominant firm in an industry with an enduringly unattractive structure.

Defining Competition

Numerous authorities have stressed the need to look beyond product to function in defining a business, to look beyond national boundaries to potential international competition, and to see beyond the ranks of one's competitors today to those that may become competitors tomorrow. Inherent in these exhortations is the fear of overlooking latent sources of competition that someday may threaten the industry. Yet the issue is an even bigger one. Many managers concentrate so single-mindedly on their direct antagonists in the fight for market share that they fail to realize that they are also competing with their customers and their suppliers for bargaining power and they are also battling the subtle threat of substitute products.

The broad view of competitive forces offered here is an antidote for such thinking. A strategist who sees rivalry as extending well beyond existing competitors will detect wider competitive threats. A strategist who understands the structural underpinnings of each competitive force will be equipped to analyze these threats. At the same time, industry-structure thinking reveals differences in customers, suppliers, substitutes, potential entrants, and rivals that demark distinct competitive arenas in which distinct strategies are needed, and sometimes an entirely different industry. In a world of more open competition and relentless change, it is more important than ever to think structurally about competition.

Exhibit 1   Histogram of Return on Invested Capital among U.S. Industries

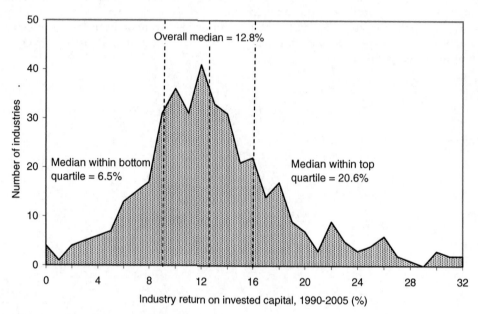

Source: Standard & Poor's Compustat, author's calculations
Note: Return on invested capital is calculated as earnings before interest and taxes divided by the sum of long-term debt,
total equity, and minority interest

Creating Corporate Advantage

by David J. Collis and Cynthia A. Montgomery

 Harvard Business Review

Reprint 98303

*How can you tell
if your company is really
more than the sum of its parts?*

CREATING
CORPORATE
ADVANTAGE

BY DAVID J. COLLIS AND CYNTHIA A. MONTGOMERY

MOST MULTIBUSINESS COMPANIES ARE the sum of their parts and nothing more. Although executives have become more sophisticated in their understanding of what it takes to achieve competitive advantage at the level of individual businesses, when it comes to creating *corporate* advantage across multiple businesses, the news is far less encouraging.

True, corporate executives face mounting pressure from their boards and from capital markets to add value. To date, however, that pressure has had the greatest impact on corporate strategy in pathological companies such as ITT, where the *destruction* of value was so great that it had to be stopped.

What has slipped under the radar are those companies – the majority, we would argue – that don't destroy value at the corporate level, but neither do they create it.

That failure is not for lack of trying. Indeed, in many of the 50 companies we studied during a six-year research project, corporate executives were struggling to create viable corporate strategies. Some were working on their core competencies, others were restructuring their corporate portfolios, and still others were building learning organizations. In each case, executives were focusing on individual elements of corporate strategy: resources, businesses, or organization. What was missing was the insight that turns those elements into an integrated whole. That insight is the essence of corporate advantage – the way a company creates value through the configuration and coordination of its multibusiness activities. Ultimately, it is what differentiates truly great corporate strategies from the merely adequate.

Choices Along
The Resource Continuum

An outstanding corporate strategy is not a random collection of individual building blocks but a carefully constructed system of interdependent parts. More than a powerful idea, it actively directs executives' decisions about the resources the corporation will develop, the businesses the corporation will compete in, and the organization that will make it all come to life.

But there's more to it than that: in a great corporate strategy, all of these elements are aligned with one another. That alignment is driven by the nature of the firm's resources – its special assets, skills, and capabilities. The firm's resources are the unifying thread, the element that ultimately determines the others. (See the exhibit "The Triangle of Corporate Strategy.")

The resources that provide the basis for corporate advantage range along a continuum – from the highly specialized at one end to the very general at the other. Sharp Corporation, the Japanese electronics company, has specialized technological

David J. Collis *is a visiting associate professor at Yale University's School of Management in New Haven, Connecticut.* ***Cynthia A. Montgomery*** *is the John G. McLean Professor of Business Administration at the Harvard Business School in Boston, Massachusetts. They are the authors of the textbook* Corporate Strategy, Resources and the Scope of the Firm *(Irwin, 1997) and "Competing on Resources" (HBR July–August 1995).*

THE TRIANGLE OF CORPORATE STRATEGY

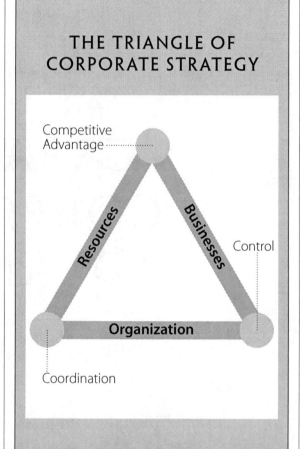

Great corporate strategies come in the first instance from strength in each side of the triangle: high-quality rather than pedestrian resources, strong market positions in attractive industries, and an efficient administrative organization. But true corporate advantage requires a tight fit at each angle as well. When a company's resources are critical to the success of its businesses, the result is competitive advantage. When the organization is configured to leverage those resources into the businesses, synergy can be captured and coordination achieved. Finally, fit between a company's measurement and reward systems and its businesses produces strategic control.

THE RESOURCE CONTINUUM

The resources that provide the basis for corporate advantage range along a continuum – from the highly specialized at one end to the very general at the other. A corporation's location on the continuum constrains the set of businesses it should compete in and limits its choices about the design of its organization along the other dimensions below.

general ← **nature of resources** → **specialized**

wide ← **scope of businesses** → **narrow**

Companies with specialized resources will compete in a narrower range of businesses than companies with more general resources.

transferring ← **coordination mechanisms** → **sharing**

The more general the resource, the more likely the company can effectively deploy it through transfer rather than sharing.

financial ← **control systems** → **operating**

As resources become more specialized, the value of moving from financial to operating controls increases.

small ← **corporate office size** → **large**

The more general the resources and the less the need for sharing, the smaller the corporate office should be.

expertise in optoelectronics that gives each of its businesses a competitive advantage. Tyco International, a conglomerate at the opposite end of the continuum, creates value for its businesses through a set of general management skills and a system of corporate governance. (See the exhibit "The Resource Continuum.")

This continuum of strategic resources is important because a corporation's location on the continuum constrains the set of businesses it should compete in and limits its choices about the design of its organization. Our research suggests that most executives think they're getting the alignment of their corporate strategies right, when in fact they are not. They mistakenly enter businesses based on similarities in products rather than similarities in the resources that contribute to competitive advantage in each business. It is a common – and costly – mistake. (See the insert "Relatedness Is About Resources, Not Products.") Moreover, instead of tailoring organizational structures and systems to the needs of a particular strategy, they create plain-vanilla corporate offices and infrastructures as if there were one best practice that every company should follow. The current fashion happens to favor a lean, minimalist corporate office – but, as we shall see, one size does not fit all.

Far from it. One can find great corporate strategies in companies all along the continuum. Some companies may fit the lean mode, while others require richer and deeper infrastructures. Consider the Newell Company, whose resources are neither exceedingly general nor specific but an attractive mixture of both.

Newell's Corporate Advantage

In 1966, Daniel Ferguson, a Stanford M.B.A., became CEO of Newell, an old-line manufacturer of brass curtain rods. The company had revenues of $14 million, a limited product line of drapery hardware, and no articulated strategy for the future. Ferguson began to develop a "build on what we do best" philosophy. At the time, Newell was selling extensively to Woolworth's and to Kresge (later Kmart). Ferguson foresaw the trend toward consolidation in the retail business and envisioned a role for Newell: "We realized we knew how to make a high-volume, low-cost product, and we knew how to relate to and sell to the large mass retailer."

In July 1967, Ferguson wrote out his strategy for Newell, identifying its focus as the market for hardware and do-it-yourself products. The company then made its first nondrapery hardware acquisition – Mirra-Cote, a producer of bath hardware – in order to gain access to new discount outlets for Newell's existing products. Over the next three decades, more than 75 acquisitions followed, all guided by Ferguson's carefully articulated strategy of 1967: "Newell defines its basic business as that of manufacturing and distributing volume merchandise lines to the volume merchandisers. A

RELATEDNESS IS ABOUT RESOURCES, NOT PRODUCTS

Mercury Measures – an actual company whose name has been disguised – makes industrial thermostats. Not long ago, growth prospects in its core markets had flattened. But not all was bleak. Mercury's head of marketing was forecasting strong growth in the demand for household thermostats. For Mercury's management team, pursuing such a natural extension of the company's current business was a no-brainer.

Three years and lots of red ink later, Mercury had to write off the business. Why? At first glance, the strategy had made good sense. Mercury would remain a thermostat producer, adding only an additional product line. But a more careful and more rigorous look reveals that the fit between the two businesses was not at all close.

Mercury had all the factors needed for success in industrial thermostats: strong R&D capabilities; expertise in strict tolerance, made-to-order production;

and a technically sophisticated sales force of industrial engineers. Although Mercury was able to leverage some of its technological know-how when it entered the household market, R&D was not critical for success in that market, nor did it constitute a significant portion of the added value.

Moreover, Mercury lacked the resources necessary to be competitive in household thermostats. It had no expertise in design, product appearance, or packaging; it lacked the capabilities for mass production; and it didn't know how to distribute products through industry representatives to mass marketers and contractors.

Like Mercury, companies often err by expanding into market segments that appear to be related to their existing businesses but in fact are quite different. In particular, they tend to make this mistake when they define relatedness according to product characteristics rather than resources.

combination or package of lines going to the large retailers carries more marketing impact than each line separately, and Newell intends to build its growth through performance and marketing leverage of this package."

Although that strategy has been reviewed annually, its basic tenets have remained largely unchanged. Steadily pursuing this vision, Newell had sales of nearly $3 billion by 1997 and was ranked twenty-second on the *Fortune* 500 in ten-year total return to shareholders. A review of Newell's corporate strategy reveals why.

Resources and Businesses. Today the products Newell makes range from propane torches to hair barrettes to office products. That may appear to be a bizarre collection of unrelated items, yet Newell is far from being a conglomerate. The relatedness across its businesses comes not from similarities in the products themselves but from the common resources they draw on: Newell's relationships with discount retailers, its efficient high-volume manufacturing, and its superior service, including national coverage, on-time delivery, and program merchandising.

How do we know that Newell has the right balance of resources and businesses? Because the firm's corporate capabilities enhance the competitiveness of every business it owns. Many of the companies Newell has acquired were subpar performers. Under its ownership, typical operating margins have increased threefold, from about 5% to 15% or more.

The company's resources define the businesses that make sense for it to own and those that do not. Newell will never compete in high-tech, seasonal, or fashion products because they require skills the company doesn't have. Nor will it enter businesses whose dominant channel of distribution is outside discount retailing. Indeed, Newell sold off Wm. E. Wright, a profitable line of home sewing products, when its distribution shifted to specialty stores. This need for fit between resources and businesses constrains the set of businesses in which a company should operate but increases the likelihood that a multibusiness strategy will actually create value.

Organization. A great corporate strategy begins with a vision of how a company's resources will differentiate it from competitors across multiple businesses. But it must also articulate how to achieve that vision. In particular, what kinds of coordination and control must the company provide in order to effectively deploy its resources?

Most corporate-level executives understand the need to add value to their businesses, yet few put in place the organizational mechanisms to make that possible. Many executives are reluctant to violate the autonomy and accountability of independent business units. Others fear they will end up with large, bureaucratic overhead structures. Companies like Newell, however, achieve the benefits of coordination with modest organizational costs.

Coordination. Newell understands that the outright sharing of resources such as a common sales force is not always the best way to capture synergies. So Newell *transfers* critical resources through-

Most executives create plain-vanilla corporate offices as if there were one best practice that every company should follow.

out the firm without undermining the independence of its business units. (See the insert "Should Corporate Resources Be Shared or Transferred?")

Much of Newell's know-how and experience is embedded in its managers. To leverage that resource, Newell deliberately moves managers across business units and from the business to the corporate level. That practice enables Newell to transfer experience and to build a skilled in-house labor pool. Job openings are publicized widely within the company and usually are filled by in-house candidates. For Newell, the benefits of such transfers can be fully realized because of the commonalities across its businesses – and that is not an accident but a result of forethought.

Other transfers of learning occur when divisional leaders convene six times a year for presidents' meetings and when they meet one another at trade shows. Annual management meetings bring together functional vice presidents for sales and marketing, operations, personnel, control, and customer service from all divisions. Each functional group has its own two-day meeting, featuring presentations and programs aimed at transferring best practices across the divisions.

In contrast to its many resource transfers, the only activity Newell *shares* among its businesses is its advanced data-management system. Meeting the needs of its demanding customers for efficient logistics, billing, and collection is so central to Newell's strategy – and the activity is so scale sensi-

SHOULD CORPORATE RESOURCES BE SHARED OR TRANSFERRED?

Deploying key resources where they are important to the competitive advantage of individual businesses is at the heart of corporate strategy. Sometimes it makes sense for businesses to share a common resource, like a sales force or an MIS system. In other cases, resources can be transferred across businesses with a minimum of coordination. Knowing whether to transfer or share resources – and which mechanisms to use – is largely a question of what kind of resource you are trying to leverage.

A useful distinction can be made between resources that we call *public goods* and those we call *private goods*. By public goods, we mean, for example, brand names or best demonstrated practices – things that can be used in several businesses simultaneously without conflict. By private goods, we mean such things as a common sales force or component-manufacturing facility – resources that are much more difficult to manage and can lead to competition and conflicts between businesses.

Transferring public goods within a company can usually be done at arm's length with little intervention and coordination by the corporate office. Indeed, it may involve few, if any, explicit organizational mechanisms. For example, simply placing the Nike brand on a new line of sporting goods may convey a substantial competitive advantage to the business with relatively little effort on the part of the corporation. Other transfers can occur through occasional cross-business meetings and limited exchanges of information. When Disney introduces a new animated cartoon character, such as Hercules, the various Disney business units, from consumer products to theme parks, just need to be aware of one another's activities so that they don't conflict. Even the transfer of best practices, such as Newell's skills in inventory man-

tive – that the corporate office itself takes responsibility for those tasks and requires the divisions to accept its terms and conditions. All other operational activities, including sales, are the responsibility of Newell's 20 independent divisions. The company explicitly chose not to form one central sales force, fearing the consequences of lost autonomy and accountability at the business level.

Control Systems. The other element of infrastructure that plays an important role in corporate strategy is a firm's control systems. Without the appropriate control systems, the corporate center can quickly lose its ability to determine strategic direction and influence performance in the individual businesses. That is why choices about what to measure and reward are so important. Broadly speaking, corporations have the choice between two types of control systems: operating or financial. Understanding which one fits a company's particular resources and businesses is critical to creating corporate advantage. (See the insert "Financial Versus Operating Control.")

Newell's system of operating controls fits its strategy of leveraging the experience of senior managers. The system focuses on 30 operating variables that management believes are critical to the success of the businesses – and because the businesses have so many similarities, a single carefully tailored system can be applied to all of them.

For example, regardless of how a business unit is organized, Newell believes its SG&A expenses should never exceed 15%. All variances are bracketed, and too many variances lead to a "brackets meeting." Similarly, even if sales are above budget, managers will intervene if the fixed-cost numbers show an unfavorable variance. Senior managers are intimately involved in the oversight and monitoring of the businesses, principally through monthly performance reviews that allow them to add value in discussions with divisional managers.

Compensation systems are always central to control systems. Again, Newell's is aligned with its strategy. To facilitate transfers, compensation is uniform across divisions; base salaries are determined by position and division size. Newell holds individual managers and operating units accountable for performance, and it rewards excellence. Managers who make it over Newell's high hurdle for bonus payouts – by achieving at least a 32.5% return on assets – are handsomely rewarded for their efforts with bonuses of up to 100% of their base compensation.

Corporate Office. A thoughtful observer would understand Newell's corporate strategy by walking around its headquarters and noting who was there and what they were doing – a simple mirror of any strategy. In 1997, there were 375 people on Newell's corporate staff. Beyond a small cadre of highly expe-

agement and program merchandising, can be relatively straightforward. Experienced managers can move to the new division or a project team can act as consultants. Because there is no conflict in their use, and because even autonomous business units will actively seek to capitalize on such truly valuable corporate resources, transferring public goods can be done with relative ease, once the means for doing so are in place.

With public goods, the challenge is often in their development and preservation. Who should be responsible for the resource? How can you ensure that the necessary investments are being made? Should new practices be developed by the corporate office or allowed to flourish in many divisions before the best one is applied everywhere? It is also important to safeguard the use of some public goods, particularly intangible ones such as brand names or sets of relationships, so that one unit does not spoil or devalue the asset.

Private goods require more explicit coordination because the same resource is shared by multiple businesses and therefore its use by one unit can affect its use by another. Consider a corporate unit that buys materials for all divisions in order to exploit economies of scale in purchasing. Should Pepsico's three restaurants, Taco Bell, Pizza Hut, and KFC – recently spun off as Tricon Global Restaurants – jointly purchase toilet paper? If they did, they would save several hundred thousand dollars per year. Believe it or not, this simple decision took more than a year to resolve. One chain wanted one-ply tissue, another wanted two-ply, and the third did not care. This example is powerful precisely because it is so trivial. If it takes a year to reach a compromise agreement on a question like this, imagine how difficult and time consuming it can be to reach consensus on sharing something important, like a sales force.

rienced senior managers who interacted frequently with the business heads, most of those people worked on the company's centralized data-management systems, which were critical to the company's operations.

From the top down, Newell maintains a culture deeply permeated by the expectation that it will be a leader in serving the needs of discount retailers. It is a source of pride that a frequently asked question in the industry is, "Do you ship as well as Newell?" Nearly all of Newell's senior managers maintain high-level relationships with customers, not to sell a particular product but to "sell Newell." As Daniel Ferguson explains, "Like everything else we do in marketing to the mass retailer, the more they see us as an effective partner, the greater the edge we have when a certain product comes up for review."

For all the value Newell adds to its businesses, it levies a corporate charge of only 2% of sales, a number far below the increase in operating margins the divisions gain by being part of Newell. That sort of tangible value has enabled Newell to achieve a ten-year total return to investors of 31% per year, compared with an 18% average for the S&P 500.

The Lessons of Newell

What are the most important lessons of Newell's long-term success?

- First, corporate strategy is guided by a vision of how a firm, as a whole, will create value. When Daniel Ferguson first laid out Newell's strategy, the company's resources were modest at best. Ferguson made the commitment to invest in and build the resources that allowed Newell to compete in a changing market.
- Second, corporate strategy is a system of interdependent parts. Its success depends not only on the quality of the individual elements but also on how the elements reinforce one another.
- Third, corporate strategy must be consistent with, and capitalize on, opportunities outside the company. Newell caught the upswing in discount retailing 30 years ago; more recently, it adjusted its domestic focus to exploit the growth of other "category killers" such as Home Depot and the office products superstores.
- Fourth, the benefits of corporate membership must be greater than the costs. Most corporate advantages are realized in the enhanced performance of the business units. While better performance is often more difficult to measure than in Newell's case, corporations must determine if they are achieving it. If they are not, they are not creating real corporate advantage.

Looking closely at how the elements of Newell's strategy work as a system, we see that its resources are the unifying thread. It is the nature of Newell's

FINANCIAL VERSUS OPERATING CONTROL

There are two fundamentally different methods for monitoring and controlling the performance of subordinates and business units. The first, *financial control*, holds managers accountable for a limited number of objective output measures, such as return on assets or aggregate sales growth. The second, *operating control*, recognizes that all sorts of events outside managers' influence, such as the bankruptcy of a major customer, may affect their performance. Rather than measuring outputs, operating control is concerned with evaluating managers' decisions and actions. Thus after an unexpected recession, financial control would punish managers because profit was below budget, while operating control might reward them for anticipating the downturn and cutting inventories, even though they missed their budget targets.

While most companies use some mix of the two, successful corporate strategies tend to emphasize one or the other. That choice depends primarily on the nature of the businesses in the portfolio and the relative expertise of corporate executives.

Financial control is most appropriate in mature, stable industries and for discrete business units. For such businesses, a few financial variables accurately reflect their strategic positions. In fast-moving industries with high levels of uncertainty, financial control is less suitable. In high-tech businesses, for example, current financial results may not capture the loss of technological leadership. Such measures may also be problematic when results across units are interdependent.

Operating control typically involves both quantitative and qualitative assessments that capture the nuances of a particular business. To use operating control effectively, corporate managers have to be very familiar with the businesses in the firm's portfolio. Often the managers themselves will have extensive relevant operating experience.

Corporate managers may monitor dozens of line items such as reject rates, delivery lead times, and conversion statistics to assess the health of a business. The trade-offs among the targets may not be fully specified and the evaluation and incentive schemes may resemble more an implicit contract than a simple objective target.

Operating control systems require far more interaction between corporate and business unit managers. Through frequent strategic-planning sessions, operating reviews, and capital-budgeting discussions, corporate management can closely observe managers' performance and act as coaches and sounding boards. Not surprisingly, such systems place more demands on an organization and generally lead to somewhat larger corporate infrastructures.

In contrast, financial control systems are the easiest to implement and place the fewest demands on corporate management. The key is to establish discrete business units, to hold management accountable for outcomes, and to provide strong incentives for managers to meet their numbers. The archetype of such systems is the LBO, in which financial targets not only are agreed to within the firm but also are bound by covenants with external providers of capital.

No control system can be assessed in isolation. Rather, its effectiveness depends on its degree of fit with the company's particular set of resources and businesses.

---

resources that determines the businesses it should compete in, the design of Newell's organization, and the role the corporate office should play in the coordination and control of its businesses.

Sharing Resources at Sharp

Sharp Corporation, a $14 billion consumer-electronics giant, sits near the specialized end of the resource continuum. Seen at one time as a second-tier competitor by its Japanese rivals, Sharp's consistent pursuit of a vision of technological creativity has pushed it to the forefront of its industry.

Resources and Businesses. Sharp's valuable resources are a set of specialized optoelectronics technologies that contributes to the competitive advantage of the company's core businesses. Its most successful technology has been liquid crystal displays (LCDs), which are critical components in nearly all Sharp's products. The competitive advantage this resource confers is illustrated by Sharp's success in video recorders. Its breakthrough Viewcam was the first to incorporate an LCD viewfinder, an innovation that propelled Sharp to capture 20% of the Japanese market within six months of the product's introduction.

Atsushi Asada, a Sharp senior executive, described Sharp's technology strategy: "We invest in the technologies that will be the nucleus of the company in the future. Like a nucleus, such technologies should have an explosive power to multiply themselves across many products." By following this strategy, Sharp can successfully extend its scope into many new businesses, as long as competitive advantage in those businesses depends on one of its core technologies. For example, as an extension of its screen technology, Sharp created the personal electronic organizer with its Wizard product.

Like most companies that operate near the specialized end of the resource spectrum, Sharp's set of businesses is fairly restricted: television and video systems, communications and audio systems, appliances, information systems, and electronic components. Unlike its competitors Sony and Matsushita, Sharp has never considered entering the movie business because it knows it has no competitive advantage outside its technology base.

Organization. Sharp's technological investments share several characteristics: they tend to be expensive, they often have substantial lead times, and the advantages they confer in products may be short-lived because of imitation or brief life cycles. To be successful in such an environment, Sharp must make good investment choices and, to recoup its investment, it must leverage new technologies quickly and broadly throughout the company.

Hence Sharp has a corporate office, not counting corporate R&D, of more than 1,500 people. Judged by today's fashion for lean corporate staff, that number is bound to appear shockingly large. Sharp's strategy, however, depends critically on extensive, intricate coordination of its shared technological activities–thus the logic behind its headquarters staffing.

Coordination. The need to share activities determines Sharp's basic structure. Unlike Newell, Sharp is divided into functional units, not product divisions. As a result, applied research and manufacturing of key components, such as LCDs, occur in a single specialized unit where scale economies can be exploited. In contrast, Honeywell, a typical U.S. company organized by product divisions, at one time had LCD research activity in seven divisions.

To prevent the functional groups from becoming vertical chimneys that obstruct effective product development, Sharp employs product managers who have responsibility–but not authority–for coordinating the entire set of value chain activities. And the company convenes enormous numbers of cross-unit and corporate committees to ensure that shared activities, including the corporate R&D unit and sales forces, are optimally configured and allocated among the different product lines. Sharp invests in such time-intensive coordination to minimize the inevitable conflicts that arise when units share important activities.

Each year, nearly one-third of Sharp's corporate R&D budget is spent on 10 to 15 Gold Badge projects. These are selected at the corporate technical strategy meeting because they involve original technologies that cut across product groups. All project members are vested with the authority of the company president and wear his gold-colored badge so that they can call on people throughout Sharp for assistance.

Control Systems. Because of the blurred accountability that results from its functional structure, Sharp requires a very different control system than a simple divisional P&L. It has to employ an operating control system that focuses more on how people behave than on the short-term financial outcomes they achieve. Promotion, therefore, rather than annual compensation, is the most powerful incentive, and employees are promoted on the basis of seniority and subtle skills exhibited over time, such as teamwork and communication. In a technologically based company with a functional organization structure, this control system is one of the few that will not unduly reward a short-term, self-interested orientation.

Like many Japanese companies, Sharp's culture reinforces the view that the company is a family or community whose members should cooperate for the greater good. In accordance with the policy of lifetime employment, turnover is very low, which encourages employees to accommodate everyone's interests and to pursue what's best for the company overall. That common outlook reduces the inevitable conflict over sharing such important resources as R&D and component manufacturing.

> # Sharp has to employ an operating control system that focuses more on how people behave than on short-term financial outcomes.

Like Newell, Sharp is successful in leveraging resources throughout its organization but, consistent with the nature of its underlying resources, it does so in very different ways. Newell's resources can be nurtured and transferred without confronting costly trade-offs across businesses. Merchandising practices used in one unit do not alter their use in another unit, and the development or deployment of those practices does not require extensive, coordinated decision making.

In contrast, Sharp's resources put greater demands on the organization. Their greatest benefits are realized when individual units collaborate and pool investments. In such a context, conflicts and trade-offs are inevitable; managing them well is critical to the success of strategies at that end of the resource continuum.

Controls and Incentives at Tyco

Tyco International represents the other end of the continuum from Sharp. Tyco is a $12 billion conglomerate built around a set of very general resources that it leverages into a wide range of businesses. Contrary to the widely held negative view of conglomerates, Tyco illustrates that a carefully conceived and implemented strategy at the far left of the continuum *can* create substantial amounts of value – even in the United States, and even in the late 1990s. Since 1993, the market capitalization of Tyco has grown from $1.2 billion to $25 billion. Return on equity in 1996 was 16%.

Resources and Businesses. "What's special about Tyco," says CEO Dennis Kozlowski, "are its financial controls, good incentive programs, strong manufacturing, and operating managers who are highly motivated by incentives and who enjoy working without a whole lot of group support." Tyco's resources are general, much like those of venture capitalists and private equity groups.

Due to the broad applicability of their resources, companies like Tyco can operate in a wide range of businesses. In 1997, the company was organized around six operating groups: fire protection, flow control, disposable medical products, Simplex Technologies, packaging materials, and specialty

mature, stable, low-tech businesses, which, compared with Sharp's, face less uncertainty and require considerably lower levels of R&D spending. Tyco could not succeed in high-tech businesses where external events can badly distort a year's financial results.

Organization. Rather than reaching for specific synergies *across* its groups, Tyco uses the general resources of the corporation to encourage the division presidents to act like entrepreneurs *within* their groups, and to focus on expanding the scope and profitability of those units. As Kozlowski explained several years ago, "While they have the backing of an old-line, financially secure, capable company, they can act like small entrepreneurs who go out and do what needs to be done without all the encumbrances of the corporation."[1]

A Tyco executive once likened the company's structure to a capitalistic system with "very little central planning. We don't tend to set up a lot of rules. We develop incentives for our people, and it works."[2] Indeed, its highly disciplined financial-control system and steep incentive schemes are at the heart of Tyco's strategy.

Tyco's managers are on the line to perform. The company's unsparing, top-down budgeting process holds divisional presidents accountable for the financial performance of their individual units – and only for that. At the same time, Tyco offers powerful incentives to achieve extraordinary results, of which there have been many. There is no cap on the bonuses for individual performance. In some cases, division heads make more money than Tyco's CEO. When a manager fails to perform, Tyco will look for a replacement with relevant industry expertise outside the organization. Because of the wide scope of its businesses, it cannot draw from an extensive internal labor pool the way Newell can.

Tyco recognizes that if you don't intend to achieve a lot of coordination across your businesses, you shouldn't have much of a corporate staff. That thinking is consistent with Tyco's "no meetings, no memos" philosophy. In 1997, only 50 of the company's 40,000 employees were on the corporate staff. Its headquarters was in a modest frame building in New Hampshire. Like the rest of the corporate infrastructure, it was unpretentious but more than adequate to get the job done.

Kozlowski is aware of the criticisms of conglomerates and of the risks and challenges of holding a company together around a very general set of resources. He explains, "At least once a year we bring

Tyco's "no meetings, no memos" philosophy is consistent with the company's corporate strategy.

products. Each of these independent product groups was headed by a president who reported directly to Kozlowski.

While there are few product similarities across Tyco's businesses, its resources – financial controls and governance structure – do set limits on the kinds of businesses it can own. Tyco confines itself to businesses in which division executives can be held strictly accountable for a limited number of financial measures. As a result, Tyco competes in

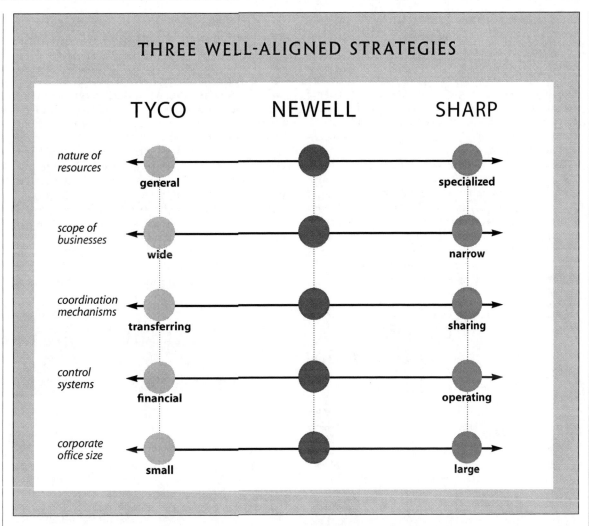

THREE WELL-ALIGNED STRATEGIES

	TYCO	NEWELL	SHARP
nature of resources	general		specialized
scope of businesses	wide		narrow
coordination mechanisms	transferring		sharing
control systems	financial		operating
corporate office size	small		large

in someone from the outside who has a lot of incentive to break up the company – someone from a JP Morgan, Merrill Lynch, or Goldman Sachs – and say to them, 'take a good look at us, break us up, and tell us what we're going to get per share for it. Then tell us if you think we should break up.' It's the only way to get an objective look at it. And they've always said that we should stay as we are." Given Tyco's impressive record of value creation, it's not a surprising conclusion.

No One Right Strategy

When we look across the spectrum of resources – from Sharp's specialized technological expertise to Tyco's general management disciplines – one thing is clear: as brilliant as any one strategy might be, it won't necessarily work well for all companies. That's because every company starts at a different

point, operates in a different context, and has fundamentally different kinds of resources. There is no best prescription for all multibusiness corporations.

What prevails instead is the logic of internally consistent corporate strategies tailored to a firm's resources and opportunities. When corporate strategy adheres to this logic, a company can create a meaningful corporate advantage. When a strategy departs from it, a company at best will coast to mediocrity. At worst, the lack of consistency could be the iceberg that sinks the corporate ship. Consider the failure of Saatchi and Saatchi – at one time the world's largest advertising agency and now, renamed Cordiant, a shadow of its former self.

Saatchi and Saatchi rose to fame in the 1970s and early 1980s on its reputation for creative advertising and its championing of global advertisements. Those skills enabled it to build a client base that became its most valuable resource. In 1986, with the acquisition of Ted Bates, Saatchi became the world's largest advertising agency.

Within six years, the firm was on the verge of bankruptcy. Saatchi and Saatchi made many mistakes, including overpaying for acquisitions and not anticipating the end of the 1980s advertising boom. Its fate, however, was sealed by its failure to craft a coherent corporate strategy. Indeed, the company violated most of the requirements for internal alignment.

The vision for Saatchi was to be number one in its industry. However, unlike Newell or Sharp, Saatchi never established a boundary to its domain. Having reached the limit in advertising (where conflict of interest prevents one agency from becoming too large), Saatchi expanded into a number of businesses in which its relationship with a client's marketing executives provided a potential competitive advantage: marketing services, public relations,

direct marketing, and promotions firms. But when Saatchi acquired consulting firms and then bid for a British merchant bank and a commercial bank, the client relationship was no longer a valuable resource. A marketing vice president is not the buyer of logistics consulting or banking services. Indeed, a corporate reputation for edgy creativity is probably the last thing a company looks for in its choice of commercial banker.

Worse still, even where there was potential synergy, Saatchi never implemented effective processes to capture it. Cross-selling was restricted to informational meetings where each business informed the others about its services, and no financial incentives were provided for referrals. The risk of a sister company souring a relationship inhibited businesses from sharing clients. As a result, Saatchi was never able to leverage its most valuable resource – customer relationships – across businesses.

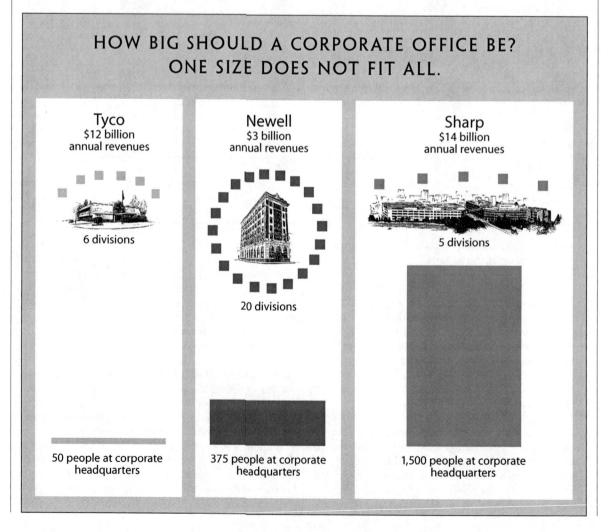

HOW BIG SHOULD A CORPORATE OFFICE BE?
ONE SIZE DOES NOT FIT ALL.

Tyco
$12 billion
annual revenues

6 divisions

50 people at corporate
headquarters

Newell
$3 billion
annual revenues

20 divisions

375 people at corporate
headquarters

Sharp
$14 billion
annual revenues

5 divisions

1,500 people at corporate
headquarters

But perhaps the worst failure came on the control side. Saatchi had developed what at the time was an advanced financial-control system for advertising agencies. But when an ex-consultant was placed in charge of both the consulting and the advertising businesses, he imposed the budgeting system from consulting on the advertising agencies. The consulting system starts not with expected client revenues, which are relatively predictable, but with desired numbers of employees. In consulting, where professionals by and large generate their own revenues, this is an adequate system. In the notoriously optimistic advertising business, it was a disaster. Agencies projected rapid growth in employees and acquired long-term leases on the office space to accommodate them. When the dust settled, Saatchi took write-offs of more than £150 million just to cover the excess floor space the company had leased. Saatchi's failure to understand the control requirements of different businesses undercut the enterprise.

Many Ways to Succeed

The fact that there are potentially an unlimited variety of effective corporate strategies does not mean that most corporate strategies are effective. Observation suggests the opposite – that many strategies do not enhance value. If executives benchmarked their corporate strategies as aggressively as they do their operations, most would discover that their strategies are far from world class.

The resource continuum and the range of strategies it encompasses provides a useful starting point for benchmarking the effectiveness of your corporate strategy. Begin by looking for companies with successful strategies built around types of resources that are similar to yours. Those companies can serve as models, while companies further away on the resource continuum can provide instructive contrasts.

The harsh moment of truth for many companies built around specialized resources comes when they discover that, despite the related appearance of their businesses, they are adding little more value to their businesses than a well-run conglomerate would. The performance of these companies, however, suffers from the drag of a larger corporate overhead than that of a conglomerate.

At the other end of the spectrum, conglomerates often find that leveraged buyout firms have even lower-cost operations and more effective means for financing and controlling sets of unrelated businesses. Alternatively, conglomerates may discover that the businesses they own could be worth more in the hands of a corporation with more specialized resources.

That is the acid test for any corporate strategy: the company's businesses must not be worth more

> The acid test for any corporate strategy is this: the company's businesses must not be worth more to another owner.

to another owner. In a dynamic, competitive environment, that threat is always lurking around the corner. To guard against it requires the continual upgrading not only of the resources on which the strategy is based but also of all the elements of the strategy triangle and their fit.

Newell, Sharp, and Tyco have all sustained corporate advantage over many years through just such a process of continual upgrading. Newell, for example, used to be proud of service levels that it would shun today. Tyco has ratcheted up the size of the acquisitions it is capable of making. Sharp has consciously fostered a feeling of crisis in the firm, a sense that the roof is falling in. Today, to respond to increased competition in some of its core markets, Sharp must be able to make another round of technology investments. The race never ends. But no company's strategy can endure without continual pressure to improve.

There are many ways to succeed. Creativity and intuition are hallmarks of great corporate strategies. So too, however, are discipline and rigor. In the companies we studied, brilliant strategies began with new ideas. These were followed by deliberate investments in resources made over many years, the development of a clear understanding of the businesses in which those resources would be valuable, and the painstaking tailoring of organizations to make the strategy a reality. Ultimately, strategies that prevail are well-constructed systems that deliver tangible benefits.

1. Mark McLaughlin, "Flat and Happy at the Top," *New England Business*, March 1990, p. 19.

2. "John Fort: CEO, Tyco Laboratories," *The Business of New Hampshire*, February 1997, p. 38.

Reprint 98303   To place an order, call 1-800-988-0886.

Harvard Business Review

CASE STUDIES AND *HARVARD BUSINESS REVIEW* ARTICLE REPRINTS

Many readers have asked for an easy way to order case studies and article reprints or to obtain permission to copy. In response, we have established a Customer Service Team to grant permission, send rush copies in paper form, deliver files in Acrobat (PDF) format electronically (*Harvard Business Review* articles only), or customize collections.

Please contact the Customer Service Team:

Phone: 617-496-1449
United States and Canada: 800-668-6780
(8 A.M. – 6 P.M. weekdays, voice mail after hours)
Fax: 617-496-1029 (24 hours, 7 days a week)
E-mail: custserv@hbsp.harvard.edu
(24 hours, 7 days a week)
Web Site: http://www.hbsp.harvard.edu

Prices (minimum order, $10):

Harvard Business Review Reprints
(Discounts apply to multiple copies of the same article.)

1–9 copies	$5 each
10–99	$4
100–499	$3.50
Electronic	$3.50 each

Harvard Business School Case Studies
$5 each

For quantity estimates or quotes on customized products, call
Frank Tamoshunas at 617-495-6198.
Fax: 617-496-8866

PERMISSIONS

For information on permission to quote or translate Harvard Business School Publishing material, contact:

Customer Service Department
Harvard Business School
   Publishing Corporation
60 Harvard Way
Boston, MA 02163

Phone: 617-496-1449
United States and Canada: 800-668-6780
Fax: 617-495-6985
E-mail: custserv@hbsp.harvard.edu

HARVARD BUSINESS REVIEW SUBSCRIPTION SERVICE

United States and Canada
Phone: 800-274-3214
Rates per year: United States, $85;
Canada, U.S.$95

International and Mexico
Phone: 44-1858-435324
Fax: 44-1858-468969
Rates per year: international, U.S.$145;
Mexico, U.S.$95
Orders, inquiries, and address changes:
Harvard Business Review
Tower House, Sovereign Park
Lathkill Street, Market Harborough
Leicestershire LE16 9EF
England

International customer service E-mail address: harvard@subscription.co.uk

Payments accepted: Visa, MasterCard, American Express; checks at current exchange rate payable to
Harvard Business Review.
Bills and other receipts may be issued.

CATALOGS

Harvard Business School Publishing Media Catalog
This 32-page, full-color catalog features more than 40 management development video and interactive CD-ROM programs.

Harvard Business School Press
This latest full-color catalog features books for the fast-paced business world where you live and work.

Harvard Business School Publishing Catalog of Best-Selling Teaching Materials
This collection of teaching materials contains those items most requested by our customers.

Harvard Business School Publishing Catalog of New Teaching Materials
Designed for individuals looking for the latest materials in case method teaching.

The Social Responsibility of Business is to Increase its Profits

Milton Friedman
A Friedman doctrine

When I hear businessmen speak eloquently about the "social responsibilities of business in a free-enterprise system," I am reminded of the wonderful line about the Frenchman who discovered at the age of 70 that he had been speaking prose all his life. The businessmen believe that they are defending free enterprise when they declaim that business is not concerned "merely" with profit but also with promoting desirable "social" ends; that business has a "social conscience" and takes seriously its responsibilities for providing employment, eliminating discrimination, avoiding pollution and whatever else may be the catchwords of the contemporary crop of reformers. In fact they are—or would be if they or anyone else took them seriously—preaching pure and unadulterated socialism. Businessmen who talk this way are unwitting puppets of the intellectual forces that have been undermining the basis of a free society these past decades.

The discussions of the "social responsibilities of business" are notable for their analytical looseness and lack of rigor. What does it mean to say that "business" has responsibilities? Only people can have responsibilities. A corporation is an artificial person and in this sense may have artificial responsibilities, but "business" as a whole cannot be said to have responsibilities, even in this vague sense. The first step toward clarity is examining the doctrine of the social responsibility of business is to ask precisely what it implies for whom.

Presumably, the individuals who are to be responsible are businessmen, which means individual proprietors or corporate executives. Most of the discussion of social responsibility is directed at corporations, so in what follows I shall mostly neglect the individual proprietor and speak of corporate executives.

In a free-enterprise, private-property system, a corporate executive is an employee of the owners of the business. He has direct responsibility to his employers. That responsibility is to conduct the business in accordance with their desires, which generally will be to make as much money as possible while conforming to the basic rules of the society, both those embodied in law and those embodied in ethical custom. Of course, in some cases his employers may have a different objective. A group of persons might establish a corporation for an eleemosynary purpose—for example, a hospital or a school. The manager of such a corporation will not have money profit as his objective but the rendering of certain services.

In either case, the key point is that, in his capacity as a corporate executive, the manager is the agent of the individuals who own the corporation or establish the eleemosynary institution, and his primary responsibility it to them.

Needless to say, this does not mean that it is easy to judge how well he is performing his task. But at least the criterion of performance is straightforward, and the persons among whom a voluntary contractual arrangement exists are clearly defined.

Of course, the corporate executive is also a person in his own right. As a person, he may have many other responsibilities that he recognizes or assumes voluntarily—to his family, his conscience, his feelings of charity, his church, his clubs, his city, his country. He may feel impelled by these responsibilities to devote part of his income to causes he regards as worthy, to refuse to work for particular corporations, even to leave his job, for example, to join his country's armed forces. If we wish, we may refer to some of these responsibilities as "social responsibilities." But in these respects he is acting as a principal, not an agent; he is spending his won money or time or energy, not the money of his employers of the time or energy he has contracted to devote to their purposes. If these are "social responsibilities," they are the social responsibilities of individuals, not of business.

What does it mean to say that the corporate executive has a "social responsibility" in his capacity as businessman? If this statement is not pure rhetoric, it must mean that he is to act in some way that is not in the interest of his employers. For example, that he is to refrain from increasing the price of the product in order to contribute to the social objective of preventing inflation, even though a price increase would be in the best interests of the corporation. Or that he is to make expenditures on reducing pollution beyond the amount that is in the best interests of the corporation or that is required by law in order to contribute to the social objective of improving the environment. Or that, at the expense of corporate profits, he is to hire "hardcore" unemployed instead of better qualified available workmen to contribute to the social objective of reducing poverty.

In each of these cases, the corporate executive would be spending someone else's money for a general social interest. Insofar as his actions in accord with his "social responsibility" reduce returns to stockholders, he is spending their money. Insofar as his actions raise the price to customers, he is spending the customers' money. Insofar as his actions lower the wages of some employees, he is spending their money.

The stockholders or the customers or the employees could separately spend their own money on the particular action if they wished to do so. The executive is exercising a distinct "social responsibility," rather than serving as an agent of the stockholders or the customers or the employees, only if he spends the money in a different way then they would have spent it.

But if he does this, he is in effect imposing taxes, on the one hand, and deciding how the tax proceeds shall be spent, on the other.

This process raises political questions on two levels: principle and consequences. On the level of political principle, the imposition o f taxes and the expenditure of tax proceeds are governmental functions. We have established elaborate constitutional, parliamentary and judicial provisions to control these functions, to assure that taxes are imposed so far as possible in accordance with the preferences and desires of the public—after all, "taxation without representation" was one of the battle cries of the American Revolution. We have a system of checks and balances to separate the legislative function of imposing taxes and enacting expenditures from the executive function of collecting taxes and administering expenditure programs and from the judicial function of mediating disputes and interpreting the law.

Here the businessman—self-selected or appointed directly or indirectly by stockholders—is to be simultaneously legislator, executive and jurist. He is to decide whom to tax by how much and for what purpose, and he is to spend the proceeds—all this guided only be general exhortations from on high to restrain inflation, improve the environment, fight poverty and so on and on.

The whole justification for permitting the corporate executive to be selected by the stockholders is that the executive is an agent serving the interests of his principal. This justification disappears when the corporate executive imposes taxes and spends the proceeds for "social" purposes. He becomes in effect a public employee, a civil servant; even though he remains in name an employee of a private enterprise. On grounds of political principle, it is intolerable that such civil servants—insofar as their action in the name of social responsibility are real and not just window-dressing—should be selected as they are now. If they are to be civil servants, then they must be selected through a political process. If they are to impose taxes and make expenditures to foster "social" objectives, then political machinery must be set up to guide the assessment of taxes and to determine through a political process the objectives to be served.

This is the basic reason why the doctrine of "social responsibility" involves the acceptance of the socialist view that political mechanisms, not market mechanisms, are the appropriate way to determine the allocation of scarce resources to alternative uses.

On the grounds of consequences, can the corporate executive in fact discharge his alleged "social responsibilities"? On the one hand, suppose he could get away with spending the stockholders' or customers' or employees' money. How is he to know how to spend it? He is told that he must contribute to fighting inflation. How is he to know what action of his will contribute to that end? He is presumably an expert in running his company—in producing a product or selling it or financing it. But nothing about his selection makes him an expert on inflation. Will his holding down the price of his product reduce inflationary pressure? Or, by leaving more spending power in the hands of his customers, simply divert it elsewhere? Or, by forcing him to produce less because of the lower price, will it simply contribute to shortages? Even if he could answer these questions, how much cost is he justified in imposing on his stockholders, customers and employees for this social purpose? What is his appropriate share and what is the appropriate share of others?

And, whether he wants to or not, can he get away with spending his stockholders', customers' or employees; money? Will not the stock holders fire him? (Either the present ones or those who take over when his actions in the name of social responsibility have reduced the corporation's profits and the price of its stock.) His customers and his employees can desert him for to her producers and employees less scrupulous in exercising their social responsibilities.

This facet of "social responsibility" doctrine is brought into sharp relief when the doctrine is used to justify wage restraint by trade unions. The conflict of interest is naked and clear when union officials are asked to subordinate the interest of their members to some more general social purpose. If the union officials try to enforce wage restraint, the consequence is likely to be wildcat strikes, rank-and-file revolts and the emergence of strong competitors for their jobs. We thus have the ironic phenomenon that union leaders—at least in the U.S.—have objected to government interference with the market far more consistently and courageously than have business leaders.

The difficulty of exercising "social responsibility" illustrates, of course, the great virtue of private competitive enterprise—it forces people to be responsible for their own actions and makes it difficult for them to "exploit" other people for either selfish or unselfish purposes. They can do good—but only at their own expense.

Many a reader who has followed the argument this far may tempted to remonstrate that it is all well and good to speak of government's having the responsibility to impose taxes and determine expen-

ditures for such "social" purposes as controlling pollution or training the hard-core unemployed, but that the problems are too urgent to wait on the slow course of political processes, that the exercise of social responsibility by businessmen is a quicker and surer way to solve pressing current problems.

Aside from the question of fact—I share Adam Smith's skepticism about the benefits that can be expected from "those who affected to trade for the public good"—this argument must be rejected on grounds of principle. What it amounts to is an assertion that those who favor the taxes and expenditures in question have failed to persuade a majority of their fellow citizens to be of like mind and that they are seeking to attain by undemocratic procedures what they cannot attain by democratic procedures. In a free society, it is hard for "good" people to do a "good," but that is a small price to pay for making it hard for "evil" people to do "evil," especially since one man's good is another's evil.

I HAVE, for simplicity, concentrated on the special case of the corporate executive, except only for the brief digression on trade unions. But precisely the same argument applies to the newer phenomenon of calling upon stockholders to require corporations to exercise social responsibility (the recent G.M. crusade, for example). In most of these cases, what is in effect involved is some stockholders trying to get other stockholders (or customers or employees) to contribute against their will to "social" causes favored by the activists. Insofar as they succeed, they are again imposing taxes and spending the proceeds.

The situation of the individual proprietor is somewhat different. If he acts to reduce the returns of his enterprise in order to exercise his "social responsibility," he is spending his own money, not someone else's. If he wishes to spend his money on such purposes, that is his right, and I cannot see that there is any objection to his doing so. In the process, he, too, may impose costs on employees and customers. However, because he is far less likely than a large corporation or union to have monopolistic power, any such side effects will tend to be minor.

Of course, in practice the doctrine of social responsibility is frequently a cloak for actions that are justified on other grounds rather than a reason for those actions.

To illustrate, it may well be in the long-run interest of a corporation that is a major employer in a small community to devote resources to providing amenities to that community or to improving its government. That may make it easier to attract desirable employees, it may reduce the wage bill or lessen losses from pilferage and sabotage or have other worthwhile effects. Or it may be that, given the laws about the deductibility of corporate charitable contribution, the stockholders can contribute more to charities they favor by having the corporation make the gift than by doing it themselves, since they can in that way contribute an amount that would otherwise have been paid as corporate taxes.

In each of these—and many similar—cases, there is a strong temptation to rationalize these actions as an exercise of "social responsibility." In the present climate of opinion, with its widespread aversion to "capitalism," "profits," the "soulless corporation" and so on, this is one way for a corporation to generate goodwill as a by-product of expenditures that are entirely justified in its own self-interest.

It would be inconsistent of me to call on corporate executives to refrain from this hypocritical window-dressing because it harms the foundations of a free society. That would be to call on them to exercise a "social responsibility"! If our institutions, and the attitudes of the public make it in their self-interest to cloak their actions in this way, I cannot summon much indignation to denounce them. At the same time, I can express admiration for those individual proprietors or owners of closely held corporations or stockholders of more broadly held corporations who disdain such tactics as approaching fraud.

WHETHER blameworthy or not, the use of the cloak of social responsibility, and the nonsense spoken in its name by influential and prestigious businessmen, does clearly harm the foundations of a free society. I have been impressed time and again by the schizophrenic character of many businessmen. They are capable of being extremely far-sighted and clear-headed in matters that are internal to their businesses. They are incredibly short-sighted and muddle-headed in matters that are outside their businesses but affect the possible survival of business in general. This short-sightedness is strikingly exemplified in the calls from many businessmen for wage and price guidelines or controls or incomes policies. There is nothing that could do more in a brief period to destroy a market system and replace it by a centrally controlled system than effective governmental control of prices and wages.

The short-sightedness is also exemplified in speeches by businessmen on social responsibility. This may gain them kudos in the short run. But it helps to strengthen the already to prevalent view that the pursuit of profits is wicked and immoral and must be curbed and controlled by external forces. Once this view is adopted, the external forces that curb the market will not be the social consciences, however highly developed, of the pontificating executives; it will be the iron fist of Government bureaucrats. Here, as with price and wage controls, businessmen seem to me to reveal a suicidal impulse.

The political principle that underlies the market mechanism is unanimity. In an ideal free market resting on private property, no individual can coerce any other, all cooperation is voluntary, all parties to such cooperation benefit or they need not participate. There are no "social" values, no "social" responsibilities in any sense other than the shared values and responsibilities of individuals. Society is a collection of individual and of the various groups they voluntarily form.

The political principle that underlies the political mechanism is conformity. The individual must serve a more general social interest—whether that is determined by a church or a dictator or a majority. The individual may have a vote and a say in what is to be done, but if he is overruled, he must conform. It is appropriate for some to require others to contribute to a general social purpose whether they wish to or not.

Unfortunately, unanimity is not always feasible. There are some respects in which conformity appears unavoidable, so I do not see how one can avoid the use of the political mechanism altogether.

But the doctrine of "social responsibility" taken seriously would extend the scope of the political mechanism to every human activity. It does not differ in philosophy form the most explicitly collectivist doctrine. It differs only by professing to believe the collectivist ends can be attained without collectivist means. That is why, in my book "Capitalism and Freedom," I have called it a "fundamentally subversive doctrine" in a free society, and have said that in such a society, "there is one and only one social responsibility of business—to use its resources and engage in activities designed to increase its profits so long as it stays within the rules of the game, which is to say, engages in open and free competition without deception or fraud."

Strategies for Asia's New Competitive Game

Peter J. Williamson
INSEAD

A fundamental strategic rethink is now required by Asian companies and Western multinationals operating in Asia alike, because Asia's competitive environment is undergoing a sea change. Repeating what worked in the past is unlikely to succeed in the face of these new realities. Change is being driven by the rapid development of China, the cumulative impact of gradual but sustained deregulation and trade liberalization across Asia, and the implications of a new generation of economic, demographic, and social forces that is beginning to reshape Asia's future. These are all long-term trends, but until now their impact on the Asian competition has been arrested by the fact that many Asian companies have been shackled by the after-effects of the 1997 financial crisis. Only recently have these shackles been removed as debt restructuring is completed or loans finally repaid, giving these Asian corporations the capital and the elbow room to respond to the pent-up pressures for change. Faced with this new economic environment in Asia and reinvigorated Asian competitors, Western multinationals will need to chart new strategies if they are to win a share of the new round of Asian growth that is now under way. Rather than cloning their global strategies or reluctantly adapting them to Asia, successful Western multinationals will adopt innovative strategies in the Asian market that allow them to more accurately pinpoint, and then to fully exploit, their own unique strengths.

This article discusses the fundamental pressures for change in Asia's new competitive game, what

Reprinted from "Strategies for Asia's new competitive game," Peter J. Williamson, *The Journal of Business Strategy* 26, no. 2 (2005), pp. 37–43. © Emerald Group Publishing Limited. Used by permission.

successful new strategies will need to look like. It is about grasping the challenges and exploiting the opportunities that the changing face of Asian competition is bringing in its wake.

FOUR MAJOR SHIFTS IN THE ASIAN COMPETITIVE ENVIRONMENT

Understanding the drivers of change in the Asian environment and what they mean for the way Asian competition will work in the next round is the first step toward creating the new kinds of strategies and companies that will succeed in the future. Four shifts occurring in today's Asia are particularly significant: the demise of asset speculators, China's scattering of the pattern of orderly Asian "flying geese" development, the breakdown of national economic "baronies," and the decay of "me-too" strategies.

The Demise of the Asset Speculators

Profitable strategies are supposed to draw their lifeblood from creating new value by finding ways to provide customers with goods and services that either better fit their needs or do so more efficiently than competitors. If we are honest, however, that was not the way a lot of companies in Asia made money during the 1990s boom. Instead, they grew rich through asset speculation: buying assets ranging from real estate to acquiring rival firms or building large manufacturing facilities and letting the rising prices of these assets swell the market value of their companies. Even as they continued to benefit from asset price inflation, too many senior managers in Asian companies were happy to bask in the illusion that they were creating new value through world-beating competitiveness and thriving in a dynamic, open market. The same was true for many of their multinational counterparts operating in the region whose management was more inclined to attribute their success to brilliant strategy and execution, than to favorable market conditions.

The Asian financial crisis of 1997 shattered those illusions because, almost at a stroke, it removed the windfall of rising asset prices that had been the unspoken secret of success in many Asian businesses. Instead of capital gains as asset prices rose year after year, Asian management was faced with a sustained period of asset price deflation. As banks and asset management companies were forced to share in the burden, the impact has been delayed for years. But now, as Asian balance sheets have been reconstructed leaving the investment community chastened, the upper hand is shifting to those who can add the most value to the assets and resources they use and away from simply adding new capacity. The next round will reward those who can do more with less, and do it differently, not those who build the largest corporate empires in Asia or assemble the biggest caches of assets on which to speculate. The drive for sheer volume is being replaced with a drive for value-added.

China Scatters the "Flying Geese"

A second major force of change in Asia's next round of competition is the China factor. Asia's traditional model of economic development was often described as "flying geese" in formation. Each country began by manufacturing and exporting simple, labor-intensive products like garments and shoes and assembly of low-end products. As it accumulated more capital and know-how, it moved through products of intermediate complexity, and then to high-value-added products and services. As one country moved on to the next level of value-added, another developing country would take its place as at the lower-value end. Japan led the flock, followed by Hong Kong, Singapore,

South Korea, and Taiwan. Then came Malaysia, Thailand, the Philippines, Indonesia, and Vietnam in the tail. Albeit somewhat simplistic, this concept of national geese flying in formation underlay many a government policy and corporate strategy. It shaped the pattern of what diversified Asian-owned companies invested in next and where multinationals located their activities in Asia.

Then along came China. *The Economist* magazine aptly summed up the result with a cartoon. It depicted a jet aircraft, piloted by a panda, zooming straight through the flock of Asian geese.[1] China wasn't flying in the cozy formation; by the new millennium it was undertaking activities that ranged from simple manufacturing to design and manufacture of high-technology components and equipment, from making rag dolls and molding plastic toys through to fabrication of semiconductors and specialized machinery. And China is doing this on a scale large enough to redraw the competitive map.

Now that the flying geese model of where to locate low- and high-end operations, respectively, has been exploded and the neat formation is in disarray, companies will have to reevaluate the roles of each of their subsidiaries across Asia. With China now a key part of the Asian game, the winners will be those who can restructure their operations into a more integrated Asian jigsaw where each subsidiary in Asia supplies specialized components or focuses on particular activities within the overall supply chain.

This development represents a fundamental change in the Asian competitive environment. When companies review the footprint of their existing operations through the new lens of a more integrated Asian supply chain, they will often discover that their existing subsidiaries are in the wrong places, with too much vertical integration and possibly specializing in the wrong things.

> *A fundamental strategic rethink is now required by Asian companies and Western multinationals operating in Asia alike, because Asia's competitive environment is undergoing a sea change.*

Semiconductor companies are a good example of the kind of new strategy that will be necessary. Leading companies in this industry have had to abandon the historic setups where they made high-end chips in one country and low-end ones in another.

They have had to replace it with a new structure where a subsidiary in one Asian country does the circuit design, another photolithography, and a different location the so-called "back-end packaging" of the final chip. These kinds of pressures for redrawing the map of Asia have huge implications for the strategies that will succeed in the future.

The Breakdown of National Economic Baronies

Asia's division into highly segregated national markets, separated from each other by a mix of tariff and nontariff barriers, cultural and language differences, divergent choices about local standards, and regulatory differences between countries is legendary. Within this environment it made sense for companies to approach each national market pretty much as a separate competitive playing field. This behavior was reinforced by various forms of preference given by governments to their local companies through the allocation of licenses, preferential access to finance, and other kinds of direct and indirect support. Likewise, multinationals historically approached Asia as a collection of separate national markets.

In this environment, local "country managers" often became local barons: each in charge of a highly autonomous subsidiary within the Asian network. Each baron fought for investment of more resources in their business unit and argued the case against sharing functions from procurement and manufacturing to distribution and marketing on the grounds that any such moves would reduce their ability to respond to the peculiarities of the local market. The result was a set of largely independent subsidiaries spanning Asia under the umbrella of a "global" parent.

Today each of these country subsidiaries is under threat from the rapid growth of cross-border competition in Asia. A potent cocktail of falling trade barriers, deregulation of national markets, and falling costs of transport and communication is now opening the door to new sources of competitive advantage based on cross-border economies of scale and coordination. The results are striking. Trade among Asian countries is now growing more than twice as fast as the area's trade with the rest of the world, reflecting a rapid increase in direct cross-border competition. And perhaps even more significantly, Asian companies have invested an average of almost $50 billion every year in building or acquiring operations in other countries since 1995 (despite the setback of the 1997 financial crisis).[2] Much of this investment is in building beachheads in other Asian markets from which to mount attacks on yesterday's national baronies. In the face of this onslaught, yesterday's fragmented Asian strategies will become untenable.

The Decay of "Me-Too" Strategies

Primary consumer demand—from the first-time purchasers of everything from cars to washing machines and mobile phones—accounts for a large part of the market when economic growth in an economy first takes off. During this phase, consumers are willing to accept standardized, basic consumer goods. If you have never owned a refrigerator before, the most basic box that keeps things cool at reasonable cost is acceptable. But once consumers move on to become second- or third-time purchasers, they look for features such as the exact performance, styling, color, and so on that suits their individual needs. Consumers begin to demand higher product quality and variety, not simply more volume. Whirlpool's experience when it entered the Chinese market for domestic appliances a few years ago is a good example of this change. Contrary to its initial expectations, it quickly found Asian consumers rejected last year's American designs and technologies. Instead, they demanded environmentally friendly CFC-free refrigerators, washing machines with state-of-the-art electronic controls, and integrated, wall-mounted air-conditioners instead of the standard type that hung precariously from a window space.[3]

Asian consumers rejected last year's American designs and technologies. Instead, they demanded environmentally friendly CFC-free refrigerators, washing machines with state-of-the-art electronic controls, and integrated, wall-mounted air-conditioners.

The same is true of fast-moving consumer goods like food or cosmetics and services: once your basic needs are satisfied by the range of products and services you consume, you start to look for particular varieties, flavors, sizes, and presentations or services customized to your individual needs. Even Asia's humble instant noodle now comes in more than 20 different flavors and a range of packaging from paper to styrofoam cups, not to mention pink "Valentine's day" and red and gold "Chinese New Year limited edition" varieties.[4] These trends are a simple fact of life that goes right back to Maslow's hierarchy of needs: as consumers become richer they want better and more customized offerings, not "more of the same."

These trends are now reaching much beyond Asia's wealthy elite. Throughout much of Asia the mass market has now reached a stage of development where consumers are no longer satisfied with reliable but standard, often boring, products and services. Even in China and India, countries with huge rural populations (estimated at 900 million and 700 million, respectively) that have been little touched by consumerism, there are hundreds of millions of urban consumers who are now sophisticated buyers who demand goods and services with the innovative features, variety, and customization that precisely fit their individual needs. Companies unable to provide more innovative, flexible products will literally be left on the shelf.

In parallel, a new generation of Asian consumers is entering the market. Unlike their parents, today's so-called "X" and "Y" generations have never lived through real hardship; they were born into a consumer society. As a result, they take abundance of goods and services largely for granted. Their choices reflect a complex mix of demand for higher quality, fashion, a desire to express more individualism, and a "what's new?" mentality. While the precise implications of serving this new consumer generation will vary by industry, it is safe to say that they will demand even greater variety, customization, and innovation from suppliers than today's mainstream consumers.

Despite all these changes, the Asian consumer is unlikely to abandon his or her traditional nose for value. Nor are Asian business buyers going to forget their historic emphasis on costs. But in the next round of competition in Asia, a strategy based solely on churning out high standard products in high volumes is unlikely to be a winner—even if the price is low. The new environment will demand that winning companies succeed in pursuing a strategy of being different from competitors, as well as better; decisively setting themselves apart from the competition with a wider range of product options, better customer segmentation and more customized offerings and stronger brands to signal differentiation from competitors.

STRATEGIC RESPONSES

The fundamental changes in Asia's competitive environment described above together demand new strategies. Clearly there is no single recipe for winning the new competitive game in Asia. But the new reality of Asia demands that managers stake out their territory based on four core ingredients: improved productivity, local brand and service, innovation, and internationalization that is designed to reshape the Asian playing field and reap cross-border synergies. Figure 1 lays out the strategic options.

Figure 1   **Strategic Choices for Winning in Asia's Next Round of Competition**

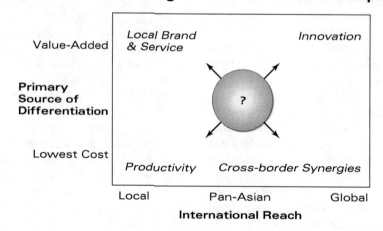

A New Productivity Drive

Given the demise of asset speculation as a way of underpinning Asian profits and increasingly intense competition from local companies in China and cross-border rivalry within Asia, a key element in future Asian strategy must be to enhance efficiency of Asian operations through productivity gains—especially in neglected "overhead" areas beyond the factory gate, like administration, sales, and distribution.

In a recent study I conducted on a sample of consumer-goods multinationals operating in Asia, I found that at an average of $75 million sales their unit overhead was a staggering 300 percent higher than Chinese rivals of comparative size. In fact, in a number of cases the overhead burden a foreign subsidiary expended just in dealing with their foreign headquarters was higher than the total overhead of the local Chinese competitors!

In many multinationals, overhead burdens rose during 1990s when expansion was the name of the game, at almost any cost. Companies recruited armies of staff to make sure support functions such as sales, administration, and distribution did not create bottlenecks or hinder the running of their expensive new factories. But as we enter a new round of Asian competition, it will not be enough for companies to rely on high productivity in manufacturing and routine operations alone. Multinationals will have to be more assiduous about deploying advanced systems—in customer relationship management, logistics, and administration: "soft technologies"—to bring their Asian operations up to world best-practice productivity outside core manufacturing and basic service operations. They will no longer be able to afford to follow the old adage that "Asia's different" as an excuse for inefficient administration and low-productivity support and service activities.

Renewed Focus on Brand Building and Service Quality

As "me-too" strategies decay and Asian consumers demand more variety, customization, and service, there will be a growing need for the capability to deliver an improved product or service experience "on the ground" to each and every individual customer in Asia. Simultaneously there will be a need to signal improved service quality to consumers and to differentiate offerings from competitors by strengthening the equity of the brands in Asia market by market and customer by customer. The need for strategies to strengthen brand differentiation will be given further impetus as local Asian companies start to build or acquire their own brands—a trend that is well under way.

In the next round of competition, multinationals won't be able to take their brand premium for granted. To exploit this potential advantage multinationals will have to increase their investment in brands in Asia. Better localization of branding, marketing, and service will also be required.

Reaping Cross-Border Synergies and Driving Consolidation

The relentless competitive pressure on yesterday's protected national baronies in the new Asian competitive game will demand better exploitation of cross-border synergies between different subsidiaries in Asia. This will mean accelerating pan-Asian and global integration, leaving behind yesterday's scatter of isolated national subsidiaries, and facing up to country barons who resist loss of independence.

As China continues to scatter the flying geese, companies will need to rethink the role of different subsidiaries and locations within the overall Asian jigsaw. Rather than a loosely connected portfolio of largely self-sufficient national companies, each subsidiary will need to be refocused on more specialized sets of activities within a new Asian network that leverages the specific advantages and knowledge within each location.

In many industries succeeding in the new competitive game in Asia will also mean taking advantage of the window of opportunity that is opening up to drive consolidation of Asia's fragmented supply base. This window for industry consolidation is opening because more intense competition from China and the elimination of the protective barriers around national markets are putting increasingly intense pressure on Asian companies to become more efficient and more focused about where they invest their resources in the future. This means that more and more companies will be forced, however reluctantly, to dispose of businesses where they lack the scale and the prospect of building sufficient depth of

567

capabilities to compete in the next round.[5] This will create a new supply of businesses for consolidators to mop up that wasn't there in the past. Here strategies for quickly identifying, assessing, and executing overseas acquisitions and then reshaping these into a fully integrated business will become critical.

Innovating in Asia

With the decay of me-too strategies and the resulting increased emphasis on innovation amongst their local Asian rivals, multinationals will not only have to exploit transfer innovative technologies and products into Asia more rapidly, they will also have to ramp up their own innovation activities in Asia. Rather than just exporting innovations and new technology developed at home, American and European multinationals will need to restructure their innovation processes to benefit from the availability of high-quality researchers and engineers at lower cost, as well as to learn more from their Asian operations.[6]

Too often in the past, multinationals have only seen Asia as a manufacturing base or a source of customers in a growing market. Too few multinational companies have seen the potential of leveraging innovations from their Asian operations across other markets. Even those who have done so frequently fail to recognize Asia as an important, ongoing source of innovation. The primacy of the home base and the "parent" organization as the font of innovation die hard.

Forward-thinking multinationals are, however, beginning to reassess the potential role of Asia in their global innovation strategies. The global drinks group Diageo (owners of Smirnoff Vodka, J&B Scotch, and Bailey's Irish Cream), for example, has an innovation group in Hong Kong whose role is to seek out emerging trends and technologies within the region for global innovations. Johnson & Johnson has begun to deploy innovative manufacturing processes designed in Asia across their subsidiaries in the region, rather than implementing solutions born in the West. Over the last few years, more than 100 global R&D centers have been established in China by leading multinationals such as HP, Microsoft, and Motorola. Others need to follow these pioneers.

The new reality of Asia demands that managers stake out their territory based on four core ingredients: improved productivity; local brand and service; innovation; and internationalization that is designed to reshape the Asian playing field and reap cross-border synergies.

ASIA'S NEW COMPETITIVE GAME

There should be no doubt that it will take a different kind of company to succeed in Asia's next round of competition. Unquestionably this will require determined efforts among multinationals operating in Asia to raise their game in the four key areas of strategy discussed above: a new productivity drive, renewed focus on brand building and service quality, reaping cross-border synergies and driving consolidation, and innovating in Asia. The mix of these strategies will vary by industry and individual company. But whatever route a company chooses to take into Asia's future, the new reality of competition in Asia is unavoidable; Amid renewed opportunity, there will be a sharper divide between the winners and losers. Only one question remains: In which group will your company end up?

Notes

1. See "A panda breaks the formation," *The Economist,* August 25, 2001, p. 65.

2. World Investment report 2003.

3. D. Clyde-Smith and P. J. Williamson, *Whirlpool in China (A): Entering the World's Largest Market.* INSEAD Case No. 08/2001-4950, INSEAD, Paris.

4. S. Donnan, "Indofood wants us to say it with noodles," *Financial Times,* February 14, 2000, p. 24.

5. A. Mody and S. Negishi, "Cross-border mergers and acquisitions in East Asia," *Finance and Development,* March 2001, pp. 6–11.

6. See Y. Doz, J. Santos, and P. Williamson, *From Global to Metanational: How Companies Win in the Knowledge Economy,* Harvard Business School Press, Boston, MA, 2001.

Outsourcing Strategies: Opportunities and Risks

Brian Leavy
Dublin City University Business School

A characteristic of corporate strategy in developed countries in the last 20 years has been an increasing interest in outsourcing as a potential source of competitiveness and value creation. The earliest outsourcing strategies were largely driven by the desire to lower costs in the face of intensifying global competition, typically by moving low-skilled, labor-intensive, activities offshore to Southeast Asia and other low-cost locations. In more recent years, there has been a growing awareness of the potential of outsourcing to support a range of strategies beyond that of lower cost

Corporate strategists may not be fully familiar with four of the most promising opportunities for using outsourcing strategies—focus, scale without mass, disruptive innovation, and strategic repositioning. While assessing the potential of those opportunities in specific corporate situations, strategists also need to look at two of the most significant associated risks—the risk of losing skills that could be key to competing in the future, and the risk of turning to outsourcing at the wrong stage in an industry's evolution. My goal is to widen managers' views of the strategic alternatives that outsourcing can be used to support, while making managers aware of the main risks to be weighed in the balance.

FOUR PROMISING OUTSOURCING STRATEGIES

Focus—Nike and Dell

In intensely competitive environments, many companies see outsourcing as a way to hire "best in class" companies to perform routine business functions and then focus corporate resources on key activities in their value chain where the impact will be felt the most by the customer. This is the strategy that has helped Nike to capture and sustain leadership in the athletic footwear and apparel industry for most of the last three decades.

Nike's business started as a company of athletes selling imported performance Japanese shoes to other athletes, and by the end of its first decade in 1972, sales had reached just $2 million. Despite the relatively slow growth of these early years, the founders continued to experiment with new performance designs and prototypes, based on their intimate knowledge of the market. By the end of their first decade they had already developed the core competencies in brand building and design that were soon to become the foundation for Nike's rapid growth. The company decided to focus primarily on these activities and outsource most of its production and much of its sales and distribution. As a consequence, by the end of its second decade Nike sales had rocketed to $700 million, with gross margins running at nearly 40 percent. Even before the notion of focused outsourcing was generally understood, Nike had demonstrated the potential power of such a strategy. It continues to do so today, retaining a 39 percent share of the $7.8 billion U.S. market for branded athletic footwear, and doing so in the face of very determined competition.

The strategy of focusing corporate resources mainly on those activities where clear differentiation

Reprinted from "Outsourcing Strategies: Opportunities and Risks," Brian Leavy, *Strategy and Leadership* 32, no. 6 (2004), © Emerald Group Publishing Limited. Reprinted with permission of Emerald Group Publishing Ltd.

can be developed and outsourcing much of the rest has also served many other companies well. The key often lies in knowing which of the main value drivers to concentrate on—customer intimacy, product leadership, or operational excellence. All three are key to delivering value to customers, but the organizational capabilities and cultures that promote them are not the same, and often tend to pull in different directions.[1] So, for example, Nike has tended to focus primarily on product leadership and Dell on operational excellence and customer relationship management, and both rely on the competencies of others to help them deliver value in other areas. The appeal of such a strategy continues to widen, even into some of the most traditional sectors. Today, for example, many newspapers now tend to concentrate mainly on the customer relationship area, outsourcing much of their content and most of their printing and distribution.

Scaling Without Mass—Nokia and Nortel

Another attractive feature of outsourcing is that it offers companies the opportunity to grow in market presence without a corresponding expansion in organizational size or bureaucracy. Strategic outsourcing can help a rapidly growing company avoid a premature internal transition from its informal entrepreneurial phase to a more bureaucratic mode of operation. In this way, outsourcing allows firms to retain their entrepreneurial speed and agility, which they would otherwise sacrifice in order to become efficient as they greatly expanded.

This is one of the primary benefits that companies like Nike, opting initially for a focused strategy with extensive outsourcing, tend to enjoy from the outset. For example, over the 1978–82 period, during the steepest phase in Nike's early growth, revenue scaled up nearly tenfold from $71 million to $690 million, while the employee population grew from 720 to 3,600, just half the growth rate of revenue. In fact, Nike continued to retain many of the characteristics of an entrepreneurial firm until it was almost a $1 billion company. It was not until it reached billionaire status that the lack of formal management systems became a serious impediment to the company's further development.

However, the prospect of being able to scale up without a pro-rata increase in organizational mass and complexity is an attractive reason to consider outsourcing at any stage in a company's development, not just at start-up. For example, in early 2000, when employee numbers at Nokia were increasing at the rate of 1,000 per month, and approaching the 60,000 mark, CEO Jorma Ollila decided to outsource a significant portion of its production in both its network equipment and mobile handset businesses in order to help slow down the growth in number of employees without impeding the company's momentum in the marketplace. It was a strategy that helped cushion the effects of a subsequent downturn, but the main consideration was the fear that too-rapid growth would dilute the Nokia spirit and undermine organizational coherence. At the time, Nokia was widely known as one of the least bureaucratic of global corporations, and Ollila embraced outsourcing to keep it that way.

For another large corporate example, at Nortel Networks in 1999 management recognized they were on the cusp of a "once-in-a-lifetime" market shift, with the opportunity to double their company's revenue from $20 billion to $40 billion within 24 months, if they could get their business model right. They also realized that they could not hope to avail themselves of this opportunity by remaining a traditional manufacturer. The realization produced a managerial mantra—"Why do companies fail? They fail because their processes don't scale." This insight led the Nortel management team to conclude that "we'd never be a $40B company with our existing processes" as Frank Dunn, the company's chief financial officer, later recalled. At the time, the company's return on invested capital was running at just about half that of market leader Cisco. Over the 1999–2001 period, Nortel divested 15 manufacturing sites and transferred 9,000 employees to contract manufacturers such as Solectron and Sanmina. This was part of a wider move toward a more customer-centric strategy, outsourcing production while creating in-house supply chain management teams for each major customer. The entire system was dedicated to improving end-to-end fulfillment using Internet-enabled resource management systems.[2]

Disruptive Innovation—IKEA, Canon, and Ryanair

Outsourcing is a key element in many of the most impressive examples of disruptive innovation to date. Typical examples include IKEA's entry into furniture retailing, Canon's into the photocopying market, and Ryanair's into the European airline industry. The primary aim of most disruptive innovation is to create a whole new segment at a price point well below the bottom of the current market and then to dominate this segment as it grows. This usually requires the development of an innovative business model capable of producing overall returns at least as good as those of the leading incumbents, but doing it at significantly lower cost through much higher asset productivity.[3] IKEA, Canon, and Ryanair were all late entrants into their respective industries, but all succeeded in building substantial market positions through such a strategy, and outsourcing was a common element in the development of a distinctive lower-cost/higher-asset productivity formula in all three cases.

At the time of IKEA's founding in the early 1950s, the European furniture industry was highly fragmented geographically. National department stores established exclusive relationships with local manufacturers to allow them to offer distinctive product lines, reflective of local tastes and traditions. Quality new furniture was typically priced beyond the reach of all but the relatively prosperous, and most young people setting out to furnish their first home had to rely on the secondhand market or hand-me-downs from parents. Ingvar Kamprad, and his company IKEA, set out to "democratize" this marketplace by bringing quality new furniture within reach of the many, not just the few. IKEA developed a range of simple, elegant, "modern" designs, using light-colored quality woods. This appealed to young customers of all nations. The key to delivering such attractive furniture at prices well below prevailing norms was designing for manufacturability and transport-ability, not just consumer appeal. IKEA revolutionized the European furniture industry with a novel "production-oriented retailing" business model, the competitiveness of which depended not only on the careful outsourcing of production but also on "outsourcing" final assembly and delivery to the customers themselves. The "production-oriented retailing" principle remains fundamental to the IKEA business model as the company continues to expand internationally, and, no matter how strong the pull at the retail end, the company will only enter new lines of furniture that fit with its production-oriented economics.

Outsourcing has been a prominent feature in the business models of other classic disruptive innovators over the years, not just IKEA. For example, in the case of Canon, outsourcing has always been a major element in the company's strategy in the copier market, with 80 percent of product assembled from purchased parts and only drums and toner manufactured in-house. Outsourcing is also prominent in the business model of Ryanair, the disruptive innovator in the European airline industry (the self-styled "Southwest Airlines of Europe"), where the company contracts out most of its aircraft handling, heavy maintenance, and baggage handling as part of its strategy to avoid complexity, keep cost down, and maintain productivity at levels well above industry norms.

Strategic Repositioning—IBM

Strategic repositioning is rarely easy, especially when you are a longtime industry leader like IBM. Yet one of the biggest strategic bets that Lou Gerstner made as part of the turnaround at IBM in the mid-1990s was that services, not technology, would be the major growth area going forward, particularly in the corporate computing market. As he saw it then: "If customers were going to look to an integrator to help them envision, design, and build end-to-end solutions, then the companies playing that role would exert tremendous influence over the full range of technology decisions—from architecture and applications to hardware and software choices."[4] Traditionally IBM's strategy had always stressed service as a distinguishing feature of its value proposition, but this was service tied to products. What Gerstner had in mind was consultancy and solutions integration services as a major business driver in its own right. In 1992, services was a $9.2 billion business at IBM—within 10 years IBM Global Services had grown into a $30 billion business, employing half the corporation's human resources. Recently, IBM has intensified its commitment to this strategic repositioning, as part of CEO Sam Palmisano's e-business "on-demand" vision.

Outsourcing is central to IBM's repositioning—both as a driver and an enabler. Under the new strategy IBM has become both an extensive provider of outsourcing services to others as part of its offering as a solutions integrator (primarily in the IT area), while at the same time becoming a more extensive user of outsourcing services itself (primarily in the product area from contract manufacturers). For example, IBM's own IT outsourcing services is now one of the main revenue drivers in the company's new e-business on demand strategy and one that generated $13 billion in the European market alone in 2002. Further back its value chain, IBM's decision to outsource a growing share of its own production is helping it accelerate its ongoing migration to a services-led model and reconfigure its resources to support this strategy. Within the last two years the company has entered into a $5 billion outsourcing contract with Sanmina-SCI Corporation to manufacture its NetVista line of desktop computers, later expanded to include a significant portion of its low- to mid-range server and workstation lines, along with some distribution and fulfillment activities. Substantial transfers of assets and overheads have been involved in both of these deals, which the company sees as allowing it to "leverage the skills of the industry where it makes sense to improve our costs, and focus our own investments on areas that deliver the highest value to our customers."[5]

THE RISKS OF OUTSOURCING

Outsourcing also increases certain strategic risks. Two of the most important are the risk of losing skills key to competing for the future and the risk of making the outsourcing move at the least suitable time in an industry's evolution.

Mortgaging the Future: Losing Key Skills and Capabilities

Companies can often be attracted to outsourcing as a means to relieve intensifying competitive pressure. However, if they fail to consider the long-term implications, they may unwittingly mortgage their future opportunities for short-term advantage. For example, not too many years ago Eastman Kodak executives made a decision to exit the camcorder business because the investment challenge at the time looked too steep to stay in the game. Years later, however, they came to recognize that the skills and knowledge they would have developed in the manufacture of the major subcomponents could have been used to support a wider range of applications of the core technologies beyond the consumer market into medical imaging and other areas. In a similar way, Bulova was slow to see the wider applications that the manufacturing

skills developed in the area of miniature tuning fork technology might have beyond the watch market, an insight not lost on Citizen. In contrast, Canon chose to take a longer view and remain in the semiconductor business following its failure to make the hoped-for impact in the calculator market, a decision that in time would leave it well positioned to play in the office products market when electronic imaging later emerged as a key technology.

Like prematurely exiting a market, hasty and near-sighted outsourcing may result in the loss or unintended transfer of critical learning opportunities, as happened to General Electric in its outsourcing arrangement with Samsung in the microwave market. In the early 1980s General Electric was still investing heavily in its own manufacturing capability in Columbia, Maryland, when it decided to outsource the production of some of its models at the small to medium end of the market to Samsung, then just a modest enterprise little known outside of Korea. The initial contract was for just 15,000 units. However, GE quickly found itself on a steep dependence spiral that ultimately saw it ceding most of the investment and skills development initiative in microwave production to its outsourcer within just two years. For Samsung, the arrangement allowed it to scale up its production and engineering to levels that would not have been possible without access to GE's American consumers. This one small outsourcing contract set the stage for Samsung's emergence as a global powerhouse in consumer appliances.[6] The lesson from this and similar examples is that it pays to be mindful that strategic capabilities are rarely synonymous with discrete functions like engineering or production but tend to be deeply embedded in the collective know-how that reflects their integration.[7] That is why many extensive outsourcers like Nike still wish to retain some manufacturing activity and closely tie it to engineering and marketing in order to preserve the multifunctional capabilities they see as key to their future success.

Choosing to Outsource at the Wrong Time in a Market's Evolution

Strategists also need to know when in an industry's evolution and where along its value chain the economics favor outsourcing. They also need to be aware how this tends to change over time, particularly in technology markets. According to disruptive innovation authority, Clayton Christensen, the critical transition is when the market changes from the stage where most customers continue to desire more functionality than is currently offered to the point where the majority of customers come to see themselves as being over-served with features. This is the juncture at which the product rapidly becomes a commodity and where the primary basis of competition shifts to aspects of the value proposition beyond technology—such as price, speed, convenience, and customization.

In the PC market, for example, it is widely recognized today that IBM outsourced too early because of its anxiety to slow down the progress of Apple Computer, and in doing so allowed the initiative at the features-driven stage of the market's evolution to flow mainly to Intel and Microsoft. Later, when the personal computer became a commodity, the market favored the business model of Dell, which focused largely on customer relationship management and efficient fulfillment and used extensive outsourcing. Indeed, in migrating its model to other segments, Dell's success continues to rely on recognizing when a market's evolution has progressed beyond the features-led, technology-driven stage. To date, it has managed to get this right in the personal computer and mid-range server markets. It now believes the time is more than ripe to apply its model to inkjet printers, where market leader Hewlett-Packard continues to place its bets on its superior technological capabilities and on proprietary features. When deciding whether to make such a wager, it is important for managers to recognize that core competence, as understood in many businesses, can be "a dangerously inward-looking notion." Managers are much more likely to win their bet if they understand that competitiveness "is far more about doing what customers value than what you think you are good at."[8] Knowing the difference is one of the secrets to getting the timing of outsourcing strategy right, as the following insight from a senior supply chain executive at Hewlett-Packard makes clear:

> How do you spot early that you are losing your protected differentiation with the customer in terms of product, process or performance? Every company likes to believe that it has a superior product. It takes skill to recognize that others are catching up. In the inkjet printer market we always have to ask ourselves

are we still producing products that the customer values on an ongoing basis? Are things going horizontal? Sooner or later, you get to a point of diminishing returns where the market no longer fully values say an improvement in speed from 25 to 30 pages per minute or where the next improvement in photo quality resolution reaches the point where only a measuring instrument will detect it. When further improvements have a negligible impact on the customer, in terms of perceived value, you are not too far from being commoditized or horizontalized. How do you then operate in a different mode? How do you transition to a different model? This is when outsourcing tends to become a serious option for a business to consider.[9]

KNOW YOUR OPTIONS AND CONSIDER THE TIMING AND RISK

Outsourcing as a strategy has the potential to drive competitiveness and value creation in many ways beyond the narrow goal of cost reduction alone. Achieving greater focus, scaling without mass, fueling disruptive innovation, and enabling strategic repositioning are just four of the many promising options that outsourcing as a strategy can offer and support. However, managers considering any such outsourcing options will always need to ask themselves whether the timing is right and also what strategic skills and capabilities they might be putting at risk.

Notes

1. For a full discussion of these value drivers see Treacy, M. and Wiersema, F. (1993), "Customer intimacy and other value disciplines," *Harvard Business Review,* January–February, pp. 84–93. For a closer look at the inherent tensions among them, see also Hagel, J. and Singer, M. (1999), "Unbundling the corporation," *Harvard Business Review,* March–April, pp. 133–41.

2. For more on the Nortel case see Fisher, L. M. (2001), "From vertical to virtual: how Nortel's supplier alliances extend the enterprise," *Strategy + Business,* Quarter 1.

3. The term disruptive innovation is used here in the sense defined by Clay Christensen—see Christensen, C. M. and Raynor, M. E. (2003), *The Innovator's Solution,* Harvard Business School Press, Boston, MA.

4. Quote from Gerstner, L. V. (2003), *Who Says Elephants Can't Dance?* HarperBusiness, New York, NY.

5. Bob Moffat, general manager of IBM's Personal & Printing Systems Group, quoted in an IBM press release, "IBM signs agreement with Sanmina-SCI to manufacture its NetVista desktop PCs in US and Europe," January 8, 2002.

6. For more on the GE/Samsung case see Magaziner, I. C. and Patinkin, M. (1989), "Fast heat: how Korea won the microwave war," *Harvard Business Review,* January–February, pp. 83–91. For more examples of the risk of losing key skills and learning opportunities, see Lei, D. and Slocum, J. W. (1992), "Global strategy, competence-building and strategic alliances," *California Management Review,* Fall, pp. 81–97.

7. For more on the embedded and integrated nature of core competencies see Prahalad, C. K., Fahey, L. and Randall, R. M. (2001), "Creating and leveraging core competencies," in Fahey, L. and Randall, R. M. (Eds), *The Portable MBA in Strategy,* 2nd ed, Wiley, New York, NY, pp. 236–52.

8. For more on this risk, see Christensen, C. M. and Raynor, M. E. (2003), *The Innovator's Solution,* Harvard Business School Press, Boston, MA (especially chapters 5 and 6—the quote comes from Chapter 6).

9. Maurice O'Connell, Materials Director of Hewlett-Packard's inkjet printer business, in conversation with the author at the HP plant in Dublin, July 2, 2004.

The Integration of Lean Management and Six Sigma

Edward D. Arnheiter
Rensselaer Polytechnic Institute

John Maleyeff
Rensselaer Polytechnic Institute

INTRODUCTION

Over the last two decades, American industrial organizations have embraced a wide variety of management programs that they hope will enhance competitiveness. Currently, two of the most popular programs are Six Sigma and lean management. Six Sigma was founded by Motorola Corporation and subsequently adopted by many U.S. companies, including GE and AlliedSignal. Lean management originated at Toyota in Japan and has been implemented by many major U.S. firms, including Danaher Corporation and Harley-Davidson. Six Sigma and lean management have diverse roots. The key issue driving the development of Six Sigma was the need for quality improvement when manufacturing complex products having a large number of components, which often resulted in a correspondingly high probability of defective final products. The driving force behind the development of lean management was the elimination of waste, especially in Japan, a country with few natural resources.

Both Six Sigma and lean management have evolved into comprehensive management systems. In each case, their effective implementation involves cultural changes in organizations, new approaches to production and to servicing customers, and a high degree of training and education of employees, from upper management to the shop floor. As such, both systems have come to encompass common features, such as an emphasis on customer satisfaction,

Reprinted from "The integration of lean management and Six Sigma," Edward D. Arnheiter, John Maleyeff, *The TQM Magazine*, Vol. 17, No. 1, 2005. Used by permission of Emerald Group Publishing Ltd.

high quality, and comprehensive employee training and empowerment.

With disparate roots but similar goals, Six Sigma and lean management are both effective on their own. However, some organizations that have embraced either Six Sigma or lean management might find that they eventually reach a point of diminishing returns. That is, after reengineering their operating and supporting systems for improvement by solving major problems and resolving key inefficiencies, further improvements are not easily generated, as illustrated in Figure 1. These organizations have begun to look elsewhere for sources of competitive advantage. Naturally, lean organizations are examining Six Sigma and Six Sigma organizations are exploring lean management. The term *lean Sigma* has recently been used to describe a management system that combines the two systems (Sheridan, 2000). In this paper, the term *lean, Six Sigma (LSS) organization* will be used to describe an entity that integrates the two systems.

The purpose of this paper is to eliminate many misconceptions regarding Six Sigma and lean management by describing each system and the key concepts and techniques that underlie their implementation. Since these misconceptions may tend to discourage the education necessary for proponents of one system to become educated into the key elements of the other system, the misconceptions will be addressed one-by-one. This discussion will be followed by a description of what lean organizations can gain from Six Sigma and what Six Sigma organizations can gain from lean management. Finally, some suggestions will be

Figure 1   **Improvements over Time with Six Sigma or Lean Management Alone**

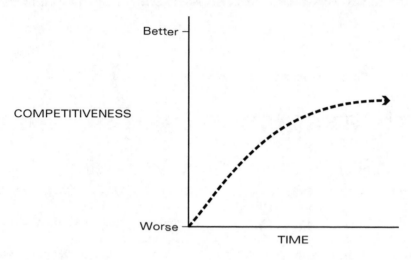

OVERVIEW OF SIX SIGMA

The roots of Six Sigma can be traced to two primary sources: total quality management (TQM) and the Six Sigma statistical metric originating at Motorola Corporation. Today, Six Sigma is a broad long-term decision-making business strategy rather than a narrowly focused quality management program.

From TQM, Six Sigma preserved the concept that everyone in an organization is responsible for the quality of goods and services produced by the organization. Other components of Six Sigma that can be traced to TQM include the focus on customer satisfaction when making management decisions, and a significant investment in education and training in statistics, root cause analysis, and other problem solving methodologies. With TQM, quality was the first priority. The main tools of TQM included the seven tools of quality: control charts, histograms, check sheets, scatter plots, cause-and-effect diagrams, flowcharts, and Pareto charts; and the seven management tools of quality: affinity diagrams, interrelationship digraphs, tree diagrams, matrix diagrams, prioritization matrices, process decision program charts, and activity network diagrams (Sower et al., 1999).

The six-sigma metric was developed at Motorola in 1987 in response to substandard product quality traced in many cases to decisions made by engineers when designing component parts. Traditionally, design engineers used the "three-sigma" rule when evaluating whether or not an acceptable proportion of manufactured components would be expected to meet tolerances. When a component's tolerances were consistent with a spread of six standard deviation units of process variation, about 99.7 percent of the components for a centered process would be expected to conform to tolerances. That is, only 0.3 percent of parts would be nonconforming to tolerances, which translates to about 3,000 nonconforming parts per million (NCPPM).

At Motorola, as products became more complex, defective products were becoming more commonplace while at the same time customers were demanding higher quality. For example, a pager or cell phone included hundreds of components. Each component typically included numerous important quality characteristics. It was not uncommon for a product to include thousands of opportunities for defects (OFDs) in each product sold (Harry and Schroeder, 2000). Traditional three-sigma quality for each OFD was no longer acceptable. For example, consider a product that contains 1,000 OFDs. If, for each OFD, three-sigma quality levels are achieved, only about 5 percent of the products would be defect free. The calculation used to obtain this probability requires raising the fraction conforming (0.997) to the power of 1,000, and is based on the binomial probability distribution (Devore, 2000).

The formula used to determine the probability of defect-free products provides only an approximate guideline for two reasons. Since three-sigma is the

Figure 2 **Process Average Shifting ± 1.5 Sigma Units**

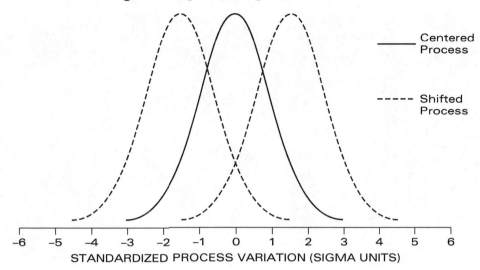

minimum design standard, it would be expected that many products would surpass the three-sigma standard. On the other hand, the 0.997 conformance probability assumes a centered process and it would be expected that many processes would not be centered every time a component is produced. The calculation does, however, effectively illustrate the challenge inherent in producing defect-free products. Assuming 1,000 OFDs, only 37 percent of products will be free of defects if the quality level at each OFD averaged 99.9 percent, and 90 percent of products will be free of defects if the quality level at each OFD averaged 99.99 percent.

Other industries face similar challenges in achieving superior quality. In addition to the consumer electronics industry, other products with a large number of OFDs include automobiles, engines, airframes, and computers. Many industries where products are less complex also face similar challenges. Manufacturers of medical devices and other products where defects in the field may cause harm must achieve almost perfect quality. Companies that manufacture less complex products but sell them in very large volumes also need to be focused on achieving superior quality.

At Motorola, when studying the relationship between component quality and final product quality it was discovered that, from lot to lot, a process tended to shift a maximum of 1.5 sigma units (McFadden, 1993). This concept is shown graphically in Figure 2, which shows a centered process and processes shifted 1.5 sigma units in both directions. Table I provides the relationship between component quality

and final product quality, assuming that the full 1.5 sigma shift takes place. In Table I, Sigma level is the standardized process variation (see Figure 2), OFD quality is the NCPPM if the process shifts a full 1.5 sigma units, and the probabilities in the table provide the proportion of final products that will be free of defects. For example, if the company sets a goal for final product quality of 99.7 percent and products include about 1,000 OFDs, then the 3.4 NCPPM corresponding to the Six-Sigma metric would became the standard against which all decisions were made.

In late 1999, Ford Motor Company became the first major automaker to adopt a Six Sigma strategy. At Ford, each car has approximately 20,000 OFDs. Therefore, if Ford were to attain Six Sigma quality, approximately 1 car in every 15 produced would contain a defect (Truby, 2000). It is interesting to note in Table I that if Ford operated at a 5.5 sigma level, about 50 percent of their cars would include at least one defect.

Today, Six Sigma is a combination of the Six Sigma statistical metric and TQM, with additional innovations that enhance the program's effectiveness while expanding its focus. The main components of Six Sigma retained from TQM include a focus on the customer, recognition that quality is the responsibility of all employees, and the emphasis on employee training. The Six Sigma metric is also used, but in an expanded fashion.

With Six Sigma, the value of an organization's output includes not just quality, but availability, reliability, delivery performance, and after-market

Table I   **Final Product Quality Level (percentage conforming)**

Sigma Level	OFD Quality (NCPPM)	Number of OFDs per Product				
		100 (%)	500 (%)	1,000 (%)	5,000 (%)	20,000 (%)
2.5	158,655	0.0	0.0	0.0	0.0	0.0
3.0	66,807	0.1	0.0	0.0	0.0	0.0
3.5	22,750	10.0	0.0	0.0	0.0	0.0
4.0	6,210	53.6	4.4	0.2	0.0	0.0
4.5	1,350	87.4	50.9	25.9	0.1	0.0
5.0	233	97.7	89.0	79.2	31.2	1.0
5.5	32	99.7	98.4	96.9	85.3	53.1
6.0	3.4	100.0	99.8	99.7	98.3	93.4
6.5	0.29	100.0	100.0	100.0	99.9	99.4
7.0	0.019	100.0	100.0	100.0	100.0	100.0
7.5	0.0010	100.0	100.0	100.0	100.0	100.0

service. Performance within each of the components of the customer's value equation should be superior. Hence, the Six Sigma metric is applied in a broad fashion, striving for near perfect performance at the lowest level of activity. In addition, Six Sigma programs generally create a structure under which training of employees is formalized and supported to ensure its effectiveness. All employees involved in activities that impact customer satisfaction would be trained in basic problem solving skills. Other employees are provided advanced training and required to act as mentors to others in support of quality improvement projects.

OVERVIEW OF LEAN MANAGEMENT

The concept of lean management can be traced to the Toyota production system (TPS), a manufacturing philosophy pioneered by the Japanese engineers Taiichi Ohno and Shigeo Shingo (Inman, 1999). It is well known, however, that Henry Ford achieved high throughput and low inventories, and practiced short-cycle manufacturing as early as the late 1910s. Ohno greatly admired and studied Ford because of his accomplishments and the overall reduction of waste at early Ford assembly plants (Hopp and Spearman, 2001). The TPS is also credited with being the birthplace of just-in-time (JIT) production methods, a key element of lean production, and for

this reason the TPS remains a model of excellence for advocates of lean management.

By contrast, the traditional U.S. production system was based on the "batch-and-queue" concept. High production volumes, large batch sizes, and long non-value-added queue times between operations characterize batch-and-queue production. Batch-and-queue techniques developed from economy of scale principles, which implicitly assumed that setup and changeover penalties make small batch sizes uneconomical. These methods typically result in lower quality since defects are usually not discovered until subsequent operations or in the finished product.

Lean management emphasizes small batch sizes and, ultimately, single-piece flow (i.e., transfer batch size = 1). The term pull is used to imply that nothing is made until it is needed by the downstream customer, and the application of a make-to-order (MTO) approach whenever possible. In some industries, such as the personal computer business, MTO production has become the de facto business model. The Dell "direct sales model," for example, quickly converts customer orders into finished personal computers ready for shipment (Sheridan, 1999). The initial "pull" on the Dell production line is the telephone or electronic order from the customer. The direct sales model also allows Dell to customize each unit to the customer's specifications.

The lean production goal of eliminating waste (*muda* in Japanese), so that all activities along the value stream create value, is known as perfection.

Efforts focused on the reduction of waste are pursued through continuous improvement or *kaizen* events, as well as radical improvement activities, or *kaikaku*. Both *kaizen* and *kaikaku* reduce *muda,* although the term *kaikaku* is generally reserved for the initial rethinking of a process. Hence, perfection is the goal and the journey to perfection is never ending (Womack and Jones, 1996).

Another element of lean management is the reduction of variability at every opportunity, including demand variability, manufacturing variability, and supplier variability. Manufacturing variability includes not only variation of product quality characteristics (e.g., length, width, weight), but also variation present in task time (e.g., downtime, absenteeism, operator skill levels). Lean management attempts to reduce task time variation by establishing standardized work procedures. Supplier variability includes uncertainties in quality and delivery times. The reduction in supplier variability is often achieved through partnerships and other forms of supplier–producer cooperation.

Lean production practices will often reduce lead times so drastically that it becomes feasible to practice MTO production, and still provide on-time deliveries. Even when a make-to-stock (MTS) approach is required (e.g., a high-volume consumer products company filling large supply and distribution channels), reducing lead times improves replenishment times, thereby lowering inventories throughout the supply network, and making the supply chain more respondent to demand uncertainties.

It should be mentioned that individual processes do exist for which batch-and-queue systems are still currently necessary. This is often the case when performing operations such as chrome plating, where large batches are placed in plating tanks. In wrench manufacturing, for example, steel forgings might move in a single-piece flow through a U-shaped machining cell, but then accumulate into a large batch at the end of the cell before being moved to a chrome plating station. In fact, very few lean manufacturers have pure single-piece-flow systems throughout their entire operation.

Lean management also applies to indirect and overhead activities. Any policy or procedure having a goal of optimizing the performance of a single portion of a company risks violating lean management rules. For example, a purchasing manager who is given a reward for cutting costs of component parts may sacrifice quality to achieve his or her goal. Accounting systems that measure efficiency of output for individuals or departments may encourage the generation of products when no demand exists.

Quality management practices in lean production emphasize the concept of zero quality control (ZQC). A ZQC system includes mistake proofing (poka-yoke), source inspection (operators checking their own work), automated 100 percent inspection, stopping operations instantly when a mistake is made, and ensuring setup quality (Shingo, 1986). Typically, inspections are performed quickly using go–no go gages rather than more time consuming variable measurement methods.

Quality practices in batch-and-queue generally emphasize acceptance sampling performed by dedicated inspectors, product quality audits, and statistical process control (SPC). Thus, for equivalent process quality levels, poor quality in a batch-and-queue system would result in high external failure costs, whereas poor quality in a lean production system would cause high internal failure costs (see Figure 3).

MISCONCEPTIONS REGARDING LEAN MANAGEMENT AND SIX SIGMA

It is clear that lean management and Six Sigma were derived from two different points of view. Lean production was derived from the need to increase product flow velocity through the elimination of all non-value-added activities. Six Sigma developed from the need to ensure final product quality by focusing on obtaining very high conformance at the OFD level. In order for proponents of one program to learn from the other program, some common misconceptions should be dispelled. The key misconceptions are described below.

Key Misconceptions Regarding Lean Management

The most common misconception of lean management is lean means layoffs. While this misconception may be due to the term *lean* (especially in the context of *lean and mean*), it is a misinterpretation of the term. In lean management, if an employee were performing non-value-added activities within his or her job, management and the employee would

Figure 3   **Batch-and-Queue Versus Lean Quality Systems**

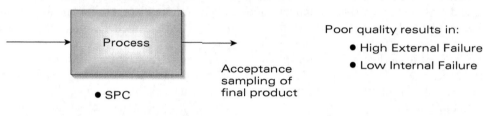

Batch-and-Queue Quality Systems

Process

• SPC

Acceptance sampling of final product

Poor quality results in:
• High External Failure
• Low Internal Failure

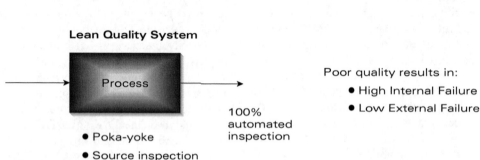

Lean Quality System

Process

• Poka-yoke
• Source inspection

100% automated inspection

Poor quality results in:
• High Internal Failure
• Low External Failure

work together to find a better way to perform the job to eliminate the non-value-added activities. Laying off the employee would be counterproductive since a knowledgeable person would no longer be available and the remaining employees would be reluctant to take part in future waste elimination projects. Hence, layoffs cannot take place in the context of lean management, unless it becomes an absolute necessity and every effort to reassign or retrain the employee fails (Emiliani, 2001).

Another misconception is that lean only works in Japan, because of their unique culture. This view is unsubstantiated. In fact, lean management is not a universal system in Japan and some of the most successful lean management implementations have been within non-Japanese companies (Emiliani, 2003). The source of the misconception may be the belief that Japanese workers are by nature more frugal than their international counterparts. Even if this statement were true, eliminating waste and being frugal often conflict, such as when an engineer designs an inferior part to save money.

Another key misconception is that lean is for manufacturing only. Even in a manufacturing environment, lean management views each step in the process as a service step, where customer value is added with minimal waste. Within this framework, processing claims in the insurance industry, evaluating loan applications at a bank, and treating patients in a hospital all involve performing activities synonymous with the lean management viewpoint.

In any business where customers exist and activities take place to satisfy those customers, lean management can be practiced successfully.

A final misconception is that lean only works within certain environments. This view is heard from managers in operations that are traditionally large batch operations as well as from managers of diverse job-shop operations. While these types of operations may never conform to the "lot size of one" principle, lean management encompasses much more than manufacturing process design. If attempts were made to identify and eliminate all non-value-added activities throughout the organization, these companies would be practicing important aspects of lean management. These companies could also pursue other elements of lean management, by continuously attempting to follow lean principles when adopting new manufacturing technologies. For example, new technologies have become available that allow for small lot sizes on processes that traditionally require long setup or cycle times, including semiconductor wafer cleaning (Lester, 2000), coating/laminating (Friedman, 2000), and chemical testing (Anné, 2000).

Key Misconceptions Regarding Six Sigma

The most common misconception of Six Sigma is that it is the new flavor of the month, pushed by quality consultants in a way similar to the way Deming Management, TQM, business process reengineering

(BPR), and ISO 9000 were pushed in the recent past. Unfortunately, there will always be consultants who jump onto any bandwagon, take a seminar and proclaim themselves experts in a program. Six Sigma is no exception to this phenomenon. However, Six Sigma should be considered state-of-the-art in terms of quality management, in that it borrows from previous programs, especially Deming's management philosophies and TQM's focus on the customer, and adds new features such as a comprehensive training structure and a broad definition of value from a customer's perspective to include not only quality, but service and delivery. It is fair to say that while the name of Six Sigma may change in the future, the main features will be carried over to subsequent programs and new and improved versions will emerge.

Another misconception of Six Sigma is that the goal of 3.4 NCPPM is absolute and should be applied to every opportunity tolerance and specification, regardless of its ultimate importance in the customer's value expression. While the 3.4 NCPPM was derived at Motorola based on the characteristics of its products, Six Sigma programs do not use this metric as an absolute goal in all cases. As part of Six Sigma, the Pareto principle is applied so that improvement projects will focus on the "lowest hanging apple" and make improvements where they matter the most. Since no company's business remains static very long, new products and services will generally provide a never-ending source of low-hanging apples. Alternatively, examples can be found where a goal of 3.4 NCPPM will never be good enough and the target must be set at a higher sigma level. For example, the nuclear power, medical device, and aerospace industries all require the pursuit of exceptional quality to prevent catastrophic loss of human life.

As a related point, proponents of ZQC systems may conclude that ZQC is preferred to Six Sigma given that ZQC results in zero NCPPM rather than "settling" for 3.4 NCPPM. This point is invalid for two reasons. First, as shown in Figure 4, the six-sigma metric is applied to the output from a process, before inspection takes place. The "zero" in the ZQC system applies to output from processes after an inspection takes place. Second, many inspection systems are prone to inspection errors. Studies have shown that some inspection systems pass nonconforming items at alarming rates. These inspection errors will be especially prevalent on sensory inspections. For example, a study at an automotive manufacturer found that trained inspectors passed 73 percent of nonconforming items based on a sensory inspection (Burke et al., 1995). Hence, ZQC does not necessarily mean zero defects escaping the inspection.

A final misconception of Six Sigma is that it is a quality only program. As described earlier, the concept of Six Sigma "quality" relates to the entire customer value equation. Its applicability is broad, encompassing manufacturing, delivery, service, and maintenance components.

INTEGRATING LEAN MANAGEMENT AND SIX SIGMA

It was pointed out earlier that companies practicing either lean management or Six Sigma alone might reach a point of diminishing returns. In this section, benefits that may be derived by combining the

Figure 4   **Typical Measurement Points in the Six-Sigma and ZQC Philosophies**

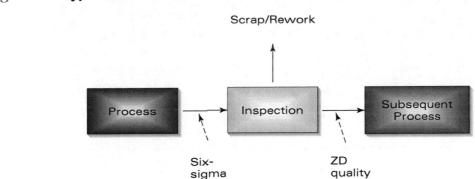

programs are described. In addition, recommendations are made that will help companies practicing one of the programs to integrate the programs via evolutionary, rather than revolutionary, changes.

What Can Lean Organizations Gain from Six Sigma?

Lean organizations should make more use of data in decision making and use methodologies that promote a more scientific approach to quality. For example, when quality problems occur within a lean management system, defects are likely to be identified internally via the ZQC system. When this occurs, waste is incurred in a number of ways. First, there is a loss of opportunity for the production of that component since operation times are synchronized with demand via the pull system of production control. Second, cost is added through rework or scrap. Third, indirect personnel and other overhead must be available to handle the scrap and rework, such as a repair department.

As an example, consider a manufacturing cell with a two-minute cycle time. The cell operates for two 8-hour shifts, resulting in a target production of 480 units per day. Work in the cell consists of 20 individual tasks, and each unit of product possesses a total of 100 OFDs. In this cell, when the 480-unit daily target is not met due to system variations (e.g., defects, machine downtime, power failures), overtime must be utilized. Table II lists the average number of overtime hours that would need to be scheduled per day to accommodate the quality level noted. For example, if component quality at the

OFD level were 1,000 NCPPM (0.1 percent), then on average 1.5 hours of overtime would be required per day. If this were the case, the company could allow for buffer quantities to be preproduced, but this practice also creates waste and is undesirable.

The ZQC system also has the potential to cause reliability and quality problems due to the interaction of tolerances in complex products. An example involving Ford transmissions illustrates the problem caused by relying on tolerance-based pass/fail criteria during inspections. Ford had a problem with warranty claims for automatic transmissions. The transmissions were made at both the Ford Batavia (Ohio, USA) facility and at a Mazda facility in Japan. Data showed that customer satisfaction was higher for the Mazda-built transmissions. Subsequently, samples of both Ford and Mazda transmissions were disassembled and each component part was measured (Gunter, 1987). The Ford transmissions all conformed to tolerances, but exhibited a much higher level of dimensional variation than the Mazda transmissions. With a product as complex as a transmission, the interaction of the parts caused more failures in the Ford transmissions. In order for a lean producer to ensure that this problem is not repeated, less dependence would need to be placed on pass/fail attribute inspections and more on keeping processes on target.

The Ford transmission example illustrates a phenomenon that is likely to occur whenever attribute, or go–no go, inspections are used to judge quality, as is often the case in ZQC systems. By collecting and analyzing variable measurements using control charting methods, processes can be effectively kept on target. In cases where variable measurements are

Table II   **Average Number of Overtime Hours versus Quality Levels**

Sigma Level	OFD-Level Quality (NCPPM)	Percentage Defect-Free Products	Average Overtime Hours/Day
3.8	10,000	36.40	10.1
4.6	1,000	90.48	1.5
5.2	100	99.01	0.2
5.8	10	99.90	0.0
6.0	3.4	99.97	0.0
6.3	1	99.99	0.0

costly or time consuming, narrow limit gauging may be used to keep processes on target (Ott and Schilling, 1990). Alternatively, precontrol, also known as stoplight control, may be used within the context of ZQC (Salvia, 1988). A comparison of control charts and precontrol shows that under most conditions, control charts are better suited for keeping processes on target (Maleyeff and Lewis, 1993).

What Can Six Sigma Companies Gain from Lean Management?

A competitive company must have both high-quality goods and provide a high quality of service. For example, a company that operates in a batch-and-queue mode runs the risk of providing poor service to customers even if quality is at Six Sigma levels. By reducing manufacturing lead times, a company that is producing to order will enhance competitiveness by achieving faster deliveries or by meeting promised due dates a higher proportion of the time. A company that is producing to stock will gain from reduced lead times by decreasing the horizon of their forecasts and by replenishing stocks more often, thereby increasing the company's revenues and inventory turnover rate. Six Sigma organizations should include training in lean management methods that eliminate all forms of waste, such as *kaizen,* reducing setup times, and mapping the value stream. Two examples will be used to show how Six Sigma organizations may get to a point of diminishing returns (illustrated in Figure 1), due to the nonuse of certain lean management methodologies.

Consider the following scenario, adapted from a Harvard Business School case study (Wong and Hammond, 1991). A manufacturing company that includes a children's knitwear division is using a process-oriented layout (i.e., the plant is organized by machine type). For this product, the average number of operations is 10 and the average processing time per operation is one minute. Like many companies run in this traditional batch-and-queue mode, processing is done in batches since machine setup times and the reluctance to risk idle machinery cause the company to accumulate large WIP inventories on the shop floor. In the case, it is noted that an average of 30,000 garments of work-in-process inventory exists

on the shop floor and the average manufacturing lead time is 15 days. The 15-day lead time results in a percent value added time of 0.14 percent.

Table III shows that, by reducing WIP inventory, thereby increasing the proportion of value-added time, the lead time can be reduced dramatically. For example, the lead time can be reduced to 17 hours by increasing the value added proportion to just 1 percent. It is within lean management that Six Sigma organizations will learn how to increase the value added time of their operations.

Consider an alternative example involving a typical Six Sigma improvement project where an organization is experiencing too many missed due dates. Efforts to address the problem might begin with the "Five whys" root cause analysis, an appro-ach also often practiced in a lean organization. The result of the "Five whys" series of questions are:

1. Problem is missing due dates—why?
2. Lead times are long—why?
3. Not enough capacity—why?
4. Long setup times—why?
5. Die adjustment is time-consuming.

At this point, two types of decisions are possible:

1. Increase capacity by purchasing additional machinery.
2. Increase capacity by reducing the setup times.

The latter alternative is preferable in terms of cost and would be the obvious choice in a lean organization. In this case, the real root cause in this situation may be that the lack of lean production knowledge

Table III   **Effect of Percent Value-Added Time on Manufacturing Lead Time**

Percent Value-Added Time	Lead Time (hours)	Lead Time (days)
0.14	119.9	15.0
0.5	33.3	4.2
1	16.7	2.1
5	3.3	0.4
10	1.7	0.2
25	0.7	0.1

within the organization has perpetuated and institutionalized long setup times.

The Intersection of Lean Management and Six Sigma

The performance of a business is determined by the complex interactions of people, materials, equipment, and resources in the context of the program that manages these interactions. It is fair to say that management theory regarding operating systems is still evolving. While both Six Sigma and lean management represent the state of the art, each system gives priority to certain facets of organizational performance. Therefore, in a highly competitive environment, diminishing returns may result when either program is implemented in isolation. A thorough analysis of the two programs provides some likely reasons why the programs alone may fail to achieve absolute perfection.

Figure 5 summarizes the nature of improvements that may occur in organizations that practice lean management or Six Sigma, and the corresponding improvements that an integrated program could offer. The horizontal axis represents the customer's perspective of value, including quality and delivery performance. The vertical axis represents the producer's cost to provide the product or service to the customer. Under either system, improvements will

be made, but these improvements will begin to level off at a certain point in time. With Six Sigma alone, the leveling off of improvements may be due to the emphasis on optimizing measurable quality and delivery metrics, but ignoring changes in the basic operating systems to remove wasteful activities. With lean management alone, the leveling off of improvements may be due to the emphasis on streamlining product flow, but doing so in a less than scientific manner relating to the use of data and statistical quality control methods.

CONCLUSIONS

A lean, Six Sigma (LSS) organization would capitalize on the strengths of both lean management and Six Sigma. A LSS organization would include the following three primary tenets of lean management:

1. It would incorporate an overriding philosophy that seeks to maximize the value-added content of all operations.
2. It would constantly evaluate all incentive systems in place to ensure that they result in global optimization instead of local optimization.
3. It would incorporate a management decision-making process that bases every decision on its relative impact on the customer.

Figure 5 **Nature of Competitive Advantage**

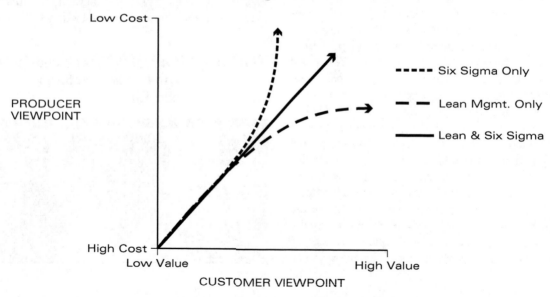

A LSS organization would include the following three primary tenets of Six Sigma:

1. It would stress data-driven methodologies in all decision making, so that changes are based on scientific rather than ad hoc studies.

2. It would promote methodologies that strive to minimize variation of quality characteristics.

3. It would design and implement a companywide and highly structured education and training regimen.

References

Anné, D. C. (2000), "Modern mobile laboratories," *Pollution Engineering,* Vol. 32 No. 8, pp. 37–9.

Burke, R. J., Davis, R. D., Kaminsky, F. C. and Roberts, A. E. P. (1995), "The effect of inspector errors on the true fraction nonconforming: an industrial experiment," *Quality Engineering,* Vol. 7 No. 3, pp. 543–50.

Devore, J. L. (2000), *Probability and Statistics for Engineering and the Sciences,* 5th ed., Duxbury Press, Pacific Grove, CA, pp. 119–26.

Emiliani, M. L. (2001), "Redefining the focus of investment analysts," *The TQM Magazine,* Vol. 13 No. 1, pp. 34–50.

Emiliani, M. L. (2003), *Better Thinking, Better Results,* The Center for Lean Business Management, Kensington, CT.

Friedman, S. (2000), "Where materials and minds meet," *Package Printing and Converting,* Vol. 47 No. 2, pp. 24–5.

Gunter, B. (1987), "A perspective on the Taguchi methods," *Quality Progress,* Vol. 20 No. 6, pp. 44–52.

Harry, M. and Schroeder, R. (2000), *Six Sigma,* Doubleday, New York, NY, p. 65.

Hopp, W. J. and Spearman, M. L. (2001), *Factory Physics,* 2nd ed., Irwin/McGraw-Hill, New York, NY, p. 25.

Inman, R. R. (1999), "Are you implementing a pull system by putting the cart before the horse?," *Production and Inventory Management Journal,* Vol. 40 No. 2, pp. 67–71.

Lester, M. A. (2000), "Quick drying enables single-wafer cleans," *Semiconductor International,* Vol. 23 No. 12, p. 54.

McFadden, F. R. (1993), "Six-Sigma quality programs," *Quality Progress,* Vol. 26 No. 6, pp. 37–42.

Maleyeff, J. and Lewis, D. A. (1993), "Pre-control or X-bar charts: an economic evaluation using alternative cost models," *International Journal of Production Research,* Vol. 31 No. 2, pp. 471–82.

Ott, E. R. and Schilling, E. G. (1990), *Process Quality Control,* Ch. 7, McGraw-Hill, New York, NY.

Salvia, A. A. (1988), "Stoplight control," *Quality Progress,* Vol. 21 No. 9, pp. 39–42.

Sheridan, J. H. (1999), "Focused on flow," *Industry Week,* Vol. 248 No. 19, pp. 46–8.

Sheridan, J. H. (2000), "Lean Sigma synergy," *Industry Week,* Vol. 249 No. 17, pp. 81–2.

Shingo, S. (1986), *Zero Quality Control—Source Inspection and the Poka-yoke System,* Productivity Press, Cambridge, MA.

Sower, V. E., Savoie, M. J. and Renick, S. (1999), *An Introduction to Quality Management and Engineering,* Prentice Hall, Upper Saddle River, NJ, pp. 33–45.

Truby, M. (2000), "Nasser, Ford embrace data-driven quality plan," *Detroit News,* 26 January, p. F1.

Womack, J. P. and Jones, D. T. (1996), *Lean Thinking,* Simon & Schuster, New York, NY, pp. 90–8.

Wong, A. and Hammond, J. H. (1991), *Doré-Doré,* Harvard Business School Publishing, Cambridge, MA.

9-193-029
REV: SEPTEMBER 13, 2004

WILLIAM BRUNS

Introduction to Financial Ratios and Financial Statement Analysis

There is almost always a reason why someone picks up an organization's financial statements and begins to analyze them. Lenders or creditors may be interested in determining whether they will be repaid money they have lent or may lend to the organization. Investors may be interested in comparing a potential investment in one organization with that of another. Employees may want to compare the current performance or financial status of their employer with earlier periods. Regulatory agencies often need to assess organizational or industry financial health and performance. Financial analysis is always based on a set of questions, and the specific questions requiring answers depend on who the financial statement user is and the reasons for his or her analysis.

Financial analyses based on accounting information consistently involve comparisons. Amounts or ratios may be compared with industry norms, the same measurement in a prior period, the same measurement in a competitor's organization, or with planned and budgeted amounts previously established. Figuring out which comparisons will best answer the questions motivating the analysis is one of the necessary steps in making the best use of accounting information.

Financial ratios can help describe the financial condition of an organization, the efficiency of its activities, its comparable profitability, and the perception of investors as expressed by their behavior in financial markets. Ratios often permit an analyst or decision maker to piece together a story about where an organization has come from, its current condition, and its possible future. In most cases, the story is incomplete, and important questions may remain unanswered.

Even though the analyst or decision maker is better informed as a result of doing the ratio analysis, the indiscriminate use of financial ratios can be extremely dangerous. Decision rules that rely on a specific or minimum value of a ratio can easily lead to missed opportunities or losses. Even the best ratio is not always indicative of the health, status, or performance of an organization. Ratios between apparently similar measurements in financial statements may be affected by differences in accounting classifications or by deliberate manipulation.

The ease with which ratios can be manipulated and the danger in using them as criteria lead many analysts to concentrate on trends in ratio measurements rather than on the absolute value or proportion expressed by the ratio itself. When a trend in the value of a ratio between financial attributes is observed, questions can be raised about why the trend is occurring. The answers to such questions provide new information, not necessarily contained in financial reports, but perhaps highly relevant and useful to the decision maker and the problem at hand.

Professor Professor William Bruns prepared this case. HBS cases are developed solely as the basis for class discussion. Cases are not intended to serve as endorsements, sources of primary data, or illustrations of effective or ineffective management.

Similarly, comparisons of firms only on the basis of ratios can lead to erroneous conclusions. The diversity inherent in available accounting practices and principles can lead to differences in ratios between organizations being compared. Comparisons between companies can be made, but they must be made with care and with full attention to the underlying differences in basic accounting methods used in the reports as well as in the companies themselves. With these cautions in mind, we can proceed to examine briefly some commonly used financial ratios.

Profitability Ratios

Profitability ratios seek to associate the amount of income earned with either the amount of resources used or the amount of activity that has taken place. These correspond to efficiency measures often used in economic and engineering theory. Ideally, the firm should produce as much income as possible with a given amount of resources or a satisfactory amount of income using as few resources as possible.

Return on Investment (ROI)

Dividing net income by the amount of investment expresses the idea of economic efficiency. Return on assets (ROA), return on investment capital (ROIC), and return on owners' equity (ROE) are all used in financial analysis as measures of the effectiveness with which assets have been employed.

Return on assets (ROA) relates net income to the investment in all of the financial resources at the command of management. It is most useful as a measure of the effectiveness of resource utilization without regard to how those resources have been obtained and financed. The formula for this ratio is:

$$\text{Return on Assets (ROA)} = \frac{\text{Income}}{\text{Assets}}$$

The consolidated statement of earnings, consolidated balanced sheets, and consolidated statements of cash flows for the Gillette Company and Subsidiary Companies (hereafter the Gillette Company) are shown in **Exhibit 1**. These financial statements will be used as a basis for illustrating the calculation of each financial ratio in this introduction. For 2003 return on assets for the Gillette Company was:

$$\text{Return on Assets (ROA)} = \frac{\$1,385}{\$9,955} = 13.9\%$$

Return on invested capital (ROIC) relates all net income to all resources committed to the firm for long periods of time. It is calculated by dividing net income by the total amount of noncurrent liabilities and stockholders' equity. The formula for this ratio is:

$$\text{Return on Invested Capital (ROIC)} = \frac{\text{Net Income}}{\text{Total Liabilities and Stockholders' Equity - Current Liabilities}}$$

Return on invested capital in 2003 for the Gillette Company was:

$$\text{Return on Invested Capital (ROIC)} = \frac{\$1,385}{\$9,955 - \$3,658} = 22.0\%$$

587

Two variations in these two ratios are often observed. Because their purpose is to compare how efficiently a pool of capital has been used—a pool that includes long-term debt as well as stockholders' equity—the after-tax interest expense is often added back to income in the numerator. This can be easily calculated by the formula:

$$\text{Interest expense} \times (1 - \text{tax rate}) = \text{After-tax interest expense}$$

The amount of the adjustment is the net interest cost. Interest expense is tax deductible, and the formula calculates the after-tax interest expense by multiplying the total interest expense by the complement of the tax rate. The rationale for this adjustment is that it is a better measure of the income flow generated by management, considering all of the sources of long-term financing it has chosen to use. Without the adjustment, the income understates the earnings generated by the total pool of capital.

A second variation is appropriate when the amount of assets or invested capital is changing. Since income is earned over a period of time, the appropriate denominator in the two ratios above is probably average assets or average invested capital. This is easily approximated by adding the beginning and ending measurements together and dividing by two. The analyst has to decide if these refinements to the ratios will improve his or her ability to answer the questions at hand.

Return on equity (ROE) relates net income to the amount invested by stockholders. It is a measure of the efficiency with which the stockholders' investment through their original capital contributions and earnings retained in the business have been used. The formula for this ratio is:

$$\text{Return on Equity (ROE)} = \frac{\text{Net Income}}{\text{Stockholders' Equity}}$$

Return on equity in 2003 for the Gillette Company was:

$$\text{Return on Equity (ROE)} = \frac{\$1,385}{\$2,224} = 62.3\%$$

Note that for this ratio stockholders' equity is the correct denominator because the ratio is an attempt to understand what the investment by the owners alone has earned. (For Gillette, the return on equity is higher than other companies often report, because Gillette has been buying its own stock, called treasury stock, for several years.)

Earnings per Share (EPS)

Because corporations have many owners, not all of whom own an equal number of shares, it is quite common to express earnings of a company on a per-share basis for those who wish to calculate their proportional share of earnings. The calculation of earnings per share can be complicated if there is more than one class of ownership, each with differing claims against the income of the firm. Preferred stock or other securities that are convertible into common shares are often treated as common stock equivalents in making this calculation. In published financial reports, this ratio is required to be presented, often in several variations such as "basic" or "diluted" (a very conservative form) EPS. Although the actual formulas for EPS are usually very complex, a simplified formula showing the basic common elements is:

$$\text{Earnings per Share (EPS)} = \frac{\text{Net Income - Preferred Stock Dividends}}{\text{Number of Shares of Common Stock + Equivalents}}$$

Net earnings per share for the Gillette Company for 2003 were $1.35.

Profit Margin

This ratio, which gives a rate of return on sales, relates two statement of income measurements to each other. For this reason, it is not a measure of efficiency, but instead, gives some indication of the sensitivity of income to price changes or changes in cost structure. The formula for this ratio is:

$$\text{Net Profit} = \frac{\text{Net Income}}{\text{Net Sales}}$$

It is important to note that neither a high nor low profit margin necessarily means good performance. A company with a high profit margin but high investment may not be returning a great amount to investors. A firm with a very low profit margin may have required only a very small investment so that it proves highly profitable to those who invest in it.

The profit margin in 2003 for Gillette was:

$$\text{Net Profit} = \frac{\$1,385}{\$9,252} = 15.0\%$$

Activity Ratios

Activity ratios provide an indication of how well assets are utilized by the organization. Efficiency in using assets minimizes the need for investment by lenders or owners. Activity ratios provide measurements of how well assets or capital are being utilized.

Asset Turnover

This ratio measures the company's effectiveness in utilizing all of its assets. The formula for this ratio is:

$$\text{Asset Turnover} = \frac{\text{Net Sales}}{\text{Total Assets}}$$

For the Gillette Company in 2003, the asset turnover was:

$$\text{Asset Turnover} = \frac{\$9,252}{\$9,955} = .929$$

Since different industries require very different asset structures, comparing asset turnover ratios from one industry to those in another is potentially meaningless and must be done with caution. Likewise, when an organization participates in many industries, the exact meaning of an asset turnover ratio can be obscured, and the most valid comparisons of an asset turnover ratio at one date may be to that of the same firm at another recent date.

Asset turnover ratios can be calculated for any group of assets. Accounts receivable, inventory, and total working capital are all asset classifications for which comparison of turnover is potentially interesting and important.

Days' Receivables

Evidence about the amount of time that lapses between sales and receipt of payment from customers can be important information about the financial structure of a company. An approximation of the number of days that elapse can be obtained by dividing the amount of accounts receivable (and notes receivable if these are related to customer accounts) by the average day's sales. In cases where cash sales are a significant portion of the total, the amount of charge sales must be estimated for use in judging the length of collection.

The collection period for accounts receivable can be calculated by first dividing net sales by 365 days to determine average sales per day.

$$\text{Average Day's Sales} = \frac{\text{Net Sales}}{365}$$

Then calculate the collection period using the following formula:

$$\text{Day's Receivables} = \frac{\text{Accounts Receivable}}{\text{Average Day's Sales}}$$

Days' receivables in 2003 for the Gillette Company was:

$$\text{Average Day's Sales} = \frac{\$9,252}{365} = \$25.3 \text{ million}$$

$$\text{Day's Receivables} = \frac{\$920}{\$25.3} = 36 \text{ days}$$

Inventory Turnover

Determining the number of times that inventory is sold during the year provides some measure of its liquidity and the ability of the company to convert inventories to cash quickly if that were to become necessary. When turnover is slow, it may indicate that inventories are not a liquid asset and suggest they should be excluded from that category for analytical purposes. On the other hand, when turnover is quite rapid, that is when inventory is sold several times each year, the liquid character of inventory can provide funds if needed in the short term and may protect the firm against inventory obsolescence.

Inventory turnover is calculated by dividing the cost of goods sold by the inventory cost. The average inventory for the year should be calculated or approximated if there has been a significant change in inventory cost from the beginning to the end of the period. Usually it is sufficient simply to add the beginning and ending inventory amounts and to use one-half of that total as the average inventory for the year. Once the inventory turnover is determined, it can be converted to days' inventory by dividing inventory turnover into 365 days.

$$\text{Inventory Turnover} = \frac{\text{Cost of Goods Sold}}{\text{Average Inventory}}$$

$$\text{Inventory Turnover Period in Days} = \frac{365}{\text{Inventory Turnover}}$$

In some financial reports issued for stockholders, the cost of goods sold is not revealed. In these cases, it is necessary to use sales as the numerator of the ratio, which gives the appearance of providing faster inventory turnover. If the relationship between price and cost does not change, the trend in turnover period would be approximately the same between two periods. Nevertheless, it is wise to use the ratio of sales to inventory with somewhat greater care.

Inventory turnover in 2003 for the Gillette Company was:

$$\text{Inventory Turnover} = \frac{\$3,708}{(\$1,094 + \$928) \div 2} = 3.6$$

$$\text{Days' Inventory} = \frac{365}{3.6} = 100 \text{ days}$$

Working Capital Turnover

Working capital turnover is a measure of the speed with which funds are provided by current assets to satisfy current liabilities. The formula for this ratio is:

$$\text{Working Capital Turnover} = \frac{\text{Net Sales}}{\text{Average Current Assets} - \text{Average Current Liabilities}}$$

Working capital turnover in 2003 for the Gillette Company was:

$$\text{Working Capital Turnover} = \frac{\$9,252}{(\$3,723.5 - \$3,573.0)} = 61.5x$$

Solvency and Leverage Ratios

When an organization is unable to meet its financial obligations, it is said to be insolvent. Because insolvency leads to organizational distress, or even to bankruptcy or organization extinction, ratios to test solvency are often used by investors and creditors. By measuring a company's ability to meet its financial obligations as they become current, solvency ratios give an indication of the liquidity of the company.

Current Ratio

This ratio is commonly used for testing liquidity or solvency. The formula for this ratio is:

$$\text{Current Ratio} = \frac{\text{Current Assets}}{\text{Current Liabilities}}$$

The size of the current ratio that a healthy company needs to maintain is dependent upon the relationship between inflows of cash and the demands for cash payments. A company that has a continuous inflow of cash or other liquid assets, such as a public utility or taxi company, may be able to meet currently maturing obligations easily despite the fact that its current ratio may be small. On the other hand, the manufacturing firm with a long product development and manufacturing cycle may need to maintain a larger current ratio.

The current ratio at the end of 2003 for the Gillette Company was:

$$\text{Current Ratio} = \frac{\$3,650}{\$3,658} = 1.0$$

Acid Test Ratio

In cases where there is a desire or a need to confirm the absolute liquidity of an organization, the current ratio is modified by eliminating from current assets all that cannot be liquidated on very short notice. Typically, then, this ratio consists of the ratio of so-called "quick" assets (cash, marketable security, and some forms of accounts receivable) to current liabilities.

$$\text{Acid Test Ratio} = \frac{\text{Quick Assets}}{\text{Current Liabilities}}$$

For 2003, add the cash, short-term investments, and receivables to calculate the acid test ratio for the Gillette Company.

$$\text{Acid Test Ratio} = \frac{\$1,952}{\$3,658} = .53$$

Debt Ratio

The degree to which the activities of a company are supported by liabilities and long-term debt as opposed to owner contributions is referred to as leverage. A firm that has a high proportion of debt to stockholder contributions would be referred to as being highly leveraged. The advantage to the owners of the firm of having high debt is that profits earned after payment of interest accrue to a smaller group of owners. On the other hand, when a firm is highly leveraged, risk rises when profits and cash flows fall. A company can be forced to the point of insolvency by the cost of interest on the debt.

The debt ratio is widely used in financial analysis because it reveals the effect of financial leverage. The debt ratio is calculated in different ways, and we will illustrate two here. First,

$$\text{Debt Ratio} = \frac{\text{Total Debt}}{\text{Total Assets}}$$

Alternatively, the debt-to-equity ratio is sometimes calculated by dividing total liabilities by the amount of stockholders' equity. The formula for this ratio would be:

$$\text{Debt - to - Equity Ratio} = \frac{\text{Total Liabilities}}{\text{Owners' Equity}}$$

Care must be taken in interpreting either of these ratios because there is no absolute level that can be referred to as being better than another. In general, as the ratio increases in size, returns to owners are higher but so also is risk higher. The trend in this ratio may reveal important management decisions about the financing of activities comparing two organizations. Differences in the size of the ratio may reveal management attitude toward risks and alternative strategies toward financing the activities of the respective entities.

Using the second of the two formulas above, the 2003 debt-to-equity ratio for the Gillette Company was:

$$\text{Debt - to - Equity Ratio} = \frac{\$9,955 - \$2,224}{\$2,224} = 3.5$$

Times Interest Earned

Almost every firm has continuing commitments that must be met by future flows if the company is to remain solvent. Interest payments are an example of such commitments. The common ratio that measures the ability of a company to meet its interest payments is times interest earned. The formula for this ratio is:

$$\text{Times Interest Earned} = \frac{\text{Pretax Operating Income} + \text{Interest Expense}}{\text{Interest}}$$

The number of times interest payments are covered by current earnings offers some measure of the degree to which income could fall without causing insolvency in this account. In many cases, this is not so much a test of solvency as a test of staying power under adversity. Times interest earned for 2003 for the Gillette Company was:

$$\text{Times Interest Earned} = \frac{\$1,964 + \$54}{\$54} = 37.4\text{x}$$

Market-Related and Dividend Ratios

Two ratios are affected by the market price for shares of ownership in corporations. These are the price earnings ratio and the dividend yield ratio. In addition, analysts sometimes calculate a dividend payout ratio as a measure of the degree to which the firm is likely to be able to continue its dividend payments provided there is fluctuation in future income.

Price Earnings Ratio (PE)

The relationship of the market price of shares of stock to the earnings of the company is of great interest to investors. Companies that are growing rapidly and are thought to have good potential for future growth often find that their shares are traded at a multiple of earnings per share much higher than companies thought to have less promise. The price earnings ratio is often included in stock market tables in investment information prepared by analysts. The formula for this ratio is:

$$\text{Price Earnings Ratio (PE)} = \frac{\text{Market Price per Share of Stock}}{\text{Earnings per Share}}$$

Since the market price of shares frequently fluctuates, this ratio is sometimes calculated using an average market price for a period of time. If the average price of a share of Gillette stock in 2003 was $34.00, the price earnings ratio would have been 25.2%.

$$2003 \ \text{Price Earnings Ratio} = \frac{\$34.00}{\$1.35} = 25.2$$

Dividend Yield Ratio

The dividend yield to common shareholders is dependent upon the market price originally paid for the share and is calculated by dividing dividends received by the market price originally paid for the shares. For a prospective investor, dividend yield is the dividend per share divided by the current market price of the stock.

$$\text{Dividend Yield} = \frac{\text{Dividends per Share}}{\text{Market Price per Share}}$$

If the market price of shares in the Gillette Company was $34.00, the dividend yield in 2003 when dividends per share of $.65 were paid to shareholders would have been:

$$\text{Dividend Yield} = \frac{\$.65}{\$34.00} = 1.9\%$$

Dividend Payout

The dividend payout ratio shows the proportion of net income that was paid in dividends. Both the dividend yield and dividend payout ratio are useful for forecasting future dividend streams to investors in the company's common stock. The formula for this ratio is:

$$\text{Dividend Payout} = \frac{\text{Dividends}}{\text{Net Income (available to common shareholders)}}$$

For the Gillette Company in 2003, dividends paid to common stockholders totaled $666.0 million; therefore the dividend payout was:

$$\text{Dividend Payout} = \frac{\$666}{\$1,385} = 48\%$$

Using Ratios to Think about Management Strategies

Sometimes it is useful when conducting a financial analysis to think about the interrelationships between ratios and to use them to think about the strategies that management has adopted or might adopt. One well-known algebraic construction using ratios is known as the du Pont model because financial analysts at the E. I. du Pont de Nemours & Co. are credited with its development and use during the 1920s. The du Pont model multiplies profit margin times asset turnover times a ratio of assets over equity to calculate return on stockholders' equity. If we look at this algebraic construction, we can see why it is so useful.

$$\frac{\text{Income}}{\text{Sales}} \times \frac{\text{Sales}}{\text{Assets}} \times \frac{\text{Assets}}{\text{Owners' Equity}} = \text{Return on Owners' Equity}$$

The first ratio, profit margin, can be used to focus management's attention on the relationship between the price and cost of products or services sold. The second ratio, asset turnover, emphasizes the efficient use of resources in producing products and services. The third ratio, assets over equity, focuses on the ability of management to leverage the firm properly to provide maximum return to stockholders. Each of these major classes of decisions that managers must make can be examined in light of its ability to provide the overall objective of increasing return to stockholders.

Common Size Financial Statements

In order to examine the changing financial structure of a firm through time and the changing nature of operations, many analysts like to create common size financial statements in which the balance sheet and the statement of income are prepared in the percentage format. In a common size balance sheet, each asset, liability, and owners' equity amount is expressed as a percentage of total assets. In a common size statement of income, sales is set at 100%, and each item is expressed as a percentage of sales.

Common size financial statements facilitate the comparison of firms of a different size as well. Although firms may be in the same industry, they may be of significantly different sizes, and common size statements allow an analyst to focus on the efficiency with which managements of different firms have created a capital structure and have achieved efficient operations.

Common size balance sheets and statements of income for the Gillette Company are presented in **Exhibit 2**.

Exhibit 1 The Gillette Company and Subsidiary Companies—Consolidated Statement of Income for Years Ended December 31, 2003, 2002, and 2001 (dollars in millions, except per share amounts)

	Year Ended December (millions, except per share amounts)		
	2003	2002	2001
Net Sales	$9,252	$8,453	$8,084
Cost of Sales	3,708	3,511	3,407
Gross Profit	5,544	4,942	4,677
Selling, General, and Administrative Expenses	3,541	3,172	3,007
Restructuring, Asset Impairment and Other	--	(39)	172
Profit from Operations	2,003	1,809	1,498
Nonoperating Charges (Income)			
Interest income	(12)	(25)	(4)
Interest expense	54	84	145
Other charges (income)—net	(3)	(2)	15
	39	57	156
Income from Continuing Operations before Income Taxes	1,964	1,752	1,342
Income Taxes	589	543	432
Income from Continuing Operations	1,375	1,209	910
Income from Discontinued Operations, net of tax	10	7	--
Net Income	$1,385	$1,216	$910
Net Income Per Common Share, Basic			
Continuing Operations	$1.35	$1.15	$.86
Discontinued Operations	.01	--	--
Net Income	$1.36	$1.15	$.86
Net Income Per Common Share, Assuming Full Dilution			
Continuing Operations	$1.34	$1.14	$.86
Discontinued Operations	.01	.01	--
Net Income	$1.35	$1.15	$.86
Adjusted Net Income, assuming the adoption of SFAS 142 for 2001	$1,385	$1,216	$934
Adjusted Net Income per Common Share, assuming the adoption of SFAS 142 for 2001			
Basic	$1.36	$1.15	$.89
Assuming full dilution	$1.35	$1.15	$.88
Weighted average number of common shares outstanding			
Basic	1,021	1,055	1,055
Assuming full dilution	1,024	1,059	1,058

Exhibit 1 (continued)   The Gillette Company and Subsidiary Companies—Consolidated Balance Sheets, December 31, 2003 and 2002 (dollars in millions except per share amounts)

At December 31	2003	2002
Assets		
Current Assets		
Cash and cash equivalents	$ 681	$ 801
Trade receivables, less allowances: 2003—$53; 2002—$73	920	1,202
Other receivables	351	311
Inventories	1,094	928
Deferred income taxes	322	380
Other current assets	282	175
Total current assets	3,650	3,797
Property, plant and equipment, net	3,642	3,565
Goodwill	1,023	962
Intangible assets, net	496	400
Other assets	1,144	1,139
Total assets	$9,955	$9,863
Liabilities and Shareholders' Equity		
Current Liabilities		
Loans payable	$ 117	$ 673
Current portion of long-term debt	742	527
Accounts payable and accrued liabilities	2,506	2,054
income taxes	293	234
Total current liabilities	3,658	3,488
Long-term debt	2,453	2,457
Deferred income taxes	626	692
Other long-term liabilities	929	920
Minority Interest	65	46
Stockholders' Equity		
Common stock, par value $1 per share		
Authorized: 2,320 shares		
Issued 2003—1,374 shares; 2002—1,370 shares	1,374	1,370
Additional paid-in capital	1,273	1,197
Earnings reinvested in the business	7,333	6,608
Accumulated other comprehensive loss	(1,088)	(1,523)
Treasury stock, at cost		
2003—367 shares; 2002—326 shares	(6,665)	(5,392)
Deferred stock-based compensation	(3)	--
Total stockholders' equity	2,224	2,260
Total liabilities and stockholders' equity	$9,955	$9,863

Exhibit 1 (continued) The Gillette Company and Subsidiary Companies—Common Size Balance Sheets, December 2003 and 2002 (%)

At December 31	2003	2002
Assets		
Current Assets		
Cash and cash equivalents	6.8	8.1
Trade receivables, less allowances: 2003—$53; 2002—$73	9.2	12.2
Other receivables	3.5	3.2
Inventories	11.0	9.4
Deferred income taxes	3.2	3.9
Other current assets	2.8	1.8
Total current assets	36.5	38.6
Property, plant and equipment, net	36.6	36.1
Goodwill	10.3	9.8
Intangible assets, net	5.0	4.1
Other assets	11.5	11.5
Total assets	100.0	100.0
Liabilities and Shareholders' Equity		
Current Liabilities		
Loans payable	1.2	6.8
Current portion of long-term debt	7.5	5.3
Accounts payable and accrued liabilities	25.2	20.8
income taxes	2.9	2.4
Total current liabilities	36.8	35.3
Long-term debt	24.6	24.9
Deferred income taxes	6.3	7.0
Other long-term liabilities	9.3	9.3
Minority Interest	.7	.5
Stockholders' Equity		
Common stock, par value $1 per share		
Authorized: 2,320 shares		
Issued 2003—1,374 shares; 2002–1,370 shares	13.8	13.9
Additional paid-in capital	12.8	12.1
Earnings reinvested in the business	73.7	67.0
Accumulated other comprehensive loss	(10.9)	(15.4)
Treasury stock, at cost		
2003—367 shares; 2002—326 shares	(67.0)	(54.7)
Deferred stock-based compensation	0.0	0.0
Total stockholders' equity	23.3	22.9
Total liabilities and stockholders' equity	$100.0	$100.0

Note: Columns do not add because of rounding.

Exhibit 1 (continued)   The Gillette Company and Subsidiary Companies—Consolidated Statements of Cash Flows for Years Ended December 31, 2003, 2002, and 2001 (dollars in millions)

Years Ended December 31	2003	2002	2001
Operating Activities			
Income from continuing operations	$1,375	$1,209	$910
Adjustments to reconcile income from continuing operations to net cash provided by operating activities:			
Restructuring and asset impairment charge (recovery)	--	(9)	172
Depreciation and amortization	578	500	509
Funding of company pension loans	(72)	(525)	(35)
Pension expense	143	70	46
Deferred income taxes	(49)	162	45
Other	7	8	(18)
Changes in assets and liabilities, excluding effects of acquisitions and divestitures:			
Accounts receivable	286	364	622
Inventories	(43)	123	101
Accounts payable and accrual liabilities	334	188	(191)
Other working capital items	38	(137)	(20)
Other noncurrent assets and liabilities	43	124	(49)
Net cash provided by operating activities	2,640	2,077	2,092
INVESTING ACTIVITIES			
Additions to property, plant and equipment	(408)	(405)	(624)
Disposals of property, plant and equipment	45	43	59
Acquisition of business, net of cash acquired	(161)	--	--
Other	6	--	1
Net cash used in investing activities	(518)	(362)	(564)
FINANCING ACTIVITIES			
Purchase of treasury stock	(1,273)	(427)	(12)
Proceeds from sale of put options	--	15	9
Proceeds from exercise of stock option and purchase plans	80	57	53
Proceeds from long-term debt	709	1,174	525
Repayment of long-term debt	(534)	(458)	(684)
Increase (decrease) in loans payable	(567)	(1,565)	56
Dividends paid	(666)	(685)	(686)
Settlements of debt-related derivative contracts	1	45	4
Net cash used in financing activities	(2,250)	(1,844)	(735)
Effect of Exchange Rate Changes on Cash	8	5	(1)
Net Cash Provided (Used) by Discontinued Operations	--	(22)	93
Increase (Decrease) in Cash and Cash Equivalents	(120)	(146)	885
Cash and Cash Equivalents at Beginning of Year	801	947	62
Cash and Cash Equivalents at End of Year	$681	$801	$947
Supplemental disclosure of cash paid for:			
Interest	$59	$83	$154
Income taxes	$563	$345	$232

Exhibit 2 The Gillette Company and Subsidiary Companies—Common Size Statement of Income for Years Ended December 31, 2003, 20021, and 2001 (%)

	2003	2002	2001
Net Sales	100.0	100.0	100.0
Cost of Sales	40.1	41.5	42.1
Gross Profit	59.9	58.5	57.9
Selling, General, and Administrative Expenses	37.3	37.5	37.2
Restructuring, Asset Impairment and Other	--	(.5)	2.1
Profit from Operations	22.6	21.5	18.6
Nonoperating Charges (Income)			
Interest income	(.1)	(.3)	0
Interest expense	.6	1.0	1.8
Other charges (income)—net	0	0	.2
	.4	.7	1.9
Income from Continuing Operations before Income Taxes	21.2	20.7	16.6
Income Taxes	6.4	6.4	5.3
Income from Continuing Operations	14.9	14.3	11.3
Income from Discontinued Operations, net of tax	.1	0	0
Net Income	15.0	14.3	11.3

Note: Columns do not add because of rounding.